Contents

Cape Naturaliste 134
Yallingup 135
Margaret River 137
Caves Road 141
Augusta & Around 144
Southern Forests 146
Nannup 146
Bridgetown 146
Manjimup.............. 147
Pemberton............. 148

SOUTH COAST WA.................151

Walpole & Nornalup..... 153
Denmark 154
Albany 157
Mt Barker.............. 161
Porongurup National Park 162
Stirling Range National Park 163
Bremer Bay............ 164
Fitzgerald River National Park 165
Hopetoun.............. 166
Esperance 166

MONKEY MIA & THE CENTRAL WEST 169

Batavia Coast 171
Dongara-Port Denison....171
Geraldton.............. 172
Kalbarri 175
Kalbarri National Park... 178
Shark Bay 179
Shark Bay Road 179
Denham 180
Monkey Mia............ 182
Gascoyne Coast 183
Carnarvon 183
Quobba Coast.......... 185

NINGALOO COAST & THE PILBARA 187

Ningaloo Coast....... 190
Coral Bay 190
Exmouth............... 191
Exmouth Region........ 195
Ningaloo Marine Park ... 197
Cape Range National Park 199
The Pilbara 200
Karratha...............200
Dampier...............203
Port Hedland..........203
Karijini National Park ...205

BROOME & THE KIMBERLEY... 209

The Kimberley........ 212
Broome 212
Dampier Peninsula......222
Derby 224
Devonian Reef National Parks 227
Gibb River Road 228
Great Northern Highway...............230
Kununurra 233
Purnululu National Park & Bungle Bungle Range 236
Wyndham..............238

UNDERSTAND

History 240
Local Produce, Wine & Craft Beer 248
Mining & the Environment 253
Indigenous Art in Western Australia..... 258

SURVIVAL GUIDE

Directory A–Z 262
Transport 272
Index................ 279
Map Legend.......... 286

SPECIAL FEATURES

Off the Beaten Track Map 36
Discover Margaret River & the Southwest.......... 38
West Coast Australia Outdoors... 42
Local Produce & Wineries Map 250

Welcome to West Coast Australia

Unfettered and alive, West Coast Australia is 12,500km of truly spectacular coastline. There's a freedom and optimism here that the rest of Australia can't replicate.

Where Is Everybody?

If the vast expanse of Western Australia (WA) was a separate nation, it would be the world's 10th largest (bigger than Algeria, smaller than Kazakhstan). Most of WA's population clings to the coast – yet you can wander along a beach without seeing another footprint, or be one of a few campers stargazing in a national park. The state's fertile southwest features white-sand coves, rampant wildflowers and lush forests abuzz with native wildlife. Up north in the big-sky, red-dirt Pilbara and Kimberley, you'll encounter ancient gorges and mesmerising waterfalls – and no one else for kilometres.

On Your Plate, in Your Glass

Perth and Fremantle are laid-back, sunny cities in which the tradition of a nightly 'sundowner' (sunset drink) is culturally ingrained. The cafe and restaurant scenes here, from bohemian to white-linen wonderful, make any visit a culinary delight. After dark, small bars simmer with typical WA decadence, while excellent local craft beers flow through pub taps. Further afield, the Margaret River and Great Southern wine regions produce world-class drops, complemented by inventive menus in regional restaurants. Truffles also grow down south, and WA's seafood is consistently sublime.

Action Attractions

Time to get active! Block out a chunk of your calendar to hike the epic 1000km Bibbulmun Track or tackle a day walk – perhaps a section of the Cape to Cape Track on Cape Naturaliste or a wildflower walk through Stirling Range National Park. Mountain bikers can wheel through the forests of Margaret River or careen along the Munda Biddi Trail (also 1000km). Dive and snorkel in marine parks and around shipwrecks, surf at Margaret River, or kitesurf and windsurf off Lancelin's blowy beaches.

All Creatures Great & Small

WA's native wildlife is ever present: you won't have to venture too far from Perth to see kangaroos, emus, colourful parrots and lesser-known locals such as quokkas, bilbies and potoroos. Each year 30,000 whales cruise the coast-hugging 'Humpback Hwy', while Bremer Bay near Albany is known for its orcas. Ningaloo Marine Park is home to the world's largest fish, the whale shark, while dolphins proliferate at Rockingham, Bunbury and Monkey Mia. With a bit of research you can make an ethical choice about how you choose to interact.

Why I Love West Coast Australia

By Charles Rawlings-Way, Writer

There's something fundamentally liberated about West Coast Australia – a frontier spirit that's free from the baggage of east-coast history. Western Australians have an extroverted world view, gazing (and travelling) across the Indian Ocean to India, Sri Lanka, Indonesia, Mauritius, the Maldives, South Africa... Perth may be the most isolated city of its size on the planet, but locals are connected to their international neighbours in a way that introspective Melburnians struggle to countenance. Within the city and beyond, this is an ancient land: Aboriginal culture here has a mainstream presence that the rest of Australia is a long way from matching.

For more about our writers, see p288

Above: Kangaroo with a joey, Lucky Bay (p166), Cape Le Grand National Park

West Coast Australia

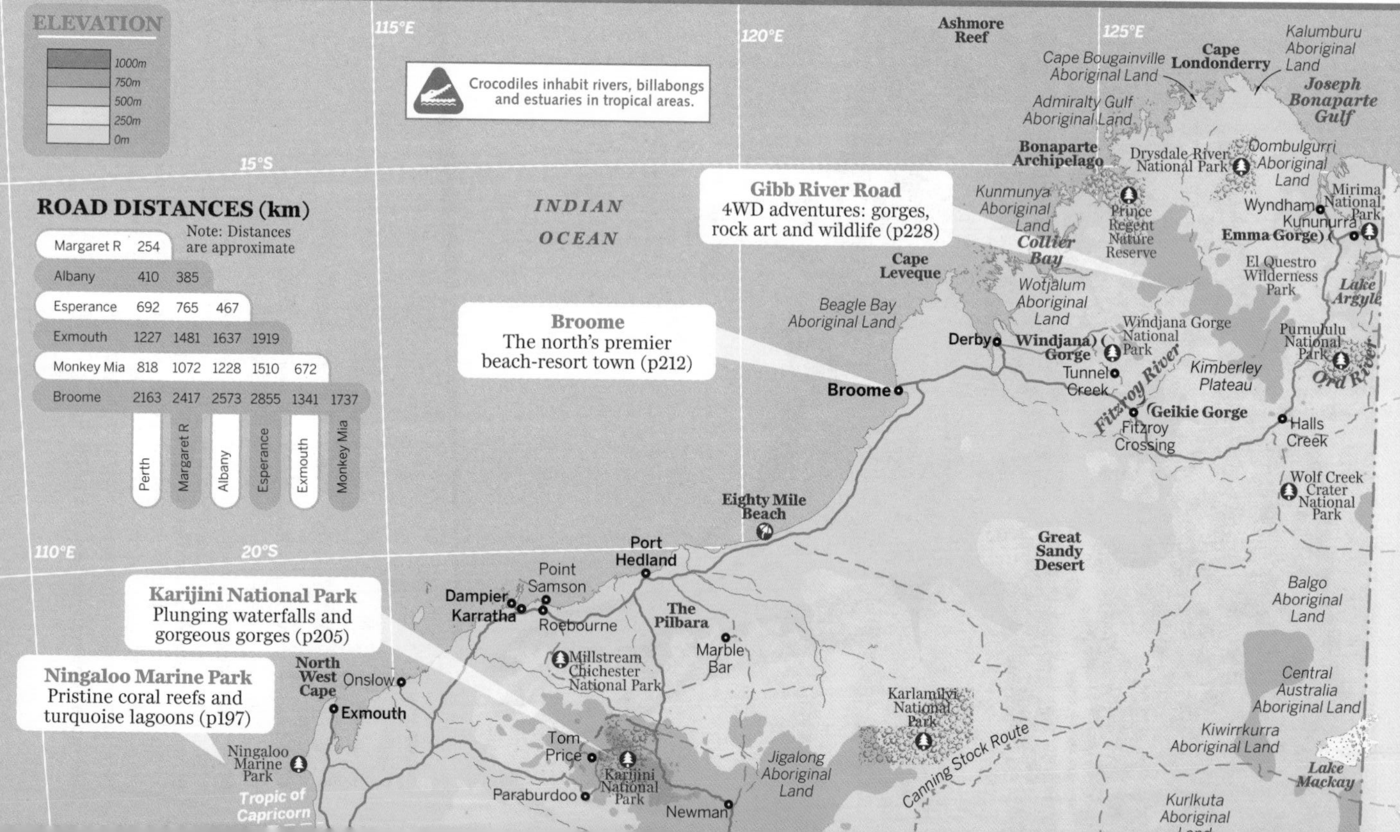

ROAD DISTANCES (km)

Note: Distances are approximate

	Perth	Margaret R	Albany	Esperance	Exmouth	Monkey Mia
Margaret R	254					
Albany	410	385				
Esperance	692	765	467			
Exmouth	1227	1481	1637	1919		
Monkey Mia	818	1072	1228	1510	672	
Broome	2163	2417	2573	2855	1341	1737

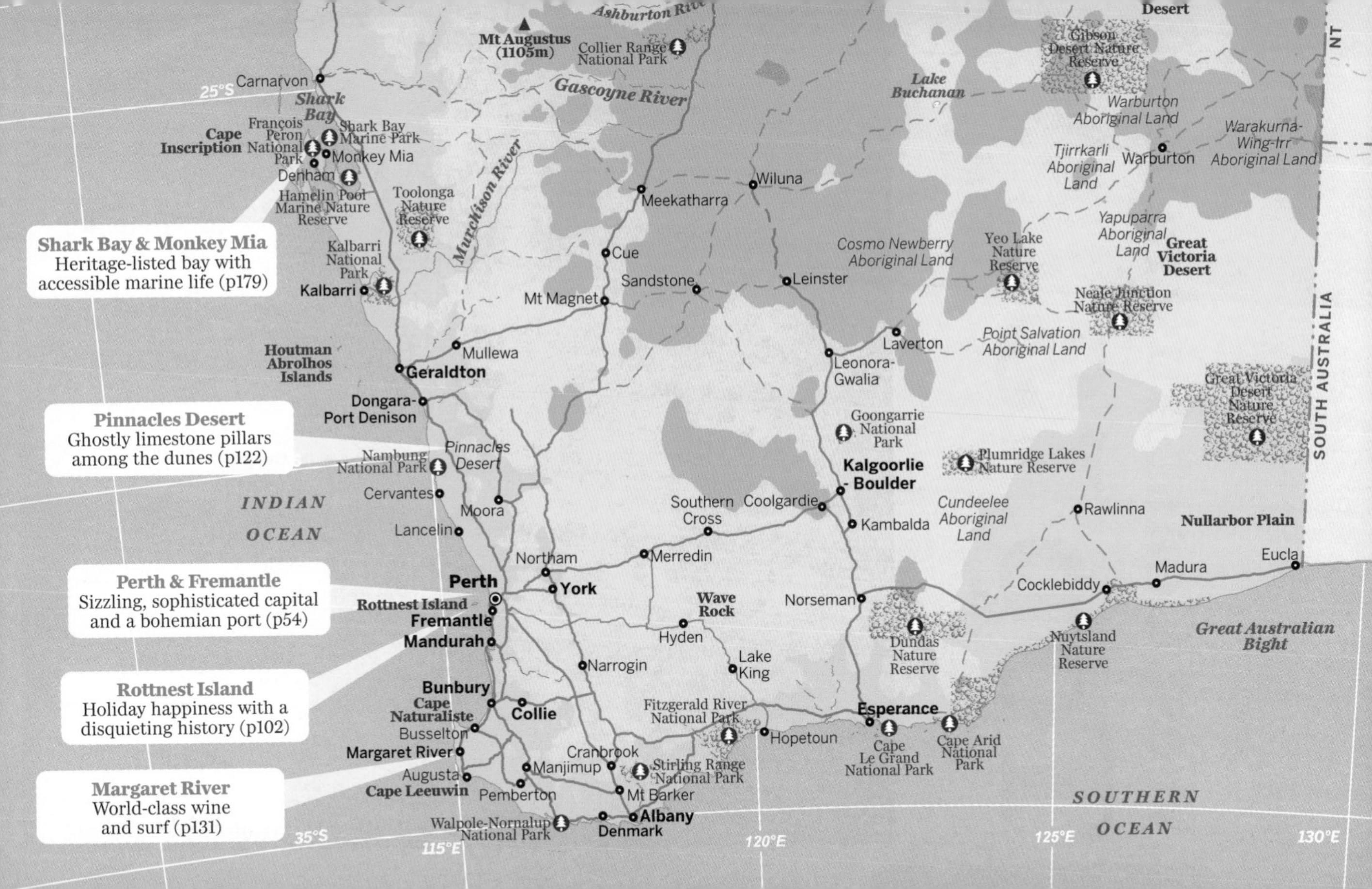
Shark Bay & Monkey Mia
Heritage-listed bay with accessible marine life (p179)
Pinnacles Desert
Ghostly limestone pillars among the dunes (p122)
Perth & Fremantle
Sizzling, sophisticated capital and a bohemian port (p54)
Rottnest Island
Holiday happiness with a disquieting history (p102)
Margaret River
World-class wine and surf (p131)
INDIAN OCEAN
SOUTHERN OCEAN
Great Australian Bight
SOUTH AUSTRALIA
NT
Mt Augustus (1105m)
Collier Range National Park
Ashburton River
Gascoyne River
Murchison River
Carnarvon
Shark Bay
Cape Inscription
François Peron National Park
Shark Bay Marine Park
Monkey Mia
Denham
Hamelin Pool Marine Nature Reserve
Toolonga Nature Reserve
Kalbarri National Park
Kalbarri
Houtman Abrolhos Islands
Geraldton
Mullewa
Dongara-Port Denison
Nambung National Park
Pinnacles Desert
Cervantes
Moora
Lancelin
Perth
Rottnest Island
Fremantle
Mandurah
Bunbury
Cape Naturaliste
Busselton
Margaret River
Augusta
Cape Leeuwin
Collie
Manjimup
Pemberton
Walpole-Nornalup National Park
Denmark
Albany
Mt Barker
Cranbrook
Stirling Range National Park
Narrogin
Northam
York
Merredin
Southern Cross
Wave Rock
Hyden
Lake King
Fitzgerald River National Park
Hopetoun
Esperance
Cape Le Grand National Park
Cape Arid National Park
Dundas Nature Reserve
Norseman
Coolgardie
Kalgoorlie - Boulder
Kambalda
Goongarrie National Park
Leonora-Gwalia
Laverton
Leinster
Sandstone
Mt Magnet
Cue
Meekatharra
Wiluna
Cosmo Newberry Aboriginal Land
Lake Buchanan
Gibson Desert Nature Reserve
Desert
Warburton Aboriginal Land
Warburton
Tjirrkarli Aboriginal Land
Warakurna-Wing-Irr Aboriginal Land
Yapuparra Aboriginal Land
Great Victoria Desert
Yeo Lake Nature Reserve
Neale Junction Nature Reserve
Point Salvation Aboriginal Land
Great Victoria Desert Nature Reserve
Plumridge Lakes Nature Reserve
Cundeelee Aboriginal Land
Rawlinna
Nullarbor Plain
Eucla
Madura
Cocklebiddy
Nuytsland Nature Reserve
25°S
35°S
115°E
120°E
125°E
130°E

West Coast Australia's Top 13

1

Perth & Fremantle

1 Perth may be remote, but it's far from a backwater. Studded across the city (p54) are chic Mod Oz restaurants, moody cocktail bars and restored heritage buildings. Soulful inner-city suburbs thrum with guitars, turntable buzz and the sizzle of woks. The shimmering Swan River and fabulous city beaches remain constants. Just downstream, the raffish port of Fremantle has a pub on just about every corner, most of which pour craft brews from around Western Australia and the world. Don't miss the World Heritage–listed Fremantle Prison while you're here. Cottesloe Beach (p61), Perth

Margaret River Wine Region

2 The pleasure of drifting from winery to craft brewery along country roads shaded by gum trees is hard to do justice in one paragraph – perhaps it's suffice to say that this is Australia's most beautiful wine region (p131). Right on its doorstep are the white sands of Geographe Bay, and closer to the vines are the world-famous surf breaks of Yallingup and Margaret River Mouth. And then there are the caves – magical subterranean palaces of limestone, scattered along the main wine-tasting route. Sip, swim, surf, spelunk – the only difficulty is picking which one to do first. Dining at Cullen Wines (p144)

BENNY MARTY/SHUTTERSTOCK ©

2

CATHERINE SUTHERLAND/LONELY PLANET ©

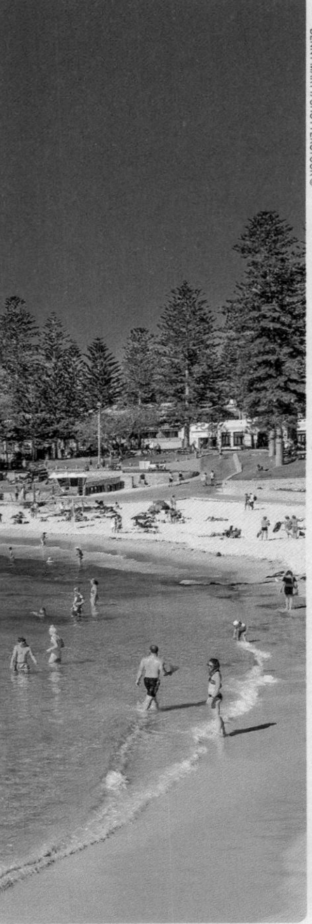

Indigenous Art

3 From upmarket city galleries to centuries-old rock carvings in wild places, the culture and spirit of WA's original inhabitants deeply infuses this land. Browse the excellent commercial galleries in Perth and Fremantle (p96), while in the far northern reaches of the Kimberley you can visit local art cooperatives such as Waringarri or Mowanjum (p225), before peering across aeons at the Wandjina and Gwion Gwion rock-art sites. Aboriginal culture here is close to the surface and in some ways easier to engage with than anywhere else in the country. Wandjina rock art (p259)

Shark Bay & Monkey Mia

4 The aquamarine waters of Shark Bay (p179) teem with astoundingly diverse marine life, from Monkey Mia's famous dolphins to the ancient stromatolites of Hamelin Pool. National parks here provide simple coastal camping (just you, the sand and the stars); and excellent Indigenous cultural tours explain how to care for and understand this country. Explore remote, wind-blown Edel Land, Australia's westernmost tip, with towering limestone cliffs; cross over to intriguing Dirk Hartog Island; or set sail alongside seagrass-munching dugongs. Dolphins, Monkey Mia

3

Ningaloo Marine Park

5 The sight of an enormous whale shark basking just below the surface is something to file in your memory banks under 'Once in a Lifetime'. This World Heritage–listed marine park (p197) on the Coral Coast also offers the chance to snorkel and dive among pristine coral and surf off seldom-visited reefs. Rivalling the Great Barrier Reef for beauty, Ningaloo is also much more accessible: you can wade into shallow, turquoise snorkelling lagoons straight from the beach. Development is very low-key, so be prepared to camp, or day-trip from Exmouth and Coral Bay.

CATHERINE SUTHERLAND/LONELY PLANET ©

Gibb River Road

6 Launch yourself into Australia's last frontier on a wild drive down this old cattle road (p228) into the heart of the Kimberley. The Gibb River Road is not for the faint-hearted; you'll need a serious 4WD, good planning and plenty of fuel, spares, food and water (not to mention healthy doses of self-reliance, flexibility and humour). Your rewards are astonishing gorges, hidden waterholes, incredible rock art and amazing wildlife, and you'll gain a first-hand insight into life in the Australian outback. Did we mention there are also flies, dust and relentless heat? Bell Gorge (p228)

Rottnest Island

7 A short ferry ride from either Perth or Fremantle, 'Rotto' (p102), or Wadjemup to the Noongar people, has been the go-to escape for city slickers for generations. It encapsulates all that's good about WA: beaches, surf, rampant wildlife, a brilliant waterside pub... But it has a tragic history too: between 1838 and 1931 thousands of Aboriginal prisoners suffered here and hundreds died, while offshore reefs have claimed many lives. Rotto's schism between holiday happiness and untold misery is intriguing – it's both a cultural touchstone for generations past and a way marker for reconciliation. Quokka (p103)

Broome

8 You can moan about the price of beer or how long your twice-cooked pork belly takes to arrive, but one thing is for certain: when that boiling crimson sun sinks slowly behind a conga-line of camels into the languid Indian Ocean at Cable Beach, you'll realise that this is a truly unique part of the planet. One of the world's great cultural and physical crossroads, Broome (p212) is a melting pot of travellers. You'll find everything you need (though perhaps not everything you want) in the backstreets, bars and markets, and on the hostel noticeboards. Cable Beach (p212)

8

Bushwalking

9 WA has an impressive 63 national parks, plus dozens of other nature reserves and regional parks. That's a whole lotta nature to explore! Pull on your hiking boots and hit the track. The Bibbulmun Track (p159), the mother of them all, starts on the outskirts of Perth and meanders 1000km to Albany on the south coast, sheltered by the cooling southern forests. At the Valley of the Giants you can walk the 40m-high Tree Top Walk. Other excellent walks, short and long, criss-cross the state: even within Perth you can bushwalk though Kings Park. Tree Top Walk, Valley of the Giants (p153)

CHAKKRAPHONG JINTHAWET/SHUTTERSTOCK ©

9

West Coast Wildlife

10 Say hello to WA's unique menagerie of species. Visit the endangered numbats, woylies, bilbies and boodies of the Dryandra Woodland, the quokkas of Rottnest Island, or the freshwater crocodiles of Windjana Gorge National Park (p227). Avian species include the migratory shorebirds of Parry Lagoons Nature Reserve, and the beautiful red-tailed tropic birds of WA's southwest coast. Oceanic attractions include migrating humpback whales and orcas, dolphins at Monkey Mia and mesmerising whale sharks at Ningaloo Reef. Freshwater crocodile, Windjana Gorge (p227)

Karijini National Park

11 Deep in the heart of the Pilbara, the shady pools and plunging waterfalls of Karijini (p205) offer cool respite from the oppressive heat of the surrounding ironstone country. Booking an adventure trip will take you beyond the easily accessible areas to abseil, swim, dive, climb and paddle through deep water-worn passages. Above gorge level, witness an amazing spring transformation as wildflowers carpet the plains, and get some altitude on the state's highest peaks, including the impressive Punurrunha (Mt Bruce; 1235m). Hancock Gorge (p205)

12

13

Pinnacles Desert

12 It could be mistaken for the surface of Mars, but scattered among the dunes of Nambung National Park, thousands of ghostly limestone pillars rise from the surrounding plain like a vast, petrified alien army. One of Australia's most bizarre landscapes, the Pinnacles (p122) attract thousands of visitors each year. Although it's easily enjoyed as a day trip from Perth, staying overnight in nearby Cervantes allows for multiple visits to experience the full spectrum of colour changes at dawn, sunset and full moon, when most tourists are back in their hotel beds.

Surfing the Shoreline

13 If you can't catch a wave on Western Australia's 12,500km-long coastline, then mate, you're doing something wrong. In which case, head straight to one of WA's excellent surf schools (Scarborough in Perth is a good place to start) and leave Margaret River and Gnaraloo waves to the pros, where breaks with nicknames such as Tombstones (p186) and Suicides beckon the fearless. Diving and snorkelling are also excellent in many spots along the WA shore, while windsurfers and kitesurfers shoot the breeze off gusty Lancelin and Geraldton. Surfing, Margaret River region (p131)

First Time West Coast Australia

For more information, see Survival Guide (p261)

Checklist

- Check whether you need a visa to visit Australia.
- Check that your passport has at least six months' validity.
- If you're flying into Perth, check which terminal you'll be landing at: there are four, with different domestic/international transfer and public-transport considerations.

What to Pack

- Decent walking shoes.
- An international driving permit and your valid local licence: there are a lot of long, empty kilometres out there...
- A 'rashie' swimming top to combat sunburn on WA's glorious beaches.
- Broad-rim hat and sunglasses (see sunburn, above).
- Umbrella for rainy-season downpours in the north.

Top Tips for Your Trip

- The WA sun kicks like a mule, even in spring and autumn: slap on sunscreen, some shades and a hat.
- WA is massive: if you're driving anywhere, don't expect to get there in a flash.
- A cooler box (aka 'esky') is handy for storing cold drinks and produce from local farmers markets.
- Everybody wears flip-flops ('thongs') here, but pack some walking shoes if you want to tackle forest and clifftop trails.
- Listen to the lifesavers: plenty of people drown here every year.

What to Wear

Western Australians aren't the planet's most stylish cohort: the weather is usually pretty good here, and the locals dress for the beach (T-shirts, shorts, thongs...). That said, dressing up for high-end restaurant meals, the theatre and cocktail bars is a good idea. Layer up in the southwest as the weather here can be changeable: stuff a raincoat in your backpack.

Sleeping

Accommodation in Western Australia ranges from remote national-park campgrounds to high-end boutique hotels. Since the WA boom went off the boil, Perth is no longer an absurdly expensive place in which to stay.

Hotels Perth and Fremantle have some terrific boutique and design hotels.

Hostels WA's backpacker hostels range from from scuzzy to beachy to downright stylish.

Camping & caravan parks Almost every sizeable WA town has a caravan park, usually with cabins or units.

Pubs Affordable rooms with the bathroom down the hall.

B&Bs Upmarket bedrooms in historic houses, with breakfast to boot.

Perth Public Transport

If you're in Perth for a while, consider buying a SmartRider card, covering bus, train and ferry travel. It's $10 to purchase, then you add value to your card. Tap in and tap out (touch your card to the electronic reader) every time you travel, including within the Free Transit Zone (FTZ). The SmartRider works out 10% to 20% cheaper than buying single tickets and automatically caps itself at the DayRider rate if you're avoiding the morning rush hour.

Bargaining

Bargaining is not part of commercial culture in Western Australia. But you can always try!

Tipping

Tipping is not the cultural norm in WA, but around 10% is appropriate if you feel service in a restaurant has been exemplary. Many cafes have a tip jar on the counter for loose change and this is usually shared between all the staff.

Francois Peron National Park (p182)

Etiquette

Although largely informal in their everyday dealings, Western Australians do observe some (unspoken) rules of etiquette.

Greetings Shake hands when meeting someone for the first time and when saying goodbye. Female friends are often greeted with a single kiss on the cheek.

Invitations If you're invited to someone's house for a barbecue or dinner, don't turn up empty-handed: bring a bottle of wine or some beers.

Shouting No, not yelling. 'Shouting' at the bar means buying a round of drinks: if someone buys you one, don't leave without buying them one too.

Eating

Eating your way around Western Australia is like experiencing a two-speed economy: there's some absolutely superb high-end stuff using regional produce in Perth, the southwest and select restaurants and resorts elsewhere; but below this is a strata of small-town, white-bread and chips-with-everything culinary culture that's hard to shake. In between you'll find consistently good cafes, craft breweries serving creative beery bites, and, as you'd expect with a coastline this long, terrific seafood (with chips) pretty much everywhere. When all else fails, there's always the local pub for a steak or a schnitzel, and the bakery for a ham-and-salad roll or lamington.

What's New

Here's the low-down on what's new and interesting around West Coast Australia. From big-city highlights and designer hotels to little bars in little towns, from fine things to eat to glam camping retreats, there's plenty of new stuff happening here to impress first-time and repeat visitors alike.

Perth's New Stadium

It's finally open! Perth's glam new riverfront Optus Stadium (p95) now hosts AFL football games for both of Perth's teams – the West Coast Eagles and the Fremantle Dockers – plus international rugby, cricket and big-ticket concerts. The new Perth Stadium train station and Matagarup Bridge, a scenic walk across the Swan River, get the fans there.

New Museum for Western Australia

From 2020, the fabulous New Museum for Western Australia – part of the Perth Cultural Centre – will pick up where the Western Australian Museum (p60) left off. Look forward to an inspiring, dynamic and progressive institution (full of interesting old things).

Rottnest Glamping

The first new accommodation offering on Rottnest Island in 30 years, Discovery Rottnest Island (p105) offers some extremely lovely tents (and a pool!) behind the dunes at Pinky Beach. Rottnest is a short ferry ride from Fremantle, but this new operator will make you feel like you're worlds away.

Small Towns, Small Bars

Sick of going to the pub? Bunbury (p129), Busselton (p131), Pemberton (p150) and Jurien Bay (p124) all now have small, shopfront-sized bars to go along with their trad taverns – a welcome alternative for a classy sundowner or mid-afternoon pick-me-up.

LOCAL KNOWLEDGE

WHAT'S HAPPENING IN WEST COAST AUSTRALIA

Charles Rawlings-Way, Lonely Planet writer

You might imagine that with the cooling of Western Australia's mining boom and the subsequent downturn in the state's real-estate sector, that West Coast Australians might be feeling a little glum. Far from it. Optimism seems to be ingrained in WA society – which can sometimes seem brash and abrasive, but is actually just plain ol' self-confidence. The local sports teams are certainly walking the talk: the West Coast Eagles won the national AFL (Australian Football League) comp in 2018, while the Perth Wildcats won the NBL (National Basketball League) title in 2019, both for the umpteenth time. Beyond the city, the Margaret River Wine Region is booming, with as many brilliant new craft-beer breweries and distilleries as progressive wineries. The Perth Hills and Rottnest Island are luring record numbers of visitors, while in the north, Broome continues to occupy a near-mythical niche in the Australian holiday consciousness: a tropical Shangri-La destination to rival Byron Bay.

Biodynamic Winemaking

Plenty of wineries in southwest WA's bountiful Margaret River Wine Region are focusing on creating interesting biodynamic and organic output, bottling-up good stuff that's not bad for the earth: try Blind Corner (p131), Amiria (p143), Stormflower Vineyard (p141) and Cullen Wines (p144; possibly not all on the same day...oh alright, go on then).

Bilya Koort Boodja

In the Avon Valley northwest of Perth, Northam's stylish new Bilya Koort Boodja Aboriginal cultural centre (p115) celebrates the history, culture and environmental savvy of the Avon Valley's Ballardong tribes. After a a 'welcome to country' introduction, an artfully designed sequence of spaces highlights the Ballardong's seasons, arts and legends.

Lobster Shack

The formerly low-key Lobster Shack (p122) in Cervantes, one of the main hubs for crayfishing along WA's Turquoise Coast, has expanded its offering to include a vast new restaurant with Indian Ocean views. Take a factory tour and retreat to the terrace for half a cray and a bottle of something cold.

Cider Scenes

Western Australians love their craft beer (actually, their beer), but there are a couple of new kids on the booze block here that are taking a more fruity approach. Funk Cider (p252) in the Swan Valley and Core Cider (p110) in the Perth Hills are doing wonderful things with apples and pears.

Perth Hotels

Not only have Perth accommodation prices slumped to a 10-year low, there's a slew of sassy new designer and international hotels here in which you can now stay for moderate outlay: try the Melbourne Hotel (p75), QT Perth (p75), Tribe Hotel (p77) and Westin Perth (p76) on for size.

Fremantle Festival goes Wintry

Fremantle's excellent three-day festival (p73) expanded to a 10-day format in 2019, and shifted from October to July. What else are you going to do when the winter chills blow through the old town?

Camping with Custodians

This new government initiative has established tourist campgrounds on WA Indigenous lands. In the Kimberley, open during the Dry, you can camp at Imintji on the Gibb River Road, and Mimbi Caves off the Great Northern Hwy – authentic, intimate and educational experiences.

LISTEN, WATCH & FOLLOW

For inspiration and up-to-date news, visit www.lonelyplanet.com/news/australia

Perth is OK (www.instagram.com/perthisok) Inspiring images from Perth, Fremantle and beyond.

ABC Radio Perth (www.abc.net.au/radio/perth/) Tune in to the national broadcaster's Perth channel.

Western Australia (https://twitter.com/westaustralia) Tourism Western Australia's official Twitter account.

So Perth (https://soperth.com.au) On-trend articles, interviews and stories from Australia's wild-western capital.

FAST FACTS

Food trend Crayfish: it's pricey, but it's everywhere (especially the Turquoise Coast)

Length of coastline 12,500km, not including islands

Urban life 86% of West Coast Australia's population lives in Perth, reaffirming Australia's status as one of the world's most urbanised countries

Pop 2.5 million

population per sq km

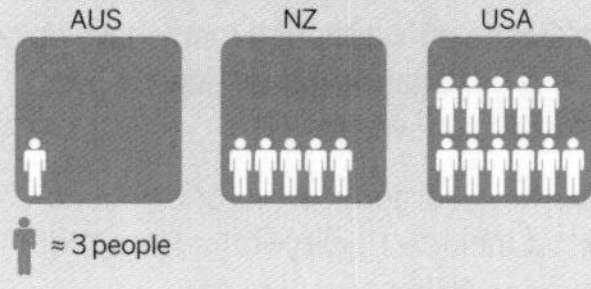

Accommodation

Find more accommodation reviews throughout the On the Road chapters (from p54)

Accommodation Types

Hotels There are some great boutique and design hotels in Perth and Fremantle. Interestingly, the economic slowdown in Western Australia has seen accommodation prices have dropped, making Perth a more affordable place to stay.

Hostels WA's backpacker hostels range in quality and style, from basic to designer. In Perth, most of the hostels are in Northbridge (near all the bars… coincidence?).

Camping & Caravan Parks Youll find a caravan park, including with cabins or units, in most sizeable towns. Beyond the urban reaches, remote national-park campgrounds are often blissfully people-free.

Pubs Affordable rooms, usually upstairs, with the bathroom down the hall. Most small towns have at least one old-time pub, although many have opted out of the accommodation game. Beware live bands downstairs on weekends!

B&Bs Upmarket bedrooms in historic houses, with breakfast included, everywhere from the Perth suburbs to little country towns.

Motels Drive-up midrange ubiquity and predictability. Frustratingly, it's hard to find good (or actually, any) handily located motels in Perth.

SLEEPING PRICE RANGES

The following price ranges refer to a double room with bathroom in high season (summer in the south, winter in the north):

$ less than $130

$$ $130 to $250

$$$ more than $250

Best Places to Stay

Best Designer Hotels

Perth is flush with boutique hotels delivering a high-end design experience, often for a midrange outlay. Expect attentive service, uniquely decorated rooms and plenty of chic style.

- Alex Hotel (p76), Perth
- Como The Treasury (p76), Perth
- Aqua (p130), Busselton
- Hougoumont Hotel (p79), Fremantle
- Beach House at Bayside (p159), Albany

Best B&Bs

B&B options range from rooms in heritage buildings to a bedroom in a family home. A full cooked breakfast is not the norm; more often these days you'll receive a hamper with DIY ingredients (bread, cereals, fruit, coffee, jam, butter etc).

- McAlpine House (p218), Broome
- Gecko Lodge (p176), Kalbarri
- Lakeside B&B (p77), Perth
- Manuel Towers (p107), Rockingham
- Denmark Waters B&B (p155), Denmark

Best for Families

Families touring around West Coast Australia will find plenty of distractions, good times and thoughtful extras in beachside caravan parks, resorts and far-flung farmstays. The further you get from the big smoke, the more native wildlife there'll be to keep you company.

- Goombaragin Eco Retreat (p223), Dampier Peninsula
- Broome Beach Resort (p219), Broome

- Big 4 Beachlands Holiday Park (p130), Busselton
- Parry Creek Farm (p238), Parry Creek
- BIG4 Ledge Point Holiday Park (p121), Lancelin

Best on a Budget

From downtown backpackers to far-flung caravan parks, WA has some top places to stay if you're doing it on the cheap. Some hostels – especially in Perth – are the go-to accommodation for short-term 'fly-in, fly-out' (FIFO) workers, which can change the travellers' vibe (preliminary assessment required).

- Beaches of Broome (p218) Broome
- Fonty's Chalets & Caravan Park (p148), Manjimup
- Hostel G (p76), Perth
- 1849 Backpackers (p159), Albany
- Tingle All Over YHA (p153), Walpole

BEN CLARK/500PX ©

Splendid fairywrens, Cape Naturaliste (p134)

Booking

Accommodation availability and pricing on Australia's West Coast is heavily influenced by the seasons. Down south, school holiday periods (Christmas, January and Easter, especially) get hectic – book well in advance and expect to pay top dollar. Conversely, up north, summer is low season and a great time to bag a deal...or come back in peak season (April to October, roughly) and pay a lot more.

Lonely Planet (lonelyplanet.com/hotels) Find independent reviews, as well as recommendations on the best places to stay – and then book them online.

Australian Bed & Breakfast (www.australianbedandbreakfast.com.au) B&B listings, plus some self-catering and farmstay options. Expect to pay $150 to $250.

Bed & Breakfast (www.bedandbreakfast.com.au) Clickable WA regional maps. Prices in the $150-to-$250 range.

Caravan Industry Association WA (www.caravanwa.com.au) WA's holiday parks offer everything from unpowered tent sites to powered van sites, chalets and motel units. Prices range from $30 to $150.

National Parks Camping (https://parks.dpaw.wa.gov.au/park-stay) Some national park camp sites can be booked online. Basic sites start at $8/3 per adult/child. You'll often need to pay park entrance fees too ($13 per car).

Stayz (www.stayz.com.au) Holiday home listings across WA. Prices drift between $100 and $300.

Getting Around

For more information, see Transport (p272)

Travelling by Car

Travelling up and down the Western Australian coast is an indulgence as much as an adventure. There are few places in the world that can deliver refined, urbane experiences (wineries, cities, boutique hotels) alongside pristine wilderness (beaches, forests, caves, reefs), all within in the space of a few hundred kilometres. Of course, the driving distances can be colossal here, too: exploring by car gives you the freedom to bite off as much or as little of this amazing coastline as you like.

Driving Licence

If you're visiting from overseas, you can drive in WA with your home country's driving licence, as long as it has your photo on it and is written in English. If not, you'll need to get hold of an International Driving Permit (IDP) from your home country's automobile association (a handy thing to have, regardless).

Car Hire

Hiring a car in WA is straightforward: all the big-name international operators (Avis, Hertz, Europcar, Budget etc) have desks at Perth Airport, and at many towns and regional airports. You'll also find local operators up and down the coast, generally offering cheaper rates. The catch here is that local outfits often restrict how far you can travel in their vehicles without incurring steep costs: when the landscape is this epic, an unlimited-kilometre deal is probably

RESOURCES

Mainroads (p276) Provides statewide road-condition reports, updated daily (and more frequently if weather conditions are changing rapidly).

Royal Automobile Club of Western Australia (p274) Advice on statewide motoring, including road safety, local regulations and buying/selling a car. Also offers car insurance and various discounts to members, and reciprocal rights with affiliated auto clubs around Australia and beyond.

Cycle Touring Association of WA (www.ctawa.asn.au) Information on touring around WA, including suggested routes, road conditions and cycling maps.

Department of Planning, Lands and Heritage (p274) For permits to travel through Aboriginal land in WA.

what you'll require. One-way hires are also a possibility: shop around.

Driving Conditions

The main highways and roads around West Coast Australia are sealed and in good condition, interlinked by a complex web of dirt roads. A regular 2WD car can usually cope, but for more hardcore explorations you're going to need a 4WD.

- Keep your speed below 80km/h on dirt roads to maintain control.
- Expect flooded roads up north in the wet season (summer).
- Road trains (trucks up to 53m long) are commonplace: overtake with caution.
- Long distances can lead to driver fatigue: take regular breaks.
- Watch out for kangaroos, emus, cattle etc, especially around dusk and dawn.

No Car?

Air

You can cover WA's vast distances quickly with Australia's major domestic airlines or smaller regional operators. It's totally feasible to fly from Perth to Esperance, Exmouth or Broome, then rent a car once you get there.

Bus

Relatively frequent services run between most traveller hotspots, up and down the WA coast. There are good links from Perth to Margaret River and the southwest, and north to Geraldton and Exmouth.

Train

A good option for day trips from Perth to Mandurah and Rockingham, on Perth's suburban train network. Suburban trains also make Fremantle a worthwhile base for exploring Perth. Further afield there are services running from Perth into rural WA, extending all the way to Sydney (the famous *Indian Pacific*).

Bicycle

Cycling around West Coast Australia can be a terrific adventure. Helmets are compulsory, as are white front lights and red rear lights.

Remote riding needs thorough planning, with access to drinking water the key issue. There are no such issues in Perth, but there aren't many on-road bike lanes here: head for the parks and coastal pathways instead.

Public Transport

Perth has an excellent integrated bus, train and ferry network, including free Central Area Transit (CAT) buses looping through the CBD and Fremantle.

DRIVING FAST FACTS

- Drive on the left.
- All vehicle occupants must wear a seatbelt; children need an approved safety seat.
- Talking on a handheld mobile phone while driving is illegal.
- Minimum unsupervised driving age is 17.
- Maximum speed 110km/h on highways and 60km/h in built-up areas, unless signed otherwise.
- Blood alcohol limit 50mg per 100ml (0.05%).

ROAD DISTANCES (KMS)

	Perth	Albany	Broome	Esperance	Exmouth	Kalgoorlie
Albany	420					
Broome	2250	2600				
Esperance	725	500	2725			
Exmouth	1275	1675	1375	1950		
Kalgoorlie	600	825	2350	400	1800	
Margaret River	280	360	2500	725	1525	875

If You Like...

Beaches

Western Australia has some of Australia's biggest and best beaches – and away from the cities and towns, chances are the only footprints in the sand will be yours.

Cottesloe Perth's iconic beach, with cafes and bars close at hand – plenty of footprints here! (p61)

Bunker Bay Brilliant white sand edged by bushland; you'll have to look hard to spot the few houses scattered about. (p134)

Hellfire Bay Sand like talcum powder in the middle of Cape Le Grand National Park, which is precisely in the middle of nowhere. (p166)

Turquoise Bay A beautiful bay in Ningaloo Marine Park, with wonderful snorkelling. (p198)

Cable Beach Surely the most famous, camel-strewn, sunset-photographed beach in WA. (p212)

Cape Leveque Red cliffs and super-duper sunsets on the Dampier Peninsula. (p222)

The Basin A natural sandy swimming pool on Rottnest Island, fringed by reefs. (p102)

Beer & Wine

WA's established wine industry is complemented by a booming craft-beer scene, while vineyard restaurants and providores also abound.

Swan Valley Within suburban Perth's northeastern grasp, the Swan Valley's wineries and microbreweries are packed with city folk on the run. (p112)

Fremantle The traditional home of WA craft beer, from established Little Creatures to more recent players like The Monk. (p92)

Margaret River Known for its Bordeaux-style varietals, chardonnay and sauvignon blanc, as well as a growing number of craft breweries. (p131)

Pemberton Another esteemed wine area, producing highly quaffable pinot noir, chardonnay and sauvignon blanc. (p148)

Denmark Notable wineries and craft breweries dot this picturesque part of the cool-climate Great Southern wine region. (p154)

Mt Barker & Porongurup The most significant subregion of the Great Southern, producing cool-climate riesling, pinot noir and cabernet sauvignon. (p161)

Aboriginal Art & Culture

Around 77,000 Aboriginal people call WA home, comprising many different Indigenous peoples, speaking many distinct languages.

Art Gallery of Western Australia A treasure trove of Indigenous art. (p60)

Wula Gura Nyinda Eco Adventures Offers bushwalks and kayak tours, and you'll learn some local Malgana language. (p180)

Djurandi Dreaming Aboriginal cultural walking tours around Elizabeth Quay precinct in downtown Perth. (p72)

The Kimberley View artists' cooperatives, visit ancient rock art, and get to know 'Country' on a cultural tour. (p209)

Ngurrangga Tours Cultural and rock-art tours in Murujuga National Park in the Pilbara. (p201)

Wundargoodie Aboriginal Safaris Offering a women-only Kimberley Spiritual Experience. (p228)

East Pilbara Arts Centre This striking centre in Newman beautifully showcases the acclaimed works of the Martumili artists. (p205)

Top: Hellfire Bay (p166), Cape Le Grand National Park.

Bottom: Gnaraloo Station (p186), Quobba Coast

Bushwalking

The state's dozens of national parks are laced with hundreds of walking tracks, heading along the coast, deep into forests, through gorges and up mountainsides.

Bibbulmun Track This is the big one, stretching 1000km from the edge of Perth through the southern forests to Albany. (p159)

Cape to Cape Track Enjoy Indian Ocean views on this 135km trail from Cape Naturaliste to Cape Leeuwin. (p142)

Stirling Range National Park Climb every mountain...or maybe just one or two in this luscious range, known for its flora and chameleon-like ability to change colour. (p163)

Punurrunha (Mt Bruce) In Karijini National Park tackle WA's second-highest peak and scan the show-stopping views along the ridge. (p207)

Mitchell Falls (Punamii-unpuu) The 8.6km track heads through spinifex, woodlands and gorges, passing Aboriginal rock art on the way. (p229)

Foodie Touring

People don't necessarily travel to WA for the cuisine, but there are plenty of foodie surprises in the state's gastronomic hotspots.

Perth No longer the poor cousin to the eastern capitals, the Perth restaurant scene is consistently exciting and continually evolving. (p80)

Swan Valley Dubbed the 'Valley of Taste' (who comes up with these things?), with winery restaurants, cafes and providores. (p112)

Margaret River Wine Region Enjoy marvellous meals, beautiful scenery and often audacious architecture in WA's top wine region. (p131)

Manjimup Hunt for truffles at the Wine & Truffle Co, and dine from a menu infused with this pungent fungus. (p147)

Lobster Shack In Cervantes, this slick seafood operation puts some crayfish in your dish. (p122)

Broome Mango Festival Held in November, the harvest is celebrated with the Great Chefs of Broome Cook-Off. (p218)

Getting off the Beaten Path

In a destination so varied and expansive, there are plenty of spectacular opportunities to craft your own journey of discovery.

Mornington Wilderness Camp The 95km stretch from the Gibb River Road to this riverside oasis is some of WA's most exquisite, lonely country. (p229)

Dryandra Woodland Less than two hours from Perth, but a world away, with endangered populations of endemic wildlife. (p113)

Gnaraloo Station Come for a night and stay for a month as your skills are put to work on this sustainable station. (p186)

Guilderton A locals' holiday haunt north of Perth at the mouth of the Moore River: surfing, fishing, swimming...all the good things. (p120)

Middle Lagoon Life doesn't get much more laid-back than at this Dampier Peninsula beachside campground far from anywhere in particular. (p223)

Duncan Road A real outback adventure without the masses, Duncan Road is both a destination itself and a 'long cut' to the Northern Territory. (p232)

Diving & Snorkelling

Reefs and wrecks are plentiful around WA and the marine life abundant, providing a smorgasbord of options for geared-up diving pros or gung-ho first-time snorkellers.

Mettams Pool Suburban snorkelling in Perth's northern suburbs. (p61)

Rottnest Island Over a dozen wrecks and two underwater snorkelling trails make this an excellent destination for snorkel fans. (p102)

Busselton Lots to see around the southern hemisphere's longest timber jetty, plus the wreck of a decommissioned navy destroyer not far offshore. (p130)

Albany Keep an eye out for leafy sea dragons among the coral reefs. (p159)

Houtman Abrolhos Islands Dive, snorkel, bushwalk or fish around these historic islands, which rarely see tourists. (p174)

Surfing & Windsurfing

Wax the board and fire up the Kombi: WA's surf is legendary.

Trigg Beach Perth surfers head to the city's northern beaches after work to catch a few waves. (p63)

Lancelin A mecca for windsurfers and kitesurfers, and a great spot to learn. (p121)

Yallingup/Margaret River 'Yals' and 'Margs' are the hub of the WA surf scene – with a major pro competition held here every year. (p135)

Ocean Beach You might find yourself sharing this beautiful Denmark bay with the odd whale. (p154)

Geraldton The surrounding beaches are a hotspot for both wind- and wave-powered surfers. (p172)

Gnaraloo Surfers flock here in winter to try their luck at the famous Tombstones break; in summer the windsurfers get their turn. (p186)

Marine Mammals

Make an informed, ethical choice about interacting with WA's creatures of the deep: humanity owes them a little peace and quiet!

Perth & Fremantle Thirty thousand whales cruise past between mid-September and early December. (p54)

Rockingham Cruise out into Shoalwater Islands Marine Park to spy dolphins and seals. (p106)

Dampier Peninsula Excellent whale-watching from a viewing platform. (p222)

Bunbury Wild dolphins regularly approach the shoreline. (p127)

Albany Between July and mid-October the bay turns into a whale nursery, with mothers and calves easily spotted from the beach. (p158)

Monkey Mia Watch dolphins feeding in the shallows and take a dugong-spotting cruise. (p182)

Month by Month

TOP EVENTS

Perth Festival, February

Fremantle Festival, July

Kings Park Festival, September

Margaret River Gourmet Escape, November

Blues at Bridgetown Festival, November

January

The peak of the summer school holidays sees families head to the beach en masse. Days are hot and dry, except in the far north, where the wet season is in full force.

Perth Cup

Perth's high-society players flock to the annual Perth Cup, a party-prone day of high-heels, expensive suits, champagne and fascinators (oh, and there's a few horse races happening too). (p73)

Lancelin Ocean Classic

In early January tiny Lancelin's legendary bluster attracts thousands for its world-famous windsurfing event. Held over four days, the event hosts wave sailing alongside jet-skiing, beach runs and good stuff to eat and drink. (p121)

Fringe World Festival

A month-long arts fest in Perth, dipping into weird, quirky, embarrassing, hilarious and sometimes-offensive terrain. How refreshing! Runs from mid-January into mid-February. (p73)

February

The kids head back to school, freeing up some room at the beach and taking some of the pressure off coastal accommodation. It's still hot and dry in the south, and soggy in the north.

Laneway Festival

International bands on the rise, mostly with a boho indie vibe, entice WA students and hipsters to Freo's West End for the annual Laneway Festival. (p73)

Leeuwin Concert

Leeuwin Estate in Margaret River hosts top-flight performers (James Taylor, Diana Krall, Sting, Paul Kelly) on its winery stage during this annual event in mid-February; other concerts run from January to April. (p144)

Perth Festival

Held over 25 days from mid-February, the Perth Festival attracts an international line-up, spanning theatre, classical music, jazz, visual arts, dance, film, literature – the whole gamut. It's worth scheduling your trip around it. (p73)

March

It's still beach weather, but it's not quite so swelteringly hot down south. It's steamy in the north, however, and the rain is still bucketing down. Accommodation prices shoot up over Easter.

Nannup Music Festival

The sleepy southwest forest town of Nannup erupts into life with this annual festival, which hosts up to 30,000 fans of folk, blues and world music. Buskers make the most of the opportunity. (p146)

April

A peerless month in Perth, with temperatures dropping to the mid-20s and a little refreshing rainfall. Up north they're finally starting to dry out; it's a great time for a Kimberley fly-over.

May

Temperatures creep down and Broome and Exmouth both finally drop below the 30s, making them particularly appealing – especially now the box jellyfish have retreated. Autumn showers are more common in the south.

Ord Valley Muster

For 10 days Kununurra hits overdrive during the annual Ord Valley Muster, a collection of sundry sporting, charity and cultural events leading up to a large outdoor concert under the full moon on the banks of the Ord River. (p234)

Margaret River Pro

This World Surf League (WSL) event sees the world's top surfers duke it out in the epic surf at Margaret River (...unless there are sharks around, as there were in 2018 when the event was cancelled). (p139)

June

Winter hits Perth with plenty of rain and even the occasional dusting of snow on the Stirling Range further south. The warm, dry north, however, heads into peak season. Whales arrive offshore from Augusta.

Festival of Voice

Rousing choruses banish the winter blues in the south-coast town of Denmark during the Festival of Voice, held over the June long weekend. The town is flooded with soloists, duos, choristers and their admirers. It's accompanied by a workshop program. (p155)

July

It's wet and cold in the south and beautiful in the north – sparking a winter-break exodus from Perth. Whales congregate in the bays around Albany.

Kullarri Naidoc Week

Aboriginal art exhibitions and performances take place throughout WA during National Aboriginal & Islander Day Observance Committee week (Naidoc; www.naidoc.org.au), which celebrates the history, culture and achievements of Aboriginal people. One of the best happens in Broome. (p217)

Fremantle Festival

Ten days of parades, performances, music, dance, comedy, visual arts, street theatre and workshops. Founded in 1905, it's Australia's longest-running festival. Highlights include the Kite Extravaganza on South Beach and the Wardarnji Indigenous Festival. (p73)

Boab Festival

Little Derby in the northwest goes big-time berserk with concerts, mud footy, horse and mudcrab races, film festivals, poetry readings, art exhibitions, street parades and a dinner out on the mudflats. (p226)

August

Lovely in the north, but still damp and cold in the south, though temperatures do start to edge up. Manjimup truffles come into season, to the delight of Perth's chefs and their customers; whales continue to hang out along the south coast.

Avon Descent

Northam and Toodyay both crank up the festivities to coincide with the Avon Descent, a gruelling 124km white-water-rafting event for powerboats, kayaks and canoes between the two towns. Toodyay's party takes a foodie turn: the Toodyay International Food Festival. (p115)

Broome Race Round

The local fillies and stallions dress up and drink insensible amounts as the Broome Race Round climaxes with the Kimberley Cup, Ladies Day and the Broome Cup – all held in early August. (p217)

CinéfestOz

The snoozy southwest town of Busselton assumes a cinematic sheen with this festival celebrating Australian and French cinema, lifting the lid on winter.

Look forward to events and screenings in venues around town. (p130)

September

Spring brings a frisson of excitement across WA, with wildflowers blooming and whales shimmying up the coast. Broome pops back into the 30s and the tourists turn around and drive south.

Shinju Matsuri Festival of the Pearl

Starting in either late August or early September, Broome's Shinju Matsuri festival celebrates the town's pearl industry and multicultural heritage with a carnival of nations, a film festival, art exhibitions, food, concerts, fireworks and dragon-boat races. (p218)

Kings Park Festival

In September and early October, Perth's Kings Park & Botanic Garden are in bloom with technicoloured wildflowers in the annual Kings Park Festival, celebrating WA's unique and spectacular flora. Expect plenty of walks, talks and live-music shindigs. (p75)

Red Earth Arts Festival

Over 10 days, Karratha and the surrounding coastal Pilbara towns kick into gear with the Red Earth Arts Festival, an eclectic mix of live music, theatre, comedy, visual arts (film, photography, sculpture) and storytelling. (p201)

October

The last of the whales depart the south coast and hit the west-coast leg of the Humpback Hwy. The weather is noticeably warmer and drier now, the WA crayfishing season opens and the wildflowers are bloomin' marvellous.

Perth Royal Show

The country comes to the city for the west's biggest agricultural show. For the local kids it's a week of funfair rides, too much sugar, creepy toothless carnies and showbags full of plastic junk. (p75)

Sunshine Festival

It started in 1959 as a tomato festival, but now Geraldton's solar celebrations include dragon-boat races, parades, sand sculptures and parties. It's held over a week in early October. Sunshine guaranteed. (p173)

Blessing of the Fleet

This popular traditional Catholic festival, marking the traditional opening of the crayfish season, was introduced to Fremantle by young Italian fishermen in 1948. It includes the procession of statues from St Patrick's Basilica to Fishing Boat Harbour, where the blessing takes place. (p75)

November

A great time to be in Fremantle, with temperatures in the mid-20s, very little rain and a convoy of whales passing by. In the far north, it's the start of the box-jellyfish season. Look before you leap.

Blues at Bridgetown Festival

Now into its third decade, one of Western Australia's longest-running music festivals infuses the south-western centre of Bridgetown with blues, folk and roots music on the second weekend of November. (p146)

Margaret River Gourmet Escape

The culinary world's heavy hitters (Nigella Lawson, Rick Stein, Heston Blumenthal et al) descend on Margaret River for four days of culinary inspiration. Australia's growing crew of celeb chefs usually put in an appearance as well. (p139)

Mango Festival

Broome celebrates the mango harvest with four days of mango-themed everything: a quiz night, a fashion parade and a Great Chefs of Broome Cook-Off. If you don't come away with sticky fingers and an orange stain on your shirt, you ain't doing it right. (p218)

December

Ring the bell – school's out! Summer arrives in WA and the kids hit the beach, while a Christmas shopping frenzy ensues in downtown Perth. Rain clouds gather up north: here comes the wet.

Itineraries

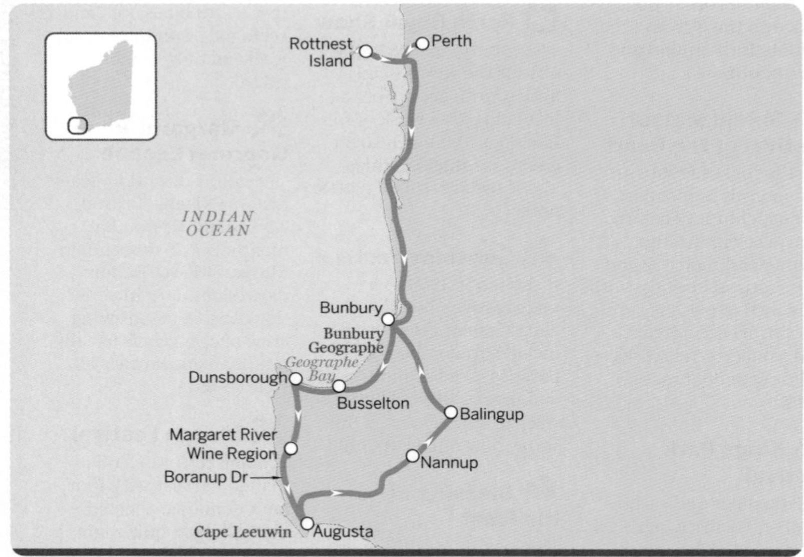

A Southwest Short Circuit

Pressed for time? This itinerary offers a taste of the best of the state – city life, colonial history, beaches, wildlife, wine, forests and lonesome rural roads.

Base yourself in **Perth**, either in the city centre or Fremantle, and spend three days exploring: don't miss Fremantle Prison, Cottesloe Beach and Kings Park. Is the New Museum for Western Australia open yet? Ferry out for a day on **Rottnest Island**, then hire a car and head south, stopping first at **Bunbury** for a visit to the Dolphin Discovery Centre. Continue on to **Bunbury Geographe**, basing yourself in either **Busselton** or **Dunsborough**, and spend the rest of the day at the beach. Pick up a map of the **Margaret River Wine Region** and spend day six checking out the wineries, surf beaches and caves, all of which are close by. Sleep in the Margaret River township that night. The next morning, head to **Augusta** via Caves Rd and take the scenic detour through the karri forest along unsealed **Boranup Drive**. Visit **Cape Leeuwin**, where the Indian and Southern Oceans collide, before heading back to Bunbury on a picturesque rural drive through **Nannup** and **Balingup**. From here it's a two-hour drive back to Perth.

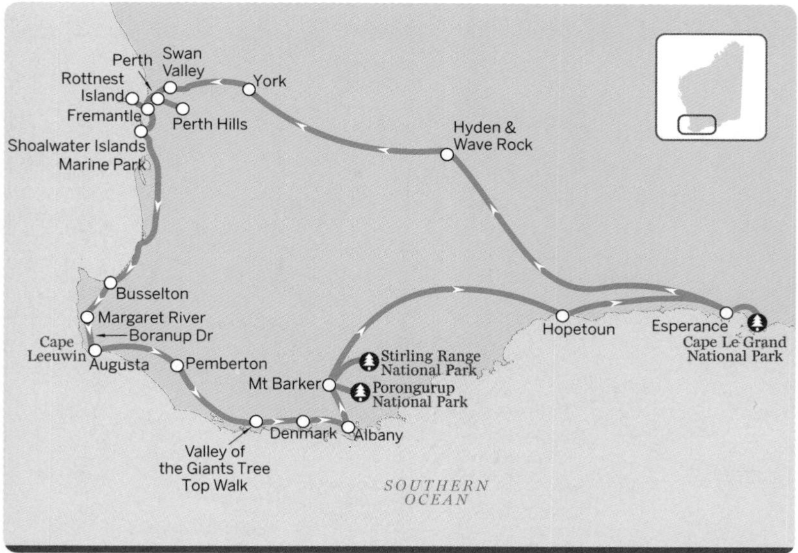

3 WEEKS

The Southwest Uncut

Western Australia's southwest is a magical corner of the continent. This itinerary checks off the main highlights over three weeks - give it a month to really relax into it.

Spend three days in **Perth** and **Fremantle** – the WA Shipwrecks Museum is a must – then beach yourself for a day on **Rottnest Island** or hit the wineries in the underrated **Perth Hills**. Truck south to Geographe Bay – stopping at Rockingham to wade out to **Shoalwater Islands Marine Park** – before overnighting in **Busselton**. After a morning walk along the town's epic jetty, continue for two nights in **Margaret River** township, exploring the local breweries, wineries, surf beaches and caves.

The following morning head to **Augusta** via Caves Rd, detouring along scenic **Boranup Drive** with its karri trees. At **Cape Leeuwin**, pinpoint the exact spot where the Indian and Southern Oceans meet, then continue to sleepy **Pemberton**. Don't miss the Karri Forest Explorer scenic drive. The next day, visit the extraordinary **Valley of the Giants Tree Top Walk** near Walpole and overnight in hippie-meets-city **Denmark**. Assess the beaches, wineries, breweries and restaurants here, before two days in history-rich **Albany**.

Head north for more Great Southern wineries at **Mt Barker** before tracking east to **Porongurup National Park**. Spend the next day (or two) tackling the mountainous tracks either here or at **Stirling Range National Park**.

Continue to the South Coast Hwy and at Ravensthorpe hop down to **Hopetoun** – it's a three-hour drive from the Stirling Range (spend the afternoon at the beach). The following day, head back to the South Coast Hwy and continue east around 2½ hours for two days in **Esperance** and **Cape Le Grand National Park**.

Back on the South Coast Hwy, turn north just past Ravensthorpe for **Hyden** and the curvilicious granite of **Wave Rock** – around four hours.

The following day, head west to the Avon Valley and classically colonial **York**. On your final day back to Perth, stop at the **Swan Valley** for craft beer and wineries.

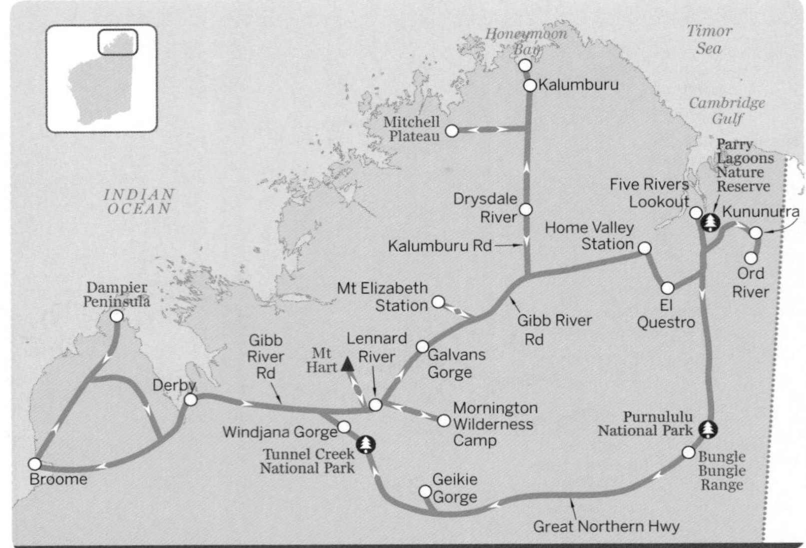

Kimberley Outback

This is the biggest adventure in the west, leaving Broome during the dry season and traversing the rugged heart of Kimberley by 4WD.

From **Broome**, the first stop is the **Dampier Peninsula**, with its Aboriginal communities, beautiful beaches and mud crabs. It's also your last saltwater swim. Take the back road to **Derby** and its boabs, then roll onto the **Gibb River Road**. **Lennard River** is the first of many inviting gorges here. Explore wildlife and more gorges at **Mt Hart** and remote **Mornington Wilderness Camp**, and look for examples of Wandjina art at **Galvans Gorge** and **Mt Elizabeth Station**. Turn off onto the **Kalumburu Road**, check the road conditions at **Drysdale River** and drive on to the **Mitchell Plateau**, with its forests of *livistona* and astonishing waterfalls. Discover the area's ancient rock art before hitting the northern coast for some top-flight fishing at **Honeymoon Bay**, just beyond the mission community of **Kalumburu**.

Retrace your route back to the Gibb, then turn left for wonderful **Home Valley Station**, where soft beds make a happy change from camping. Nearby **El Questro** has gorges aplenty, none more beautiful than Emma Gorge near the resort. Soon you're back on asphalt, but not for long as you take in the amazing birdlife of **Parry Lagoons Nature Reserve**. Let Wyndham's **Five Rivers Lookout** blow your mind, before heading for the civility of **Kununurra**, with its excellent eateries. Canoe down the mighty **Ord River**, or jump back behind the wheel for the wonders of **Purnululu National Park** and the orange-domed **Bungle Bungle Range**.

Darwin and the Northern Territory are beckoning, or you can follow the Great Northern Hwy back to Broome, stopping in at beautiful **Geikie Gorge** for a relaxing boat cruise: any freshwater crocs? There are plenty at nearby **Windjana Gorge**, sunning themselves on the riverbanks. En route, grab your torch and wade through the icy waters of **Tunnel Creek National Park**, with its bats and rock art. From Windjana, plant the pedal back to Broome, where the price of beer probably won't bother you as much as it did a month ago.

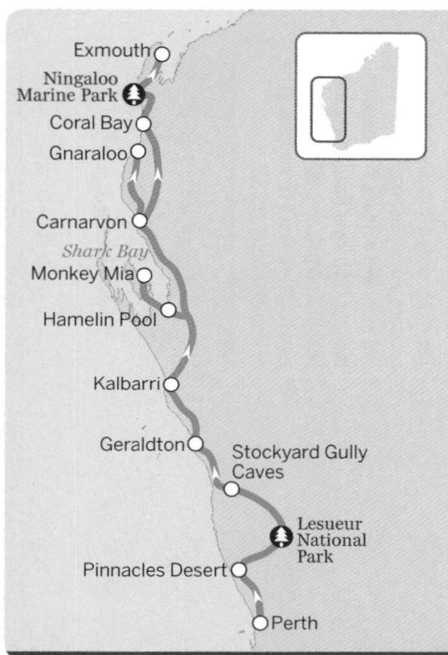

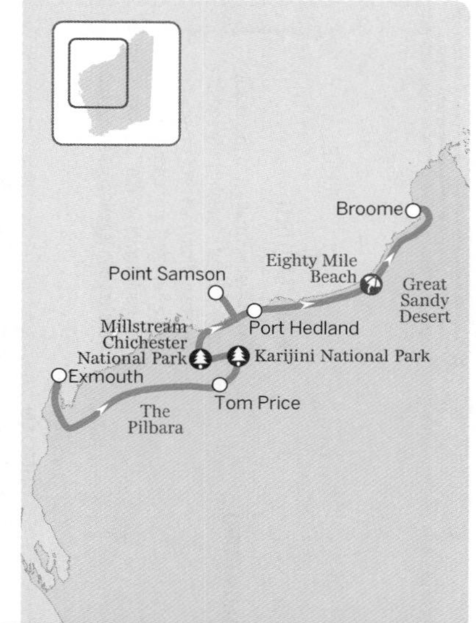

2 WEEKS Indian Ocean Dreaming

Beautiful beaches, spectacular sunsets and diverse wildlife are your constant companions on this coastal cruise.

Take Indian Ocean Dr north from **Perth** to Cervantes for a crayfish dinner and sunset over the otherwordly **Pinnacles Desert**. Assess the native blooms at **Lesueur National Park**, take your 4WD to the **Stockyard Gully Caves**, then hit the cafes and museums of **Geraldton**. Try kitesurfing on for size, then move on to the wonderful **Kalbarri** coastline. Paddle a canoe in the gorges before the long drive to World Heritage–listed **Shark Bay**. Spy some dolphins and dugongs at **Monkey Mia**, and sign up for an Indigenous cultural tour. Check out the stromatolites of **Hamelin Pool** before hitting **Carnarvon**. Drop into **Gnaraloo** for world-class waves before arriving at tiny **Coral Bay** and **Exmouth**, where whale sharks, humpback whales, manta rays and turtles inhabit the exquisite **Ningaloo Marine Park**. Fly out of Exmouth, drive back to Perth, or push on to the gorgeous gorges of Karijini.

1 WEEK Jewels of the Pilbara

You'll camp most of the way on this missing link between Ningaloo and Broome, with long empty beaches, shady pools and some surprisingly good food.

From **Exmouth**, take Burkett Rd back to the highway and head north, turning off at Nanutarra for the long, scenic haul up to **Tom Price**. After stocking up, spend the next few days camped in **Karijini National Park**, exploring sublime gorges and engaging in a spot of peak-bagging among the state's highest mountains. Don't miss a swim at Hamersley Gorge en route to the relaxing, shady pools in **Millstream Chichester National Park**. Check out the mesas and breakaways of the Chichester Range before dropping down to the coast, assessing the petroglyphs at Murujuga, then on to lovely **Point Samson** for snorkelling. Take the North West Coastal Hwy directly to **Port Hedland** and indulge in some urban eats before camping at remote **Eighty Mile Beach**, where you might spot nesting turtles. Your last leg is a long stretch of nothingness (how amazing!) as you skirt the **Great Sandy Desert** to arrive in tropical **Broome**.

Off the Beaten Track - West Coast Australia

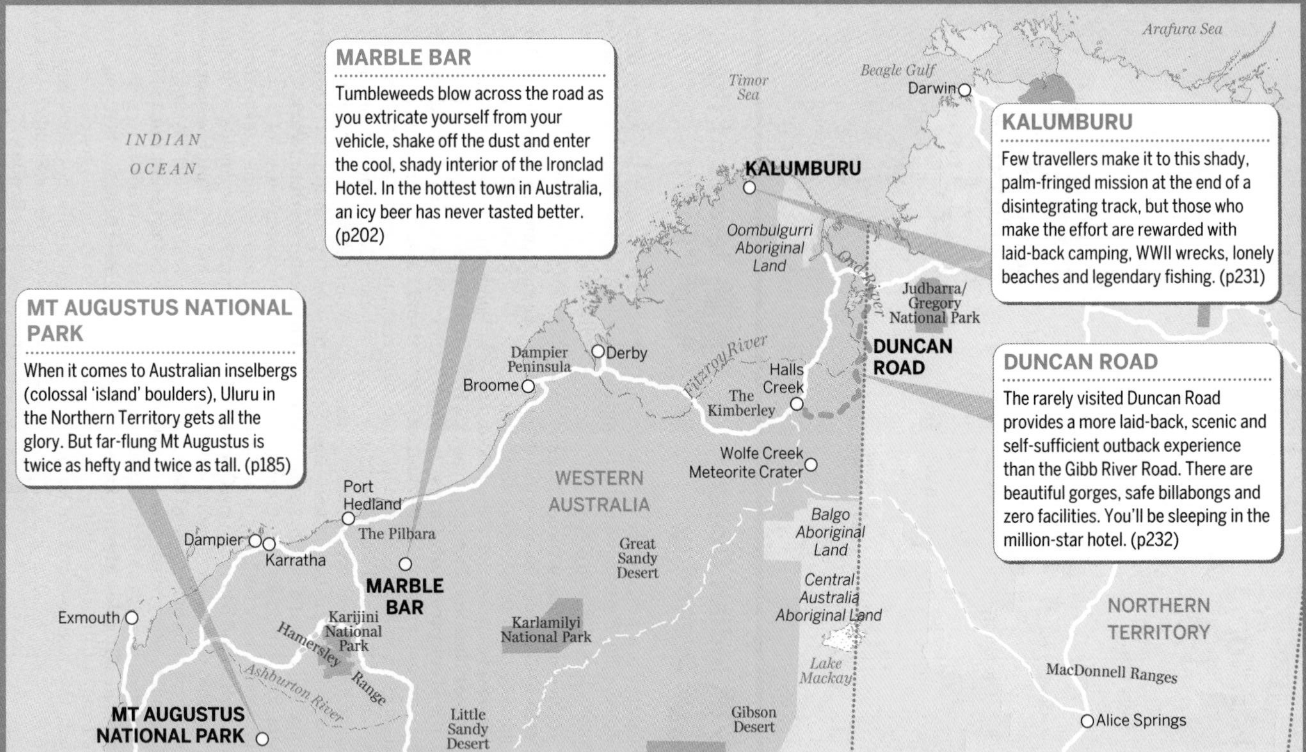

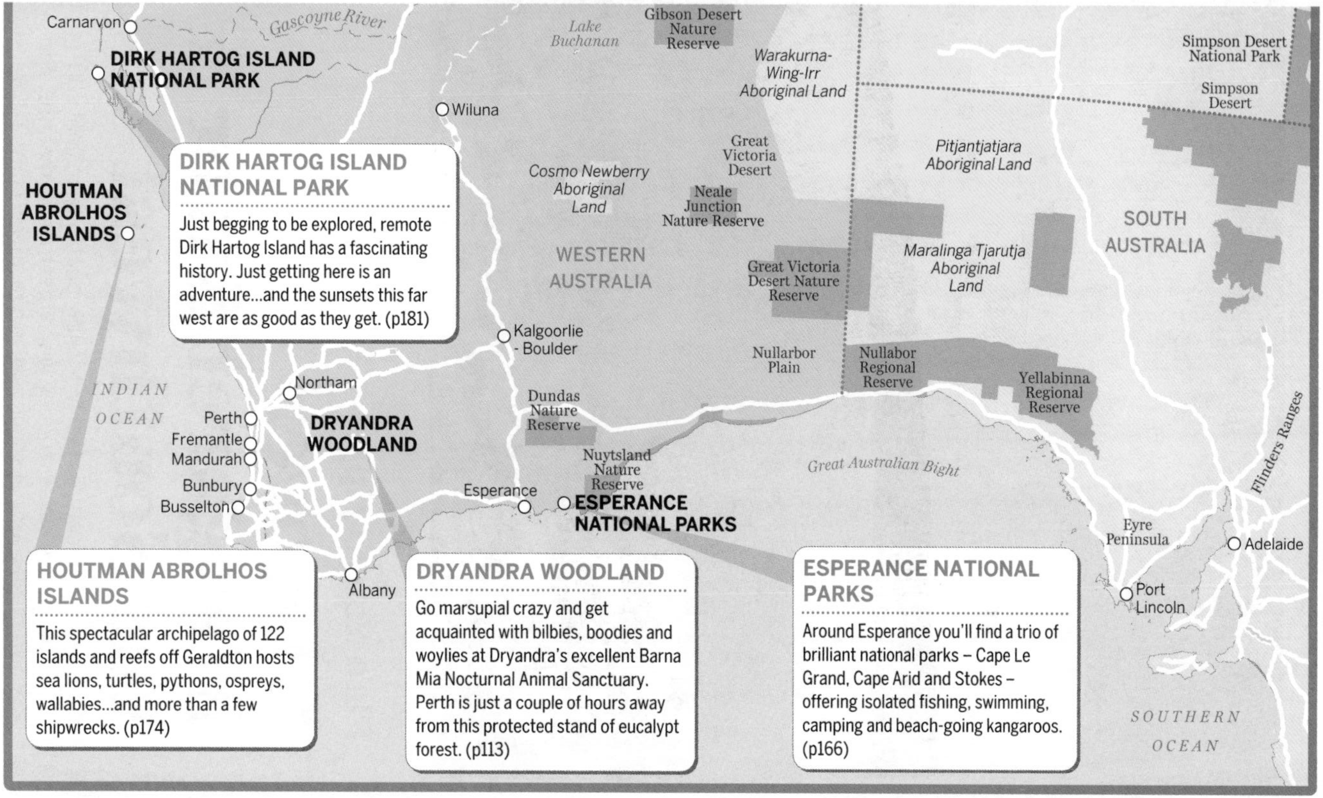

DIRK HARTOG ISLAND NATIONAL PARK

Just begging to be explored, remote Dirk Hartog Island has a fascinating history. Just getting here is an adventure...and the sunsets this far west are as good as they get. (p181)

HOUTMAN ABROLHOS ISLANDS

This spectacular archipelago of 122 islands and reefs off Geraldton hosts sea lions, turtles, pythons, ospreys, wallabies...and more than a few shipwrecks. (p174)

DRYANDRA WOODLAND

Go marsupial crazy and get acquainted with bilbies, boodies and woylies at Dryandra's excellent Barna Mia Nocturnal Animal Sanctuary. Perth is just a couple of hours away from this protected stand of eucalypt forest. (p113)

ESPERANCE NATIONAL PARKS

Around Esperance you'll find a trio of brilliant national parks – Cape Le Grand, Cape Arid and Stokes – offering isolated fishing, swimming, camping and beach-going kangaroos. (p166)

Margaret River bea

Plan Your Trip

Discover Margaret River & the Southwest

Margaret River features family-friendly beaches, brilliant surfing, labyrinthine caves studded with limestone formations, and a world-class gourmet scene – all in a relatively compact area. Vineyards segue into rural back roads punctuated with craft breweries, provedores, dairies, chocolate shops and art galleries.

Best Times to Be Here

For a beach holiday December to March.

For surfing Any time, but the big Surf Pro is in March.

For wineries, breweries and caves All year.

For whale watching June to September from Augusta, September to December from Dunsborough.

For peak gourmet November's Gourmet Escape.

...And Best Times to Avoid

Beach towns in January Unless you've booked accommodation in advance, as this is the busiest time for families.

Dunsborough in November End-of-school revellers descend though it's well managed most of the time.

Margaret River town weekends Accommodation prices are higher and there are always loads of people – but at least everything will be open.

The Lay of the Land

The sheltered white sands of Geographe Bay start south of Bunbury and arch along to Cape Naturaliste. Busselton and Dunsborough are the bay's main towns. At Cape Naturaliste the coastline pirouettes and runs nearly due south to Cape Leeuwin. The wine region runs parallel to this coast with the Margaret River itself cutting roughly east to west through the centre, passing through the town of the same name to the beach with the same name. Wineries are scattered all around, but the biggest concentration is found north of the river.

Things to See & Do

Much of the Margaret River experience is based on indulgence – the wineries, craft-beer breweries and distilleries here are world class – but to balance the virtue-vs-vice ledger, get active amid the region's stunning scenery. Surfing, swimming and walking are obvious choices, but there's also caving, diving and kayaking – to name a few.

Wineries

Wine time? Pick up one of the excellent free wine-region maps from local visitor centres, squabble over who's going to be the nondrinking driver, and dive right in. Look forward to sampling some excellent chardonnays and Bordeaux-style reds. The other alternative is to take a tour – public transport isn't a workable option.

Most of the wineries here offer tastings between 10am and 5pm daily. At busy times (this includes every weekend), consider booking ahead for lunch before you set out.

The pick of the bunch:

Amiria (p143) Down-a-dirt-road delight, with fabulous meals and organic and biodynamic wines.

Cape Mentelle (p137) A real stayer on the Margs wine scene (since 1970!) with outdoor movies to boot.

Stormflower Vineyard (p141) Rustic and laid-back, with a catchy name you won't soon forget.

Thompson Estate (p142) One for the architecture fans among us.

Voyager Estate (p141) A major player with a highly rated restaurant.

Surfing

Known to surfers as 'Yals' (around Yallingup) and 'Margs' (around the mouth of the Margaret River), the beaches between Capes Naturaliste and Leeuwin offer powerful reef breaks, mainly left-handers (the direction you take after catching a wave). The surf at Margs has been described by surfing supremo Nat Young as 'epic', and by world surfing champ Mark Richards as 'one of the world's finest'.

As is the way with such hotspots, surfers can be quite territorial, so respect the etiquette and defer to locals if you're

Fairy-floss topped doughnut, Voyager Estate (p141)

Margaret River vineyard

unsure. If you're planning on spending a lot of time on the breaks, call in to the surf shops and get to know some locals.

Around Dunsborough, the better locations include Rocky Point (short left-hander) and the Farm and Bone Yards (right-handers), which are between Eagle and Bunker Bays. Near Yallingup there are the Three Bears (Papa, Mama and Baby, of course), Rabbits (a beach break towards the north of Yallingup Beach), Yallingup (reef with breaks left and right), and Injidup Car Park and Injidup Point (right-hand tube on a heavy swell; left-hander). You'll need a 4WD to access Guillotine/Gallows (right-hander), north of Gracetown. Also around Gracetown are Huzza's (an easy break within the beach), South Point (popular break) and Lefthanders (the name says it all). The annual surfer pro is held around Margaret River Mouth and Southside ('Suicides') in April.

Pick up a surfing map from one of the visitor centres.

Surfing is never without its risks. People have been killed by sharks in the vicinity of Gracetown and a shark attacked an inflatable boat near Dunsborough a few years back.

SOUTHWEST SURPRISES

- Street art and work by celebrated visual artists are found in Bunbury (p127).
- A highly rated French-Australian film festival, CinéfestOZ (p130), is held annually in beachy Busselton.
- A colony of red-tailed tropicbirds (p136) roosts off Cape Naturaliste.
- Most vineyard restaurants aren't open after dark; this is a daytime region.

Beer is the New Wine

West Coast Australia has been fully swept away by the global craft-beer tide, with an innovative generation of local brewers proving there's more to beer than innocuous Euro lagers. Around Margaret River, look forward to a global array of styles including IPAs, Belgian ales and meaty chocolate porters. Many breweries serve

Lake Cave (p141)

bar snacks and lunch. As per the wineries, brewery tours are a great way to go.
The Caves Rd and Busselton Hwy areas, extending north and northwest of Margaret River township, host a particularly interesting collection of breweries in which to while away a lazy afternoon (or two):

Beer Farm (p143) Kids, foods, dogs and IPA – all the good things in life.

Bootleg Brewery (p143) Putting a US spin on the local scene...plus live music!

Caves Road Collective (p143) Black Brewing Company delivers the goods, in cahoots with a local distiller and winemaker.

Cheeky Monkey (p143) Lakeside eats and sips, including a cheeky cider.

Cowaramup Brewing Company (Map p132; ☎08-9755 5822; www.cowaramupbrewing.com.au; North Treeton Rd, Cowaramup; ⏲11am-6pm) A mod operator with primo pilsner and pale ale.

Going Underground

The main cave complexes are spread, perhaps unsurprisingly, along Caves Rd. Ngilgi Cave (p134) sits by itself near Yallingup, but the other main complexes are between Margaret River township and Augusta. Lake Cave (p141), Jewel Cave (p145) and Mammoth Cave (p142) can be seen on a combined ticket.

Other Attractions

Beaches And lots of them; they're particularly beautiful between Dunsborough and Cape Naturaliste.

Walking There are excellent tracks around Cape Naturaliste and between the capes.

Diving Trips leave from Busselton and Dunsborough to explore local wrecks and reefs.

Whale watching Cruises leave from Augusta (starting in June) and Dunsborough (starting in September).

Lighthouses Both capes have them and both can be visited. From Cape Leeuwin you can watch the Indian and Southern Oceans collide.

Adventure sports From mountain biking to climbing and canoeing.

Murchison River, Kalbarri National Park (p17

Plan Your Trip

West Coast Australia Outdoors

With incredible landscapes and seascapes, intriguing native wildlife and all that brilliant sunshine, West Coast Australia is the perfect playground for outdoor enthusiasts, with tracks to hike, waves to surf and reefs to explore.

Best Daredevil Activities

Scramble, abseil, slide and dive through the gorges of the Karijini National Park, or ride the surge in a speedboat on the Horizontal Waterfalls near Derby. Kite- and wind-surfing at Lancelin is also heart-pumping, especially when the breeze gets its game on. You can also try abseiling at the Perth Observatory (p110) in the Perth Hills.

Best Wildflower Spots

Kings Park and Botanic Garden (p60) Perth.

Fitzgerald River National Park (p165) Between Albany and Esperance.

Porongurup National Park (p162) North of Albany.

Stirling Range National Park (p163) North of Albany.

Kalbarri National Park (p178) On the Batavia Coast.

Wildflower Way (p118) Between Wongan Hills and Geraldton.

Lesueur National Park (p123) On the Turquoise Coast.

Bushwalking

WA's excellent bushwalking terrain includes the southwest's cool forests, the blister-inducing 1000km Bibbulmun Track (p159) and the north's rugged national parks.

See www.trailswa.com.au and www.bushwalkingwa.org.au for walk and bushwalking club details. To contact potential walking buddies, or to buy and sell gear, see the forums on www.bushwalk.com.

For tips on responsible bushwalking, see the camping and bushwalking guidelines online at https://parks.dpaw.wa.gov.au.

Perth & Surrounds

With hiking and camping facilities, **John Forrest National Park** (☎08-9290 6100; www.parks.dpaw.wa.gov.au/park/john-forrest; via Park Rd, Hovea; per car $13; ⏲24hr) in the Perth Hills has an easy 15km walk to waterfalls and the must-do 340m walk through the brick-lined Swan View Tunnel. The rugged **Walyunga National Park** (☎08-9290 6100; www.parks.dpaw.wa.gov.au/park/walyunga; per vehicle $13; ⏲8am-5pm), also in the Perth Hills, features a medium-to-hard 18km walk that fords the Avon River and has excellent wildlife viewing. Yanchep National Park (p120) north of the city has short strolls and challenging full-day walks. The 28km Yaberoo Budjara Heritage Trail here follows an Aboriginal walking trail.

Down South

Serious walkers gravitate to the ruggedly beautiful Stirling Range National Park (p163). Top walks here include the Bluff Knoll climb (6km, three to four hours). Visit from September to November for the park's flowering glory (1500 species) and be prepared for wind chill and rain (and sometimes snow!) in winter.

North of Albany is the smaller Porongurup National Park (p162), with spectacular granite rocks and dense karri forest. Trails here include the 10-minute Tree in the Rock stroll, the medium-grade Hayward and Nancy Peaks hike (three hours), and the challenging three-hour Marmabup Rock hike. Wildflowers and bird buzz make springtime the peak season for Porongurup, but it can be visited year-round.

For some amazing coastal highlights, walk through Walpole-Nornalup, Fitzgerald River and Cape Le Grand National Parks. The Cape to Cape Track (p142) follows the coastline 135km from Cape Naturaliste to Cape Leeuwin, taking five to seven days, and features wild campsites en-route.

Albany, also down south, is the terminus of the Bibbulmum Track.

Up North

Summer's no picnic in the sweltering, remote national parks of WA's north, so high season for many bushwalkers here is from April to October. The arid terrain can be treacherous, so research carefully, be prepared with water and supplies, and check

THE BIBBULMUN TRACK

Taking around eight weeks, the 1000km Bibbulmun Track (p159) goes from Kalamunda, 20km east of Perth in the Perth Hills, through mainly natural environment to Walpole and Albany.

Terrain includes jarrah and marri forests, wildflowers, granite outcrops, coastal heath country and eye-popping coastlines.

Comfortable campsites are spaced regularly along the track. The best time to tackle it is from August to October, before things get too hot.

in with local rangers just after you lace up your boots.

Kalbarri National Park (p178) showcases scenic gorges, thick bushland and rugged coastal cliffs. A popular six-hour loop features dramatic seascapes, including spectacular Nature's Window.

Rugged, sometimes-hazardous treks can be taken into the dramatic gorges of Karijini National Park (p205). The walk to the Punurrunha (Mt Bruce) summit (9km, five hours) is popular with experienced bushwalkers.

Visitors to the Kimberley's Purnululu National Park (p236) come to see the striped beehive-shaped domes of the World Heritage–listed Bungle Bungles. Walks include the easy Cathedral Gorge walk, and the more difficult overnight trek to Piccaninny Gorge. The park is only open from April to November.

Cycling

WA's southwest offers good cycle touring, and while there are thousands of kilometres of flat, virtually traffic-free roads elsewhere in the state, the distances between towns makes it difficult to plan (not to mention actually cycle).

Perth is a relatively bike-friendly city, with plenty of recreational bike paths, including routes that run along the Swan River to Fremantle and along the coast between Cottesloe and Scarborough, and paths overlooking the city through Kings Park. Spinway WA (p98) is Perth's bike-hire kiosk system, at 14 handy locations around the city.

Seals, Rottnest Island (p102)

Cyclists rule on mostly car-free Rottnest Island (p106), with long stretches of empty roads circumnavigating the island and its beaches. Geraldton (p172) also has great cycle paths.

The most exciting route for mountain bikers is the Munda Biddi Trail (p108), meaning 'path through the forest' in the Noongar Aboriginal language. The 1000km mountain-biking equivalent of the Bibbulmun Track runs all the way from Mundaring in the Perth Hills to Albany on the south coast. Camp sites are situated a day's easy ride apart, and maps are available online and at visitor centres.

Surfing & Windsurfing

Beginners, intermediates, wannabe pros and hardcore renegade surfers will all find excellent conditions to suit their skill levels. WA gets huge swells (often over 3m), so it's critical to align the surf and the location with your ability. Look out for strong currents, sharks and territorial

Bungle Bungle Range (p236), Purnululu National Park

local surfers (they bite too). For surf cams and reports, check out www.coastalwatch.com/surf-cams-surf-reports/wa.

WA's traditional surfing home is the southwest, particularly from Yallingup (p135) to Margaret River (p137). This stretch has many different breaks to explore.

Around Perth the surf is smaller, but there are often good conditions at bodyboard-infested Trigg (p63) and Scarborough (p61). If the waves are small, head to Rottnest Island (p103) for (usually) bigger and better waves. Check out Strickland Bay.

Heading north, there are countless reef breaks waiting to be discovered (hint: take a 4WD). Best known are the left-hand point breaks of Jakes Bay (p176) near Kalbarri; Gnaraloo Station (p186), 150km north of Carnarvon; and **Surfers Beach** (Dunes Beach; Mildura Wreck Rd) at Exmouth. Buy the locals a beer and they might share a few secret world-class locations.

Windsurfers and kitesurfers have plenty of choice with excellent flat-water and wave sailing. Kitesurfers appreciate the long, empty beaches and offshore reefs.

After Perth's city beaches, head to Lancelin (p121), home to a large summer population of surfers. Flat-water and wave sailing are excellent here. Further north, Geraldton (p172) has the renowned Coronation Beach. The Shark Bay (p179) area has excellent flat-water sailing and Gnaraloo Station is also a world-renowned wave-sailing spot.

NATIONAL PARKS PASSES

Thirty of WA's 60-plus national parks charge vehicle entry fees (per car/motorcycle $13/7), which are valid for any park visited that day. If you're camping within the park, the entry fee is only payable on the first day (camping fees are additional). If you plan to visit more than three WA parks with entry fees – quite likely if you're travelling outside Perth – get the four-week Holiday Pass ($44). All Department of Parks & Wildlife offices (https://parks.dpaw.wa.gov.au) sell them, and if you've already paid a day-entry fee in the last week (and have the voucher to prove it), you can subtract it from the cost of the pass.

WHALE WATCHING

Watching whales and other marine mammals (dolphins, sea lions, dugongs) cavorting offshore is big business here, and an undeniable thrill. So many southern right and humpback whales (upwards of 30,000) cruise along this coast every year, that it's become known as the Humpback Hwy. But be aware that research suggests that human interaction with sea mammals potentially alters their behavioural and breeding patterns. If you do head out to see them in a boat, do some research to ensure you're going with a licenced, environmentally savvy operator, and keep your distance – humanity owes these species a little peace and quiet!

Diving & Snorkelling

WA's fascinating diving and snorkelling locations include amazing marine parks and shipwrecks.

Close to Perth, divers can explore wrecks and marine life off the beaches of Rottnest Island (p102), or explore the submerged reefs and historic shipwrecks of the **West Coast Dive Park** (☎08-9592 3464; www.westcoastdivepark.com.au; permits per day/week $25/50) within Shoalwater Islands Marine Park, near Rockingham. You can take a dive course in Geographe Bay with companies based in Dunsborough (p131) or Busselton (p130); the bay offers excellent dives under Busselton Jetty (p130), on Four Mile Reef (a 40km limestone ledge about 6.5km off the coast) and around the scuttled HMAS *Swan*.

Other wrecks include the HMAS *Perth* (at 36m), deliberately sunk in 2001 in King George Sound near Albany; and the *Sanko Harvest,* near Esperance (p166). Both the wrecks' artificial reefs teem with marine life.

Divers seeking warmer waters should head north. Staggering marine life can be found just 100m offshore within the Ningaloo Marine Park (p197), fantastic for both diving and snorkelling. In Turquoise Bay, underwater action is equally accessible, and one of the planet's most amazing underwater experiences is diving or snorkelling alongside the incredible whale shark, the world's largest fish. Tours leave from Exmouth (p193) and Coral Bay (p190). Book ahead.

There's also excellent diving and snorkelling around the Houtman Abrolhos Islands (p174).

Fishing

From sailfish in the north to trout in the south, all types of fishing are on offer along WA's immense coastline. Fishing is the state's largest recreational activity, with many locals catching dinner nearly every time.

Close to Perth, Rottnest Island has plentiful schools of wrasse and Western Australian dhufish (previously called jewfish).

South of Perth, popular fishing hotspots include Mandurah (p107), with options for deep-sea fishing, catching tailor from the beach or nabbing Mandurah's famed blue manna crabs and king prawns in the estuaries. In Augusta (p144) you can chase salmon in the Blackwood River or whiting in the bay; or drop a line from Busselton Jetty (p130).

Popular spots at sunny Geraldton (p172) include Sunset Beach and Drummond Cove, and fishing charters go to the nearby Houtman Abrolhos Islands (p174). There's great fishing all along the coast, and lots of charters in the hotter, steamier northwest. There's a good chance to hook a monster fish at Exmouth (p191), the Dampier Archipelago (p203) and the game-fishing nirvana of Broome (p212). The northern Kimberley is good for barramundi.

Buy a Recreational Fishing Licence (RFL; $50) if you intend to catch marron (freshwater crayfish) or rock lobsters; if you use a fishing net; or if you're freshwater angling in the southwest. If you're fishing from a motorised boat, someone on the boat will need to have a Recreational Fishing from Boat Licence (RFBL; $40). Licences can be obtained online from the Department of Fisheries (www.fish.wa.gov.au) or from Australia Post offices. Note that there are strict licence, bag and size limits – see the Fisheries website for specific details.

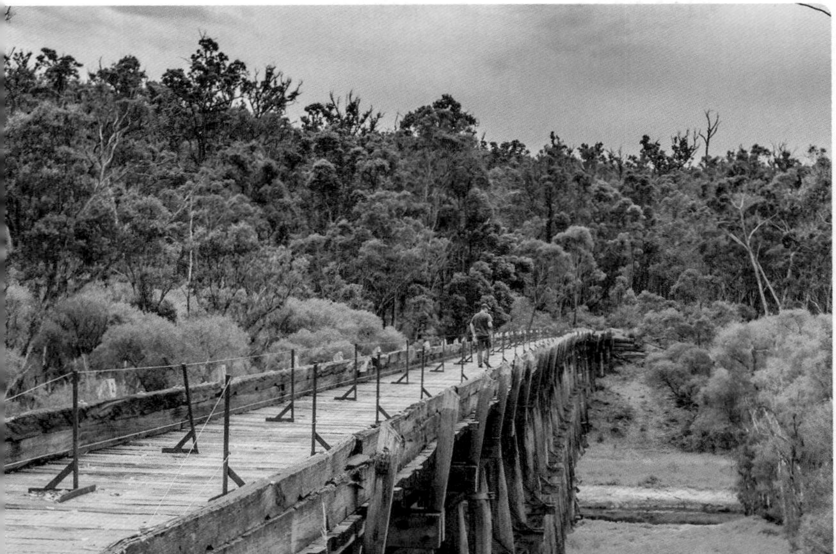

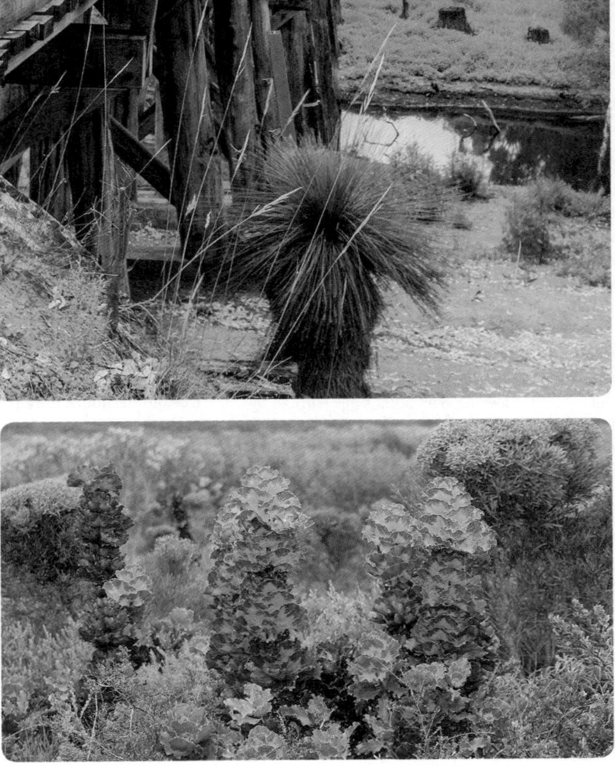

INES PORADA/SHUTTERSTOCK ©

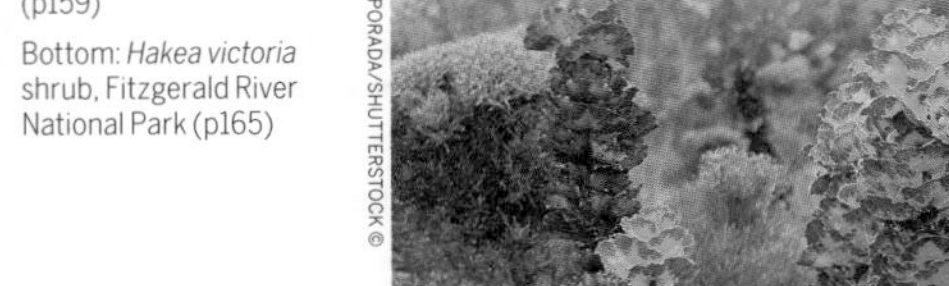

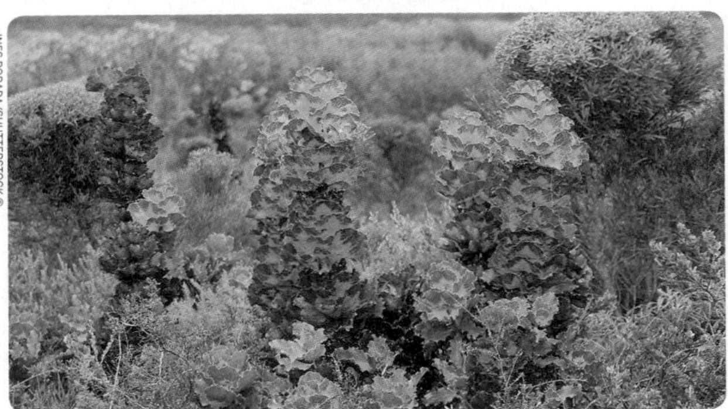

Top: Bibbulmun Track (p159)

Bottom: *Hakea victoria* shrub, Fitzgerald River National Park (p165)

Plan Your Trip

Family Travel

With good weather, beaches and big open spaces, West Coast Australia is a wonderful place to travel with the kids. Australians are famously laid-back and their generally tolerant, 'no worries' attitude extends to children having a good time and perhaps being a little bit raucous.

Keeping Costs Down

Discounts

Child concessions (and family rates) often apply for tours and admission fees, with discounts as high as 50% of the adult rate. Babies and kids under four or five will often get into sights for free. Note that the definition of 'child' can vary from under 12 to under 18 years.

Accommodation

Concessions generally apply to children under 12 years old, sharing the same room as adults. WA's caravan parks are a great budget option with kids: sleep in a cute cabin (or tent!), then hit the surf/ swimming pool/games room/giant trampoline/ minigolf...

Airlines

On the major airlines kids aged two and under travel for free (they sit on an adult's lap, with a special seat belt). Child fares usually apply between three and 11 years. The major players also let you bring your own car seats, strollers (prams) and port-a-cots as 'oversized baggage' for free.

Eating

In pub dining rooms, dedicated kids' menus are the norm (even if selections are unimaginative: ham-and-pineapple pizza, fish fingers, chicken nuggets...). WA also has a proliferation of free electric BBQs in parks, or there's always fish and chips by the beach.

Children Will Love...

Surfing & Swimming

Scarborough Beach Surf School (p72) Lessons in Perth for kids aged 11 and over.

Yallingup Surf School (p135) 'Microgrom' lessons for the under-10s.

Scarborough Beach Pool (p68) Perth's best swimming pool, if it's too windy to surf.

Sorrento Beach Enclosure (p68) Safe swimming in the sea in Perth's northern reaches.

Midwest Surf School (p172) Teach the kids to carve it up on Geraldton's back beaches.

Wildlife Parks & Zoos

Perth Zoo (p57) Such a well-planned zoo; you'll want to stay all day.

Bunbury Wildlife Park (p127) Marsupial and avian encounters, with a swamp to explore across the road.

Caversham Wildlife Park (p113) Excellent wildlife meet-and-greet in the Swan Valley on Perth's northeastern fringe.

Malcolm Douglas Wilderness Park (p213) Tropical crocs and jabirus populate this park near Broome.

Barna Mia Nocturnal Animal Sanctuary (p113) Torchlight tours to see rare marsupial bilbies, quendas, dalgytes, boodies, woylies, wurrups; south of Perth in the Peel Region.

Eating Out

Green's & Co (p87) There are kids' games out the back in this hip Leederville cafe.

Ocean & Paddock (p160) Kid-focused seafood in Albany (the best fish and chips in WA?).

Parkerville Tavern (p111) Kids hit the sandpit at this cheery historic pub in the Perth Hills.

Jetty Seafood Shack (Map p177; 08-9937 1067; Grey St; meals $11-25, burgers $9-14; 4.30-8.30pm;) Fab and fast fish and chips in Kalbarri, with outdoor tables for messy consumption.

Town Beach Cafe (Map p214; 08-9193 5585; www.restaurantsnapshot.com/townbeachcafe; Robinson St, Town Beach; dishes $12-23; 7am-2pm Tue-Sun Mar-Nov;) Kid-conducive cafe fare in Broome, with fabulous bay views to boot.

Amusement Parks, Water Parks & Rides

Adventure World (p67) White-knuckle rides including the 'Black Widow' and the 'Kraken', plus pools and water rides at this Perth amusement park.

Perth Royal Show (p75) Funfair rides, show bags and farm animals.

Elizabeth Quay Water (p67) Hyperactive spraying jets and fountains at Perth's redeveloped riverfront precinct.

Hyde Park Playground (p67) Fabulous fun times (a lake, a water park and lots of lawns) in Highgate (Perth).

Whale Watching

Timing If you're on the right part of the coast at the right time of year, you'll definitely see whales from the shore: see www.whalewatchwesternaustralia.com for info.

Tours Organised whale-watching boat trips depart from Perth, Fremantle, Dunsborough, Augusta, Albany, Bremer Bay, Coral Bay, Broome, Kalbarri, Exmouth and the Dampier Peninsula.

Ethics If you are heading out in a boat, make an informed choice that allows you to keep your distance: research suggests that human interaction with sea mammals potentially alters their behavioural and breeding patterns.

Region by Region

Perth

Perth (p54) is blessed with brilliant weather, drawing local families outside to play in the parks and playgrounds, and on the beaches and bike paths. Or, if it is raining (it does happen!), many big-ticket attractions – the likes of the Aquarium of Western Australia, the Western Australian Museum – Maritime, Fremantle Arts Centre and the Art Gallery of Western Australia – have hands-on exhibits and run excellent school-holiday programs for the little 'uns.

Perth Region

Trucking out of the city, kids will love a trip to Rottnest Island (p102) to swim, cycle, snorkel and check out the resident quokkas. There are also safe swimming beaches around Mandurah (p107) and Rockingham (p106), and wild ocean shores (great beachcombing) further north along the Turquoise Coast (p121). Natural highlights like Wave Rock (p111) and the Pinnacles (p122) are rewarding day trips, while among the Swan Valley (p112) vines you'll find wildlife parks, playgrounds and curio-filled transport museums.

Margaret River & the Southwest

Margaret River (p125) has a deserved rep for adult indulgences, but there's plenty around here to keep the kids happy too. Geographe Bay features broad beaches, Yallingup has a surf school, while local breweries and wineries are often kitted-out for kids (so mum and dad can enjoy a sneaky drink). You might even spy some whales off the coast.

Southern WA

This part of West Coast Australia is just far enough to dissuade Perth day trippers but close enough for weekending families to take some interest. Consequently, there's plenty for the kids to see and do here. Highlights include the Historic Whaling Station (p159) near Albany, the lofty Tree Top Walk at the Valley of the Giants (p153), eco cruises on Nornalup Inlet (p153) and orca spotting at Bremer Bay (p164).

Monkey Mia & the Central West

If a visit to meet the world-famous dolphins of Monkey Mia (p182) isn't enough to elicit waves of rapturous excitement from the family, we're not sure what will. You can also feed the pelicans at Kalbarri and learn about Indigenous culture on a guided tour.

Ningaloo Coast & the Pilbara

Coral Bay has plenty of long empty stretches of sand on which small people can blow off steam or swim safely...and there are whale sharks at Ningaloo Reef (p197)! Whale sharks! The very prospect may just be enough to sustain them on the long road trip.

Broome & the Kimberley

While WA's northern reaches (p209) feature wildlife interaction like camel rides and crocodile-park tours, it's the camping, gorge swimming and Indigenous culture that kids will really remember – particularly on the Dampier Peninsula and along the remote Gibb River Road.

Good to Know

Look out for the icon for family-friendly suggestions throughout this guide. For all-round information and advice, check out Lonely Planet's *Travel with Children*.

Accommodation Many hotels can supply cots and (sometimes) baby baths – larger hotels may also have child-minding services. B&Bs are often kid-free.

Breastfeeding Most Western Australians have a relaxed attitude about breastfeeding in public.

Change rooms Cities and most major towns have centrally located public rooms – in parks, libraries or department stores – where parents can go to nurse their baby or change a nappy. Check with local tourist offices. If you're caught short, don't worry: a parent using the open boot of a car as a nappy-changing platform is a common sight!

Child care WA's numerous licensed childcare agencies offer babysitting services. Check with local tourist offices.

Child safety seats Major car-hire companies can supply child safety seats for a fee; install them yourself (or BYO). Call taxi companies in advance to organise child safety seats; kids aged seven and over can use adult seatbelts in cabs.

Eating out Many cafes, pubs and restaurants supply kids' meals; many also supply high chairs.

In the sun Stop the kids from getting too cripsy with 'rashie' shirts at the beach, plus high-protection sunscreen (SPF 30-plus) and broad-rim hats.

Medical services and facilities Standards of GP and hospital care are predictably high; baby food, formula and disposable nappies are widely available.

Playgrounds Plentiful throughout WA; see www.playgroundfinder.com.

Prams Despite plenty of dirt roads, there's good pram access in most WA towns – this isn't a land of cobblestones. Search for 'pram hire' on www.gumtree.com.au.

Useful Resources

Lonely Planet Kids (www.lonelyplanetkids.com) Loads of activities and great family travel blog content.

My Family Travel Map: Australia (shop.lonelyplanet.com) Unfolds into a colourful and detailed poster for kids to personalise with stickers to mark their family's travels. Ages five to eight.

LetsGoKids (www.letsgokids.com.au/westernaustralia) Touring advice and highlights across most of Australia, including Western Australian coverage.

Kids Holidays Online (www.kidsholidaysonline.com.au/australia.htm) Bookings for kid-friendly accommodation nationwide, including WA.

Regions at a Glance

Perth

Architecture
Beaches
Drinking

Heritage Buildings

Relics of the colonial era and gold rushes abound. Fremantle, in particular, offers frozen-in-time Victorian streetscapes with sea-salty historic ambience. The big drawcard here is convict-built Fremantle Prison, its grim stories brought to life through engaging guided tours.

Urban Retreats

They may not offer the solitude and pristine beauty of WA's more remote beaches, but Perth's sandy shores act as urban retreats for surfers, snorkellers and swimmers.

Small Bars & Craft Beer

Drinking in Perth is whole lotta fun, especially now the city has fully embraced small-bar culture in its secretive laneways. Big ol' heritage pubs are still here too, these days catering to more erudite craft-beer drinkers than in the past.

p54

Perth Region

Coastline
Wildlife
Day Trips

Beaches

Raggedy Rottnest Island is ringed by gorgeous beaches that are often deserted. Mandurah, Rockingham and Yanchep are beach 'burbs with busy cafes and marinas. Guilderton sits on a sandy estuary, while Lancelin is windsurfing nirvana.

Native Species

Whales, dolphins, sea lions, seals, penguins, kangaroos, possums, quokkas, bilbies, boodies, woylies – it's amazing how much native wildlife lives so close to the big smoke.

Heritage Towns

The photogenic townships in the forests, hills and river valleys surrounding Perth are perfect day-trip terrain. York is a standout, with contiguous rows of historic buildings evoking gold-rush atmosphere.

p100

Margaret River & the Southwest

Coastline
Wine
Nature

Surf & Sand

The sandy beaches of Geographe Bay are perfect for a bucket-and-spade family holiday. The top spots are near Cape Naturaliste. The state's primo surf breaks also roll ashore to the south.

Margaret River Wine Region

Australia's most beautiful wine region also produces some of the country's best wine. The cool-climate vineyards around Pemberton are worth exploring too.

Southwest Forests

Studded with tuart and karri, WA's tall-tree forests are a truly impressive sight. Some of the larger specimens are rigged with spikes, allowing the fit and fearless to climb up to 68m into the canopy.

p125

South Coast WA

Coastline
Wine
Nature

Isolated Bays

Glorious, isolated bays of powdery white sand are spread all along this stretch of coast. On many of them you'll be more likely to spot a whale than another human.

Great Southern Wine Region

The cold-climate wineries of the Great Southern region are growing in stature, producing lovely drops in the clean southern airs. Sip your way from Denmark to Mt Barker and on to Porongurup.

National Parks

This region's national parks encompass the dramatic Tree Top Walk in Walpole-Nornalup and the silky sands of Cape Arid. Don't miss the rugged Porongurup and the Stirling Range National Parks, or the vast wild heath of Fitzgerald River.

p151

Monkey Mia & the Central West

Coastline
Adventure
History

White-Shell Beaches

The white-shell beaches of Shark Bay – with the famous Monkey Mia dolphins – are just part of a turquoise coastline stretching from Port Denison to Gnaraloo Station.

Outdoor Exploits

Surfers and windsurfers flock to Geraldton and Gnaraloo for winter swells and summer winds, while fisherfolk and explorers head west to remote Edel Land. Bushwalkers trudge through Kalbarri in winter.

Shipwrecks & Settlements

Historic artefacts, shipwrecks and 19th-century buildings stud this rugged coastline. Highlights include Greenough's pioneer settlement and the 1629 wreck of the *Batavia*.

p169

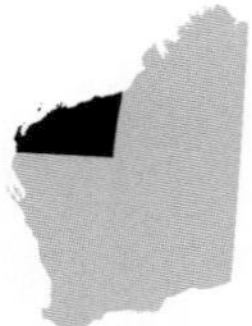

Ningaloo Coast & the Pilbara

Coastline
Adventure
Wildlife

Isolated Beaches

Superb, isolated beaches lead down to shallow lagoons hemmed by World Heritage–listed Ningaloo Marine Park. Fabulous snorkelling and diving are only a short wade from shore, with camping right behind the dunes.

Remote Explorations

Karijini National Park is the Pilbara's adventure playground, with deep, narrow gorges inviting exploration, and the state's highest peaks.

Native Species

Whale sharks, manta rays, turtles and whales all visit Ningaloo, while inland birds flock to the oasis pools of Millstream Chichester National Park. Pythons and rock wallabies hide in the shadows of Karijini.

p187

Broome & the Kimberley

Coastline
Culture
Adventure

Picturesque Beaches

Don't miss sunset camel rides on Cable Beach and the 'Staircase to the Moon' illusion on the tidal flats. Equally spectacular are the Dampier Peninsula's seldom-visited beaches.

Aboriginal Culture

Learn traditional practices from the Aboriginal communities of the Dampier Peninsula or follow Broome's Lurujarri Dreaming Trail. before exploring the Kimberley's amazing Wandjina and Gwion Gwion images.

Remote Explorations

Canoe the Ord River, drive the bone-shaking Gibb River Rd, detouring to Mitchell Falls and remote Kalumburu, or ride a speedboat to the Horizontal Waterfalls.

p209

On the Road

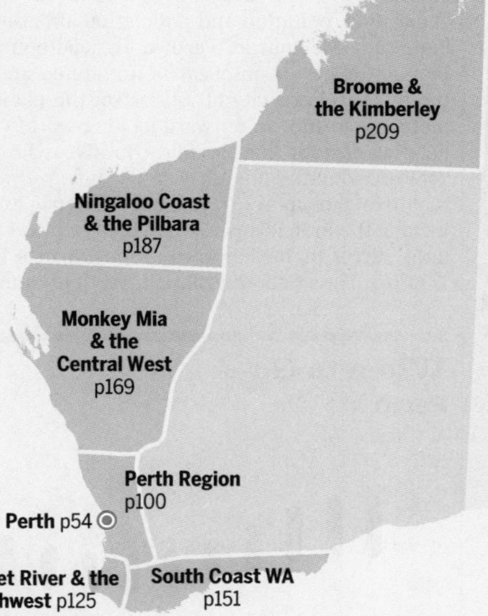

Broome & the Kimberley p209

Ningaloo Coast & the Pilbara p187

Monkey Mia & the Central West p169

Perth Region p100

Perth p54

Margaret River & the Southwest p125

South Coast WA p151

Perth

08 / POP 2.14 MILLION

Includes ➡

Sights 56
Activities 66
Tours. 72
Festivals & Events 73
Sleeping. 75
Eating 80
Drinking & Nightlife . . . 89
Entertainment. 93
Shopping 95
Information 96
Getting There & Away . . 97
Getting Around 98

Best Places to Eat

- Wildflower (p81)
- Bread in Common (p88)
- Pinchos (p87)
- Sayers Sister (p83)
- Il Lido (p88)

Best Places to Stay

- Como The Treasury (p76)
- Alex Hotel (p76)
- Hostel G (p76)
- Cottesloe Beach Hotel (p78)
- Lakeside B&B (p77)

Why Go?

In Wadjuk country, way out west in the Indian Ocean breeze, Perth regularly attracts that most easy-going of adjectives – 'livable'. Under a near-permanent canopy of blue sky, life here unfolds at a pleasing pace. Throw in superb beaches, global eats and booming small-bar and street-art scenes, and Perth seems downright progressive. Free from the pressures of congestion, pollution and population afflicting Sydney, Brisbane and Melbourne, Perth and neighbouring port town Fremantle are uncomplicated, unfettered and alive. Yes, it's the most isolated city of its size on the planet, but this remoteness fosters an outward-looking world view. Instead of heading east for their holidays, locals – who suffer the ugly, geologic-sounding moniker of 'Perthites' – travel to Bali, the Maldives, Singapore, Sri Lanka... Currency-exchange reports include the Indian rupee, while the Perth-to-London 'Dreamliner' direct flight delivers Europe's virtues in a tick under 17 hours. Forget about isolation: Perth is going places.

When to Go

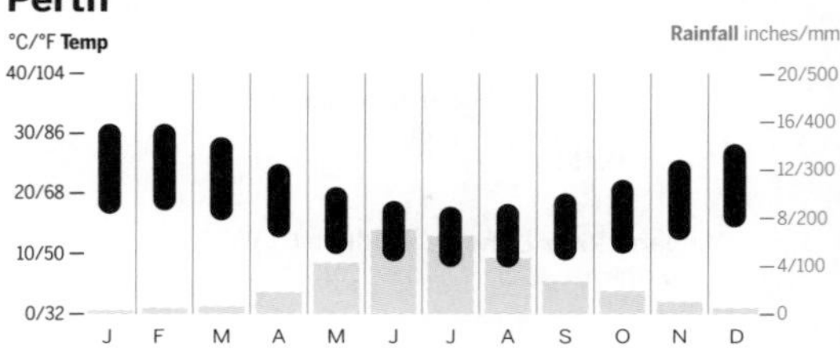

Feb The arty Perth Festival is happening and school starts – the beaches begin to empty.

Mar Warm and dry with clear blue skies – perfect beach weather.

Sep Kings Park wildflowers, the Perth Royal Show and the Listen Out festival – what's not to like?

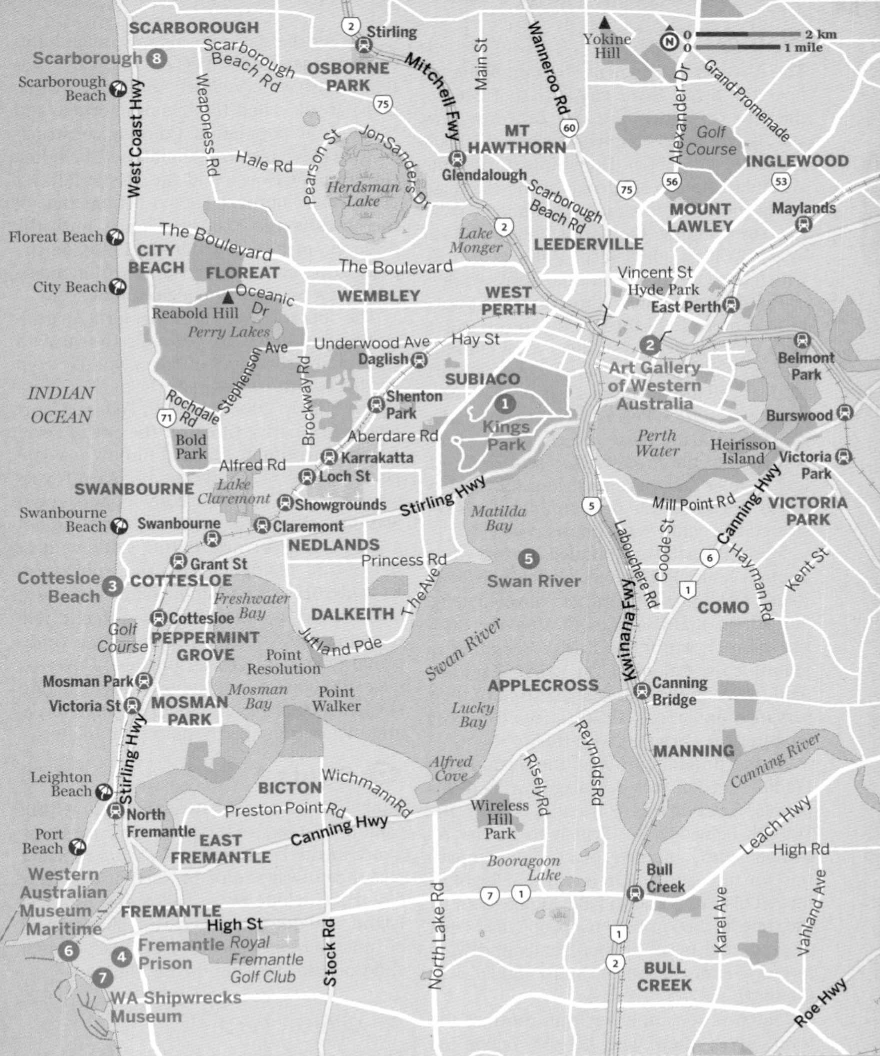

Perth Highlights

1 Kings Park (p60) Stretching out on the lawn with the glittering city spread out below you.

2 Art Gallery of Western Australia (p60) Viewing this trove of WA art, including an Aboriginal collection.

3 Cottesloe Beach (p61) Sipping a sundowner after a hard day on the sand at Perth's best beach.

4 Fremantle Prison (p65) Creeping yourself out at this World Heritage–listed former jail.

5 Swan River (p56) Chugging up or down Perth's broad, sparkling estuary on a ferry or cruise boat.

6 Western Australian Museum – Maritime (p65) Exploring Perth's relationship with the ocean.

7 WA Shipwrecks Museum (p65) Refloating WA's maritime history.

8 Scarborough (p61) Surfing and swimming at this beach 'burb.

History

The discovery of ancient stone implements near the Swan River suggests that Mooro, the site on which the city of Perth now stands, has been occupied for around 40,000 years. In indigenous Dreaming stories, the Wadjuk people, a subgroup of the Noongar, tell of the Swan River (Derbal Yaragan) and the surrounding landforms being shaped by two Wargal (giant serpentlike creatures), which lived under present-day Kings Park.

Fast-forward many thousands of years: in December 1696 three ships in the Dutch fleet commanded by Willem de Vlamingh anchored off Rottnest Island. On 5 January 1697 a well-armed party landed near present-day Cottesloe Beach. They tried to make contact with the local people to ask about survivors of the *Ridderschap van Holland*, lost in 1694, but were unsuccessful, so they sailed north. It was de Vlamingh who bestowed the name Swan on the river.

Modern Perth was founded in 1829 when Captain James Stirling established the Swan River Colony, and (rather obsequiously) named the main settlement after the Scottish home town of the British Secretary of State for the Colonies. The original settlers paid for their own passage and that of their servants, and received 200 acres for every labourer they brought with them.

At the time, Mooro was the terrain of a Wadjuk leader called Yellagonga and his people. Relations were friendly at first, the Wadjuk believing the British to be the returned spirits of their dead, but competition for resources led to conflict. Yellagonga moved his camp first to Lake Monger, but by the time he died in 1843 his people had been dispossessed of all of their lands and were forced to camp around swamps and lakes to the north.

Midgegooroo, an elder from south of the Swan River, along with his son Yagan, led a resistance campaign against the British invasion. In 1833 Midgegooroo was caught and executed by firing squad, while Yagan was shot a few months later by some teenage settlers whom he had befriended. Yagan's head was removed, smoked and sent to London, where it was publicly displayed as an anthropological curiosity. Yagan's head was buried in an unmarked grave in Liverpool in 1964, before being exhumed in 1993 and eventually repatriated to Australia and finally laid to rest in the Swan Valley in 2010, 177 years after his murder.

Life for the new arrivals was much harder than they had expected. The early settlement grew very slowly until 1850, when convicts alleviated the labour shortage and boosted the population. Convicts constructed the city's substantial buildings, including Government House and the Town Hall. Yet Perth's development lagged behind that of the cities in the eastern colonies until the discovery of gold inland in the 1890s. Perth's population increased by 400% within a decade and a building bonanza commenced.

The mineral wealth of Western Australia has continued to drive Perth's growth and prosperity. Too often excluded from Perth's race to riches have been the Noongar people. In 2006 the Perth Federal Court recognised native title over the city of Perth and its surrounds, but this finding was appealed by the WA and Commonwealth governments. In December 2009 an agreement was signed in WA's parliament, setting out a time frame for negotiating settlement of native-title claims across the southwest. In mid-2015 a $1.3-billion native-title deal was settled by the WA government recognising the Noongar people as the traditional owners of WA's southwest. Covering over 200,000 sq km, the settlement region stretches from Jurien Bay to Ravensthorpe, and includes the Perth metropolitan area.

Sights

Many of Perth's main attractions are within walking distance of the inner city, and several are in the Perth Cultural Centre precinct past the railway station in Northbridge. Easy day trips include Swan Valley and Rottnest Island, and don't miss Perth's brilliant string of Indian Ocean beaches, with Scarborough and Cottesloe beaches the highlights.

Central Perth

The **Swan River** cuts through the core of Perth, splitting the city into north and south and providing oodles of waterfront for locals who choose river over sea. It's where ferries journey to Fremantle and on to Rottnest, where yachts cruise and catamarans jibe, where dolphins bob and kayaks skim. On windy days, you might even see wind- and kitesurfers on the shallow expanse. The river is very swimmable, and grassy stretches perfect for picnicking mean Perth folk often edge its pretty shores.

PERTH IN...

Two Days

Kick off with a leisurely cafe breakfast in Mount Lawley or central Perth, then spend your first morning exploring the Perth Cultural Centre – don't miss the superb **Art Gallery of Western Australia** (p60). Grab lunch and browse the shops in hip the Leederville 'hood before exploring verdant and view-catching **Kings Park** (p60) – a huge parkland area close to the city. The following day, discover the lustrous riches of the **Perth Mint** before catching the **Little Ferry Co** (p72) from **Elizabeth Quay** to view the city from the water. A night drinking cocktails in the city's laneway bars, or craft beer in the Northbridge pubs awaits...

Four Days

Follow the two-day itinerary then head for the beach. Pick up provisions for a picnic at **Cottesloe** (p61) or **City Beach** (p61), or truck further north to booming **Scarborough** (p61), with its brilliant swimming pool, precipitous skate bowl and rolling surf (and surf lessons). On your final day, visit Fremantle, Perth's raffish, soulful port town. Two of WA's best museums are here – the **Western Australian Museum – Maritime** (p65) and **WA Shipwrecks Museum** (p65) – plus the disquieting, World Heritage–listed **Fremantle Prison** (p65). Take your pick, then conclude your Perth adventure with some chilly pints at **Little Creatures** (p92).

Elizabeth Quay AREA

(Map p62; www.elizabethquay.com.au; Barrack St) A vital part of the city's urban redevelopment is Elizabeth Quay, at the bottom of Barrack St. Luxury hotels and apartments – including the Ritz – are nearing completion, joining waterfront cafes and restaurants. With a busport, train station and ferry terminal, the area is also a busy transport hub. Cross the spectacular Elizabeth Quay pedestrian bridge and splash in the water park.

Bell Tower LANDMARK

(Map p62; ☎08-6210 0444; www.thebelltower.com.au; Barrack Sq; adult/child $18/9 incl bell-tower chiming experience; ⏰10am-4pm, ringing noon-1pm Mon, Thu & Sun) This pointy glass spire fronted by copper sails contains the royal bells of London's St Martin-in-the-Fields, the oldest of which dates from 1550. The 12 bells were given to WA by the British government in 1988, and are the only set known to have left England. Clamber to the top for 360-degree views of Perth by the river.

Perth Zoo ZOO

(Map p58; ☎08-9474 0444; www.perthzoo.wa.gov.au; 20 Labouchere Rd; adult/child $32/15.50; ⏰9am-5pm) Part of the fun is getting to this zoo – take a ferry across the Swan River from Elizabeth Quay Jetty (p99) to Mends St Jetty (every half hour) and walk up the hill. Zones include Australian Bushwalk (kangaroos, emus, koalas, dingos), Reptile Encounter (all those Aussie snakes you want to avoid), peaceful Australian Wetlands (black swans, brolgas, blue-billed ducks) and the usual international animals from giraffes and lions to elephants and orangutans. Another transport option is bus 30 or 31 from Elizabeth Quay Bus Station.

Perth Mint HISTORIC BUILDING

(Map p62; ☎08-9421 7222; www.perthmint.com.au; 310 Hay St; adult/child $19/8; ⏰9am-5pm) Dating from 1899, the compelling Mint displays a collection of coins, nuggets and gold bars. You can caress bullion worth over $700,000, mint your own coins and watch gold pours (on the half hour, from 9.30am to 3.30pm). The Mint's Gold Exhibition features a massive, Guinness World Record–holding 1 tonne gold coin, worth a staggering $60 million.

Whipper Snapper Distillery DISTILLERY

(Map p62; ☎08-9221 2293; www.whippersnapperdistillery.com; 139 Kensington St, East Perth; tours & tastings $20-55; ⏰7am-5pm Mon-Fri, 8am-4pm Sat, from 11am Sun) Look for the vintage aircraft logo on the exterior wall as you visit this combination of urban whisky distillery and sunny coffee shop, in an out-of-the-way location. The whisky is crafted from 100% WA ingredients, something you'll hear a lot about on an entertaining and informative distillery tour (from $20 per person).

Perth

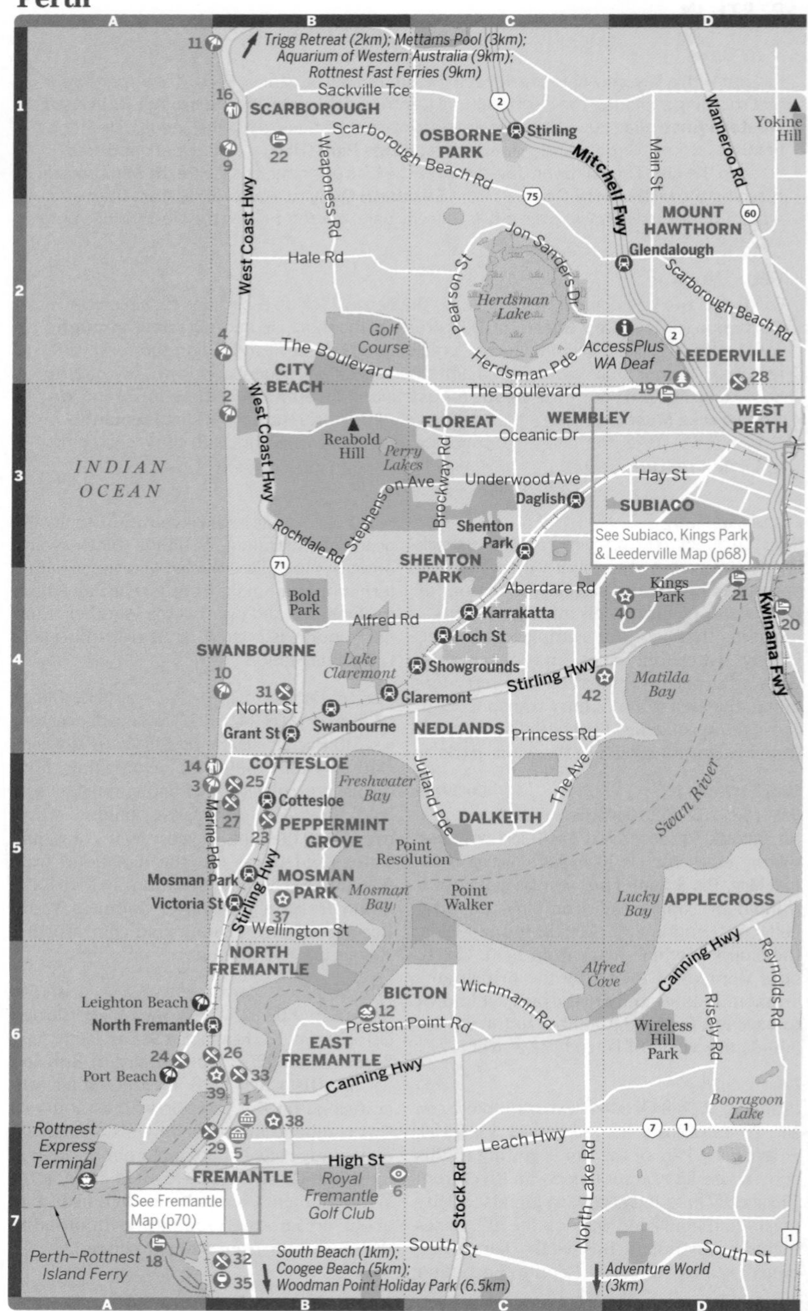

Trigg Retreat (2km); Mettams Pool (3km); Aquarium of Western Australia (9km); Rottnest Fast Ferries (9km)
Sackville Tce
SCARBOROUGH
Scarborough Beach Rd
OSBORNE PARK
Stirling
Mitchell Fwy
Main St
Wanneroo Rd
Yokine Hill
Weaponess Rd
West Coast Hwy
MOUNT HAWTHORN
Glendalough
Jon Sanders Dr
Hale Rd
Pearson St
Herdsman Lake
Scarborough Beach Rd
Golf Course
The Boulevard
AccessPlus WA Deaf
LEEDERVILLE
CITY BEACH
Herdsman Pde
The Boulevard
WEMBLEY
WEST PERTH
FLOREAT
Reabold Hill
Perry Lakes
Oceanic Dr
INDIAN OCEAN
Underwood Ave
Hay St
Stephenson Ave
Brockway Rd
Daglish
SUBIACO
Rochdale Rd
Shenton Park
See Subiaco, Kings Park & Leederville Map (p68)
SHENTON PARK
Aberdare Rd
Kings Park
Bold Park
Alfred Rd
Karrakatta
Kwinana Fwy
Loch St
SWANBOURNE
Lake Claremont
Showgrounds
Stirling Hwy
Matilda Bay
North St
Claremont
Swanbourne
NEDLANDS
Princess Rd
Grant St
COTTESLOE
Freshwater Bay
Jutland Pde
The Ave
Cottesloe
Marine Pde
PEPPERMINT GROVE
DALKEITH
Swan River
Point Resolution
Mosman Park
MOSMAN PARK
Mosman Bay
Point Walker
Lucky Bay
APPLECROSS
Victoria St
Stirling Hwy
Wellington St
NORTH FREMANTLE
Canning Hwy
Reynolds Rd
Alfred Cove
BICTON
Wichmann Rd
Leighton Beach
Preston Point Rd
North Fremantle
Risely Rd
Wireless Hill Park
EAST FREMANTLE
Port Beach
Canning Hwy
Booragoon Lake
Rottnest Express Terminal
Leach Hwy
High St
FREMANTLE
Royal Fremantle Golf Club
Stock Rd
North Lake Rd
See Fremantle Map (p70)
South St
South St
Perth–Rottnest Island Ferry
South Beach (1km); Coogee Beach (5km); Woodman Point Holiday Park (6.5km)
Adventure World (3km)

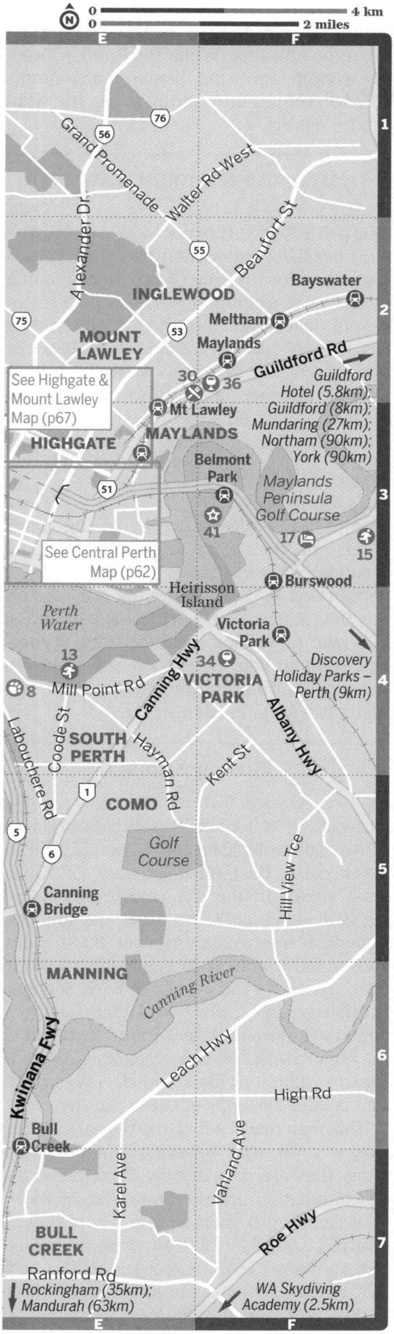

Perth

Sights

1 Army Museum of WA B6
2 City Beach B3
3 Cottesloe Beach B5
4 Floreat Beach B2
5 Fremantle Arts Centre B7
6 Fremantle Cemetery B7
7 Lake Monger D2
8 Perth Zoo E4
9 Scarborough Beach B1
10 Swanbourne Beach B4
11 Trigg Beach B1

Activities, Courses & Tours

12 Bicton Baths B6
13 Funcats E4
14 Fun's Back Surf B5
15 iFly Indoor Skydiving F3
16 Scarborough Beach Surf School B1

Sleeping

17 Aloft Perth F3
18 Be.Fremantle A7
Cottesloe Beach Hotel .... (see 14)
19 Lakeside B&B D3
20 Peninsula D4
21 Quest Mounts Bay Road D4
22 Western Beach Lodge B1

Eating

23 Boatshed Market B5
Canvas .... (see 5)
24 Coast A6
25 Cott & Co Fish Bar B5
26 Flipside B6
27 Il Lido B5
28 Kitsch D2
29 Mantle B7
30 Mrs S E2
31 North Street Store B4
32 Ootong & Lincoln B7
33 Propeller B6

Drinking & Nightlife

34 Dutch Trading Co F4
Mrs Browns .... (see 26)
35 Percy Flint's Boozery & Eatery B7
36 Swallow F2
Twenty9 .... (see 23)

Entertainment

37 Camelot Outdoor Cinema B5
38 Duke of George B6
39 Mojos B6
40 Moonlight Cinema D4
41 Optus Stadium F3
42 Somerville Auditorium C4

Shopping

Found .... (see 5)

Northbridge

★ Art Gallery of Western Australia GALLERY

(Map p62; ☎08-9492 6622; www.artgallery.wa.gov.au; Perth Cultural Centre; ⏲10am-5pm Wed-Mon) FREE Founded in 1895, this excellent gallery houses the state's preeminent art collection as well as regular international exhibitions that, increasingly, have a modern, approachable bent. The permanent collection is arranged into wings, from contemporary to modern, historic to local and Aboriginal. Big-name Australian artists such as Arthur Boyd, Russell Drysdale and Sidney Nolan are there, as are diverse media including canvases, bark paintings and sculpture. Check the website for info on free tours running most days at 11am and 1pm.

Nostalgia Box MUSEUM

(Map p62; ☎08-9227 7377; www.thenostalgiabox.com.au; 16 Aberdeen St; adult/child/family $17/12/50; ⏲11am-4pm Sun-Mon & Wed-Fri, to 5pm Sat; 👪) Ease into poignant, low-pixel childhood memories of Atari, Nintendo and Super Mario at this surprisingly interesting collection of retro 1970s and '80s gaming consoles and arcade games. Along the way you'll learn about the history of gaming, and there are plenty of consoles to try out and see if the old skills are still there from a few decades back.

Perth Institute of Contemporary Arts GALLERY

(PICA; Map p62; ☎08-9228 6300; www.pica.org.au; Perth Cultural Centre; ⏲10am-5pm Tue-Sun) FREE PICA (*pee*-kah) may look traditional – it's housed in an elegant 1896 red-brick former school – but inside it's one of Australia's principal platforms for contemporary art, including installations, performance, sculpture and video. PICA actively promotes new and experimental art, and it exhibits graduate works annually. From 10am to late, Tuesday to Sunday, the **PICA Bar** is a top spot for a coffee or cocktail, and has occasional live music.

Western Australian Museum – Perth MUSEUM

(Map p62; ☎08-6552 7800; www.museum.wa.gov.au; Perth Cultural Centre; ⏲9.30am-5pm) FREE The state's museum is a six-headed beast, with branches in Albany, Geraldton and Kalgoorlie as well as two in Fremantle. This main branch in Northbridge is closed for renovations and is due to reopen as the renamed New Museum for WA in 2020. See online for an outline of the project – it's going to be amazing. While the hub is closed, key exhibits are being displayed as pop-ups at other venues around town; see the website for details.

Highgate & Mount Lawley

Hyde Park PARK

(Map p67; William St, Highgate; 👪) One of Perth's most beautiful parks, suburban Hyde Park is a top spot for a picnic or lazy book-reading on the lawn, as fountains flow. A path traces a split lake, and sprawling Moreton Bay figs provide plenty of shade. Kids love the playground and free water park. It's within walking distance of Northbridge; continue northeast along William St.

Leederville

Lake Monger PARK

(Map p58; Lake Monger Dr) In spring black swans and their cygnets waddle about the grounds – a meeting place for local birdlife – nonplussed by joggers circling the lake on the flat, 3.5km path surrounded by grass. The lake is walking distance from Leederville train station; exit on the side opposite the shops, turn right onto Southport St and veer left onto Lake Monger Dr.

Kings Park & Subiaco

★ Kings Park & Botanic Garden PARK

(Map p68; ☎08-9480 3600; www.bgpa.wa.gov.au; ⏲free guided walks 10am, noon & 2pm) FREE The 400-hectare, bush-filled expanse of Kings Park, smack in the city centre and enjoying epic views, is Perth's pride and joy. The Botanic Garden contains over 3000 plant species indigenous to WA, including a giant boab tree that's 750 years old. Each September there's a free festival displaying the state's famed wildflowers. A year-round highlight is the **Federation Walkway**, a 620m path leading to a 222m-long glass-and-steel sky bridge that crosses a canopy of eucalyptus trees.

The main road leading into the park, Fraser Ave, is lined with towering lemon-scented gums that are dramatically lit at night. At its culmination are the State War Memorial, a cafe, a gift shop, **Fraser's restaurant** (Map p68; ☎08-9481 7100; www.frasersrestaurant.com.au; mains $32-45; ⏲noon-late Mon-Fri, from 11.30am Sat & Sun) and the Kings Park Visitor Centre. Free guided walks leave from here.

It's a good spot for a picnic or to let the kids off the leash in one of the playgrounds. Its numerous tracks are popular with walkers and joggers all year round, with an ascent of the steep stairs from the river rewarded with wonderful views from the top.

Scitech MUSEUM
(Map p68; ☎08-9215 0700; www.scitech.org.au; City West Centre, Sutherland St; adult/child $19/12; ⏲9am-4pm Mon-Fri, 9.30am-5pm Sat & Sun; 👪) Scitech is an excellent rainy-day option for those travelling with children. It has over 160 hands-on, large-scale science and technology exhibits. Tickets are discounted later in the afternoon.

Scarborough to Cottesloe

Cottesloe Beach BEACH
(Map p58; Marine Pde; 👪) Perth's safest swimming beach, Cottesloe has cafes, pubs, pine trees and fantastic sunsets. From Cottesloe train station (on the Fremantle line) it's 1km to the beach; there's a free shuttle that runs between the stop and the sand during the annual Sculpture by the Sea exhibition in March. Bus 102 ($4.80) from Elizabeth Quay Busport goes straight to the beach.

Aquarium of Western Australia AQUARIUM
(AQWA; ☎08-9447 7500; www.aqwa.com.au; Hillarys Boat Harbour, 91 Southside Dr; adult/child $30/18; ⏲10am-5pm) Dividing WA's vast coastline into five distinct zones (Far North, Coral Coast, Shipwreck Coast, Perth and Great Southern), AQWA features a 98m underwater tunnel showcasing stingrays, turtles, fish and sharks. (The daring can snorkel or dive with the sharks with the aquarium's in-house divemaster.) By public transport, take the Joondalup train to Warwick Station and then transfer to bus 423. By car, take the Mitchell Fwy north and exit at Hepburn Ave.

Scarborough Beach BEACH
(Map p58; The Esplanade; 👪) This is a popular young surfers' spot, so be sure to swim between the flags, as waves can be powerful. A $100-million revitalisation of the beachfront has adorned it with a new public pool, grassed sunset-viewing hill, skate park, free BBQs, massive playground and restaurants and cafes. From Perth Busport, take bus 990 to the beach.

City Beach BEACH
(Map p58; Challenger Pde) Offers swimming, surfing, lawn and amenities. Following a significant redevelopment, there are two restaurants (we like Odyssea) and a pizzeria, public change rooms with hot showers and free outdoor seating. On the beach's northern end, old faithful Clancy's pub is another fine option with gorgeous views. Take bus 81 or 82 from Perth Busport.

Mettams Pool BEACH
(West Coast Dr; 👪) On calm days, it's like a turquoise paddling pool with some of Perth's best snorkelling – think mottled reef with swaying seaweeds and similarly coloured fish. Avoid the water, particularly the outer reef, during rough weather as it has proven dangerous in the past. There's a wheelchair-accessible path leading to a beach shelter and another to the sand.

PERTH FOR CHILDREN

With a usually clement climate and plenty of open spaces and beaches to run around on, Perth is a great place to bring the kids. Of the beaches, Cottesloe is the safest and a family favourite. Otherwise, the netted Sorrento Beach Enclosure (p68) offers secure waves. With older kids, arrange two-wheeled family expeditions along Perth's riverside bike paths or Coastal Trail (p66) north or south from Scarborough. Kings Park has playgrounds and walking tracks.

The Perth Royal Show (p75) is an ever-popular family day out, with breakfast-reintroducing rides, kitsch show bags and proudly displayed poultry. Many of Perth's big-ticket attractions also cater well for young audiences, especially the Aquarium of Western Australia, the fabulous Perth Zoo (p57) and the Art Gallery of Western Australia.

A good rainy-day option is Scitech, which has more than 160 hands-on, large-scale science and technology exhibits. For artificial rain, try the squirting water jets at Hyde Park Playground (p67) or the Elizabeth Quay Water Park (p67) by the river.

Fremantle is super kid-focused, with excellent events at Fremantle Arts Centre (p65) and the awesome WA Shipwrecks Museum (p65) and Western Australian Museum – Maritime (p65). Little Creatures (p92) brewery has a big sandpit full of toy trucks.

Central Perth

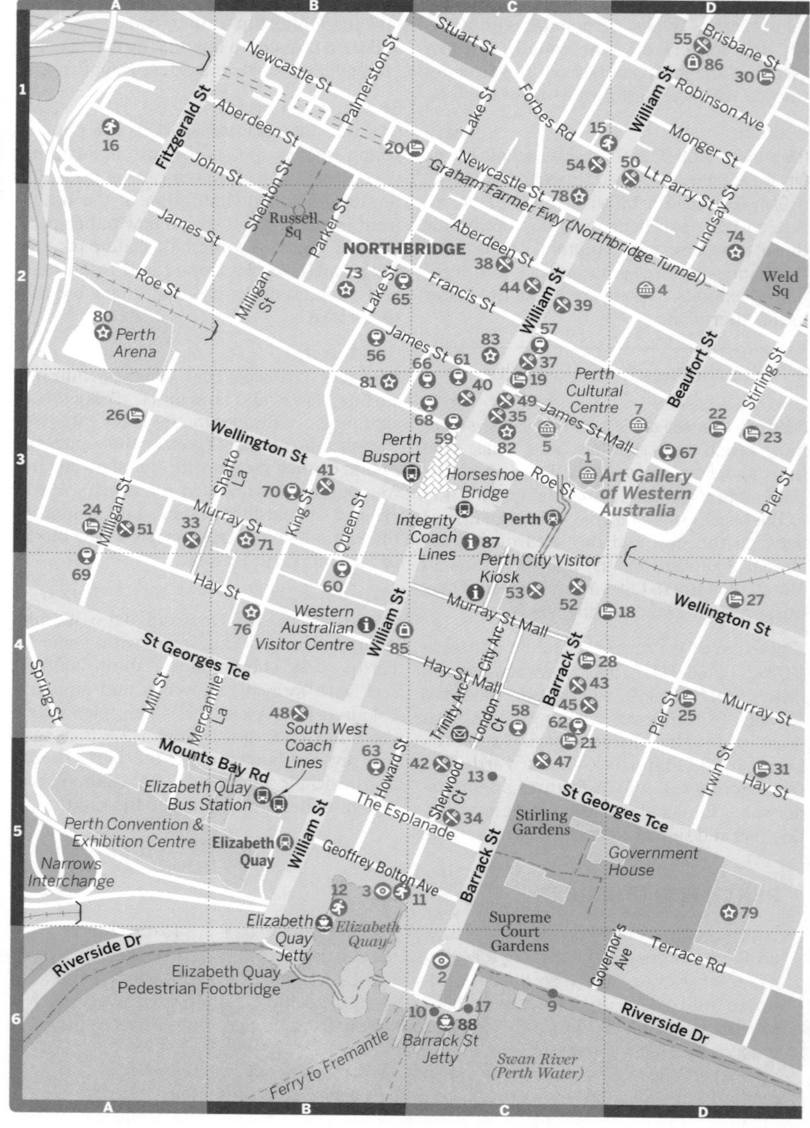

Floreat Beach BEACH

(Map p58; West Coast Hwy;) A generally uncrowded beach, but waves can be on the dumpy side. There's decent swimming, surfing, a cafe, playground and a grassy, free BBQ area. Catch bus 81, 82 or 83 from Perth Busport to City Beach and walk north 1km.

Swanbourne Beach BEACH

(Map p58; Marine Pde) Safe swimming, and an unofficial nude and gay beach. From Grant St train station it's a 1.5km walk to the beach (2km from Swanbourne Station). Or catch bus 102 from Elizabeth Quay Bus Station and get off at Marine Pde. The flashy Shore-

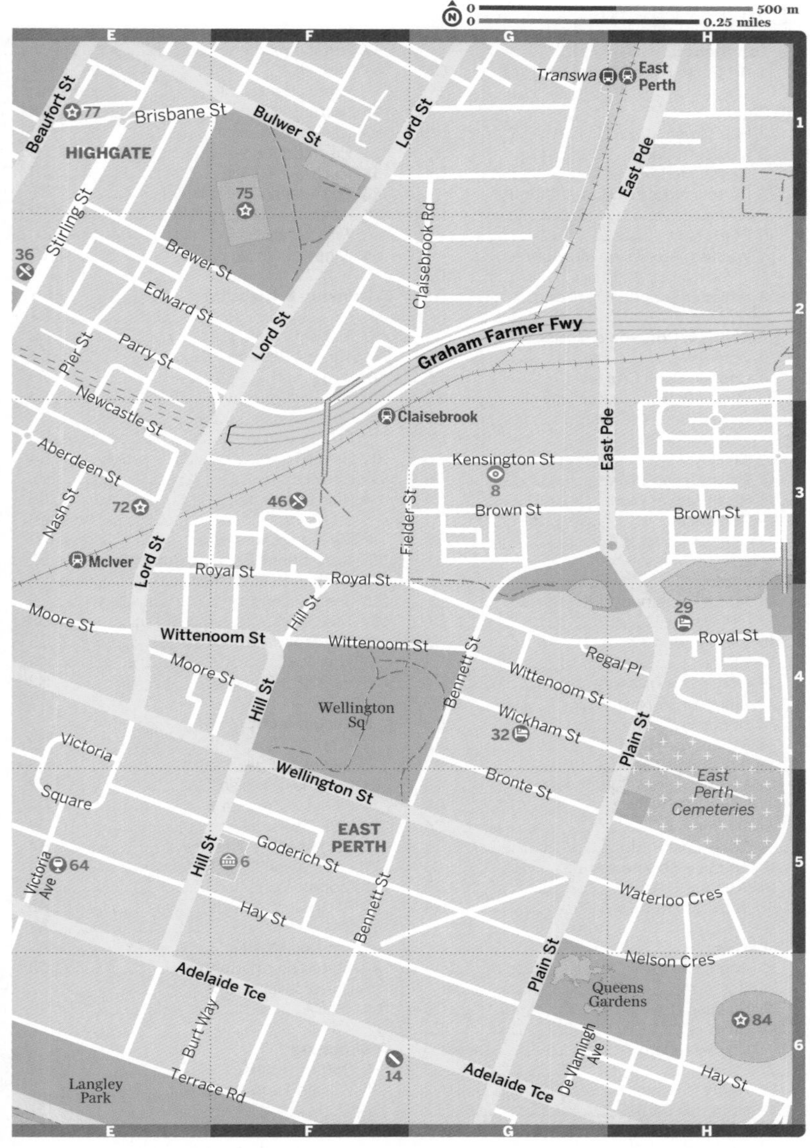

house restaurant has excellent ocean views and a playground out the front.

Trigg Beach BEACH

(Map p58; West Coast Hwy) Good surf, with a hardcore group of locals who come out when the surf's up; dangerous when rough and prone to rips – always swim between the flags. Middle Eastern–inspired restaurant Island Market is a fantastic lunch or sunset option, or go more casual with Canteen's poke bowls, next door.

Central Perth

Top Sights
1 Art Gallery of Western Australia C3

Sights
2 Bell Tower C6
3 Elizabeth Quay B5
4 Nostalgia Box D2
5 Perth Institute of Contemporary Arts C3
6 Perth Mint F5
7 Western Australian Museum – Perth D3
8 Whipper Snapper Distillery G3

Activities, Courses & Tours
9 Camel West C6
10 Captain Cook Cruises C6
11 Elizabeth Quay Water Park B5
12 Gondolas on the Swan B5
Little Ferry Co .... (see 12)
13 Oh Hey WA C5
14 Perth Ocean Diving F6
15 Perth Steam Works C1
16 Rockface A1
17 Segway Tours WA C6

Sleeping
18 Adina Apartment Hotel Barrack Plaza C4
19 Alex Hotel C3
20 Attika C1
21 Como The Treasury C4
22 Emperor's Crown D3
23 Hostel G D3
24 Melbourne Hotel A3
25 Pensione Hotel D4
26 Peppers Kings Square Hotel A3
27 Perth City YHA D4
28 QT Perth C4
29 Sebel East Perth H4
30 Shiralee Backpackers D1
31 Westin Perth D5
32 Wickham Retreat G4

Eating
33 Angel Falls Grill A3
34 Balthazar C5
35 Bivouac Canteen & Bar C3
36 Brika E2
Chicho Gelato .... (see 35)
37 Flipside C2
38 Henry Summer C2
39 Hummus Club C2
40 Kakulas Bros C3
41 La Veen B3
42 Lalla Rookh C5
43 Le Vietnam C4
44 Little Willys C2
Long Chim .... (see 47)
45 Nao C4
46 Perth City Farm F3
47 Petition Kitchen C5
48 Print Hall B4
Santini Bar & Grill .... (see 28)
49 Sauma C3
50 Tak Chee House D1
51 Tiisch Cafe Bistro A3
52 Toastface Grillah C4
53 Twilight Hawkers Market C4
54 Viet Hoa C1
Wildflower .... (see 21)
55 Wines of While D1

Drinking & Nightlife
56 Air B2
57 Alabama Song C2
58 Alfred's Pizzeria C4
59 Bird C3
60 Cheeky Sparrow B4
61 Connections C3
Ezra Pound .... (see 40)
62 Halford C4
63 Helvetica B5
64 Hula Bula Bar E5
LOT 20 .... (see 49)
Mechanics Institute .... (see 37)
65 Northbridge Brewing Company B2
Petition Beer Corner .... (see 47)
66 Sneaky Tony's C3
67 The Court D3
68 The Standard C3
69 Tiny's A4
70 Varnish on King B3

Entertainment
71 Amplifier B3
72 Badlands Bar E3
73 Cinema Paradiso B2
74 Ellington Jazz Club D2
75 HBF Park F1
76 His Majesty's Theatre B4
77 Lazy Susan's Comedy Den E1
78 Moon C2
79 Perth Concert Hall D5
80 RAC Arena A2
81 Rooftop Movies B3
82 State Theatre Centre C3
83 Universal C2
84 WACA H6

Shopping
85 Boffins Books B4
86 William Topp D1

Information
87 Department of Planning, Lands and Heritage C3

Transport
Rottnest Express .... (see 88)
88 Rottnest Express Terminal C6

Fremantle

★**Fremantle Prison** HISTORIC BUILDING

(Map p70; 08-9336 9200; www.fremantleprison.com.au; 1 The Terrace; day tour adult/child $22/12, combined day tour $32/22, Torchlight Tour $28/18, Tunnels Tour $65/45; 9am-5pm) With its forbidding 5m-high walls, the old convict-era prison dominates Fremantle. Various daytime tours explore the jail's maximum-security past, give insights into criminal minds and allow you into solitary-confinement cells. Book ahead for the Torchlight Tour through the prison, with a few scares and surprises, and the 2½-hour Tunnels Tour (minimum age 12 years), venturing into subterranean tunnels and doing an underground boat ride.

Entry to the gatehouse, including the Prison Gallery, gift shop and Convict Cafe is free. In 2010 the prison's cultural status was recognised as part of the Australian Convict Sites entry on the Unesco World Heritage list.

The first convicts were made to build their own prison, constructing it from beautiful pale limestone dug out of the hill on which it was built. From 1855 to 1991, 350,000 people were incarcerated here, although the highest numbers held at any one time were 1200 men and 58 women. Of those, 43 men and one woman were executed on-site, the last of which was serial killer Eric Edgar Cooke in 1964.

★**WA Shipwrecks Museum** MUSEUM

(Map p70; 1300 134 081; www.museum.wa.gov.au; Cliff St; suggested donation $5; 9.30am-5pm) Located within an 1852 commissariat store, the Shipwrecks Museum is considered the finest display of maritime archaeology in the southern hemisphere. The highlight is the **Batavia Gallery**, where a section of the hull of Dutch merchant ship *Batavia,* wrecked in 1629, is displayed. Nearby is a stone gate, intended as an entrance to Batavia Castle, which was carried by the sinking ship.

Other items of interest include the inscribed pewter plate left on Cape Inscription by Willem de Vlamingh in 1697, positioned next to a replica of the plate left by Dirk Hartog in 1616 during the first confirmed European landing in WA.

★**Western Australian Museum – Maritime** MUSEUM

(Map p70; 1300 134 081; www.museum.wa.gov.au; Victoria Quay; adult/child museum $15/free, submarine $15/7.50; 9.30am-5pm) Significant West Australian boats are suspended from the rafters of this sail-shaped museum building. There's the yacht that won the America's Cup race in 1983, pearl luggers and an Aboriginal bark canoe. Take an hour-long tour of the submarine HMAS *Ovens;* the vessel was part of the Australian Navy's fleet from 1969 to 1997. Tours leave every half hour from 10am to 3.30pm. Book ahead.

While not an ocean-going vessel, a classic 1970s panel van (complete with fur lining) makes the cut – because of its status as the surfer's vehicle of choice.

Fremantle Arts Centre GALLERY

(Map p58; 08-9432 9555; www.fac.org.au; 1 Finnerty St; 10am-5pm) FREE An impressive neo-Gothic building surrounded by lovely elm-shaded gardens, the Fremantle Arts Centre was constructed by convict labourers as a lunatic asylum in the 1860s. Saved from demolition in the 1960s, it houses interesting exhibitions and the excellent **Canvas cafe** (Map p58; 08-9335 5685; www.fac.org.au/about/cafe; mains $16-28; 8am-3pm Mon-Fri, to 4pm Sat & Sun;). During summer there are concerts (free on Sunday afternoons), courses and workshops.

Fremantle Markets MARKET

(Map p70; www.fremantlemarkets.com.au; cnr South Tce & Henderson St; 8am-8pm Fri, to 6pm Sat & Sun) FREE Originally opened in 1897, these colourful markets were reopened in 1975 and today draw slow-moving crowds combing over souvenirs. A few younger designers and artists have introduced a more vibrant edge. The fresh-produce section is a good place to stock up on supplies and there's an excellent food court featuring lots of global street eats.

Round House HISTORIC BUILDING

(Map p70; 08-9336 6897; www.fremantleroundhouse.com.au; Captains Lane; admission by donation; 10.30am-3.30pm) Completed in 1831, this 12-sided stone prison is WA's oldest surviving building. It was the site of the colony's first hangings, and was later used for holding Aboriginal people before they were taken to Rottnest Island for incarceration. At 1pm daily, a time ball and cannon-blasting ceremony just outside reenacts a historic seamen's alert. Book ahead to fire the cannon.

Walyalup Aboriginal Cultural Centre CULTURAL CENTRE
(Map p70; ☎08-9430 7906; www.fremantle.wa.gov.au/wacc; 12 Captains Lane; ⏲10am-3pm Thu-Sat) Various classes and workshops, including language, art and crafts, are held at this interesting Aboriginal cultural centre. Booking ahead for most is encouraged, so check the program online. As it's part of the **Bathers Beach Art Precinct** (Map p70; www.facebook.com/bathersbeachartsprecinct; Captains Lane; ⏲hours vary) there are also regular Aboriginal art exhibitions, with works available for purchase and proceeds going directly to the artists.

PS Arts Space ARTS CENTRE
(Map p70; ☎08-9430 8145; www.facebook.com/pg/pakenhamstreetartspace; 22 Pakenham St; ⏲gallery 11am-4pm Tue-Sat) Independent WA artists display often-challenging work in this repurposed heritage warehouse. Occasional events, including pop-up opera, fashion shows and concerts, fill the spacious interior after dark. Drop by or check the Facebook page for what's on.

Leighton Beach BEACH
(Map p58; Leighton Beach Blvd) Flat, white-sand beach with tiny waves and no current, just north of Fremantle. Loved by families.

Bathers Beach BEACH
(Map p70) In late 2016 Bathers became the first beach in WA to be granted an alcohol licence – you can drink cocktails on the sand if you're in a deckchair in front of **Bathers Beach House** (Map p70; ☎08-9335 2911; www.bathersbeachhouse.com.au; 47 Mews Rd; mains $22-36, grazing boards $49-78; ⏲11am-late; ❄👪) restaurant. It's the closest beach to central Fremantle and also has an art trail. You can swim here, but **South Beach** (Ocean Dr) or **Port Beach** (Map p58; Port Beach Rd) are nicer options.

Esplanade Reserve PARK
(Esplanade Park; Map p70; Marine Tce) A large park shaded by Norfolk Island pines between the city and Fishing Boat Harbour. Attractions include a soaring Ferris wheel and a skateboard park. Live-music gigs and festivals are often held here.

Fremantle Train Station HISTORIC BUILDING
(Map p70; Phillimore St) Built from Donnybrook sandstone in 1907; no one can say why the swans are white (rather than black), given that only black swans exist in WA.

Army Museum of WA MUSEUM
(Map p58; ☎08-9430 2535; www.armymuseumwa.com.au; 2 Burt St; adult/child $12/9; ⏲10.30am-1pm Wed-Sun) Situated within the imposing Artillery Barracks, this little museum pulls out the big guns, literally. Howitzers and tanks line up outside, while inside you'll find cabinets full of uniforms and medals. The WWI galleries were completely redeveloped for the centenary of the war in 2014. Photo ID is required at entry.

Activities

With weather this good, it should really come as no surprise that Perth is an active, outdoorsy kinda town: locals are up and about early in the morning, jogging, swimming, surfing, riding bikes and paddling stand-up paddleboards across the broad Swan River estuary.

Climbing

Rockface CLIMBING
(Map p62; ☎08-9328 5998; www.rockface.com.au; 63b John St; climbing with/without gear hire adult $30/20, child $27/17; ⏲10am-10pm Mon-Fri, 9am-6pm Sat & Sun; 👪) Inside an old brick warehouse abutting the Mitchell Fwy, Rockface has an impressive array of indoor climbing walls, bouldering areas, slabs and overhangs. Don your nifty rubber shoes, clip your rope to your harness and up you go. Good fun for kids too.

Cycling

Perth can get a bit hilly, but cycling is still an excellent way to explore the city. Kings Park (p60) has some good bike tracks and there are cycling routes along the Swan River, running all the way to Fremantle, and a Coastal Trail tracking north to Sorrento. For route maps, see www.transport.wa.gov.au/cycling or call into a bike shop. For bike hire, try Spinway WA (p98), the city's bike-kiosk system, or Cycle Centre (p98) for longer rentals.

Coastal Trail CYCLING
(Scarborough Beach Foreshore, Scarborough) FREE Feel like a ride? There's a fabulous cycling/walking trail running continuously north from the Scarborough foreshore, tracing the Indian Ocean clifftops all the way to Hillarys Boat Harbour 10km to the north. The trail extends southwards too, delivering you eventually (with a few detours) to Fremantle, 20km away.

Highgate & Mount Lawley

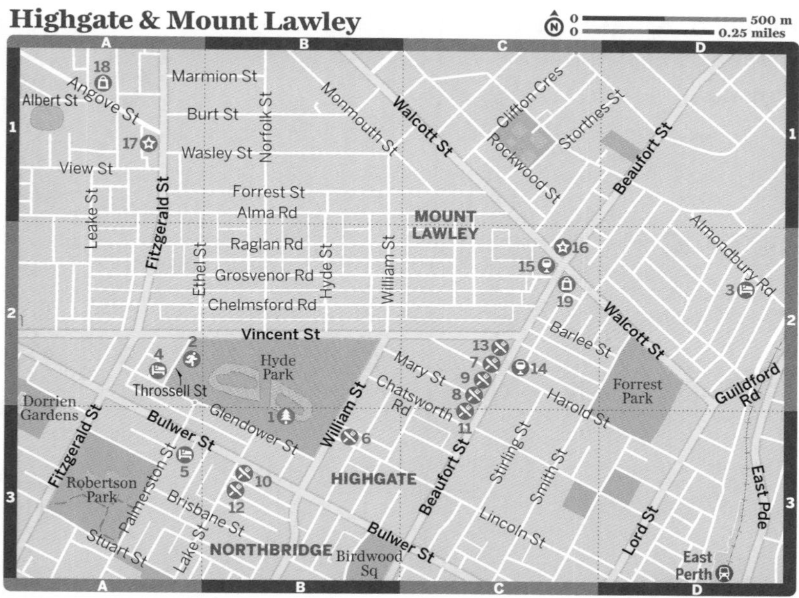

Highgate & Mount Lawley

Sights
1 Hyde Park....B3

Activities, Courses & Tours
2 Hyde Park Playground....A2

Sleeping
3 Durack House....D2
4 Pension of Perth....A2
5 Witch's Hat....A3

Eating
6 Chu Bakery....B3
7 El Público....C2
8 Mary Street Bakery....C2
9 Must Winebar....C2
10 Sayers Sister....B3
11 St Michael 6003....C3
12 Tarts....B3
13 Veggie Mama....C2

Drinking & Nightlife
14 Five Bar....C2
15 Flying Scotsman....C2
Must Winebar....(see 9)

Entertainment
16 Astor....C2
17 Rosemount Hotel....A1

Shopping
18 Future Shelter....A1
19 Planet Books....C2

Parks & Playgrounds

Elizabeth Quay Water Park PLAYGROUND
(Map p62; 08-6557 0700; www.mra.wa.gov.au; Geoffrey Bolton Way; 10am-10pm daily Dec-Feb, to 6pm Wed-Mon Mar-Nov;) FREE Cool off with the kids at this free waterside splash park, a curvy sunken terrace with water jets squirting upwards for 50 minutes on the hour.

Hyde Park Playground PLAYGROUND
(Map p67; 08-9273 6000; www.vincent.wa.gov.au/parks-and-facilities/item/hyde-park; Throssell St, Highgate; daylight hours;) FREE Highgate's reverently named Hyde Park may not have its London namesake's grandeur, but it does have a fabulous water park (squirting jets, happy kids), a big playground, open lawns, ice-cream trucks and a lake with turtles in it. If the kids can't find something here to keep them entertained, we give up.

Adventure World AMUSEMENT PARK
(08-9417 9666; www.adventureworld.net.au; 351 Progress Dr, Bibra Lake; adult/child/family $59.50/49.50/185; 10am-7pm Sun-Fri, to 6pm

Subiaco, Kings Park & Leederville

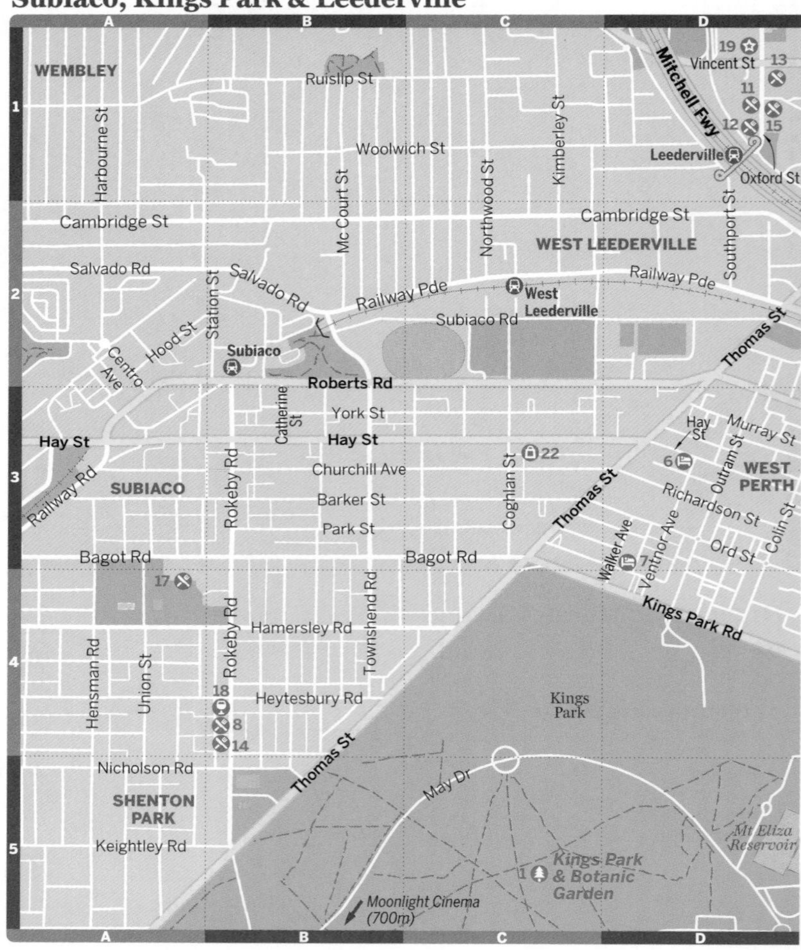

Sat Dec-Jan, reduced hours mid-Sep–Nov & Feb-Apr; 👪) Highlights of Adventure World's 28 rides are the Abyss roller coaster; the Black Widow, a G-force-defying spinning wonder; and (release) the Kraken, the world's longest and steepest funnel water slide, navigable in four-person rafts. Other water- and theme-park attractions include rapids, go-karts, Australian wildlife, a castle and the lofty Sky Lift.

Swimming

★ **Scarborough Beach Pool** SWIMMING

(☎08-9205 7560; www.scarboroughbeachpool.com.au; 171 The Esplanade, Scarborough; swimming adult/child $7/4.30; ⏲5.30am-9pm Mon-Fri, 6.30am-8pm Sat, from 7.30am Sun, reduced winter hours; 👪) This superb outdoor, oceanside swimming pool is the place to be when the Fremantle Doctor blows in and flattens out the Scarborough surf. Bikinis, buff bods, squealing kids and general West Coast ebullience – it's quite a scene. Cafe on-site.

Sorrento Beach Enclosure SWIMMING

(☎08-9400 4000; www.joondalup.wa.gov.au; West Coast Dr, Sorrento; ⏲daylight hours; 👪) FREE A lot of beaches around southwest WA have a bad rep for things that bite. But at Sorrento Beach in the city's northern reaches there's a large, fully netted, safe-swimming

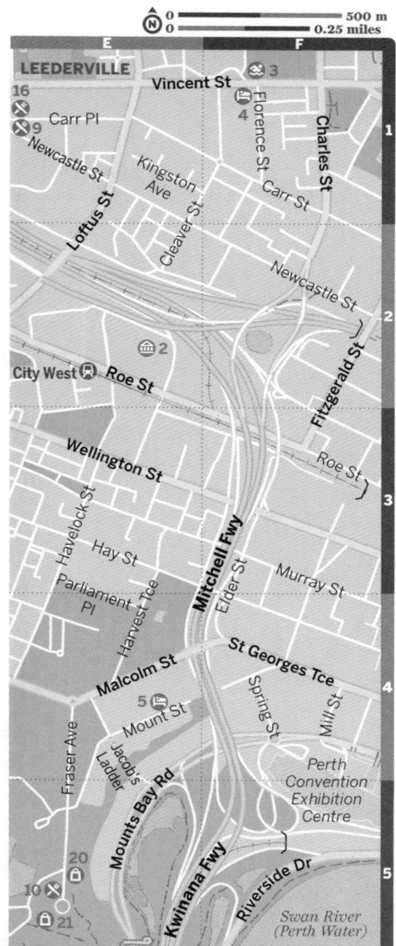

Subiaco, Kings Park & Leederville

Top Sights
1 Kings Park & Botanic Garden C5

Sights
2 Scitech E2

Activities, Courses & Tours
3 Beatty Park Leisure Centre F1

Sleeping
4 Beatty Lodge F1
5 Riverview 42 Mt St Hotel E4
6 Sage Hotel D3
7 Tribe Hotel D3

Eating
8 Boucla B4
9 Duende E1
10 Fraser's E5
11 Green's & Co D1
12 Kailis Bros D1
13 Low Key Chow House D1
14 Meeka B4
15 Pinchos D1
16 Sayers E1
17 Subiaco Farmers Market A4

Drinking & Nightlife
18 Juanita's B4
Leederville Hotel .... (see 13)

Entertainment
19 Luna D1

Shopping
20 Aboriginal Art & Craft Gallery E5
21 Aspects of Kings Park E5
Atlas Divine .... (see 11)
22 Mossenson Galleries – Indigenart C3

enclosure where you can frolic in the Indian Ocean waves without the risk of becoming something's lunch. There's another (more sheltered) safe-swimming area nearby at the **Sorrento Quay Boardwalk**.

Bicton Baths SWIMMING
(Map p58; ☎08-9364 0666; www.melvillecity.com.au; 80 Blackwall Reach Pde, Bicton; ⏲daylight hours; 👪) FREE A lovely neighbourhood salt-water swim-spot, the Bicton Baths occupy a sheltered corner of the Swan River south of the city. Even if you don't fancy a swim, take a stroll around the boardwalk enclosure with its splashing kids, fit-bods swimming laps and families picnicking on the lawns.

Beatty Park Leisure Centre SWIMMING
(Map p68; ☎08-9273 6080; www.beattypark.com.au; 220 Vincent St, North Perth; swimming adult/child $7/5; ⏲5.30am-9pm Mon-Fri, 6.30am-7pm Sat & Sun; 👪) Built for the Commonwealth Games, hosted by Perth in 1962, this complex has indoor and outdoor pools, water slides and a huge gym. Turn left at the top of William St and continue on Vincent St to just past Charles St.

Skating

Snake Pit SKATING
(☎08-6557 0700; www.mra.wa.gov.au/see-and-do/scarborough/attractions/snake-pit; The Esplanade,

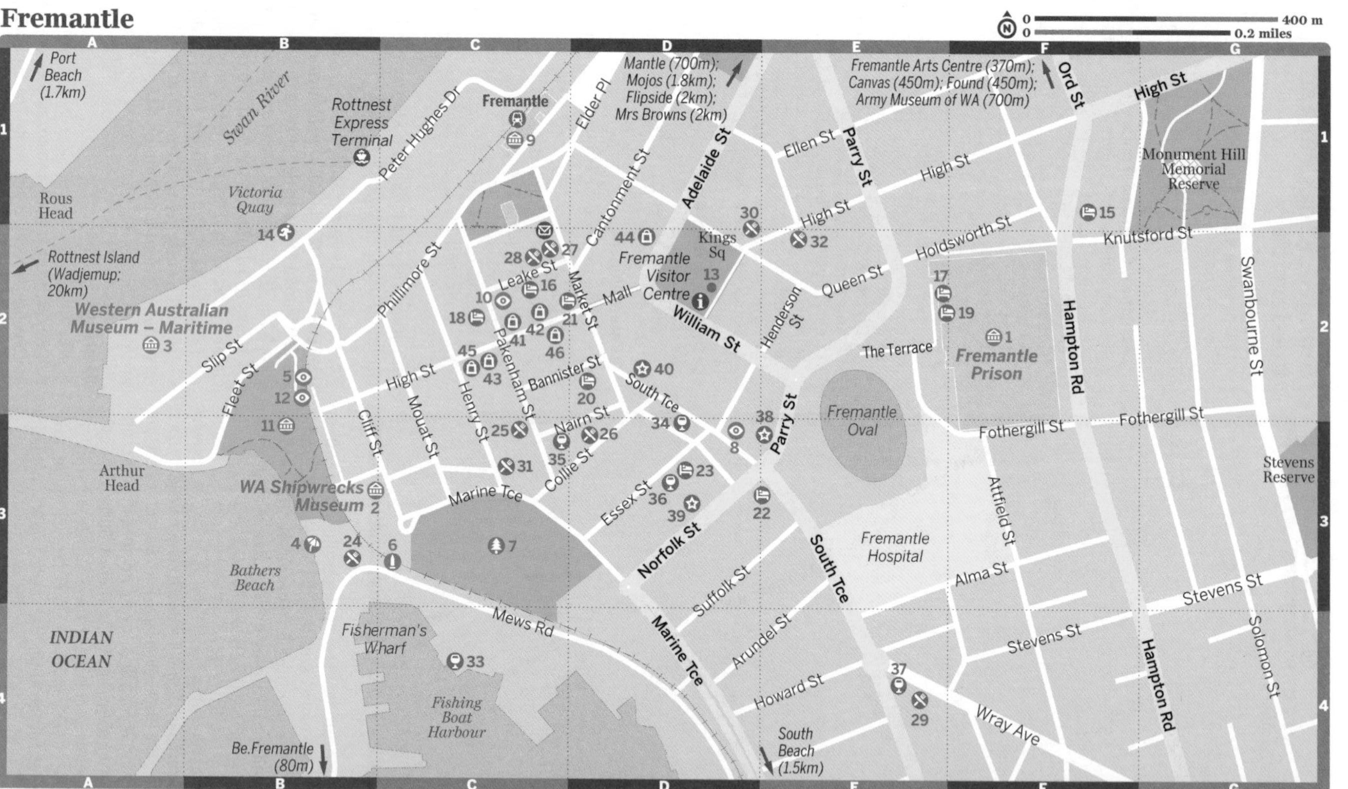
Fremantle
400 m
0.2 miles
Port Beach (1.7km)
Swan River
Rottnest Express Terminal
Peter Hughes Dr
Fremantle
Elder Pl
Mantle (700m); Mojos (1.8km); Flipside (2km); Mrs Browns (2km)
Fremantle Arts Centre (370m); Canvas (450m); Found (450m); Army Museum of WA (700m)
Ord St
High St
Monument Hill Memorial Reserve
Rous Head
Victoria Quay
Ellen St
Parry St
Adelaide St
Cantonment St
Kings Sq
Knutsford St
Holdsworth St
Rottnest Island (Wadjemup; 20km)
Phillimore St
Leake St
Market St
Mall
Fremantle Visitor Centre
Queen St
Henderson St
Swanbourne St
Western Australian Museum – Maritime
William St
The Terrace
Fremantle Prison
Hampton Rd
Slip St
Fleet St
High St
Pakenham St
Bannister St
South Tce
Mouat St
Cliff St
Henry St
Nairn St
Fremantle Oval
Fothergill St
Collie St
Arthur Head
WA Shipwrecks Museum
Marine Tce
Essex St
Stevens Reserve
Norfolk St
South Tce
Fremantle Hospital
Attfield St
Bathers Beach
Alma St
Suffolk St
Stevens St
Mews Rd
INDIAN OCEAN
Fisherman's Wharf
Arundel St
Marine Tce
Solomon St
Howard St
Fishing Boat Harbour
Wray Ave
South Beach (1.5km)
Be.Fremantle (80m)

Fremantle

Top Sights

1	Fremantle Prison	F2
2	WA Shipwrecks Museum	B3
3	Western Australian Museum – Maritime	A2

Sights

4	Bathers Beach	B3
5	Bathers Beach Art Precinct	B2
6	Bon Scott Statue	C3
7	Esplanade Reserve	C3
8	Fremantle Markets	D3
9	Fremantle Train Station	C1
10	PS Arts Space	C2
11	Round House	B3
12	Walyalup Aboriginal Cultural Centre	B2

Activities, Courses & Tours

13	Fremantle Tram Tours	D2
14	STS Leeuwin II	B2

Sleeping

15	Fothergills of Fremantle	F1
16	Fremantle Apartment	C2
17	Fremantle Colonial Cottages	E2
18	Fremantle Hostel	C2
19	Fremantle Prison YHA Hostel	E2
20	Hougoumont Hotel	D2
21	National Hotel	C2
22	Norfolk Hotel	E3
23	Port Mill B&B	D3

Eating

24	Bathers Beach House	B3
25	Bread in Common	C3
26	Duck Duck Bruce	D3
27	Kakulas Sister	C2
28	Leake St Cafe	C2
29	Little Concept	E4
30	Manuka Woodfire Kitchen	D1
31	Moore & Moore	C3
32	Raw Kitchen	E2

Drinking & Nightlife

33	Little Creatures	C4
34	Monk	D3
	Norfolk Hotel	(see 22)
35	Strange Company	C3
36	Whisper	D3
37	Who's Your Mumma	E4

Entertainment

38	Freo.Social	E3
39	Luna on SX	D3
40	Newport Hotel	D2

Shopping

41	Bodkin's Bootery	C2
42	Common Ground Collective	C2
43	Japingka	C2
44	Mills Records	D2
45	New Edition	C2
46	Record Finder	C2

Scarborough; daylight hours) FREE A highlight of the redeveloped Scarborough Beach foreshore is this epic 3.6m-deep concrete skate bowl, named after an open-air rock-and-roll dance joint which stood here in the 1950s. There's also a quarter pipe, and stairs, ramps and rails. Do skaters still say 'rad'?

Skydiving

iFly Indoor Skydiving SKYDIVING
(Map p58; 1300 366 364; www.ifly.com.au; 143 Great Eastern Hwy, Rivervale; 2/4 flights Mon-Fri $89/129, Sat & Sun $109/149; 9am-9pm Mon-Fri, 8.30am-8pm Sat & Sun;) It's hard to imagine the sheer amount of updraft it takes to suspend a human body midair – plenty! The jumbo wind generators here do the job with ease: don a natty jumpsuit, step into the wind chamber and fly.

WA Skydiving Academy SKYDIVING
(1300 137 855; www.waskydiving.com.au; 2 Mustang Rd, Jandakot Airport, Jandakot) Hurl yourself out of a perfectly good aeroplane high above Perth, Mandurah or Pinjarra. Tandem jumps from 6000/8000/10,000/12,000ft start at $260/350/390/430. Flights depart from Jandakot Airport 22km south of Perth.

Walking

Fremantle Trails WALKING
(www.fremantlestory.com.au/explore) Pick up trail cards from the visitor centre (p97) or find them online for 11 self-guided walking tours: there's a street-art trail, one on pubs, past and present, and another covering retro and vintage shops. Local heritage, creativity and Aboriginal history is also covered. Kick off with the discovery trail, covering major tourist attractions. Most walks take less than one hour.

Water Sports

Water Wanderers KAYAKING
(0412 101 949; www.waterwanderers.com.au) Guided and self-guided kayak tours around the Swan River in central Perth – a watery perspective that most locals never experience. Tours run at dawn ($55, 75 minutes), in the morning ($60, 90 minutes) and at twilight ($79, two hours). Self-guided tours for experienced kayakers are $160 for two paddlers.

STS Leeuwin II BOATING

(Map p70; ☎08-9430 4105; www.sailleeuwin.com; Berth B, Victoria Quay; adult/child $99/40; ⊙Nov–mid-Apr) Take a three-hour sailing trip on a 55m, three-masted, 1850s-style tall ship; see the website for details of morning, afternoon and twilight sails. Sailings are usually Saturday and Sunday, but dates vary, so check online. No experience necessary, and just a low level of fitness.

Gondolas on the Swan BOATING

(Map p62; ☎0414 746 867; www.gondolasontheswan.com.au; Elizabeth Quay; 15/30min cruise $15/30; ⊙11am-5pm Wed-Sun) Thinking about popping the question? It ain't Venice, but these short gondola rides around Elizabeth Quay evoke a passably romantic vibe (just don't drop the ring). One-hour cruises available seven days (from $250).

Funcats BOATING

(Map p58; ☎0408 926 003; www.funcats.com.au; Coode St Jetty, South Perth; per hour $45; ⊙10am-6.30pm Oct-Apr) These easy-to-sail catamarans are for hire on the South Perth foreshore (international ocean-going yacht mastery not a prerequisite). Each boat holds up to three mariners. Stand-up paddleboards and kayaks also for hire. Book online, or bring cash.

Perth Ocean Diving DIVING

(Map p62; ☎0450 005 381; www.perthocean.com; 143 Adelaide Tce, East Perth; ⊙8am-6pm) Scuba diving for beginners and experienced submariners, including fully supervised introductory dives ($149), PADI courses, and day-trip dives at Rottnest Island and further south at Dunsborough.

Scarborough Beach Surf School SURFING

(Map p58; ☎08-9448 9937; www.surfschool.com; Scarborough Beach, Scarborough; lessons $70; ⊙Oct-May) Longer-than-usual lessons (2½ hours) at Scarborough Beach, including boards and wetsuits; bookings essential. From June to September the operation moves to Leighton Beach just north of Fremantle.

Fun's Back Surf SURFING

(Map p58; ☎08-9284 7873; 120 Marine Pde, Cottesloe; ⊙9am-5pm) Is fun really back? Hire a stand-up paddleboard ($50 per half-day) and find out. Surfboards ($25), bodyboards ($20) and snorkelling gear ($20) also available, plus wetsuits ($15) if the Cottesloe brine is a tad brisk.

Tours

Go Cultural Aboriginal Tours CULTURAL

(☎0459 419 778; www.gocultural.com.au) Small-group, Aboriginal-run walking tours of Yagan Sq (one hour, $40) and Elizabeth Quay (90 minutes, $60) in central Perth. Tours peel back the layers of the city to understand the cultural and physical landscape of Aboriginal life here, now and in ancient times. Three-hour tours also available ($120).

Oh Hey WA WALKING

(Map p62; ☎0408 995 965; www.ohheywa.com.au; 45 St Georges Tce; tours from $35) Highly rated central Perth walking tours, zeroing in on the city's booming street-art scene, hip small bars, throbbing nightlife zones and architectural heritage. Self-guided audio tours and two-hour bike tours also available.

Two Feet & A Heartbeat WALKING

(☎1800 459 388; www.twofeet.com.au; tours from $35) Crime, culture, coffee and cocktails – these excellent guided walking tours of Perth and Fremantle cover all the bases, running both during the day and after dark. Kids will enjoy the three-hour Scavenger Hunt ($35); three-hour nocturnal bar tours take in some lesser-known booze rooms ($55).

Food Loose Tours FOOD & DRINK

(☎0467 542 437; www.foodloosetours.com.au; ⊙tours from $39) Entertaining, informative walking tours negotiating flavour-packed Perth routes, taking in restaurants, quick-fire cafes and hard-to-find small bars in Perth and Fremantle. Italian- and Asian-themed tours also available.

Djurandi Dreaming CULTURAL

(☎0458 692 455; www.djurandi.com.au; tours adult/child $45/35) Aboriginal walking tours around the booming Elizabeth Quay precinct in central Perth: 45 minutes of Nyungar cultural immersion, focusing on stories of the Dreaming, art, native flora and fauna, traditional diet, seasons and family structures.

Little Ferry Co BOATING

(Map p62; ☎0488 777 088; www.littleferryco.com.au; Elizabeth Quay; 1/2/3 stops adult $12/18/22, child $10/16/20, day pass adult/child $32/28; ⊙10am-5.30pm) This heritage-style electric ferry travels between the Elizabeth Quay terminal and the cafes and restaurants of Claisebrook Cove – an excellent Swan River snapshot. Either take a return trip, or bus it back to the city on the free CAT bus. Also connects to Optus Stadium (p95) on big-game days.

Perth Explorer BUS
(☎08-9370 1000; www.perthexplorer.com.au; 24hr ticket adult/child/family $40/12/95) Hop-on, hop-off double-decker bus tour, with a looping route taking in the central city, Kings Park and Northbridge. Buy tickets on board, or shave a few dollars off the price if you purchase online; 48-hour tickets also available. Other package options include a two-day bus and Rottnest Island experience, and an add-on river cruise to Fremantle.

Camel West HORSE RIDING
(Map p62; ☎0437 404 037; www.camelwest.com.au; Riverside Dr; adult/child $45/30; ⏱10am-1pm Wed-Sun; 👪) OK, so the idea of riding a camel in the middle of a major Australian city is a little odd…but without camels, the early white Western Australian colonies would never have been able to trade and move goods from one remote point to another. Catch the humpy vibe on 30-minute waterfront ride, departing near Barrack St Jetty.

Captain Cook Cruises CRUISE
(Map p62; ☎08-9325 3341; www.captaincookcruises.com.au; Pier 3, Barrack St Jetty; adult/child from $40/23) Mainstream sightseeing river cruises upstream to the Swan Valley or downstream to Fremantle, with a whole swathe of add-ons including meals, craft beer, wine tastings and tram rides. Departs from Barrack St Jetty near Elizabeth Quay.

Segway Tours WA TOURS
(Map p62; ☎08-9325 5790; www.segwaytourswa.com.au; Barrack St Jetty) How *do* these nifty two-wheel scooter-thingies work? Find out on a 90-minute Foreshore and City or Kings Park tour (adult/child $129/115) or one-hour Riverside tour ($89/79). There's a full training session before you get rolling. Tours depart Barrack St Jetty.

Fremantle Tram Tours BUS
(Map p70; ☎08-9473 0331; www.fremantletrams.com.au; city circuit adult/child $27/4, ghostly tour $85/65) Looking like a heritage tram, this bus departs from the Town Hall on an all-day hop-on, hop-off circuit around the city. The Ghostly Tour, departing 6.45pm and returning 10.30pm Friday, visits the prison (p65), Round House (p65), former asylum Fremantle Arts Centre (p65) and the Fremantle Cemetery (p78) – where AC/DC rocker Bon Scott is buried – by torchlight.

Rottnest Air Taxi SCENIC FLIGHTS
(☎0421 389 831; www.rottnest.aero; Eagle Dr, Jandakot Airport, Jandakot) Thirty-minute joy flights over the city, Swan River, Kings Park and Fremantle (per person from $88), and transfers to Rottnest Island (return from $106). Flights leave from Jandakot Airport, 22km south of Perth.

Festivals & Events

Perth Cup SPORTS
(www.perthracing.org.au; Ascot Racecourse; ⏱5 Jan) Perth's biggest day at the races, with the party people heading to 'Tentland' for DJs and daiquiris.

Fringe World Festival PERFORMING ARTS
(☎08-9227 6288; www.fringeworld.com.au; varies by performance; ⏱Jan-Feb) If you're challenged by nudity, offended by swearing and hate being drawn from the audience into a show, look away now. At Perth's cheekiest arts festival, hundreds of international and Australian artists perform in parks, pubs and playhouses for a month across January and February, delivering a party vibe with boundary-pushing comedy, circus, burlesque and theatre shows – many are free.

Australia Day Skyworks FIREWORKS
(www.perth.wa.gov.au; ⏱26 Jan) Around 300,000 people come to the riverside for a whole day of largely free, family entertainment, culminating in a 30-minute firework display at 8pm. Activities spread across Langley Park and on the South Perth foreshore, while views of the fireworks are best from Kings Park.

Laneway Festival MUSIC
(http://fremantle.lanewayfestival.com; ⏱early Feb) Open-air party with the planet's up-and-coming indie acts. The ubercool festival takes place around Fremantle's West End and Esplanade Reserve.

Perth Festival ART
(www.perthfestival.com.au; ⏱mid-Feb–early Mar) Artists such as Laurie Anderson, Dead Can Dance and Sleater-Kinney perform alongside top local talent. Held over 26 days, the festival spans theatre, classical music, jazz, visual arts, dance, immersive experiences (many free), international films and a writers' week. Worth scheduling a trip around, especially for nocturnal types.

Fremantle Festival CULTURAL
(www.fremantlefestival.com.au; ⏱Jul) In winter the city's streets and concert venues come

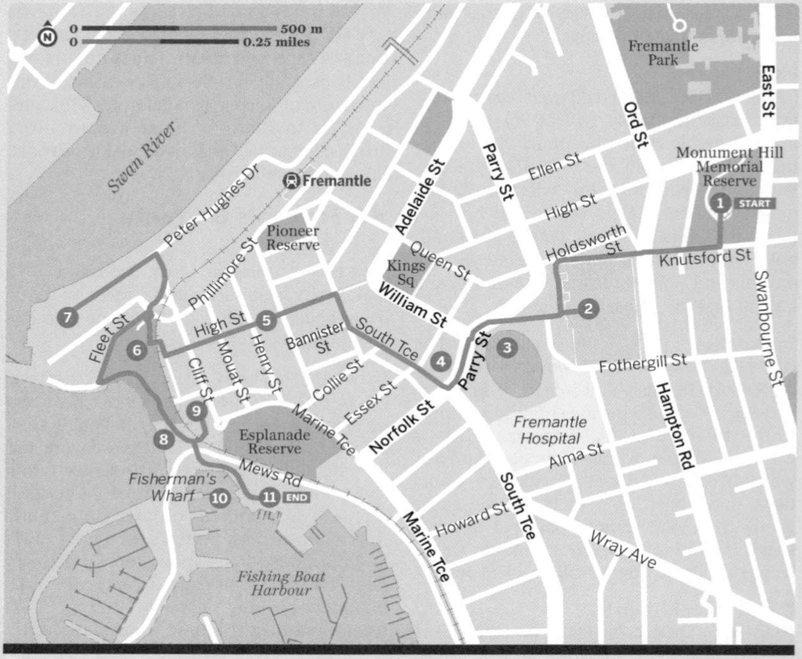

City Walk Fremantle on Foot

START MONUMENT HILL
END LITTLE CREATURES
LENGTH 4KM; TWO HOURS

Check out Fremantle's big-ticket sights on this atmospheric amble, and absorb the town's nautical vibes en route.

Get the lay of the land (and sea) from atop 1 **Monument Hill**, a lofty peak just east of the old town. Take a deep breath of sea air then head downhill to Knutsford St, turn right and cross Hampton Rd. The towering limestone walls of 2 **Fremantle Prison** (p65) are ahead. Tours here are grimly fascinating.

From the front of the prison, take Fairburn St to Parry St past the historic 3 **Fremantle Oval** (home to the Fremantle Dockers women's team), then turn right onto South Tce, dubbed 'Cappuccino Strip' in less cosmopolitan days. The historic 4 **Fremantle Markets** (p65) are on your right: duck inside for a quick-fire bite and an earful of buskers.

Continue along South Tce and turn left on 5 **High St**, the heart of the West End, lined with atmospherically weathered Victorian and Edwardian port buildings. At the end of the street over the rail line is the 1831 6 **Round House** (p65), a former prison and WA's oldest building.

Stay west of the rail line, following it around to Peter Hughes Dr and the excellent 7 **Western Australian Museum – Maritime** (p65) on Victoria Quay; the museum illuminates Freo's timeless bond with the sea.

Backtrack to Peter Hughes Dr, veer right onto Fleet St and head down to 8 **Bathers Beach** (p66) – the only beach in WA with an alcohol licence. Abstain for now and follow the foreshore south. Cross the rails again to the excellent 9 **WA Shipwrecks Museum** (p65), a captivating space in which to wreck a few hours.

Recross the rail line and follow the waterside boardwalk around 10 **Fishing Boat Harbour** to 11 **Little Creatures** (p92), one of Australia's pioneering craft-beer breweries and the perfect spot to end your hike with a pizza and a pale ale.

alive with parades and performances in Australia's longest-running festival.

Kings Park Festival CULTURAL

(www.kingsparkfestival.com.au; ⌚ Sep) Perth's largest inner-city green space, Kings Park is planted with thousands of native wildflowers each year, which bloom each September. To coincide with the Botanic Garden (p60) displays, the festival includes live music every Sunday, nature exhibitions, wellness events, guided walks and talks.

Perth Royal Show FAIR

(www.perthroyalshow.com.au; Claremont Showground; ⌚ late Sep-early Oct) A week of funfair rides, spun sugar and show bags full of plastic junk. Oh, and farm animals.

Blessing of the Fleet RELIGIOUS

(www.facebook.com/fremantleblessingofthefleet; Fishing Boat Harbour, Esplanade Reserve; ⌚ late Oct) A tradition since 1948, this event was brought to Fremantle by immigrants from Molfetta, Italy. It includes the procession of the Molfettese *Our Lady of Martyrs* statue and the Sicilian *Madonna di Capo d'Orlando* from St Patrick's Basilica to Fishing Boat Harbour, where the blessing takes place.

Sleeping

Perth's hotel options have improved greatly in recent years, with a slew of luxury and designer hotels opening in Northbridge and the CBD. Most of Perth's hostels are in Northbridge; some cater to long-term residents working in Perth, which can skew the ambience for travellers. But some good news: accommodation prices here have collapsed since the WA mining boom went bust. Perth is now an affordable city for sleepy people.

Central Perth

Pensione Hotel BOUTIQUE HOTEL $

(Map p62; ☎ 08-9325 2133; www.pensione.com.au; 70 Pier St; d $105-175; P ❄ ≈) The central-city 98-room Pensione delivers a bit of budget boutique sheen. The standard rooms definitely veer towards cosy and (very) compact, but classy decor, reasonable prices and a good location are redemptive. Spend a few dollars more on a Premium King room for some extra elbow room. Parking $28.

Perth City YHA HOSTEL $

(Map p62; ☎ 08-9287 3333; www.yha.com.au; 300 Wellington St; dm from $25, d/f $90/120, d without bathroom $70; ❄ ≈ ≋) Occupying an impressive 1939 sandstone art deco building by the train tracks, Perth's YHA corridors have a boarding-school feel, but the rooms are clean and there's a pool, gym and generous kitchen. The 'Fun Starts Here' declares a sign on a faux-turf wall, but like most YHAs the vibe is low-key after dark (good or bad, depending on your interests).

Wickham Retreat HOSTEL $

(Map p62; ☎ 08-9325 6398; www.facebook.com/wickhamretreat; 25-27 Wickham St, East Perth; dm from $30; ❄ ≈) Nooked into a residential 'hood east of the CBD, arty, independent Wickham Retreat has a quieter vibe than many Perth hostels. Most guests are international travellers, drawn by the colourful dorms, relaxed vibe and funky AstroTurf garden. Free pasta extends travel budgets; so too the free CAT bus nearby. Tight reception hours (8am to 10am and 7pm to 9pm).

★ **Melbourne Hotel** BOUTIQUE HOTEL $$

(Map p62; ☎ 08-9320 3333; www.melbournehotel.com.au; 33 Milligan St; d/ste from $180/280; P ❄ ≈) The new section of the Melbourne Hotel looms above the original 1897 heritage pub like a parasitic black Darth Vader. But fear not – it's actually an extremely stylish addition to the old dame, itself thoroughly upgraded. Room prices in either the old or new sections are comparable: it's just a question of taste. Parking from $18.

QT Perth DESIGN HOTEL $$

(Map p62; ☎ 08-9225 8000; www.qthotelsandresorts.com/perth; 133 Murray St; d from $285; P ❄ ≈) With a lobby decorated with potted cacti, polished concrete and jarrah, retro furniture and a sparkling cafe/cocktail bar, you'll be forgiven for feeling like you're on a James Bond film set. Rooms dip into a similar 'industrial luxe' designer grab bag: it's a really funky high-end product, enhanced by a superb rooftop bar. Valet parking $40.

Peppers Kings Square Hotel HOTEL $$

(Map p62; ☎ 08-9483 9600; www.peppers.com.au/kings-square; 621 Wellington St; d/f from $190/320; P ❄ ≈) Australia's tallest modular hotel has perforated metal sunshades and sabres of blue neon dancing on its 17-storey facade by night, though the rooms are less imaginative. Concrete-jungle views are guaranteed; fast wi-fi, pod coffee and free bottled water are other sweeteners. The downstairs lobby restaurant has decent breakfast, but there are better options nearby for dinner. Parking from $30.

Adina Apartment Hotel Barrack Plaza APARTMENT $$
(Map p62; ☎08-9267 0000; www.tfehotels.com/brands/adina-apartment-hotels; 138 Barrack St; 1/2 bedroom apt from $249/289; P❄📶🏊) With a curved facade shining in the bright sun, Adina's meticulously decorated, apartment-sized hotel rooms are minimalist yet welcoming. One-bedroom rooms have balconies, with rooms fronting Barrack St enjoying more natural light. Barack St below is a bit of a downer (sex shops, tattoo joints etc) – but maybe you don't mind a bit of urban grit? Rooftop pool. Parking $30.

★ **Como The Treasury** BOUTIQUE HOTEL $$$
(Map p62; ☎08-6168 7888; www.comohotels.com/thetreasury; State Bldgs, 1 Cathedral Ave; r from $445; P❄📶🏊) A regular on lists of 'World's Best Hotels', Como the Treasury has 48 luxury rooms that fill the baroque splendour of the historic State Buildings, vacant for 20 years before the Como opened in 2016. Despite the heritage backdrop, the property is wonderfully contemporary, with tasteful art, supercourteous staff, a superb spa and indoor pool. Valet parking from $40.

Westin Perth HOTEL $$$
(Map p62; ☎08-6559 1888; www.marriott.com; 480 Hay St; d/f/ste from $280/370/520; P❄📶) A glam glass tower, straight outta downtown Houston, this slick internationalist could easily have defaulted to carbon-copy global style. But with the breezy outdoor lounges and cafes on adjacent Hibernian Pl, native plantings and fabulous Aboriginal art installations (sculptures, weavings, paintings and imprinted concrete panels), the Westin manages to feel very 'WA'. One of Perth's top hotels. Valet parking $55.

Sebel East Perth APARTMENT $$$
(Map p62; ☎08-9223 2500; www.thesebel.com/western-australia/the-sebel-east-perth; 60 Royal St, East Perth; apt from $240; P❄📶🏊) Modern, chic apartments with self-contained kitchenette and a classy hotel vibe. Hit the BBQ terrace at night, or adjacent Claisebrook Cove has a few nights' worth of restaurants, cafes and bars to explore. Parking from $20.

Northbridge

★ **Hostel G** HOSTEL $
(Map p62; ☎0402 067 099; www.hostelgperth.com; 80 Stirling St; dm/d/f from $26/96/120; ❄📶) Hostel G is a snappy refit of an old office block, with designer interiors by esteemed architects Woods Bagot. Beanbag-strewn communal areas revolve around a central bar/cafe (burgers, pizza, pasta), with a cinema wall, pool tables and yoga studio. The quiet en suite rooms are graded in ascending order of niceness: good, great, glam and greatest, priced accordingly. Excellent!

Shiralee Backpackers HOSTEL $
(Map p62; ☎08-9227 7448; www.theshiralee.com; 107 Brisbane St; dm/d $30/70; ❄📶) Beyond a high wooden fence and sociable front porch, this international backpackers (no Aussie fly-in/fly-out workers) extends a long way back from the street. Myriad dorms and doubles, decent bathrooms and an impressive commercial-standard kitchen eventually cede territory to a bricky rear BBQ courtyard.

Emperor's Crown HOSTEL $
(Map p62; ☎08-9227 1400; www.emperorscrown.com.au; 85 Stirling St; dm from $19, d/tr $75/99, d without bathroom from $65; P❄📶) One of Perth's best hostels is also one of the most keenly priced, with friendly staff, high housekeeping standards and a primo position (close to the Northbridge scene without actually being in it). Over several levels and awash with orange doors, it's an entirely tidy operation. Parking $10.

★ **Alex Hotel** BOUTIQUE HOTEL $$
(Map p62; ☎08-6430 4000; www.alexhotel.com.au; 50 James St; d from $209; ❄📶) A vision of robust contemporary design, the Alex is stylish evidence of Northbridge's social evolution. Classy, compact rooms are decked out in neutral colours, and stacked with fine linen and electronic gear. Relaxed shared spaces include a hip mezzanine lounge (honesty bar and muffins!) and fab city-view roof terrace. Shadow, Alex's street-front wine bar, channels Euro bistro vibes. Excellent stuff.

Attika APARTMENT $$
(Map p62; ☎08-6168 8598; www.attikahotel.com; 279 Newcastle St; apt from $190; P❄📶) Sophisticated, grey-hued Attika features 22 contemporary studio and one-bedroom apartments over two levels, a short wobble from the William St action (just far enough from the boozy mayhem). Expect good security and compact kitchenettes making clever use of space. It's popular with business bods, so weekend rates are cheaper. Greek eats downstairs; parking $25.

Highgate & Mount Lawley

Pension of Perth B&B $

(Map p67; ☎08-9228 9049; www.pensionperth.com.au; 3 Throssell St, Highgate; s/d from $135/150; P ❄ 📶) Pension of Perth lays the belle époque luxury on thick, with rich floral rugs, brocade curtains, open fireplaces and gold-framed mirrors. It's a 120-year-old red-brick house, with two bay-window en suite doubles looking out onto a magnificent Moreton Bay fig across the street in Hyde Park (p60), which has a good kids' playground, and a third room with spa bath. Free on-street parking. Includes continental breakfast.

Witch's Hat HOSTEL $

(Map p67; ☎08-9228 4228; www.witchs-hat.com; 148 Palmerston St, Highgate; dm $24-30, tw & d $60-75; P ❄ @ 📶) Like something out of a fairy tale, this 1897 building could be mistaken for a gingerbread house, with its stained glass, lovely old floorboards and the witch's hat itself (a terracotta-tiled Edwardian turret) standing proudly out the front, beckoning the curious to step inside. Dorms are light and uncommonly spacious, and there's a red-brick barbecue area out the back.

Durack House B&B $$

(Map p67; ☎08-9370 4305; www.durackhouse.com.au; 7 Almondbury Rd, Mount Lawley; r $195-215; P ❄ 📶) It's hard to avoid words like 'delightful' when describing this white-painted Federation house, set on a peaceful Mount Lawley street behind a brick-paved garden and rose-adorned picket fence. The two guest rooms have boundless old-world charm, paired with mod bathrooms. It's only 250m from Mount Lawley station. Rates include breakfast: cooked (menu changes daily) or continental (fruit, yoghurt, juice, cereal).

Leederville

★ **Lakeside B&B** B&B $

(Map p58; ☎08-9381 7257; www.lakesideperth.com.au; 130 St Leonards Ave, West Leederville; d with/without breakfast from $160/140; P ❄ 📶 🏊) Lakeside B&B is close to Lake Monger, with its ducks, jogging paths and BBQs, but once you're inside this lovely wisteria-hung Federation home you'll lose interest in lakes. The two guest rooms are tastefully styled with interesting antiques, and there's a pool and shady verandah demanding the consumption of G&Ts. The guest rooms share a bathroom, but that's the only catch.

THE FREMANTLE DOCTOR

Huh? Who's a doctor? And why are they the only one in Fremantle? No – this medic is actually Perth's famous summer sea breeze, which cools down the city and provides sweet relief to the gasping, sun-stroked locals. The science is simple: the air over Perth heats up in the sunshine and rises into the sky, sucking in cool air from over the Indian Ocean to fill the void – a classic sea-breeze scenario. The Doctor peaks between noon and 3pm, reaching wind speeds of up to 20 knots (about 37km/h) and blustering as far inland as York by late afternoon. Local tip: hit the beach in the morning, before the Doctor flattens out the surf and blows sand in your face.

Beatty Lodge HOSTEL $

(Map p68; ☎08-9227 1521; www.beattylodge.com.au; 235 Vincent St, West Perth; dm/s/tw/d from $23/60/65/70; P ❄ 📶 🏊) Built to house athletes competing at the 1962 Perth Commonwealth Games – swimming events happened at Beatty Park Leisure Centre (p69) across the street – Beatty Lodge is now a trim-and-tidy backpackers hostel with 130 beds over three floors. It's a big and rather spartan setup, with good security, a cavernous kitchen and a fab swimming pool in the centre of the complex.

Kings Park & Subiaco

★ **Riverview 42 Mt St Hotel** APARTMENT $

(Map p68; ☎08-9321 8963; www.riverviewperth.com.au; 42 Mount St, West Perth; apt $110-210; P ❄ 📶) There's a lot of brash new money on Mount St, but character-filled Riverview stands out with a bit of old-school personality. Its refurbished 1960s bachelor pads sit neatly atop a buzzy cafe and foyer hung with Persian rugs. Rooms (all with kitchenette) are sunny and simple; the ones at the front have river views, while the rear ones are quieter.

Tribe Hotel DESIGN HOTEL $$

(Map p68; ☎08-6247 3333; www.tribehotels.com.au; 4 Walker Ave, West Perth; r from $170; P ❄ 📶) Join the tribe of fans who list Tribe as their fave Perth hotel, a stylin' multistorey addition to the accommodation offerings around Kings Park, barely 100m away. Looking like the black-box flight recorder from some giant crash-landed spaceship – all black perforated-metal panels and jaunty sunshades – Tribe ticks the style boxes inside too. Hip defined.

Quest Mounts Bay Road APARTMENT $$
(Map p58; 08-9480 8100; www.questapartments.com.au; 130 Mounts Bay Rd, Kings Park; d from $200, 1-bedroom apt from $260;) On a tree-lined boulevard at the base of the steep escarpment rising up to Kings Park, seven-storey Quest delivers consistent, reliable, stylish serviced apartments. Next to the hotel, the Jacob's Ladder steps (242 of them) climb up to the park: sit in Quest's on-site cafe and silently mock the sweaty joggers parading past. Parking is off-site.

Sage Hotel DESIGN HOTEL $$
(Map p68; 08-6500 9100; www.nexthotels.com/sage/west-perth; 1309 Hay St, West Perth; r from $190; P) Handily placed for both the CBD and Kings Park, Sage's eccentrically patterned concrete tower offers sassy rooms with big TVs, cleverly designed bathrooms and work stations. Amenities include a gym in which to iron out your aeroplane-seat kinks, and **Julio's Italian Restaurant** (mains $28 to $47) in a 100-year-old heritage house out the front. Free off-site parking.

Scarborough to Cottesloe

Western Beach Lodge HOSTEL $
(Map p58; 08-9245 1624; www.westernbeach.com; 6 Westborough St, Scarborough; dm/d without bathroom from $28/60; P) A real surfer hang-out, this sociable, rather shaggy hostel has a low-key, guitar-strumming, hammock-swinging vibe. Discounts kick in for stays of three nights or longer. Surfboards and bodyboards are ready to go ('At the beach' says the sign, if the owner's not around).

ROCKIN' BON SCOTT

Legendary hellraiser and frontman of Australian hard-rock band AC/DC, Ronald Belford Scott (1946–80), known universally as 'Bon', moved to Fremantle from Scotland with his family in 1956. He spent his teen years strutting around Freo, and the city still adores him. Down by Fishing Boat Harbour, check out Bon's **statue** (Map p70; Carrington St & Leach Hwy, Palmyra) by local artist Greg James, in classic rock pose (it's a petite rendition – surely not life-size?). Bon's ashes are interred in **Fremantle Cemetery** (Map p58; Carrington St): enter near the corner of High and Carrington Sts – Bon's plaque is 15m along the path on the left.

★ **Cottesloe Beach Hotel** PUB $$
(Map p58; 08-9383 1000; www.cottesloebeachhotel.com.au; 104 Marine Pde, Cottesloe; d from $195;) The old art deco Cottesloe is a mighty charming pub on Cottesloe Beach, with bars and cafes downstairs (perfect Indian Ocean sunset-watching territory) and 13 lovely rooms upstairs. Far above usual pub accommodation standards, each room has a bathroom, double glazing, balcony and effortless beachy style. Angle for a sea view if you can. On-street parking only.

Ramada Vetroblu Scarborough Beach APARTMENT $$
(08-6248 7000; www.ramadavetrobluscarboroughbeach.com; 48a Filburn St, Scarborough; d from $185, 1-/2-bedroom apt from $220/380; P) A couple of blocks back behind the monolithic Rendezvous Grand, the eight-tier Ramada does things with a little more subtlety. Some of the apartments in the building are residential, so construction, security and cleaning standards are sky-high. All apartments have kitchenettes, stylish interiors and whisper-quiet double glazing. Cafe on-site; parking $15.

Seashells Scarborough Beach APARTMENT $$
(08-9341 9600; www.seashells.com.au/resorts/scarborough; 178 The Esplanade, Scarborough; 1-/2-/3-bedroom apt from $265/280/405; P) Seashells is a local WA chain with a few other properties around the state, but Scarborough is their flagship, with two pools and nothing between you and the deep blue sea but a road and a glass-fronted balcony. Inside, the apartments aren't up-to-the-minute hip, but they're spacious, secure and private. Free parking is a bonus.

Quest Scarborough APARTMENT $$
(08-6140 3500; www.questapartments.com.au; 4 Brighton Rd, Scarborough; d from $250, 1-/2-bedroom apt from $280/460; P) If you're seduced by muted colour schemes, polite service and corporate stylings, the Quest chain generally delivers. Predictable and unremarkable, maybe...but also fabulously located, reliable, secure and quiet: seven storeys of rock-solid slumbering. Book car parks in advance (from $20).

Fremantle

Fremantle Hostel HOSTEL $
(Map p70; ☎08-9430 6001; www.fremantlehostel.com.au; 15 Packenham St; dm $22-29;) A lofty warehouse encloses this bright, airy, clean hostel of dorms and shared bathrooms only. It has free bikes to borrow, a free food night, a hammock, gym, BBQ, pool table and a chilled lounge area. Street art graces the walls and there's an in-house cafe doing drinks and desserts. Buffet breakfast included. Upstairs rooms have air-conditioning.

Fremantle Prison YHA Hostel HOSTEL $
(Map p70; ☎08-9433 4305; www.yha.com.au; 6a The Terrace; dm $24-29, d & tw from $96, f/cottages from $122/250; ⊙7am-11pm reception;) Fremantle's former women's prison is a hostel with clean dorm-style accommodation, private rooms and family-friendly **cottages** (Map p70; www.fremantlecottages.com.au; cottages $250), once guards' homes. Stay in one of the spartan cells and read the photo boards sharing inmate and prison stories. Well located, with excellent communal spaces and plenty of social activities such as free movies, team sports and wine nights.

Norfolk Hotel HOTEL $
(Map p70; ☎08-9335 5405; www.norfolkhotel.com.au; 47 South Tce; d $150, s/d with shared bathroom $90/120;) While eucalypts and elms stand quietly in the sun-streaked beer garden, the old limestone Norfolk harbours a secret upstairs: its nine rooms. Far above your standard pub digs, they've all been tastefully decorated in muted tones and crisp white linen, and there's a communal sitting room. It can be noisy on weekends, but the bar closes at midnight.

Woodman Point Holiday Park CAMPGROUND $
(☎08-9434 1433; www.discoveryholidayparks.com.au; 132 Cockburn Rd; sites for 2 people $38-43, d $99-159;) A lovely caravan and camping spot 10km south of Fremantle. It's usually quiet, and feels more summer beach holiday than outer-Freo staging post. Kids will gravitate to the bouncing pillow, playground and pool, dogs are welcome and there are BBQs, a camp kitchen and a kiosk. It's a 15-minute drive into Fremantle and there's a public bus stop out the front.

★ **Fremantle Apartment** APARTMENT $$
(Map p70; www.thefremantleapartment.com; 7 Leake St; apt $110-160;) Arrayed across three floors and featuring a New York–loft vibe, this spacious apartment is right in Fremantle's heritage precinct. A massive leather couch and big-screen TV combine with a well-equipped kitchen, and the fridge is usually stocked with a few complimentary chocolate nibbles. Friendly owners Cam and Terri have plenty of ideas on how best to enjoy Fremantle.

★ **Hougoumont Hotel** BOUTIQUE HOTEL $$
(Map p70; ☎08-6160 6800; www.hougoumonthotel.com.au; 15 Bannister St; d $173-275;) Named after a historic convict ship, this boutique hotel's spotlessly clean rooms are cleverly constructed from sea containers. Standard 'cabins' are compact, but stylish and efficiently designed; state rooms are bigger. Top-end toiletries, a breezy ambience and complimentary late-afternoon wine and snacks reinforce the centrally located Hougoumont's refreshing approach to accommodation. Service from the multinational team is relaxed but professional.

National Hotel BOUTIQUE HOTEL $$
(Map p70; ☎08-9335 6688; www.nationalhotelfremantle.com.au; 98 High St; d $189-376;) Not only does this boutique hotel have Fremantle's best (and only) rooftop bar, but its classic, heritage-style rooms are also exceedingly comfortable. The historic hotel was burnt to the ground and restored; now, chic bathrooms with huge baths that face a wall TV add allure. Lower-level rooms will feel and hear the vibrations from weekend live music in the anchoring pub.

Fothergills of Fremantle B&B $$
(Map p70; ☎08-9335 6784; www.fothergills.net.au; 18-22 Ord St; r $195-245;) Naked bronze women sprout from the front garden, while a life-size floral cow shelters on the verandah of these neighbouring mansions on the hill. Internal decor is in keeping with the buildings' venerable age (constructed 1892), including wonderful Aboriginal art and a superb collection of heritage maps of Australia. Breakfast is served in a sunny conservatory and there's free parking.

Be.Fremantle APARTMENT $$
(Map p58; ☎08-9430 3888; www.befremantle.com.au; Challenger Harbour, 43 Mews Rd; studio/apt from $189/199;) At the end of a wharf, these 4.5-star sandstone studios and one- to three-bedroom apartments have had a stylish makeover to reopen as the Be.Fremantle complex. The more expensive Marina View apartments enjoy the best ocean vistas, and

bikes are available to explore Fremantle. A further 24 new apartments opened in mid-2017, so ask about scoring one of those.

Port Mill B&B B&B $$
(Map p70; 08-9433 3832; www.portmillbb.com.au; 3/17 Essex St; r $199-299;) One of the most luxurious B&Bs in town, Port Mill is clearly the love child of Paris and Freo. Crafted from local limestone (it was built in 1862 as a mill), inside it's all modern French style, with gleaming taps, wrought-iron balconies and French doors opening out to the sun-filled decks, where the included breakfast is often served.

Other Areas

Discovery Holiday Parks – Perth Airport CARAVAN PARK $
(08-9453 6877; www.discoveryholidayparks.com.au; 186 Hale Rd, Forrestfield; powered sites $39-47, cabin without bathroom from $88, cabins & units with bathroom $95-169;) This well-kept holiday park with plenty of trees, 15km out of the city and 7km from the airport (closer to terminals 1 and 2 than 3 and 4), has a wide range of cabins and smart-looking units with decks. The rather grand terracotta-roofed entranceway delivers a dose of establishment.

Aloft Perth HOTEL $$
(Map p58; 08-6147 2468; www.marriott.com/hotels/travel/peral-aloft-perth; 27 Rowe Ave, Rivervale; d/f/ste from $180/210/345;) Lofty Aloft delivers city-style boutique vibes with airport proximity for your early-morning flight to the east coast (commonly known as the 'red-eye'). It's a towering white edifice near the southern banks of the Swan River, with stylish, generously sized rooms and a kitchen and bar on-site. Parking starts at $10.

Peninsula APARTMENT $$
(Map p58; 08-9368 6688; www.thepeninsula.net; 53 South Perth Esplanade, South Perth; 1-/2-bedroom apt from $170/250;) While only the front few apartments have full-on views, the Peninsula's waterfront location lends itself to lazy ferry rides and sunset strolls along the riverbank (swimming beach, bike track, fastidiously mown lawns). It's a sprawling, older-style, parchment-coloured complex, but it's kept in good nick. The apartments all have kitchenette and there's a communal laundry.

Eating

The slowing of WA's resources boom means that Perth's restaurant prices have eased a little. However, it can still be an expensive city for the hungry. The happening 'hoods for eating are Northbridge, Leederville and Mount Lawley, while nowhere does beachy fish and chips like Fremantle. Look forward to some cool cafes, brilliant bakeries and top seafood across the board.

Central Perth

Le Vietnam VIETNAMESE $
(Map p62; 08-6114 8038; www.facebook.com/levietnamcafe; 1/80 Barrack St; snacks $7; 7.30am-3pm Mon-Fri;) The best banh mi (Vietnamese baguettes) in town are served in this tiny, central spot. Classic flavour combos blend pork slivers, pâté, chilli and lemongrass, while newer spins feature pulled pork, roast pork and crackling. Interesting drinks include Vietnamese coffee and lychee lemonade, and a hearty breakfast or lunch will only cost around 10 bucks.

Nao JAPANESE $
(Map p62; 08-9325 2090; www.naojapaneserestaurant.com.au; Equus Arcade, shop 191/580 Hay St; mains $11-14; 11.30am-6pm Mon-Thu, to 9pm Fri, noon-5pm Sat & Sun) Asian students, CBD desk jockeys and savvy foodies gravitate to this spot serving the best Japanese-style ramen in town. At peak times you'll need to battle a small queue, but the silky combinations of broth, roast *chashu* pork and noodles are definitely worth the wait.

Twilight Hawkers Market STREET FOOD $
(Map p62; http://twilighthawkersmarket.com; Forrest Chase; snacks & mains around $10-15; 4.30-9.30pm Fri Nov-Mar) Ethnic food stalls bring the flavours and aromas of the world to central Perth on Friday nights in spring and summer. Combine your Turkish *gözleme* (savoury crepe) or Colombian empanadas (deep-fried pastries) with regular live music from local Perth bands.

Toastface Grillah CAFE $
(Map p62; 0409 115 909; www.toastfacegrillah.com; Grand Lane; sandwiches $5-9; 7am-4pm Mon-Fri, from 9am Sat) Vibrant street art, excellent coffee and a sneaky laneway location combine with interesting toasted sandwiches such as the 'Pear Grillz' with blue cheese, pear and lime chutney. All this and a not-so-subtle Wu-Tang Clan reference too.

Petition Kitchen AUSTRALIAN $$

(Map p62; 08-6168 7771; www.petitionperth.com/kitchen; cnr St Georges Terrace & Barrack St; small plates $12-22, large plates $17-60; 7am-11pm Mon-Fri, from 8am Sat & Sun;) One of Perth's most polished warehouse bistros, Petition manages to impress across all meal sittings with its inventive approach to local and seasonal ingredients, sometimes woven with indigenous produce such as finger lime or pepper berry. Breakfast is punchy, lunch wows with squid-ink linguine, pipis and Pernod, while dinner keeps the party going with charred zucchini, stracciatella and curry leaf.

Angel Falls Grill VENEZUELAN $$

(Map p62; 08-9481 6222; www.angelfallsgrill.com.au; Shop 16, Shafto Lane; mains $18-50; 11am-late) The pick of Shafto Lane's ethnic restaurants, Angel Falls Grill brings a taste of South America to WA. Salads and meat dishes are served with arepas (flat breads), and starters include empanadas and savoury-topped plantains. Grilled meat dishes from the *parrillada* (barbecue) are flavour-packed, and surprising breakfast options also make Angel Falls a great place to start the day.

La Veen CAFE $$

(Map p62; 08-9321 1188; www.laveencoffee.com.au; 90 King St; mains $13-25; 6.30am-3pm Mon-Fri, 7.30am-2pm Sat & Sun) La Veen's sunny brick-lined space, around the corner from fashion and design stores, showcases some of the city's best breakfast and lunch dishes – and it does excellent coffee. This being Australia, of course shakshuka (baked eggs) is on the menu, but La Veen's version, topped with *dukkah* and yoghurt and served with ciabatta toast, is one of Perth's best.

Tiisch Cafe Bistro CAFE $$

(Map p62; 0452 239 121; www.tiisch.com.au; 938 Hay St; mains $14-24; 7am-3pm Mon-Fri, 8am-2pm Sat & Sun) High ceilings and white walls inspire a European ambience at this leafy CBD cafe. A serious drinks list includes cold-brew coffee, matcha latte and artisan teas, and the breakfast and lunch menus are equally on trend. Start with macadamia-nut granola, or come later for mushroom orecchiette pasta with Parmesan velouté. It also does a bottomless brunch ($65) on weekends.

Lalla Rookh WINE BAR $$

(Map p62; 08-9325 7077; www.lallarookh.com.au; lower ground fl, 77 St Georges Tce; pizzas from $18, shared plates from $15; 11.30am-midnight Mon-Fri, from 5pm Sat) Escape down a hole in the CBD pavement to this subsurface restaurant specialising in modern Italian food. The fare encourages relaxed grazing with a tableful of shared dishes and local wine from the thoughtfully compiled wine list.

COTTESLOE PINES

Aside from the drop-dead gorgeous beach, the defining features of Cottesloe are its towering ranks of extremely healthy-looking Norfolk Island pine trees (*Araucaria heterophylla*) lining the streets. First planted along John St in 1915 when the Cottesloe Roads Board procured 168 pint-sized pines, the 18-inch saplings did so well that the pine-planting scheme soon expanded to incorporate most of the streets behind the beach. John St and Broome St remain the prime exemplars – cast an eye skywards as you wander by.

Perth City Farm MARKET $$

(Map p62; 08-9221 7300; www.perthcityfarm.org.au; 1 City Farm Pl; mains $13-21.50; 8am-noon Sat, cafe 7am-3pm Mon-Fri, to noon Sat) Local organic producers sell eggs, fruit, vegetables and bread at the Saturday-morning markets, and there's an excellent cafe on-site from Monday to Saturday. It's interesting to roam the grounds, looking at the community-run veggie gardens.

★ **Wildflower** MODERN AUSTRALIAN $$$

(Map p62; 08-6168 7855; www.wildflowerperth.com.au; State Bldgs, 1 Cathedral Ave; mains $42-49, 5-course tasting menu without/with wine $145/240; noon-2.30pm & 6pm-late Tue-Fri, 6pm-late Sat) Filling a glass pavilion atop the restored State Buildings, Wildflower offers fine-dining menus inspired by the six seasons of the Indigenous Noongar people of WA. There's a passionate focus on West Australian produce: dishes often include Shark Bay scallops or kangaroo smoked over jarrah embers, as well as indigenous herbs and bush plants like lemon myrtle and wattle seed.

★ **Long Chim** THAI $$$

(Map p62; 08-6168 7775; www.longchimperth.com; State Bldgs, cnr St Georges Tce & Barrack St; mains $25-45; noon-late;) Australian chef David Thompson is renowned for respecting the authentic flavours of Thai street food, and with dishes like a tongue-burning chicken *laap* (warm salad with fresh herbs) and roast red-duck curry, there's definitely no dialling back the flavour for Western palates. The prawns with toasted coconut and betel leaves may well be the planet's finest appetiser.

Santini Bar & Grill ITALIAN **$$$**
(Map p62; ☎08-9225 8000; www.santinibarandgrill.com.au; QT Perth, 133 Murray St; small plates $14-24, large plates $23-58; ⊙6.30am-late; ❄) Classy, fine-dining-style Italian food is served in the undeniably cool interiors of the QT hotel (p75). The pasta is made in-house (the duck 'Bolognese' with crackling is a thing of beauty), the fish is ocean-fresh (try the tuna crostini) and the perfectly seasoned steak sublime. The pizzas are cracking too. Have a pre or post drink across the hall.

Print Hall MODERN AUSTRALIAN **$$$**
(Map p62; ☎08-6282 0000; www.printhall.com.au; 125 St Georges Tce; shared plates $12-20, mains $25-49; ⊙11.30am-midnight Mon-Fri, from 4pm Sat) This sprawling complex in the Brookfield Pl precinct includes the Apple Daily, featuring Southeast Asian–style street food, the perfect-for-leaning Print Hall Bar and a swish Italian restaurant called Gazette. Don't miss having a drink and a burger or pizza in the rooftop Bob's Bar, named after Australia's larrikin former prime minister Bob Hawke.

Balthazar MODERN AUSTRALIAN **$$$**
(Map p62; ☎08-9421 1206; www.balthazar.com.au; 6 The Esplanade; small plates $21-28, large plates $36-57; ⊙noon-midnight Mon-Fri, from 6pm Sat) Low-lit, discreet and sophisticated, with a cool soundtrack and charming staff, Balthazar has an informal vibe that's matched by exquisite food and a famously excellent wine list. The menu is refreshingly original, combining European flavours with an intensely local and seasonal focus. Younger owners have reinvented Balthazar as a refined yet relaxed option with superior shared plates.

Northbridge

★ **Wines of While** AUSTRALIAN **$**
(Map p62; ☎08-9328 3332; www.winesofwhile.com; 458 William St; mains $10-24; ⊙noon-midnight Tue-Sat, to 10pm Sun) A 50-seater wine bar that's fast become known for its great value and incredibly flavoursome food. Surprisingly, the bar's run by a young, qualified doctor who still works as a surgical assistant on Mondays. His true passion is natural wine, but he's a phenomenal cook. Get the ricotta-zucchini salad, the house-baked bread and zesty lemon white beans.

★ **Chicho Gelato** GELATO **$**
(Map p62; www.chichogelato.com; 180 William St; from $5; ⊙noon-10pm Sun-Wed, to 11pm Thu-Sat) Hands down Perth's best gelato. With innovative flavours like avocado with candied bacon, and everything made from real ingredients (no fake flavourings here), it's easy to see why. Expect queues in the evening – don't worry, the line moves quickly – and ask about current collaborations with local chefs. Do pay $1 extra to have melted chocolate poured into your waffle cone.

Tak Chee House MALAYSIAN **$**
(Map p62; ☎08-9328 9445; 1/364 William St; mains $11-18; ⊙11am-9pm Tue-Sun) With Malaysian students crammed in for a taste of home, Tak Chee is one of the best Asian cheapies along William St. If you don't have a taste for satay, Hainan chicken or *char kway teo* (fried noodles), Thai, Vietnamese, Lao and Chinese flavours are all just footsteps away. Cash only; BYO wine or beer.

Little Willys CAFE **$**
(Map p62; ☎08-9228 8240; 267 William St; mains $10-19; ⊙6am-4pm Mon-Fri, from 8am Sat & Sun) The name here pertains to the cafe's petite size, and the fact it's on William St – don't get any funny ideas. Grab a footpath table and tuck into robust treats such as the city's best breakfast burrito and Bircher muesli. It's also a preferred coffee haunt for the hip Northbridge indie set. BYO skinny jeans.

Kakulas Bros DELI **$**
(Map p62; ☎08-9328 5285; www.kakulasbros.com.au; 183 William St; ⊙8am-5pm Mon-Sat, 11am-4pm Sun; ✎) A local institution since 1929, this fragrant provisions store overflows with sacks and vats of legumes, nuts, dried fruits and olives, plus a deli counter that's well stocked with cheese and meats. The coffee beans are roasted on-site. There's another branch, **Kakulas Sister** (Map p70; ☎08-9430 4445; www.kakulassister.net.au; 29-31 Market St; ⊙9am-5.30pm Mon-Fri, to 5pm Sat, from 11.30am Sun; ✎), in Fremantle.

★ **Bivouac Canteen & Bar** CAFE **$$**
(Map p62; ☎08-9227 0883; www.bivouac.com.au; 198 William St; small plates $9-19, large plates $28-34; ⊙noon-late Tue-Sat) Flavour-jammed, Middle Eastern–influenced cuisine partners with a good wine list, craft beers and artisanal ciders. Always-busy Bivouac's white

walls are adorned with a rotating roster of work from local artists. The lamb ribs in a lemon glaze are a great way to kick off the meal, followed by the Palestinian-style nine-spice chicken with toasted buckwheat and smoky yoghurt.

Henry Summer AUSTRALIAN **$$**
(Map p62; www.lavishhabits.com.au/venues/henry-summer; 69 Aberdeen St; ⌚noon-midnight Sun-Thu, to 2am Fri & Sat; 🐾; 🚌free CAT) The size of a pub with the feel of a small bar, Henry Summer woos with cascading plants and fronded canopies, open-air spaces and a welcoming vibe. The menu blends premixed cocktails with wood-fired meats and raw salads. Collect your dishes from a pink neon sign declaring 'Pick up spot' and see what – or who – else you encounter.

Hummus Club MIDDLE EASTERN **$$**
(Map p62; ☎08-9227 8215; www.thehummusclub.com; 258 William St; mains $14-18; ⌚5-10pm Tue-Thu & Sun, from noon Fri & Sat; 🍷) If you can nab a seat on the open-air balcony, consider yourself lucky. Hummus Club has become one of Northbridge's coolest foodie haunts, not least for its creamy hummus served with spiced beef and toasted almonds, lamb kofta, falafel and watermelon fattoush salad. Cocktails using local craft spirits and Lebanese Almaza beer complement a fun vibe.

Sauma INDIAN **$$**
(Map p62; ☎08-9227 8682; www.sauma.com.au; 200 William St; mains $16-29; ⌚5-10pm Tue & Wed, 11am-10.30pm Thu & Sun, to 11pm Fri & Sat) Punchy Indian street-food flavours feature at this corner location in Northbridge that always has the windows open wide. Interesting antiques surround the main bar dispensing Indian-inspired cocktails and Swan Valley beers, while the shared tables are crowded with diners tucking into chai-smoked oysters, chargrilled chilli-squid salad and a terrific, rustic goat curry.

Brika GREEK **$$**
(Map p62; ☎0455 321 321; www.brika.com.au; 3/177 Stirling St; meze & mains $12-35; ⌚5pm-late Mon-Thu, from noon Fri-Sun) Presenting a stylish spin on rustic Greek cuisine, off-the-main-drag Brika is a load of fun. The whitewashed interior is enlivened by colourful traditional fabrics. Menu highlights include creamy smoked-eggplant dip, slow-cooked lamb and charred calamari. Definitely leave room for a dessert of *loukoumades* (Greek doughnuts).

Viet Hoa VIETNAMESE **$$**
(Map p62; ☎08-9328 2127; www.viethoa.com.au; 349 William St; mains $10-23; ⌚10am-10pm Mon-Sat, to 9pm Sun) Don't be fooled by the bare-bones ambience of this corner Vietnamese restaurant, or you'll miss out on the fresh rice-paper rolls and top-notch, steaming-hot pho. Greenery creeping up the beams gives the busy place an offbeat feel.

Highgate & Mount Lawley

Chu Bakery CAFE, BAKERY **$**
(Map p67; ☎08-9328 4740; www.instagram.com/chubakery; 498 William St, Highgate; snacks from $5; ⌚7am-4pm Tue-Sun) Chu makes a great stop before or after exploring nearby Hyde Park (p60). The coffee is excellent, the doughnuts superb, and the sourdough bread recommended if you're planning a beach picnic at Cottesloe or City Beach. For a picnic lunch, a favourite outdoor combo is takeaway espresso and toast topped with creamy avocado, whipped feta and sriracha sauce.

★**Sayers Sister** CAFE **$$**
(Map p67; ☎08-9227 7506; www.sayerssister.com.au; 236 Lake St, Highgate; mains $14-28; ⌚7am-4pm Mon-Fri, to 3pm Sat & Sun) Top-notch brunch options – including leek and Parmesan croquettes in dreamy leek cream with poached eggs – combine with eclectic interiors that are said to be inspired by the long-time owners' home. Plonk down in an armchair or perch on the bench table for fine-quality, seasonal fare a short walk from leafy Hyde Park (p60). Breakfast cocktails add to the fun.

Mary Street Bakery CAFE **$$**
(Map p67; ☎0499-509-300; www.marystreetbakery.com.au; 507 Beaufort St, Highgate; mains $13-24; ⌚7am-4pm) Crunchy and warm baked goods, artisan bread and interesting cafe fare combine with what may be Perth's best chocolate-filled doughnuts at this spacious, sunny addition to the casual dining scene in Mount Lawley. It's a good way to start the day – particularly if you order the fried-chicken buttermilk pancakes – before exploring the area's eclectic retail scene.

Mrs S CAFE **$$**
(Map p58; ☎08-9271 6690; www.mrsscafe.com.au; 178 Whatley Cres, Maylands; mains $11-23; ⌚7am-4pm Mon-Fri, from 8am Sat & Sun) Mrs S has a quirky retro ambience, the perfect backdrop for beautifully decorated cakes, a healthy breakfast or a lazy brunch.

1

CATHERINE SUTHERLAND/LONELY PLANET ©

2

4

BMPHOTOGRAPHER/SHUTTERSTOCK ©

1. Varnish on King (p90)
This cocktail bar, which specialises in American whiskey, is located on hip lower King St.

2. Elizabeth Quay (p57)
Home to luxury hotels and waterfront restaurants, plus waterside sculpture *Spanda* by Christian de Vietri, this redeveloped area is more than a transport hub.

3. Cafe, Beaufort St, Highgate (p83)
Highgate is home to plenty of eateries offering tasty baked goods, seasonal fare and fancy bread.

4. Federation Walkway, Botanic Garden (p60)
A highlight of the gardens is the Federation Walkway, designed by architects Donaldson and Warn, leading to a glass-and-steel sky bridge that passes over a eucalyptus canopy.

FLEUR BAINGER/LONELY PLANET ©

1am Fri, to 2am Sat) Old-style pub that attracts the Beaufort St indie crowd. A good spot for a drink before a comedy show or music gig up the road at the **Astor** (Map p67; 08-9370 1777; www.astortheatreperth.com; 659 Beaufort St, Mount Lawley) theatre.

Leederville

Leederville Hotel PUB
(Map p68; 08-9202 8282; www.leedervillehotel.com; 742 Newcastle St; 11am-late) Cool decor and good food ensure nights are huge at the Garden, the Leederville's stab at a 21st-century gastropub. It's the summery, open-air section to the enormous pub: the rest is filled by Bill's Bar, a polished-concrete and couches zone, while out the back is the popular Blue Flamingo, which heaves after dark. Live music plays upstairs at Babushka.

Kings Park & Subiaco

Juanita's BAR
(Map p68; 08-9388 8882; www.facebook.com/juanitasbarsubiaco; 341 Rokeby Rd, Subiaco; 2-10pm Tue, to 11pm Thu, from noon Fri, from 2pm Sat, 3-9pm Sun) Welcome to Perth's most neighbourly small bar. Tapas, shared platters (terrines, pâtés and fries – the co-owner chef often works the floor) and a concise selection of beer and wine partner with mismatched chairs and couches inside, and packed clusters of tables outside. It's all thoroughly local, very charming and a refreshing antidote to the flash, renovated pubs elsewhere in Subiaco.

Scarborough to Cottesloe

Twenty9 BAR
(Map p58; 08-9284 3482; 29 Napoleon St, Cottesloe; 7am-9pm Tue-Wed, to 10pm Thu-Sun) In the swanky retail street of Cottesloe, away from the chilled-out beach strip, Twenty9 is a casual, family-friendly joint playing Foxtel sport and serving easy-to-please dishes (mains $20).

Fremantle

★ **Little Creatures** BREWERY
(Map p70; 08-6215 1000; www.littlecreatures.com.au; Fishing Boat Harbour, 40 Mews Rd; 10am-late Mon-Fri, from 9am Sat, to 11pm Sun;) Try everything on tap – particularly the Pale Ale and Rogers. The floor's chaotic and fun, and the wood-fired pizzas ($20 to $24) are worth the wait. Shared plates ($8 to $27) include kangaroo with tomato chutney and marinated octopus. There's a sandpit out the back for kids and free bikes for all, plus regular brewery tours ($20). No bookings.

★ **Norfolk Hotel** PUB
(Map p70; 08-9335 5405; www.norfolkhotel.com.au; 47 South Tce; 11am-midnight Mon-Sat, to 10pm Sun) Slow down to Freo pace at this 1887 pub. Interesting guest beers wreak havoc for the indecisive drinker, and the food and pizzas are very good (share plates $9-24, mains $19-40). The heritage limestone courtyard is a treat, especially when sunlight dapples through elms and eucalypts. Downstairs, the Odd Fellow channels a bohemian small-bar vibe and has live music Wednesday to Saturday from 7pm.

Strange Company COCKTAIL BAR
(Map p70; www.strangecompany.com.au; 5 Nairn St; small plates $9-15, mains $14-23; noon-midnight) Fabulous cocktails (try the spiced daiquiri), WA craft beers and slick, good-value food make Strange Company a sophisticated alternative to the raffish pubs along South Tce. It's still very laid-back, though – this is Freo, after all – and after-work action on the sunny terrace segues into after-dark assignations in Strange Company's cosy wooden interiors. It's worth staying for dinner.

Percy Flint's Boozery & Eatery BAR
(Map p58; 08-9430 8976; www.facebook.com/percyflintsouthfreo; 211 South Tce; 4pm-midnight Tue-Thu, from noon Fri-Sun) A relaxed neighbourhood watering hole, Percy Flint is very popular with locals. The tap-beer selection is one of Freo's most interesting, with brews from around WA, and shared plates with Mediterranean or Asian flavours are best enjoyed around the big tables in the garden courtyard.

Mrs Browns BAR
(Map p58; 08-9336 1887; www.mrsbrownbar.com.au; 241 Queen Victoria St, North Fremantle; 4.30pm-midnight Mon-Thu, from noon Fri & Sat, to 10pm Sun) Exposed bricks and a copper bar combine with retro and antique furniture to create North Fremantle's most atmospheric drinking den. The music could include all those cult bands you thought were *your* personal secret, and an eclectic menu of beer, wine and tapas targets the more discerning, slightly older bar hound. Ordering burgers from **Flipside** (Map p58;

☎08-9433 2188; www.flipsideburgers.com.au; 239 Queen Victoria St; burgers $8-16; ⏰11.30am-9pm) next door is encouraged.

Who's Your Mumma BAR

(Map p70; ☎08-9467 8595; www.facebook.com/whosyourmummabar; cnr Wray Ave & South Tce; ⏰4pm-midnight Mon-Thu, from noon Fri & Sat) Industrial-chic lightbulbs and polished-concrete floors are softened by recycled timber at chilled Who's Your Mumma. An eclectic crew of South Freo locals gathers for excellent cocktails, craft beer and moreish bar snacks, including duck spring rolls and steamed pork buns.

Whisper WINE BAR

(Map p70; ☎08-9335 7632; www.whisperwinebar.com.au; 1/15 Essex St; ⏰3pm-late Tue-Thu, from noon Fri-Sun) In a lovely heritage building, this classy French-themed wine bar also does shared plates of charcuterie and cheese.

Other Areas

Dutch Trading Co CRAFT BEER

(Map p58; ☎08-6150 8329; www.thedutchtradingco.com.au; 243 Albany Hwy, Victoria Park; ⏰4pm-midnight Tue-Thu, from noon Fri & Sat, to 10pm Sun) Located in an up-and-coming eating-and-drinking strip, the Dutch Trading Co combines rustic bar leaners and repurposed sofas with tattooed and bearded bartenders slinging the best of Aussie craft beers. Besides the ever-changing taps, there's a fridge full of international brews, and bar snacks include croquettes with mustard, spicy buttermilk chicken and hearty steak sandwiches.

☆ Entertainment

Check the *West Australian* newspaper for what's on. Book through www.ticketek.com.au or www.ticketmaster.com.au.

Cinema

Rooftop Movies CINEMA

(Map p62; ☎08-9227 6288; www.rooftopmovies.com.au; 68 Roe St; online/door $16/17; ⏰Tue-Sun late Oct-late Mar) Art-house films, classic movies and new releases screen under the stars on the 6th floor of a Northbridge car park. Beanbags, wood-fired pizza and craft beer all combine for a great night out. Booking ahead online is recommended and don't be surprised if you're distracted from the on-screen action by the city views. Score $14 tickets on cheap Tuesdays.

Somerville Auditorium CINEMA

(Map p58; ☎08-6488 2000; www.perthfestival.com.au; 35 Stirling Hwy, Crawley; ⏰Nov-Mar) A quintessential Perth experience, the Perth Festival's international film program is held outdoors, on the University of WA's beautiful grounds, surrounded by pines and strings of lights. Picnicking before the film is a must. Bring a cushion as the deckchair seating can be uncomfortable.

Cinema Paradiso CINEMA

(Map p62; ☎08-6559 0490; www.palacecinemas.com.au/cinemas/cinema-paradiso; 164 James St) Art-house, independent and foreign movies are shown at this cinema in the heart of Northbridge.

Luna CINEMA

(Map p68; ☎08-9444 4056; www.lunapalace.com.au; 155 Oxford St) Fully licensed, art-house cinema in Leederville with Monday double-header features and a bar. The vintage cinema has been renovated with four new screens alongside the original building. Cheap tickets on Wednesday ($12 to $14). During summer there's an outdoor screen.

Camelot Outdoor Cinema CINEMA

(Map p58; ☎08-9386 3554; http://camelot.lunapalace.com.au; Memorial Hall, 16 Lochee St, Mosman Park; ⏰Dec-Easter) Seated open-air cinema where you can BYO picnic (no booze). It has free live music ahead of the 8.15pm film screening on Wednesdays, ranging from jazz to folk and blues.

Moonlight Cinema CINEMA

(Map p58; www.moonlight.com.au; May Dr Parklands, Kings Park; ⏰1 Dec-31 Mar) In summer bring a blanket and a picnic and enjoy a romantic moonlit movie. Booking ahead online is recommended.

Luna on SX CINEMA

(Map p70; ☎08-9430 5999; www.lunapalace.com.au; Essex St; adult/child $20/14.50; 👪) Art-house cinema between Essex and Norfolk Sts. Cheaper tickets on Wednesday ($12/14 before/after 6pm).

Comedy

Lazy Susan's Comedy Den COMEDY

(Map p62; ☎08-9328 2543; www.lazysusans.com.au; Brisbane Hotel, 292 Beaufort St, Highgate; ⏰8pm Tue, Fri & Sat) Shapiro Tuesday offers a mix of first-timers, seasoned amateurs and pros trying out new shtick (for a very reasonable $5). Friday is for more grown-up stand-ups, including some interstate visitors ($25).

Saturday is the Big Hoohaa – a team-based, improv-meets-theatre laugh-fest ($25).

Live Music

Freo.Social LIVE MUSIC

(Map p70; www.freo.social; Parry St, Fremantle; 11am-midnight Wed-Sun;) Part live-music haunt, part microbrewery, part food-truck and beer-garden hang-out, Freo.Social is difficult to pigeonhole. Open since March 2019, the evolving venue with capacity for 550 people fills a historic space in central Fremantle. It favours big-name local talent, from San Cisco to John Butler and the Waifs, but also leans towards the experimental and has DJ sets.

★ **Duke of George** JAZZ

(Map p58; 08-9319 1618; www.dukeofgeorge.com.au; 135 George St, East Fremantle; plates $18-29, dinner show $35-65 plus gig ticket; 5pm-midnight Thu-Fri, from noon Sat, to 10pm Sun;) Newly opened in the historic Brush Factory, this is a fun, lively, hugely approachable jazz bar where dancing between the tables (there's no designated dance floor) is encouraged. Saturday's dinner and show is highly recommended (excellent value too), but you can keep things simple with the à la carte menu of dishes inspired by America's deep south.

Moon LIVE MUSIC

(Map p62; 08-9328 7474; www.themoon.com.au; 323 William St; 5pm-1am Mon-Thu, noon-late Fri-Sun) A low-key, late-night cafe that's been running for more than 20 years and is regarded as a local institution, particularly by students. It has singer-songwriters on Wednesday night, jazz on Thursday and poetry slams on Saturday afternoon from 2pm.

Badlands Bar LIVE MUSIC

(Map p62; 0498 239 273; www.badlands.bar; 3 Aberdeen St; 6pm-2am Fri & Sat) Located on the fringes of Northbridge, Badlands has shrugged off its previous incarnation as a retro 1950s-inspired nightclub to be reborn as an edgy rock venue. The best WA bands are regulars, and if an up-and-coming international band is touring, Badlands is the place to see them before they become really famous. Check online for listings.

Mojos LIVE MUSIC

(Map p58; 08-9430 4010; www.mojosbar.com.au; 237 Queen Victoria St, Fremantle; 5.30pm-midnight Mon & Tue, from 5pm Wed, to 1am Thu-Sat, 4-10pm Sun) Local and national bands (mainly Aussie rock and indie) and DJs play at this small place, and there's a sociable beer garden out the back. First Friday of the month is reggae night, every Monday is open-mic night and local music stars on Tuesdays. It's slightly dingy and dog-eared in that I-want-to-settle-in-all-night kind of way. Locals love it.

RAC Arena LIVE MUSIC

(Perth Arena; Map p62; 08-6365 0700; www.pertharena.com.au; 700 Wellington St) Used for big concerts by major international acts such as Rhianna and the Rolling Stones. It's also used by the Perth Wildcats NBL basketball franchise and is home to West Coast Fever netball.

Newport Hotel LIVE MUSIC

(Map p70; 08-9335 2428; www.thenewport.com; 2 South Tce; noon-10pm Mon-Tue, to midnight Wed-Thu, to 1am Fri & Sat, 11am-10pm Sun) Local bands and DJs gig out the back from Friday to Sunday, while there's musical bingo and trivia on quieter nights in this nautically themed pub. The Tiki Beat Bar is worth a kitsch cocktail or two.

Amplifier LIVE MUSIC

(Map p62; 08-9321 7606; www.amplifiercapitol.com.au; rear 383 Murray St) The good old Amplifier is one of the best places for live (mainly indie) bands. (Part of the same complex as Capitol, used mainly for DJ gigs.)

Perth Concert Hall CONCERT VENUE

(Map p62; 08-9231 9999; www.perthconcerthall.com.au; 5 St Georges Tce) Home to the **Western Australian Symphony Orchestra** (WASO; 08-9326 0000; www.waso.com.au), this brutalist-style building also hosts big-name international acts, musicals and comedians.

Universal LIVE MUSIC

(Map p62; 08-9227 6771; www.universalbar.com.au; 221 William St; 3pm-1am Wed & Thu, 11.30am-2am Fri, from 4pm Sat, to midnight Sun) The unpretentious Universal is one of Perth's oldest live-music bars and much loved by soul, R & B and blues enthusiasts. All ages hit their groove on the dance floor. It ain't pretty, but it is fun.

Rosemount Hotel LIVE MUSIC

(Map p67; 08-9328 7062; www.rosemounthotel.com.au; cnr Angove & Fitzgerald Sts; 11am-late) Local and international bands play regularly in this spacious art deco pub with a laid-back beer garden.

IT'S JUST NOT CRICKET

Feared and respected by cricketers the world over, Perth's WACA Ground – the Western Australian Cricket Association's HQ on the edge of central Perth – is famous for its rock-hard batting surfaces. Test cricket was first played here in the 1970–71 season, and for many decades, local fast-bowling firebrands like Dennis Lillee, Terry Alderman and Rodney Hogg sent down thunderbolts here. The WACA pitch and outfield were *fast* – and beating Australia here took some serious doing. But now, the WACA's ageing infrastructure and the shifting tastes of Australia's cricket-watching public have spawned the Optus Stadium across the river. Will the pitch live up to the WACA tradition, or will spongy new 'drop-in' pitches change the way the cricketing world thinks about playing in Perth? Either way, for Perth's cricket fans, the times are a-changin'.

Ellington Jazz Club JAZZ
(Map p62; ☎08-9228 1088; www.ellingtonjazz.com.au; 191 Beaufort St; ⏲6.30-10pm Mon-Thu, to 1.30am Fri & Sat, 5.30-9pm Sun) There's live jazz nightly in this handsome, intimate venue staging professional-level jazz in all its forms. Standing-only admission is $10, or you can book a table (per person $15 to $20) for tapas and pizza.

Sport

Optus Stadium STADIUM
(Perth Stadium; Map p58; www.optusstadium.com.au; Victoria Park Dr, Burswood) Perth's new 60,000-seat riverside stadium and its surrounding, family-friendly park (think playground, BBQs, sculptures) opened in January 2018. Big concerts, AFL games and international sport fixtures including cricket and rugby are held here. A new Perth Stadium train station services incoming crowds, while the Matagarup bridge links the stadium precinct with East Perth, enabling pedestrian access across the Swan River.

WACA STADIUM
(Western Australian Cricket Association; Map p62; ☎08-9265 7222; www.waca.com.au; Nelson Cres) Main venue for interstate and international cricket, and home to the Perth Scorchers. Since 2018, one-day internationals have been held at Optus Stadium.

HBF Park STADIUM
(Perth Oval; Map p62; ☎08-9422 1500; www.hbfpark.com.au; 310 Pier St) Home to soccer (football) team **Perth Glory** (☎08-9492 6000; www.perthglory.com.au) and rugby team **Western Force** (☎08 6280 0168; www.westernforce.com.au).

Theatre

His Majesty's Theatre THEATRE
(Map p62; ☎08-6212 9292; www.ptt.wa.gov.au/venues/his-majestys-theatre; 825 Hay St) The majestic home to the **West Australian Ballet** (☎08-9214 0707; www.waballet.com.au) and **West Australian Opera** (☎08-9278 8999; www.waopera.asn.au), as well as lots of theatre, comedy and cabaret.

State Theatre Centre THEATRE
(Map p62; ☎08-6212 9292; www.ptt.wa.gov.au/venues/state-theatre-centre-of-wa; 174 William St) This stunning complex filled with gold tubes hanging from the ceiling includes the 575-seat Heath Ledger Theatre and the 234-seat Studio Underground. It hosts performances by the Black Swan State Theatre Company, Yirra Yaakin Theatre Company and the Barking Gecko young people's theatre. Serious, challenging and deeply artistic performances are regularly held.

Shopping

Visit Northbridge for vintage and retro stores, and Leederville for design shops and galleries. In the city, the William St mall offers major retailers, while King St is home to independent clothing designers. Down in Fremantle, books and music shops prevail, plus some quirky arts-and-crafts hubs. The historic Fremantle Markets (p65) are always worth a look, if only for the buskers!

Boffins Books BOOKS
(Map p62; ☎08-9321 5755; www.boffinsbooks.com.au; 88 William St; ⏲9am-5.30pm Mon-Thu, to 8pm-Fri, to 5pm Sat, noon-4pm Sun) Locally adored, Boffins' technical and specialist range includes travel.

William Topp DESIGN
(Map p62; ☎08-9228 8733; www.williamtopp.com; 452 William St; ⏲10.30am-5.30pm Mon-Fri, 10am-5pm Sat, 11am-4pm Sun) Cool designer knick-knacks, one-off finds, handmade ceramics and framed tea towels. If you need a quirky gift, this is your spot.

Future Shelter HOMEWARES
(Map p67; ☎08-9228 4832; www.futureshelter.com; 56 Angove St, North Perth; ⏰10am-5pm Mon-Sat, noon-3pm Sun) Quirky clothing, gifts and homewares designed and manufactured locally. Surrounding Angove St is an emerging hip North Perth neighbourhood with other cafes and design shops worth browsing.

Atlas Divine CLOTHING
(Map p68; ☎08-9242 5880; www.facebook.com/atlasdivine; 121 Oxford St; ⏰10am-5pm Sat-Wed, to 9pm Thu & Fri) Hip women's and men's clobber: jeans, quirky tees, dresses etc.

Planet Books BOOKS, MUSIC
(Map p67; ☎08-9328 7464; www.planetbooks.com.au; 638 Beaufort St, Mount Lawley; ⏰10am-late) Cool bookshop with prints, posters and a good range of Australian-themed titles.

Aspects of Kings Park ART, SOUVENIRS
(Map p68; ☎08-9480 3900; www.aspectsofkingspark.com.au; Fraser Ave, Kings Park; ⏰9am-5pm) Australian art, homewares, chunky jewellery and coffee-table books with an emphasis on handcrafted pieces and organic shapes.

Aboriginal Art & Craft Gallery ART
(Map p68; ☎08-9481 7082; www.aboriginalgallery.com.au; Fraser Ave, Kings Park; ⏰10.30am-4.30pm Mon-Fri, 11am-4pm Sat & Sun) Work from around WA; more populist than high end or collectible. The gallery is slightly hidden below the Kaarta Gar-up lookout.

Mossenson Galleries – Indigenart ART
(Map p68; ☎08-9388 2899; www.mossensongalleries.com.au; 115 Hay St, Subiaco; ⏰11am-4pm Wed-Sat) Serious Aboriginal art from around Australia but with a focus on WA artists. Works include weavings, paintings on canvas, bark and paper, and sculpture.

New Edition BOOKS
(Map p70; ☎08-9335 2383; www.newedition.com.au; cnr High & Henry Sts; ⏰9am-9pm) Celebrating a sunny corner location for the past 30 years, this bookworm's dream has comfy armchairs for browsing, and a superb collection of Australian fiction and nonfiction tomes for sale. Author events, poetry readings and literary launches are common; check the website for the shop's latest book reviews.

Common Ground Collective DESIGN
(Map p70; ☎0418 158 778; www.facebook.com/cmmngrnd; 82 High St; ⏰10am-5pm Mon-Sat, from 11am Sun) An eclectic showcase of jewellery, apparel and design, much of it limited edition and mainly from local Fremantle artisans and designers. The coffee at the in-house cafe is pretty damn good too.

Found ARTS & CRAFTS
(Map p58; ☎08-9432 9569; www.fac.org.au/shop; Fremantle Arts Centre, 1 Finnerty St; ⏰9am-5pm) The Fremantle Arts Centre (p65) shop stocks an inspiring range of WA art and craft, from textiles and jewellery to prints and woodwork.

Japingka ART
(Map p70; ☎08-9335 8265; www.japingka.com.au; 47 High St; ⏰10am-5.30pm Mon-Fri, noon-5pm Sat & Sun) Specialising in ethical Aboriginal fine art from WA and beyond. Purchases come complete with extensive notes about the works and the artists who created them.

Record Finder MUSIC
(Map p70; ☎08-9335 2770; www.truelocal.com.au/business/the-record-finder/fremantle; 87 High St; ⏰10am-5pm) A treasure trove of old vinyl, including niche editions and music styles as well as collectibles.

Bodkin's Bootery SHOES
(Map p70; ☎08-9336 1484; www.bodkinsbootery.com; 72 High St; ⏰9am-5.30pm Mon-Thu, to 6pm Fri, to 6.30pm Sat, noon-6pm Sun) Handcrafted boots and hats. Aussie as.

Mills Records MUSIC
(Map p70; ☎08-9335 1945; www.mills.com.au; 22 Adelaide St; ⏰9am-5.30pm Mon-Fri, to 5pm Sat, from 11am Sun) Music, including some rarities (on vinyl and CD); instruments from harmonicas to acoustic guitars; and concert tickets. Check out the 'Local's Board' for recordings by Freo and WA acts.

ℹ Information

EMERGENCY & IMPORTANT NUMBERS

Emergency (police, fire, ambulance) ☎000

Directory assistance ☎1223

Perth Police Station (☎emergency 000, non-emergency 08-9422 7111; www.police.wa.gov.au; 2 Fitzgerald St; ⏰24hr)

INTERNET ACCESS

Perth City offers free wi-fi access in Murray St Mall between William St and Barrack St.

Fremantle City Library (☎08-9432 9766; www.frelibrary.wordpress.com; Fremantle Oval, 70 Parry St; ⏰9am-6pm Mon-Thu, to 5pm Fri, to 1pm Sat, 11am-3pm Sun; 📶)

State Library of WA (☎08-9427 3111; www.slwa.wa.gov.au; Perth Cultural Centre, 25

Francis St; ⌚9am-8pm Mon-Thu, to 5.30pm Fri, from 10am Sat & Sun; 📶)

MEDIA

Newspapers Perth's daily paper is the *West Australian*, aka the *West*, although the *Australian* and *Financial Review* are also widely available. There's also a Sunday tabloid called the *Sunday Times*.

Websites See www.perthnow.com.au for breaking news, and www.xpressmag.com.au or www.scenestr.com.au/perth for live music and culture.

MEDICAL SERVICES

Chemist Discount Centre (☎08-9321 5391; www.chemistdiscountcentre.com.au; 93 William St; ⌚7am-7pm Mon-Thu, to 9pm Fri, 9am-6pm Sat, 11am-5pm Sun) Handy city pharmacy.

Fremantle Hospital (☎08-9431 3333; www.fhhs.health.wa.gov.au; Alma St; ⌚24hr) At the edge of central Fremantle.

Lifecare Dental (☎08-9221 2777; www.lifecaredental.com.au; 419 Wellington St; ⌚8am-8pm) In Forrest Chase.

Royal Perth Hospital (☎08-9224 2244; www.rph.wa.gov.au; 197 Wellington St; ⌚24hr) In central Perth.

Sexual Assault Resource Centre (☎08-6458 1828, free call 1800 199 888; www.kemh.health.wa.gov.au/services/sarc; ⌚24hr) Provides a 24-hour emergency service.

Travel Medicine Centre (☎08-9321 7888; www.travelmed.com.au; 5 Mill St; ⌚8am-5pm Mon-Thu, to 4pm Fri, 8.30am-12.30pm Sat) Travel-specific advice and vaccinations.

MONEY

ATMs are plentiful, and there are currency-exchange facilities at the airport and major banks in the CBD.

POST

Australia Post Office (Map p62; ☎13 76 78; www.auspost.com.au; 66 St Georges Tce; ⌚8am-5pm Mon-Fri)

Fremantle Post Office (Map p70; ☎13 13 18; www.auspost.com.au; 1/13 Market St; ⌚9am-5pm Mon-Fri, to 12.30pm Sat)

TOURIST INFORMATION

Fremantle Visitor Centre (Map p70; ☎08-9431 7878; www.visitfremantle.com.au; Town Hall, Kings Sq; ⌚9am-5pm Mon-Fri, to 4pm Sat, from 10am Sun) Accommodation and tour bookings; bike rental.

Perth City Visitor Kiosk (Map p62; www.visitperth.com.au; Forrest Pl, Murray St Mall; ⌚9.30am-4.30pm Mon-Thu & Sat, to 8pm Fri, 11am-3.30pm Sun) Volunteers here answer questions and run walking tours.

WA Visitor Centre (p270) Excellent resource for information across WA.

ℹ Getting There & Away

AIR

Around 10km east of Perth, **Perth Airport** (☎08-9478 8888; www.perthairport.com.au; Airport Dr) is served by numerous airlines, including **Qantas** (QF; ☎13 13 13; www.qantas.com.au), with daily flights to and from international and Australian destinations. There are four terminals: T1 and T2 are 15 minutes from T3 and T4. T1 handles most international flights, along with Virgin Australia interstate flights. T2 handles regional WA flights for Alliance Airlines, Tigerair, Virgin Australia and Regional Express. T3 handles all Jetstar flights; T4 handles all Qantas flights. A free terminal transfer bus operates around the clock.

BUS

Transwa (Map p62; ☎13 62 13; www.transwa.wa.gov.au; East Perth Station, West Pde, East Perth; ⌚office 8.30am-5pm Mon-Fri, to 4.30pm Sat, 10am-4pm Sun) operates services from the bus terminal at East Perth train station to/from many destinations around the state. These include the following.

- SW1 to Augusta ($55, six hours) via Mandurah, Bunbury, Busselton and Dunsborough.
- SW2 to Pemberton ($57, 5½ hours) via Bunbury, Balingup and Bridgetown.
- GS1 to Albany ($66, six hours) via Mt Barker.
- GE2 to Esperance ($98, 10 hours) via Mundaring, York and Hyden.
- N1 to Geraldton ($69, six hours) and on to Northampton and Kalbarri.

South West Coach Lines (Map p62; ☎08-9753 7700; www.southwestcoachlines.com.au) focuses on the southwestern corner of WA, running services from **Elizabeth Quay Bus Station** (Map p62; ☎13 62 13; www.transperth.wa.gov.au; Mounts Bay Rd) to most towns in the region. Destinations include Bunbury ($58, three hours), Busselton ($63, 3¾ hours), Dunsborough ($77, 4½ hours), Margaret River ($77, 4½ hours) and Manjimup ($79, five hours).

Integrity Coach Lines (p121) runs northbound and southbound services linking Perth to Broome and stopping at key coastal travellers' destinations en route. It also runs inland services between Perth and Port Hedland via Mt Magnet, Cue, Meekatharra and Newman.

TRAIN

Transwa runs the following services from Perth into rural WA.

- *Australind* (twice daily) Perth Station to Pinjarra ($18.05, 1¼ hours) and Bunbury ($33.50, 2½ hours).

➡ *MerredinLink* (daily) East Perth Station to Toodyay ($18.05, 1¼ hours), Northam ($21.15, 1½ hours) and Merredin ($48.60, 3¼ hours).

➡ *Prospector* (daily) East Perth to Kalgoorlie-Boulder ($91.80, 5¾ hours).

Great Southern Rail (1800 703 357; www.greatsouthernrail.com.au) runs the *Indian Pacific* train between Perth and Sydney – a four-day, three-night, 4352km cross-continental epic. Fares start at $2239 one way, including all meals, drinks and off-train excursions.

Getting Around

TO/FROM THE AIRPORT

Taxi fares to the city from the airport are around $45 from all terminals.

Just Transfers (0400 366 893; www.justtransfers.com.au) runs prebooked shuttle buses between Perth Airport and the city/Fremantle (one way per person from $17.50/60, cheaper for multiple travellers).

Transperth bus 40 travels regularly to T3 and T4 from Elizabeth Quay Bus Station; bus 380 runs regularly to T1 and T2, also from Elizabeth Quay Bus Station (both routes $4.90, 45 minutes).

BICYCLE

Riding in the central city can be a drag (traffic, hills, no bike lanes) but Perth has some great bike tracks around the river, around Kings Park and along the beach-suburb coastline. Bikes can be taken free of charge on ferries at any time and on trains outside weekday peak hours (7am to 9am and 4pm to 6.30pm) – with a bit of planning you can pedal as far as you like in one direction then return via public transport. Bikes can't be taken on buses, except some regional coaches (for a small charge). For route maps, see www.transport.wa.gov.au/cycling or call into a bike shop.

Spinway WA (0413 343 305; www.spinwaywa.bike; per 1/4/24hr from $11/22/33) has 14 self-serve bicycle-hire kiosks in handy spots around central Perth, Kings Park, South Perth, Scarborough and Fremantle. Bikes cost $11 for one hour, $22 for four hours, or $33 for 24 hours. Swipe your credit card and follow the prompts. Helmets and locks are included, available from partner businesses (often hotel reception desks) where bikes are parked outside. Alternatively, rent a bike from **Cycle Centre** (08-9325 1176; www.cyclecentre.com.au; 326 Hay St; bike hire per day/week from $25/65; 9am-5.30pm Mon-Fri, to 4pm Sat, from 1pm Sun).

About Bike Hire (08-9221 2665; www.aboutbikehire.com.au; 305 Riverside Dr, East Perth; per hour/day/week from $10/24/64; 8am-6pm Nov-Mar, reduced hours Apr, May & Oct) Road, off-road and hybrid bikes for hire at reasonable rates. Also hires kayaks and stand-up paddleboards; see the website for details.

Free Wheeling Fremantle (08-9431 7878; www.fremantle.wa.gov.au/visit/getting-around/cycling; Fremantle Visitor Centre, Kings Sq; 9am-5pm Wed-Sun) Bike rental.

CAR & MOTORCYCLE

Driving in the city takes a bit of practice, as some streets are one way and many aren't signposted. There are plenty of (expensive) car-parking buildings in the central city but no free places to park. For unmetered street parking you'll need to look well away from the main commercial strips and check the signs carefully.

A fun way to careen about the city is on a moped. **Scootamoré** (08-9380 6580; www.scootamore.com.au; 356a Rokeby Rd, Subiaco; hire 1/3/7 days $60/150/300; 8.30am-5.30pm Mon-Fri, 9am-1pm Sat) hires 50cc scooters with helmets (compulsory) and insurance included (for those over 21).

Car-rental companies big and small proliferate in Perth, including the following:

Avis (08-9237 0022; www.avis.com.au; 960 Hay St; 7.30am-6pm Mon-Fri, to 1pm Sat & Sun)

Backpacker Car Rentals (08-9430 8869; www.backpackercarrentals.com.au; 284 Hampton Rd, South Fremantle)

Bayswater (08-9325 1000; www.bayswatercarrental.com.au; 160 Adelaide Tce; 7am-6pm Mon-Fri, 8am-3.30pm Sat & Sun)

Budget (08-9237 0022; www.budget.com.au; 960 Hay St; 8am-5pm Mon-Fri, to 11am Sat, to 10am Sun)

Campabout (08-9858 9126; www.campaboutoz.com.au)

Hertz (08-9321 7777; www.hertz.com.au; 475 Murray St; 7am-6pm Mon-Thu, to 6.30pm Fri, 8am-1pm Sat & Sun)

Sunset (08-9245 2466; www.sunsetrentacar.com.au; 6 Scarborough Beach Rd, Scarborough; 8am-5pm Mon-Fri, to 1pm Sat)

Thrifty (08-9225 4466; www.thrifty.com.au; 198 Adelaide Tce; 8am-4.45pm Mon-Fri, to 11.45pm Sat & Sun).

Britz (08-9479 5208; www.britz.com/au) hires out fully equipped 4WDs fitted out as campervans, popular on the roads of northern WA; it has offices in all the state capitals, as well as Perth and Broome, so one-way rentals are possible.

PUBLIC TRANSPORT

Transperth (13 62 13; www.transperth.wa.gov.au) operates Perth's excellent network of public buses, trains and ferries. There are Transperth information offices at Perth Station (Wellington St), Perth Busport (between Roe St and Wellington St), Perth Underground Station (off Murray St) and Elizabeth Quay Bus Station

(Mounts Bay Rd). There's a serviceable online journey planner.

Bus

Perth's central **Free Transit Zone** (FTZ) is served by regular buses and is well covered during the day by the four free **Central Area Transit** (CAT) services. The Yellow and Red CATs operate east–west routes, with Yellow sticking mainly to Wellington St, and Red looping roughly east on Murray St and west on Hay St. The Blue CAT does a figure eight through Northbridge and the southern end of the city; this is the only one to run late – to midnight on Friday and Saturday only. The Green CAT connects Leederville Station and Elizabeth Quay Bus Station via West Perth and St Georges Tce. There are also free Red and Blue CATs in Fremantle: Red loops north of the central area, Blue to the south.

Pick up a copy of free CAT timetables (widely available on buses and elsewhere) for the exact routes and stops. Buses run roughly every five to 15 minutes, more frequently on weekdays. Digital displays at the stops advise when the next bus is due.

The broader metropolitan area is serviced by a wide network of Transperth buses. Pick up timetables from any Transperth information centre or use the online journey planner. Most buses leave from the underground **Perth Busport** (Map p62; ☎13 62 13; www.transperth.wa.gov.au/perthbusport; via Yagan Sq; ⏰ info centre 7.30am-5.30pm Mon-Fri, 8am-1pm Sat), located between the CBD and Northbridge.

Ferry

A ferry runs every 20 to 30 minutes between **Elizabeth Quay Jetty** (Map p62; ☎13 62 13; www.transperth.wa.gov.au; off William St, Elizabeth Quay) and Mends St Jetty in South Perth – a great way to get to Perth Zoo or for a bargain from-the-river glimpse of the Perth skyline. Little Ferry Co (p72) runs scheduled services linking Elizabeth Quay and Claisebrook Cove, also connecting to Perth Stadium on big-game days.

The highly professional Rottnest Express (p106) runs ferries to Rottnest Island from both Elizabeth Quay (p106) and Fremantle – stops at **Victoria Quay** (Map p70; B Shed, Victoria Quay; ⏰ 6.45am-5.15pm) and Rous Head (p106). All kinds of bike-hire, island-tour and accommodation packages are available.

Train

Transperth (☎13 62 13; www.transperth.wa.gov.au) operates five train lines from around 5.20am to midnight weekdays and to about 2am Saturday and Sunday. Your rail ticket can also be used on Transperth buses and ferries within the ticket's zone. You're free to take your bike on the train during nonpeak times. The lines and useful stops include the following:

Armadale Thornlie Line Perth, Burswood

Fremantle Line Perth, City West, West Leederville, Subiaco, Swanbourne, Cottesloe, North Fremantle, Fremantle

Joondalup Line Elizabeth Quay, Perth Underground, Leederville

Mandurah Line Perth Underground, Elizabeth Quay, Rockingham, Mandurah

Midland Line Perth, East Perth, Mount Lawley, Guildford, Midland

Perth Station (☎13 62 13; www.transperth.wa.gov.au; Wellington St) is the main hub with access to all lines (some via the linked Perth Underground Station).

Elizabeth Quay Station (☎13 62 13; www.transperth.wa.gov.au; off William St, Elizabeth Quay) is serviced by the Joondalup and Mandurah lines.

Fares

From the central city, the following fares apply for all public transport.

Free Transit Zone (FTZ) Covers the central commercial area, bounded (roughly) by Fraser Ave, Kings Park Rd, Thomas St, Newcastle St, Parry St, Lord St and the river (including the City West and Claisebrook train stations, to the west and east respectively).

Zone 1 Includes the city centre and the inner suburbs ($3.10).

Zone 2 Fremantle, Guildford and the beaches as far north as Sorrento ($4.80).

Zone 3 Hillarys Boat Harbour (AQWA), the Swan Valley and Kalamunda ($5.60).

Zone 5 Rockingham ($9.40).

Zone 7 Mandurah ($11.10).

DayRider Unlimited travel after 9am weekdays and all day on the weekend in any zone ($12.80).

FamilyRider Lets two adults and up to five children travel for a total of $12.80 on weekends, after 6pm weekdays and after 9am on weekdays during school holidays.

Buy cash tickets from ticket machines at train stations and ferry jetties, or from bus drivers.

TAXI

Perth has a decent system of metered taxis, though the distances make frequent use costly and on busy nights you may have trouble flagging a taxi down in the street. The two main companies are **Swan Taxis** (☎13 13 30; www.swantaxis.com.au) and **Black & White Cabs** (☎08-9230 0440; www.blackandwhitecabs.com.au); both have wheelchair-accessible cabs. Uber also operates throughout Perth.

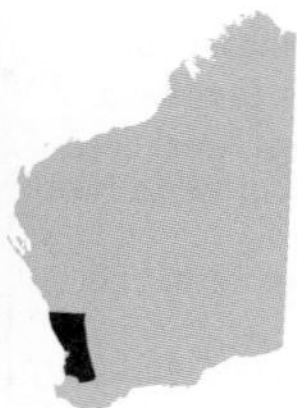

Perth Region

Includes ➡

Rottnest Island......102
Rockingham........106
Peel Region.........107
Mandurah..........107
Dwellingup..........108
Perth Hills..........110
Swan Valley.........112
Avon Valley.........115
New Norcia.........118
Wildflower Way......118
Sunset Coast.......120
Turquoise Coast.....121

Why Go?

You don't have to travel too far from Perth for a taste of the rest of Western Australia. Just a day trip away, venturing into the lands of the Noongar nation, are the oceanic activities and breezy cafes of Mandurah, and the hyperactive winery, craft-beer and foodie scenes of the Swan Valley and Perth Hills (Wajuk tribal country). The heritage-listed towns of the underrated Avon Valley (Ballardong homelands) are also nearby. If you prefer more natural detours, head for the astonishing granite swell of Wave Rock on Nyaki-Nyaki lands; the brilliant swim spots and resident quokkas on Rottnest Island (Wadjemup); the people-free shores of the Sunset Coast and Turquoise Coast (Yuat lands); or the lonesome highways and long-lost wheat towns along Wildflower Way (also Ballardong country), which burst into a blaze of native blooms in spring.

Best Places to Eat

- Flic's Kitchen (p108)
- Ostro Eatery (p107)
- Core Cider (p110)
- Hotel Rottnest (p105)
- Rose & Crown (p113)

Best Places to Stay

- Lancelin Lodge YHA (p121)
- Centre Break Beach Stay (p124)
- Manuel Towers (p107)
- Discovery Rottnest Island (p105)
- Dukes Inn (p115)

When to Go

Mandurah

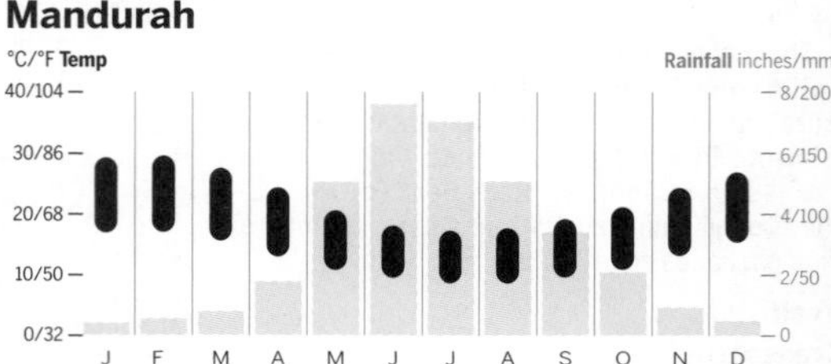

Mar Lingering beach weather lures you up the coast to Guilderton, Lancelin and beyond.

Aug Wildflowers start to bloom; brave paddlers take on the Avon River Descent.

Nov Catch the ferry to Rottnest Island and beat the summer crowds.

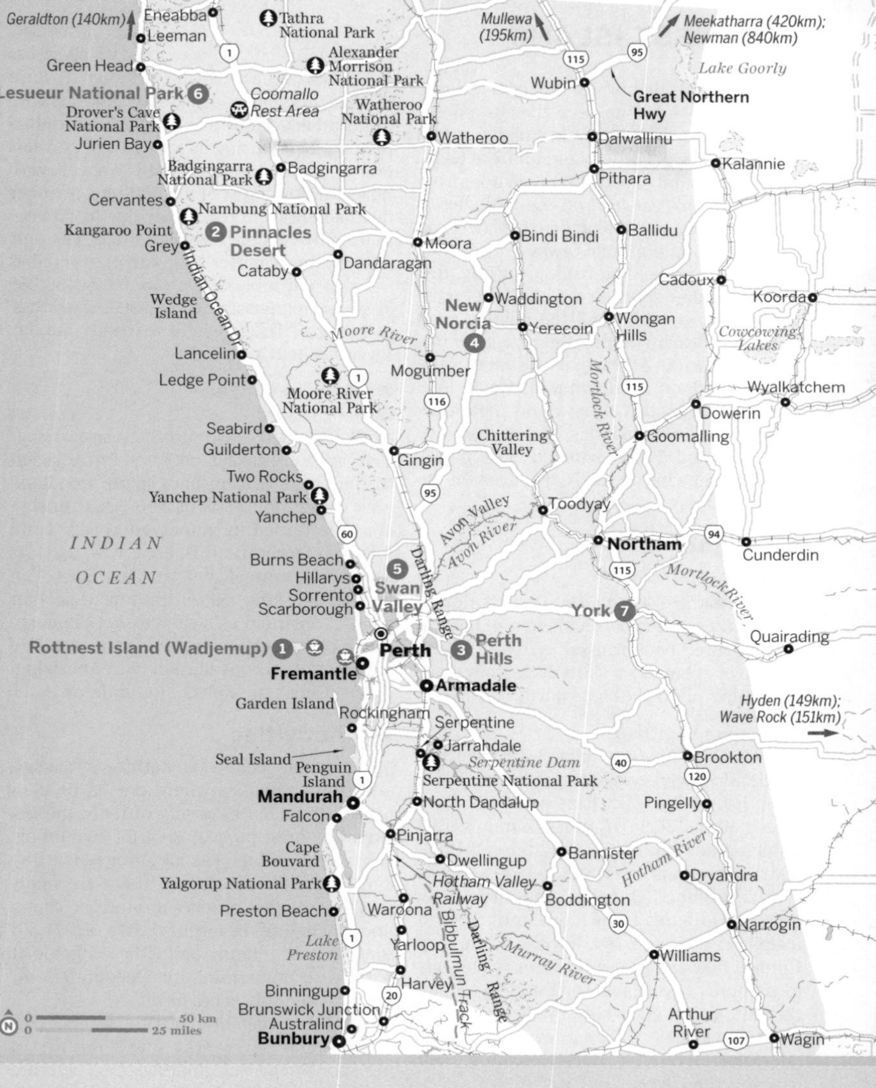

Perth Region Highlights

❶ **Rottnest Island** (p102) Cycling to a private slice of coastal paradise to swim and snorkel.

❷ **Pinnacles Desert** (p122) Exploring these other-worldly limestone prongs in Nambung National Park.

❸ **Perth Hills** (p110) Cruising between winery cellar doors and tracts of forest in the hills east of Perth.

❹ **New Norcia** (p118) Stumbling upon this bizarre monastery town with some rather astonishing architecture.

❺ **Swan Valley** (p112) Getting your food and booze fix at vineyards, breweries and artisan producers.

❻ **Lesueur National Park** (p123) Immersing yourself in a seasonal wildflower wonderland.

❼ **York** (p116) Time-travelling back to another architectural era in this heritage-listed Avon Valley town.

ROTTNEST ISLAND

☎08 / POP 340

'Rotto' – or Wadjemup to Noongar Aboriginal people – has long been the go-to destination for Perth families on holiday, and a coming-of-age promised land for local teens. Although it's only about 19km offshore from Fremantle, this car-free, off-the-grid slice of paradise, ringed by secluded beaches and bays, feels a million miles away

Cycling, snorkelling, fishing, surfing, diving and wildlife spotting are excellent on the island. But overriding all the holiday good times and beachy leisure, there's a grim history here: 3700 Aboriginal prisoners were incarcerated on Wadjemup between 1838 and 1931. Around 370 boys and men died, many from flu or measles, and at least five were executed. People suffered here: there's a disquieting vibe on the island, even on the sunniest of days.

Sights

★The Basin BEACH

(off Kings Way; 24hr;) The Basin is Rotto's top family swim spot – a sheltered, natural sandy-floored pool, fringed by reefs to keep the waves at bay. It's a short cycle from main township: follow the signs north.

Wadjemup Lighthouse LIGHTHOUSE

(☎08-9372 9730; www.rottnestisland.com/see-and-do/Island-tours/wadjemup-lighthouse; Wadjemup Hill, off Digby Dr; tours adult/child $9/4; tours 10am-2.30pm) Rottnest's unmissable human-made landmark, the 20m-tall Wadjemup Lighthouse was built in 1849 and was WA's first stone lighthouse. Tours run daily every 30 minutes from 10am until 2.30pm inclusive, operated by Rottnest Voluntary Guides. Take the Island Explorer (p106) bus to get here or cycle, but don't underestimate the ride: it can get windy by the salt lakes, and there are more than a few hills to conquer. There's often a coffee caravan parked here to aid recovery.

Rottnest Museum MUSEUM

(☎08-9372 9703; www.rottnestisland.com/see-and-do/island-tours/museums-and-galleries; Kitson St; by donation; 10am-3.30pm) Housed in the old hay-store building built by Aboriginal prisoners in 1857, this engaging little museum tells of the island's natural and human history, not shirking from grim tales of shipwrecks and Aboriginal incarceration.

Quod HISTORIC SITE

(☎08-9432 9300; www.ria.wa.gov.au/sustainability/social-sustainability/quod; Kitson St) Built in 1864, this hefty octagonal building with a central courtyard was once the Aboriginal prison block. During its time as a prison several men would share a 3m by 1.7m cell, with no sanitation (most of the 300-plus prisoner deaths here were reportedly due to disease; at least five people were executed). The only part of the complex that can be visited is a small whitewashed **chapel** (☎0435 065 326; www.rottnestisland.com/whats-on/weddings; 9am-5pm) FREE, where a weekly Sunday service is held at 9.30am.

Wadjemup Aboriginal Burial Ground CEMETERY

(☎08-9372 9730; www.rottnestfoundation.org.au/aboriginal-burial-ground; off Kitson St) Adjacent to the Quod is a hushed, shady woodland area where hundreds of Aboriginal prisoners were buried in unmarked graves. Until relatively recently, this area was used as a camping ground, but it's now fenced off with signs asking visitors to show respect for what is regarded as a sacred site. Plans are under consideration to convert the area into a memorial, in consultation with Aboriginal Elders. Check the website for updates.

Activities

Most visitors come for Rottnest's beaches and briny activities (there are 63 beaches here!). Protected by a ring of reefs, the Basin is the most popular spot for swimming. Other good swim spots are **Longreach Bay** and **Geordie Bay**, though there are many smaller secluded beaches around the shoreline, including beautiful **Little Parakeet Bay**. There's a handy online beach guide at www.westernaustralia-travellersguide.com/rottnest-island-beaches.html.

Excellent visibility, warm waters, coral reefs and shipwrecks make Rottnest a top spot for getting underwater. There are snorkel trails with underwater plaques at Little Salmon Bay and Parker Point. The Basin, Little Parakeet Bay, Longreach Bay and Geordie Bay are also worth a gander. **Pedal & Flipper** (☎08-9292 5105; www.rottnestisland.com/see-and-do; cnr Bedford Way & Welch Rd; bikes per half-/full day from $16/30; 8am-6pm) hires out masks, snorkels and fins, as well as bodyboards, paddleboards and scooters. The only wreck that's accessible to snorkellers without a boat is at Thomson Bay.

The best surf breaks are at Strickland, Salmon and Stark Bays, towards the western end of the island. Hire bodyboards and wetsuits from Pedal & Flipper; BYO surfboards.

Skydive Geronimo SKYDIVING
(☎1300 449 669; www.skydivegeronimo.com.au; Rottnest Airport, Brand Way; 10,000/14,000/15,000ft $349/449/499; ⏲by appointment) Take a tandem leap of faith (15,000ft is the highest legal jump height in Australia) and land on a Rottnest beach. Ferry-and-skydive packages also available.

Oliver Hill Train & Tour RAIL
(☎08-9432 9300; www.rottnestisland.com/see-and-do/Island-tours/oliver-hill; Oliver Hill Battery, off Defence Rd; adult/child $29/16.50) This trip, departing from the Settlement Train Station (Brand Way) at 1.30pm, takes you by train to historic **Oliver Hill Battery** (☎08-9372 9730; tours adult/child $9/4; ⏲tours hourly 10am-2pm) and includes the Gun & Tunnels tour run by Rottnest Voluntary Guides. The gun in question is a military remnant from WWII, with an impressive 9.2in calibre (never fired in defence or anger).

Rottnest Air-Taxi SCENIC FLIGHTS
(☎0421 389 831; www.rottnestairtaxi.com.au/joy-flights; Rottnest Airport, Brand Way; per adult 10/20/35min $65/95/145) Spectacular joy flights over the island (joyous!), departing from Rottnest Airport.

Tours

Rottnest Voluntary Guides WALKING
(☎08-9372 9757; www.rvga.asn.au) FREE
Themed walks take place daily, with topics including History, Reefs, Wrecks and Daring Sailors, **Vlamingh Lookout** (off Digby Dr; ⏲24hr) and Salt Lakes, and the Quokka Walk. The outfit also runs tours of Wadjemup Lighthouse (adult/child $9/4) and Oliver Hill Gun & Tunnels (adult/child $9/4); you'll need to make your own way there for the last two.

Sea Kayak Rottnest KAYAKING
(☎08-6219 5164; www.rottnestkayak.com.au; 2hr tour adult/child $49/39; 👪) Guided paddles in sheltered bays, peering into the brine though glass panels beneath your bum (!). Kids as young as six can join in – it's a very safe, low-impact session. Call for bookings and pick-up locations.

QUOKKAS

Rottnest's tame little fur-bundles have suffered a number of indignities over the years. First Willem de Vlamingh's crew mistook them for rats as big as cats. Then the British settlers misheard and mangled their name (the Noongar word was probably *quak-a* or *gwaga*). But, worst of all, a cruel trend of 'quokka soccer' by sadistic louts in the 1990s saw many kicked to death before a $10,000 fine was imposed; occasional cases are still reported. On a more positive note, the phenomenon of 'quokka selfies' has illuminated the internet since 2015, and shows no signs of abating (Margot Robbie and Roger Federer in glorious Instagram quokka-company!). Don't be surprised if a quokka approaches looking for a morsel. Politely decline: human food isn't good for them.

Discover Rottnest BUS
(☎1300 467 688; www.rottnestexpress.com.au/tours-and-services/island-tours.html; adult/child $49/25; ⏲departs 11.20am & 1.50pm) Ninety-minute tours of the island with informative and entertaining commentary. Coaches depart from the main bus stop in Thomson Bay. Run by Rottnest Express (p106) ferries.

Sleeping

Rotto is wildly popular in summer and during school holidays, when accommodation books out months in advance and prices skyrocket. Most accommodation is in cottages run by the Rottnest Island Authority: book via www.rottnestisland.com. Other privately run accommodation can also be booked via this website.

Rottnest Campground CAMPGROUND $
(☎08-9432 9111; www.rottnestisland.com; off Strue Rd; unpowered sites $39) Rottnest Island Authority (p105) runs this simple, sandy, 43-site camping ground en route to the Basin, with barbecue pavilions and an amenities block. Be vigilant about your belongings, especially your food – insolent quokkas have been known to help themselves.

Rottnest Hostel HOSTEL $
(☎08-9432 9111; www.rottnestisland.com; Kingstown Rd; dm/f $53/117) This rather austere backpackers occupies a 1937 art deco army barracks that still has an institutional vibe

Rottnest Island (Wadjemup)

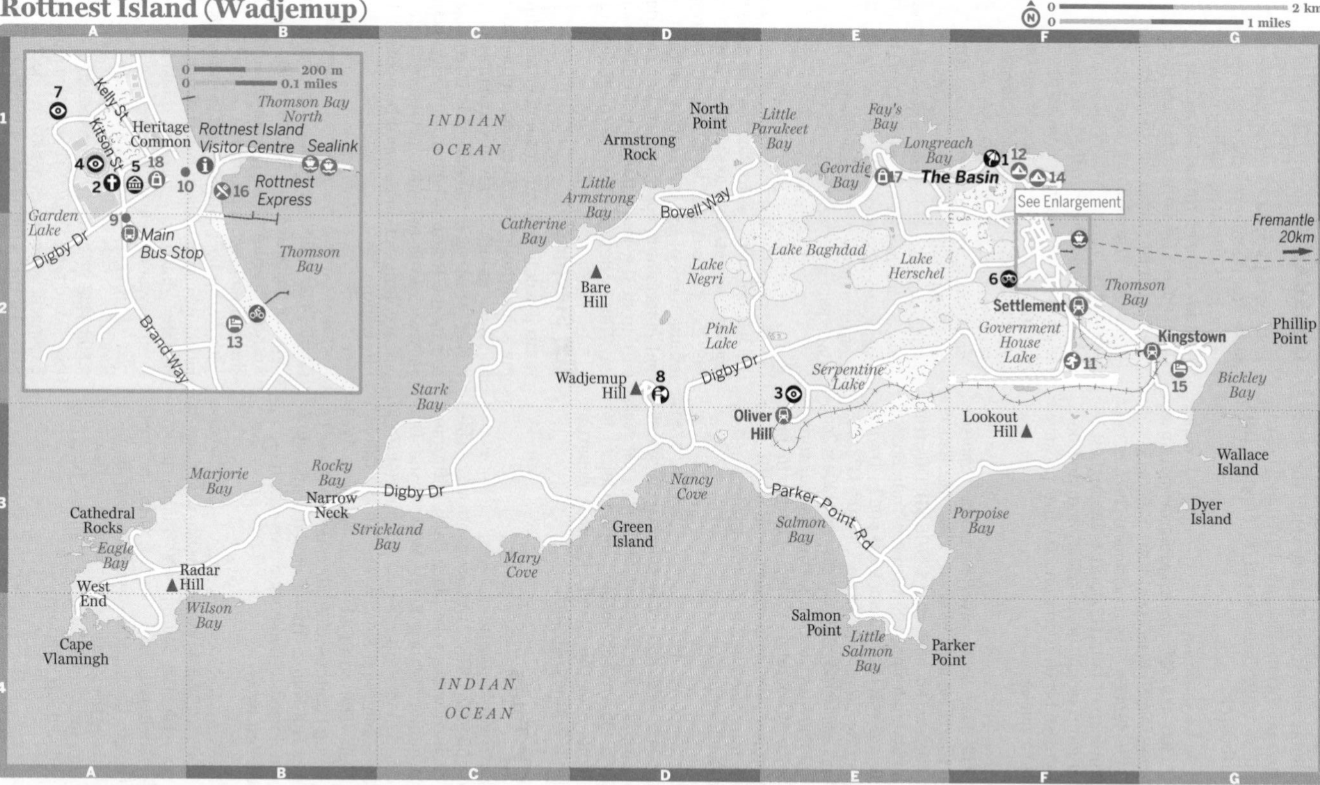

Rottnest Island (Wadjemup)

Top Sights
1 The Basin.......F1

Sights
2 Historic Chapel.......A1
3 Oliver Hill Battery.......E2
4 Quod.......A1
5 Rottnest Museum.......A1
6 Vlamingh Lookout.......F2
7 Wadjemup Aboriginal Burial Ground.......A1
8 Wadjemup Lighthouse.......D2

Activities, Courses & Tours
9 Discover Rottnest.......A2
Island Explorer.......(see 9)
Oliver Hill Train & Tour.......(see 3)
Rottnest Air-Taxi.......(see 11)
10 Rottnest Voluntary Guides.......A1
11 Skydive Geronimo.......F2

Sleeping
12 Discovery Rottnest Island.......F1
13 Hotel Rottnest.......B2
14 Rottnest Campground.......F1
15 Rottnest Hostel.......G2

Eating
Hotel Rottnest.......(see 13)
16 Thomsons.......B1

Shopping
17 Geordie Bay General Store.......E1
18 Rottnest General Store.......A1

and limited good-time opportunities. The defunct clock tower is stuck in an eternal 4pm. Check in at the visitor centre before you make the 1.8km walk, bike or bus trip to Kingston. There's a simple cafe on-site.

★**Discovery Rottnest Island** TENTED CAMP **$$**
(☎08-6350 6170; www.discoveryholidayparks.com.au/discovery-rottnest-island; Strue Rd; tents d/f from $150/270;) The first accommodation option to hit Rottnest in decades, this fabulous safari-tent park is nooked into the dunes behind Pinky Beach. Accommodation takes the form of 83 en suite safari tents, with muted colour schemes, luxe beds, roll-up walls and (in the deluxe versions) sea views. There's also a brilliant swimming pool, restaurant and bar. Wonderful!

Rottnest Island Authority Cottages COTTAGE **$$**
(☎08-9432 9111; www.rottnestisland.com; cottages $120-385;) Most of the accommodation on the island is run by the Rottnest Island Authority. There are more than 250 villas and cottages for rent: some have magnificent beachfront positions and are palatial; others are more like beach shacks. Prices jump by around $60 on Fridays and Saturdays, and higher in peak season. Check online for the labyrinthine pricing schedule.

Eating

Most overnight visitors to Rotto self-cater. The **general store** (☎08-9292 5017; www.rottnestgeneralstore.com.au; Digby Dr; 8am-8pm) is a small supermarket (and also stocks liquor) – and there's a similar store at **Geordie Bay** (☎cafe 08-9292 5411, supermarket 08-9292 5068; www.rottneststore.myfoodlink.com; 1 Geordie Bay Rd; 8am-7pm) – but if you're staying a while, it's better to bring supplies with you.

★**Hotel Rottnest** PUB FOOD **$$**
(☎08-9292 5011; www.hotelrottnest.com.au; 1 Bedford Ave; mains $21-35; 11am-late) It's difficult to imagine a more inviting place for a sunset pint of Little Creatures than the front terrace at this chic waterfront pub. A big open-sided glass pavilion creates an inviting interior space; bistro-style food and pizzas are reasonably priced given the location and ambience. Bands and DJs regularly bolster the laid-back island mood during summer. Hard to beat.

There's high-end hotel **accommodation** (r $249-400;) here too.

Thomsons SEAFOOD **$$**
(☎08-9292 5171; www.thomsonsrottnest.com.au; Colebatch Ave; mains $19-39; 11.30am-late) With mod boathouse vibes in a primo waterfront position (only compromised by netting to keep the seagulls out), Thomsons is Rotto's most upmarket option. Seafood is the name of the game: prise open some chilli mussels, dip into a chowder, or push the boat (way) out with a seafood platter for two ($160).

Information

Rottnest Island Visitor Centre (☎08-9372 9730; www.rottnestisland.com; Thomson Bay; 7.30am-6pm Sat-Thu, to 7pm Fri) Handles check-ins for all of the island authority's accommodation, and hands out maps, directions and general advice with good cheer. Your first point of call for all Rotto info.

Getting There & Away

AIR

Rottnest Air-Taxi (☎0421 389 831; www.rottnestairtaxi.com.au) Flies to Rottnest from Jandakot Airport in Perth's southern suburbs. Return prices start at around $120 per per person with a full plane (six passengers).

Rotorvation Helicopters (☎08-9414 8584; www.rotorvation.com.au) Flies to Rotto from Jandakot Airport and Hillarys Boat Harbour in Perth's northern suburbs, from around $300 per person one way.

BOAT

Rottnest Express (☎1300 467 688; www.rottnestexpress.com.au; return ex-Fremantle adult/child from $64/30, ex-Perth from $103/49) Regular ferries from Perth's **Barrack Street Jetty** (Map p62; pier 2, Barrack St Jetty, Elizabeth Quay; 1¾ hours, once daily), Shed B on Victoria Quay in **Fremantle** (Map p62; 30 minutes, seven times daily) and Rous Head in **North Fremantle** (Map p58; 1 Emma Pl, Northport, Rous Head; ⊙7.30am-5pm; 30 minutes, four times daily). A huge array of packages is on offer.

Rottnest Fast Ferries (☎08-9246 1039; www.rottnestfastferries.com.au; adult/child return from $86.50/49) Departs from Hillarys Boat Harbour (40 minutes, four times daily), around 40 minutes' drive north of Perth. All kinds of packages are available. Reduced winter services.

Sealink (☎1300 786 552; www.sealinkrottnest.com.au; adult/child return from $64/30) A major player, with two to six daily departures from Shed B on Victoria Quay in Fremantle, year-round, with lots of tour add-ons.

Getting Around

BICYCLE

Rottnest is just big enough (and has just enough hills) to make a day's ride a good workout. The ferry companies all hire bikes and helmets (per day around $30/15 per adult/child) as part of their island packages, and have them waiting for visitors on arrival. The visitor centre (p105) hires bikes too.

BUS

A free **shuttle bus** runs between Thomson Bay and the main accommodation areas (and the airport on request), departing roughly every 30 minutes from 7.30am, with the last bus at 6pm (8pm on Friday and Saturday).

The **Island Explorer** (☎08-9432 9300; www.rottnestisland.com; adult/child/family $20/15/50; ⊙departs every 30min 8.30am-3pm) is a handy hop-on/hop-off coach service stopping at 19 locations around the island. Between Geordie Bay and Thomson Bay it's free.

ROCKINGHAM

☎08 / POP 125,120

Just 46km south of Perth on Wajuk homelands, Rockingham is finding its feet as a seaside destination. Wedged between the Shoalwater Islands Marine Park to the south (home to colonies of dolphins, sea lions and penguins), and the vast industrial estates, port works and naval facilities of Kwinana and Garden Island to the north, the town has a cheery cafe strip and a strung-out waterfront park, backing onto a lovely safe swimming beach.

Sights

Shoalwater Islands Marine Park NATURE RESERVE
(☎08-93037700; www.parks.dpaw.wa.gov.au/park/shoalwater-islands; off Arcadia Dr, Shoalwater; ⊙daylight hours, closed for nesting Jun–mid-Sep) FREE Just a few minutes' paddle, swim or boat ride away from the shore 5km south of Rockingham is strictly protected **Penguin Island**, home to penguins, silver gulls, boardwalks, beaches and picnic tables. Apart from birdwatching (pied cormorants, pelicans, crested and bridled terns, oystercatchers), day visitors can also swim, paddle in the rock pools and snorkel.

It's free to wade the few hundred metres out to the island across the sandbar at low tide, but make sure you keep one eye on the sea – people have drowned here after being washed off the bar during strong winds and high tides. Otherwise, the **Penguin Island Ferry** (☎08-9591 1333; www.penguinisland.com.au/penguin-island-ferry; Mersey Point Jetty, 153 Arcadia Dr, Shoalwater; adult/child/family $18/14/56, with penguin feeding $27/20/85; ⊙hourly 9am-3pm mid-Sep–May) can chug you out there and back: fares can include a penguin-feeding session at the Discovery Centre on the island, run by **Rockingham Wild Encounters** (☎08-9591 1333; www.penguinisland.com.au; cnr Arcadia Dr & Penguin Rd, Shoalwater; ⊙8.30am-4.30pm mid-Sep–May). Sea-kayaking tours with **Capricorn Seakayaking** (☎0427 485 123; www.capricornseakayaking.com.au; adult/child $180/162; ⊙late Sep-late Apr) explore the marine park in more depth.

Sleeping & Eating

★ Manuel Towers B&B $$

(☎08-9592 2698; www.manueltowers.com.au; 32 Arcadia Dr, Shoalwater; d with/without breakfast from $205/155; P ❄ 📶) Manuel? He's from Barcelona... *Fawlty Towers* gags aside, this five-room waterfront B&B near Penguin Island is the real deal, with rough-hewn limestone walls, terracotta tiles, chunky beams, wrought-iron balustrades, fig trees and a Spanish host (OK, he's from Morocco, but he grew up across the Med). The downstairs breakfast room is marvellously atmospheric – a little slice of Catalonia in Shoalwater.

★ Ostro Eatery CAFE $$

(☎08-9592 8957; www.ostroeatery.com.au; 11a Rockingham Beach Rd; mains breakfast $13-20, lunch & dinner $16-34; ⏲7.30am-3pm Mon-Thu & Sun, to late Fri & Sat) This arty waterfront cafe with broad shared tables morphs into an effervescent evening option on weekends. The pulled-pork breakfast burger will kick-start your day, while nocturnal options range from house-cured salmon with apple and fennel to classy fish and chips. Cold-pressed juices, hemp-seed protein shakes and house-made sodas complement a concise beer and wine selection (Bloody Mary mix to take away).

Information

Visitor Information Centre (☎08-9592 3464; www.rockinghamvisitorcentre.com.au; 19 Kent St; ⏲9am-5pm Mon-Fri, to 4pm Sat & Sun) Has accommodation listings and all the local low-down.

Getting There & Away

Rockingham is on the Mandurah line on the Transperth (p99) public-transport network. Regular trains depart Perth Underground for Rockingham ($8.40, 35 minutes).

PEEL REGION

Taking in swathes of jarrah forest, historic towns and the increasingly glitzy coastal hub of Mandurah, the Peel Region can easily be tackled as a day trip from Perth, or as the first stopover on a longer expedition down the South Western Hwy (Rte 1).

As you enter the Peel, you'll pass out of Wadjuk country and into that of their fellow Noongar neighbours, the Pinjarup (or Bindjareb) people.

Mandurah

☎08 / POP 80,820

Shrugging off its fusty retirement-haven image, Mandurah – Mandjoogoordap in Pinjarup dialect – has made a good fist of reinventing itself as an upmarket beach enclave, taking advantage of the easy train link to Perth. And, although the town's network of interlinked marinas, canals and precincts is shamelessly artificial, and despite well-documented social problems (local rates of methamphetamine use are some of the highest in regional Australia) most people here seem to be enjoying themselves!

Sights & Activities

Mandurah Museum MUSEUM

(☎08-9550 3682; www.mandurah.wa.gov.au/facilities/museum; 3 Pinjarra Rd; by donation; ⏲10am-4pm Tue-Fri, 11am-3pm Sat & Sun) Mandurah's community-run museum is an engaging little repository of all things aged and olden – it's one of WA's better regional collections. Unless you're walking, park behind the museum in the car park off Leslie St: if you try to drive any closer on Pinjarra Rd, there's nowhere to stop and you'll be funneled across the Mandurah Bridge, never to return...

Mandurah Cruises CRUISE

(☎08-9581 1242; www.mandurahcruises.com.au; 73 Mandurah Tce) Take a one-hour Dolphin & Scenic Canal Cruise (adult/child $32/18), half-day Murray River Lunch Cruise ($89/55) or Sunset Cruise ($30/15). Fish and chips on the canal and dolphin cruises are $12 extra. Book online. Indo-Pacific bottlenose dolphins come close to the boat; note that research suggests that human interaction with sea mammals potentially alters their behavioural and breeding patterns.

Mandjoogoordap Dreaming CULTURAL

(☎0408 952 740; www.mandurahdreaming.com.au; adult/child $35/15) Explore Mandurah's foreshore with local Pinjarup guide George – a 90-minute interpretation of the land and sea through Indigenous eyes. Book ahead; meet at the **Mandurah Performing Arts Centre** (ManPAC; ☎08-9550 3900; www.manpac.com.au; Ormsby Tce; ⏲box office 9am-5pm Mon-Fri, 10am-4pm Sat, from noon Sun). Bus tours and longer explorations around the Peel Inlet are also available.

OFF THE BEATEN TRACK

YALGORUP NATIONAL PARK

Fifty kilometres south of Mandurah is this beautiful 12,000-hectare coastal **park** (08-9303 7750; www.parks.dpaw.wa.gov.au/park/yalgorup; via Preston Beach Rd, Preston Beach; 24hr) FREE, consisting of 10 tranquil lakes and their surrounding woodlands and dunes. The park is recognised as a wetland of international significance for seasonally migrating waterbirds, with 130 species winging-in on the breeze. Also here are globular **thrombolites** at Lake Clifton, descendants of the earliest living organisms on earth (they are the only life form known to have existed over 650 million years ago). There's a viewing platform on Mt John Rd off Old Coast Rd; keep an eye out for long-neck tortoises below the boardwalk. A 5km **walking track** starts from here and loops around the lake. There's no public transport to the park – BYO vehicle.

Sleeping & Eating

★Mandurah Ocean Marina Chalets MOTEL $$
(08-9535 8173; www.marinachalets.com.au; 6 The Lido; d/f unit from $120/140;) Embrace Mandurah by staying right in the middle of it: pitched-roof chalets here are spotless and modern, with full-kit kitchens and little decks, all revolving around a central BBQ pavilion and crab-cooking facility. It's a tightly arranged complex, but is beautifully landscaped with eucalypts and neat hedges. There's no pool, but Mandurah's **Swimming Beach** (Keith Holmes Reserve, The Lido; daylight hours;) FREE is right across the Lido. Great value.

★Flic's Kitchen BISTRO $$
(08-9535 1661; www.flicskitchen.com; 3/16 Mandurah Tce; breakfast $10-25, share plates $21-27; 8am-late;) Perfectly aligned to snare the afternoon sun, fabulous Flic's is infused with city cool, with outdoor seating and a versatile menu spanning breakfast to dinner. Consider a breakfast beer (how fabulously indecent!) to accompany your smoked pork collar with charred corn, chilli scramble and whipped feta. Vegan and paleo options too. Winner!

★Three Rivers Brewing Company CRAFT BEER
(0411 823 870; www.3riversbrewing.com.au; 2/6 Harlem Pl, Greenfields; 2-8pm Fri-Sun) Murray, Serpentine, Harvey: Mandurah's three rivers all flow into the Peel Inlet, which in turn empties into the Indian Ocean. It's a cyclic environmental image, setting a sustainable tone at this cheery craft brewery in the industrial backblocks. There's no gimmickry here, just traditionally brewed English, European and American ales. The Tomahawk American pale ale (APA) rules the roost. Tasting paddles $10.

Information

Mandurah Visitor Centre (08-9550 3999; www.visitpeel.com.au; 75 Mandurah Tce; 9am-4pm) On the estuary boardwalk.

Getting There & Away

BUS

Transwa (1300 662 205; www.transwa.wa.gov.au) SW1, SW2 and SW3 buses roll into Mandurah most days from East Perth ($18.05, 1¼ hours), continuing south.

TRAIN

Mandurah sits within the outermost zone (7) of the Transperth (p99) public-transport system on the end of the Mandurah line, with direct trains to/from Perth Underground ($11.10, 50 minutes).

Dwellingup

08 / POP 560

Dwellingup is a small, timber-shrouded township between Pinjarup and Wiilman lands 100km south of Perth, with a forest-load of character. Its rep as an activity hub has been enhanced by the hardy long-distance walkers and cyclists trucking through town on the epic Bibbulmun Track (p159) and **Munda Biddi Trail** (08-6336 9699; www.mundabiddi.org.au) respectively. There's a petrol station, a pub and a police station here too – the three pillars of society in rural WA.

Sights & Activities

★Wine Tree Cidery WINERY
(08-9538 1076; www.winetreecidery.com.au; 46 Holyoake Rd; 1-7pm Fri, from 10am Sat & Sun)

Wine, cider, apples, trees...the name almost hangs together, conceptually. Regardless, this cavernous steel space (a former apple shed) is a cheery spot for a tasting paddle of the house ciders ($16: classic, dry and fruity), a look at the vintage motorcycle collection, a cheese board ($30), or all of the above. Ben the Labrador is on duty.

Forest Discovery Centre NATURE RESERVE
(☎08-9538 1395; www.forestdiscoverycentre.com.au; 1 Acacia St; adult/child/family $5/3/13; ⏱10am-3pm Mon-Fri, to 4pm Sat & Sun; 👪) Tucked into the jarrah forest on the edge of town, this interesting rammed-earth building takes the shape of three interlinked gum leaves. Inside are displays about the forest's flora and fauna, and a shop selling beautiful pieces crafted by local and visiting woodworkers. Short trails, including an 11m-high canopy walk, meander off into the woods. There's a cafe and kids' nature-play areas here too.

Lane Pool Reserve NATURE RESERVE
(☎08-9538 1078; www.parks.dpaw.wa.gov.au/park/lane-poole-reserve; Banksiadale Rd; per vehicle $13; ⏱24hr) The vast Lane Poole Reserve, on the jarrah-lined banks of the Murray River, is an ace place to stop for a barbecue, a picnic, bushwalk or (in summer, when the waters are calmer) a swim. The best swim spots are Island Pool and near the Baden-Powell water spout. To get here, head south of Dwellingup on 2WD-friendly Nanga Rd for 10km. You can camp in eight riverside spots (adult/child $8/3). **Trees Adventure** (☎08-9463 4063; www.treesadventure.com.au/park/lane-poole-park; off Nanga Rd; adult/child $48/38; ⏱10am-5pm Tue-Fri, from 9am Sat & Sun; 👪) climbing park is here too.

Dwellingup Adventures ADVENTURE SPORTS
(☎08-9538 1127; www.dwellingupadventures.com.au; cnr Marinup & Newton Sts; 1-person kayaks & 2-person canoes per day $50, mountain bikes $40; ⏱8.30am-5pm Sat & Sun, by appointment Mon-Fri) A one-stop shop for canoe, kayak, raft, camping-gear and mountain-bike hire to explore the terrain on and around the beautiful Murray River. Or sign up for a supported (but self-guided) paddling or cycling tour (from $125 per person). White-water-rafting tours are also available from June to October (from $150 per person).

Eating

★ **Blue Wren Cafe** CAFE $$
(☎08-9538 1234; www.facebook.com/dwellingupbluewrencafe; 53 McLarty St; mains $15-20; ⏱6am-5pm Sat-Thu, to 7.30pm Fri) Corrugated iron, hessian hangings and rustic timber collude to create a happy vibe at this cosy corner cafe, offering stonking homemade sausage rolls and regular specials (pulled-pork pies!). The coffee is worthy of a flash cafe in the big smoke, and there's a roaring wood heater for chilly Dwellingup winters (it gets down to -3°C here sometimes).

Information

Dwellingup History & Visitor Information Centre (☎08-9538 1108; www.dwellingupwa.com.au; Marinup St; ⏱9am-3.30pm; 📶) Lots of local info, including interesting displays about the 1961 bushfires that wiped out the town, destroying 75 houses but taking no lives. The website lists accommodation options.

Getting There & Away

There's no regular public transport to Dwellingup: hit the road, Jack.

WORTH A TRIP

JARRAHDALE & SERPENTINE NATIONAL PARK

Cut from the forest in 1871, Jarrahdale (www.jarrahdale.com) is an old mill village reached by a leafy 6km drive east from the South Western Hwy. The town sits on the northern fringes of **Serpentine National Park** (☎08-9525 2128; www.parks.dpaw.wa.gov.au/park/serpentine; via Falls Rd, Serpentine; per vehicle $13; ⏱8.30am-5pm), a forested area with walking tracks, picnic spots and the spectacular **Serpentine Falls**. This 15m sluice of water feathers down the face of a smooth granite escarpment. Signs warn of the dangers of swimming in the cool pools below the falls, but don't expressly forbid it – and on a hot afternoon the temptation is significant! If you succumb, don't swim alone, don't dive in and don't climb the falls or jump off – several people have expired doing so over the years. If you don't want to pay the entry fee, you can walk in for free – it's around 1km from the gates to the falls.

PERTH HILLS

Wait...Perth has hills? Who knew! Technically known as the Darling Range, this forest-covered escarpment to the city's east is Beelu country, and provides a green backdrop with some great spots for picnicking, bushwalking, mountain biking and hanging with the local kangaroos. Better yet, nooked into a lush Hills' vale, the Bickley Valley plays host to a dozen or so wineries with attendant cellar doors, B&Bs and cafes. Perth locals are discovering the pleasures of an indulgent Hills weekend away. Kalamunda (pop 57,450) and Mundaring (pop 38,000) are the main towns hereabouts.

Sights & Activities

★Core Cider WINERY

(☎08-9293 7583; www.corecider.com.au; 35 Merrivale Rd, Pickering Brook; tours adult/child tractor $30/23, walking $25/18; ⏰10am-4pm Wed-Sat, to 5pm Sun) This hidden valley in Pickering Brook has sustained apple orchards since 1939. Take a one-hour tour through the trees on a tractor-pulled carriage, a 45-minute walking tour, or book a table at the excellent bistro (mains $27 to $32) or casual cider garden (mains $12 to $25) for lunch. But of course, the main deal here is cider: its 'Core Range' (ha-ha) includes outstanding sparkling apple and pear offings. Head to the Harvest Room for tastings (from $10).

Perth Observatory OBSERVATORY

(☎08-9293 8255; www.perthobservatory.com.au; 337 Walnut Rd, Bickley; tours adult/child day $20/15, night $40/30; ⏰admission by tour only) Check the website for regularly scheduled day and night tours of the Perth Observatory, sitting pretty atop a Perth Hills' peak near the Bickley Valley wineries. Check the website for times and bookings. They've been stargazing here for 120 years, over which time local astronomers have discovered 29 minor planets, 30 supernovae and the rarely seen rings around Uranus. You can also abseil down the concrete tower (adult/child $35/25).

Brookside Vineyard WINERY

(☎08-9291 8705; www.brooksidevineyard.com.au; 5 Loaring Rd, Bickley; ⏰11am-4pm Sat & Sun) Follow the sounds of lilting jazz down a shady, poplar-lined driveway to Brookside, a rustic farm-shed cellar door. Enjoy a couple of glasses of cab sav, chardonnay or sparkling white on the terrace by the namesake babbling brook. The **Vineyard Kitchen** (☎08-9227 7715; www.thevineyardkitchen.net.au; mains $29-33; ⏰noon-3pm Thu-Sun) restaurant is here too, serving masterful Mod Oz.

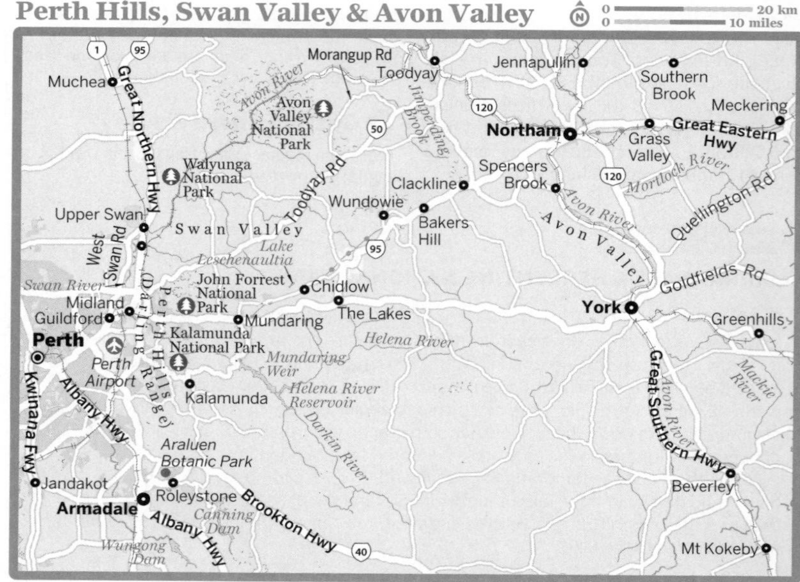

Mundaring Weir DAM
(☎08-9290 6645; www.goldenpipeline.com.au; Mundaring Weir Rd, Mundaring; ⊙daylight hours) FREE Restraining the Helena River, Mundaring Weir is a concrete dam built in 1903 to the designs of engineer CY O'Connor as part of a dazzlingly ambitious scheme to supply water to the Kalgoorlie goldfields 560km to the east (the longest freshwater pipeline in the world...and it worked!). The reservoir is a blissful spot, with walking trails, kangaroos and a well-positioned pub (☎08-9295 1106; www.mundaringweirhotel.com.au; cnr Hall & Mundaring Wier Rds; r $125-150, extra adult/child $40/20; P ☎ ≋). The best dam view is from the lookout just off Mundaring Weir Rd near the dam's southern end.

Rock 'n' Roll Mountain Biking MOUNTAIN BIKING
(☎0410 949 182; www.facebook.com/rockandroll mtb; 361 Paulls Valley Rd, Paulls Valley; bike hire per half-/full day/weekend from $45/60/100; ⊙9am-noon Thu & Fri, 8am-2pm Sat & Sun, by appointment Mon-Wed) Right on the Bibbulmun Track, these two-wheeled rock 'n' rollers can kit you out with a top-quality mountain bike, upon which you can blaze local trails from easy to 'Black Diamond' (extremely difficult). They also run courses and have an in-house repair shop.

Tours

Up Close & Local Tours WINE
(☎0423 126 254; www.upcloseandlocaltours.com.au; half-/full-day tours $79/129) Bickley Valley specialists offering a half-day (afternoon) tour from Perth, visiting two wineries and Core Cider (p110), with plenty of sightseeing in between. There's also a full-day option called the 'Cider, Wine & Whiskey' tour, getting a bit more of the good stuff into your glass.

Sleeping & Eating

Bickley Valley Cottage B&B $$$
(☎0437 616 869; www.bickleyvalleycottage.com; 15 Glenisla Rd, Bickley; d from $270, extra person $40; P ❄ ☎) A three-bedroom heritage cottage built in 1914, this little timber B&B offers valley views and buckets of charm. Breakfast comes in an overflowing DIY hamper (with a bottle of wine...not necessarily for breakfast, but why not?). The interior design is cottagey, but without erring on the side of chintz. There are a couple of good wineries located within walking distance of the cottage.

★ **Parkerville Tavern** PUB FOOD $$
(☎08-9295 4500; www.parkervilletavern.com.au; 6 Owen Rd, Parkerville; pizzas $15-20, mains $22-34; ⊙11.30am-late Mon-Sat, from 8am Sun; ☎ ♿) Built in 1896, this cheery red-brick pub 3km northwest of Mundaring is a surprising find. Pub grub is the main lure (brilliant BLTs, perfect parmas), plus there's a pool table, a blazing pizza oven in the beer garden (weekends only) and a kids' sandpit. All-day kitchen Friday to Sunday; noon to 2.30pm and 5.30pm to 8.30pm Monday to Thursday.

Information

The **Perth Hills Visitor Centre** (☎08-9257 9998; www.experienceperthhills.com.au; 50 Railway Rd; ⊙9am-4pm Mon-Fri, from 10am Sat & Sun) is in Kalamunda, with all the requisite maps and brochures including the handy *Kalamunda to Mundaring Self-Drive Tourist Map*, *Perth Hills Winery Guide* and *Bickley Valley Wine Trail* maps.

Getting There & Away

The Hills are most easily accessed with your own set of wheels (great wiggly roads for motorcycle touring!) but Transwa (p108) buses and trains from Perth do link with Kalamunda and Mundaring.

HYDEN & WAVE ROCK

☎08

Stark granite outcrops dot the Central and Southern Wheat Belt regions, rising incongruously from the fields of nodding wheat like big bald balloons. The most famous of these is undoubtedly the sensually weather-sculpted Wave Rock, deep into Nyaki-Nyaki country – it's nowhere near as big as Uluru, but remains an essential WA icon. The nearest town is little Hyden (population 380), 5km to the west – a sleepy bush settlement with a tavern-motel, a bakery, swimming pool and petrol station.

Sights & Activities

★ **Wave Rock** NATURAL FEATURE
(☎08-9880 5182; www.waverock.com.au; Wave Rock Rd, Wave Rock; per vehicle/adult/child $12/5/3; ⊙24hr) The multicoloured cresting swell of Wave Rock, 336km east of Perth, formed some 60 million years ago by

weathering and water erosion. Streaked with colours created by run-off from local mineral springs, it's actually one edge of a larger granite outcrop called Hyden Rock. It's not gargantuan – just 15m high and 110m long – but it's nonetheless impressive. And when the wind is whispering in the sheoaks, it's a quietly moving place – as it has always been for the Nyaki-Nyaki people.

To get the most out of Wave Rock, pick up the *Walk Trails at Wave Rock and The Humps* brochure from the **visitor centre** (9am-5pm). A steep walk leads up around the summit of Hyden Rock, passing a dazzlingly insensitive concrete-block wall built along the crest of Wave Rock to stop stone-surfers from plunging to their deaths (you can't see the wall from the base of the rock). There's another good trail to **Hippo's Yawn** (per vehicle/adult/child $12/5/3; 24hr) along a shady 1km track from the base of Wave Rock.

Parking at Wave Rock is $12 per car (pay at the parking meter); or you can save a few bucks by parking out on Wave Rock Rd or the visitor centre and walking in a few hundred metres – pay pedestrian fees at the **caravan-park kiosk** (08-9880 5022; www.waverock.com.au/business/accommodation/wave-rock-caravan-park; 1 Wave Rock Rd, Wave Rock).

★Mulka's Cave & the Humps CAVE
(off Bates Rd, Wave Rock; daylight hours) FREE
Amazing Mulka's Cave is an important Nyaki-Nyaki rock-art site, with 452 recorded stencils and handprints, some produced as recently as 400 years ago. Astonishingly, it's free to access with no protective measures in place: visitors are trusted to be respectful. Not all the stencils are immediately apparent, but as your eyes adjust to the half-light, more and more start to emerge from the gloom. The cave is 19km north of Wave Rock (p111), the last 1.5km on an unsealed road.

Sleeping

Wave Rock Country Cottage RENTAL HOUSE $$
(0400 488 821; www.waverockaccommodation.com.au; 5 Smith Loop, Hyden; d from $140, extra adult/child $20/10; P ❄) This modest kid-friendly cottage (toys, cot, unbreakable crockery, DVDs) isn't flashy, but it fills a void in the Wave Rock accommodation scene, with three bedrooms, a full-kit kitchen and plenty of space to do your own thing. Walking distance to the pool and the pub.

Getting There & Away

Like most of WA, this region is best explored with your own vehicle. Wave Rock is 336km east of Perth.

Transwa (p108) runs bus GE2 from East Perth to Hyden ($56.90, five hours) and on to Esperance ($59.55 from Hyden, five hours) every Tuesday, Thursday and Sunday...but how are you going to get to Wave Rock itself, 5km east of Hyden?

Western Travel Bug (08-9486 4222; www.travelbug.com.au; adult/child incl lunch $185/135; Tue, Thu & Sat) offers a long one-day tour from Perth three times a week.

SWAN VALLEY

Perth locals love to swan around this semirural vale on the city's northeastern suburban fringe. This is Wadjuk country – the inland extension of the river valley that becomes a vast estuary as it flows past Perth. Any visit to the Swan Valley inevitably revolves around wine – there are more than 40 vineyards here. Perhaps in tacit acknowledgement that its wines will never compete with the state's more prestigious regions (it doesn't really have the ideal climate), the Swan Valley compensates with plenty of galleries, breweries, provedores and restaurants. Online, see www.swanvalley.com.au.

Guildford

08 / POP 2020

Guildford is the Swan Valley's gateway town. It's part of Perth's suburban sprawl these days, but historically the town was a separate colony (founded 1829), and before that an important meeting hub for the local Wadjuk people. Today, the centre of town is Stirling Sq, at the intersection of Swan and Meadow Sts. There's a cluster of historic buildings opposite the square and a grand colonial mansion just east of town, by the river. Eating and drinking in Guildford is a pleasure, with some terrific old pubs and cafes on offer.

Eating

Cafe Poste CAFE $
(08-9379 2333; www.facebook.com/postegardendesigncentre; 24 Stirling St; mains $10-19; 9am-4pm Mon-Sat) Guildford's faded old post office is an Italianate 1897 edifice, reborn as a garden cafe. Horticulture and interior de-

sign are the main thrust here – the interior is decorated with antiques and heirloom artefacts – but you can sit amid the ferns and ficuses for a potent coffee, a slab of coconut, pistachio and ginger cake or a French breakfast brioche.

★**Rose & Crown** PUB FOOD $$
(☎08-9347 8100; www.rosecrown.com.au; 105 Swan St; mains breakfast $13-24, lunch & dinner $22-46; ⊙7am-late Mon-Fri, from 8am Sat & Sun) WA's oldest still-operating pub (1841) has a rambling beer garden and quirky heritage corners to explore inside. Have a beer in the enticingly dim cellar bar, where there's a convict-built well, and check out the sealed-off tunnel that used to connect the hotel with the river. The fat rabbit pie with a pint of Feral Brewing's 'The Local' is unbeatable.

There's also accommodation here, in the form of heritage hotel rooms in the pub and tastefully styled motel rooms out the back (with pool). Rates include breakfast and start at $170.

Information

Swan Valley Visitor Centre (☎08-9207 8899; www.swanvalley.com.au; Guildford Courthouse, cnr Swan & Meadow Sts, Guildford; ⊙9am-4pm) Information and maps, plus an interesting display on local history.

Getting There & Away

Guildford falls within Zone 2 of Perth's public-transport system: it costs only $4.80 to get here by bus or train on the Midland line from Perth, East Perth or Mt Lawley Station.

Swan Valley Wine Region

The valley's vineyards are mainly concentrated along busy West Swan Rd leading north from the Guildford and the Great Northern Hwy, running parallel to the east – the Swan River runs between these two main thoroughfares. Look for the free *Swan Valley Visitor Guide* and map at the Swan Valley Visitor Centre in Guildford.

Sights

Sandalford Wines WINERY
(☎08-9374 9374; www.sandalford.com; 3210 West Swan Rd, Caversham; tours $25, mains $35-45; ⊙10am-5pm, tours noon, restaurant noon-3pm) Sandalford is one of the oldest Swan Valley wineries (1840) and hosts high-society weddings and major concerts (Sting, Tom Jones, Lionel Richie) on its expansive lawns. Sip some semillon at the cellar door, take a tour, or book a seat at the elegant restaurant for creative Mod Oz mains (the likes of barramundi with preserved lemon, pomegranate, beetroot, feta and maple dressing).

OFF THE BEATEN TRACK

DRYANDRA WOODLAND

Within the Dryandra Woodland (www.parks.dpaw.wa.gov.au/park/dryandra-woodland), an isolated 28,000-hectare remnant eucalypt forest 164km southeast of Perth, the excellent **Barna Mia Nocturnal Animal Sanctuary** (☎08-9881 9200; www.parks.dpaw.wa.gov.au/site/barna-mia-nocturnal-wildlife-experience; Marri Rd, Dryandra; adult/child/family $22/11/55) is a predator-free sanctuary, home to endangered marsupial bilbies, boodies, woylies, dalgytes, wurrups and quendas (don't worry, we hadn't heard of some of these either). Ninety-minute after-dark torchlight tours provide a rare opportunity to see these critters doing their thing in the dark. Book through Parks & Wildlife for postsunset tours on Monday, Wednesday, Friday and Saturday (Friday and Saturday only December to February)

Houghton WINERY
(☎08-9274 9540; www.houghton-wines.com.au; 148 Dale Rd, Middle Swan; ⊙10am-5pm) The Swan's oldest and best-known winery is surrounded by stroll-worthy grounds, including a jacaranda grove (check out the insanely purple blooms from late spring to early summer). There's a gallery in the cellar where bushranger Moondyne Joe was caught, and a small display of old winemaking equipment. Oh, and the wine's good too!

Whiteman Park PARK
(☎08-9209 6000; www.whitemanpark.com.au; off Lord St, West Swan; ⊙8.30am-6pm, visitor centre 10am-4pm, water park 10am-3pm; 👪) FREE Located in Caversham in West Swan, at 26 sq km this is Perth's heftiest park – a marvellous grassy reserve with over 30km of walkways and bike paths, a free kids' **water park**, sports ovals and dozens of picnic and barbecue spots. You'll also find the **Caversham Wildlife Park** (☎08-9248 1984; www.cavershamwildlife.com.au; off Whiteman Dr E; adult/child $29/13; ⊙9am-5.30pm, last entry 4.30pm; 👪), **Revolutions Transport**

Museum (08-9209 6040; Village Junction; by donation; 10am-4pm;), the **Motor Museum of Western Australia** (08-9249 9457; www.motormuseumofwa.asn.au; Whiteman Village; adult/child/family $15/10/35; 10am-4pm Mon-Fri, to 5pm Sat & Sun;), a **tractor museum** (08-9209 3480; www.facebook.com/tmofwa; off Whiteman Dr E; by donation; 10am-4pm Wed & Fri-Sun), **train rides** (08-9534 3215; www.bbr.org.au; Village Junction; adult/child/family $8/4/20; 11am-1pm Wed & Thu, to 4pm Sat & Sun) and **tram rides** (08-9443 1945; www.pets.org.au; Village Junction; adult/child/family return $5/2.50/13; 11am-1.30pm Tue & Fri-Sun, daily in school holidays) for the kids. It's a massive place: pick up a map from the visitor centre.

Tours

Out & About Wine Tours WINE

(08-9377 3376; www.outandabouttours.com.au; half-/full-day tours from $85/115) An experienced local operator running full-day, half-day and evening tours of the Swan Valley wineries, including lunch and plenty of tastings. There's a river-cruise option from Perth too ($155). Ex-Perth.

d'Vine Wine Tours WINE

(08-9244 5323; www.dvinetours.com.au; half-/full-day tours from $87/110) Good-humoured wine tours, either quick-fire or relaxed, with more good things to eat and drink than your body probably requires. Customised tours also available. Ex-Perth or Guildford.

Sleeping & Eating

Keller's B&B B&B $$

(08-9274 8500; www.kellersbedandbreakfast.com.au; 104 Victoria Rd, Dayton; d $140-210; P) Amid a remnant patch of farmland near the (it has to be said) awful Dayton suburban housing subdivision, Keller's is a charming limestone farmhouse with two en suite guest rooms, each with a private entrance. It's a working farm with lots of cows, pigs and sheep – but it's not really set up for kids. Generous continental breakfast included.

Lamont's TAPAS $$

(08-9296 4485; www.lamonts.com.au; 85 Bisdee Rd, Millendon; tapas $9-27; 10am-5pm Thu-Sun) Look forward to lazy tastings and heaving plates of tapas (shaved pastrami with black-olive salsa, coconut crumbed prawns) under the wide WA sky. The wine's top-notch too, much of it grown at Lamont's Margaret River vineyard. Little Lamont's cafe is down the road at 660 Great Northern Hwy, Herne Hill.

RiverBank Estate BISTRO $$$

(08-9377 1805; www.riverbankestate.com.au; 126 Hamersley Rd, Caversham; mains $29-65; cellar door 10am-4pm, lunch 11.30am-2.30pm) The pick of the region's winery restaurants, rustic RiverBank delivers excellent Mod Oz cuisine on its wrap-around verandah (or inside if it's hot). It's a little better dressed than the competition (hot tip: you too) and there's regular live jazz. There's also Sunday breakfast on the lawns from 7.30am to 10.30am (mains $16 to $25).

Drinking & Nightlife

★ **Homestead Brewery** CRAFT BEER

(08-6279 0500; www.mandoonestate.com.au/eat-drink/homestead-brewery; 10 Harris Rd, Caversham; 10am-8.30pm Mon-Fri, 7.30am-10.30pm Sat & Sun) Located in the grounds of the award-winning Mandoon Estate winery (aren't they all award-winning?), progressive Homestead's standout brews include Kaiser's Choice, a zingy Bavarian wheat beer, and Thunderbird, an American pale ale. Food runs all day, from baked eggs with chorizo and coriander to mussels in Homestead apple cider to chickpea and black-bean burgers with mustard mayo. Winner!

★ **Feral Brewing Company** CRAFT BEER

(08-9296 4657; www.feralbrewing.com.au; 152 Haddrill Rd, Baskerville; 11am-5pm Sun-Thu, to late Fri & Sat) The regularly lauded, always-interesting craft beers at Feral include a Hop Hog pale ale and barrel-aged and sour brews that pair nicely with a robust pub-grub menu (mains $22 to $36). Try the fruity Karma Citra India black ale with some beer-fried cheese.

Information

The Swan Valley Visitor Centre (p113) is in Guildford.

Getting There & Away

Guildford (p113) is the gateway to the Swan Valley. For Whiteman Park, catch the train to Bassendean Station. Switch to the 353 or 955 bus to Ellenbrook and get off at Lord St (bus stop 15529). There are also myriad tour companies – ferry and minibus – who can show you around.

Getting Around

To get around the Swan Valley your best options are to drive or take a tour.

Another option is to rent a **bike** (☎0401 077 405; 1235 Great Northern Hwy, Upper Swan; standard/electric bikes per day $35/45), but the area is surprisingly spread out and the roads are usually busy. Pick up the *Cycling in the Swan Valley & Guildford* brochure/map from the Swan Valley Visitor Centre (p113).

There's also the hop-on/hop-off **Swan Valley Explorer** (☎1300 551 687; www.adamspinnacletours.com.au/full-day-tours/swan-valley-explorer-bus-service; adult/child/family $20/15/50) service, running two handy loops around the valley from Guildford train station, departing every 30 minutes from around 10am. Book online.

AVON VALLEY

The meandering – and before summer takes hold, lush and green – Avon Valley is Ballardong country. European settlers moved into the area in early 1830 after food shortages forced Governor Stirling to dispatch Ensign Dale to search the Darling Range for arable land. What he found was the upper reaches of the Swan River, which he presumed was a separate waterway (which is why the river's name changes from the Swan to the Avon in Walyunga National Park). And so, just a year after Perth was founded, homesteads began to appear in the newly named Avon Valley. Many historic stone buildings still stand in the towns and countryside here: it's an atmospheric place, with Ballardong culture still esteemed and celebrated.

Northam

☎08 / POP 6550

The major town in the Avon Valley and a stronghold of Ballardong culture, Northam is a busy commercial hub on the Avon River – a likable enough place with a couple of good cafes and old pubs, but a down-on-its-luck main street and little to warrant a lengthy stay. The railway line from Perth once ended here and miners had to make the rest of the weary trek to the Kalgoorlie goldfields by road; the line now continues all the way to Sydney, traversed by the iconic *Indian Pacific*. The most stimulating time to be in town is during the hectic Avon Descent in early August.

Sights

★Bilya Koort Boodja CULTURAL CENTRE

(☎08-9622 2170; www.bilyakoortboodja.com; 2 Grey St; adult/child/family $10/5/25; ⏲9am-4pm) Next to the 117m pedestrian suspension bridge over the Avon, this striking black-clad centre honours the history, culture and environmental know-how of local Ballardong tribes and the broader Noongar nation. A sequence of spaces includes a 'Welcome to Country' introduction, an explanation of the six Noongar seasons, artefacts, artworks and a storytelling session. It's an impressive celebration of this living culture.

Northam Silo Art PUBLIC ART

(☎08-9226 2799; www.publicsilotrail.com; Northam-Toodyay Rd; ⏲24hr) FREE Part of WA's series of seven brilliant silo-art installations, spangled across the southwest wheat-belt region, Northam's towering rank of 16 silos has a fabulously weird future-fantasy scene on one end by London artist Phlegm, and a dazzlingly colourful Aboriginal-inspired mural by Atlanta artist Hense at the other. Head out of town on the road to Toodyay – you can't miss it.

Festivals & Events

Avon Descent SPORTS

(www.avondescent.com.au; ⏲Aug) A street parade, markets and fireworks are followed by the Avon Descent, a gruelling 124km white-water event for power dinghies, kayaks and canoes down the river in all its winter-flow glory. General chaos ensues – great fun!

Sleeping & Eating

★Dukes Inn MOTEL $$

(☎08-9670 3450; www.dukesinn.com.au; 197 Duke St; d with/without bathroom from $130/90, 1-/2-bedroom apt from $180/190; P❄📶) Northam has a handful of rambling old pubs, most of which have seen better days. But the two-tier red-brick 1907 Dukes Inn in the backstreets raises the bar with a zappy renovation and superior pub grub (mains $15 to $35). Choose from upstairs rooms with shared bathrooms (and access to the balcony) or apartments in the renovated stables out the back.

Cafe Yasou CAFE $$

(☎08-9622 3128; www.cafeyasou.com.au; 175 Fitzgerald St; mains $14-24; ⏲8am-4pm Mon-Fri, to noon Sat) This sunny cafe serves excellent coffee and a Med-inspired menu, including a grilled-halloumi and peach salad, crispy fish tortillas with apple slaw and turmeric, and a stonking eggs Benedict. Sandwiches, cakes and a Greek goddess mural complete the picture. Be sure to pick up a slice of baklava to take away.

Information

Visitor Centre (08-9622 2100; www.avonvalleywa.com.au; 2 Grey St; 9am-4pm;) Overlooking a picturesque slice of the Avon River, with pelicans, parrots and a little island, Northam's info centre is a helpful operation. **RiversEdge Cafe** (08-9622 5635; www.riversedgecafe.com.au; 2 Grey St; mains $13-25; 7.30am-2.30pm Tue-Sun) is here too. Pick up the *Northam Walking Tracks* pamphlet detailing a few good walks around town.

Getting There & Away

Transwa (p108) coach GS2 runs between Northam and East Perth ($21.15, 1½ hours).

Northam is a stop on the Transwa (p108) AvonLink, MerredinLink and Prospector lines, with regular trains to/from East Perth ($21.15, 1½ hours).

York

08 / POP 3610

Only 97km from Perth on Ballardong land, National Trust–listed York is the Avon Valley's most appealing town. It's the oldest inland town in WA, settled by white farmers in 1831, just two years after the Swan River Colony. The homesick settlers here drew parallels between Avon Valley and their native Yorkshire, so Governor Stirling bestowed the name York. These days York is an affable country town with plenty to keep you out of trouble for a day or two.

Sights & Activities

Mt Brown Lookout VIEWPOINT
(off Pioneer Dr; 24hr) FREE For a cracking view over York, the Avon River and the surrounding hills and wheatfields, find your way out past the town cemetery on the eastern side of the river, continuing to the end of Pioneer Dr and the summit of Mt Brown (342m). Pick up a map at the visitor centre.

York Motor Museum MUSEUM
(08-9641 1288; www.yorkmotormuseum.com; 116 Avon Tce; adult/child $10/3; 9.30am-4pm) A must for old-car enthusiasts (vintage, veteran and classic – do you know the difference?), York's main-street motor museum has everything from a basic billycart to a hippy-painted 1951 Ford Prefect and a 1966 Valiant ute, as seen in the film *Crocodile Dundee* and autographed by Paul Hogan.

Skydive York SKYDIVING
(1300 815 241; www.skydive.com.au; 3453 Spencers Brook Rd; 14,000ft tandem jumps from $279) The Avon Valley is WA's skydiving epicentre; the drop zone is about 3km out of town. Weekdays usually offer the best rates.

Festivals & Events

York Festival CULTURAL
(www.yorkfestival.com.au; Sep-Oct) This month-long arts and culture fest injects plenty of life (and dollars) into York every September, banishing the winter blues in favour of workshops, concerts, markets, foodie events, exhibitions and installations.

Sleeping & Eating

York Palace Hotel MOTEL $$
(08-9641 2454; www.theyork.com.au; 145 Avon Tce; d hotel/motel from $165/210;) Choose between lavishly restored heritage rooms upstairs at the silver-turreted York Palace (one of York's fine old pubs, built in 1909), or one of 15 very tidy, contemporary motel-style rooms in the terraces out the back. It comes down to what kind of person you are: frills, or no-frills.

Jules Cafe CAFE $
(08-9641 1832; 121 Avon Tce; mains $19-21; 8am-4pm Mon-Fri, to 3pm Sat & Sun;) Putting a hippy spin on heritage York since 1990 (Che Guevara poster, World Wildlife Fund sticker, trance tunes, patchouli incense...you get the picture), Jules Cafe channels Lebanese heritage with top-notch kebabs, falafel and Middle Eastern salads, wraps and sandwiches. Expect myriad organic, veggie and gluten-free options, plush freshly smashed juices and summery fruit smoothies.

Information

Visitor Centre (08-9641 1301; www.avonvalleywa.com.au; Town Hall, 81 Avon Tce; 9.30am-12.30pm & 1.30-3.30pm) Closes for lunch every day (how quaint).

Getting There & Away

Regular Transwa (p108) coaches arrive from East Perth ($18.05, 1½ hours).

Toodyay

08 / POP 1410

Historic Toodyay, on the Avon River just 85km northeast of Perth, is a hit with wandering city weekenders, browsing the bric-a-brac shops and ducking into the bakery for a citrus tart or two. As you'd expect of a National Trust–classified town, there are plenty of endearing old stone buildings here, most notably a jail, church and downtown mill. Originally known as Newcastle, Toodyay (pronounced '2J') came from the Ballardong Aboriginal word *duidgee* (place of plenty); the name was adopted around 1910.

Sights

Newcastle Gaol Museum MUSEUM

(08-9574 9380; www.toodyay.com; 17 Clinton St; adult/family $5/12; 10am-3pm Mon-Fri, to 3.30pm Sat & Sun) Built in the 1860s using convict labour, this stone complex includes a courtroom, cells and stables, and operated as the Toodyay (then Newcastle) lock-up until 1907. The whole place then fell into ruin until it was restored in the 1960s and '70s (local school kids dug the mud out of the well). A gallery tells the story of famed local bushranger Moondyne Joe.

Festivals & Events

Moondyne Festival CULTURAL

(www.moondynefestival.com.au; Stirling Tce; May) Costumed heritage high jinks in honour of Moondyne Joe, aka Joseph Bolitho Johns, the infamous Avon Valley bushranger, who had a penchant for stealing cheese, illegally branding horses and escaping from prison (which he did with inspiring frequency).

Sleeping & Eating

Toodyay Caravan Park CARAVAN PARK $

(08-9574 2612; www.toodyaycaravanpark.com.au; 122 Railway Rd; unpowered/powered sites $32/37, cabins $105-155; P) A palm-fringed saltwater pool is the highlight at this raffish riverside caravan park, about 1km west of town. Cabins and amenities are basic but clean; campers will need heavy-duty pegs and a serious mallet to bust into the rock-solid ground.

★ **Toodyay Bakery** CAFE $

(08-9574 2617; www.facebook.com/toodyaybakery; 123 Stirling Tce; items $4-8; 7am-3pm) Toodyay Bakery has been here since 1980, but recent refurbishment brings a little city-style artisan sheen to Toodyay. Excellent sourdough loaves and chicken-and-mushroom pies are famous around the Valley: stock up for on-the-road picnics, or grab a sunny outdoor table and see what you can accomplish after an espresso and a lemon-curd tart.

Information

Visitor Information Centre (08-9574 2435; www.toodyay.com; 7 Piesse St; 9am-4pm) Tourist information and accommodation bookings. **Connor's Mill** (08-9574 9380; www.toodyay.com; cnr Stirling Tce & Piesse St; adult/family $5/12; 10am-3.30pm) is right next door. Pick up the *Bilya Walking Track* brochure, charting a 5.6km amble along the Avon River.

Getting There & Away

Toodyay is on the Transwa (p108) AvonLink, Prospector and MerredinLink train lines, with regular connections to East Perth ($18.05, 1¼ hours).

BUSTING OUT WITH MOONDYNE JOE

Joseph Bolitho Johns (aka Moondyne Joe; 1826–1900) was WA's most illustrious bushranger. Sent to WA for pilfering cheese, he arrived in Fremantle in 1853 and was granted an immediate ticket of leave for good behaviour. This good behaviour lasted until 1861, when he was arrested on a charge of illegally branding a horse; however, he escaped that night from Toodyay jail on the horse he rode in on, sitting snugly on the magistrate's new saddle. He was recaptured and sentenced to three years' imprisonment. Between November 1865 and March 1867 he made four attempts to escape, three of them successful. When eventually captured he was placed in a special reinforced cell with triple-barred windows in Fremantle, but later that year he managed to escape from the prison yard while breaking rocks. He served more time in Fremantle Prison when recaptured and was conditionally pardoned in 1873. After release he worked in the Vasse district and kept his nose relatively clean, but he suffered from poor mental health later in life until his death in 1900. You can see his grave at Fremantle cemetery.

NEW NORCIA

08 / POP 100

A bizarre architectural vision in the dry hills 132km north of Perth, the monastery settlement of New Norcia is a cluster of ornate, Spanish-style buildings cast incongruously in the Australian bush. Founded in 1847 by Spanish Benedictine monks as an Aboriginal mission, the working monastery today holds prayers and retreats, alongside a business producing boutique breads and curating a marvellous museum and art gallery. White-robed monks meet for lunch at the town's hotel, then return to their pious single-file movements from church to chambers. It's all very cinematic, and at once gloriously tranquil and deeply unnerving: looking at the faces in the old photographs on display at the museum, it's easy to believe that as many people have suffered as been saved here. Either way, it's a fascinating place.

Sights

★New Norcia Museum & Art Gallery MUSEUM

(08-9654 8056; www.newnorcia.wa.edu.au/museum/museum; New Norcia Rd; adult/child/family $12.50/7.50/30, with Town Tour $25/15/60; 9.30am-4.30pm) Over three levels, New Norcia's marvellously musty Museum & Art Gallery traces the history of the monastery and houses and has an impressive art collection. Contemporary Australian works recast traditional religious styles, alongside one of the country's largest collations of post-Renaissance religious art (including a genuine Raphael). The gift shop sells souvenirs, honeys, preserves and monk-baked breads. **Town Tours** (11am & 1.30pm) leave from here too.

Abbey Church CHURCH

(08-9654 8056; www.newnorcia.wa.edu.au; Old Geraldton Rd; 9.30am-4.30pm) Creak open the door of New Norcia's 1850s Georgian-meets-Latvian Abbey Church, flanked by slender palms. Spot the kangaroos in the sgraffito murals, depicting the Stations of the Cross (look hard – there's also an astronaut). It's a sombre, hushed interior, the wind whispering in the eaves: you'll be forgiven for feeling that you're not alone in here (we made a hurried exit).

Sleeping

New Norcia Hotel HOTEL $

(08-9654 8034; www.newnorcia.wa.edu.au/hotel/hotel; New Norcia Rd; s/d with shared bathroom incl breakfast from $80/100, extra person $27; meals noon-2pm & 6-8pm; P) The white colonnades of the noble New Norcia Hotel hark back to a more genteel time (1927, actually), with sweeping staircases, high ceilings, simple rooms and wide verandahs. Better-than-decent pub food (mains $20 to $28) is available at the bar or in the elegant dining room. Don't bypass the dips with New Norcia's own olive oil and wood-fired sourdough.

Monastery Guesthouse GUESTHOUSE $

(08-9654 8002; www.newnorcia.wa.edu.au/accommodation/individuals-groups/guesthouse; Old Geraldton Rd; s & tw incl meals per person $80) The abbey offers lodging in the Monastery Guesthouse, within the walls of the southern cloister. Guests can join in prayers with the monks (and men can dine with them). Some rooms have bathrooms, some have shared facilities. Air-con also filters through to some of the rooms. Various other cottages and colleges are also available for groups – ask when you book.

Getting There & Away

Transwa (p108) bus N2 runs in each direction between New Norcia and East Perth ($24.15, two hours) on Tuesday, Thursday, Saturday and Sunday.

WILDFLOWER WAY

Extending north from the towns of Moora and Wongan Hills in WA's northern wheatfields (Ballardong lands) to meet the coast at Geraldton, WA's Wildflower Way joins the dots between a series of humble farming towns: Ballidu, Pithara, Dalwallinu, Wubin, Buntine, Latham, Perenjori and Morawa... most of which have a wheat silo, a pub and a caravan park. But you're not necessarily here to drink beer and pitch a tent: the main game here is native wildflowers, which burst into glorious bloom between August and September. Collectively, Western Australia's annual wildflower bloom is the largest such event on earth, including more than 12,000 species – more than 60% are found nowhere else. Online, check out www.wildflowercountry.com.au.

Moora

08 / POP 1780

Tall gums, a broad grid of streets, pubs with deep verandahs, a couple of cafes, a good caravan park and a railway line (wheat trains only) define this agricultural service hub – all of which make it a good base for wildflower explorations into the surrounding area.

The Visitor Information Centre can supply a map of the local wildflower-watching sites and other nearby sites, including Jingemia Cave in **Watheroo National Park**.

Sleeping & Eating

★Moora Shire Caravan Park CARAVAN PARK $

(08-9651 0000; www.moora.wa.gov.au/accommodation; end of Dandaragan St; unpowered/powered sites from $20/30, cabins $120-180; P ❄) Down by the Moore River, the tastefully designed, comfortable cabins at Moora's caravan park are council-owned, and benefit from high civic maintenance standards. Book online, or pay/collect keys at the Shire of Moora administration building (34 Padbury St) or the Gull Service Station across the street from the caravan park. Camping is run separately: call 0409 511 400 to book.

Jeanne d'Moore CAFE $

(0497 857 975; www.jeannedmoore.com.au; 97 Gardiner St; mains $7-20; 7am-4pm Mon-Fri, 8am-1pm Sat) This little Gallic slice in far-flung Moora is a real curio, hung with plastic plants and faux-vines creeping across the shopfront windows. It's mostly a gift shop (clothes, books, baskets, ceramics) but doubles as a cafe, plating-up French-inspired crepes, tarts, pastries, wraps and baguettes. Sit at a retro table and bite into a roast-vegetable baguette with cheesy béchamel sauce.

Information

Visitor Information Centre (08-9653 1053; www.moora.wa.gov.au; Moora Railway Station, 34 Padbury St; 9am-4pm Mon-Thu, to 3pm Fri) Fully in sync with the needs, questions and curiosities of wandering wildflower spotters, Moora's info centre doles out maps and directions with a smile. Ask about other nearby attractions including Jingemia Cave in Watheroo National Park, and an interesting self-guided town walk that takes in Moora's heritage buildings and murals.

Getting There & Away

From Moora, Transwa (p108) buses run to East Perth ($33.50, three hours) on Tuesday, Thursday, Saturday and Sunday; and to and from Geraldton ($51.40, four hours) on the same days.

Wongan Hills

08 / POP 900

With the first wheat crop budding forth here in 1905, unassuming little Wongan Hills isn't as old as many towns in WA's wheat belt. But with its gently undulating countryside, hiking trails and myriad verticordias (aka featherflowers), it makes a pleasant change from the flatter farming towns to the south. In fact, the wildflowers here are extremely diverse: more than 1400 species, with 24 found only around Wongan Hills. Heading north, the Wildflower Way proper begins: drive towards Dalwallinu and into the blooms.

Sights

To get the lay of the land, drive to the top of the **Wheatbelt Lookout** atop Mt O'Brien (424m), 11km west of Wongan Hills.

Wongan Hills' visitor centre (p120) has maps for popular wildflower walks such as **Mt Matilda** (8km return), 12km west of Wongan Hills, and **Christmas Rock** (behind the caravan park, 2km return). Around 29km north of Wongan Hills, the **Reynoldson Nature Reserve** walk (1km one way) has spectacular verticordias.

Sleeping & Eating

Wongan Hills Caravan Park CARAVAN PARK $

(08-9671 1009; www.wonganhillscaravanpark.com.au; 65 Wongan Rd; unpowered/powered sites from $22/28, cabins from $110; P ❄) Wongan Hills' unremarkable caravan park has plenty of hard-stand sites separated by scrubby rows of squat gum trees, plus a good kitchen, a few modern units and the odd cactus studded here and there. A short walk to the pub.

Wongan Hills Hotel PUB FOOD $$

(08-9671 1022; www.facebook.com/wonganhillshotel; 5 Fenton Pl; mains $18-30) Meals at the curvilicious art deco Wongan Hills Hotel are typical country-pub fare, including decent pizzas and the odd international guest (mango chicken curry, lamb rogan josh). Upstairs are classic pub rooms (single/double with shared bathroom from $70/90), some opening onto the verandah; or there are newer motel rooms in a separate building out the back (doubles from $120).

Information

Visitor Information Centre (08-9671 1973; www.wongantourism.com.au; The Station, Wongan Rd; 9am-5pm Mon-Sat, to 12.30pm Sun Mar–mid-Dec) Also books accommodation.

Getting There & Away

Transwa (p108) runs N3 bus services from East Perth to Wongan Hills ($33.50, 2¾ hours) continuing to Geraldton ($68.40, six hours) on Mondays and Thursdays, and in the opposite direction on Tuesdays and Fridays.

SUNSET COAST

The coast road north of Perth follows the Indian Ocean shores to some popular spots for travellers. Within an hour's drive, Perth's outer suburbs give way to the bushland oasis of Yanchep National Park, with its hyperactive wildlife and walking trails. Further north at the tannin-stained mouth of the Moore River, Guilderton offers excellent swimming and fishing; while if [insert deity of choice] had a plan, he/she no doubt tagged the breezy beaches at Lancelin for windsurfing, kitesurfing and sandboarding. On Wajuk and Yuat lands, this is laid-back camping and fishing terrain, with very few urban trimmings.

Guilderton

08 / POP 170

Some 43km north of Yanchep, beyond pine plantations and scrubby dune country, Guilderton is a staggeringly beautiful family-holiday spot where the meandering Moore River empties into the sea. Kids paddle out to the pontoon on the river, parents cast a line into the brine, and teens hit the surf on the ocean beach. For much of the year the river mouth is dammed by a natural sandbar, until winter rains bust it open. For river explorations try **Explorer Boat Hire** (0488 984 942; www.members.iinet.net.au/~rokhor/canoe/moorehire.html; Edwards St; 9am-4pm Sat & Sun, daily school holidays).

Sleeping & Eating

Guilderton Caravan Park CARAVAN PARK $
(08-9577 1021; www.guildertoncaravanpark.com.au; 2 Dewar St; unpowered/powered sites $30/45, cabins $140-170; P ❄) Backing onto the dunes down by the estuary, Guilderton's caravan park gets crazy-busy in summer, and has plenty of level sites and 10 simple self-contained cabins (BYO linen).

Guilderton Country Club PUB FOOD $$
(08-9577 1013; www.guildertoncc.wixsite.com/guildertoncc; Wedge St; mains $16-35; noon-2pm Sat & Sun, 6-8.30pm Wed & Thu, 5-8pm Fri-Sun;) The closest thing Guilderton has to a pub, the Country Club (golf, bowls, tennis) has a roomy bar/dining space and serves pub-grub meals (burgers, schnitzels, fish and chips) five days a week. Or just stop by

WORTH A TRIP

YANCHEP NATIONAL PARK

Within easy reach of Perth, the woodlands and wetlands of **Yanchep National Park** (08-9303 7759; www.parks.dpaw.wa.gov.au/park/yanchep; cnr Indian Ocean Dr & Yanchep Beach Rd; per vehicle $13; visitor centre 9.15am-4.30pm) are home to rampant populations of native fauna, including koalas, kangaroos, emus and cockatoos. Trails range from the 20-minute Dwerta Mia walk to the four-day Coastal Plain walk. To ogle some koalas, stroll along the 240m-long **Koala Boardwalk**. The park also features the splendid limestone **Crystal Cave**, which you can check out on daily 45-minute tours (adult/child/family $15/7.50/37.50).

On Sundays (and occasional Tuesdays and Thursdays), local Wajuk guides run an excellent 45-minute **Aboriginal Experience** (adult/child/family $15/7.50/37.50, prior booking essential) showcasing traditional culture, including the importance of the park's plants and animals and spear and boomerang demonstrations. **Trees Adventure** (08-6365 1833; www.treesadventure.com.au/park/yanchep-park; Ghost House Rd; adult/child $48/38; 9.30am-5pm Tue-Fri, from 8.30am Sat & Sun;) is here too – up to 25m above terra firma and festooned with tricky nets, swings, platforms, ropes and flying foxes.

for a beer and a chat. As per other estimable country clubs around the world, the dress-code standards here are sky-high (shoes).

Information

Guilderton Visitor Information Centre (☎0414 631 273; www.guildertonwa.com.au; 2 Dewar St; ⏰9am-12.30pm Sat & Sun, daily school holidays) When it's open (which isn't often enough), this volunteer-run info hub does a good job proffering local advice. It's next to the entrance to the caravan park.

Getting There & Away

You'll need your own transport to get to Guilderton, 7km off the main highway.

Lancelin

☎08 / POP 730

Afternoon offshore winds and a protective outlying reef make raffish little Lancelin a heaven-sent destination for windsurfing and kitesurfing, attracting wind-worshippers from around the planet. In January the **Lancelin Ocean Classic** (www.lancelinoceanclassic.com.au; ⏰Jan) windsurfing race kicks off at Ledge Point not far to the south. Back on dry land, the mountainous white dunes on the edge of town are prized sandboarding terrain. For sandboard and snorkelling gear hire try **Have a Chat General Store** (☎08-9655 1054; 104 Gingin Rd; sandboard hire per 2hr $10; ⏰5am-5pm Mon-Fri, from 6am Sat, 7am-4pm Sun). Online, see www.lancelin.com.au.

Sleeping & Eating

★**Lancelin Lodge YHA** HOSTEL $
(☎08-9655 2020; www.lancelinlodge.com.au; 10 Hopkins St; dm/d/f from $33/90/135; P❄📶🏊) This laid-back, flag-adorned hostel on the edge of town is well equipped and welcoming, with deep verandahs and lots of indoor/outdoor communal spaces. Facilities include a big kitchen, BBQ, wood-fired pizza oven, enticing swimming pool, hammocks and free bikes and bodyboards. Stylistically it's big, boxy and bricky, but remains one of WA's best hostels. Self-contained suite also available (from $250). Kayaks and sandboards are available for hire.

BIG4 Ledge Point Holiday Park CARAVAN PARK $
(☎08-9655 2870; www.ledgepointholidaypark.com; 742 Ledge Point Rd, Ledge Point; unpowered/powered sites from $20/24, cabins from $115; P❄📶) About a 10-minute drive south of Lancelin, Ledge Point's BIG4 has super-tidy facilities, immaculate lawns and spotless accommodation ranging from caravan and camping sites to white weatherboard cabins and studios. Family-friendly attractions include pedal carts and a jumping pillow (there's not much else to do in Ledge Point...). The beach is about 1km away.

★**Endeavour Tavern** PUB FOOD $$
(☎08-9655 1052; www.endeavourtavern.com.au; 58 Gingin Rd; mains $19-39; ⏰10.30am-10pm Sun-Thu, to midnight Fri & Sat, meals noon-2pm & 6-8pm) The Endeavour is a classic Aussie beachfront beer bunker, with a big grassy terrace overlooking the Indian Ocean. The kitchen cooks up hefty pub-grub standards (chips with everything), including BLTs and burgers in buns from the Lancelin **bakery** (☎08-9655 1457; 8 Rock Way; items $4-8; ⏰10am-6pm Fri-Wed). As you'd expect, the seafood is magic: order the grilled sweetlip snapper (with chips). Live bands on weekends.

Lobster Trap CAFE $$
(☎08-9655 1127; www.lobbstertrap.com; 91 Gingin Rd; mains $12-32; ⏰8am-3pm Thu-Mon) On Lancelin's rather aimless main street, Lobster Trap has the best coffee in town, plus wraps, salads, curries and lobster (aka crayfish) served myriad ways: lobster linguine, lobster wraps, lobster sliders... Trap yourself in the shady garden and ponder your next move. Opening hours can vary: call ahead if you're making a dedicated voyage to eat here.

Getting There & Away

From Perth en route to Geraldton on Friday and Sunday, Transwa (p97) N5 buses stop at Lancelin ($24.15, two hours). En route to Broome from Perth, **Integrity Coach Lines** (Map p62; ☎08-9274 7464; www.integritycoachlines.com.au; cnr Wellington St & Horseshoe Bridge) also stops at Lancelin ($34, two hours).

TURQUOISE COAST

Cruising up Indian Ocean Dr from Lancelin into Cervantes and beyond, the chilled-out Turquoise Coast – traditional Yuat lands, and Amangu country further north – is studded with soporific fishing villages, sweeping stretches of beach, extraordinary geological formations, craggy national parks and wildflower blooms. Not far offshore, marine parks and island nature reserves provide safe breeding havens for Australian sea lions, while crayfishing brings in the big bucks (there's a distinct 'have' and 'have not' social divide here, between the crayfishers and the landlubbers). If you've been craving some time to reconnect with the natural realm, do some beachcombing (this coastline is shipwreck central) or just chew through your airport novel, the Turquoise Coast is waiting for you.

Cervantes & Pinnacles Desert

08 / POP 530

Laid-back crayfishing town Cervantes, 198km north of Perth, makes a handy overnight stop with easy access to the Pinnacles Desert, the Kwongan wildflowers and the heaths of Lesueur National Park and Badgingarra National Park, plus some beaut beaches. Only established in 1963, the town is scruffy, sprawling and charmless – even the Spanish street names, taking their cue from the 1844 wreck of the *Cervantes* nearby, do little to elevate the vibe. But things could be worse: the waterlogged survivors of the *Cervantes* wreck had to walk to their salvation in Fremantle, 216km away.

Sights

Many Perth-based companies offer day trips to the Pinnacles, including the following:

Explore Tours Perth (08-9308 2211; www.exploretoursperth.com.au; day tour adult/child $169/119)

Kandu Perth Tours (0419 935 677; www.kanduperthtours.com.au; day tour adult/child from $175/130)

Travel Western Australia Tours (08-6267 0701; www.twatours.com.au; day tour per person $165)

★ **Nambung National Park** NATIONAL PARK
(08-9652 7913; www.parks.dpaw.wa.gov.au/park/nambung; Pinnacles Dr, off Indian Ocean Dr; per vehicle $13; daylight hours, visitor centre 9.30am-4.30pm) Around 14km from Cervantes, Nambung is home to the eye-popping **Pinnacles Desert**, a vast, alien-like plain studded with thousands of jaunty limestone pillars. Rising eerily from the desert floor, some of them 3.5m tall, these columns are remnants of a compacted seashell layer that once covered the plain and, over millennia, has slowly eroded. The one-way Pinnacles Desert Dr loop road runs through the formations, but it's more fun on foot, especially in the crepuscular evening light when crowds evaporate.

Sleeping & Eating

Lobster Lodge HOSTEL $
(08-9652 7377; www.lobsterlodge.com.au; 91 Seville St; dm $35, d with/without bathroom $135/95, 3-bedroom apt $300; P ❄) Refurbished in early 2019 and managed by the same folks who run the Lobster Shack, this unhurried hostel behind the dunes near Thirsty Point has a fantastic front terrace hung with a lazy hammock or two, small and tidy dorms, a chipper communal kitchen and a snug lounge. Bright, spacious en suite rooms, some with views, occupy the building next door.

RAC Cervantes Holiday Park CARAVAN PARK $
(08-9652 7060; www.parksandresorts.rac.com.au/park/cervantes-holiday-park; 35 Aragon St; unpowered/powered sites $36/46, 2-/3-bedroom cabins $200/250; P ❄) In a fantastic location right behind the dunes with plenty of shady, grassy sites and an on-site **cafe** (www.parksandresorts.rac.com.au/cervantes/park-info/cafe-and-shop; mains $8-20; 8am-4pm), this auto-club park is open to all comers (RAC members receive a $5 discount). The spanking-new cabins circling around the swimming pool are a highlight. Kids scoot around pathways lined with native plants, and to the playground across the street.

★ **Lobster Shack** SEAFOOD $$
(08-9652 7010; www.lobstershack.com.au; 37 Catalonia St; mains $17-43; shop 8am-5pm, cafe 11am-3pm, tours noon-3pm) Craving some cray? They don't come much fresher than at this lobster-factory-turned-lunch spot, where half a grilled lobster, chips and salad will set you back around $38. Fish burgers, prawn buckets, abalone, oysters, beer and wine complete the picture. Self-guided factory tours ($10) and takeaway also available; B-52s' 'Rock Lobster' sing-alongs mandatory.

Information

Grab a copy of the *Turquoise Coast Self Drive Map* from Cervantes' **Visitor Information Centre** (08-9652 7700; www.visitpinnaclescountry.com.au; 14-16 Cadiz St; 9am-5pm), which also supplies accommodation and tour info.

KWONGAN WILDFLOWERS

Take any road inland from the Turquoise Coast and you'll soon enter the Kwongan heathlands, where, depending on the season (broadly July to January), the roadside verges erupt with native wildflowers: banksia, grevillea, hakea, calothamnus, kangaroo paw, smokebush... Lesueur National Park, northeast of Jurein Bay, is the main go-to zone for all things botanical hereabouts, but the following options are also bloomin' marvellous.

Badgingarra National Park (www.parks.dpaw.wa.gov.au/park/badgingarra) Around 50km inland from Cervantes, with 3.5km of walking trails, kangaroo paws, banksias, grass trees, verticordia and a rare mallee.

Alexander Morrison National Park (www.parks.dpaw.wa.gov.au/park/alexander-morrison) Named after WA's first botanist, this park is 50km inland from Green Head. Expect to see dryandra, banksia, grevillea, smokebush, leschenaultia and honey myrtle.

Tathra National Park (www.parks.dpaw.wa.gov.au/park/tathra) Tathra has similar flora to Alexander Morrison National Park, and the drive between the two is rich with banksia, kangaroo paw and grevillea.

Alternatively, take a guided day tour from Leeman with **Kwongan Country Tours** (☎0427 042 557; day tours per person $165). Exploring further inland, don't miss the **Wildflower Way** between Wongan Hills and Geraldton.

Getting There & Away

Integrity Coach Lines (p121) runs from Perth to Cervantes on Tuesday and Thursday ($42, three hours). Also chugging out of Perth on Friday and Sunday, Transwa (p108) N5 buses stop at Cervantes ($36.60).

Jurien Bay

☎08 / POP 1760

Big enough to have an op shop, a supermarket and a tattoo parlour, rough-and-tumble Jurien Bay has been booming over the past decade, after being selected as a regional 'SuperTown' by WA's Department of Primary Industries & Regional Development in 2011 and earmarked for population growth. Home to a hefty fishing fleet and lots of garish big houses, it's already rather spread out and disjointed; however, there's a long swimming beach, a fishing jetty and some great snorkelling and diving sites.

Sights & Activities

Lesueur National Park NATIONAL PARK

(☎08-9688 6000; www.parks.dpaw.wa.gov.au/park/lesueur; off Cockleshell Gully Rd, Hill River; per vehicle $13; ⏲24hr) This botanical nirvana, 30km northeast of Jurien Bay, protects 900 plant species, many of them rare and endemic, such as the pine banksia *(Banksia tricupsis)* and Mt Lesueur grevillea *(Grevillea batrachioides)*. Late winter sees the heath erupt into a mass of colour: cruise the 18km Lesueur scenic drive and check it out, stopping at picnic areas and lookouts (maybe you'll spot an endangered Carnaby's black cockatoo). A jaunt to the flat top of **Mt Lesueur** (4km return) delivers panoramic coastal views.

Jurien Bay Underwater Interpretive Snorkel & Dive Trail SNORKELLING

(☎08-9652 0870; www.trailswa.com.au/trails/jurien-bay-underwater-interpretive-trail; foreshore; ⏲daylight hours) FREE Around 25m off the beach near the piles of Jurien Bay's old jetty, this underwater trail guides snorkellers around an artificial reef, slowly becoming inhabited by marine flora and fauna. Interpretive plinths on the sea floor (up to 6m deep) provide info. For gear hire try **Jurien Bay Adventure Tours** (☎1300 462 383; www.jurienbayadventuretours.com.au; tours per person $29-99).

Sleeping & Eating

Jurien Bay Tourist Park CARAVAN PARK $

(☎08-9652 1595; www.jurienbaytouristpark.com.au; 1 Roberts St; powered sites $38, cabins $125-160; P❄📶) Down on the Jurien Bay foreshore you'll find these natty navy-and-cream one- and two-bedroom chalets. Most are right behind the beach, although the tent sites are set back against the main road. The **Jetty Cafe** (☎08-9652 1999; meals $11-19; ⏲7.30am-5pm) is on hand for burgers and coffee.

★ **Murray St Grill** BISTRO $$

(☎08-9652 2114; www.facebook.com/murrayst grill; 1/12 Murray St; mains $20-39; ⊙11am-9pm Tue-Thu, to 10pm Fri & Sat, to 8pm Sun;) This slick bistro is a breath of fresh Indian Ocean air for Jurien Bay, with savvy interior design, amiable staff, quick-fire tapas plates (cheese-stuffed jalapeños, pork-belly bites, lemon-pepper squid) and meatier mains (steaks, burgers, lamb cutlets, battered red-spot emperor). The double-beef burger is challengingly weighty. Full bar, all-day kitchen, good coffee and kickin' apple mojitos. Nice one!

Information

Turquoise Coast Visitor Centre (☎08-9652 0870; www.visitturquoisecoast.com.au; 67 Bashford St; ⊙9am-5pm Mon-Fri, to 1pm Sat;) Jurien Bay's excellent visitor centre can advise on activities, transport and accommodation in 'JB' and the surrounding Dandaragan Shire.

Getting There & Away

Integrity Coach Lines (p121) runs from Perth to Jurien Bay on Tuesday and Thursday ($44, 3¼ hours). Also leaving Perth on Friday and Sunday, Transwa (p108) N5 buses stop at Jurien Bay ($42.60, 30 minutes).

Green Head & Leeman

☎08

On the way to Green Head from Jurien Bay, stop at **Grigson Lookout** for a superscenic view along the coast and of the Kwongan heathlands (p123). Tiny, flat **Green Head** itself (population 300) was only gazetted in 1966, and has very little going on (just how we like it). There are several beautiful bays here; the horseshoe-shaped **Dynamite Bay** is your best bet if you fancy a dip, but it's often awash with great wads of floating seagrass. There's good fishing, snorkelling, surfing and windsurfing here, and at little **Leeman** (population 250, gazetted 1961) 15 minutes' drive further north.

Sights & Activities

Stockyard Gully Caves CAVE

(☎08-9688 6000; www.parks.dpaw.wa.gov.au/park/stockyard-gully; off Cockleshell Gully Rd, Warradarge; ⊙daylight hours) FREE Got a 4WD and a torch? Detour 35km northeast of Green Head (via Coorow-Green Head Rd) to Stockyard Gully National Park, where this limestone-cave complex awaits in darkened silence. The main cave here is a vast, 300m-long walk-in cavern with a sandy floor, used by stockmen up until the the 1950s to corral their cattle. Amazing!

Three Bays Walkway WALKING

(☎08-9952 0100; www.coorow.wa.gov.au; off Ocean View Dr, Green Head; ⊙24hr) FREE This 2.5km foreshore trail at Green Head actually connects five bays – South, Hunters, Dynamite, Rocky and Anchorage – tracing craggy limestone cliffs through low coastal heath. Look for ospreys and ancient Aboriginal middens in the dunes along the way. The southern trailhead is at the South Bay Lookout off Ocean View Dr.

Sleeping

★ **Centre Break Beach Stay** MOTEL $$

(☎08-9953 1896; www.facebook.com/centrebreak beachstay; Lot 402, Ocean View Dr, Green Head; dm/d/f from $35/150/190, 1-/2-bedroom apt from $250/300; P) Near Dynamite Bay, two-tier Centre Break has rooms for everyone, from clean, small dorms to a two-bedroom apartment. The on-site licensed **Osprey Bar & Lounge** (meals $18 to $40) has a beachy dining room and BBQ deck, and serves burgers, seafood and steaks for lunch and dinner. The set-up is surprisingly stylish! Kayaks, snorkelling gear and sandboards for hire too.

Getting There & Away

Integrity Coach Lines (p121) runs from Perth to Green Head on Tuesday and Thursday ($48, four hours), continuing north. Also leaving Perth on Friday and Sunday, Transwa (p108) N5 buses stop at Green Head ($45.60, 4¼ hours) and Leeman ($8.55 from Green Head, 15 minutes).

Margaret River & the Southwest

Includes ➡

Bunbury............127
Busselton...........130
Dunsborough........131
Cape Naturaliste....134
Yallingup...........135
Margaret River......137
Caves Road.........141
Nannup.............146
Manjimup...........147

Best Places to Eat

- ➡ Market Eating House (p129)
- ➡ Tokyo Jack's (p129)
- ➡ Miki's Open Kitchen (p140)
- ➡ Blue Ocean Fish & Chips (p145)
- ➡ Yarri (p134)

Best Places to Stay

- ➡ Acacia Chalets (p143)
- ➡ Burnside Organic Farm (p139)
- ➡ Forest Rise (p139)
- ➡ Wildwood Valley Cottages (p136)
- ➡ Fonty's Chalets & Caravan Park (p148)

Why Go?

The farmland, forests, rivers and coast of the lush, green southwestern corner of Western Australia (WA), traditionally the land of the Wardandi and Bibbulmun people, contrast vividly with the stark, sunburnt terrain of much of the state. On land, world-class wineries and craft breweries beckon, and tall trees provide shade for walking trails and scenic drives. Offshore, dolphins and whales frolic, and devoted surfers often find their perfect break.

Unusually for WA, distances between the many attractions are surprisingly short, making it a fantastic area to explore for a few days – you will get much more out of your stay here if you have your own wheels. Summer brings hordes of visitors, but in the wintry months from July to September the cosy pot-bellied stove rules and visitors are scarce, and while opening hours can be somewhat erratic, prices are much more reasonable.

When to Go

Margaret River

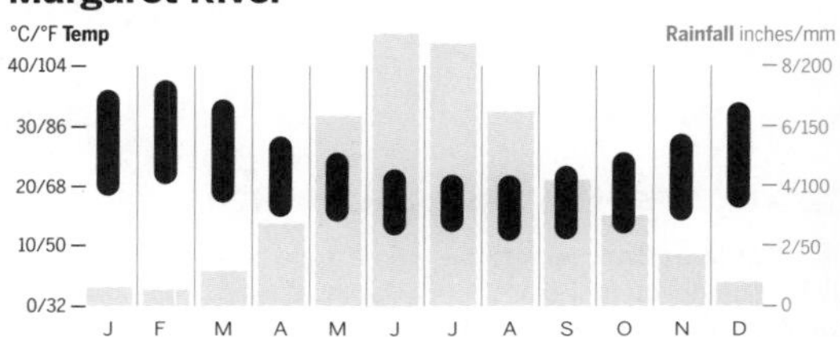

Mar–Apr Catch the surf festival in Margaret River, and the Nannup Music Festival.

May–Aug Whale watching along the coast; cosy fireside evenings in forest accommodation.

Nov Gourmet Escape brings foodies to the wineries and otherwise empty beaches.

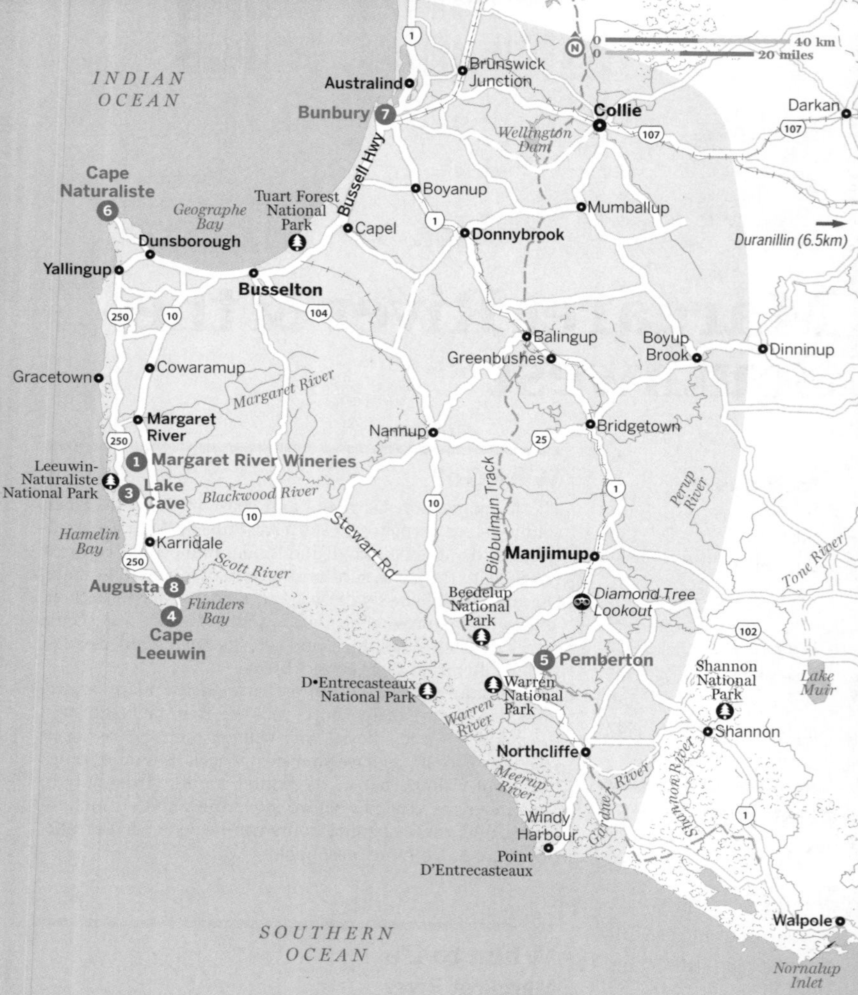

Margaret River & the Southwest Highlights

1 Margaret River wineries (p137) Sampling first-class wine and tucking into excellent seasonal produce.

2 Get outdoors (p39) Walking, swimming, canoeing, cycling, diving in dramatic sea- and landscapes.

3 Lake Cave (p141) Exploring the labyrinthine limestone caverns along Caves Rd.

4 Cape Leeuwin Lighthouse (p145) Fronting up to the confluence of the Indian and Southern Oceans.

5 Pemberton (p148) Walking through the dappled depths of the karri forests surrounding this timber town.

6 Cape Naturaliste (p134) Revelling in wild and beautiful coastal scenery.

7 Bunbury (p127) Taking in this arty small city with its theatre, street art and dolphin discovery centre.

8 Fish & chips (p145) Eating fresh fish and chips by the sea in sleepy Augusta.

BUNBURY GEOGRAPHE

Turquoise waters and 30km of excellent swimming beaches define this gorgeous bay. Positioned between the Indian Ocean and hills of wine, the beachside towns of Busselton and Dunsborough attract hordes of holidaymakers. By West Australian standards, attractions are close together, making it perfect for leisurely touring.

For 55,000 years the area from Geographe Bay to Augusta was inhabited by the Wardandi, one of the Noongar peoples. They lived a nomadic life linked to the six seasons here, heading to the coast in summer to fish, and journeying inland during the wet winter months.

The French connection to many of the current place names dates from an early-19th-century expedition by the ships *Le Géographe* and *Naturaliste*. Thomas Vasse, a crewman who was lost at sea, is remembered in the name of a village, river, inlet and Margaret River winery.

Bunbury

08 / POP 81,389

Both a busy port and beachside holiday spot, Bunbury has much to recommend it. Holidaymakers mostly stop here to see the local dolphins, but with an excellent local history museum, regional art gallery, street art, international cuisine and opportunities to learn about the Aboriginal culture, it's definitely worth a longer visit.

Inhabited by the Wardandi, before the Dutch, French and then Brits sailed in (the Brits later returning to claim ownership in 1838), the bay was named after Nicolas Baudin's ship *Le Géographe* in 1803; British Governor James Stirling renamed the township after a lieutenant in charge of the original military outpost.

Today Bunbury features a mishmash of architectural styles: heritage buildings around Victoria St, deco and some late-20th-century monsters, plus spanking-new waterfront developments along the estuary and ocean-facing beach.

Sights

★Dolphin Discovery Centre SCIENCE CENTRE
(08-9791 3088; www.dolphindiscovery.com.au; Koombana Beach; adult/child $18/10; 9am-2pm May-Sep, 8am-4pm Oct-Apr; P) Around 60 bottlenose dolphins live in the bay year-round, their numbers increasing in summer. This community-led centre teaches visitors about the dolphins and their habitat, with lots of hands-on experiences. To meet the wild dolphins in real life, head to the beachside zone early in the day. The experience is carefully supervised by well-trained volunteers for the safety of the dolphins.

★Bunbury Museum & Heritage Centre MUSEUM
(www.bunburymuseum.com.au; 1 Arthur St; 10am-4pm Tue-Sun;) FREE A fabulous small museum, packed full of information on the original inhabitants here, the Wardandi people, explorers who visited and the colonisers who moved in. Relies a lot on multimedia, but there are some interesting artefacts and an old school room. Ask about the wreck buried under Bunbury somewhere.

Bunbury Regional Art Gallery GALLERY
(08-9792 7323; www.brag.org.au; 64 Wittenoom St; 10am-4pm; P) FREE Housed in a restored late-19th-century convent, now painted a dusty pink, this excellent gallery is arranged over two floors and exhibits new works as well as pieces from its collection.

Bunbury Wildlife Park ZOO
(08-9721 8380; www.bunburywildlifepark.com.au; Prince Philip Dr; adult/child $10.50/5.50; 10am-5pm; P) A simple wildlife park to introduce the kids to Australian wildlife including kangaroos, wallabies, possums, parrots, owls and emus with some hands-on feeding possible. Across the road, the **Big Swamp** wetlands also has good walking tracks and stops for birdwatching.

Activities

Geographe Alternative Wine Trail WINE
(https://visitbunburygeographe.com.au/geographe-alternative-wine-trail) Get off the beaten track and tour this lesser-known wine region. The visitor centre has copies of the self-drive maps, which are also available online. Meet innovative winemakers working with 12 alternative wine varieties for the region, from barbera to tempranillo.

Dolphin Swim Tour & Eco Cruises WILDLIFE WATCHING
(https://dolphindiscovery.com.au; 3hr swim tour $165, 1½hr eco tour adult/child $54/40; 8am & noon;) Rise early for the opportunity to swim with dolphins in what many say is a life-changing experience, although animal welfare experts are wary. Alternatively, meet

Bunbury

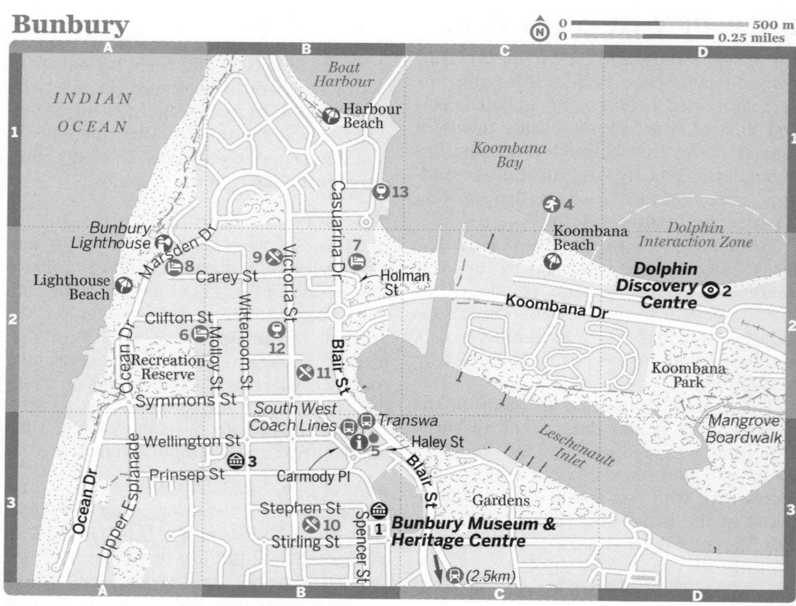

Bunbury

Top Sights
1 Bunbury Museum & Heritage Centre B3
2 Dolphin Discovery Centre D2

Sights
3 Bunbury Regional Art Gallery B3

Activities, Courses & Tours
4 Dolphin Swim Tour & Eco Cruises C1
5 Ngalang Wongi Aboriginal Cultural Tours B3

Sleeping
6 Clifton A2
7 Mantra B2
8 Quality Hotel Lighthouse A2

Eating
9 Market Eating House B2
10 No. 140 .... B3
11 Tokyo Jack's B2

Drinking & Nightlife
12 Lost Bills B2
13 Mash B1
Yours or Mine .... (see 11)

at midday for an informative boat cruise spotting some of Bunbury's playful dolphins in the wild.

Tours

Ngalang Wongi Aboriginal Cultural Tours CULTURAL
(0457 360 517; www.ngalangwongi.com.au; Bunbury Visitor Centre; adult/child from $50/25;) Don't leave Bunbury without learning about its pre- and post-colonial history and sites of cultural significance. A gifted storyteller, local Noongar man Troy Bennell runs a two-hour city walking tour, plus a morning around the estuary and Collie River including wildlife and bush foods.

Sleeping

Bunbury Glade Caravan Park CARAVAN PARK **$**
(08-9721 3800; www.glade.com.au; Timperley Rd; sites per 2 people $40, cabins $100-150;) This spotless park is a five-minute drive from the centre of town. Family friendly with good BBQ facilities and a small fenced playground.

Quality Hotel Lighthouse BOUTIQUE HOTEL **$$**
(08-9781 2700; http://lighthousehotel.com.au; 2 Marlston Dr; r from $150;) With a commanding location looking towards the

Indian Ocean, this newish hotel is across the road from the ocean beach and a short walk to the estuary. It has excellent modern facilities, but is small enough to have a boutique vibe.

Clifton MOTEL $$
(☎08-9721 4300; www.theclifton.com.au; 2 Molloy St; r from $135;) For heritage accommodation with a dose of luxury, go for the top-of-the-range rooms in the Clifton's historic Grittleton Lodge (1885). Good-value motel rooms are available in a separate building.

Mantra APARTMENT $$$
(☎08-9721 0100; www.mantra.com.au; 1 Holman St; apt from $210;) The Mantra has sculpted a set of modern studios and apartments around four grain silos by the estuary. Deluxe rooms have spa baths and full kitchens.

Eating

Bunbury Farmers Market MARKET
(https://bunburyfarmersmarket.com.au; 2 Vittoria Rd; ⊙7.30am-6.30pm, 8am-5.30pm Sat & Sun) Fresh local produce, as well as sushi and self-catering platters for picnickers.

No. 140 CAFE $$
(☎08-9721 2254; https://oneforty.com.au; 140 Victoria St; mains $13-32; ⊙7am-4pm Mon-Fri, 8am-2pm Sat & Sun) Hip, onto-it staff make this welcoming cafe a top spot for a leisurely Bunbury breakfast with a twist – try the cured pork kedgeree omelette or an iced coffee in a jar. Lunches include burittos, platters and grilled sandwiches.

★**Market Eating House** MODERN AUSTRALIAN $$$
(☎08-9721 6078; www.marketeatinghouse.com.au; 9 Victoria St; shared plates $12-18, mains $35-42; ⊙5.30pm-late Wed & Thu, noon-late Fri & Sat, 9am-4pm Sun) Focuses on a custom-made wood-fired grill that is used for everything from chicken and fish to pork and beef. Turkish and Middle Eastern flavours underpin many dishes, and smaller shared plates include plump ricotta dumplings and hummus topped with lamb.

★**Tokyo Jack's** JAPANESE $$$
(www.tokyo-jacks.com.au; 54 Victoria St; small share plates $5-18, large plates $29-38; ⊙11am-10pm;) With a contemporary fit-out, polished concrete and a mural, Tokyo Jack's offers *izakaya* (bar) style Japanese tapas. Moreish highlights include popcorn shrimp and Wagyu beef croquettes, while the broader menu includes sushi and sashimi as well as all your Japanese classics.

Drinking & Nightlife

Yours or Mine BAR
(☎08-97918884; www.facebook.com/yoursormine1; 26 Victoria St; ⊙noon-3pm & 5pm-midnight Mon-Thu, noon-midnight Sat & Sun) Yours or Mine continues Bunbury's small-bar scene but with tasty shared plates ($18 to $28) and chesterfield sofas. The South American–influenced menu (mains $24 to $42), including pulled-pork tacos, is worth the wait when its busy. Check the website for nightly specials and occasional live gigs.

Lost Bills COCKTAIL BAR
(www.lostbills.com; 41 Victoria St; ⊙4-11pm Wed-Thu, 3pm-midnight Fri & Sat, 2-8pm Sun) Lost Bills' compact brick-lined space is enlivened by quirky artwork. A good wine and cocktail list and four guest taps with beer and cider from around WA are also valid reasons to visit Bunbury's answer to the small bar in Sydney or Melbourne.

Mash CRAFT BEER
(☎08-9721 6111; www.mashbrewing.com.au; 2/11 Bonnefoi Blvd; ⊙11am-9pm, from 7.30am Fri-Sun) This waterfront microbrewery turns out seven regular beers, plus always interesting seasonal concoctions. Try the Copycat AIPA, champion brew at the Australian International Beer Awards in 2014. The food is typical pub grub – and it does breakfasts too – but service can be hit and miss.

Information

Visitor Centre (☎08-9792 7205; www.visitbunburygeographe.com.au; Carmody Pl; ⊙9am-5pm Mon-Sat, 10am-2pm Sun) Located in the historic train station (1904). Bikes can be rented and there are free historic walking tours every Wednesday at 10am.

Getting There & Away

South West Coach Lines (☎08-9261 7600; www.southwestcoachlines.com.au) Runs to/from Perth's Elizabeth Quay Busport to Busselton, Dunsborough and Bridgetown.

Transwa (☎1300 662 205; www.transwa.wa.gov.au) Runs buses to most neighbouring cities and towns and down to Albany and Denmark.

Bunbury is the terminus of the Transwa Australind train line, with two daily services to Perth ($31.45, 2½ hours).

Busselton

08 / POP 38,300

Unpretentious and uncomplicated, Busselton is what passes for the big smoke in these parts. Surrounded by calm waters and white-sand beaches, its outlandishly long jetty is its most famous attraction. The family-friendly town has plenty of diversionary activities for lively kids, including sheltered beaches, water slides and animal farms.

Sights

Busselton Jetty LANDMARK

(08-9754 0900; www.busseltonjetty.com.au; adult/child $4/free; 8.30am-6pm Oct-Apr, 9am-5pm May-Sep;) Busselton's 1865 timber-piled jetty – the southern hemisphere's longest (1841m) – reopened in 2011 following a $27 million refurbishment. A little **train** (adult/child $13.50/8.50) chugs along to the **Underwater Observatory** (adult/child incl train $34/20; 9am-4.25pm;), where tours take place 8m below the surface; bookings essential. There's also an Interpretive Centre, in an attractive building in the style of 1930s bathing sheds, about 50m along the jetty. You can also explore the underwater world around the jetty's historic piles with **Dive Busselton Jetty** (1800 994 210; www.divebusseltonjetty.com.au; underwater walks $179, snorkelling/diving from $20/99; underwater walks Dec-Apr), wearing a self-contained breathing apparatus called a SeaTREK helmet.

Tuart Forest National Park FOREST

(www.parks.dpaw.wa.gov.au;) The tuart is a type of eucalypt that only grows on coastal limestone in southwest WA. This 20-sq-km strip squeezed between the Bussell Hwy and the Indian Ocean just outside Busselton is the last tuart forest left after decades of logging. There is a self-guided 1.5km walk in the forest designed for night-time possum spotting. Bring your own torch.

Capel Vale WINERY

(08-9727 1986; www.capelvale.com.au; Mallokup Rd; cellar door 10am-4.30pm, restaurant 11.30am-3pm Thu-Mon) Geographe Bay wine region's best-known winery is conveniently located halfway between Bunbury and Busselton. Capel Vale offers free tastings and has a restaurant overlooking the vines. It's off the Bussell Hwy on the opposite side of the highway from Capel village.

Wonnerup House HISTORIC BUILDING

(08-9752 2039; www.nationaltrust.org.au/places/wonnerup; 935 Layman Rd; adult/child $8/5; 10am-4pm Thu-Mon, closed Jul;) A whitewashed National Trust homestead (1859) and nearby school house in a bucolic setting, but with a tragic colonial history. Visitors are provided with an information sheet for a self-guided tour of the property.

ArtGeo Cultural Complex GALLERY

(08-9751 4651; www.artgeo.com.au; 6 Queen St; 10am-4pm) Grouped around the old courthouse (1856), this complex includes tearooms, an artist-in-residence and the Busselton Art Society's exhibition space, selling work by local artists from ceramics to fine jewellery.

Festivals & Events

CinéfestOZ FILM

(www.cinefestoz.com; late Aug) Busselton briefly morphs into Cannes with this oddly glamorous festival of French and Australian cinema, including lots of Australian premieres and the odd Aussie starlet.

Sleeping

Big 4 Beachlands Holiday Park CARAVAN PARK $

(Map p132; 08-9752 2107; www.beachlands.com.au; 10 Earnshaw Rd, West Busselton; sites per 2 people $53, chalets $145-215;) This excellent family-friendly park offers a wide range of accommodation – grassy tent sites to deluxe villas – amid shady trees, palms and flax bushes. A playground, pool, bikes, stand-up paddleboards and pedal go-carts will keep kids happy.

Observatory Guesthouse B&B $$

(08-9751 3336; www.observatoryguesthouse.com; 7 Brown St; d from $150;) A five-minute walk from the jetty, this friendly B&B has four bright, cheerful rooms. They're not overly big, but you can spread out on the communal sea-facing balcony and front courtyard.

★ **Aqua** DESIGN HOTEL $$$

(Map p132; 08-9750 4200; www.theaquaresort.com.au; 605 Bussell Hwy; apt $420-1400;) Down a driveway framed by peppermint trees and with direct beach access, the luxury beach town houses at Aqua are a grand option for families or a pair of couples travelling together. Bedrooms and bathrooms are stylish and understated, but the real wow factor comes from the stunning lounges and living areas. Facilities include a beachfront infinity pool and a spa and sauna.

Eating

Goose CAFE $$
(08-9754 7700; www.thegoose.com.au; Geographe Bay Rd; breakfast $13-22, share plates & mains $11-35; 7am-10pm;) Next to the jetty, stylish Goose is a cool and classy cafe, bar and bistro. The drinks list bubbles away with WA craft beer and wine, and a versatile menu kicks off with eggy breakfasts, before graduating to share plates using local ingredients, including Vietnamese pulled-pork sliders, and larger dishes such as steamed mussels and seafood chowder.

Vasse Bar + Kitchen PUB FOOD $$
(08-9754 8560; www.vassebarkitchen.com.au; 44 Queen St; mains $17-32; 10am-late) The pub menu mainstays include hearty pizza, pasta, steaks and pale-ale-battered fish. There's a good range of beers on tap, and the outdoor tables are perfect for people-watching. Check out the listings for live music on the window.

Coco's Thai THAI $$
(08-9754 7222; 55 Queen St; mains $16-23; 5pm-late;) A little place serving tasty Thai favourites and more adventurous dishes such as a delicious fish curry with apple. Loaded with fresh herbs, the prawn salad is also great. It's BYO, and often recommended for its friendly service.

Drinking & Nightlife

Darleen's BAR
(www.facebook.com/pg/Darleens; 43 Prince St; noon-midnight Wed-Sat, to 8pm Sun) Taking over from the much-loved Laundry 43, Darleen's brings the karaoke, vinyl and beer-yoga vibes to Busselton. Exposed brick walls form the backdrop for Margaret River beers and wines, plus dishes.

Fire Station CRAFT BEER
(08-9752 3113; www.firestation.bar; 68 Queen St; 11.30am-9.30pm, till late Fri & Sat) Park yourself in the cosy interior or outside under the market umbrellas and enjoy one of the southwest's best selections of wine and craft beer. The tasty food menu includes classic drinking dishes like spicy chicken wings and cheese and chilli croquettes, and weekly specials include Thursday's Bao & Beer deal and Asian steamed buns from 4pm.

Information

Visitor Centre (08-9752 5800; www.margaretriver.com; end of Queen St, Busselton foreshore; 9am-5pm, to 4.30pm Sat & Sun) On the waterfront near the pier. Loans out helmets for cycle hire.

Getting There & Around

South West Coach Lines (p129) and Transwa (p129) buses link Busselton to the north and south.

Busso is fairly spread out; if you don't have a car, hire a **bike** (www.spinwaywa.bike; 1 hr/day $15/33) to get around.

MARGARET RIVER REGION

With vineyard restaurants, artisan food producers, and some of Australia's most spectacular surf beaches and rugged coastline, the Margaret River wine region packs attractions aplenty into a compact area. Sleepy Yallingup conceals excellent beaches, restaurants and luxe accommodation, Margaret River township is the region's bustling foodie heart, and the best of the area's wineries are focused around Cowaramup and Wilyabrup. Throughout the area, an excellent craft-beer scene bubbles away, and the road further south to the windswept Cape Leeuwin Lighthouse at Augusta is studded with spectacular underground caves with particular significance to the traditional custodians of this land, the Wardandi.

Dunsborough

08 / POP 5320

Dunsborough is a gentle township with a well-heeled resident base. It's a good spot to base yourself to explore Cape Naturaliste's bushland and beaches, with excellent shopping and dining options. Family holiday houses line the bayside waterfront, and its YHA has one of the best backyards in Australia. The name Dunsborough first appeared on maps in the 1830s, but to the Wardandi people it was always Quedjinup, meaning 'place of women'.

Sights & Activities

Blind Corner WINERY
(Map p132; www.blindcorner.com.au/blogs/cellar-door/cellar-door; 1105 Vasse-Yallingup Siding Rd;

Margaret River Wine Region

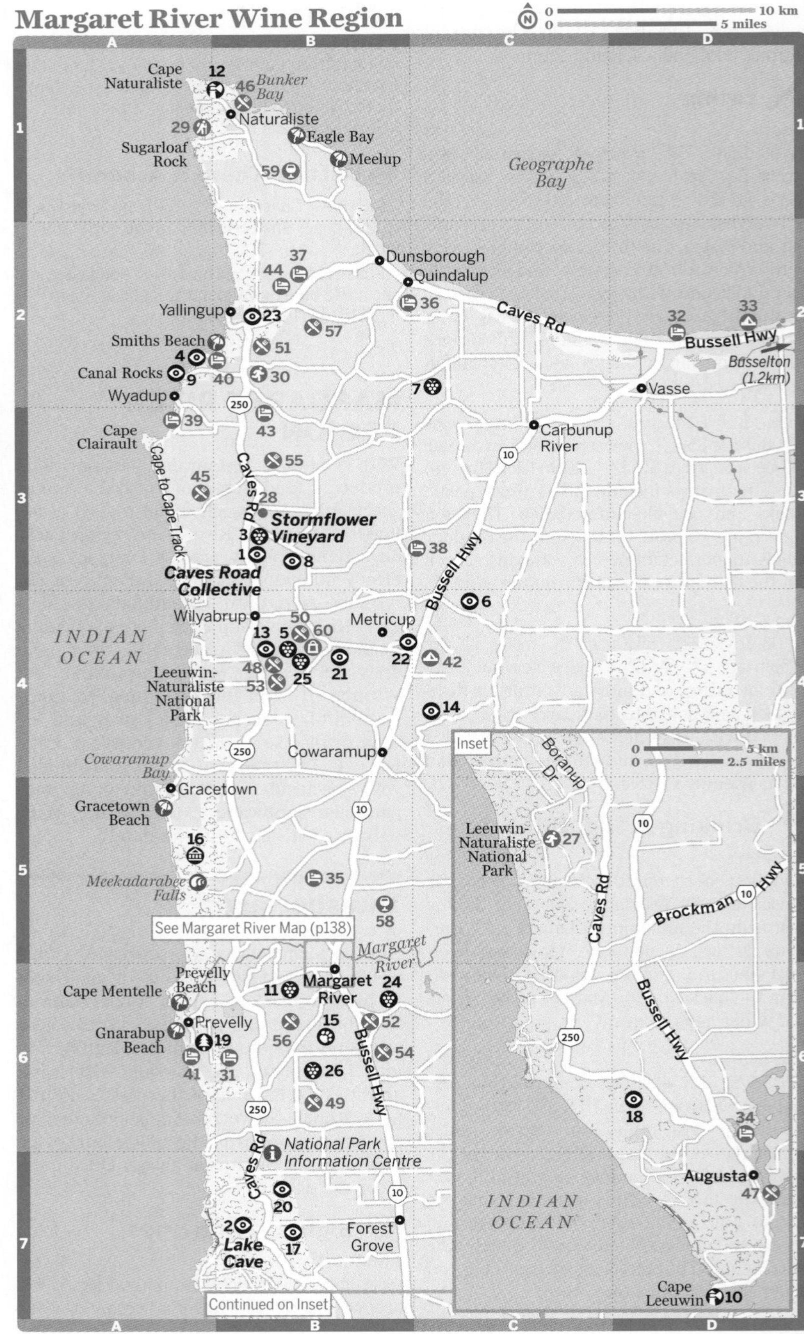

Margaret River Wine Region

Top Sights
1 Caves Road Collective B3
2 Lake Cave B7
3 Stormflower Vineyard B3

Sights
4 Aquarium A2
5 Ashbrook B4
6 Beer Farm C4
7 Blind Corner C2
8 Bootleg Brewery B3
9 Canal Rocks A2
10 Cape Leeuwin Lighthouse D7
11 Cape Mentelle B6
12 Cape Naturaliste Lighthouse B1
13 Cheeky Monkey B4
14 Cowaramup Brewing Company C4
15 Eagles Heritage B6
16 Ellensbrook Homestead A5
17 Giants Cave B7
18 Jewel Cave D6
19 Leeuwin-Naturaliste National Park A6
20 Mammoth Cave B7
21 Margaret River Chocolate Company B4
22 Margaret River Dairy Company B4
23 Ngilgi Cave B2
24 Stella Bella B6
25 Thompson Estate B4
26 Voyager Estate B6

Activities, Courses & Tours
27 Boranup Drive C5
28 Cape Lodge B3
29 Cape to Cape Track A1
30 Premalaya B2
Wildwood Valley Cooking School .... (see 43)

Sleeping
31 Acacia Chalets B6
32 Aqua D2
33 Big 4 Beachlands Holiday Park D2
34 Blackwood River Houseboats D6
35 Burnside Organic Farm B5
36 Dunsborough Rail Carriages & Farm Cottages B2
37 Empire Retreat & Spa B2
38 Forest Rise C3
39 Injidup Spa Retreat A3
Llewellin's .... (see 31)
40 Smiths Beach Resort B2
41 Surfpoint A6
42 Taunton Farm Holiday Park C4
43 Wildwood Valley Cottages B3
44 Yallingup Lodge & Spa B2

Eating
45 Amiria A3
46 Bunkers Beach Cafe B1
47 Colourpatch Café D7
48 Cullen Wines B4
49 Leeuwin Estate B6
50 Rustico at Hay Shed Hill B4
51 Studio Bistro B2
52 Temper Temper B6
The Common .... (see 41)
53 Vasse Felix B4
54 Watershed Premium Wines B6
White Elephant Cafe .... (see 41)
55 Wills Domain B3
56 Xanadu B6
57 Yallingup Woodfired Bread B2

Drinking & Nightlife
58 Colonial Brewing Co B5
59 Eagle Bay Brewing Co B1

Shopping
60 Providore B4

10am-4pm Mon-Sat) Newcomers to the region, the winemakers at Blind Corner are shaking things up with a super-approachable cellar door experience (no question too embarrassing) and producing biodynamic hand-picked wines. Plans to get a pizza oven will see people lingering longer.

Naturaliste Charters WHALE WATCHING
(08-9750 5500; www.whales-australia.com.au; 25/27 Dunn Bay Rd; adult/child $90/50; 10am & 2pm Sep–mid-Dec) Two-hour whale-watching cruises. From December to January, the emphasis switches to an Eco Wilderness Tour showcasing beaches, limestone caves with Aboriginal art, and wildlife, including dolphins and seals.

Cape Dive DIVING
(08-9756 8778; www.capedive.com; 222 Naturaliste Tce; 9am-5pm) There is excellent diving in Geographe Bay, especially since the decommissioned Navy destroyer HMAS *Swan* was purposely scuttled in 1997 for use as a dive wreck. Marine life has colonised the ship, which lies at a depth of 30m, 2.5km offshore. Trips include Busselton Jetty (p130) too.

Sleeping

Dunsborough Beachouse YHA HOSTEL $
(08-9755 3107; www.dunsboroughbeachouse.com.au; 205 Geographe Bay Rd; dm $34-36, s/d $57/88; P) This friendly, well-run hostel has lawns stretching languidly to the beach. Welcoming, though popular with

longer-term stayers too, it's an easy 2km cycle from the town centre; bike hire available.

Dunsborough Central Motel MOTEL **$$**
(☎08-9756 7711; www.dunsboroughmotel.com.au; 50 Dunn Bay Rd; dm $40, r $180-220;) Centrally located, this motel is good value with dorm beds as well as motel rooms. A good option if you want to dine, drink or just mooch in town.

Dunsborough Rail Carriages & Farm Cottages COTTAGE **$$**
(Map p132; ☎08-9755 3865; www.dunsborough.com; Commonage Rd; rail carriages/cottages from $145/490;) Refurbished rail carriages are dotted about this big bush block near Quindalup, as are self-contained timber cottages, which are spacious for families. Kids will have fun with the friendly sheep and chooks.

Eating & Drinking

Occy's Food & Brews PUB FOOD **$$**
(www.occys.com.au; 34 Dunn Bay Rd; meals $20-38; 11.30am-9pm;) Best bet for families or large groups, Occy's does not disappoint, from its colourful street front to its friendly staff serving crowd-pleasers such as crispy whole snapper, pizza and burgers. Most of the seating is outdoors, but heaters and blankets keep punters warm when the temperature drops.

Wild & Woods CAFE **$$**
(☎08-9755 3308; www.wildandwoods.com.au; 2/237 Naturaliste Tce; mains $12-25; 8am-4pm Tue-Fri, to 3pm Sat, to 2pm Sun) Wild & Woods' Australia-meets-Scandinavia decor is a relaxing backdrop for excellent breakfasts and counter food like falafel wraps for lunch. Fresh juices and smoothies provide a healthy balance to the region's vineyards and craft breweries.

Pourhouse Bar & Kitchen GASTROPUB **$$**
(☎08-9759 1720; www.pourhouse.com.au; 26 Dunn Bay Rd; mains $19-34; 11am-late) An unpretentious modern pub, with comfy couches, weekend DJs and an upstairs terrace, the **Elevator Bar**. The pizzas are varied, and burgers come in a locally baked sourdough bun. A considered approach to beer includes rotating taps from the best of WA's craft breweries and lots of bottled surprises.

Yarri AUSTRALIAN **$$$**
(https://yarri.com.au; 6/16 Cyrillean Way; mains $18-40; P) The talk of the region when we visited, this elegant restaurant serves a modern Australian menu aligned with the seasons and using indigenous ingredients. You're as likely to have dishes with emu as marron (freshwater crayfish). Food is paired with wines from Snake + Herring.

Blue Manna ASIAN **$$$**
(☎08-9786 5051; www.bluemannabistro.com.au; 1/16 Cyrillean Way; mains $20-38; noon-late, closed public holidays; P) Pan Asian–style bistro specialising in seafood dishes with excellent staff who manage well given its buzzing popularity. Dishes range from mouth-watering salt and pepper blue manna crab to Balinese betutu duck.

Eagle Bay Brewing Co BREWERY
(Map p132; ☎08-9755 3554; www.eaglebaybrewing.com.au; Eagle Bay Rd; 11am-5pm) Offers a lovely rural outlook; interesting beers and wines served in modern, spacious surroundings; and excellent food, including crisp wood-fired pizzas. Keep an eye out for single batch specials.

Information

Visitor Centre (☎08-9752 5800; www.margaretriver.com; 1/31 Dunn Bay Rd; 9am-5pm Mon-Fri, 9.30am-4.30pm Sat & Sun) Information and bookings.

Getting There & Away

South West Coach Lines (p129) and Transwa (p129) buses link Dunsborough north to Perth and further south through Margaret River to Albany and the southwest.

Cape Naturaliste

☎08

Northwest of Dunsborough, Cape Naturaliste offers the secluded white-sand beaches of **Meelup**, **Eagle Bay** and **Bunker Bay**, a lighthouse with breathtaking views and the oft-photographed Sugarloaf Rock. There are plenty of short walks and lookouts along the cape to explore; pick up brochures from Dunsborough's visitor centre before heading out of town. Whales like to hang out on the edge of Bunker Bay, where the continental shelf drops 75m. There's also excellent snorkelling at Shelley Cove and the HMAS *Swan* wreck offshore.

Sights & Activities

Ngilgi Cave CAVE
(Map p132; ☎08-9755 2152; www.margaretriver.com; Yallingup Caves Rd; adult/child $22.50/12;

9am-5pm; P) This 500,000-year-old cave is associated in Wardandi spirituality with the victory of the good spirit Ngilgi over the evil spirit Wolgine. A whitefella first stumbled upon the site in 1899 while looking for his horse. Today semi-guided tours of the caves, which allow you to explore at your own pace, depart every half-hour. Last tour at 4pm.

More adventurous caving options are available as well as multi-cave passes for the four main sites in the region. Highly recommended are the cultural immersion tours of the caves and neighbouring region with Koomal Dreaming (p136). The 'Above & Below' ticket (adult/child $30/15) includes entry to the Cape Naturaliste Lighthouse, a short drive away.

Cape Naturaliste Lighthouse LIGHTHOUSE
(Map p132; 08-9780 5911; www.margaretriver.com/members/cape-naturaliste-lighthouse; adult/child $14/7; 9.30am-4pm; P) Built in 1903, this lighthouse can only be visited as part of the guided tours, which run half-hourly and help fund the upkeep of the site. The view of two oceans meeting is spectacular. A museum and cafe are also on-site.

Southwest Eco Discoveries ECOTOUR
(0477 049 722, 0477 030 322; www.southwestecodiscoveries.com.au; tours $55-95) Brothers Ryan and Mick White run tours exploring Geographe Bay and Cape Naturaliste. Options include morning tours of the stunning coastline, afternoon tours with a wine and gourmet focus, and evening outings to see endangered woylies and other nocturnal marsupials. Tour pick-ups can be made from accommodation in Busselton, Dunsborough and Cowaramup, and from Margaret River by availability and arrangement.

Eating

Bunkers Beach Cafe CAFE $$
(Map p132; 08-9756 8284; www.bunkersbeachcafe.com.au; Farm Break Lane; breakfast $14-25, lunch $18-38; 8am-11am & noon-3pm Thu-Mon; P) In a staggeringly good location, just metres from the sand, this breezy cafe has limited hours, but a great menu, excellent wine list and sophisticated options for kids.

Getting There & Away

No public transport runs to Cape Naturaliste, so visitors need their own transport, or else will need visit on a pre-booked tour.

Yallingup

08 / POP 1029

Huddled on an ocean-facing hillside, the township of Yallingup is a quiet spot favoured by surfers and coastal walkers. It's mostly residential, with a wellness, yoga and family-holidays vibe. The dramatic surf-battered coastline is overlooked by a cascade of residential houses huddled together surrounded by trees. Yallingup means 'place of love' in the Wardandi Noongar tongue. Beautiful well-marked walking trails follow the coast over rocky outcrops and through treed hills overlooking the aquamarine ocean.

Sights & Activities

Aquarium NATURAL POOL
(Map p132; Smiths Beach Rd; 24hr; P) FREE Protected from the pounding surf, this natural rock pool is a top spot for swimming and snorkelling. It's a walk along the Cape to Cape Track to the rock pool – ask locally for exact directions. Wild swimming precautions should be taken.

Canal Rocks NATURAL FEATURE
(Map p132; https://parks.dpaw.wa.gov.au/site/canal-rocks; Canal Rocks Rd; P) Photo opportunities abound with the new bridge across the natural canal here. The Wardandi called it Winjee Sam.

Premalaya YOGA
(Map p132; www.premalaya.com.au/wellness; 1701 Wildwood Rd; yoga $20; classes Mon-Sat) Just outside Yallingup, this family-run yoga and meditation studio (with accommodation attached) offers a range of classes in a large comfortable studio looking over eucalypts and a small dam. Catch some sun rays on the deck outside after.

Yallingup Surf School SURFING
(08-9755 2755; www.yallingupsurfschool.com) Grab a 1½-hour group lesson for beginners or private coaching sessions. Also offers six-day surf and yoga safaris for women at www.escapesafaris.com.au.

Courses

Wildwood Valley Cooking School COOKING
(Map p132; 08-9755 2120; www.wildwoodvalley.com.au; 1481 Wildwood Rd, Wildwood Valley Cottages; classes per person $140; Dec-Mar) Set amid the shaded grounds of Wildwood Valley Cottages (p136), the cooking school with Sioban and Carlo Baldini offers hands-on classes in

RED TAILS IN THE SUNSET

Between Cape Naturaliste and Cape Leeuwin is the most southerly breeding colony of the red-tailed tropicbird *(Phaethon rubricauda)* in Australia. From September to May, look for it soaring above Sugarloaf Rock, south of Cape Naturaliste. The viewpoint can be reached by a 3.5km walk from the Cape Naturaliste lighthouse or by taking Sugarloaf Rd.

The tropicbird is distinguished by its two long, red tail streamers – almost twice its body length. Bring binoculars to watch this small colony soar, glide, dive and then swim with their disproportionately long tail feathers cocked up.

Thai or Italian cuisine. Sioban's CV includes cooking at Longrain and living in Tuscany. Cooking classes include Wood Fired cooking and Taste of Tuscany and are wildly popular with Perth visitors, so check the schedule online and book early. Most classes occur on a Wednesday, Friday or Saturday, but this does vary.

Tours

Koomal Dreaming TOURS
(☎0413 843 426; www.koomaldreaming.com.au; adult/child from $78/44) Charismatic Yallingup local and Wardandi man Josh Whiteland runs a range of tours showcasing Indigenous food, culture and music, including walks and exploration of the Ngilgi Cave (p134). Don't leave the region without learning about its Aboriginal cultural story.

Sleeping

Yallingup Beach Holiday Park CARAVAN PARK $
(☎08-9755 2164; www.yallingupbeach.com.au; Valley Rd; sites per 2 people $32-54, cabins $90-285;) You'll fall asleep to the sound of the surf here, with the beach just across the road. Prices vary with the seasons.

Yallingup Lodge & Spa RETREAT $$
(Map p132; ☎08-9755 2411; https://yallingup lodge.com.au; 40 Hemsley Rd; glamping $170, r $200-550;) On a secluded property between Dunsborough and Yallingup with the comforts of a lodge – a cosy lounge area around an open fire and a large deck, plus a swimming pool and day spa. Accommodation is mostly in the main residence, but the glamping option includes an outdoor shower, and waking to birdsong with the sunrise.

★**Wildwood Valley Cottages** COTTAGE $$$
(Map p132; ☎08-9755 2120; www.wildwoodvalley.com.au; 1481 Wildwood Rd; cottages from $250;) Luxury cottages trimmed by native bush are arrayed across 48 hectares, and the property's main house also hosts the Wildwood Valley Cooking School (p135) with Sioban and Carlo Baldini. Look out for grazing kangaroos as you meander up the unsealed road to reception.

Injidup Spa Retreat BOUTIQUE HOTEL $$$
(Map p132; ☎08-9750 1300; www.injidupspa retreat.com.au; Cape Clairault Rd; ste from $650;) The region's most stylish and luxurious accommodation, Injidup perches atop an isolated cliff south of Yallingup. A striking carved concrete and iron facade fronts the car park, while inside there are heated polished-concrete floors, 'eco' fires and absolute sea views. Each of the 10 suites has its own plunge pool. It's off Wyadup Rd.

Empire Retreat & Spa SPA HOTEL $$$
(Map p132; ☎08-9755 2065; www.empireretreat.com; Caves Rd; ste $295-575;) Everything about the intimate Empire Retreat is stylish, from the cool Scandi-inspired design to the attention to detail and service. The rooms are built around a former farmhouse, and a rustic but sophisticated ambience lingers. Check online for good packages combining accommodation and spa treatments.

Smiths Beach Resort RESORT $$$
(Map p132; ☎08-9750 1200; www.smithsbeach resort.com.au; Smiths Beach Rd; apt from $350;) This is a large complex of tastefully plush one- to four-bedroom apartments by a very beautiful beach – which it nearly has all to itself. A restaurant, cafe, deli and bottle shop are on-site, but the apartments also have full kitchens. Other accommodation options include poolside and ocean-view villas ($450 to $550).

Eating & Drinking

Yallingup Woodfired Bread BAKERY $
(Map p132; 189 Biddle Rd; bread from $4; 7am-6pm Mon-Sat) Look out for excellent sourdough, rye bread and fruit loaves at local shops and the Margaret River Farmers Market (p140), or pick up some still-warm loaves at the bakery near Yallingup.

Wills Domain BISTRO $$$
(Map p132; ☎08-9755 2327; www.willsdomain.com.au; cnr Brash & Abbey Farm Rds; mains $29-40, 7-course menu $110; tastings 10am-5pm,

lunch noon-3pm) A restaurant and gallery with wonderful hilltop views over vines. An innovative seven-course tasting menu (with or without matching wines) is also available.

Studio Bistro MODERN AUSTRALIAN **$$$**
(Map p132; ☎08-9756 6164; www.thestudiobistro.com.au; 7 Marrinup Dr; small plates $16-22, mains $35-55; ⊙noon-5pm, also 6pm-late Sat; ✎) Studio Bistro's gallery focuses on Australian artists, while the garden restaurant showcases subtle dishes such as pan-fried fish with cauliflower cream, radicchio, peas and crab meat. Five-course tasting menus are offered on Saturday nights. Bookings recommended.

Caves House BEER GARDEN
(Hotel Yallingup; ☎08-9750 1888; www.caveshousehotelyallingup.com.au; 18 Yallingup Beach Rd;) This restored heritage hotel is the main congregation spot for Yallingup locals. Pub food, a sprawling beer garden with plenty of shade, big screens showing Australian sport, and live music on summer afternoons draw in the families who are mostly content to let their kids run riot.

Getting There & Away

Transwa (p129) buses linking Perth and Albany stop in Yallingup, but to explore fully you'll need your own transport.

Margaret River

☎08 / POP 4500

Although tourists usually outnumber locals, Margaret River still feels like a country town. The advantage of basing yourself here is that after 5pm, once the wineries shut up shop, it's one of the few places with any vital signs. Plus, it's close to the incredible surf of Margaret River Mouth and Southside, and the swimming beaches at Prevelly and Gracetown.

Margaret River spills over with tourists every weekend and gets very, *very* busy at Easter and Christmas. Accommodation prices tend to be cheaper midweek.

Sights

Cape Mentelle WINERY
(Map p132; www.capementelle.com.au; 331 Walcliffe Rd; tours from $30; ⊙10am-5pm;) Offers a cellar door, wine tours and tastings (with optional and food pairings), petanque, and an outdoor cinema in summer. This Margaret River winery is one of the originals from 1970.

Margaret River Distilling Company DISTILLERY
(Map p138; ☎08-9757 9351; www.distillery.com.au; Maxwell St, off Carters Rd; ⊙10am-6pm, to 7pm Fri & Sat;) Limeburners single malt whisky, Tiger Snake sour mash, Great Southern gin and White Shark vodka can all be sampled at this edge-of-the-forest tasting room. There are also local beers to take away with pizzas and shared platters.

Stella Bella WINERY
(Map p132; ☎08-9758 5000; www.stellabella.com.au; 205 Rosa Brook Rd; ⊙10am-5pm) Excellent wines at a pretty cellar door (BYO picnic). This outfit boasts the more interesting label designs in the region.

Margaret River Dairy Company CHEESE
(Map p132; ☎08-9750 6600; www.margaretriverdairy.com.au; 8063 Bussell Hwy; ⊙9.30am-5pm) Take a break from the wineries and try artisan cheeses in Cowaramup dairy country.

Activities

Margaret River SUP WATER SPORTS
(☎0419 959 053; www.margaretriversup.com.au; adult/child $79/49) See a different side to Margs on a two-hour stand-up paddleboarding (SUP) tour of the river in the nearby national park. Guides teach you the skills, and provide all the equipment required. Kids over eight welcome.

Dirty Detours MOUNTAIN BIKING
(☎08-9758 8312; www.dirtydetours.com; per person $80-105) Runs guided mountain-bike rides, including through the magnificent Boranup Forest, as well as a Sip 'n' Cycle cellar-door tour. Multiday tours are also available.

Margaret River Adventure Company ADVENTURE SPORTS
(☎0418 808 993; www.margaretriveradventure.com.au; half-/full day $80/160) Mountain biking, reef snorkelling and 'coasteering' – a combination of rock climbing, shore scrambling and leaping off cliffs into the ocean – all combine in these fun and active tours with an excellent guide.

Margaret River Surf School SURFING
(☎0401 616 200; www.margaretriversurfschool.com; group/individual lessons from $50/120, 3-/5-day course from $120/185) Group and individual lessons for both surfing and stand-up paddleboards. Three- and five-day courses are the best option if you're serious about learning to surf.

Margaret River

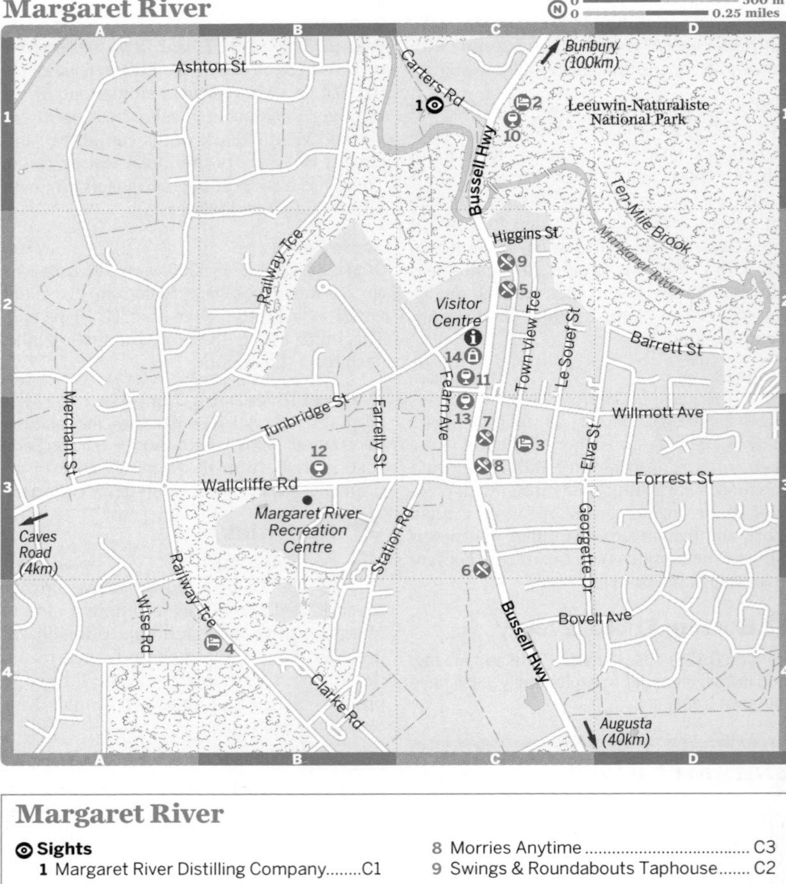

Margaret River

Sights

1 Margaret River Distilling Company........C1

Sleeping

2 Edge of the Forest........C1
3 Margaret River Backpackers YHA........C3
4 Margaret River Lodge........B4

Eating

5 Margaret River Bakery........C2
6 Margaret River Farmers Market........C3
7 Miki's Open Kitchen........C3
8 Morries Anytime........C3
9 Swings & Roundabouts Taphouse........C2

Drinking & Nightlife

10 Brewhouse........C1
11 Settler's Tavern........C2
12 The River Hotel........B3
13 Yonder........C3

Shopping

14 Margaret River Artisan Store........C2

Dirt Skills MOUNTAIN BIKING

(0402 305 104; www.dirtskillsmargaretriver.com; per person $65-70; Sat) If you're keen to get into Margaret River's growing mountain-biking scene, consider a training hook-up with these guys. Beginner and intermediate riders are welcome; a special trail-guiding session will help you find the region's best tracks. Bikes can also be hired.

Margaret River Kitesurfing & Windsurfing KITESURFING

(0419 959 053; www.mrkiteandsail.com.au; 2hr for 2 people from $220) Instruction and gear rental. Lessons take place on flat and sheltered waters around the coast. Then say a prayer while watching the experts at Surfers Point.

Tours

Margaret River Brewery Tours FOOD & DRINK
(☎0458 450 120; www.mrbt.com.au; per person $70-110; ⊙noon-6pm) Four craft breweries are visited on these small-group minibus tours helmed by the super-friendly Jules. The $70 'Mid Strength' option allows participants to buy their own drinks as they go, while the $110 'Full Strength' tour includes a six-brew tasting paddle at each stop. Both options include an excellent lunch, and cider drinkers can also be catered for.

Cape to Cape Tours WALKING
(☎0459 452 038; www.capetocapetours.com.au; per couple from $1300) Negotiate the entire route or just parts of the stunning Cape to Cape coastal walk on self-guided and guided itineraries. Trips include camping or lodge accommodation and excellent meals, and options from three to eight days are available. Various day tours exploring the Margaret River region are also offered.

Wine for Dudes WINE
(☎0427 774 994; www.winefordudes.com; per person $105) Includes a brewery, a chocolate factory, four wineries, a wine-blending experience and lunch.

Margies Big Day Out WINE
(☎0416 180 493; www.margaretrivertourswa.com.au; per person $95) Three wineries, two breweries, cheese, chocolate and lunch.

Festivals & Events

Gourmet Escape FOOD & DRINK
(www.gourmetescape.com.au; ⊙late Nov) From Rick Stein, Nigella Lawson and Heston Blumenthal to *MasterChef Australia*'s George Calombaris and Matt Preston, the Gourmet Escape food and wine festival attracts the big names in global and Australian cuisine. Look forward to three days of food workshops, tastings, vineyard events and demonstrations.

Margaret River Pro SPORTS
(www.worldsurfleague.com; ⊙May-Jun;) FREE Top ranked male and female surfers compete over a 12-day period, plus there are gigs, surf workshops and exhibitions.

Sleeping

Prevelly Caravan Park CARAVAN PARK $
(☎08-9757 2374; http://prevellycaravanpark.com.au; sites from $30; P) A well-run family-friendly caravan park with shady tent sites near the beach rather than town. There's a well-stocked shop, plus the **Sea Garden** cafe on-site is a great spot for some sundowners.

Margaret River Backpackers YHA HOSTEL $
(Map p138; ☎08-9757 9572; www.margaretriverbackpackers.com.au; 66 Town View Tce; dm $30-33;) A short walk from Margaret River town centre, this central backpackers is popular with seasonal workers. Dorms are spartan, but there's table tennis and a big deck out the back – perfect for socialising.

Margaret River Lodge HOSTEL $
(Map p138; ☎08-9757 9532; www.margaretriverbackpackers.com.au; 220 Railway Tce; dm $30-32, r with/without bathroom $87/76;) About 1.5km southwest of the town centre, this well-run hostel has a pool, volleyball and plenty of intel on what to do locally. Dorms share a big communal kitchen, and a quieter area with private rooms has its own little kitchen and lounge.

Edge of the Forest MOTEL $$
(Map p138; ☎08-9757 2351; www.edgeoftheforest.com.au; 25 Bussell Hwy; r $135-175;) Just a pleasant stroll from Margaret River township, the rooms here have stylish bathrooms and a chic Asian theme. The friendly owners have lots of local recommendations, and the leafy shared garden is perfect for an end-of-day barbecue. The spacious front unit is a good option for families. At busy times a two-night minimum stay is required.

★**Forest Rise** CHALET $$$
(Map p132; www.forestrise.com.au; Yelverton Rd; cabins from $260;) Award-winning luxury self-contained cabins are spread across a large tree-filled property. So gorgeous and relaxing you probably won't want to leave.

★**Burnside Organic Farm** BUNGALOW $$$
(Map p132; ☎08-9757 2139; www.burnsideorganicfarm.com.au; 287 Burnside Rd; d from $300;) Welcome to the perfect private retreat after a day cruising the region's wine, beer and food highlights. Bungalows made from rammed earth and limestone have spacious decks and designer kitchens, and the surrounding farm hosts a menagerie of animals and organic orchards. Guests can pick vegetables from the garden. Minimum two-night stay.

Eating

Temper Temper SWEETS $
(Map p132; ☎08-9757 3763; www.tempertemper.com.au; 2 Rosa Brook Rd; ⊙9am-5pm;) This

elegant shrine to chocolate features a tasting area where you can try loads of free samples showcasing the difference between cacao from Cuba, Venezuela, Sumatra and Madagascar, and also enticingly rich slabs with thoroughly adult and addictive flavours like pink peppercorn or liquorice. If you're buying souvenirs for the folks back home, you could certainly do worse. Vegan options.

Margaret River Farmers Market MARKET **$**
(Map p138; 0438 905 985; www.margaretriverfarmersmarket.com.au; Lot 272 Bussell Hwy, Margaret River Education Campus; 8am-noon Sat;) The region's organic and sustainable artisan producers come to town every Saturday. It's a top spot for breakfast. Check the website for your own foodie hit list.

Margaret River Bakery CAFE **$**
(Map p138; 08-9757 2755; www.margaretriverbakery.com.au; 89 Bussell Hwy; mains $10-18; 7am-4pm Mon-Sat;) Retro furniture and kitsch needlework art – the MRB is a rustic, playful bakery producing quality pastries and big breakfasts.

Morries Anytime CAFE **$$**
(Map p138; 08-9758 8280; www.morries.com.au; 2/149 Bussell Hwy; tapas $11-14, mains $21-34; noon-late) Settle into the intimate clubby atmosphere of Morries for lunch, or come back later for expert cocktails and Asian-style tapas for dinner. Local beers from Colonial Brewing are on tap, and the service here is impeccable.

Swings & Roundabouts Taphouse BISTRO, WINE BAR **$$**
(Map p138; 08-9758 7155; www.swings.com.au; 85 Bussell Hwy; shared plates $13-32, pizzas $22-25; 3pm-late) Wine from its nearby vineyards and craft beer are served with tapas plates and gourmet pizzas, making this a popular cosmopolitan option at the northern end of Margaret River township. The kitchen closes at 9pm, but the bar is open later.

★ Miki's Open Kitchen JAPANESE **$$$**
(Map p138; 08-9758 7673; www.facebook.com/mikisopenkitchen; 131 Bussell Hwy; small plates $12-17, large plates $31-36; 6pm-late Tue-Sat) Secure a spot around the open kitchen and enjoy the irresistible theatre of the Miki's team creating innovative Japanese spins on the best of WA's seafood and produce. Combine a Margaret River wine with the $60 multicourse tasting menu for the most diverse experience. Bookings recommended.

Drinking & Nightlife

Yonder BAR
(Map p138; www.yonderbar.com; 124 Busselton Hwy; 5pm-midnight Wed-Sat, to 10pm Sun) Tucked behind the shops off the Busselton Hwy, this American-style saloon bar serves an extensive range of beers plus classic cocktails.

The River Hotel PUB
(Map p138; www.theriverhotel.com.au; 40 Wallcliffe Rd; noon-late;) Exposed brick walls give a warm feel inside, while tables and chairs on the grass out the front are the perfect place to catch some rays at this large country tavern that also hosts live music.

Colonial Brewing Co BREWERY
(Map p132; 08-9758 8177; www.colonialbrewingco.com.au; 56 Osmington Rd; 11am-6pm, to 10pm Fri) This modern microbrewery has rural views and an excellent range of beers, including a wheat beer with coriander and mandarin, and a hop-fuelled India pale ale (IPA). Our favourite is the refreshing German-style kölsch. Look for seasonal special brews and settle in with a pizza on the deck.

Brewhouse MICROBREWERY
(Map p138; 08-9757 2614; www.brewhousemargaretriver.com.au; 35 Bussell Hwy; 11am-7pm, to 9pm Fri-Sun;) A craft-beer place you can walk to! Brewhouse is nestled amid karri forest with a rustic bar and restaurant serving three guest beers and six of its own brews. Try the Inji Pale Ale with the chilli salt squid, and check out live music on Friday nights and Sunday afternoons.

Settler's Tavern PUB
(Map p138; 08-9757 2398; www.settlerstavern.com; 114 Bussell Hwy; 11am-midnight, from 10am Sat) There's live entertainment Thursday to Sunday at Settler's, so pop in for good pub grub (mains $16 to $35) and a beer, or choose a wine from the extensive list. Then wait for the locals to let their hair down.

Shopping

Margaret River township has design shops and galleries. To fully explore the region's excellent makers scene, pick up the *Margaret River Artisans Cape to Cape Guide* at the visitor centre. This map lists artists' and designers' studios across the region. Online, see www.margaretriverartisans.com.au.

Margaret River Artisan Store ARTS & CRAFTS
(Map p138; 0448 733 799; www.margaretriverartisanstore.com; 2/110 Bussell Hwy; 10am-5pm,

to 1pm Sun) Clothing, design and arts and crafts all feature at this eclectic shop where the majority of items are sourced from local Margaret River designers, jewellers and artists.

Margaret River Regional Wine Centre WINERY
(☎08-9755 5501; www.mrwines.com; 9 Bussell Hwy, Cowaramup; ⏲10am-7pm Mon-Sat, noon-6pm Sun) A one-stop shop for buying up a selection of 600 Margaret River wines and craft beers in nearby Cowaramup.

Information

Visitor Centre (Map p138; ☎08-9780 5911; www.margaretriver.com; 100 Bussell Hwy; ⏲9am-5pm) Bookings and information plus displays on local wineries.

Getting There & Away

Margaret River is linked by regular buses north to Bunbury and Perth, and also further south to Pemberton, Denmark and Albany. During summer, the **Margaret River Beach Bus** (☎08-9757 9532; www.margaretriverbackpackers.com.au) links the township with the beaches around Prevelly.

Caves Road

☎08

West of the Margaret River township, the coastline provides spectacular surfing opportunities and long coastal forest walks. Prevelly is the main settlement, with a few places to sleep and eat. Most of the sights are on Caves Rd or just off it.

Sights

★Stormflower Vineyard WINERY
(Map p132; www.stormflower.com.au; 3503 Caves Rd, Wilyabrup; ⏲11am-5pm) Rustic and relaxed, with beautiful Australian natives in the garden, this is the antidote to some of Margaret River's more grandiose tasting rooms and formal wine estates. The compact organic vineyard is just 9 hectares, and Stormflower's cabernet shiraz is highly regarded.

★Lake Cave CAVE
(Map p132; ☎08-9757 7411; www.margaretriver.com/members/lake-cave; Conto Rd, Forest Grove; adult/child $22.50/12; ⏲9am-5pm; 👪) The main ticket office for Lake, Mammoth (p142) and Jewel Caves (p145) has excellent displays about caves, cave conservation and local fossil discoveries. You'll also find an authentic model cave and a 'cave crawl' experience.

WORTH A TRIP

COWARAMUP

Cowaramup (Cow Town to those who cannot pronounce it) is 10 minutes up the road from Margaret River on the Busselton Hwy and an excellent option for accommodation if Margs is full or too pricey. Cow Town is a thriving regional centre with a strong local community; check out the website (www.cowaramup.com.au) to see what we mean. Cow puns and cow sculptures abound. The area is famous for its dairy offerings, but if you're not into ice cream there are other sweets, plus cafes and local wineries to check out too.

Behind the centre is Lake Cave, the prettiest of them all, where limestone formations are reflected in an underground stream. Tours depart hourly from 9.30am to 3.30pm.

Voyager Estate WINERY
(Map p132; ☎08-9757 6354; www.voyagerestate.com.au; Stevens Rd, Margaret River; ⏲10am-5pm) The formal gardens and Cape Dutch–style buildings delight at Voyager Estate. Tours of the estate include the kitchen garden that Rick Stein also loved. Wine flight tastings start at $9, or stay for a seven-course tasting menu at the award-winning restaurant.

Leeuwin-Naturaliste National Park NATIONAL PARK
(Map p132; https://parks.dpaw.wa.gov.au/park/leeuwin-naturaliste; Caves Rd) Despite the vast areas of aridity it contains, WA also boasts a startling variety of endemic wildflowers. The Leeuwin-Naturaliste National Park explodes with colour in the spring months. The leached, sandy soils of WA produce a surprising variety of vividly coloured wildflowers.

The demanding environment prevents any one species predominating, leaving a gorgeous array of fantastically evolved orchids, sundews, kangaroo paws and the like to flourish in their exclusive niches. Their striking colours and shapes developed as a means of attracting the attention of the few pollinators found in the area. Walking in the 155-sq-km Leeuwin-Naturaliste National Park in spring (September to November), it's possible to see orchids, banksias, clematis, cowslips and many other species, including the improbably named prickly moses.

Giants Cave CAVE
(Map p132; www.parks.dpaw.wa.gov.au; Caves Rd, Boranup; adult/child $18/9; ⏲10am-1pm Oct-Apr, 9.30am-3.30pm school & public holidays; 👪) This self-guided cave is managed by the Parks & Wildlife Service, which provides helmets and torches. Features steep ladders and scrambles. See it on a combined ticket with other caves on the cape.

Ashbrook WINERY
(Map p132; ☎08-9755 6262; www.ashbrookwines.com.au; 379 Tom Cullity Dr, Wilyabrup; ⏲10am-5pm) Ashbrook grows all of its grapes on-site. Its award-winning rieslings are rightly lauded.

Thompson Estate WINERY
(Map p132; ☎08-9755 6406; www.thompsonestate.com; 299 Tom Cullity Dr, Wilyabrup; ⏲10.30am-4.30pm) A small-scale producer with an architectural-award-winning tastings and barrel room.

Ellensbrook Homestead HISTORIC BUILDING
(Map p132; ☎08-9755 5173; www.nationaltrust.org.au; Ellen Brook Rd, Margaret River; adult/child $4/2; ⏲10am-4pm Thu-Sat; 👪) Around 8km northwest of Margaret River, Ellensbrook (1857) was the first home of settlers Alfred and Ellen Bussell. The Wardandi people welcomed them, gave them Noongar names and led them to this sheltered site. The basic ramshackle house is constructed of paperbark, driftwood, timber, lime, dung and hair. Between 1899 and 1917, Edith Bussell, who farmed the property alone for many years, established an Aboriginal mission. Children were taught to read and write, and two became beneficiaries of Edith's will.

Mammoth Cave CAVE
(Map p132; www.margaretriver.com; Caves Rd; adult/child $22.50/12; ⏲9am-5pm; 👪) Mammoth Cave boasts a fossilised jawbone of *Zygomaturus trilobus*, a giant wombat-like creature, as well as other fossil remains and the impressive Mammoth Shawl formation. Visits are self-guided; an MP3 audio player is provided.

Margaret River Chocolate Company SWEETS
(Map p132; ☎08-9755 6555; www.chocolatefactory.com.au; Harman's Mill Rd, Metricup; ⏲9am-5pm; 👪) The original factory of this local maker opened here in 1999. Watch chocolate truffles being made and sample the flavours.

Eagles Heritage WILDLIFE RESERVE
(Map p132; ☎08-9757 2960; www.eaglesheritage.com.au; 341 Boodjidup Rd, Margaret River; adult/child $18/12; ⏲10am-4pm; 👪) Housing Australia's largest collection of raptors, this centre, 5km south of Margaret River, rehabilitates many birds of prey each year. There are free flight displays at 11am and 1.30pm.

Activities

Cape to Cape Track WALKING
(Map p132; www.capetocapetrack.com.au) Stretching from Cape Naturaliste to Cape Leeuwin, the 135km Cape to Cape Track passes through the heath, forest and sand dunes of the Leeuwin-Naturaliste National Park (p141), with Indian Ocean views. Most walkers take about seven days to complete the track (staying in a combination of national park campsites and commercial accommodation). You can walk it in five days, or break up the route into a series of day trips.

Boranup Drive SCENIC DRIVE
(Map p132) This 14km diversion runs along an unsealed road through Leeuwin-Naturaliste National Park's beautiful karri forest. Near the southern end there's a lookout offering sea views.

Courses

Cape Lodge COOKING
(Map p132; ☎08-9755 6311; www.capelodge.com.au; 3341 Caves Rd, Wilyabrup; from $145) Cooking classes and cooking demonstrations using local produce are a hands-on foodie experience. Overnight accommodation packages at this lovely country lodge are also available.

Sleeping

Taunton Farm Holiday Park CARAVAN PARK $
(Map p132; ☎1800 248 777; www.tauntonfarm.com.au; Bussell Hwy, Cowaramup; sites $45, cottages $130-160; 📶) There are plenty of farm animals for the kids to meet at one of Margaret River's best family-oriented campgrounds. For caravan and tenting buffs, the amenities blocks are spotless, and farm-style self-contained cottages are also scattered about.

Surfpoint GUESTHOUSE $$
(Map p132; ☎08-9757 1777; www.surfpoint.com.au; Reidle Dr, Gnarabup; d with/without bathroom from $140/95; @📶🏊) This airy place offers the beach on a budget. The rooms are clean and well presented, and there's an enticing little pool. Private rooms with en-suite facilities are good value, and the energetic new

owners have done a great job with recent renovations. Shared spaces include a very comfortable lounge and a full kitchen. Stylish apartments nearby are also available.

Noble Grape Guesthouse B&B $$
(☎08-9755 5538; www.noblegrape.com.au; 29 Bussell Hwy, Cowaramup; s $140-160, d $150-190; ❄📶) Noble Grape is more like an upmarket motel than a traditional B&B. Rooms offer a sense of privacy and each has a verdant little garden courtyard.

★ **Acacia Chalets** CHALET $$$
(Map p132; ☎08-9757 2718; www.acaciachalets.com.au; 113 Yates Rd, Margaret River; d $240-280; ❄) Private bushland conceals three luxury chalets that are well located to explore the region's vineyards, caves and rugged coastline. Limestone walls and honey-coloured jarrah floors are combined in some of the area's best self-contained accommodation. Spacious decks are equipped with gas barbecues.

Llewellin's B&B $$$
(Map p132; ☎08-9757 9516; www.llewellinsguesthouse.com.au; 64 Yates Rd, Margaret River; r $208-268; 📶) It may be a Welsh name, but the style is French provincial in the four upmarket yet homey guest rooms.

Eating

Arimia WINERY $$
(Map p132; ☎08-9755 2528; https://arimia.com.au; 242 Quininup Rd, Wilyabrup; 2-course menu $55) Down an unsealed road you'll find this organic and biodynamic winery and restaurant creating excellent seasonal meals with ingredients almost entirely sourced from the property.

The Common BISTRO $$
(Map p132; ☎08-9757 1586; www.thecommonbistro.com.au; 1 Resort Pl, Gnarabup; mains $18-38; ⏲4pm-late, from noon Sat & Sun) Pizza, burgers and hearty mains come with a side order of salty maritime breezes at this relaxed bistro a short walk from the surf at Gnarabup. Pair the barramundi fillet and garlic roasted potatoes with a glass of Margaret River sauvignon blanc, or settle with craft beer and cocktails on the huge outdoor deck with ocean views.

White Elephant Cafe CAFE $$
(Map p132; ☎08-9757 1990; www.whiteelephantcafe.com.au; Gnarabup Rd, Gnarabup; mains $13-24; ⏲7.30am-3pm) Combining a simple pavilion and a spacious deck, White Elephant's location just metres from the cobalt waters of Gnarabup beach offers some of the best dining views around Margaret River. Wraps

CAVES ROAD CRAFT BEER

The Margaret River region's wine credentials are impeccable, but the area – and around Caves Rd in particular – is also a destination for craft-beer fans. Here are some of the best:

Caves Road Collective (Map p132; ☎08-9755 6500; https://cavesroadcollective.com.au; 3517 Caves Rd, Wilyabrup; tasting paddles from $20; ⏲11am-5pm; Ⓟ👪) A spectacular location on a private lake, Black Brewing Company, Ground to Cloud winery and Dune Distilling have joined forces at this tastings temple with an excellent restaurant, and a kids' playground to boot. Beers are approachable: try the crisp and citrusy extra pale ale (XPA). Dune boasts local botanicals, and the on-site winery produces a small but confident list.

Bootleg Brewery (Map p132; ☎08-9755 6300; www.bootlegbrewery.com.au; Puzey Rd, off Yelverton Rd, Wilyabrup; ⏲11am-5pm) More rustic than some of the area's flashier breweries, but lots of fun with a pint in the sun – especially with live bands on Saturday. Try the award-winning Raging Bull Porter – a West Australian classic – or the US West Coast–style Speakeasy IPA. The food is also very good.

Beer Farm (Map p132; ☎08-9755 7177; www.beerfarm.com.au; 8 Gale Rd, Metricup; ⏲11am-6pm, to 10.30pm Fri, to 7pm Sat; 👪) Located in a former milking shed down a sleepy side road, the Beer Farm is Margaret River's most rustic brewery. Loyal locals crowd in with their children and dogs, supping on the Beer Farm's own brews – try the hoppy Rye IPA – and there's a food truck and plenty of room for the kids (and dogs) to run around.

Cheeky Monkey (Map p132; ☎08-9755 5555; www.cheekymonkeybrewery.com.au; 4259 Caves Rd, Margaret River; ⏲10am-6pm) Set around a pretty lake, Cheeky Monkey has an expansive restaurant and lots of room for the kids to run around. Try the Hatseller Pilsner with bold New Zealand hops or the Belgian-style Hagenbeck Pale Ale. Decent food and apple and pear ciders mean you'll make a day of it.

and burgers go well with good smoothies and juices, and the cafe is open later in summer for the best of Indian Ocean sunsets.

Rustico at Hay Shed Hill TAPAS **$$$**
(Map p132; ☎08-9755 6455; www.rusticotapas.com.au; 511 Harmans Mill Rd, Wilyabrup; shared plates $17-28, pizzas $27-29, 6-course tasting menu from $65; ⏲11am-5pm) Vineyard views from Rustico's deck provide the background for a Spanish-influenced menu using the best of southwest Australian produce. Albany rock oysters are paired with Margaret River riesling, pork belly comes with Pedro Ximinéz sherry, and paella is crammed with chicken from Mt Barker and local seafood. Consider a leisurely six-course tasting menu with wine matches from Hay Shed Hill vineyard.

Vasse Felix BISTRO **$$$**
(Map p132; ☎08-9756 5050; www.vassefelix.com.au; cnr Caves Rd & Tom Cullity Dr, Cowaramup; mains $37-39; ⏲10am-3pm, cellar door to 5pm; P ❄) Vasse Felix winery is considered by many to have the best fine-dining restaurant in the region, with a big wooden dining room reminiscent of an extremely flash barn. The grounds are peppered with sculptures, while the gallery displaying a revolving exhibition from the Holmes à Court collection is worth a visit. Vegans catered for with 24 hours' notice.

Xanadu BISTRO **$$$**
(Map p132; ☎08-9758 9531; www.xanaduwines.com; Boodjidup Rd, Margaret River; mains $34-38; ⏲10am-5pm, restaurant from noon) Escape into your own personal pleasure dome in the hip and chic restaurant filling Xanadu's vast space. The menu of small and larger shared plates changes seasonally – we had terrific kangaroo with black garlic, cheddar and macadamia. Definitely leave room for dessert.

Watershed Premium Wines BISTRO **$$$**
(Map p132; ☎08-9758 8633; www.watershedwines.com.au; cnr Bussell Hwy & Darch Rd, Margaret River; mains $34-42; ⏲10am-5pm) Famous for its 'Awakening' cabernet sauvignon, and regularly rated one of WA's best vineyard restaurants, Watershed offers dining options that include an informal cafe and a classier restaurant with expansive views of a compact lake and trellised vines.

Leeuwin Estate WINERY **$$$**
(Map p132; ☎08-9759 0000; www.leeuwinestate.com.au; Stevens Rd, Margaret River; mains $32-45; ⏲10am-5pm, also 6-9pm Sat) An impressive estate with tall trees and lawns gently rolling down to the bush, Leeuwin Estate offers behind-the-scenes tours, wine flights and tastings, plus regular international open-air concerts. Don't miss visiting the downstairs gallery of excellent Australian art that has been used on Leeuwin's colourful labels. The winery's Art Series chardonnay is one of Australia's best.

Cullen Wines BISTRO **$$$**
(Map p132; ☎08-9755 5656; www.cullenwines.com.au; 4323 Caves Rd, Cowaramup; mains $25-38; ⏲10am-4pm Fri-Tue) Grapes were first planted here in 1966, and Cullen has an ongoing commitment to organic and biodynamic principles in both food and wine. Celebrating a relaxed ambience, Cullen's food is excellent, with many of the fruits and vegetables sourced from its own gardens. Booking ahead is recommended, especially on weekends.

Shopping

Providore DELI
(Map p132; ☎08-9755 6355; www.providore.com.au; 448 Tom Cullity Dr, Wilyabrup; ⏲9am-5pm) Voted one of Australia's Top 100 Gourmet Experiences by *Australian Traveller* magazine – given its amazing range of artisan produce, including organic olive oil, tapenades and preserved fruits, we can only agree. Look forward to loads of free samples.

Information

National Park Information Centre (Map p132; ☎08-9757 7422; www.parks.dpaw.wa.gov.au; Calgardup Cave, Caves Rd, Boranup; ⏲9am-4.15pm)

Getting There & Away

Buses link to Margaret River township, but to further explore the area you'll need to join a tour, or have your own transport with one designated driver. As they say round here, 'Who's the Skipper?'

Augusta & Around

☎08 / POP 1392

Augusta is positioned at the mouth of the Blackwood River just north of Cape Leeuwin. The vibe is pure nostalgia as if you've stepped back in time to slowed-down beach holidays of yesteryear where kids ride bikes without supervision, families languidly fish from the pier, or puddle around on boats, and no one is trying to sell you anything but the opportunity to relax.

Sights

Jewel Cave CAVE

(Map p132; ☎08-9780 5911; www.margaretriver.com; Caves Rd; adult/child $22.50/12; ⏲9.30am-3.30pm) The most spectacular of the region's caves, Jewel Cave has an impressive 5.9m straw stalactite. Fossil remains of a Tasmanian tiger (thylacine), believed to be 3500 years old, were discovered here. It's near the south end of Caves Rd, 8km northwest of Augusta. Access to the cave is by guided tours that run hourly.

Cape Leeuwin Lighthouse LIGHTHOUSE

(Map p132; ☎08-9780 5911; www.margaretriver.com; tour adult/child $20/14; ⏲8.45am-4.30pm) Wild and windy Cape Leeuwin, where the Indian and Southern Oceans meet, is the most southwesterly point in Australia. It takes its name from a Dutch ship that passed here in 1622. The lighthouse (1896), WA's tallest, offers magnificent views of the coastline. Whale-watching opportunities abound in the migration season. There is a good cafe on-site too.

Augusta Historical Museum MUSEUM

(☎08-9758 0465; Blackwood Ave; adult/child $5/2; ⏲11am-4pm) Interesting local exhibits run by volunteer staff. The building belies the museum inside. Pick up a Heritage Trail booklet and ask about the portrait gallery in town.

Activities

Augusta Boat Hire WATER SPORTS

(www.margaretriver.com/members/augusta-boat-hire; Ellis St Pier; per hr $25;) This old-school outfit hires canoes, boats and stand-up paddleboards so you can get out on the river and explore. Safety gear also provided.

Augusta River Tours CRUISE

(www.augustarivertours.com.au; Ellis St Pier; from $35; ⏲Sep-Jun;) Spot waterbirds such as black swans, cormorants and pelicans on a 1½-hour cruise up the Blackwood River with the knowledgeable skipper Graeme Challis.

Naturaliste Charters WHALE WATCHING

(☎08-9750 5500; www.whales-australia.com.au; from $90; ⏲mid-May–Aug) This operator runs two-hour whale-watching cruises departing Augusta from mid-May to August. During May, the emphasis switches to an Eco Wilderness Tour showcasing beaches and wildlife, including dolphins, seals and lots of seabirds.

Sleeping & Eating

Baywatch Manor HOSTEL $

(☎08-9758 1290; www.baywatchmanor.com.au; 9 Heppingstone View; dm $38, d from $130, without bathroom $100; @) Clean rooms have cream brick walls and pieces of antique furniture. There is a bay view from the deck and, in winter, a roaring fire in the communal lounge. Some doubles have compact balconies.

Blackwood River Houseboats HOUSEBOAT $$$

(Map p132; ☎08-9758 0181; www.blackwoodriverhouseboats.com.au; Westbay; 3 nights $1000-1900, per week $2300-3800; P) Why not take care of your accommodation, river cruising, dining and fishing trip all at once with a houseboat break from Augusta? Houseboats are easy to cruise with some common sense. Bird spotting and a natural swimming pool around you come for free.

Blue Ocean Fish & Chips FISH & CHIPS $

(73 Blackwood Ave; ⏲11.30am-2pm & 5-8pm; P) Oft-rated best fish and chips ever eaten (no overstatements here obviously), this very basic blue-plastic-chairs and simple-wall-menu fast-food joint boasts excellent locally caught fish, perfectly crisp batter and optional chicken salt on your chips. At night there are not many other options in sleepy Augusta.

Deckchair Gourmet CAFE $

(☎08-9758 0700; Blackwood Ave; mains $10-22; ⏲8am-3pm Mon-Sat, to noon Sun;) Excellent coffee and good food. Try the bacon-and-egg wrap for breakfast while southern sunshine streams through the windows.

Colourpatch Café CAFE $$

(Map p132; ☎08-9758 1295; 38 Albany Tce; snacks & mains $15-34; ⏲9am-6pm; P) The self-styled 'last eating house before the Antarctic': you can get breakfast, lunch or fish and chips by the Blackwood River mouth here. Note it can sometimes close earlier than the stated hours.

Information

Visitor Centre (☎08-9780 5911; www.margaretriver.com; cnr Blackwood Ave & Ellis St; ⏲9am-5pm) Information and bookings. Ask about seeing local wildflowers, boat trips and local entertainment options.

Getting There & Away

Augusta is on bus routes with South West Coach Lines (p129) and Transwa (p129) linking Perth with Albany.

SOUTHERN FORESTS

The tall forests of WA's southwest are simply magnificent, with towering gums (karri, jarrah, marri) sheltering cool undergrowth. Between the forests, small towns bear witness to the region's history of logging and mining. Many have redefined themselves as small-scale tourist centres where you can take walks, wine tours, canoe trips and fishing expeditions.

Nannup

08 / POP 1327

Nannup's historic weatherboard buildings and cottage gardens have an idyllic bush setting on the Blackwood River. The town has a nuts-and-berries vibe: wood crafts, organic food and a gentle pace.

Sights & Activities

Nannup Clock Tower LANDMARK
(www.thenannupclocktower.com.au; 12 Forrest St; adult/child $14/7; 9am-5pm;) A passionate local named Kevin Bird designed and built the world's largest wooden clock. You can marvel at the dream and the craftsmanship with a self-guided audio tour.

Barrabup Swimming Pool SWIMMING
(off Mowen Rd; 24hr) FREE Wild swimming spot with decking and a picnic area, located 10km out of town and surrounded with forest.

Festivals & Events

Nannup Music Festival MUSIC
(08-9756 1511; www.nannupmusicfestival.org; early Mar) Held in early autumn, focusing on folk and world music. Buskers are encouraged. It's the one weekend when this town is busy.

Sleeping & Eating

Holberry House B&B $$
(08-9756 1276; www.holberryhouse.com; 14 Grange Rd; r $165-220;) The decor might lean towards granny-chic, but this large house on the hill has charming hosts and comfortable rooms. It's surrounded by large gardens dotted with quirky sculptures.

Melo Velo CAFE $
(www.melovelo.com.au; 8 Warren St; snacks $5-15; 7am-3pm;) A red-brick heritage house on the main road has been turned into a cycling hub and cafe. Does excellent coffee, simple dishes and smoothies.

Nannup Bridge Cafe CAFE $$
(08-9756 1287; www.facebook.com/nannupbridgecafe; 1 Warren Rd; breakfast & lunch $9-24, dinner $16-34; 9am-2pm Tue-Sun, plus 6-8pm Thu-Sat) This gorgeous riverfront cafe morphs into an evening bistro from Thursday to Saturday. Standout dishes include the pork belly and the smoky duck pancakes. Breakfasts until 11am only.

Shopping

Wild Eyed ARTS & CRAFTS
(www.wildeyedpress.com.au; 33 Warren Rd; 10am-5pm, closed Wed) Eclectic gift shop selling natural soaps, stationery and unique jewellery – plus colourful locally published books, specialising in children's titles. It's worth visiting Nannup just to shop here for Australian souvenirs crafted with care.

Getting There & Away

There is no regular public transport to Nannup. Visitors need their own vehicle.

Bridgetown

08 / POP 2400

Historic Bridgetown is surrounded by karri forests and farmland, and spread around the Blackwood River. Weekends are busy, and the popular Blues at Bridgetown Festival occurs annually in November.

Sights

Bridgedale House HISTORIC BUILDING
(Hampton St; by donation; 10am-2pm Sat & Sun) Bridgedale House is one of Bridgetown's oldest buildings, built of mud and clay by the area's first settler in 1862, and since restored by the National Trust.

Festivals & Events

Blues at Bridgetown Festival MUSIC
(08-9761 2921; www.bluesatbridgetown.com.au) Held on the second weekend of November, with occasional big-name acts.

Sleeping & Eating

Bridgetown Hotel HOTEL $$
(08-9761 1034; www.bridgetownhotel.com.au; 157 Hampton St; r $165-250;) This main-street 1920s gem features large modern bedrooms (some with balconies) with spa baths, and art deco interior features. Also a

good spot for a bite, it's open for lunch and dinner with quirky dishes like satay prawn pizzas ($24).

Bridgetown Riverside Chalets CHALET $$
(☎08-9761 1040; www.bridgetownchalets.com.au; 11347 Brockman Hwy; chalets from $150) On a rural riverside property, 5km up the road to Nannup, these four stand-alone wooden chalets (complete with pot-bellied stoves and washing machines) sleep up to six in two bedrooms.

Barking Cow CAFE $$
(☎08-9761 4619; www.barkingcow.com.au; 88 Hampton St; breakfast $11-18, lunch $13-21; ⏲8am-2.30pm Mon-Sat; ✍) Colourful, cosy and serving the best coffee in town, the Barking Cow is also worth stopping at for daily vegetarian specials and world-famous-in-Bridgetown gourmet burgers.

Cidery CAFE $$
(☎08-9761 2204; www.thecidery.com.au; 43 Gifford Rd; mains $10-25; ⏲11am-4pm, to 8pm Fri) Craft beer from the Blackwood Valley Brewing Company, cider and light lunches are all enjoyed on outdoor tables. On Friday nights from 5.30pm there's live music. Our favourite brew is the easy-drinking mid-strength Summer Ale.

Information

Visitor Centre (☎08-9761 1740; www.bridgetown.com.au; 154 Hampton St; ⏲9am-5pm Mon-Fri, 10am-3pm Sat, 10am-1pm Sun) Includes apple-harvesting memorabilia and a surprisingly interesting display of jigsaws from around the world in the attached heritage museum.

Getting There & Away

Bridgetown is a regular stop for South West Coach Lines (p129), with departures heading from Perth to Manjimup via Bunbury.

Manjimup

☎08 / POP 4349

Manjimup is a regional centre for the timber and agricultural industries. It's a working town, so the centre is not rich with tourist delights, but the region has much to explore. For foodies, in particular, it's known for something very different: truffles. During August especially, Manjimup's black Périgord truffles make their way onto top Australian menus.

OFF THE BEATEN TRACK

BALINGUP & GREENBUSHES

The 1960s hippie era is alive and well in Balingup (population 450), where coloured flags, herbal remedies and murals of fairies keep the spirit alive. Stop and rummage around eclectic stores, pick up some local produce or tap into the wellness vibes at the herbal remedies shop. On the road to Nannup stop at the lavender farm (www.lavenderbalingup.com.au) for gorgeous summer photo opportunities, especially in November, and to purchase some essential oils.

Greenbushes (population 342) is a mining town, 10km south of Balingup. Some splendid historic buildings from the boom days line the road. A series of walks loop around town and out to join the Bibbulmun track.

Sights

Truffle & Wine Co FARM
(☎08-9777 2474; www.truffleandwine.com.au; Seven Day Rd; ⏲10am-4pm, cafe 11am-3pm) To discover how the world's most expensive produce is harvested, follow your nose here. Join a 2½-hour truffle hunt with clever truffle-hunting Labradors from Friday to Sunday (June to August only and book ahead). Throughout the year there are plenty of truffle products to sample, and the attached provedore and cafe serves up tasting plates and truffle-laced mains ($25 to $40).

Four Aces FOREST
(Graphite Rd) These four 300-plus-year-old karri trees sit in a straight line; stand directly in front and they disappear into one. There's a short loop walk through the surrounding karri glade, and a 1½-hour loop bushwalking trail from the Four Aces to One Tree Bridge.

One Tree Bridge & Glenoran Pool BRIDGE
(Graphite Rd) In a forest clearing 22km from Manjimup are the remains of One Tree Bridge. It was constructed from a single karri log carefully felled to span the width of the river, but was rendered unusable after floods in 1966. Adjacent is gorgeous Glenoran Pool, a popular swimming hole.

Diamond Tree Lookout VIEWPOINT
Nine kilometres south of Manjimup along the South Western Hwy is the Diamond Tree Lookout. Metal spikes allow you to climb this 52m karri, and there's a nature trail nearby.

Timber & Heritage Park PARK
(cnr Rose & Edward Sts; ⏲9am-5pm) Located in town this park has a little lake, an excellent playground for kids, plus a tiny museum and logging paraphernalia.

Activities

Great Forest Trees Drive SCENIC DRIVE
(https://trailswa.com.au/trails/great-forest-trees-drive) A 48km one-way loop with walks that include the easy 3.5km walk to the Shannon Dam and the 8km Great Forest Trees Walk across Shannon River. On the southern section of the drive, hop out to tread boardwalks over giant karri at Snake Gully and Big Tree Grove or take the path to a lookout point over Lane Poole Falls.

Sleeping & Eating

★ **Fonty's Chalets & Caravan Park** CARAVAN PARK $
(www.fontyspool.com.au; 699 Seven Day Rd; sites from $33;) An excellent well-run caravan park a short drive from town through busy orchards. It is blessed with a natural swimming pool for the summer months, which is also a popular day trip for locals.

Diamond Forest Cottages COTTAGE $$
(☎08-9772 3170; www.diamondforest.com.au; 29159 South Western Hwy; chalets $180-220;) South of Manjimup, before the turn-off to Pemberton, is this collection of well-equipped wooden chalets with decks, scattered around a farm. Turkeys and sheep wander around, and it has a petting zoo and daily animal-feeding for the kids. Sunday to Thursday stays offer the best rates.

Tall Timbers BISTRO $$
(☎08-9777 2052; www.talltimbersmanjimup.com.au; 88 Giblett St; tapas $10-19, mains $19-44; ⏲9am-10pm, from 8am Sat & Sun) The upmarket pub food stretches from gourmet burgers to confit duck, but the real point of difference is wines from all over southwest Australia. More than 40 wines are available, many from boutique vineyards that don't have cellar doors. A special dispensing system allows visitors to purchase samples from just 25mL and pair them with tapas or cheese platters.

Information

Department of Parks & Wildlife (☎08-9771 7988; www.parks.dpaw.wa.gov.au; Brain St) Good for information for exploring local forests.

Visitor Centre (☎08-9771 1831; www.manjimupwa.com; Giblett St; ⏲9am-5pm) Located in Manjim Park and offering accommodation and transport bookings.

Getting There & Away

South West Coach Lines (p129) has regular departures linking Manjimup to Perth via Bunbury.

Pemberton

☎08 / POP 974

Hidden deep in the karri and jarrah forests, tiny Pemberton is blessed with a multitude of activities, from canoeing and mountain-bike riding to just sipping a whisky by a wintry fire. The last whistle at the South West timber mills blew in 2016, and thankfully the national parks circling Pemberton and beyond to D'Entrecasteaux National Park remain deeply impressive. Spend a day or two driving the well-marked Karri Forest Explorer tracks, walk forest trails, and 'forest bathe' among the gigantically tall trees standing here.

Pemberton also produces excellent cooler climate wines: chardonnay and pinot noir, among other varietals. Wine tourism isn't developed here, but you can grab a free map listing cellar-door opening hours from the visitor centre (p150).

Sights

Pemberton Fine Woodcraft Gallery ARTS CENTRE
(☎08-9776 1741; www.pembertonfwg.com.au; Dickinson St; ⏲9am-5pm) In lush gardens, this small gallery has truly exquisite pieces for sale, all mastercrafted from salvaged timber. Even if a table isn't going to fit in your luggage, a bottle stopper or wood clock might be the souvenir from Pemberton that you need.

Activities

Big Brook Dam SWIMMING
(https://parks.dpaw.wa.gov.au/site/big-brook-dam; ⏲24hr) FREE Signposted from town, this large dam is a great spot to cool off in summer, with a picnic area and a small sandy beach for little ones to wade in the water.

Pemberton Mountain Bike Park MOUNTAIN BIKING
(www.pembertonvisitor.com.au/pages/pemberton-mountain-bike-park;) Near Pemberton Pool is the trailhead for tracks making up the Pemberton Mountain Bike Park graded by difficulty. Trail maps can be downloaded from the website.

Mountford Wines & Tangletoe Cidery WINE
(☎08-9776 1345; www.mountfordwines.com.au; Bamess Rd; ⏰10am-4pm) 🍃 The wines and ciders produced here are all certified organic, plus there's a gallery on-site. It's north of Pemberton and is easily incorporated into the Karri Forest Explorer circuit.

Pemberton Pool SWIMMING
(Swimming Pool Rd) Surrounded by karri trees, this natural pool is popular on a hot day – despite the warning sign (currents, venomous snakes). They breed them tough around here. Nearby is the trailhead for tracks making up the Pemberton Mountain Bike Park.

Pemberton Tramway RAIL
(☎08-9776 1322; www.pemtram.com.au; adult/child $28/14; ⏰10.45am & 2pm Mon-Sat; 👪) Built between 1929 and 1933, the tram route travels through lush karri and marri forests to Warren River. A commentary is provided and it's a fun – if noisy – 1¾-hour return trip for the whole family.

Tours

Donnelly River Cruises CRUISE
(☎08-9777 1018; www.donnellyrivercruises.com.au; adult/child $75/45) 🍃 Cruises through 12km of D'Entrecasteaux National Park to the cliffs of the Southern Ocean.

Pemberton Discovery Tours TOURS
(☎08-9776 0484; www.pembertondiscoverytours.com.au; 12 Brockman St; tours per person from $95) 🍃 Half-day 4WD tours to the Yeagarup sand dunes and the Warren River mouth. Other tours focus on local vineyards, breweries and cideries, and the wild coastal scenery of D'Entrecasteaux National Park. Visit its central Pemberton location for local information and mountain-bike hire, including details of nearby tracks and recommended rides.

Pemberton Hiking & Canoeing CANOEING
(☎08-9776 1559; www.hikingandcanoeing.com.au; adult/child $50/25; 👪) 🍃 Offers environmentally sound tours in Warren and D'Entrecasteaux National Parks. Specialist tours (wildflowers, frogs, rare fauna) are also available, as are night canoeing trips to spot nocturnal wildlife.

Sleeping

Pemberton Backpackers YHA HOSTEL $
(☎08-9776 1105; www.yha.com.au; 7 Brockman St; dm from $31.50; 📶) Pemberton's only budget digs is sometimes busy with seasonal workers, so book ahead if you're planning to stay. There's a main building plus a cute weatherboard cottage, all of it comfortable enough for the price, and it's centrally located.

RAC Karri Valley Resort CABIN $$
(☎08-9776 2020; https://parksandresorts.rac.com.au/karri-valley; Vasse Hwy; cabins from $185; 📶🏊) A recently refurbished forest resort next to a lush body of deep water where kangaroos and local fisherfolk also congregate. Cabins are self-contained, and not too close to each other. There's a restaurant on-site with beautiful views, especially after dark when the lakeside trees are lit up. It's a decent drive into Pemberton township for more things to see and do.

Pemberton Lodge Resort LODGE $$
(☎08-9776 1113; www.forestlodgeresort.com.au; Vasse Hwy; r from $135) A well-managed lodge with accommodation in the main building, and self-contained cabins. The lounge opens onto outdoor decks to enjoy meals or a drink overlooking the lake. Board games and DVDs available. A short walk back into town (good if you want to have a drink), but take a torch. It's dark here in the forest.

Pump Hill Farm Cottages COTTAGE $$
(☎08-9776 1379; www.pumphill.com.au; Pump Hill Rd; cottages $145-305; 📶) Families love this farm property, where kids are taken on a hay ride each day to feed the animals. Child-free folk will enjoy the ambience of the private, well-equipped cottages too.

Marima Cottages COTTAGE $$
(☎08-9776 1211; www.marima.com.au; 388 Old Vasse Rd; cottages from $195) Right in the middle of Warren National Park, these four country-style rammed-earth-and-cedar cottages with pot-bellied stoves and lots of privacy are luxurious getaways. Look forward to marsupial company at dusk.

Old Picture Theatre Holiday Apartments APARTMENT $$
(☎08-9776 1513; www.oldpicturetheatre.com.au; cnr Ellis & Guppy Sts; apt $170-220; ❄📶) The town's old cinema has been revamped into well-appointed, self-contained, spacious apartments with lots of jarrah detail and black-and-white movie photos. It offers good value for money and includes an on-site spa.

Foragers COTTAGE $$$
(☎08-9776 1580; www.foragers.com.au; cnr Roberts & Northcliffe Rds; cottages $250-350; ❄) 🍃 Choose between very nice, simple karri

WORTH A TRIP

KARRI FOREST EXPLORER

Punctuated by glorious walks, magnificent trees and picnic areas, the Karri Forest Explorer tourist drive wends its way along 86km of scenic (partly unsealed) roads through three national parks (vehicle entry per park $12; four-week holiday pass $44).

Attractions include the **Gloucester Tree**, a fire-lookout tree laddered with a spiral metal stairway. If you're fit and fearless, climb 58m to the top.

The **Dave Evans Bicentennial Tree**, tallest of the 'climbing trees' at 68m, is in Warren National Park, 11km southwest of Pemberton. Its tree-house cage weighs 2 tonnes and can sway up to 1.5m in either direction in strong winds. The Bicentennial Tree one-way loop leads via **Maiden Bush** to the **Heartbreak Trail**, passing through 250-year-old karri stands. Nearby Drafty's Camp and Warren Campsite are great for overnighting (sites per adult/child $7.50/2.20).

The enchanting **Beedelup National Park**, 15km west of Pemberton on the Vasse Hwy (Rte 104), includes a scenic walk that crosses Beedelup Brook near **Beedelup Falls**. There are numerous bird species to be found in the tall trees. North of town, **Big Brook Arboretum** (24hr) FREE features 'big' trees from all over the world.

The track loops on and off the main roads, so you can drive short sections at a time. Pick up a brochure from Pemberton's visitor centre.

cottages and luxury eco-chalets. The latter are light and airy, with elegant, contemporary decor, eco-conscious waste-water systems and a solar-passive design. It's a drive out of town.

Eating

Forest Fresh Marron MARKET

(0428 887 720; www.forestfreshmarron.com.au; Pump Hill Rd; 10.30am-4.30pm Mon-Fri, 1-4pm Sun) Live, sustainably farmed marron for sale. Transport packs – to keep the wee beasties alive for up to 30 hours – and cooking pots are also available. You'll need to order marron at least a day prior to pick-up.

Holy Smoke CAFE $

(https://pembertonfwg.com.au/cafe; 6 Dickinson St; dishes $8-25; 9.30am-3.30pm;) A gourmet cafe outpost for Holy Smoke, the gourmet food suppliers in nearby Manjimup. This small garden cafe serves the best coffee in town plus a sumptuous tasting platter of smoked salmon, chicken and trout, complemented by local seasonal goodies like pickled walnuts, quince paste and cheeses.

Treehouse Tapas & Wine TAPAS $$

(www.treehousewinebar.com.au; 50b Brockman St; 4-10pm Thu-Sat, 4-9pm Sun;) A relaxed owner-run tapas restaurant serving up excellent small dishes, a decent wine list and good nonalcoholic drink choices including local sparkling apple juices.Try the lightly fried cauliflower, marinated octopus, marron, or the local avocado options (including avocado desserts). Furnishings include formica chairs and soft armchair spaces. Board games and children's books are welcome distractions.

Drinking & Nightlife

Jaspers BAR

(www.jasperspemberton.com; 23 Brockman St; 3-8pm Mon-Wed, noon-10.30pm Thu-Sat, noon-10pm Sun) The latest addition to Pemberton town centre, this stylish new whisky bar boasts an extensive list and a cosy fire for an evening in.

Jarrah Jacks CRAFT BEER

(08-9776 1333; www.jarrahjacks.com.au; Lot 2 Kemp Rd; 11am-5pm Thu-Sun) A popular craft brewery with vineyard views, six craft beers and tasty locally sourced food from a seasonal menu. Try the Swinging Axe Ale, a robust 6% Red Ale, or take it easy with the mid-strength 2.9% Arthur's Hop Ale. Sampling trays are also available, and you can also try wines from Pemberton's Woodsmoke Estate.

Information

Visitor Centre (08-9776 1133; www.pembertonvisitor.com.au; Brockman St; 9am-4pm) Includes a pioneer museum and karri-forest discovery centre.

Getting There & Away

Transwa (p129) bus services all travel to Pemberton from Perth. For self-drive travellers, the roads in here are winding and kangaroos are a common sight.

South Coast WA

Includes ➡

Walpole & Nornalup . . 153
Denmark 154
Albany 157
Mt Barker 161
Porongurup National Park 162
Stirling Range National Park 163
Bremer Bay 164
Esperance 166

Best Places to Eat

- Maleeya's Thai Cafe (p163)
- Emu Point Cafe (p160)
- Loose Goose (p168)
- Pepper & Salt (p156)
- Mean Fiddler (p160)

Best Places to Stay

- Cape Howe Cottages (p155)
- Beach House at Bayside (p159)
- Esperance B&B by the Sea (p168)
- Denmark Waters B&B (p155)
- The Lily Dutch Windmill (p163)

Why Go?

Standing above the waves and cliffs of the rugged south coast is an exhilarating experience. On calm days, the sea is aquamarine and white-sand beaches lie pristine and welcoming. Even busy summer holiday periods in the Great Southern are relaxed. Winter months bring pods of migrating whales, while the spectacular tingle trees of Walpole's Valley of the Giants are more super-sized evidence of nature's wonder.

For a change from the great outdoors, Albany – the state's earliest European settlement – has colonial and Anzac history, and Denmark has excellent wine, craft beer and good food. Inland, the peaks and plains of Stirling National Park are enlivened by wildflowers from September to November, while orca visit remote Bremer Bay from February to April.

Further west, Esperance is the gateway to some of Australia's best beaches.

When to Go

Esperance

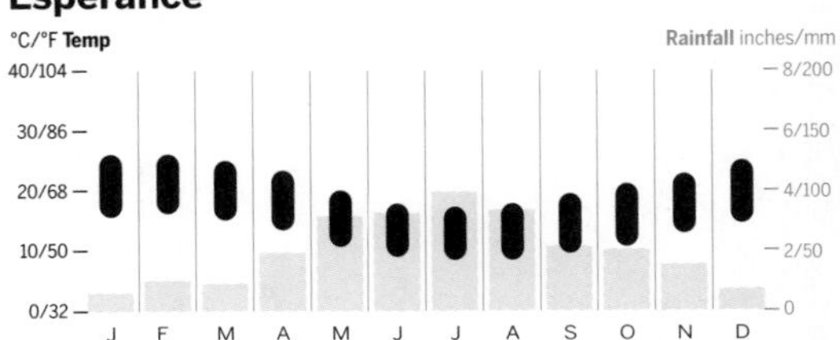

Jan The best beach weather – and it's not as hot or crowded as the west coast.

Sep Go wild for wildflowers and whales.

Dec Ideal time for hiking in the Stirling Range and Porongurup National Parks.

South Coast WA Highlights

1. **Cape Le Grand National Park** (p166) Swimming and surfing at some of Australia's best beaches.
2. **Valley of the Giants** (p153) Walking among and above the giant tingle trees along the Tree Top Walk.
3. **National Anzac Centre** (p157) Paying your respects to the sacrifice made by soldiers more than 100 years ago.
4. **Porongurup National Park** (p162) Hiking among immense karri trees and spectacular granite outcrops.
5. **Denmark** (p154) Touring the superb wineries, meadery and brewery near this laid-back seaside town.
6. **Cape Arid National Park** (p166) Deserted, pristine beaches and good bushwalking.
7. **King George Sound** (p158) Competing to see who can spot the most whales.
8. **Fitzgerald River National Park** (p165) Wandering through wildflowers.

Walpole & Nornalup

08 / POP 330

On traditional Minang Noongar land, the peaceful twin inlets of Walpole and Nornalup make good bases from which to explore the heavily forested Walpole Wilderness Area – an immense wilderness incorporating a rugged coastline, several national parks, marine parks, nature reserves and forest conservation areas – covering a whopping 3630 sq km. Walpole is the bigger settlement, and it's here that the South Western Hwy (Hwy 1) becomes the South Coast Hwy.

Sights

★Valley of the Giants NATURE RESERVE

(08-9840 8263; www.valleyofthegiants.com.au; Valley of the Giants Rd, Walpole; Tree Top Walk adult/child $21/10.50; 9am-5pm) The spectacular Tree Top Walk consists of a 600m-long ramp rising from the valley, allowing visitors access high into the canopy of the giant tingle trees. At its highest point, the ramp is 40m above the ground. It's on a gentle incline so it's easy to walk and is accessible by assisted wheelchair. At ground level, the Ancient Empire boardwalk (admission free) meanders through veteran red tingles, up to 16m in circumference and 46m high.

Walpole-Nornalup National Park NATIONAL PARK

(https://parks.dpaw.wa.gov.au/park/walpole-nornalup; off South Coast Hwy) Giant trees include red, yellow and Rate's tingles (all types of eucalypt, or gum, trees). Good walking tracks include a section of the **Bibbulmun Track**, which passes through Walpole to Coalmine Beach. Scenic drives include the **Knoll Drive**, 3km east of Walpole; the Valley of the Giants Rd; and through pastoral country to Mt Frankland, 29km north of Walpole. Here you can climb to the summit for panoramic views or walk around the trail at its base.

Petrichor Gallery GALLERY

(0438 401 148; www.petrichorgallery.com.au; 8 Nockolds St, Walpole; 10am-4pm) Showcasing up to eight annual exhibitions by regional artists and those further afield, this gallery also sells a good selection of locally made native hardwood crafts, watercolours, glass art, jewellery, sculpture and more.

Conspicuous Cliffs LANDMARK

(Conspicuous Beach Rd) Midway between Nornalup and Peaceful Bay, Conspicuous Cliffs is a good spot for whale watching from July to November. It features a hilltop lookout and a steepish 800m walk to the beach.

Tours

★WOW Wilderness Ecocruises CRUISE

(08-9840 1036; www.wowwilderness.com.au; Jones Rd, Walpole, town pier; adult/child $45/15) The dreamy landscape of Nornalup Inlet and its wildlife are brought to life through anecdotes about Aboriginal settlement, Leo Tolstoy's Walpole connections, and shipwrecked pirates. Highlights include a stop with an optional walk to windswept Sandy Beach and the guide's mother's legendary lemon cake. The 2½-hour cruise leaves at 10am daily; book at the visitor centre (p154).

Naturally Walpole Tours ECOTOUR

(08-9840 1111; Walpole Visitor Centre) Half-day tours exploring the Walpole Wilderness (adult/child $70/35) and the Tree Top Walk ($80/40).

Sleeping

★Tingle All Over YHA HOSTEL $

(08-9840 1041; www.yha.com.au; 60 Nockolds St, Walpole; dm/s/d $30/50/70; P ❄ @ ☎) Help yourself to lemons from the garden of this motel-style option with spotless, snug rooms, a great guest kitchen and a lounge filled with DVDs and board games. Lots of advice on local walks is on offer and the owners are super-friendly.

Nornalup Riverside Chalets CHALET $$

(08-9840 1107; www.nornalupriversidechalets.com.au; Riverside Dr, Nornalup; chalets $115-190; P ❄) Stay a night in sleepy Nornalup in these comfortable, colourful self-contained chalets, just a rod's throw from the fish in the Frankland River. The chalets are well spaced out, and there are two-person canoes

THE ROAD TO MANDALAY

About 13km west of Walpole, at Crystal Springs, is an 8km gravel road to **Mandalay Beach**, where the *Mandalay*, a Norwegian barque, was wrecked in 1911. The wreck eerily appears every 10 years or so after storms. See the photos at Walpole's visitor centre. The beach is glorious, often deserted, and accessed by a boardwalk across sand dunes and cliffs. It's part of D'Entrecasteaux National Park.

($25 per hour), kayaks ($15) and stand-up paddleboards ($15) for hire.

Riverside Retreat CHALET $$
(☎08-9840 1255; www.riversideretreat.com.au; South Coast Hwy, Nornalup; chalets $170-230; P ⊖ ❄) On the banks of the beautiful Frankland River, these well-equipped chalets are great value, with pot-bellied stoves for cosy winter warmth, and tennis and canoeing as outdoor pursuits. Expect frequent visits from the local wildlife.

Eating & Drinking

Nornabar BISTRO $$
(☎08-9840 1407; http://nornabar.com; 6684 South Coast Hwy, Nornalup; tapas $12-16, mains $25-37; ⏲10am-late Wed-Sun; ❄ ⊕) This light, sunny bar and cafe soundtracked with cool jazz and enlivened by colourful local art serves playful, globally inspired dishes. There's a concise selection of local Great Southern wines available, and the menu stretches from chicken, ricotta and tarragon meatballs to spicy baby squid. A compact beer garden completes a versatile offering.

Four Sisters Cafe COFFEE
(Nockolds St, Walpole; ⏲7am-4pm) Come to this petrol station cafe for good coffee and muffins against a backdrop of stunning Aboriginal art.

Information

Walpole Visitor Centre (☎08-9840 1111; www.walpole.com.au; South Coast Hwy, Walpole; ⏲9am-5pm) Plenty of info on the region. Book your WOW cruise tickets (p153) here.

Getting There & Away

Walpole and Nornalup sit on the South Coast Hwy (Hwy 1).

Departing from the visitor centre, Transwa (www.transwa.wa.gov.au) bus GS3 heads daily to/from Bunbury ($49, 4½ hours), Bridgetown ($27, three hours), Pemberton ($21, 1¾ hours), Denmark ($15, one hour) and Albany ($24, 1¾ hours).

Denmark

☎08 / POP 2557

Denmark's beaches and coastline, river and sheltered inlet, forested backdrop and hinterland have attracted a varied, arty and environmentally aware community. Farmers, fishers and families all mingle during the town's four market days each year, and Denmark makes a terrific base for visiting some of the top Great Southern wineries.

This sleepy, pleasant little town was established by European settlers to supply timber to the early goldfields. Known by the Minang Noongar people as Koorabup (place of the black swan), there's evidence of early Aboriginal settlement in the 3000-year-old fish traps found in Wilson Inlet.

Sights

William Bay National Park NATIONAL PARK
(https://parks.dpaw.wa.gov.au/park/william-bay; William Bay Rd) William Bay National Park, about 20km west of town, offers sheltered swimming in gorgeous **Greens Pool** and off nearby **Elephant Rocks**, and has good walking tracks.

West Cape Howe National Park NATIONAL PARK
(https://parks.dpaw.wa.gov.au/park/west-cape-howe; Lower Denmark Rd) Midway between Denmark and Albany, this 35-sq-km coastal park is a playground for naturalists, bushwalkers, rock climbers and anglers. Inland are areas of coastal heath, lakes, swamp and karri forest. With the exception of the road to Shelley Beach, access is restricted to 4WDs, mostly travelling through sand dunes, to explore the wild coast.

Camping is permitted at Shelley Beach, although campfires are banned.

Activities

To get your bearings, walk the **Mokare Heritage Trail** (a 3km circuit along the Denmark River), or the **Wilson Inlet Trail** (12km return, starting at the river mouth), which forms part of the longer **Nornalup Trail**. The **Mt Shadforth Lookout** has fine coastal views, and lush **Mt Shadforth Road**, running from town to the South Coast Hwy west of town, makes a great scenic drive. A longer pastoral loop is via **Scotsdale Road**. Attractions include alpaca farms, wineries, dairy farms and arts-and-crafts galleries.

Surfers and anglers should head to ruggedly beautiful **Ocean Beach**. Accredited local instructor Mike Neunuebel gives **surfing lessons** (☎0401 349 854; www.southcoastsurfinglessons.com.au; Ocean Beach; 2hr lesson incl equipment from $60). Rent kayaks and stand-up paddleboards at the Denmark Rivermouth Caravan Park for a paddle up Denmark River.

Tours

Poornarti Aboriginal Tours CULTURAL
(☎0412 786 588, 0415 840 216; www.poornarti.com.au; 27 Strickland St; adult/child $150/60; ⏰9.30am-5pm) Joey leads engaging day tours that focus on the Noongar cultural history of Kwoorabup (Denmark) and Stirling Range National Park, and include foraging and tasting bush tucker, as well as local art and traditional song and dance. Vibrational healing day tours are also available, incorporating ancient Noongar healing techniques.

Denmark Wine Lovers Tour WINE
(☎0427 482 400; www.denmarkwinelovers.com.au) Full-day tours taking in Denmark wineries ($88 per person, two-person minimum) or heading further afield to Porongurup/Mt Barker ($90 per person, four-person minimum). Check out the website to see which vineyards can be included in the mix. Pick-up arranged.

Festivals & Events

Market Days FAIR
(www.denmarkarts.com.au/markets; Berridge Park; ⏰Dec, Jan & Easter) Four times a year (mid-December, early and late January and Easter) Denmark hosts riverside market days with craft stalls, music and food.

Festival of Voice MUSIC
(www.denmarkfestivalofvoice.com.au; ⏰Jun) Performances and workshops on the WA Day long weekend, which incorporates the first Monday in June.

Sleeping

Denmark Rivermouth Caravan Park CARAVAN PARK $
(☎08-98481262; www.denmarkrivermouthcaravanpark.com.au; Inlet Dr; camping per person $17.50, cabins & chalets $140-220; P❄) Ideally located for nautical pursuits, this caravan park sits along Wilson Inlet beside the boat ramp. Some of the units are properly flash, although they are quite tightly arranged. It also has a kids' playground and kayaks and stand-up paddleboards for hire. Look forward to pelicans cruising the nearby estuary most afternoons.

Blue Wren Travellers' Rest YHA HOSTEL $
(☎08-9848 3300; www.denmarkbluewren.com.au; 17 Price St; dm/s/d/f $30/50/70/120; ❄) Great info panels cover the walls, and it's small enough (just 20 beds) to have a homey feel. Bikes can also be rented – $20 per day – and the friendly new owner is an affable South African who reckons Denmark is a great place to call home.

★**Denmark Waters B&B** B&B $$
(☎0409 038 300; www.denmarkwaters.com.au; 9 Inlet Dr; r $180-190; P❄📶) Run by the delightful Maria, a treasure trove of local knowledge, this intimate, three-room B&B sits in a quiet location overlooking the sound, just south of town. Spotless rooms come with separate sleeping and living areas with complimentary decanters of port.

★**Cape Howe Cottages** COTTAGE $$
(☎08-9845 1295; www.capehowe.com.au; 322 Tennessee Rd S; cottages $179-289; P❄📶) For a remote getaway, these five cottages in bushland southeast of Denmark really make the grade. They're all different, but all come with well-equipped kitchens, TVs and iPod docks. The best is only 1.5km from dolphin-favoured Lowlands Beach and is properly plush – with a BBQ on the deck.

31 on the Terrace BOUTIQUE HOTEL $$
(☎08-9848 1700; www.denmarkaccommodation.com.au; 31 Strickland St; r $145-165, apt $199; ❄) Travel from Windsor to Havana inside these stylish, individually decorated en-suite rooms – some with balconies – that fill this renovated corner pub in the centre of town. Compact apartments sleep up to five people.

Celestine Retreat CHALET $$$
(☎08-9848 3000; www.celestineretreat.com; 413 Mt Shadforth Rd; r $250-300; P❄) With just four spa chalets scattered over 13 hectares, there are stunning ocean and valley views at this luxury retreat. Romance is also on the agenda, with private spas, fluffy bathrobes and high-end bathroom goodies. There is usually a two-night stay minimum.

Eating

★**Ravens Coffee** CAFE $
(☎08-9848 1163; www.ravenscoffee.com; 1/7 South Coast Hwy; mains $17-20; ⏰8am-6pm; ❄📶) Denmark's best coffee, as well as the most creative breakfasts – from avo crisp to poached eggs with a spicy, Tunisian-style tomato sauce.

Mrs Jones CAFE $
(☎0467 481 878; www.mrsjonescafe.com; 12 Mt Shadforth Rd; mains $13-20; ⏰7am-4pm; ❄📶) Settle in with locals and tourists at this spacious spot with high ceilings and exposed beams. There's interesting cafe fare, often with an Asian or a Mediterranean spin.

Albany

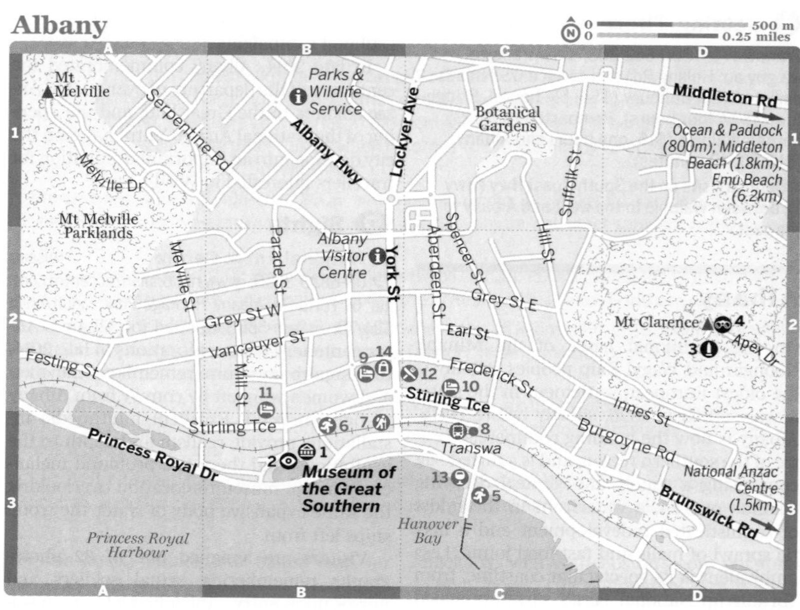

Albany

Top Sights
1 Museum of the Great Southern B3

Sights
Albany Residency Museum .... (see 1)
2 Brig Amity B3
3 Desert Mounted Corps Memorial D2
4 Mt Clarence D2

Activities, Courses & Tours
Albany Ocean Adventures .... (see 5)
5 Albany Whale Tours C3
6 Alkoomi Wines B3
7 Bibbulmun Track B3
8 Busy Blue Bus C3

Sleeping
9 1849 Backpackers B2
10 Albany Foreshore Guest House C2
11 Albany Harbourside B2

Eating
Gourmandise & Co .... (see 10)
12 Mean Fiddler C2

Drinking & Nightlife
13 Due South C3
White Star .... (see 10)

Shopping
14 South Coast Woodwork Gallery B2

availability – include tastings, and there's a cafe offering tapas, local beer and snacks.

Mt Clarence VIEWPOINT
(Apex Dr) There are fine views over the coast and inland from Mt Clarence, which sits atop the Albany Heritage Park. On top of Mt Clarence is the **Desert Mounted Corps Memorial** (Albany Heritage Park).

Princess Royal Fortress HISTORIC SITE
(Forts Rd; incl with entry to National Anzac Centre; ⏲9am-5pm) As a strategic port, Albany was historically regarded as being vulnerable to attack. Built in 1893 on Mt Adelaide, this fort was initially constructed as a defence against potential attacks from the Russians and French, and the restored buildings, gun emplacements and views are very interesting. From the fortress take the Convoy Walk for excellent views of King George Sound and signage showing where each ship was anchored before its departure to the Egypt and Gallipoli campaigns of WWI.

Activities

After whaling ended in 1978, whales slowly began returning to the waters of Albany. Now southern right and humpback whales gather near the bays and coves of King George Sound from July to mid-October. You can sometimes spot them from the beach. Both **Albany Ocean Adventures** (☎0428 429 876; www.whales.com.au; 5a Toll Pl; adult/child $100/60; ⊗Jul-Oct) and **Albany Whale Tours** (☎08-9845 1068; www.albanywhaletours.com.au; 5d Toll Pl; adult/child $98/58; ⊗Jun-Oct) run whale-watching trips in season.

Albany's appeal as a top-class diving destination grew after the 2001 scuttling of the warship HMAS *Perth* to create an artificial reef for divers. **Southcoast Diving Supplies** (☎08-9841 7176; www.divealbany.com.au; 84b Serpentine Rd; 4-day open water course $595; ⊗9am-5pm Mon-Fri, 8.30am-1pm Sat) can show you the underwater world.

Bibbulmun Track HIKING
(www.bibbulmuntrack.org.au; Princess Royal Dr) Taking around eight weeks, the 963km Bibbulmun Track runs from Albany to Kalamunda, 20km east of Perth, through mainly natural environment. Terrain includes jarrah and marri forests, wildflowers, granite outcrops, coastal heath country and spectacular coastlines. Comfortable campsites are spaced regularly along the track. The best time to do it is from August to October.

SUPLime WATER SPORTS
(☎0475 090 404; www.facebook.com/suplimewa; 6 Middleton Rd; ⊗6am-7pm) Fun stand-up paddleboarding (SUP) outings, SUP lessons and SUP hire ($25 per hour). Locations vary; check its Facebook page for updates.

Tours

Busy Blue Bus BUS
(☎08-9842 2133; www.busybluebus.com.au; old train station, Proudlove Pde; ⊗adult/child from $109/103) Full- and half-day tours taking in Albany's Anzac history, the city's whaling heritage, or further afield to the Great Southern vineyards or Castle Rock and the Granite Skywalk in the Porongurup National Park. Pick-ups from the old train station.

Sleeping

★**1849 Backpackers** HOSTEL $
(☎08-9842 1554; www.albanybackpackersaccommodation.com.au; 45 Peels Pl; dm/s/d $33/77/99; ❄@📶) Big flags from many nations provide a colourful international welcome at this well-run hostel. A huge, modern kitchen; info on local attractions splashed across walls; sunny rooms; and a laid-back social ambience make this one of WA's best places to stay for budget travellers. Homemade pancakes for breakfast every morning.

WORTH A TRIP

ALBANY DAY TRIPS

On a peninsula directly south of Albany, the **Historic Whaling Station** (☎08-9844 4021; www.discoverybay.com.au; 81 Whaling Station Rd; adult/6-15yr/family $32/12/75; ⊗9am-5pm; 👪) and **Torndirrup National Park** (https://parks.dpaw.wa.gov.au/park/torndirrup; off Frenchman Bay Rd; per motorcycle/car $7/13) are easy and popular half-day trips from town. East of Albany, **Two Peoples Bay** (https://parks.dpaw.wa.gov.au/park/two-peoples-bay; Two Peoples Bay Rd) and **Waychinicup National Park** (https://parks.dpaw.wa.gov.au/park/waychinicup; Waychinicup South Rd; camp site adult/child $8/2.30) FREE beckon with their beaches, bushwalking and canoeing opportunities.

Albany Foreshore Guest House B&B $
(☎08-9842 8324; http://albanyforeshoreguesthouse.com.au; 86 Stirling Tce; ⊗s/d from $100/120; ❄📶) Housed inside a 19th-century former bank, this five-room B&B has more character than most in the region. Expect sky-high ceilings, heavy drapes, a collection of vintage cameras and replicas of famous paintings peering out at you at every angle. Hearty breakfast included.

Albany Harbourside APARTMENT $$
(☎08-9842 1769; www.albanyharbourside.com.au; 8 Festing St; d $169-279; P❄📶) Albany Harbourside's portfolio includes spacious and spotless apartments on Festing St, and three other self-contained options arrayed around central Albany. Decor is modern and colourful, and some apartments have ocean views.

★**Beach House at Bayside** BOUTIQUE HOTEL $$$
(☎08-9844 8844; www.thebeachhouseatbayside.com.au; 33 Barry Ct, Collingwood Park; r $310-435; P❄📶) Positioned right by the beach and the golf course in a quiet cul-de-sac, midway between Middleton Beach and Emu Point, this 10-room hotel offers wonderful service. Rates include breakfast, afternoon tea, and evening port and chocolates. The friendly owners have their fingers on the pulse of Albany's dining scene, and a second property a few doors away is equally comfortable.

Eating

★Gourmandise & Co BAKERY $
(☎08-9847 4005; www.gourmandiseandco.com.au; 56 Stirling Tce; cakes from $6; ⏲7.30am-3pm Mon-Sat; ❄) Squeeze inside this bright and cheerful little French bakery and help yourself to quiche, freshly baked croissants and bread, organic coffee and all manner of sweet goodies.

★Emu Point Cafe CAFE $
(☎08-9844 7207; http://emupointcafe.com.au; 1 Mermaid Ave; mains $8-23; ⏲7.30am-4pm Mon-Fri, to 5pm Sat & Sun; ❄✍👪) This locally legendary breakfast joint does everything right: from Albany's best cup of coffee and cold-pressed juices to imaginative morning offerings, such as poached eggs with chimichurri and garlicky yoghurt, freshly baked muffins and jalapeño corn fritters. Eat inside or on the breezy seafront terrace.

Ocean & Paddock FISH & CHIPS $
(☎08-9842 6212; www.oceanandpaddock.com.au; 116 Middleton Ave; mains $12-19; ⏲3-9pm Wed & Thu, 11am-9pm Fri-Sun; ❄👪) Winners of the 'best fish and chips in WA' award, these guys serve up perfectly cooked, lightly battered ocean goodies. Not a pescatarian? There are moreish beef brisket, pulled pork and southern chicken rolls as well. Kiddie menu too.

Oyster Shack SEAFOOD $
(1 Swarbrick St; half-dozen oysters $10; ⏲9am-5pm Mon-Fri, 9am-noon Sat) No-frills oyster shack with a couple of picnic tables and inexpensive oysters fished right out of the bay.

Mean Fiddler MODERN AUSTRALIAN $$$
(☎08-9841 1852; www.facebook.com/MeanFiddlerRestaurant; 132 York St; mains $27-48; ⏲noon-3pm & 5.30-10pm Mon-Sat; ❄👪) Making waves in Albany foodie circles, the menu at this creative new spot takes inspiration from the owner's global roamings. Expect the likes of five-spice pork belly, Vietnamese-style prawns, local oysters with a splash of strawberry vinegar and local Wilson Brewing Company craft beer.

Drinking & Nightlife

★Wilson Brewing Company MICROBREWERY
(☎08-9842 3090; www.wilsonbrewing.com.au; 47768 South Coast Hwy; ⏲10am-7pm) Just west of Albany, this nautically themed microbrewery is particularly popular for its Rough Seas pale ale, though the hoppy Stiff Mast and malty Dirty Oar are also well worth a try. Seasonal brews and session ales available.

★White Star PUB
(☎08-9841 1733; www.whitestarhotel.com.au; 72 Stirling Tce; ⏲11am-late) With the largest selection of beers on tap in town (from James Squire to the local Wilson Brewing Company), excellent pub grub (from $20), a beer garden and lots of live music, this old pub gets a gold star. Sunday-night folk and blues gigs are a good opportunity to share a pint with Albany's laid-back locals.

Due South BAR
(☎08-9841 8526; www.duesouthalbany.com.au; 6 Toll Pl; ⏲11am-late) Located inside an airy space with great sea views, Due South is the best place for a sunset drink. There are decent craft beers on tap, the wine list comprises exclusively Great Southern wines, and the pub food menu is available throughout the day – handy in a town where many places take a break between lunch and dinner.

ALBANY WINERIES

Albany is part of the Great Southern wine-growing region, and there are four wineries dotted around the area. Don't miss the following:

Oranje Tractor (☎08-9842 5175; www.oranjetractor.com; 198 Link Rd, Marbelup; ⏲11am-6pm Sun; by appointment rest of time) FREE Small organic winery, good riesling and sauvignon blanc and sparkling varieties, plus WWOOFing opportunities.

Wignalls Wines (☎08-9841 2848; www.wignallswines.com.au; 448 Chester Pass Rd; ⏲11am-4pm Thu-Mon) Family-run winery renowned for pinot noir. Also good cabernet merlot, shiraz, chardonnay and sauvignon blanc.

Montgomery's Hill (☎0407 424 455; www.montgomeryshill.com.au; 45821 South Coast Hwy, Kalgan; cheese platters $15; ⏲11am-5pm) Excellent shiraz and cabernet sauvignon; cheese platters served alongside wines.

Shopping

★ **South Coast Woodwork Gallery** ARTS & CRAFTS

(☎08-9845 2028; www.southcoastwoodworks.com.au; 135 York St; ⏲10am-4pm Mon-Fri, to 1pm Sat) If you believe that everything useful should also be beautiful, you'll find plenty of fine handcrafted kitchen utensils to captivate you here. More high-end are striking vases and other wooden art, made of sustainably harvested jarrah, sheoak and other native hardwoods.

Mount Romance Sandalwood Factory PERFUME

(☎08-9845 6888; www.mtromance.com.au; 2 Down Rd; ⏲9am-5pm) Some 8km north of town, just past the airport, Australia's largest sandalwood factory welcomes you into its sweet-scented depths. Learn about its production; purchase the scents, body butters and other skincare products; and taste sandalwood nut cheesecake at the attached cafe.

Information

Albany Visitor Centre (☎08-6820 3700; www.amazingalbany.com; 221 York St; ⏲9am-5pm) Central; lots of helpful regional info.

Parks & Wildlife Service (☎08-9842 4500; https://parks.dpaw.wa.gov.au; 120 Albany Hwy; ⏲8am-4.30pm Mon-Fri) National park information.

Getting There & Away

Albany Airport (☎08-6820 3777; Albany Hwy) is 11km northwest of the city centre. Rex Airlines (www.rex.com.au) flies to/from Perth (70 minutes) daily.

Transwa (☎1300 662 205; www.transwa.wa.gov.au; Proudlove Pde) bus services stop at the visitor centre. These include the following:

- AP6 to/from Perth ($65, six hours) and Mt Barker ($10, 39 minutes) daily.
- 488 to/from Perth ($65, eight hours), Northam ($71, 6½ hours), York ($65, six hours) and Mt Barker ($10, 41 minutes) four times a week.
- 336 to/from Bunbury ($62, six hours), Bridgetown ($49, 4¾ hours), Pemberton ($40, 3½ hours), Walpole ($24, 1¾ hours) and Denmark ($10, 47 minutes) daily.

Getting Around

The visitor centre has information on local buses to Emu Point and Middleton Beach. **Albany Bicycle Hire** (☎0428 415 168; www.albanybicyclehire.com.au; 223 Middleton Rd; half-/full day from $20/25) can deliver bicycles anywhere in town.

Mt Barker

☎08 / POP 1910

Traditionally the home of the Bibbulmun people, Mt Barker (50km north of Albany) is the gateway to the Porongurup and Stirling Range National Parks. It's also part of the Great Southern wine region. Pick up the *Mt Barker Wineries* map from the town's visitor centre in the old railway station and visit www.mountbarkerwine.com.au.

Sights

Among the coolest of the Great Southern sub-regions, Mt Barker produces world-class shiraz, cabernet sauvignon and riesling. Merlot, chardonnay and cabernet franc also thrive here. There are seven wineries dotted around Mt Barker, three of them rated five-star by James Halliday. Don't miss:

Plantagenet Wines (☎08-9851 3111; www.plantagenetwines.com; Albany Hwy; mains from $15; ⏲10am-4.30pm) Particularly good for riesling, shiraz and chardonnay, in central Mt Barker.

West Cape Howe Wines (☎08-9892 1444; www.westcapehowewines.com.au; 14923 Muir Hwy; ⏲10am-5pm Mon-Fri, 11am-4pm Sat & Sun) Award-winning cabernet sauvignon, chardonnay and shiraz; also roasts its own coffee and hosts art exhibitions.

Poacher's Ridge (☎08-9857 6066; www.poachersridge.com.au; 1630 Spencer Rd; ⏲10am-4pm Fri-Sun) Fantastic merlot, as well as marsanne, viognier and other rarer wines that few local vineyards produce.

Sleeping

Nomads Guest House GUESTHOUSE $

(☎08-9851 2131; www.nomadsguesthousewa.com.au; 12 Morpeth St; s/d/yurts/chalets $70/90/100/110; P❄📶) A surprising sight is the authentic Mongolian yurt (felt tent) and gallery of Mongolian and Chinese art in the grounds of Nomads Guest House, which also offers several singles and doubles. The owners frequently rescue orphaned joeys (baby kangaroos), so don't be surprised to see a few temporary marsupial visitors in the main house.

Getting There & Away

Mt Barker is reachable via Albany Hwy (Hwy 30) and Muir Hwy (Hwy 102).

Transwa (www.transwa.wa.gov.au) operates the following bus services:

➡ GS1 to/from East Perth ($57, 5½ hours) and Albany ($10, 39 minutes) daily.

➡ GS2 to/from East Perth ($57, 7¼ hours), Northam ($62, 5¾ hours), York ($60, 5¼ hours) and Albany ($10, 41 minutes) on Thursdays, Fridays and Sundays.

Porongurup National Park

☎ 08

The 24-sq-km, 12km-long **Porongurup National Park** (https://parks.dpaw.wa.gov.au/park/porongurup; Porongurup Rd; per car/motorcycle $13/7) has 1100-million-year-old granite outcrops, panoramic views, misty scenery, large karri trees and some excellent bushwalks. Porongurup is also part of the Great Southern wine region and there are 11 wineries in the vicinity, several of them truly excellent. See www.porongurup.com.

The Wagyl Kaip people are the traditional custodians of this area.

Sights

Castle Rock Estate WINERY
(☎ 08-9853 1035; www.castlerockestate.com.au; Porongurup Rd; ⊙10am-5pm) Family-owned winery producing award-winning riesling, shiraz, sauvignon blanc and chardonnay. Also great for pinot noir, as well as a sparkling della and the sweet dessert muscat. Intimate tasting sessions.

Zarephath Wines WINERY
(☎ 08-9853 1152; www.zarephathwines.com.au; 424 Moorialup Rd; mains from $20; ⊙11am-4pm Sat & Sun) A short drive east of Porongurup National Park, this small, family-run winery serves trophy-winning riesling and pinot noir, as well as excellent syrah, chardonnay and cabernet, all grown on the estate. Book ahead for tasty slow-food lunches.

Duke's Vineyard WINERY
(☎ 08-9853 1107; www.dukesvineyard.com; 1380 Porongurup Rd; ⊙10am-4.30pm) Particularly good for award-winning, single-vineyard shiraz, riesling and rosé, a fantastic reserve shiraz and sparkling riesling and shiraz. Cellar door combined with art gallery.

Activities

Trails include the following:

Granite Skywalk (4km return; two hours) Mostly gentle hike through the forest, followed by vertical climb up Castle Rock.

Wansborough Walk (4km one way) Easy walk through the forest from the Tree-in-the-Rock picnic area.

Devil's Slide Trail (5km return; two hours) Turn-off from Wansborough Walk, with great views from the rocky summit.

Hayward Peak & Nancy Peak Walk (5.5km loop, two to three hours) Moderately challenging ascents of two peaks on a loop from Tree-in-the-Rock.

Sleeping & Eating

There is limited accommodation around the national park. See www.porongurup.com for listings of a caravan park and B&Bs. It's only a short drive from Mt Barker, and Albany is around 54km from Porongurup.

Ironwood Estate Wines WINERY $
(☎ 08-9853 1126; www.ironwoodestatewines.com.au; 2191 Porongurup Rd; mains from $15; ⊙11am-

Porongurup National Park

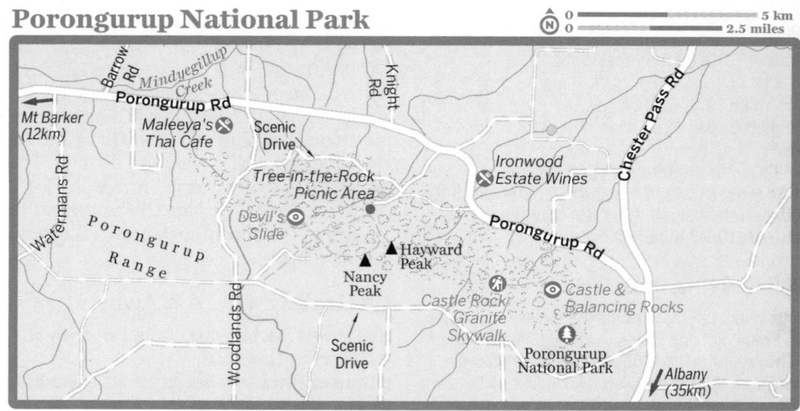

5pm Wed-Mon; ❄) Bailey, the friendly labradoodle, usually welcomes visitors who come to enjoy the stunning Porongurup views at Ironwood's tasting room, where you can sample its award-winning rosé, chardonnay and merlot. Light meals, including salmon quiche, are available along with coffee, tea and cakes.

★ **Maleeya's Thai Cafe** THAI $$
(☎08-9853 1123; www.maleeya.com.au; 1376 Porongurup Rd; mains $26-34; ⏲11.30am-3pm & 6-9pm Fri-Sun; ❄☎) Foodies and chefs venture to Porongurup for some of WA's most authentic Thai food. Curries (including the signature massaman prawn curry), soups and stir-fries all come with fresh herbs straight from Maleeya's garden. Bookings recommended.

Getting There & Away

To explore the Porongurup area you'll need your own wheels.

Stirling Range National Park

☎08

Rising abruptly from surrounding flat and sandy plains, the Stirling Range's propensity to change colour through blues, reds and purples captivates photographers during the spectacular wildflower season from late August to early December. Over 1500 plant species grow in the park, including 120 species of orchids and 87 endemics. The Noongar and Wagyl Kaip peoples are the traditional custodians of Stirling Range and recognise it as a place where the spirits of the dead return.

This 1156-sq-km **national park** (https://parks.dpaw.wa.gov.au/park/stirling-range; Chester Pass Rd; ⏲per car/motorcycle $13/7) consists of a single chain of peaks pushed up by plate tectonics to form a range 10km wide and 65km long. Running most of its length are isolated summits, some knobbly and some perfect pyramids, towering above broad valleys covered in shrubs and heath. Bluff Knoll (Bular Mai), at 1095m, is the highest point in the southwest.

Park fees are charged at the start of Bluff Knoll Rd.

Activities

The Stirlings are renowned for serious bushwalking. Trails are as follows:

Bluff Knoll (1095m; 6km return, three to four hours) The highest mountain in the park with great views.

Toolbrunup Peak (1052m; 4km return, three to four hours) Second-highest peak; some steep loose rock and scree sections near the top; 360-degree views.

Mt Hassell (848m; 3km return, three hours) Steep scramble over rock dome on approach to the summit. Great views from Toolbrunup Peak from the top.

Talyuberlup (783m; 2.6km return, three hours) Scrambles through gullies and increasingly steep climb to a rocky crag.

Mt Trio (856m; 3.5km return, two to three hours) Knee-popping steps for much of the way, then a gentle stroll; 360-degree views.

Mt Magog (856m; 7km return, three hours) Serious bushwalking through wandoo woodland and thick bush. Great summit views.

The park's most challenging trek is from Bluff Knoll to **Ellen Peak** (28.8km, three days). Alpine conditions: violent weather changes, steep ascents and descents, scrambling over rock. Two-night bivouac involved.

Sleeping & Eating

Stock up on food in Mt Barker or Albany if you're camping. There's a basic cafe 200m down the road from Stirling Range Retreat. If you're staying at the Lily, evening meals are available for in-house guests.

Stirling Range Retreat CARAVAN PARK $
(☎08-9827 9229; www.stirlingrange.com.au; 8639 Chester Pass Rd; unpowered/powered site $16/36, on-site caravan $69, cabins $95-149, units $170-195; ❄@≋) On the park's northern boundary, this shaded area offers campsites, cabins and vans, and self-contained, rammed-earth units. Wildflower and orchid bus tours and birdwatching walks (three hours, $49 per person) are conducted from mid-August to the end of October. The swimming pool only opens from November to April. Shuttle transport to Bluff Knoll arranged.

★ **The Lily Dutch Windmill** GUESTHOUSE $$
(☎08-9827 9205; www.thelily.com.au; Chester Pass Rd; cottages $159-189; ❄) These cottages, 12km north of the park, are grouped around a working windmill. Accommodation is self-contained, and meals are available for guests at the neighbouring restaurant. Call to enquire which nights the restaurant is

Stirling Range National Park

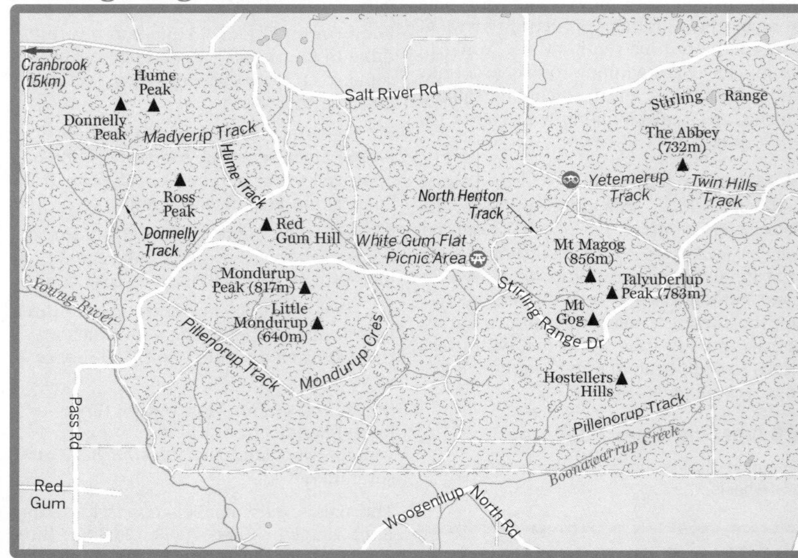

open to the public and to arrange mill tours ($50, minimum of four people). There's also private accommodation in a restored 1944 Dakota DC3 aircraft ($249).

Getting There & Away

Everything except the three campgrounds and the Bluff Knoll trailhead is accessed via decent unsealed roads. The scenic Stirling Range Dr that cuts through the park is unsealed but suitable for 2WD. Stirling Range is around 80km north of Albany.

Bremer Bay

08 / POP 373

Edged with brilliant white sand and translucent green waters, this sleepy fishing and holiday hamlet sits on the traditional lands of the Wudjari and Goreng people and is 61km from the South Coast Hwy. From July to November, the bay is a cetacean maternity ward for southern right whales, and orca are seen from January to late April.

Tours

Bremer Canyon Killer Whale Expeditions WHALE WATCHING
(08-9750 5500; www.whales-australia.com.au/bremer-killer-whales; Bremer Bay Boat Harbour; per adult/child $385/300; Jan-late Apr) From late January to mid-April, orca are regular visitors to the deep and nutrient-rich waters of the Bremer Canyon. Excursions departing from Bremer Bay wharf run from 8.30am to 4.30pm, and booking ahead is strongly recommended. Transport is available from Albany with Busy Blue Bus (p159). Operator Naturaliste Charters is supporting Riggs Australia (www.riggsaustralia.com) in passive research on the Bremer Canyon whales.

Sleeping

Tozer's Bush Camp CAMPGROUND $
(0428 371 015; www.facebook.com/Tozers-Bush-Camp-523067784473012/; Lot 52, Ocumup Rd; unpowered site per person $15) Proper bush camping outside Bremer Bay, with wonderful hosts, spotless ablution facilities and a terrific camp kitchen. Message on Facebook for directions.

Bremer Bay Beaches Resort & Tourist Park CARAVAN PARK $
(08-9837 4290; www.bremerbaybeaches.com.au; Wellstead Rd; unpowered/powered site $45/70, cabins & chalets $170-240;) This park has shady campsites and a well-equipped shared kitchen. It's a 1.5km walk through the dunes to the beach. There's also a seasonal pizzeria and very good espresso coffee.

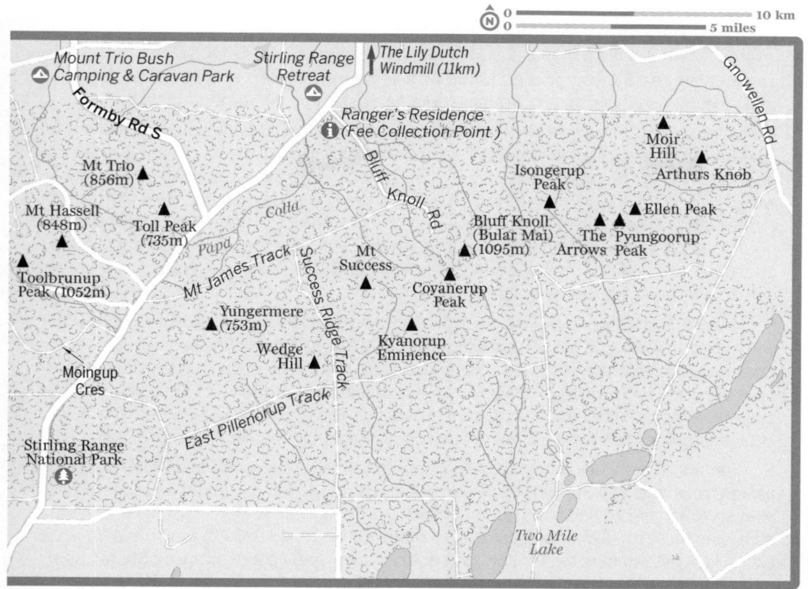

Information

Bremer Bay Visitor Centre (08-9837 4171; www.bremerbaycrc.com.au; Mary St; 9am-4pm Tue-Fri;) Internet access in the shire library, plus regional info.

Getting There & Away

Busy Blue Bus (p159) in Albany runs tours to see the orca.

Bremer Bay sits off Hwy 1, reachable via Gairdner S Rd if coming from Esperance and via Borden-Bremer Bay Rd if driving from Albany.

Fitzgerald River National Park

08

Midway between Albany and Esperance, this gem of a **national park** (https://parks.dpaw.wa.gov.au/park/fitzgerald-river; per car/motorcycle $13/7) is the traditional home of the Wudjari people and a Unesco Biosphere Reserve. Its 3300 sq km contains half of the orchid species in WA (more than 80, 70 of which occur nowhere else), 22 mammal species, 200 species of bird and 1700 species of plant (20% of WA's described flora species).

Walkers will discover beautiful coastline, sand plains, rugged coastal hills (known as 'the Barrens') and deep, wide river valleys. In season, you'll almost certainly see whales and their calves from the shore at **Point Ann**, where there's a lookout and a heritage walk that follows a short stretch of the 1164km **No 2 rabbit-proof fence**.

Bookending the park are the sleepy coastal settlements of Bremer Bay and Hopetoun, both with white sand and shimmering waters.

Sleeping & Eating

Camping is the way to see the best of the park. Camp sites (sites per adult/child $13/2.20) at St Mary Inlet (near Point Ann) and Four Mile Beach can be reached by 2WD. Others at Hamersley Inlet, Whale Bone Beach, Quoin Head and Fitzgerald Inlet are accessible by 4WD or on foot. There's also a nearby homestead. The nearest supermarket is at Ravensthorpe (to the northeast of the park).

Quaalup Homestead CAMPGROUND $
(08-9837 4124; www.whalesandwildflowers.com.au; 1 Gairdner Rd; camping per person $13, cabins $115-130;) This German-owned 1858 homestead is secluded deep within the park's southern reaches. Electricity is solar generated, and forget about mobile-phone coverage. Accommodation includes a bush camp site with gas BBQs and cosy units and chalets. Full board an extra $36.

OFF THE BEATEN TRACK

ESPERANCE NATIONAL PARKS

The area around Esperance is endowed with some tremendous white-sand beaches, as well as good bushwalking and fishing, spread across three different national parks.

Cape Le Grand National Park (https://parks.dpaw.wa.gov.au/park/cape-le-grand; off Fisheries Rd; entry per car/motorcycle $13/7, campsites adult/child $11/3) Good fishing, swimming and camping can be found at **Lucky Bay** – arguably Australia's top beach, complete with beach-going kangaroos – and **Le Grand Beach**, and day-use facilities at gorgeous **Hellfire Bay**. Make the effort to climb **Frenchman Peak** (a steep 3km return, allow two hours), as the views from the top and through the rocky 'eye', especially during the late afternoon, are superb. The beautiful 15km **Le Grand Coastal Trail** links the bay, or you can do shorter stretches between beaches.

Cape Arid National Park (https://parks.dpaw.wa.gov.au/park/cape-arid; off Fisheries Rd; entry per car/motorcycle $13/7, campsites adult/child $11/3) Whales (in season), seals and Cape Barren geese are seen regularly here. Much of the park is 4WD-accessible only, although the Thomas River Rd leading to the shire campground suits all vehicles and you can reach most of the beautiful, deserted beaches either via 2WD or on foot. There's a challenging walk to the top of Tower Peak on Mt Ragged (3km return, three hours).

Stokes National Park (https://parks.dpaw.wa.gov.au/park/stokes; off South Coast Hwy; entry per car/motorcycle $13/7) Most of this park's 107 sq km is covered in scrub and coastal heath, sheltering kangaroos and birds. You might also spot seals. Stokes Inlet is popular with anglers, and there's a bush **campground** (campsites adult/child $11/2.20), which is 2WD accessible. Highlights include the Moir Homestead ruins and great shore diving off Shoal Cape.

Getting There & Away

You'll need your own transport; a 4WD vehicle is strongly recommended. The three main 2WD entry points to the park are from the South Coast Hwy (Quiss Rd and Pabelup Dr), Hopetoun (Hamersley Dr) and Bremer Bay (along Swamp and Murray Rds). All roads are gravel, and likely to be impassable after rain, so check locally before you set out.

Hopetoun

08 / POP 871

The traditional home of the Wudjari people, Hopetoun is now a sleepy little beach town once more due to closure of the nearby nickel mine. From the jetty at the end of the main drag (Veal St) there are wonderful views. Beside it is a child-friendly beach with a swimming pontoon. The old train route between Ravensthorpe and Hopetoun is now a **heritage walking track**.

The world's longest fence – the 1833km-long **No 1 rabbit-proof fence** – enters the sea at Starvation Bay, east of Hopetoun; it starts at Eighty Mile Beach on the Indian Ocean, north of Port Hedland. The fence was built during the height of the rabbit plague between 1901 and 1907. However, the bunnies beat the fence-builders to the west side, so it wasn't as effective a barrier as hoped.

Sleeping & Eating

Hopetoun Motel & Chalet Village MOTEL $$
(08-9838 3219; www.hopetounmotel.com.au; 458 Veal St; r $150-170; P) Rammed-earth complex with comfy beds and spacious rooms, some with kitchenettes.

Simon's Market Cafe CAFE $$
(0487 907 162; www.facebook.com/SimonsMarketCafe6390; Veal St; lunch $12-18, dinner $26-30; 8.30am-2.30pm & 5.30-8pm Tue-Sat, to 2pm Sun) This friendly combination cafe and gift shop offers burgers, pasta and other light meals.

Getting There & Away

Albany is reachable via Hwy 1 from the Ravensthorpe turn-off, while Jerdacuttup Rd is a useful shortcut if driving to or from Esperance. Bus transport to Hopetoun is limited to the midweek GE4 service of **Transwa** (www.transwa.wa.gov.au), linking Albany and Esperance.

Esperance

08 / POP 10,420

Framed by aquamarine waters and pristine white beaches, Esperance sits on traditional Wudjari land in solitary splendour on the Bay of Isles. But despite its isolation, families still travel from Perth or Kalgoorlie just to plug into the easy-going vibe and great beach life. For travellers taking the coastal route east across the continent, it's the last sizeable town before the Nullarbor.

Picture-perfect beaches dot the even more remote national parks to the town's southeast, and the pristine environment of the 105 islands of the offshore Recherche Archipelago are home to fur seals, penguins and seabirds.

Sights

There are numerous stunning beaches within easy reach of Esperance, strung out along the Great Ocean Dr – all pristine white sand and crystal-clear cerulean waters. Many, including **West Beach**, **Salmon Beach**, **Fourth Beach** and **Twilight Beach**, are great for walking and sunbathing, but swimmers must heed the rip current warnings: West Beach waters are particularly dangerous. The best beach for swimming is **Blue Haven**, but it also gets occasional strong currents.

Esperance Museum MUSEUM
(☎08-9071 1579; cnr James & Dempster Sts; adult/child $8.50/3.50; ⏲1.30-4.30pm) This warehouse is filled with everyday objects from yesteryear, as well as Aboriginal weaponry, a vintage locomotive and a 19th-century train carriage you can climb aboard. Other big items include boats, a train carriage and the remains of the USA's spacecraft *Skylab*, which made its fiery re-entry at Balladonia, east of Esperance, in 1979.

Activities

★**Great Ocean Drive** SCENIC DRIVE
(Twilight Beach Rd) Many of Esperance's most dramatic sights can be seen on this well-signposted 40km loop. Starting from the waterfront, it heads southwest along the breathtaking stretch of coast that includes a series of popular surfing and swimming spots, including Blue Haven Beach and **Twilight Cove**. Stop at rugged **Observatory Point**, the lookout on **Wireless Hill** and the Lucky Bay Brewery (p168).

Great Ocean Trail CYCLING
(Twilight Beach Rd) Stretching from Castletown Beach in Esperance proper all the way to Twilight Beach, 17km west, this is a terrific seafront trail for cycling or hiking, with wonderful sea views throughout.

Esperance Diving & Fishing DIVING, FISHING
(☎08-9071 5111; www.esperancedivingandfishing.com.au; 72 The Esplanade) Takes you wreck diving on the *Sanko Harvest* (two-tank dive including all gear $270) or charter fishing throughout the archipelago. Also gear hire and PADI dive courses available.

Tours

Esperance Island Cruises BOATING
(☎08-9071 5757; www.esperancecruises.com.au; 72 The Esplanade; adult/child $100/65; ⏲9am-12.30pm) Scenic half-day wildlife cruises for spotting sea lions, New Zealand fur seals, dolphins, Cape Barren geese and sea eagles. Snorkelling equipment and a light morning tea provided.

Eco-Discovery Tours DRIVING
(☎0407 737 261; www.esperancetours.com.au) Runs 4WD tours along the sand to Cape Le Grand National Park (half-/full day $105/195, minimum two/four people) and two-hour circuits of Great Ocean Dr (adult/child $60/45).

Woody Island Tours BOATING
(☎0484 327 580; www.woodyisland.com.au; Taylor St Jetty; full-day ferry adult/child $95/30, half-day guided trip $95/68/55; ⏲mid-Dec–Jan, mid-Apr–early May) Half-day boat trips incorporating a guided walk on this small island with dramatic topography – part of the Recherche Archipelago. Tours also include snorkelling, morning tea and the opportunity to spot fur seals, sea lions, dolphins and Cape Barren geese. Alternatively, for independent swimming and bushwalking on the island, catch a ferry at 7am and return at 3pm.

Sleeping

Woody Island Eco-Stays CAMPGROUND $
(☎0484 327 580; www.woodyisland.com.au; camping $42, 2-/4-person tent $100/135, safari tent $155; ⏲mid-Dec–Jan, mid-Apr–early May; ❄) Sleeping options at this appealing campground include leafy campsites (BYO camping equipment), as well as pre-prepped tents and canvas-sided two-person safari huts. Power is mostly solar, and rainwater supplies the island – both are highly valued. Allow for an $80 return ferry transfer as well.

Driftwood Apartments APARTMENT $
(☎0428 716 677; www.driftwoodapartments.com.au; 69 The Esplanade; apt $120-260; P❄📶) Each of these seven smart blue-and-yellow apartments, right across from the waterfront, has its own BBQ and outdoor table setting. The two-storey, two-bedroom units have decks and a bit more privacy.

Clearwater Motel Apartments MOTEL $
(☎08-9071 3587; www.clearwatermotel.com.au; 1a William St; s/d/f/apt from $120/140/160/160; P ❄ 📶) Centrally located, the bright and spacious rooms and apartments here have balconies and are fully self-contained, and there's a well-equipped shared BBQ area.

Blue Waters Lodge YHA HOSTEL $
(☎08-9071 1040; www.yha.com.au; 299 Goldfields Rd; dm/s/d $30/45/70; P ❄) On the beachfront about 1.5km from the town centre, this rambling place is popular with groups, and many guests are long-stay residents working in the area. Bikes can be hired.

★ **Esperance B&B by the Sea** B&B $$
(☎08-9071 5640; www.esperancebb.com; 34 Stewart St; r $130-190, f $360; P ❄ 📶) This great-value beachhouse has a private guest wing and the views from the deck overlooking Blue Haven Beach are breathtaking, especially at sunset. It's just a stroll from the ocean and a five-minute drive from central Esperance.

Eating & Drinking

★ **FishFace** SEAFOOD $
(☎08-9071 1601; www.facebook.com/FishFace Esperance; 1 James St; mains $15-20; ⏲4.30-8.30pm Thu-Tue; ❄) Seafood is the star at FishFace. One half is a busy fish-and-chip takeaway, with punters lining up for superior battered snapper, whiting and cod. The other half is a restaurant with brisk, friendly service and lively conversation around the tables fuelled by seafood risotto, with the slurping of raw oysters and the crunch of crispy batter.

Taylor St Quarters CAFE $$
(☎0457 232 039; www.facebook.com/taylorst quarters; Taylor St Jetty; mains $17-36; ⏲9am-11pm Tue-Fri, 8am-11pm Sat & Sun; ❄ 📶) This sprawling cafe by the jetty serves fish tacos, burgers, seafood and salads. Locals hang out at the tables on the grass or on the covered terrace. It's good for a glass of wine or chilled pint of Lucky Bay Brewing's refreshing kölsch beer. Ask about occasional live music – usually on Sunday afternoons.

★ **Loose Goose** MODERN AUSTRALIAN $$$
(☎08-9071 2320; www.loosegooseesperance.com.au; 9a Andrew St; 1/2/3 courses $35/60/80; ⏲4pm-midnight Mon-Sat, to 10pm Sun; ❄) Easily the most creative restaurant in town, the Goose also doubles as a lively bar that serves its own lager plus a handful of craft beers on tap. It's all minimalist black and chrome and teardrop lamps, with creative fare ranging from sashimi scallops to spicy, blackened catch of the day on fresh pasta.

★ **Lucky Bay Brewery** MICROBREWERY
(☎0447 631 115; www.facebook.com/luckybay brewing; Barook Rd; tastings $10-15; ⏲2-6pm) Look for Lucky Bay's beers in bars around Esperance or make the journey 12km west to this simple brewery and tasting room. Two-litre growlers are available for takeaway, and the friendly brewmasters will guide you through beers, including the refreshing Skippy Rock kölsch, award-winning Thistle Cove Scottish ale, smoky Black Jack porter or hoppy Cyclops IPA.

Shopping

★ **Karnpi Designs Art Gallery** ART
(☎08-9072 1688; www.facebook.com/karnpi designs; cnr Dempster & Kemp Sts, Museum Village; ⏲10am-4pm Tue-Fri, to 2pm Sat) Desert reds and ochres meet ocean blues in the stunning Aboriginal artworks displayed at this gallery by the likes of award-winning artist Sophia Ovens, as well as owner Pauline. Also for sale are silk ties and bags with Aboriginal designs, clapping sticks, maps of Aboriginal Australia and much more, with a substantial part of the sales going directly to artists.

Information

Parks & Wildlife (☎08-9083 2100; https://parks.dpaw.wa.gov.au; 92 Dempster St; ⏲8am-4.30pm Mon-Fri) National park information.

Visitor Centre (☎08-9083 1555; www.visitesperance.com; cnr Kemp & Dempster Sts; ⏲9am-5pm Mon-Fri, to 4pm Sat, to 2pm Sun) In the museum village with handy 24-hour information on the outside wall.

Getting There & Away

Esperance Airport (www.esperance.wa.gov.au/airport; Coolgardie-Esperance Hwy) is 18km north of the town centre. Rex Airlines (www.rex.com.au) flies between Perth and Esperance daily.

Transwa (☎1300 662 205; www.transwa.wa.gov.au; cnr Kemp & Dempster Sts) bus services stop at the visitor centre, with services to/from Albany, Perth, Kalgoorlie-Boulder and beyond.

Getting Around

Avis (☎08-9071 3998; www.avis.com.au; 63 The Esplanade; ⏲8.30am-5pm Mon-Fri, to noon Sat) Has a branch in town and at the airport.

Dempster Sporting (☎08-9071 1823; 65 Dempster St; ⏲8.30am-5pm Mon-Fri, to 1pm Sat) Mountain bikes for hire.

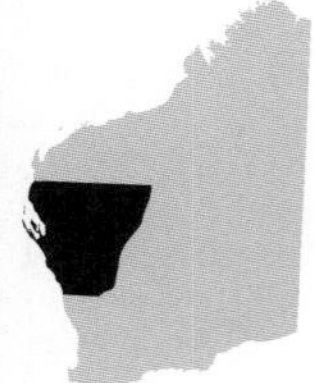

Monkey Mia & the Central West

Includes ➡

Batavia Coast 171
Dongara-Port Denison 171
Geraldton........... 172
Kalbarri National Park 178
Shark Bay 179
Denham 180
Monkey Mia......... 182
Carnarvon 183
Quobba Coast....... 185

Best Places to Eat

- Saltdish (p175)
- Beached Barrel (p174)
- Boughshed (p183)
- Grace of Kalbarri (p176)
- Oceans Restaurant (p181)

Best Places to Stay

- Gnaraloo Station (p186)
- On The Deck @ Shark Bay (p181)
- Dongara Breeze Inn (p171)
- Red Bluff (p186)
- Eco Abrolhos (p174)

Why Go?

The pristine coastline and sheltered turquoise waters of World Heritage–listed Shark Bay draw tourists and marine life from around the world. Aside from the dolphins of Monkey Mia, the bay's submerged seagrass meadows host dugongs, rays, sharks and turtles. On land, rare marsupials take refuge in remote national parks, and limestone cliffs, red sand and salt lakes litter a stark interior.

Further south, the gorges of Kalbarri invite adventurers to explore their depths, while wildflowers carpet the plains, and ospreys wheel away from primeval Indian Ocean cliffs as humpback whales migrate south.

Veggies ripen in Carnarvon as anglers and board-riders check the tides, and windsurfers and kitesurfers wait for the 'Doctor' (strong afternoon sea breeze) to blow. In Geraldton, cool cafes, weekend markets and an excellent museum combine with Indian Ocean views along the city's wonderfully revamped foreshore.

When to Go

Monkey Mia

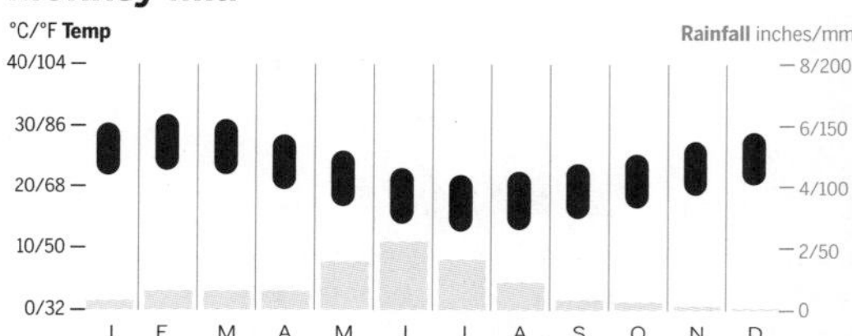

Jun–Aug The winter swells pump the surf breaks off Gnaraloo and Quobba.

Aug & Sep Kalbarri and surrounds erupt in wildflowers.

Nov–Feb Wind- and kitesurfers ride the waves from Geraldton to Carnarvon.

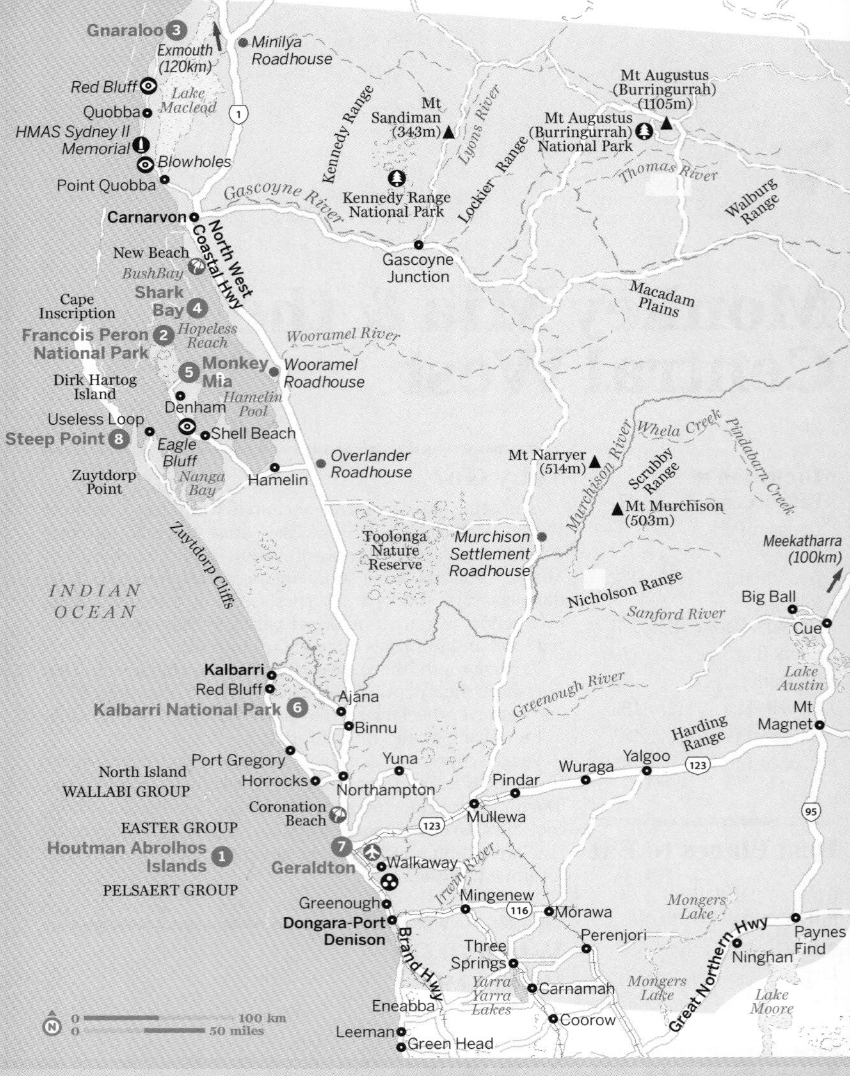

Monkey Mia & the Central West Highlights

1 **Houtman Abrolhos Islands** (p174) Diving on ancient shipwrecks or taking in the reef from the air.

2 **Francois Peron National Park** (p182) Exploring remote cliffs and beaches and spotting marine life.

3 **Gnaraloo** (p186) Surfing the wild Tombstones break or swimming at divine Gnaraloo Bay.

4 **Shark Bay** (p179) Spotting amazing stromatolites and walking on Shell Beach.

5 **Monkey Mia** (p182) Watching the wild dolphins feed on their morning visit.

6 **Kalbarri National Park** (p178) Taking in glorious viewpoints and canoeing or abseiling the deep gorges.

7 **Geraldton** (p172) Checking out the first-rate foreshore regeneration.

8 **Steep Point** (p179) Driving out to the Australian mainland's most westerly tip.

BATAVIA COAST

From tranquil Dongara-Port Denison to the remote, wind-scoured Zuytdorp Cliffs stretches a dramatic coastline steeped in history, littered with shipwrecks and rich in marine life. While the region proved the undoing of many early European sailors, today modern fleets make the most of a lucrative crayfish industry, and travellers hunt down empty beaches.

Dongara-Port Denison

08 / POP 2788

Pretty little Dongara and Port Denison, twin seaside towns some 360km from Perth, make an idyllic spot to break up a long drive. Surrounded by beautiful beaches and walking trails, the towns are divided by the Irwin River and have a laid-back atmosphere. Port Denison has good beaches and a marina filled with fishing boats, while Dongara's main street, shaded by enormous, century-old Moreton Bay fig trees, offers the best eating.

Sights & Activities

From the visitor centre, pick up the free *Thungara Trails* brochure outlining six walking trails that follow the river and/or coastline. A good place to start exploring is from the **Irwin River Estuary Nature Park** (Church St, Dongara).

There are several excellent beaches in town:

Granny's Beach (McIntyre Cove) Family-friendly, calm water, and great snorkelling in Nun's Pool at the north end.

South Beach (White Tops Dr, Port Denison) Long white-sand crescent, popular with kite- and windsurfers.

Northshore Beach (Brady Rd, Dongara) Surfers hit the waves here.

Seaspray Beach (Church St) Dune-backed, ideal for strolling.

★**Illegal Tender Rum Co** RUM
(0435 818 887; www.illegaltenderrumco.com; 35 Illyarrie Rd, Springfield; 11am-4pm Wed-Sun) This award-winning distillery crafts its 1808 Barely Legal and Spiced rums in small batches. Tours and tastings are on the hour, from 11am to 3pm.

Sleeping & Eating

★**Dongara Breeze Inn** GUESTHOUSE $
(08-9927 1332; www.breezeinn.com.au; 32 Waldeck St, Dongara; dm/s/d/tr $30/80/85/100;) The cheapest beds in town look onto a gorgeous leafy garden at this friendly, popular guesthouse, which has stylish doubles and triples (some windowless) with a chic Asian ambience, rustic dorms (in a vintage railway carriage) and free bike use for guests. All rooms share good kitchen and bathroom facilities, and the garden with its chill-out spaces holds great appeal.

Port Denison Holiday Units APARTMENT $$
(08-9927 1104; www.dongaraaccommodation.com.au; 14 Carnarvon St, Port Denison; r $130-140;) These spotless, spacious self-catering units are just a block from the marina. One- and two-bedroom options are available, with full kitchen plus an outdoor barbecue area in case you fancy throwing some steaks on the grill.

Seaspray Beach Cafe AUSTRALIAN $
(0405 400 496; 81 Church St, Dongara; mains $12-28; 7.30am-2pm;) Particularly popular for its imaginative breakfasts, Seaspray cooks up large portions of eggs Benedict with smoked salmon, scrambled eggs with spinach, and stacks of pancakes. Pair them with fresh juices or coffee while gazing out over Seaspray Beach.

Dongara Hotel Motel BISTRO $$
(08-9927 1023; www.dongarahotel.com.au; 12 Moreton Tce, Dongara; mains $22-44; 7am-10pm;) Locals love the Dongara's legendary servings of fresh seafood, steaks and 'Asian Corner' curries, mie goreng and pad thai. There's a shady outdoor terrace for drinks, plus live music ('Jammin with Charlie') on Sunday afternoons, and other live acts on Saturday nights.

The motel rooms (room/suite $145/290) are stylish and facilities are good.

Information

Dongara Visitor Centre (08-9927 1404; www.dongaraportdenison.com.au; 9 Waldeck St, Dongara; 8.30am-4.30pm Mon-Fri, 10am-1pm Sat) Plenty of information on the town and region.

Getting There & Away

Dongara-Port Denison is accessible via the Brand Hwy, Indian Ocean Dr or Midlands Rd (Rte 116).

Transwa (www.transwa.wa.gov.au) buses run daily to Perth ($60, 5¼ to 6½ hours, two daily) and Geraldton ($15, 50 minutes, two daily). **Integrity** (www.integritycoachlines.com.au) runs three times a week to Perth ($56, five hours) and Geraldton ($34, 1¼ hours), and to Exmouth ($172, 12¼ hours).

Geraldton

08 / POP 31,978

Capital of the midwest, sun-drenched 'Gero' is surrounded by excellent beaches offering myriad aquatic opportunities – swimming, snorkelling, surfing and, in particular, wind- and kitesurfing. While many travellers pass through briefly, heading for attractions further north, Geraldton is a town with a gritty maritime history and the gateway to the stunning Abrolhos Islands, and is worth a couple of days of your time. The fantastically revamped waterfront is a masterclass in creating fun public spaces, and Gero blends big-city sophistication with small-town friendliness, offering a strong arts culture and a thriving foodie scene.

Sights

★Western Australian Museum – Geraldton MUSEUM
(08-9431 8393; www.museum.wa.gov.au; 2 Museum Pl; by donation; 9.30am-3pm) At one of the state's best museums, intelligent multimedia displays relate the area's natural, cultural and Aboriginal history. The Shipwreck Gallery documents the tragic story of the *Batavia,* while 3D video footage reveals the sunken wrecks of HMAS *Sydney II* and the *Kormoran*. A highlights tour is run daily at 11.30am.

★HMAS Sydney II Memorial MONUMENT
(www.hmassydneymemorial.com.au; Gummer Ave) FREE Commanding the hill overlooking Geraldton is this moving, multifaceted memorial commemorating the 1941 loss of the *Sydney* and its 645 men after a skirmish with the German raider *Kormoran*. Note the Waiting Woman, the Pool of Remembrance and the cupola over the pillared Dome of Souls – the latter comprises 645 steel gulls, representing the lives lost. Free guided tours at 10.30am daily.

Foreshore WATERFRONT
(Foreshore Dr;) Geraldton's foreshore is a great example of waterfront redevelopment: loads of beach space and grassy spots, walking paths, picnic shelters, free barbecues, playgrounds (including a water-play park), cafes and event spaces. Check out the fun 'Rubik's cube' public toilets at the northern end, and the wonderful 'emu eggs' art sculpture from local Aboriginal artists.

Geraldton Regional Art Gallery (GRAG) GALLERY
(08-9956 6750; https://artgallery.cgg.wa.gov.au; 24 Chapman Rd; 10am-4pm Mon-Sat, from 1pm holidays) FREE With an excellent permanent collection, including paintings by Norman Lindsay and Elizabeth Durack, this petite gallery also presents provocative contemporary work and regular touring exhibitions by the best local and international artists.

Activities

Bike paths include the 10km-long coastal route from **Tarcoola Beach to Chapman River**. Grab the Local *Travelsmart* map from the visitor centre (p175). Bikes can be hired from **Revolutions** (08-9964 1399; www.revolutionsgeraldton.com.au; 268 Marine Tce; bike hire per half-/full day $25/30; 9am-5.30pm Mon-Fri, to 2pm Sat, 10am-2pm Sun).

KiteWest KITESURFING
(0449 021 784; www.kitewest.com.au; Coronation Beach; lessons per hr from $70; 9am-5pm) From October to May, KiteWest offers kitesurfing courses, surfing lessons, stand-up paddleboarding tuition and yoga. It can also arrange customised water-sports and 4WD camping tours. Lessons are held on various Gero beaches, depending on the weather.

Ultimate Watersports WATER SPORTS
(0427 645 362; www.ultimatewatersports.com.au; Foreshore; SUP hire per 30min/1hr $30/50; 9am-4pm) Based on the Foreshore from October to April, these guys rent stand-up paddleboards and kayaks and offer flyboard X ($150), wakeboarding, kneeboarding and pretty much any kind of water sport you can think of.

Midwest Surf School SURFING
(0419 988 756; www.surf2skool.com; lessons/board hire from $60/20) Year-round surfing lessons for absolute beginners and kids through to advanced surfers at Geraldton's back beaches. Stand-up paddleboarding lessons and rental also available.

Shine Aviation TOURS
(08-9923 3600; www.shineaviation.com.au; Geraldton Airport; 4/6hr Abrolhos tour $320/360)

Geraldton

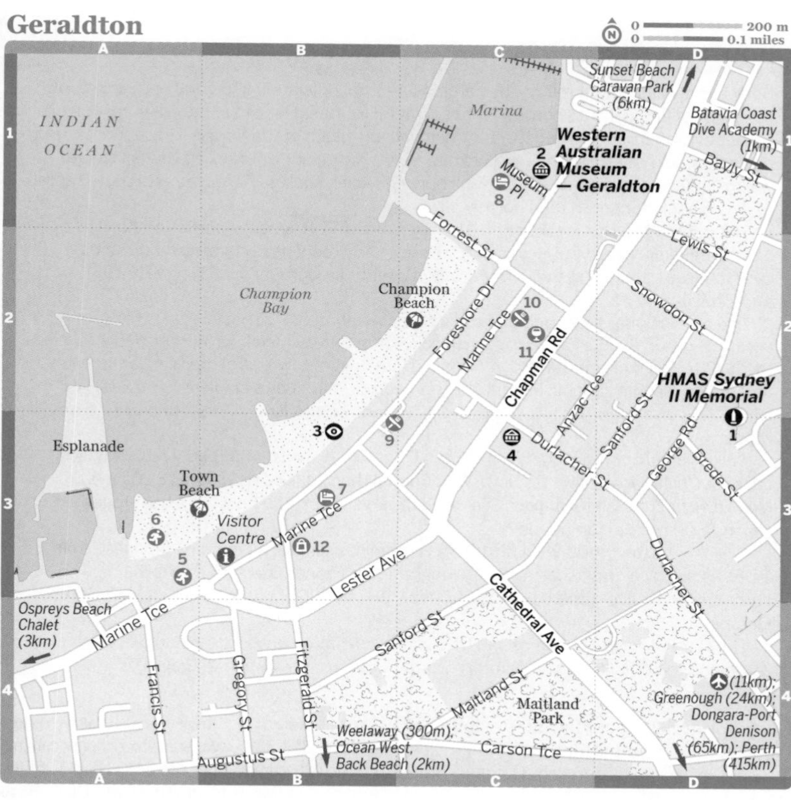

Geraldton

Top Sights
1 HMAS Sydney II Memorial D3
2 Western Australian Museum – Geraldton C1

Sights
3 Foreshore B3
4 Geraldton Regional Art Gallery (GRAG) C3

Activities, Courses & Tours
5 Revolutions A3
6 Ultimate Watersports A3

Sleeping
7 Geraldton Backpackers B3
8 Mantra Geraldton C1

Eating
9 Beached Barrel B3
10 Saltdish C2
Skeetas ..... (see 8)

Drinking & Nightlife
11 Cutler & Smith C2

Shopping
12 Yamaji Art B3

Offers excellent flightseeing tours, with the most popular option to land on the Abrolhos Islands and snorkel off the beach. There's also a cheaper flyover option (90 minutes, $290), and you can combine an Abrolhos visit with flyover of Kalbarri and Hutt Lagoon (aka Pink Lake; $495). Also offers half-hour scenic flights above Geraldton and surrounds ($110).

Festivals & Events

Sunshine Festival CULTURAL
(www.sunshinefestival.com.au; Oct) It started in 1959 as a tomato festival, but now

OFF THE BEATEN TRACK

HOUTMAN ABROLHOS ISLANDS

Better known as 'the Abrolhos', this archipelago of 122 islands and coral reefs 60km off the coast of Geraldton is home to amazing wildlife, including sea lions, green turtles, carpet pythons, ospreys and the Tammar wallaby. Much of the flora is rare, endemic and protected, and the surrounding reefs offer great diving and snorkelling thanks to the warm Leeuwin Current, which allows tropical species such as *Acropora* (staghorn) coral to flourish further south than normal.

The name Abrolhos is thought to derive from the Portuguese expression *Abre os olhos*, meaning 'keep your eyes open'. These gnarly reefs have claimed many ships over the years, including the ill-fated Dutch East India Company's *Batavia* (1629) and *Zeewijk* (1727).

Two airlines offer tours and day trips: Shine Aviation (p172) and **Geraldton Air Charter** (☎08-9923 3434; www.geraldtonaircharter.com.au; Geraldton Airport; 4/6hr Abrolhos tour $320/350) fly from Geraldton Airport, 11km east of town, and offer similar services and prices. Kalbarri Scenic Flights offers a two-hour flight and quick stop on East Wallabi ($275) or a five-hour tour including picnic and snorkelling ($299), departing from Kalbarri.

Divers should contact **Batavia Coast Dive Academy** (☎08-9921 4229; www.facebook.com/bataviacoastdive; 118 North West Coastal Hwy; 2-tank dive $200; ⏲8.30am-5pm Mon-Fri, 8am-2pm Sat, 10am-noon Sun) in Geraldton, which can help get a boat together (from $300 per person per day).

Eco Abrolhos (☎08-9964 5101; www.ecoabrolhos.com.au; 5-day cruise incl meals from $2161) is run by a crayfisherman with long-standing connections to the Abrolhos. The company offers live-aboard boat tours, departing from Geraldton between March and October.

The Geraldton visitor centre can help with information and tour bookings. Online, download the *Abrolhos Islands Information Guide* from www.fish.wa.gov.au.

Geraldton's celebrations include dragon-boat races, parades, sand sculptures and parties. It's held over a week in early October. Sunshine guaranteed.

Sleeping

★**Geraldton Backpackers** HOSTEL $
(☎08-9904 7342; www.geraldtonbackpackers.com.au; 172 Marine Tce; dm/s/d without bathroom $34/55/89; P ❄ @ ≋) This rambling central hostel is full of hidden nooks, sunny balconies and world-weary travellers. It's very close to beaches, bars and cafes, and is a good place to find a job, lift or travel buddy. It's well run too, with bright, fresh decor that's a cut above. Discounts for longer stays.

Weelaway B&B $
(☎08-9997 0356; www.weelaway.com.au; 104 Gregory St; r $88-125, 2-bedroom cottage $145; P ❄ ≋) Weelaway offers four sumptuously decorated rooms (three en suite) in a heritage-listed homestead dating from 1862. There are formal lounge rooms, shady verandahs and a well-stocked library, and it's all within walking distance of the town centre and a great beach for swimming.

Sunset Beach Holiday Park CARAVAN PARK $
(☎1800 353 389; www.sunsetbeachpark.com.au; 4 Bosley St; camping per site $41, cabins $96-186; P ❄ ≋) About 6km north of the CBD, Sunset Beach has roomy, shaded sites just a few steps from a lovely beach, and an ultramodern camp kitchen with a huge TV. Cabins range from basic with shared facilities to two-bedroom ocean chalets.

Mantra Geraldton APARTMENT $$
(☎08-9956 1300; www.mantra.com.au; 221 Foreshore Dr; apt from $219; P ❄ ≋ ≈) This is the pick of the upmarket options, for its marina-side location and proximity to museums, the foreshore and town centre. It offers modern apartments (one- to three-bedroom, all with balcony, kitchen and laundry), polished facilities and **Skeetas** (☎08-9964 1619; www.skeetas.com.au; 3/219 Foreshore Dr; mains $24-46; ⏲7am-9.30pm; ❄) restaurant downstairs.

Eating & Drinking

★**Beached Barrel** AUSTRALIAN $
(www.facebook.com/BeachedBarrel; 26 Foreshore Dr; doughie $6-19; ⏲7.30am-3pm Tue-Sun) Love doughnuts? Love burgers? This beachfront

shack combines the two in a genius move by using doughnuts instead of buns – from its lunchtime Angus Beef 'Cheesenut' to the Dirty Dawg, smothered in barbecue beans, sour cream and jalapeños. There are breakfast doughies as well as great coffee. Your arteries may not thank you, but your taste buds will.

★ Saltdish CAFE **$$**
(08-99646030; www.facebook.com/saltdishcafe; 35 Marine Tce; breakfast $8-25, lunch $22-30; 7am-4pm Mon-Fri, plus 6-11pm Fri & Sat;) The hippest cafe in town serves innovative, contemporary brekkies, light lunches and industrial-strength coffee, plus homebaked sweet treats. The menu is an ode to local produce and accomplished cooking, from Exmouth prawn and spring-pea risotto to tempura-fried Atlantic cod. Also open for dinner on Friday and Saturday nights. BYO wine or beer.

★ Burnt Barrel BARBECUE **$$$**
(08-9920 5552; www.burntbarrel.com; 305 Nanson-Howatharra Rd, Nanson; mains $28-40; 11am-4pm Fri-Sun, plus 6-9.30pm Sat (prior booking only); P) If you happen to be exploring Chapman Valley, north of Geraldton, you may be lured inside this self-proclaimed 'Outback brewBQ' by the wafting scents of pulled pork, smoked for hours on end, ribs, with the meat so tender it falls right off the bone, and the promise of ice-cold beers, brewed at the on-site microbrewery. Reservations essential.

Cutler & Smith CRAFT BEER
(08-9921 8925; www.cutlerandsmith.com.au; 41 Chapman Rd; 4pm-midnight Wed & Thu, from noon Fri & Sat, from 2pm Sun) Comfy booths, a smattering of local craft beers (including seasonal brews), a menu full of imaginative tapas (jalapeño and mozzarella arancini, pork belly with apple slaw, hot wings) and rock on the stereo make this industrial-themed joint a cool new addition to Geraldton's night scene.

Shopping

★ Yamaji Art ART
(08-9965 3440; www.yamajiart.com; 205 Marine Tce; 9am-4pm Mon-Fri) This Aboriginal-owned and -operated art gallery is a terrific place to learn about Wajarri, Noongar, Badimaya, Wilunyu and other regional art, ranging from traditional to abstract, and to purchase paintings, painted wooden emu eggs and other crafts by the 30 or so artists who are exhibited here.

Information

Visitor Centre (08-9956 6670; www.visitgeraldton.com.au; 246 Marine Tce; 9am-5pm Mon-Fri, to 1pm Sat & Sun) Helpful staff and plenty of info on the town and region. Can book Abrolhos Islands tours. Gift shop sells books on marine life and Aboriginal and military history.

Getting There & Away

Virgin Australia and Qantas both fly daily between Perth and Geraldton. Geraldton Airport is 12km east of the city centre.

Integrity (www.integritycoachlines.com.au) Runs three bus services per week linking Geraldton to Perth ($63, six hours), Carnarvon ($115, 6½ hours) and Exmouth ($156, 11½ hours).

Transwa (www.transwa.wa.gov.au) Runs buses between Perth and Geraldton ($68, six to 8½ hours).

Kalbarri

08 / POP 1351

Kalbarri is a sleepy seaside town surrounded by stunning nature – magnificent sandstone cliffs, the Murchison River and Gantheaume Bay – and there's great surfing, swimming, fishing, bushwalking, horse riding and canoeing both in town and in Kalbarri National Park (p178). To the north, the towering line of the limestone Zuytdorp Cliffs remains aloof, pristine and remote.

Sights

Just south of town are turn-offs to a string of beaches (all great for sunset watching), connected by the 8km **Melaleuca Cycle-Walk Trail**.

Blue Holes is the best place for snorkelling, while **Jakes Bay** draws surfers (Jakes Point is an elevated area for watching the surfers and any visiting dolphins). **Wittecarra Beach** draws fishing fans, and **Red Bluff Beach** is ideal for swimming. South of here is Red Bluff itself, the start of the southern section of Kalbarri National Park.

Rainbow Jungle BIRD SANCTUARY
(08-9937 1248; www.rainbowjunglekalbarri.com; Bridgeman Rd; adult/child/family $16/8/42; 9am-5pm Mon-Sat, to 4pm Sun;) Bird fans (and kids) will enjoy this bird park south of town – it's an Australian parrot breeding centre, and there are other feathered creatures

to admire (local lorikeets and cockatoos, but also South American macaws). It has a walk-through aviary, a lookout tower, a maze (adult/child/family $15/7/40) and a small cafe. Look for outdoor movie evenings at the park's Cinema Parrotiso (adult/child $18/10), held in the school holidays.

Pelican Feeding WATERFRONT
(Foreshore, off Grey St; 8.45-9.15am) FREE Kalbarri's most popular attraction takes place every morning on the waterfront. Look for the compact wooden viewing area and wait for the hungry birds to rock up.

Activities

Visitors arrive to see the **wildflowers** from mid-June into November. Look for wildflowers along Stiles Rd, the Ajana-Kalbarri Rd and near the airport. The visitor centre (p178) publishes wildflower updates in season and doles out up-to-date advice.

Kalbarri Wagoe Beach Quadbike Tours OUTDOORS
(08-9936 6060; www.kalbarriquad.com; 4043 George Grey Dr; driver/passenger from $90/45) Some 20km south of Kalbarri, offering exhilarating 2½-hour quad bike and dune buggy tours of Wagoe Beach and its dunes. You need a current driver's licence to drive.

Tours

Kalbarri Abseil CANYONING
(08-9937 1618; www.kalbarriabseil.com; adult/child $90/80) Abseil into the gorges of Kalbarri National Park, then take a dip in the river. After a morning pick-up you're driven to the Z-Bend Gorge – cliff walls range in height from 4m to 35m. A visit to Nature's Window rounds out the half-day tour. Kids need to be aged six to abseil, but all ages can join the tour (tag-alongs with no abseiling are $40).

Kalbarri Scenic Flights SCENIC FLIGHTS
(08-9937 1130; www.kalbarriaircharter.com.au; Kalbarri Airport, off Ajana-Kalbarri Rd; 5-hr Abrolhos Islands flight $299) Offers 20-minute scenic flights over the coastal cliffs, and a menu of longer flights over river gorges, the Zuytdorp Cliffs, Shark Bay and the Abrolhos Islands (including landing options at the latter two). The Pink Lake, River Gorges & Coastal Cliffs tour (1¾ hours, $299) is a spectacular combo.

Kalbarri Adventure Tours CANOEING
(08-9937 1677; www.kalbarritours.com.au; half-day canoe tour adult/child $85/60) Combine canoeing, bushwalking and swimming around the national park's Z-Bend/Loop area. Full- and half-day tours available. You can opt for more sedate half-day tours of the park highlights, and seasonal wildflower tours.

Sleeping

Pelican's Nest MOTEL $
(08-9937 1598; www.pelicansnestkalbarri.com.au; 45-47 Mortimer St; r/apt from $120/140; P ❄ 📶 🏊) In a quiet location a short walk from the beach, the Nest has a selection of neat motel-style rooms, plus apartments with kitchenette or full kitchen.

Kalbarri Backpackers YHA HOSTEL $
(08-9937 1430; www.kalbarribackpackers.com; cnr Woods & Mortimer Sts; dm/r $29/77; P ❄ @ 📶 🏊) The great location near the beach and the friendly hosts win brownie points; the facilities themselves are in real need of a spruce-up. Still, there's a pool, a barbecue and outdoor kitchen, and you can hire bikes ($20 per day), snorkels and boogie boards.

★ **Gecko Lodge** B&B $$
(08-9937 1900; www.geckolodgekalbarri.com.au; 9 Glass St; ste from $215; P ❄ 📶) If you're looking to romance your sweetie in Kalbarri, there's no better place than this intimate, luxurious B&B. The suites come with spa baths, the penthouse has its own balcony and kitchen, owners Paul and Lindley are treasure troves of local knowledge, and there are freshly baked muffins every morning.

Pelican Shore Villas APARTMENT $$
(08-9937 1708; www.pelicanshorevillas.com.au; cnr Grey & Kaiber Sts; villas $205-295; P ❄ 📶 🏊) Eighteen modern and stylish villas are dotted around a curvy pool, with the best view in town and lovely grounds. All units have full kitchen and laundry; choose from two- or three-bedroom options.

Eating

★ **Grace of Kalbarri** NORTH INDIAN $$
(0426 986 752; www.facebook.com/AuthenticIndianRestaurant; 4 Clotworthy St; mains $16-28; 11am-2pm & 5-9pm Wed-Mon; ❄ 🌱) A first-class Indian restaurant that would do any large city proud, Grace serves an excellent range of North Indian standards to please all palates, including savoury, moreish chana masala, super-fresh local fish in a punchy, fiery vindaloo or tangy Goan fish curry, and fragrant lamb biriyani.

Kalbarri

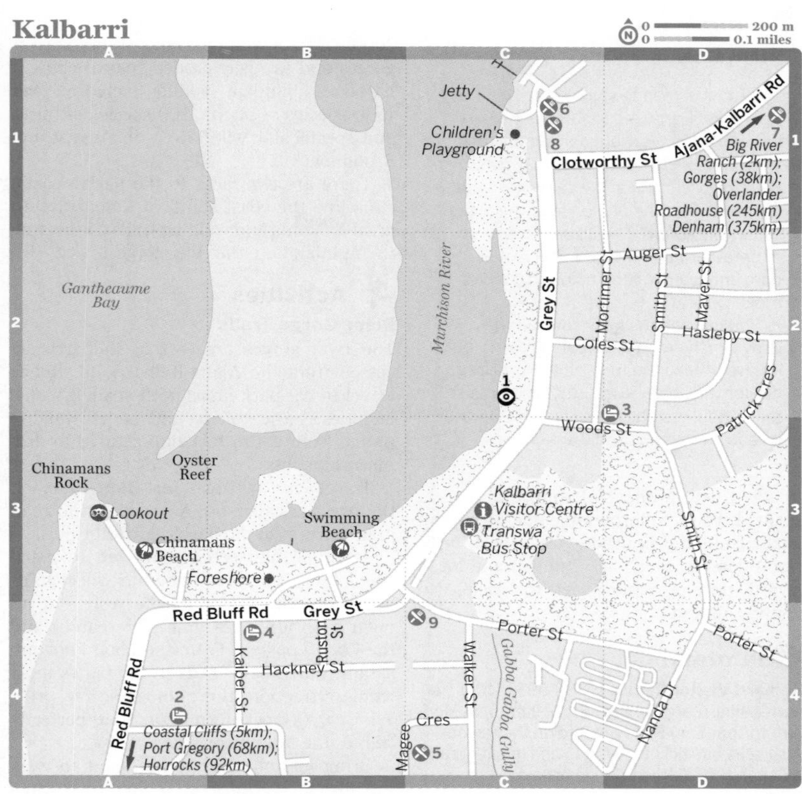

Portions are large, and service is efficient and friendly.

★**Finlay's Fresh Fish BBQ** SEAFOOD $$
(☎0438 708 429; www.facebook.com/finlays.bbq.palmresort; 24 Magee Cres; mains $15-45; ⊙5.30-10pm Tue-Sun) Fresh local seafood (chilli mussels, salt and pepper squid, catch of the day) comes simply but beautifully prepared at this super-quirky Kalbarri institution – a junkyard strewn with farming implements, buoys and shark sculptures. Wash it down with Finlay's own microbrews.

Gorges Café CAFE $$
(☎08-9937 1200; 166 Grey St; meals $10-30; ⊙7am-2pm Wed-Mon; ❄) Just opposite the jetty, Gorges has excellent breakfasts and lunches, and bright friendly service. Look forward to the best coffee in town, ace eggy breakfasts and delicious lunchtime dishes like fish cakes, Thai beef salad and club sandwiches.

Kalbarri

Sights
1 Pelican Feeding C2

Sleeping
2 Gecko Lodge A4
3 Kalbarri Backpackers YHA D2
4 Pelican Shore Villas B4
Pelican's Nest .... (see 3)

Eating
5 Finlay's Fresh Fish BBQ C4
6 Gorges Café C1
7 Grace of Kalbarri D1
8 Jetty Seafood Shack C1
9 Restaurant Upstairs C4

Restaurant Upstairs MODERN AUSTRALIAN $$$
(☎0408 001 084; www.facebook.com/Upstairs.Kalbarri; 2 Porter St; mains $33-42; ⊙11am-3pm & 5-10pm Thu-Mon; ❄) With its interior decked out with photos from the owners' global wanderings, the classiest dining spot

WORTH A TRIP

PINK LAKE

The most arresting sight in the Horrocks/Port Gregory area is Hutt Lagoon, which is more commonly referred to as **Pink Lake** (Hutt Lagoon; Port Gregory Rd). Yes, the saltwater here is pink, due to the presence of the algae *Dunaliella salina*. The algae is a source of beta-carotene, which is harvested here and used in food colouring and make-up.

You can see the lake from George Grey Dr (the road south of Kalbarri), but it pays to take the turn-off to Port Gregory for the best viewpoints. You can also take popular sightseeing flights over the lake from Kalbarri and Geraldton.

in town does wonderful things with local seafood. Exotic offerings include Moroccan goat tagine and bourbon-glazed pork belly. Good desserts (such as tiramisu) and local, award-winning wines seal the deal. No young children.

Information

Kalbarri Visitor Centre (☎08-9937 1104; www.kalbarri.org.au; Grey St; ⏰9am-5pm Mon-Sat, to 1pm Sun) Plenty of info on the region. Also sells bus tickets, fly nets and quality crafts by Aboriginal Warlukurlangu artists.

Getting There & Away

Getting to/from Perth ($85, 10 hours) and Geraldton ($30, two hours) by bus is easiest with **Transwa** (www.transwa.wa.gov.au; Grey St, Kalbarri Visitor Centre), which departs from the visitor centre on Tuesdays, Thursdays and Saturdays.

Heading to/from points further north, the only option is Integrity (www.integritycoachlines.com.au), which has three departures per week heading to Exmouth ($146, 10 hours) and on to Broome or Port Hedland. To link with these services, catch a shuttle ($45) linking Kalbarri with the Ajana-Kalbarri Rd turn-off. Shuttles should be pre-booked with Integrity or via Kalbarri Backpackers (p176).

Kalbarri National Park

☎08

With its magnificent river red gums and Tumblagooda sandstone, rugged **Kalbarri National Park** (www.parks.dpaw.wa.gov.au/park/kalbarri; admission per car $13) contains almost 2000 sq km of wild bushland, stunning river gorges and savagely eroded coastal cliffs. It harbours abundant wildlife, including over 1000 species of plants, 200 species of birds, and spectacular wildflowers in August and September.

There are two faces to the park: coastal cliffs line the coast south of Kalbarri, with great lookouts and walking trails connecting them; inland are the river gorges.

Activities

River Gorge Trails

The river gorges are east of Kalbarri, accessed from the Ajana-Kalbarri Rd. Roads travel to car-park areas with shaded picnic facilities, basic toilets and short walking paths (from 200m to 1.2km return) to dramatic lookouts.

Travel east of town for 11km to reach the first park turn-off. A sealed, 20km road grants access to the park's favourite sites.

At the T-intersection, turn left to reach **West Loop Lookout** (where a wheelchair-accessible Skywalk and cafe were due to open soon after the time of research) and the Loop Lookout. From the Loop Lookout, a 1km return path leads to the park's most iconic attraction, the photogenic **Nature's Window** (a rock formation that perfectly frames the Murchison River below).

Bring lots of water if you want to walk the unshaded **Loop Trail** (8km return, three to five hours) that continues from Nature's Window and descends into the gorge.

Turning right at the T-intersection leads to **Z-Bend** with a breathtaking viewpoint overlooking the bend in the Murchison River (1.2km return, one hour), or you can continue steeply down to the gorge bottom (2.6km return, two hours), scrambling on rocks and climbing ladders en route. The most demanding trail here is the Four Ways Trail (6km return, two to three hours), with a steep ascent up from the river.

Head back to Ajana-Kalbarri Rd and travel a further 24km east to reach the second set of sights. Turn off the road and you'll quickly reach the **Ross Graham Lookout**, with stunning gorge views and where you can access the river's edge (700m return). Nearby **Hawks Head** (200m return) has more great views – it's named after the shape of the rock structure seen from the lookout.

Coastal Cliff Trails

A string of lookouts dots the coast south of Kalbarri (accessed from George Grey Dr). Most lookouts are just a short walk from car-parking areas; Eagle Gorge, Red Bluff and Pot Alley have trails down to beaches below. From July to November, you may spot migrating whales.

For an invigorating walk, take the **Bigurda Trail** (8km one way), following the clifftops between Natural Bridge and Eagle Gorge; for a shorter walk, pick up the trail at Shellhouse Grandstand.

Pot Alley, Rainbow Valley, Mushroom Rock and Red Bluff are closer to town. **Red Bluff** is the closest part of the park to town, and is accessible via a walking trail from Kalbarri (5.5km one way). From the lookout there are wonderful views of the Zuytdorp Cliffs to the north, and sunsets here are stunning.

Information

For information, visit the Kalbarri visitor centre or the Department of Parks & Wildlife website (www.parks.dpaw.wa.gov.au). The Kalbarri tourist brochure (published annually) has excellent maps and details of all the walks. Take *lots* of water.

Getting There & Away

There is no public transport serving the park.

Without your own car, you could consider hiring a bike in Kalbarri to cover the coastal cliffs. To visit the river gorges, you could take a tour from Kalbarri.

SHARK BAY

The World Heritage–listed area of Shark Bay, stretching from Kalbarri to Carnarvon, consists of more than 1500km of dazzling coastline: turquoise lagoons, barren finger-like peninsulas, hidden bays, white-sand beaches, towering limestone cliffs and numerous islands. It's the westernmost part of the Australian mainland, and one of WA's most biologically rich habitats, with an array of plant and animal life found nowhere else on earth. Lush beds of seagrass and sheltered bays nourish dugongs, sea turtles, humpback whales, dolphins, stingrays, sharks and more.

On land, Shark Bay's biodiversity has benefited from Project Eden, an ambitious ecosystem-regeneration program that has sought to eradicate feral animals and reintroduce endemic species. Shark Bay is also home to the amazing stromatolites of Hamelin Pool.

Shark Bay Road

☎08

It can feel like a lengthy stretch driving the 130km-long Shark Bay Rd World Heritage Drive from the North West Coastal Hwy (at Overlander Roadhouse) to Denham. However, there are some excellent reasons to stop and break the journey.

Turn-offs lead to great natural attractions, including the 'living fossils' at Hamelin Pool and the stunning Shell Beach. With some preparation and a 4WD, you can also explore the Australian mainland's most westerly tip.

Sights

★Hamelin Pool MARINE RESERVE

(Hamelin Pool Rd) Twenty-nine kilometres along Shark Bay Rd from the Overlander Roadhouse is the turn-off for Hamelin Pool, a marine reserve with the world's best-known colony of stromatolites. These coral-like formations consist of cyanobacteria almost identical to organisms that existed 3.5 billion years ago; through their use of photosynthesis they are considered largely responsible for creating our current atmosphere, paving the way for more complex life.

★Eagle Bluff VIEWPOINT

(Eagle Bluff Rd) About 25km south of Denham, take the unsealed road 4km to this brilliant viewpoint, where a boardwalk allows you vistas that meld pinky-orange cliffs with the azure lagoon below. You may spot turtles, sharks or manta rays in the clear waters.

Shell Beach BEACH

(Denham Hamelin Rd) Some 55km past the Hamelin turn-off is the road to the wide sweep of Shell Beach, where tiny cockle shells, densely compacted over time, were once quarried as building material for places such as the Old Pearler Restaurant in Denham. The 1.5km Boolagoorda walking trail swings by the old quarry. The water is often warm, but very salty.

Steep Point LANDMARK

(Steep Point Track) The Australian mainland's most westerly point, accessed by 4WD only via Useless Loop Rd off Shark Bay Rd.

Sleeping

★Hamelin Outback Station Stay FARMSTAY $
(☎08-9948 5145; www.hamelinstationstay.com.au; off Denham Hamelin Rd; camping per adult/child $14/6, r $80-180; ⊙mid-Mar–Oct; P ❄) Far and away the nicest place to stay along Shark Bay Rd, Hamelin Station is a former pastoral property transformed into a 202,000-hectare conservation reserve by its owners, the NGO Bush Heritage Australia. The rooms in the converted shearers' quarters are lovely and the amenities (including the communal kitchen-dining area) are top-notch; the bush camping sites are all unpowered.

Getting There & Away

You'll need your own wheels to explore, although some tour companies visit Hamelin Pool from Denham.

There's a connecting shuttle from the Overlander Roadhouse to Denham/Monkey Mia to meet Integrity buses; it needs to be booked in advance through Shark Bay Coaches & Tours (p182).

Denham

☎08 / POP 696

Beautiful, laid-back Denham, with its aquamarine sea and palm-fringed beachfront, makes a great base for trips to the surrounding Shark Bay Marine Park, nearby Francois Peron and Dirk Hartog Island National Parks, and Monkey Mia, 26km away.

Australia's westernmost town originated as a pearling base, and the streets were once paved with pearl shell.

Sights

★Ocean Park AQUARIUM
(☎08-9948 1765; www.oceanpark.com.au; Shark Bay Rd; adult/child $25/18; ⊙9am-5pm; 👪) On a spectacular headland 8km south of Denham, this family-friendly attraction features an artificial lagoon where you can observe shark feedings, plus tanks filled with turtles, stingrays and fish (many of them being rehabilitated after rescue). It's all revealed on a funny and informative 60-minute guided tour.

The park also has a range of diving opportunities (including diving with the park's sharks), plus 4WD and boat tours. It also has an excellent restaurant.

★Little Lagoon LAGOON
(Little Lagoon Rd) Idyllic Little Lagoon, 4km from town, has picnic tables and barbecues along its small beach, and is good for a walk or swim.

Shark Bay World Heritage Discovery Centre MUSEUM
(☎08-9948 1590; www.sharkbayvisit.com; 53 Knight Tce; ⊙9am-5pm Mon-Fri,to 1pm Sat & Sun) Shark Bay's visitor centre has a gallery (free entry) that houses stunning aerial photos of the Shark Bay area, and a superb museum (adult/child $11/6) dedicated to the Unesco World Heritage Site of Shark Bay. Informative and evocative displays showcase Shark Bay's ecosystems, marine and animal life (including rare endemics), Aboriginal culture, early explorers, settlers and shipwrecks.

Tours

★Wula Gura Nyinda Eco Adventures OUTDOORS
(☎0429 708 847, 0432 029 436; www.wulagura.com.au; 2hr sunset tour adult/child $70/35) Learn how to let the Country talk to you on these excellent tours led by local Aboriginal guide Darren 'Capes' Capewell, including the secrets of bush survival and bush tucker. The campfire-at-sunset 'Didgeridoo Dreaming' tours are magical. There are also kayaking and stand-up paddleboarding tours (adult/child $199/145), plus exciting 4WD adventures into Francois Peron National Park ($199/140). Custom tours arranged.

Shark Bay Coastal Tours OUTDOORS
(☎0407 890 409; www.sharkbaycoastaltours.com.au; Post Office, Knight Tce; half-/full day $150/195) Recommended half- and full-day tours of Francois Peron National Park, full-day ventures to Steep Point and custom tours of Shark Bay.

Shark Bay 4WD OUTDOORS
(☎08-9948 1765; www.sharkbay4wd.com.au; 1 Ocean Park Rd; ⊙from $205) Day trips to Francois Peron National Park, Steep Point and Dirk Hartog Island.

Shark Bay Aviation SCENIC FLIGHTS
(☎08-9948 1773; www.sharkbayaviation.com; 2 Denham Rd; flights from adult/child $120/60) Flights from Shark Bay airport range from a 20-minute Francois Peron National Park flyover to a sensational 90-minute trip over Useless Loop, Steep Point and the Zuytdorp Cliffs (adult/child $345/160). There are also

tours available to Dirk Hartog Island, Coral Bay or Mt Augustus. Make bookings at the waterfront office.

Sleeping

Tradewinds APARTMENT $
(☎08-9948 1222; www.tradewindsdenham.com.au; Knight Tce; apt from $145; P ❄ 📶) Spacious, fully self-contained, modern, one- or two-bedroom units sit right across from the beach. Friendly owners, plus a nice outdoor dining area overlooking the sea.

★**On The Deck @ Shark Bay** B&B $$
(☎0409 481 957; www.onthedeckatsharkbay.com; 6 Oxenham Chase; r $169-186; ❄ 📶) Denham's most characterful accommodation is this luxurious B&B on the outskirts of town, overlooking scrubland and visited daily by local wildlife. Whether you're staying in one of the two individually decorated, spacious rooms upstairs, or in the garden-facing downstairs room, you have access to the heated spa, outdoor dining area, continental breakfast and helpful advice from owners Phil and Kerrie.

Denham Seaside Tourist Village CARAVAN PARK $$
(☎08-9948 1242; www.sharkbayfun.com; Knight Tce; unpowered/powered site $37/55, 1-/2-bedroom chalet $150/159; P ❄ 📶) This lovely, shady park on the water's edge is the best of the three parks in Denham, though you will need to borrow the drill for your tent pegs. Accommodation ranges from unpowered campsites to one- and two-bedroom en-suite chalets with shady decks, sleeping up to five/six people respectively. There's a handy supermarket across the road.

Oceanside Village APARTMENT $$
(☎08-9948 3003; www.oceanside.com.au; 117 Knight Tce; villa from $175; P ❄ 📶 🏊) This complex of smart self-catering cottages is perfectly located opposite the beach. Choose from one- or two-bedroom, beachfront or elevated. Kitchen and barbecuing facilities are top-notch.

Eating & Drinking

★**Oceans Restaurant** CAFE $$
(☎08-9948 1765; www.oceanpark.com.au; Ocean Park Rd; mains $14-34; ⏲9am-3pm) Overlooking aquamarine waters at Ocean Park, breakfast is served here until 11am, and you can partner craft beer and award-winning wines with the freshest seafood in Shark Bay (such as seared lemon pepper calamari and crispy-skinned barramundi). Romancing your other half? Look no further than the spectacular Ocean Park seafood platter ($60).

Old Pearler Restaurant SEAFOOD $$
(☎08-9948 1373; 71 Knight Tce; mains $26-50; ⏲from 5pm Mon-Sat; ❄) Built from shell bricks that account for the incredible acoustics, this atmospheric nautical haven serves decent seafood. There are no outdoor tables or view, but the hefty seafood platter ($100 for two people) features local snapper, whiting, crayfish, oysters, prawns and squid – some grilled, some battered and fried. BYO drinks; bookings recommended.

OFF THE BEATEN TRACK

DIRK HARTOG ISLAND NATIONAL PARK

WA's largest island is now a national park, with feral goats, sheep and cats removed, native plants replanted and endemics such as the boodie, banded hare-wallaby and rufous hare-wallaby being reintroduced. Home to the Malgana people for hundreds of years, the island is named after Dutch explorer Dirk Hartog, who landed here in 1616 – the first European to set foot in Western Australia. Hartog left a record of his landing inscribed on a pewter plate (now in Amsterdam's Rijksmuseum) nailed to a post at a site now known as Cape Inscription, in the island's far north.

There are three sleeping options here: camping at basic campsites, staying at the **Dirk Hartog Island Eco Lodge** (☎08-9948 1211; www.dirkhartogisland.com; 3 nights incl meals & transfers/with own 4WD per person $1338/996) or in a self-contained villa.

The best source of information is the website www.dirkhartogisland.com. See also the Parks & Wildlife Service's site, at http://parks.dpaw.wa.gov.au/park/dirk-hartog-island.

Shark Bay 4WD runs guided half- and full-day tours from Denham to Dirk Hartog Island using its own boat. Wula Gura Nyinda Eco Adventures can arrange custom-made, multiday tours of the island.

Shark Bay Hotel PUB

(☎08-9948 1203; www.sharkbayhotelwa.com.au; 43 Knight Tce; ⏰10am-late; 👪) Sunsets are dynamite from the front beer garden of Australia's most westerly pub, lovingly called 'the Oldie' by locals. It has a decent menu of pub classics (served noon to 2pm, and 6pm to 9pm), plus occasional live music.

Information

For information, interactive maps and downloadable permits, check out www.sharkbay.org.au. See also www.sharkbayvisit.com.au and www.experiencesharkbay.com.

Department of Parks & Wildlife (☎08-9948 2226; www.parks.dpaw.wa.gov.au; 61 Knight Tce; ⏰8.30am-4.30pm Mon-Fri) Park passes, drone permits and info about Edel Land, Dirk Hartog Island and Francois Peron National Park.

Shark Bay Visitor Centre (☎08-9948 1590; www.sharkbayvisit.com; 53 Knight Tce; ⏰9am-5pm Mon-Fri, to 1pm Sat & Sun) Books accommodation, tours and bush-camping permits for South Peron.

Getting There & Away

Tiny Shark Bay airport is located between Denham and Monkey Mia. Rex (www.rex.com.au) flies to/from Perth six times weekly.

The closest Integrity (www.integritycoachlines.com.au) buses get is the Overlander Roadhouse, 128km away on the North West Coastal Hwy. **Shark Bay Coaches** (☎0429 110 104; www.sharkbaycoaches.com.au; adult/child from $90/40) runs a connecting shuttle (book at least 24 hours ahead).

Monkey Mia

☎08

Watching the wild dolphins turning up for a feed each morning in the shallow waters of Monkey Mia, 26km northeast of Denham, is a highlight of most travellers' trips to the region.

There's not much to the place (Monkey Mia is little more than a beach and resort), but you don't need to rush off after the early feeding – the beach is lovely, the area is rich in Aboriginal history, and there are water sports and other activities.

Sights

★**Monkey Mia Marine Reserve** BAY

(adult/child/family $13/5/30; ⏰feeding at 7.45am; 👪) It's hard not to smile as Indo-Pacific bottlenose dolphins start arriving for a breakfast snack. Note that during feedings, visitors are restricted to the edge of the water, and only a lucky few people per session are selected to wade in and help feed the dolphins. The pier makes a good vantage point for it all. Rangers talk you through the history of the dolphin encounters.

The first feed is around 7.45am, though dolphins don't turn up like clockwork. They commonly come a second or third time until around noon (and the crowds are usually lighter for these later sessions). The dolphins may spend the day close to the beachfront, too.

You can volunteer to work full time with the dolphins for between four and 14 days – it's popular, so apply several months in advance and specify availability dates,

WORTH A TRIP

FRANCOIS PERON NATIONAL PARK

This 520-sq-km **national park** (http://parks.dpaw.wa.gov.au/park/francois-peron; admission per car $13) was named after the French naturalist and explorer who was the zoologist aboard Nicolas Baudin's 1801 and 1803 scientific expeditions to WA. Covering the whole peninsula north of Denham, it's a spectacular area of low scrub, salt lagoons and sandy dunes, home to the rare bilby, mallee fowl and woma python.

Two-wheel drive vehicles can travel only as far as the **Peron Heritage Precinct** (Peron Homestead Rd) FREE, which was a sheep station in the 1950s. The big attractions – **Cape Peron** with its red cliffs and dolphin population, **Skipjack Point Lookout** with rays and whales swimming below, and several gorgeous beaches, such as **Big Lagoon** and **Cattle Well** – are reachable only by high-clearance 4WD.

Five tour operators from Denham, including Shark Bay 4WD (p180) and **Naturetime Tours** (☎0427 385 178; www.naturetimetours.com; 3 Leeds Ct; half-/full-day Francois Peron $150/195), run full-day (around $200) tours of the national park. Some run half-day tours as well, but full-day ones are much more worthwhile.

though sometimes there are last-minute openings. Contact the **volunteer coordinator** (☎08-9948 1366; monkeymiavolunteers@westnet.com.au).

Tours

Wildsights ADVENTURE
(☎1800 241 481; www.monkeymiawildsights.com.au; 2½hr cruise adult/child $99/50) On the small *Shotover* catamaran you're close to the action for the 2½-hour wildlife cruise (recommended). There are also 1½-hour sunset cruises (adult/child $49/25, bring your own drinks and snacks), and a full-day 4WD trip to Francois Peron National Park (adult/child $215/140); discounts are available if you do both.

Aristocat 2 CRUISE
(☎1800 030 427; www.perfectnaturecruises.com.au; 2½hr cruise adult/child $99/49) After you've greeted the morning dolphins, step aboard this large catamaran for its 10.30am cruise around Shark Bay, where you might see dugongs, dolphins and loggerhead turtles. You'll also stop off at the Blue Lagoon Pearl Farm. Cheaper afternoon and sunset tours don't enter the dugong habitat.

Sleeping & Eating

Monkey Mia Dolphin Resort RESORT $
(☎1800 871 570; www.monkeymia.com.au; Monkey Mia Rd; unpowered/powered site $38/53, backpacker dm/r $34/145, r from $265; P ❄ ☎ ≋) With a stunning beachside location, the only accommodation option in Monkey Mia is a catch-all resort for campers, backpackers, package and top-end tourists. The backpacker rooms are good value (and have kitchen access), but the top-end rooms are expensive. It can also get quite crowded. The grounds are home to a restaurant, bar, two pools, shop and tour booking office.

Boughshed MODERN AUSTRALIAN $$
(☎08-9948 1171; www.facebook.com/boughshed; Monkey Mia Resort, Monkey Mia Rd; lunch $15-24, dinner mains $26-42; ⏲7am-8pm) The views are fabulous (and the visiting birdlife is prolific – just don't feed it!). Stylish Boughshed has plenty of areas in which to nurse a coffee or drink, and menus range from buffet/à la carte breakfast to light lunches and some creative dinner options, such as Shark Bay blue swimmer crab with linguini and twice-cooked pork belly. Reservations recommended.

Information

Monkey Mia Visitor Centre (☎08-9948 1366; Monkey Mia Rd; ⏲7am-3.30pm) Information about the area, tour bookings, plus art for sale by local Aboriginal artists. It's close to the dolphin feeding location.

Getting There & Away

There is no public transport to Monkey Mia from Denham. Hire a car in Denham, or use the transfer service ($60 return per person) operated by Shark Bay Coaches.

The resort can arrange transfers from Shark Bay airport ($15).

GASCOYNE COAST

This wild, rugged, largely unpopulated coastline stretches between two World Heritage–listed areas, Shark Bay and Ningaloo Reef, and offers excellent fishing and a killer wave that attracts surfers and kitesurfers from around the world.

Subtropical Carnarvon, the region's hub, is an important fruit- and vegetable-growing district, and farms are often looking for seasonal workers. Travellers see it as a handy place to restock before heading north from Carnarvon, either towards Shark Bay or along the stunning Quobba Coast.

Carnarvon

☎08 / POP 4429

On Yinggarda country at the mouth of the Gascoyne River, fertile Carnarvon, with its fruit and vegetable plantations and fishing industry, makes a decent stopover between Denham and Exmouth.

It's a friendly place without the tourist focus of other coastal towns, with a few quirky attractions, decent accommodation, well-stocked supermarkets and great local produce. The palm-fringed waterfront is a relaxing place to amble.

Carnarvon is also the last town of any size before you reach the turn-off for the gorgeous Quobba Coast.

Sights

You can walk or cycle 2.5km along the old tramway to the **Carnarvon Heritage Precinct** on Babbage Island, once the city's port, though its main attraction, One Mile Jetty, was closed indefinitely at research time.

★**Tombstones** SURFING

Boasting one of the longest, roundest tubes in the world, Tombstones is on most surfers' must-do lists. You have to be an expert, since it's a heavy, scary, left-hander reef break. Surfers come here mid-April to October; the rest of the time, conditions are best for hardcore kite- and windsurfers.

Sleeping

Quobba Station Homestead CAMPGROUND $
(08-9948 5098; www.quobba.com.au; off Gnaraloo Rd; unpowered/powered site per person $15/20, cottages & chalets per person $30-70) Ten kilometres north of the blowholes is Quobba Station, a huge, ocean-front pastoral property with plenty of rustic self-catering accommodation, campsites (including some generator-powered sites), a small shop and legendary fishing. The family-sized chalets are the pick for noncampers.

Quobba Station also owns the **Red Bluff Campground** (08-9948 5001; www.quobba.com.au; Red Bluff Rd; unpowered site/shack per person $15/30, eco-tent per person $80), which is some 60km north of the homestead.

★**Gnaraloo Station** CABIN $$
(08-9942 5927; www.gnaraloo.com; off Quobba-Gnaraloo Rd; camping per adult/child from $25/12.50, cabins $150-330;) At the end of the road, around 150km from Carnarvon, Gnaraloo Station is the jewel in the crown of the Gascoyne Coast. Surfers from around the world come from April to October to ride the notorious Tombstones, while hotter months bring wind- and kitesurfers trying to catch the Carnarvon Doctor, the strong afternoon sea breeze. Camp or stay at the homestead.

There are terrific campsites next to a gorgeous lagoon at **3-Mile Camp** (08-9942 5927; www.gnaraloo.com; camping per adult/child $25/12.50, r $90;), near Tombstones, or there's a range of options up at the **homestead** (5km further north of the 3-Mile turn-off) that range from the basic swaggers' camp and shearing shed to self-contained stone cabins (bathroom and kitchen) with uninterrupted ocean views – great for spotting migrating whales (between June and November) and sea eagles.

Don't leave without visiting the eye-burningly pristine Gnaraloo Bay, 7km from the homestead. Here and around 3-Mile Camp, there's excellent snorkelling close to shore.

Gnaraloo is dedicated to sustainability and has implemented a number of visionary environmental programs. The station is always looking for willing workers. Just be aware that this is a working station in the Australian outback, not a luxury resort.

Getting There & Away

From the turn-off on the North West Coastal Hwy (24km north of Carnarvon), it's 49km on a sealed road to reach the blowholes. Heading north from here, an unsealed, occasionally bumpy road takes you 75km to Gnaraloo Station, passing a couple of coastal sites and campgrounds en route. You'll need to retrace your steps to join the highway again (you can't travel north of Gnaraloo to Coral Bay).

Ask locally for advice about road conditions; the unsealed road is passable by 2WD, but there are several sandy stretches, so high clearance is a boon. The website www.gnaraloo.com/getting-here has useful info.

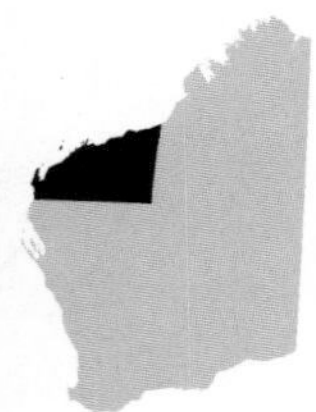

Ningaloo Coast & the Pilbara

Includes ➡

Coral Bay...........190
Exmouth............191
Ningaloo Marine Park.........197
Cape Range National Park 199
Karratha........... 200
Dampier........... 203
Port Hedland....... 203
Karijini National Park 205

Best Places to Eat

- Whalers Restaurant (p194)
- Karijini Eco Retreat Restaurant (p207)
- Esplanade Hotel (p204)
- Empire 6714 (p202)
- Fin's Cafe (p191)

Best Places to Stay

- Karijini Eco Retreat (p207)
- Mantarays Ningaloo Beach Resort (p194)
- Camping in Cape Range National Park (p199)
- Latitude20 The Dunes (p201)

Why Go?

Lapping languidly against Australia's second-largest reef, the shallow, turquoise waters of the Ningaloo Coast nurture a marine paradise. Lonely bays, deserted beaches and crystal-clear lagoons offer superb snorkelling and diving among myriad forms of sea life, including humpback whales, manta rays and loggerhead turtles. World Heritage–listed Ningaloo Reef is one of the very few places where you can swim with the gentle whale shark, as well as humpback whales. Development is low-key, towns few and far between, and seafood and sunsets legendary.

Inland, among the eroded ranges of the Pilbara, giant mining machinery delves into the depths of the earth, while ore trains snake down to a string of busy ports. Hidden away here are ancient Aboriginal rock-art sites and two beautiful national parks, home to spectacular gorges, remote peaks, tranquil pools and abundant wildlife.

When to Go

Exmouth

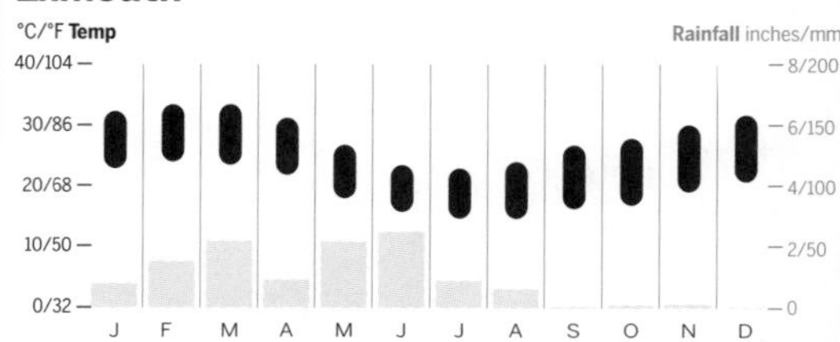

Apr–Jul Whale-shark season – don't miss the swim of a lifetime.

Aug–Oct Interact with humpback whales in Ningaloo Marine Park.

Nov–Mar Ningaloo is full of turtle love, eggs and hatchlings. Temps are very high, and cyclones are a risk.

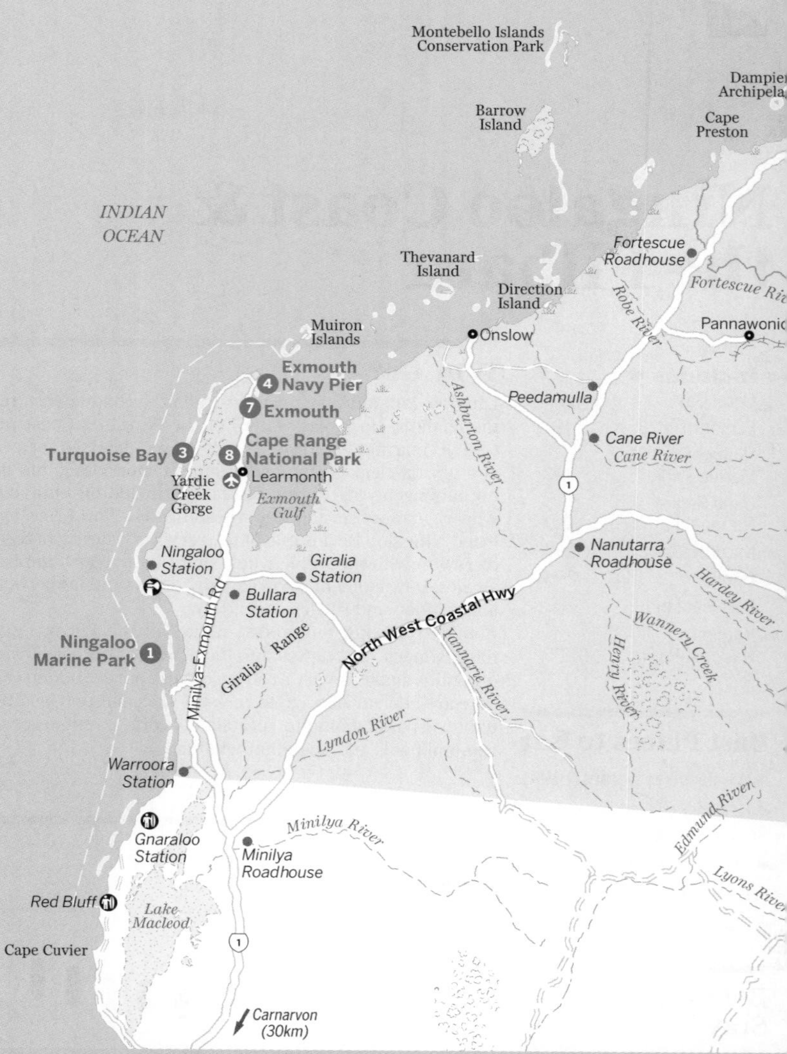

Ningaloo Coast & the Pilbara Highlights

1 Ningaloo Marine Park (p197) Swimming with whale sharks, manta rays, sea turtles or even humpbacks.

2 Karijini National Park (p205) Descending into the 'centre of the earth' on an adventure tour through the gorges.

3 Turquoise Bay (p198) Snorkelling over marine life at one of Ningaloo's finest bays.

4 Exmouth Navy Pier (p196) Scuba diving off Point Murat, one of the world's finest shore dives.

5 Millstream Chichester National Park (p208) Cooling

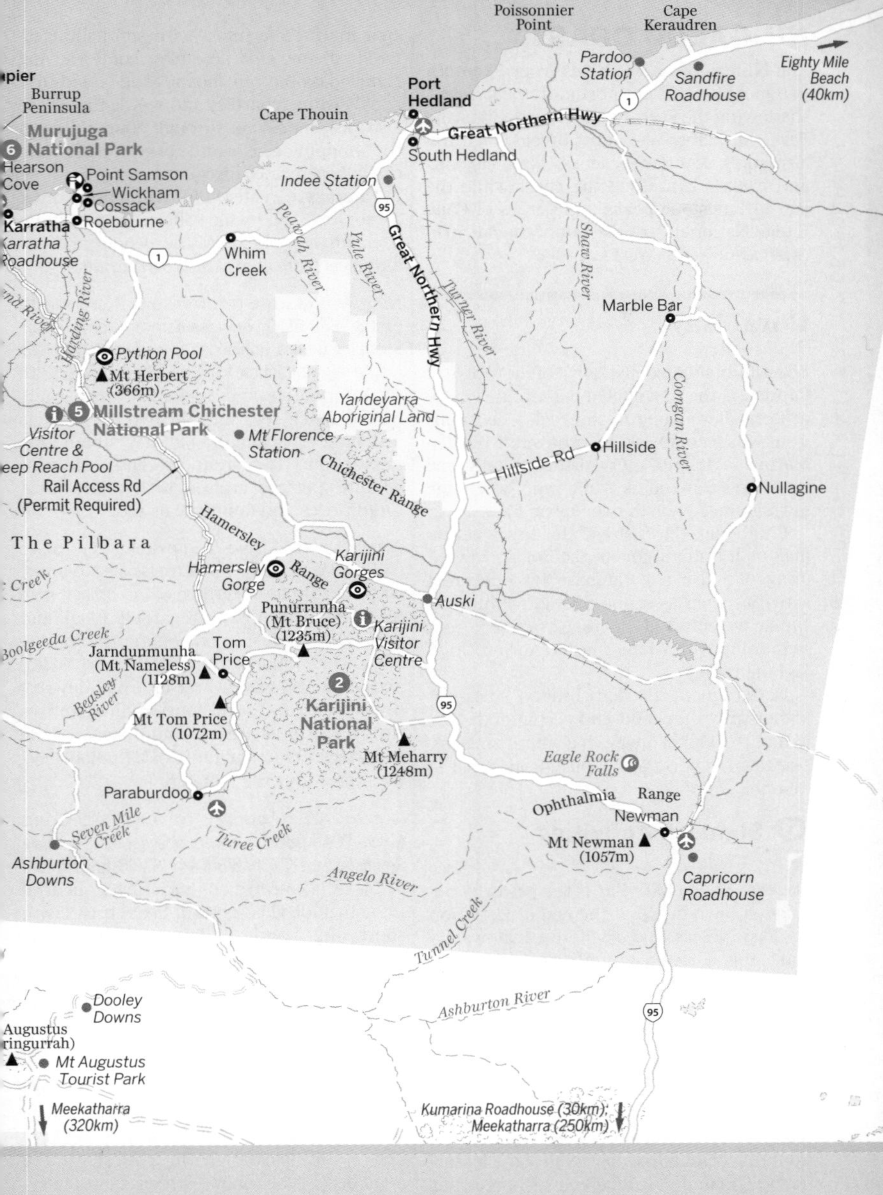

off in an idyllic waterhole after taking in spectacular views.

6 Murujuga National Park (p203) Being welcomed to Country and exploring ancient rock art on an Aboriginal cultural tour.

7 Exmouth (p191) Spending a few days indulging in good food and craft beer at this laid-back seaside town.

8 Cape Range National Park (p199) Spotting rock wallabies from a boat or bushwalking through arid gorges.

NINGALOO COAST

The Ningaloo coast extends from Exmouth to Quobba Station (north of Carnarvon), shadowing the spectacular Ningaloo Marine Park – arguably WA's most precious natural attraction. Remote beaches, bays, lagoons and islands run along the coast while the jagged limestone peaks and gorges of Cape Range National Park rise out of the flat, arid expanse of North West Cape.

Coral Bay

08 / POP 214

Beautifully situated just north of the Tropic of Capricorn, the tiny, chilled-out seaside village of Coral Bay is one of the easiest locations from which to access the exquisite Ningaloo Marine Park (p197). Consisting of only one street and a sweeping white-sand beach, the town is small enough to enjoy on foot.

Coral reefs lie just off the town beach, making it brilliant for snorkelling and swimming. It's also a great base for outer-reef activities such as scuba diving, fishing and whale watching (June to November), and swimming with whale sharks (April to July) and manta rays.

Development is strictly limited, so expect higher prices for food and accommodation. Exmouth, 152km away, has more options. The town is particularly busy from April to October.

Sights & Activities

★Bill's Bay BEACH

(Robinson St;) Bill's Bay is the perfectly positioned town beach at the end of Robinson St. Easy access and sheltered teal waters make this a favourite with everyone, from families to snorkellers. Keep to the southern end when snorkelling; the northern end (Skeleton Bay) is a breeding ground for reef sharks.

Purdy Point SNORKELLING

Walk 500m south from Bill's Bay along the coast until the 8km/h marker. Snorkelling from this point allows access to some fantastic coral bommies (submerged offshore reefs), and you can drift with the current back to the bay. Hire snorkel gear anywhere in town.

Tours

Popular tours from Coral Bay include snorkelling with whale sharks or manta rays (reduced price for observers), boat tours to spot marine life (most with snorkelling offered; diving also possible), coral viewing from glass-bottom boats, and quad-bike trips. Fishing charters and scenic flights are also possible. Book through tour offices at the shopping centre and caravan parks, and check for advance discounts.

Families are catered for with family rates. 'Observers' on whale-shark and humpback-whale tours are also welcome, and pay a reduced rate compared to swimmers.

Ningaloo Marine Interactions SNORKELLING

(08-9948 5190; www.mantaraycoralbay.com.au; Shopping Centre, Robinson St; whale watching $75, manta-ray interaction $170, wildlife spotting $210) Informative and sustainably run tours to the outer reef include two-hour whale watching (seasonal), half-day manta-ray interaction (year-round) and six-hour wildlife-spotting cruises with snorkelling. Child prices and family deals too.

Ningaloo Reef Dive & Snorkel DIVING

(08-9942 5824; www.ningalooreefdive.com; Shopping Centre, Robinson St; diving from $300) This highly regarded PADI and eco-certified dive crew offers snorkelling with whale sharks (March to July; $390) and manta rays (all year; $155), half-day reef dives ($180) and a full range of dive courses (from $300), as well as 'humpback whale in-water interaction' tours ($355). Book scenic flights over the reef here.

Coral Bay Ecotours SNORKELLING

(08-9942 5885; www.coralbayecotours.com.au; Robinson St; 1/2/3hr tours $41/57/78, full-day tour $175) Eco-certified and carbon-neutral tours include glass-bottom-boat cruises with snorkelling, and all-day wildlife-spotting trips complete with manta-ray interaction. In season, the company offers snorkelling with whale sharks ($395) and humpback-whale interaction ($365). The booking office is next to Fin's Cafe.

Ningaloo Kayak Adventures WATER SPORTS

(08-9948 5034; www.coralbay.org/kayak.htm; off Robinson St; day package $70; 8am-5pm Mon-Fri, 9am-3pm Sat) From a kiosk by the main beach, you can hire a glass-bottom kayak ($30 per hour), stand-up paddleboards (SUPs; $25 per hour), wetsuits and snorkelling gear ($15 per day). Kayaking tours with snorkelling are also available, plus one-hour guided snorkelling tours using underwater Sea-Doo scooters for propulsion ($70).

Coral Coast Tours OUTDOORS
(☎0427 180 568; www.coralcoasttours.com.au; Shopping Centre, Robinson St) A mixed bag of adventure trips: fun 4WD buggies for tours over dunes and along beach tracks (can be combined with snorkelling; tours $125 to $145); and snorkelling from the Aqua Rush RIB (rigid-inflatable 12-seater boat). The company also arranges airport transfers ($95) that continue on to Exmouth ($135).

Sleeping

Ningaloo Club Backpackers HOSTEL $
(☎08-9948 5100; www.ningalooclub.com; Robinson St; dm $29-34, r with/without bathroom $120/95; P❄📶🏊) Popular with the party crowd, this hostel is a great place to meet people, and boasts a central pool equipped for water volleyball, plus a well-equipped kitchen, an on-site bar and surprisingly swish en suite rooms. It also sells bus tickets (Integrity coaches stop outside) and discounted tours.

Bayview Coral Bay CARAVAN PARK $$
(☎08-9942 5932, reservations 08-9385 6655; www.coralbaywa.com; Robinson St; unpowered/powered sites $46/51, cabins $140, chalets & villas $190-350; P❄🏊) The town's biggest and busiest option, with camp sites and accommodation for all budgets, from unpowered sites and basic cabins (BYO linen) to two-bedroom villas and a four-bedroom house. On-site is a tour booking office and an all-day cafe-pizzeria.

Peoples Park CARAVAN PARK $$
(☎08-9942 5933; www.peoplesparkcoralbay.com; Robinson St; sites $44-54, cabins/villas from $232/258; P❄) This excellent caravan park offers grassy, shaded sites and a variety of self-contained cabins and villas. Friendly staff keep the amenities and camp kitchen spotless, and it's the only place with fresh-water showers. The hilltop villas have superb views.

Ningaloo Reef Resort HOTEL $$$
(☎08-9942 5934; www.ningalooreefresort.com.au; 1 Robinson St; r $280-450; P❄📶🏊) The cream-tile and blonde-wood decor of this resort probably won't make your social-media pics, but Coral Bay's plushest digs offer studios and various apartments (ocean views are pricier). The location is the winner: directly opposite the beach, in a slightly elevated position, making views from the outdoor areas a treat. There's a restaurant and bar here too.

Eating

★**Fin's Cafe** SEAFOOD $$
(☎08-9942 5900; www.facebook.com/finscafecb; Robinson St; mains $22-42; ⏲8am-9.30pm) Out the front of Peoples Park, Fin's is a super-casual outdoor place with an ever-changing blackboard menu giving pride of place to local seafood. Menus rove from breakfast eggs Benny to a lunchtime king snapper burger, and get interesting at dinner time: crispy soft-shell crab, chilli-scented calamari, and seafood fettuccine.

Bill's on the Ningaloo Reef MODERN AUSTRALIAN $$
(☎08-9948 5156; Robinson St; mains $18-40; ⏲noon-2.30pm & 5-9pm) The interior courtyard at Bill's is a fine spot to enjoy a menu of classic hits (burgers, fish tacos, catch of the day) prepared with flair. Try the fabulous fish curry, a selection of tapas or wash down a bucket of prawns with a boutique ale.

Information

A visitor centre was being constructed at the time of research; in the meantime, the tour operators can provide information.

Getting There & Away

The closest airport is at Learmonth (p195), 116km to the north, en route to Exmouth. Airport transfers ($95 per person) can be arranged with **Coral Coast Tours** (☎0427 180 568; www.coralcoasttours.com.au; Shopping Centre, Robinson St; adult/child $95/48). Groups should consider hiring a car.

Three times a week, **Integrity** (☎1800 226 339; www.integritycoachlines.com.au; Robinson St, outside Ningaloo Club) coaches run from Ningaloo Club to Perth ($203, 16 hours) and Exmouth ($47, 90 minutes); twice a week, services head north to Broome ($240, 18½ hours). There are weekly services to Tom Price ($162, 10½ hours) for Karijini National Park. The Flying Sandgroper (www.flyingsandgroper.com.au) offers tours that link with Integrity services and visit Ningaloo and Karijini.

Exmouth

☎08 / POP 2207

Wandering emus, palm trees laden with screeching cockatoos, and a laid-back air give Exmouth a real Australian charm. Year-round, visitors are drawn by the nearby Ningaloo Reef, with spikes in visitor numbers during the whale-shark season (from April

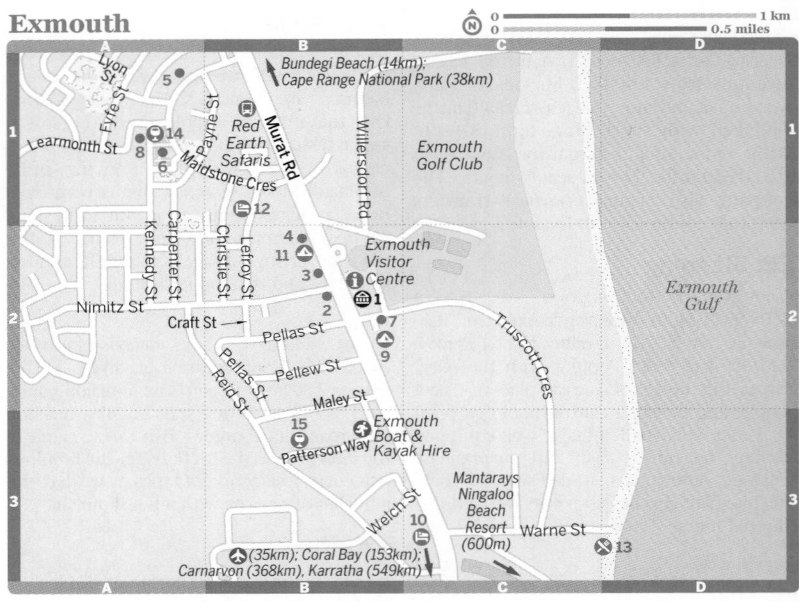

Exmouth

Sights
1 Ningaloo Interpretation Centre B2

Activities, Courses & Tours
2 Dive Ningaloo B2
3 Exmouth Adventure Co B2
4 Kings Ningaloo Reef Tours B2
5 Ningaloo Safari A1
6 Ningaloo Whaleshark-N-Dive A1
7 Ocean Eco Adventures B2
8 Three Islands Whale Shark Dive A1

Sleeping
9 Exmouth Cape Holiday Park B2
10 Exmouth Escape C3
11 Exmouth Ningaloo Caravan & Holiday Resort B2
12 Ningaloo Lodge B1

Eating
BBqFather .... (see 11)
Blue Lips .... (see 6)
13 Short Order Local D3
Social Society .... (see 6)
Whalers Restaurant .... (see 10)

Drinking & Nightlife
14 Froth Craft Brewery A1
15 Whalebone Brewing Company B3

to July) and humpback-whale season (August to October).

Whether you've come to swim with the leviathans, snorkel off the Ningaloo Reef or bushwalk in Cape Range National Park, Exmouth makes a terrific base.

Sights & Activities

Ningaloo Interpretation Centre MUSEUM
(08-9949 3000; www.ningaloocentre.com.au; Murat Rd; adult/child $19/14; 8.30am-5pm) Exmouth's showpiece houses the expanded visitor centre, plus three beautifully presented galleries. One covers the history of this young town that grew from an American air base in the 1960s. Reef to Range introduces you to the Ningaloo Reef and Cape Range fauna, while Cape Range explores the region's unique landscapes. The 55,000L Aquarium shows off 100 species of reef fish, while other displays regale you with tales of local shipwrecks.

Exmouth Boat & Kayak Hire BOATING
(0438 230 269; www.exmouthboathire.com; 7 Patterson Way; kayaks/tinnies per day $50/100) Tinnies (small dinghies) or something larger (including a skipper!) can be hired; you

can also hire kayaks, fishing gear, camping gear and 4WDs, or arrange highly regarded fishing charters. Prices drop dramatically in November and February.

 Tours

Swim with whale sharks or humpbacks, spot wildlife, dive, snorkel, kayak, surf and fish to your heart's content – the excellent visitor centre (p195) has the full list of tours available, along with all the details and availability, and can book everything. Some tours are seasonal. Note that some animal-welfare organisations counsel against swimming with dolphins and other wild marine animals.

★ Dive Ningaloo DIVING
(☎0456 702 437; www.diveningaloo.com.au; 6 Nimitz St; 2-tank dive from $200) A small, local company garnering a big reputation, Dive Ningaloo offers try dives, PADI courses, snorkelling trips (including with small Sea-Doo scooters), whale-watching cruises and great dive options. It's the only diving operator licensed to dive the world-class Navy Pier (p196) site and to do four-dive overnight trips to the Muiron Islands.

Ocean Eco Adventures SNORKELLING
(☎08-9949 1208; www.oceanecoadventures.com.au; Truscott Cres; whale-shark swim/observation from $379/219) A well-set-up operator with a luxurious vessel and its own wildlife-spotting microlight. The whale-shark swim months are followed by humpback interaction and whale-watching tours.

Three Islands Whale Shark Dive SNORKELLING
(☎1800 138 501; www.whalesharkdive.com; 1 Kennedy St; whale-shark swim adult/child $395/285; Mar-Oct) This well-respected, ecologically minded outfit consistently wins awards for its whale-shark tours, which run from mid-March to July. From August to October, it also offers humpback interaction tours (adult/13–17 years $325/295); under-13s may only observe from the boat.

Exmouth Adventure Co KAYAKING
(☎0477 685 123; www.exmouthadventureco.com.au; Exmouth Ningaloo Caravan & Holiday Resort, Murat Rd; full-day kayak, snorkel & SUP tour $250) This long-standing company has an expanding range of offerings, including multiday kayaking, snorkelling and hiking adventures (including to Karijini). Also surfing and stand-up paddleboarding lessons. Its original offerings are excellent: a half-day ($120) or full day ($230) kayaking and snorkelling in pristine Ningaloo waters.

Birds Eye View SCENIC FLIGHTS
(☎0427 996 833; www.birdseyeview.net.au; Hangar 28, Exmouth Aerodrome, Minilya-Exmouth Rd; 30/60/90min flight $199/329/439) Don't want to get your feet wet but still after adrenaline? Get some altitude on these incredible microlight flights over Ningaloo reef and (longer flights only) the Cape Range.

Kings Ningaloo Reef Tours SNORKELLING
(☎08-9949 1764; www.kingsningalooreeftours.com.au; Exmouth Ningaloo Caravan & Holiday Resort, Murat Rd; adult/2-16yr whale-shark swim $399/280) Long-time player Kings gets rave reviews for its whale-shark and humpback-whale interactions. It's renowned for staying out longer than everyone else, and has a 'next available tour' no-sighting policy.

Ningaloo Whaleshark-N-Dive DIVING
(☎1800 224 060; www.ningaloowhalesharkndive.com.au; Ross St Mall; whale-shark swim adult/child $399/299) As well as swimming with whale sharks and interaction with humpbacks (snorkelling/observer $369/195), this company arranges dives to Lighthouse Bay and the Muiron Islands.

Ningaloo Safari TOURS
(☎08-9949 1550; www.ningaloosafari.com; 11 Maidstone Cres; adult/child $240/190) This company shifts the focus away from the water to the terrain of Cape Range National Park, offering a full-day 4WD tour that includes canyons and gorges, a cruise at Yardie Creek and snorkelling at Turquoise Bay. Good for folks without their own transport.

Ningaloo Ecology Cruises BOATING
(☎1800 554 062; www.glassbottomboat.com.au; 1hr boat tour adult/child $50/25, half-day snorkelling adult/child $120/50;) Family-friendly operator with well-regarded one-hour glass-bottom-boat trips (April to October) and longer trips (all year) including snorkelling. It also offers a half- and full-day snorkelling option, and whale-watching cruises in season (adult/3–14 years $80/40).

Sleeping

Exmouth Cape Holiday Park CARAVAN PARK $
(☎1800 871 570; www.parksandresorts.rac.com.au/park/exmouth; 3 Truscott Cres; unpowered/powered sites $37/43, dm/d $33/110, cabins $120-250;) This large park offers good facilities for campers, backpackers (its

rooms are known as Blue Reef Backpackers) and families. Lots of cabin options too, from simple (some kitchen facilities, no bathroom) to deluxe family-sized units. Bike hire available.

Exmouth Ningaloo Caravan & Holiday Resort CARAVAN PARK $
(08-9949 2377; www.exmouthresort.com; Murat Rd; unpowered/powered sites $40/50, dm/d $40/84, chalets from $185;) Across from the visitor centre, this friendly, spacious park has grassy sites, self-contained chalets, backpacker dorms and doubles (shared bathrooms; known as Winston's Backpackers), an on-site restaurant and even a pet section.

Exmouth Escape APARTMENT $$
(08-9949 4800; www.exmouthescaperesort.com.au; 27 Murat Rd; apt from $199;) A collection of smart, self-contained villas that range in size (up to three bedrooms). They're set around a lovely central area with pool and garden, plus the excellent **Whalers Restaurant** (08-9949 2416; www.whalersrestaurant.com.au; mains $30-42; 5.30pm-late;). The resort also has car hire available, and package deals.

Ningaloo Lodge MOTEL $$
(08-9949 4949; www.ningaloolodge.com.au; Lefroy St; r $160;) One of the better deals in town. Motel-style rooms are compact but clean and well appointed, and the extras are great: a well-equipped communal kitchen and laundry, barbecue, shady pool and courtyard.

★ **Mantarays Ningaloo Beach Resort** RESORT $$$
(08-9949 0000; www.mantaraysningalooresort.com.au; Madaffari Dr; r/apt from $179/360;) At the marina, this resort is at the pointy end of sophistication (and expense) in Exmouth. The tastefully designed rooms are spacious and well equipped and all have balconies. They range from standard rooms to two-bedroom self-contained bungalows with ocean views. The grounds, pool, beach access and **restaurant** (lunch $17-30, dinner mains $28-43; 6.30am-late) are all top-notch.

Eating

★ **Social Society** VEGETARIAN $
(08-9949 2261; 2/5 Thew St; mains $11-21; 7am-3pm Mon-Fri, to 2pm Sat & Sun;) If you don't believe that breakfast is an exciting meal, this cafe will blow your misconceptions out of the water. Everything is vegan or vegetarian and made from organically sourced local ingredients – from poached eggs with green harissa and halloumi to banana pancake stacks. There's gourmet coffee and a shop stocking eco-conscious sunscreen and apparel designed by local artists.

★ **Short Order Local** FOOD TRUCK $
(0411 149 372; www.facebook.com/theshortorderlocal; Warne St, Town Beach; snacks $5-10; 6.30-11.30am Mon-Sat) Cute as a button, this pastel-striped food van is parked at the north end of Town Beach and rewards early risers with great coffee, toasties and fresh muffins. Tables and benches are scattered around the grassy patch next to it.

Blue Lips FISH & CHIPS $
(08-9940 1130; www.facebook.com/BlueLipsFishAndChips; Thew St; fish & chips from $19; 5-8.30pm Wed-Mon) A classic of the genre: burgers, souvlakis, milkshakes, and lots of battered or grilled fish options.

BBqFather ITALIAN $$
(Pinocchio's; 08-9949 4905; www.thebbqfather.com.au; Exmouth Ningaloo Caravan & Holiday Resort, Murat Rd; mains $21-37; 6-9pm Mon-Sat;) This popular, licensed al fresco *ristorante* serves up huge, succulent, smoky slabs of brisket and pork ribs. At the same time, the Italian owners remain true to their much-loved pizzas and homemade pastas that made them a hit originally. The servings are as legendary as ever. Locals still call it Pinocchio's. BYO wine.

Drinking & Nightlife

★ **Froth Craft Brewery** MICROBREWERY
(08-9949 1451; www.frothcraft.com; 5 Kennedy St; 11am to late;) Award-winning Froth wears many hats and we love them all. It's a cracking microbrewery where you can quench your post–Ningaloo Reef thirst with a pint of pale ale, IPA, amber ale or kölsch, grab a juicy burger, rock out to live music with a beer cocktail in hand or sip an excellent coffee.

Whalebone Brewing Company CRAFT BEER
(0498 554 406; www.whalebonebrewing.com.au; 27 Patterson Way; 4-10pm Thu-Sun;) Run by two local couples who wished to share their love of good beer with the world, this friendly microbrewery entices with its nine offerings, ranging from the hoppy Big Bone IPA

and German-style wheat beer to the malty amber ale and refreshing pale ale. Great pizza, plus a kids' play area.

Information

Exmouth Visitor Centre (08-9949 1176; www.visitningaloo.com.au; Ningaloo Centre, Murat Rd; 9am-5pm Apr-Oct, 9am-5pm Mon-Fri, to 1pm Sat & Sun Oct-Mar;) Tour bookings, bus tickets, accommodation service and parks information. It's a great first port of call, with boards and folders outlining all the tour options in the area, and friendly, helpful staff. You can hire snorkel gear here too, and purchase local Aboriginal art and stunning photos of Ningaloo.

Getting There & Away

Learmonth Airport (www.exmouth.wa.gov.au; Minilya-Exmouth Rd) is 36km south of town and has regular links with Perth courtesy of Qantas.

The **airport shuttle bus** (08-9949 4623; adult/child $40/25) must be prebooked; it costs adult/child $40/25 between Learmonth and Exmouth town.

On Tuesdays, Fridays and Sundays, Integrity (www.integrity.com.au) coaches run from the visitor centre to Perth ($240, 17½ hours) and Coral Bay ($47, 90 minutes); on Wednesdays and Fridays, services head north to Broome ($240, 16¾ hours). There are buses on Mondays to Tom Price ($146, eight hours) for Karijini National Park. The Flying Sandgroper (p207) offers tours that link with Integrity services and visit Ningaloo and Karijini.

Red Earth Safaris (1800 827 879; www.redearthsafaris.com.au; Murat Rd; $840) operates a weekly tour out of Perth, which reaches Exmouth over six days ($840, including dorm accommodation and most meals). On Sundays it departs Exmouth from the Potshot Hotel Resort at 7am, returning to Perth over two days ($200, 30 hours; price includes meals and an overnight stop).

Exmouth Region

08

North of Exmouth, the main road skirts the top of the **North West Cape** before turning and running south, passing glorious beaches until it reaches the entry to Cape Range National Park (p199).

Head north past Harold E Holt Naval Communication Station to an intersection before the VLF antenna array. Continue straight on for Bundegi Beach or turn left onto Yardie Creek Rd for the magnificent beaches and bays of the western cape and Ningaloo Reef.

STATION STAYS

Aside from the accommodation options in Exmouth, Coral Bay and en route to Cape Range National Park, there are some excellent station stays in the area offering a range of rustic accommodation – be it an exquisite slice of empty coast, dusty home paddock, basic shearers' digs or fully self-contained, air-conditioned cottages. Don't expect top-notch facilities; the more self-sufficient you are, the more enjoyable the stay.

Bullara Station (08-9942 5938; www.bullara-station.com.au; Burkett Rd; unpowered/powered sites $14/38, tw/d $110/140, cottages from $270; Apr-Oct;) A great, friendly, 2WD-accessible set-up 65km north of Coral Bay, and 6km east of the Minilya–Exmouth road junction. There are several rooms in the stylishly renovated shearers' quarters (shared kitchen and bathrooms), a couple of self-contained cottages, and camp sites with amenities (including laundry and open-air showers).

Ningaloo Station (08-9942 5936; www.ningaloostation.com.au; Minilya-Exmouth Rd; camping per person $5) The original station here offers five limited, totally self-sufficient wilderness camp sites on pristine coastline. Eco toilets are to be used by all campers (available for hire at the station). A bond of $100 per site is payable. Shearing-shed and other station accommodation available on request. Bookings required. The turn-off is 50km north of Coral Bay.

Warroora Station (08-9942 5920; www.warroora.com; Minilya-Exmouth Rd; camping per person $10, s/d $30/60, cottages $150-270) South of Coral Bay, Warroora offers 11 wilderness camp sites along the coast (14-Mile is 2WD accessible), twin-share rooms in the shearers' quarters, as well as a couple of large, self-contained homes. There are two access points off the main road – both OK for 2WD. Chemical toilets are compulsory for campers, and available for hire.

North West Cape

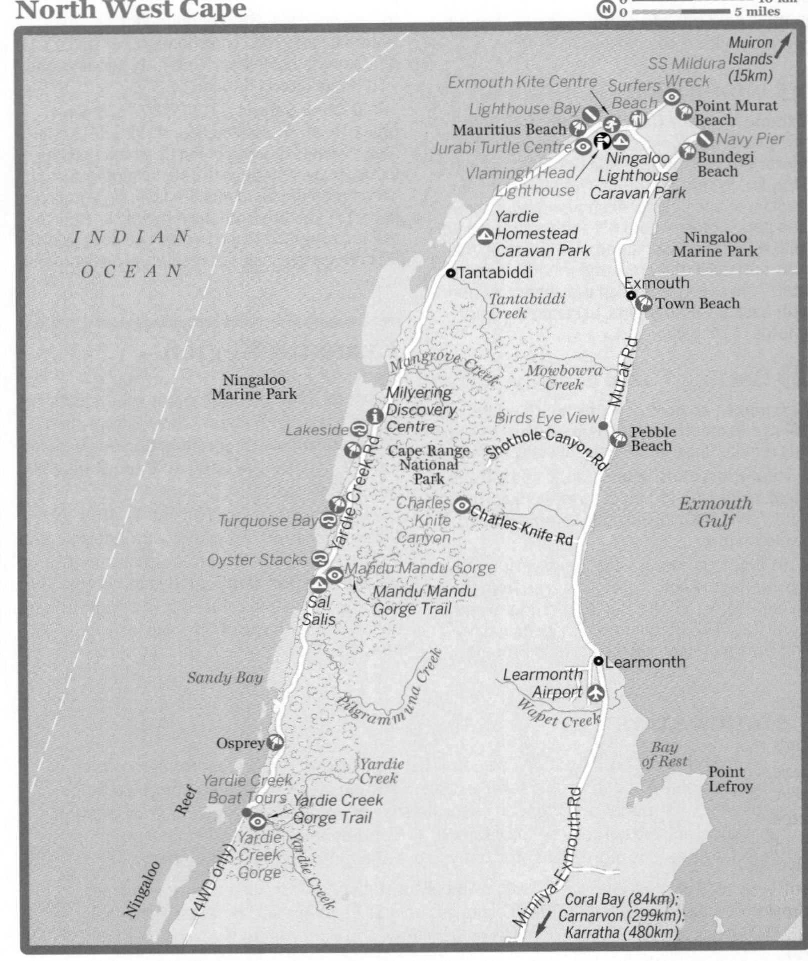

Sights

★Vlamingh Head Lighthouse LIGHTHOUSE
(Lighthouse Access Rd) It's hard to miss this hilltop lighthouse built in 1912. Spectacular views of the entire cape make it a great place for whale spotting and sunset watching.

Jurabi Turtle Centre VISITOR CENTRE
(JTC; www.ningalooturtles.org.au/jurabi.html; Yardie Creek Rd) FREE Visit this unstaffed interpretive centre by day to study turtle life cycles and obtain the Parks & Wildlife Service pamphlet *Marine Turtles in Ningaloo Marine Park*. Return at night to observe nesting turtles and hatchlings (December to March), remembering to keep the correct distance and to never shine a light directly at any animal. Guided evening **turtle-viewing tours** (adult/child $20/10; 6.30pm Mon, Wed & Fri Dec-Feb) are available.

Activities

The big swells arrive on the North West Cape between July and October and there are plenty of breaks. In the warmer months windsurfing and kiteboarding are popular.

★Exmouth Navy Pier DIVING
(0456 702 437; www.diveningaloo.com.au; Point Murat; 1-/2-tank dives $140/210) Point Murat,

named after Napoleon's brother-in-law, is home to one of the world's very best shore dives, under the Navy Pier. There's a fantastic array of marine life including nudibranchs, scorpion fish, moray eels and reef sharks. As it's on Defence territory, there are strict visitation rules and you'll need to join a tour operated by Dive Ningaloo (p193).

Exmouth Kite Centre KITESURFING
(☎0467 906 091; www.exmouthkitecentre.com.au; Yardie Creek Rd, Ningaloo Lighthouse Caravan Park; 1/3hr kitesurf lessons $100/290) Learn to kitesurf, surf or stand-up paddleboard (SUP) with this fun, expert crew based at the Ningaloo Lighthouse Caravan Park. You can take various lessons, SUP sunset tours or just rent the gear (surfboard/SUP $40/50 per day).

Sleeping & Eating

Yardie Homestead Caravan Park CARAVAN PARK $
(☎08-9949 1389; www.yardie.com.au; Yardie Creek Rd; unpowered/powered sites $35/40, cabins & chalets $160-190;) Located just outside the entrance to Cape Range National Park, this former sheep station has some nice grassy tent sites. There's a range of snug cabins plus a pool, tennis court, shop and camp kitchen. It's about 35km from Exmouth.

Ningaloo Lighthouse Caravan Park CARAVAN PARK $
(☎08-9949 1478; www.ningaloolighthouse.com; Yardie Creek Rd; unpowered/powered site $35/45, cabins $120, chalets $165-245;) Superbly located on the western cape, this park has lots of options: the clifftop, two-person chalets have fantastic views, there are plenty of shady tent sites, and a cafe opens during peak season (May to September). Sells fuel and some supplies. It's about 20km from Exmouth.

Bundegi Beach Shack CAFE $
(☎0450 887 902; www.facebook.com/beachshackexmouth; Learmonth Minilya Rd; mains $10-24; 7am-1pm & 5-8pm Thu-Sun) This beach shack with mismatched furniture is your post-diving/surfing pit stop for good coffee, ample brekkies, homemade burgers and buckets of Exmouth prawns.

Getting There & Away

The Cape Range National Park (p199) entrance station is 40km from Exmouth, and the road south is navigable by all vehicles as far as Yardie Creek (a further 50km from the entrance station).

Hire cars and boats in Exmouth.

Ningaloo Marine Park

☎08

You'll be hard-pressed to find words that do justice to the pristine, aquarium-like waters and pure sands of Ningaloo, Australia's largest fringing reef, which extends for over 300km of coastline. The fact that it abuts the arid, rugged Cape Range National Park for much of its length simply adds to the appeal, as do a couple of world-class beaches you'll find there.

World Heritage–listed Ningaloo Marine Park protects the full 300km length of Ningaloo Reef, from Bundegi on the eastern tip of the North West Cape to Red Bluff on Quobba Station far to the south. It's home to a staggering array of marine life – sharks, manta rays, humpback whales, turtles, dugongs, dolphins and more than 200 coral species and 500 fish species – and it's also easily accessible; in places it's only 100m offshore.

When to Go

Year-round marine awesomeness:

December to March Turtles – three endangered species nest and hatch in the dunes. Best seen outside Exmouth.

March and April Coral spawning – an amazing event occurring seven days after the full moon.

Mid-March to mid-August Whale sharks – the biggest fish on the planet arrive for the coral spawning. Tours out of Exmouth and Coral Bay.

May to November Manta rays – present year-round; their numbers increase dramatically over winter and spring. Snorkelling and diving tours that interact with manta rays (ie swim above them) leave from Exmouth and Coral Bay in winter, and from Coral Bay in summer.

June to November Humpback whales – breed in the warm tropics then head back south to feed in the Antarctic. Tours out of Exmouth and Coral Bay (whale watching, and also interaction tours).

September to February Reef sharks – large numbers of harmless blacktip reef sharks can be found inhabiting the shallow lagoons. Skeleton Bay near Coral Bay is a well-known nursery.

Sights

★Turquoise Bay BEACH

This perfect sweep of powdery-white sand, lapped at by cerulean waters, is considered one of the top beaches in Australia. If snorkelling at the reef near the shore, mind the posted warnings about rip currents.

The Bay Snorkel Area is suitable for all skill levels with myriad fish and corals just off the beach. The Drift Snorkel Area attracts stronger swimmers where the current carries you over coral bommies. Don't miss the exit point or you'll be carried out through the gap in the reef.

The Drift Snorkel Area is 300m south along the beach from the Drift car park; swim out for about 40m then float face down in the current. Get out before the sandy point where the current strengthens, then run back along the beach and start all over!

Activities

Most travellers visit Ningaloo Marine Park to snorkel. Always stop first at Milyering Discovery Centre (p200) for maps and information on the best spots and conditions. Check the tide chart and know your limits: currents can be dangerous, the area is remote, and there's no phone coverage or lifeguards. While not common, unseasonal conditions can bring dangerous 'smacks' of irukandji jellyfish. Milyering also rents and sells snorkelling equipment (as do many other places around Exmouth and Coral Bay).

Kayak moorings are installed at some of Ningaloo's best snorkelling sites. Tether your craft and snorkel at Bundegi, Tantabiddi and Osprey in the north, and Maud in the south (close to Coral Bay). Kayaks can be hired off the beach in Coral Bay or in Exmouth town, or you can join a tour from either destination.

Oyster Stacks SNORKELLING

(Yardie Creek Rd) These spectacular bommies (submerged offshore reefs) are just metres offshore, but they must be snorkelled at high tide to avoid damaging the reef, and reef booties are a boon since there are sharp rocks at the entry/exit point. The car park is 69km from Exmouth.

Lighthouse Bay DIVING

(Yardie Creek Rd) There's great scuba diving at Lighthouse Bay (at the northern tip of the cape) at sites such as the Labyrinth, Blizzard Reef and Helga's Tunnels. Check out the Parks & Wildlife Service book *Dive and Snorkel Sites in Western Australia* for other ideas. Dive operators in Exmouth can set you up and take you out.

Lakeside SNORKELLING

(Yardie Creek Rd) Lakeside snorkelling site is accessed from the road by Milyering Visitor Centre; it's 56km from Exmouth. Walk 500m south along the beach from the car park then snorkel out with the current before returning close to your original point. Recommended for experienced swimmers only.

Information

The Department of Parks & Wildlife (DPaW) produces an invaluable visitor guide, entitled *Ningaloo Coast World Heritage Area*. It's given out at the Cape Range National Park entrance station.

NINGALOO'S CORAL & WHALE SHARKS

Over 220 species of hard coral have been recorded in Ningaloo, ranging from bulbous brain corals found on bommies (submerged offshore reefs), to delicate branching staghorns and slow-growing massive coral. While less colourful than soft corals (which are normally found in deeper water on the outer reef), the hard corals have incredible formations. Spawning, where branches of hermaphroditic coral simultaneously eject eggs and sperm into the water, occurs after full and new moons between February and May, but the peak action is usually seven to 10 days after the March and April full moon.

It's this spawning that attracts the park's biggest drawcard, the solitary speckled whale shark *(Rhiniodon typus)*. Ningaloo is one of the few places in the world where these gentle giants arrive like clockwork each year to feed on plankton and small fish, making it an unmissable destination for marine biologists and visitors alike. The largest fish in the world, whale sharks can reach up to 18m long, and are believed to live for 70 to 100 years. Whale sharks encountered at Ningaloo are mostly between 3m and 12m (a 12m whale shark may weigh as much as 11 tonnes and have a mouth more than 1m wide).

Upload your amazing whale-shark pics to Wildbook for Whale Sharks (www.whaleshark.org), which will identify and track your whale shark.

The best visitor centres for Ningaloo are at Exmouth (p195) and Milyering (p200) – the latter is inside Cape Range National Park.

In the digital realm, see http://parks.dpaw.wa.gov.au/park/ningaloo, www.visitningaloo.com.au and the Marine Parks WA iPhone and iPad app.

Getting There & Away

Get yourself to either Exmouth or Coral Bay to make your way to the reef. Both towns have an assortment of tour operators that can get you diving, snorkelling, boating, fishing and kayaking the reef's waters.

From Exmouth, you'll probably need your own wheels to travel the western cape, and there are a few companies renting cars, campervans, scooters and boats. In Coral Bay, tours will get you out on the water.

Yardie Creek Boat Tours (p200) offers a bus service between Exmouth and Turquoise Bay ($40 per person return, including national-park entry) in peak season. Pick up in Exmouth is around 9am, and you return around 3pm, giving you four hours at the beach. Bookings are essential.

CAMPING IN CAPE RANGE NATIONAL PARK

The camping grounds (adult/child $13/2.20) are run by the Parks & Wildlife Service. All bookings must be done online, where you can also see the location and facilities of each camping ground: https://parkstay.dpaw.wa.gov.au.

The park's 12 camping grounds stretch from Neds Camp in the north to Yardie Creek in the south (note: there is no camping ground at Turquoise Bay).

Facilities and shade are minimal at the sandy grounds, though most have eco-toilets (no showers, no water) and some shelter from prevailing winds, plus possibly a picnic shelter. No campfires allowed; bring your own camp stove. There are no powered sites, though some camping grounds are for tents and campervans only. Most camping grounds have resident caretakers during peak season.

Cape Range National Park

08

It's the coastline of the rugged 506-sq-km Cape Range National Park (https://parks.dpaw.wa.gov.au/park/cape-range; admission per car $13) that gets most of the attention – after all, these are the spectacular beaches that give access to the pristine Ningaloo Marine Park (p197).

Still, the park's jagged limestone peaks and heavily incised gorges deserve acclaim – they offer relief from the otherwise flat, arid expanse of North West Cape, and are rich in wildlife, including the rare black-flanked rock wallaby, five types of bat and over 160 species of bird. Spectacular deep canyons cut dramatically into the range, before emptying out onto the wind-blown coastal dunes and turquoise waters of Ningaloo Reef.

Sights & Activities

Charles Knife Canyon GORGE

(Charles Knife Rd) On the east coast, a very scenic, partially sealed and at times dramatically narrow 11km-long road ascends a knife-edge ridge via rickety corners. A rough track (passable by 2WD) continues to **Thomas Carter lookout** (at 311m, with great views). From near the lookout, in the cooler months you can walk the 6.8km **Badjirrajirra Trail**. The signposted canyon road is 22km south of Exmouth (not suitable for caravans).

Yardie Creek Gorge GORGE

(Yardie Creek Rd) Two walking trails give access to excellent views above this water-filled gorge: the gentle **Nature Walk** is 1.2km return, or the longer, steeper trail is 2km return and takes you high above the creek. There's also the option of a more relaxing boat tour (p200). Yardie Creek is 50km from the park entry (and accessible to all vehicles).

Mandu Mandu Gorge GORGE

(Yardie Creek Rd) There's a small car park off the main road 14km south of the Milyering Discovery Centre, and from here there's a pleasant, occasionally steep 3km return walk onto the picturesque gorge rim.

Badjirrajirra Trail HIKING

(Yardie Creek Rd) This scenic 6.8km loop trail (two to three hours) starts from the car park and meanders gently through spinifex and in and out of several steep rocky gullies. There's very little shade and you *must* bring plenty of water. Don't want to do the whole loop? Do a hike to the Shothole Viewpoint (around 4km return) – the trail's scenic highlight.

Shothole Canyon Road SCENIC DRIVE

(Shothole Canyon Rd) Some 14km south of Exmouth, this 12km-long unsealed road runs deep into the heart of the eponymous canyon, meandering along a dry creek bed and passing some colourful, dramatic rock formations before reaching a picnic area and a short trail. Officially this road is 4WD only, but it's suitable for 2WDs with decent clearance during the dry months.

Yardie Creek Boat Tours BOATING

(08-9949 2920; www.yardiecreekboattours.com.au; Yardie Creek Rd; adult/child/family $40/20/90; 11am & 12.30pm on scheduled days) A relaxing one-hour cruise up the short, sheer Yardie Creek Gorge, where you're likely to spot rare black-flanked rock wallabies. It's worth checking operating days – with the company, or with Exmouth visitor centre (p195) – as these vary with season. There are no cruises from early January to late March.

Sleeping

Sal Salis TENTED CAMP **$$$**

(08-9949 1776; www.salsalis.com; off Yardie Creek Rd, South Mandu; per person per night $900-1125; mid-Mar–Oct) Want to watch that crimson Indian Ocean sunset from between 500-threadcount sheets? Pass the chablis! For those who want their camp without the cramp, this exclusive tented camp has a minimum two-night stay, 16 en-suite, fan-cooled tents, three gourmet meals a day, a free bar (!) and the same things to do as the folks staying nearby in the pop-up camper.

Information

Check out the handy visitor guide, *Ningaloo Coast World Heritage Area*. You can pick it up at the Cape Range National Park entrance station.

Milyering Discovery Centre (08-9949 2808; Yardie Creek Rd; 9am-3.45pm;) Serving both Ningaloo Marine Park and Cape Range National Park, this visitor centre has informative natural and cultural displays, maps, tide charts, camping ground photos and iPads for making camping reservations. Check here for road and water conditions. It rents out snorkelling gear (day/overnight $10/15), and sells drinks, ice cream and books on wildlife and history.

Getting There & Away

The Cape Range National Park entrance station is 40km from Exmouth, and the road south is sealed as far as Yardie Creek (91km from Exmouth). Off the main road are short access roads to beaches, camping grounds and day-use sites. The park is full of wildlife – try to avoid driving between dusk and dawn.

Exmouth also has an abundance of tour operators, plus several car- and campervan-rental companies.

THE PILBARA

Karratha and Port Hedland are the Pilbara coast's mining hubs – relatively large towns with good transport connections and a decent range of services.

Karratha in particular is full of pleasant surprises – an excellent dining scene, proximity to one of Australia's wealthiest collections of rock art, and a state-of-the-art cultural centre. Port Hedland has its own gritty outback appeal, particularly if you're interested in mining, huge cargo ships and railways. The region's ghost towns and Roebourne's terrific Aboriginal art gallery are additional draws.

Karratha

08 / POP 22,205

In the past, most travellers to Karratha ran their errands – banking, restocking, repairing stuff etc – and then got out of town before their wallet ignited. That did the town a small disservice. It's the primary base for mining and industry in the region, and it certainly has a few things worth sticking around to investigate, from excellent Aboriginal tours and ancient rock art to cafes that wouldn't look out of place in the coolest parts of Perth.

Sights & Activities

Miaree Pool LAKE

(North West Coastal Hwy) Yeah, it gets hot up here. You might have noticed. Cool off at this shady waterhole, popular with locals for picnicking and swimming. It's 30km southwest of the Karratha turn-off, on the North West Coastal Hwy (Hwy 1).

Warlu Way SCENIC DRIVE

(www.warluway.com.au; Warlu Rd) Dotted with interpretive signage, this 2500km scenic drive follows the path of the warlu, the Dreaming serpent who travelled through the Pilbara, creating waterways as he went along.

Follow it through Karratha, the Burrup Peninsula, Roebourne, Cossack and Point Samson before cutting across Karijini and

WORTH A TRIP

ROEBOURNE, COSSACK & POINT SAMPSON

Sitting on Ngarluma country, 40km east of Karratha, Roebourne (population 630) is the oldest (1866) Pilbara town still functioning. The town's **heritage trail** includes some beautiful historic buildings along the main street. Drive or hike up **Mt Welcome** (Fisher Dr) to the lookout point for the lofty views. There's also a thriving Aboriginal art scene here (www.roebourneart.com.au); the Aboriginal-run **Yinjaa-Barndi Gallery** (☎08-9182 1959; www.yinjaa-barni.com.au; Lot 3 Roe St; ⊙9am-2pm Mon-Fri or by appointment) showcases gifted Millstream artists.

Fourteen kilometres from Roebourne at the mouth of the Harding River, the scenic ghost town of Cossack was previously the district's main port, driven by the pearling industry, but was eclipsed by Point Samson and then eventually abandoned by 1950. The **Cossack Heritage Trail** is an informative (and shadeless) 5km trail linking historic sites: grab a brochure from local visitor centres.

Point Samson (population 212) is a small, industry-free seaside village 20km north of Roebourne. It's home to good seafood and clean beaches, making it one of the nicest places to stay in the area. It buzzes with 4WDs, boats and fishing fans, as it's a popular R & R spot for Pilbara workers. You'll find good swimming off **Samson Beach** (Miller Cl), plus decent snorkelling off Point Samson and the picturesque curved beach of Honeymoon Cove. Finish your explorations with a cold one at **Samson Beach Bistro & Tavern** (☎08-9187 1503; www.samsonbeach.com.au; Bartley Ct; mains $17-46; ⊙11am-2pm & 5.30-8pm).

Millstream-Chichester national parks, and on to Port Hedland, Eighty Mile Beach and Broome.

Yaburara Heritage Trail WALKING
(off Karratha Rd) The heritage trail consists of three main trail loops (2.25km to 3.75km in length), as well as a two further trails, and can be accessed either from behind the visitor centre or a car park off Dampier Hwy. Sites include Yaburara rock art, stone quarries and shell middens, plus excellent lookout points. Bring plenty of water and start your walks early.

Tours

★**Ngurrangga Tours** CULTURAL
(☎08-9182 1777; www.ngurrangga.com.au; 42 Roe St, Roeborne; half-day rock-art tour adult/child $160/80; ⊙Feb-Nov) Clinton Walker, a Ngarluma man, runs cultural tours that merit rave reviews. His half-day Murujuga National Park tour explores rock-art petroglyphs on the Burrup Peninsula near Dampier, while longer day tours explore the culturally significant areas of Millstream Chichester National Park (adult/child $300/150). Three-day Millstream camping tours are also available ($1450/500).

Helispirit SCENIC FLIGHTS
(☎08-9168 1101; www.helispirit.com.au; Bayly Ave, Karratha Airport; tours per person $195-495) If you have a large budget, splash out on a scenic helicopter flight over the Burrup Peninsula (30 minutes, $325 per person) or the Dampier Archipelago (45 minutes, $495 per person). Packages are available that combine scenic flights with rock-art tours run by Ngurrangga Tours.

Festivals & Events

Red Earth Arts Festival CULTURAL
(www.reaf.com.au; ⊙Sep) Over 10 days in mid-September, Karratha and the surrounding coastal Pilbara towns come alive for this festival, an eclectic mix of live music (all genres), theatre, comedy, visual arts and storytelling.

Sleeping

★**Latitude20 The Dunes** APARTMENT $
(☎1300 528 488; www.latitude20apartments.com.au; 2 Walcott Way; apt $110; P ❄ ☜ ≋) Spacious, spotless and equipped with a full kitchen, these fantastic studio apartments are clustered around a pool with an appealing barbecue area. They're a 3km drive from central Karratha, right by the coastal mangroves.

Discovery Parks – Pilbara, Karratha CARAVAN PARK $
(☎08-9185 1855; www.discoveryholidayparks.com.au; 70 Rosemary Rd; camping per site $29-49, motel r/studio from $88/129; P ❄ ☜ ≋) Neat and well run with good facilities, this park has all manner of options for all budgets, from sites

OFF THE BEATEN TRACK

MARBLE BAR

A long way off everybody's beaten track, Marble Bar (population 174) has burnt itself into the Australian psyche as the country's hottest town when, back in summer of 1923–24, the mercury reached 37.8°C (100°F) for 160 consecutive days. A service centre for nearby mines and full of quirky local characters, the town was (mistakenly) named after a bar of jasper beside a pool on the Coongan River, 5km southwest of the town centre.

Aside from poring over the minerals at the **Comet Gold Mine Museum** (08-9176 1015; Comet Mine Rd; $3; 9am-4pm), admiring the jasper at the **Marble Bar Pool** (Marble Bar Pool Rd) and checking out lofty views from the **Water Tank Lookout** (Water Tank Lookout Rd), there's not a great deal to do in town other than to prop yourself up at the bar and have a yarn with Foxy at the **Iron Clad Hotel** (08-9176 1066; 15 Francis St; noon-close).

The first weekend in July, the population of Marble Bar swells by around 3000 visitors for a weekend of drinking, gambling, fashion crime, country music, nudie runs and horse racing known as the **Marble Bar Cup** (www.marblebarraces.com; early Jul). The caravan park overflows and the Iron Clad is besieged as punters from far and wide come for a bit of an outback knees-up.

Marble Bar is 200km from Port Hedland via Rte 138 (a sealed road). The **East Pilbara Shire Office** (08-9176 1008; Francis St) runs a bus from Port Hedland to Marble Bar a couple of times a week in either direction. See www.eastpilbara.wa.gov.au for details.

with en suite to family-sized units and cabins. It's tucked away off the Dampier Hwy.

Ranges APARTMENT $$
(1300 639 320; www.therangeskarratha.com.au; De Witt Rd; apt $180;) This swanky complex of deluxe self-contained apartments offers a surprising level of sophistication, with king-sized beds and smart kitchen appliances. Outside are manicured grounds and a big pool and barbecue area. Service is first-rate. It's about 1km south of the visitor centre, on the road into town.

Eating

Lo's Cafe Fusion Bistro CAFE $
(0438 186 688; www.facebook.com/losbistro; 20 Sharpe Ave, The Quarter; mains $18-24; 7.30am-5pm;) This bright and breezy cafe mixes local ingredients with Asian influences to create its signature sweet-potato waffle with fried chicken, poached eggs with pork belly, banana pancakes and more. All-day breakfasts aside, there are also rice burgers and wraps with teriyaki fillings and great coffee.

★ **Empire 6714** CAFE $$
(0427 654 045; www.empire6714.com.au; Warambie Rd; mains $13-28; 5.30am-3pm;) Sure, you can get your standard bacon and eggs here, but why wouldn't you go for banana-flour waffles or tuna poke? There's lots of organic, hard-to-source goodness on the menu, and we like the playful Asian touches: bibimbap and salmon *katsu* (crumbed and fried) alongside steak sandwiches. There are also impeccable smoothies, cold-pressed juices, coffee and kombucha.

Soul Karratha CAFE $$
(08-91838278; www.facebook.com/soulkarratha; Warambie Rd, Pelago Centre; dishes $10-33; 6am-2pm Mon-Fri, from 7am Sat & Sun;) City-style sophisticated breakfasts (until 11am) are followed by an all-day menu of crowd-pleasers, from gourmet burgers to tempting share plates (sliders, quesadillas, antipasto platters). It delivers top-notch coffee, too, from its cute, bright-blue Elektra coffee machine.

Entertainment

Red Earth Arts Precinct ARTS CENTRE
(08-9186 8600; www.redearthartsprecinct.com.au; 27 Welcome Rd; 9am-5pm Mon, Wed & Fri, to 6pm Tue, to 7pm Thu, to 2pm Sat;) Combining funky architecture that draws inspiration from the surrounding wilderness with state-of-the-art facilities, Karratha's cultural centre comprises a rooftop cinema showing the latest blockbusters, a theatre with great acoustics and an excellent library.

Information

Karratha Visitor Centre (08-9144 4600; www.karrathavisitorcentre.com.au; De Witt Rd; 8.30am-4.30pm Mon-Fri, 9am-2pm Sat & Sun;) Has excellent local maps and info, supplies rail access road permits to Tom Price, and books tours. Closed during the time of research and may be moving to a new location; in the interim period, the **City of Karratha** (08-9186 8555; www.karratha.wa.gov.au; 1083 Welcome Rd; 9am-5pm Mon-Fri) office is the best place for local info.

Getting There & Away

Karratha Airport (www.karrathaairport.com.au; Hood Way), halfway between Karratha and Dampier, is well connected to Perth courtesy of Virgin Australia and Qantas. Also daily flights to Port Hedland.

Integrity (www.integritycoaches.com.au) operates twice-weekly bus services from Perth to Broome, stopping at Coral Bay, Exmouth, Karratha, Roebourne and Port Hedland.

Dampier

08 / POP 1106

Practically a suburb of Karratha, Dampier is the region's main port, 20km northwest of Karratha. Home to heavy industry, it's spread around King Bay. Dampier's most famous resident is Red Dog (who has had books written about him, and movies made), a much-loved mutt that roved the town and surrounds in the 1970s. A statue of him is at the entry to town. North of Dampier is the Burrup Peninsula, home to a pretty beach and one of Australia's wealthiest collections of Aboriginal rock paintings.

Sights

★ **Murujuga National Park** NATIONAL PARK

(http://parks.dpaw.wa.gov.au/park/murujuga; Burrup Peninsula Rd) FREE Murujuga is home to the world's largest concentration of rock art (dating back more than 30,000 years), stretched out along the rocky hills of the heavily industrialised Burrup Peninsula. The most accessible are at **Deep Gorge**, near Hearson's Cove. The engravings depict fish, goannas (lizards), turtles, ospreys, kangaroos and even a Tasmanian tiger.

The best way to see and appreciate the importance of this art is through a half-day tour out of Karratha with Ngurrangga Tours (p201).

Dampier Archipelago NATURE RESERVE

(https://parks.dpaw.wa.gov.au/park/dampier-archipelago) Offshore from Dampier, the coral waters and pristine islands of the Dampier Archipelago support a wealth of marine life, including dugongs, plus endangered marsupials (25 of the 42 islands are nature reserves). It's a popular recreational fishing and boating destination, and plenty of boat-owning locals head here for R&R. Enquire at Karratha visitor centre about fishing charters and cruises.

Hearson's Cove BEACH

(Hearson Cove Rd) A fine pebble beach with calm waters for swimming and a picnic area. Staircase to the Moon viewing (March to November) and great mudflat exploring at low tide.

Getting There & Away

Dampier is 20km northwest of Karratha.

There's a twice-daily community bus between Karratha and Dampier; see www.karratha.wa.gov.au/community-bus.

Port Hedland

08 / POP 13,828

Founded on traditional Kariyarra lands, Port Hedland is many things; it's mountains of gleaming white salt that turn pink during sunset, vast cargo ships and furnaces, the world's largest deep-water port, a dystopia of railway yards and iron-ore stockpiles, and the all-pervasive red dust that tints the buildings and passing road trains a uniform ochre. Under that red dust lurks a colourful 130-year history of mining booms and busts, cyclones, pearling and WWII action, juxtaposed against two galleries showcasing contemporary Aboriginal art and colourful street art. If you're heading north to Broome or south through the Outback, this is your last stop with real coffee, good food and a dip in the sea for quite some time.

Sights

Collect the brochure entitled *Adventure Awaits: Your Guide to Port Hedland* from the visitor centre and take a self-guided tour around the CBD and foreshore.

Goode St, near Pretty Pool, is handy to observe Port Hedland's **Staircase to the Moon** (on full-moon nights from March to October), where water caught in sand ripples reflects the moonlight, creating the effect of a staircase to the moon.

★ **Courthouse Gallery** GALLERY

(08-9173 1064; www.courthousegallery.com.au; 16 Edgar St; 9am-4.30pm Mon-Fri, to 3pm Sat) FREE More than a gallery, this leafy arts HQ is the centre of all goodness in Port Hedland. Inside are stunning, curated local contemporary and Aboriginal art exhibitions, while the shady surrounds host sporadic craft markets. Curators are happy to chat about art styles.

Cemetery Beach Park PARK

(Sutherland St;) Named for its location opposite the town's old cemetery, this grassy beachfront park is primed for barbecues and picnics, and there's a large kids' playground. From November to February, sea turtles come out to lay eggs by night; if you want to watch, follow the turtle-watching guidelines set out by the visitor centre.

Pretty Pool SWIMMING

(Matheson Dr) A popular picnicking and swimming spot (beware of stonefish), 7km east of the town centre. The best swimming spots depend on the tides – follow the locals' lead.

Tours

Harbour Tour TOURS

(08-9173 1315; www.phseafarers.org; cnr Wedge & Wilson Sts; adult/child $55/30; 9.30am Mon-Sat, 1.30pm Sun) Run by the Seafarers Centre, this hour-long tour covers the facts and figures of the port, and includes a boat tour around the harbour. Check tour times online and wear proper footwear.

BHP Billiton Iron Ore Tour TOURS

(13 Wedge St; adult/child $45/30; noon-1pm Mon, Tue & Thu Apr-Oct; on demand Nov-Mar) Popular one-hour guided tour of an iron-ore plant. Book through the visitor centre, from which the tour departs. Five person minimum; it's free for kids under 10 years.

Discover Port Hedland: West End Walking Tour WALKING

(09-9173 1711; 13 Wedge St; adult/child $20/10; 8am Tue & Thu) This engaging walking tour departs from the visitor centre and takes in historic sights such as the Pier Hotel, Old Methodist Church and the old Courthouse.

Sleeping & Eating

Discovery Holiday Caravan Park CARAVAN PARK $

(08-9173 1271; www.discoveryholidayparks.com.au; cnr Athol & Taylor Sts; camping per site $38, backpacker r $59-89, unit r $119-169;) At the town's eastern end, this caravan park offers lots of cabin options, backpacker rooms (with shared kitchen and bathroom) and well-maintained amenities. There's a nice view over the mangroves.

Esplanade Hotel HISTORIC HOTEL $$

(08-9173 9700; www.theesplanadeporthedland.com.au; 2-4 Anderson St; tw/d incl breakfast from $199/215;) One of the roughest pubs in Port Hedland in a former incarnation, the 'Nard' is now a reasonably characterful 4½-star hotel with 98 smart, well-equipped guest rooms (though they're petite and quite pricey). It's a favourite with business travellers, making the weekend rates considerably cheaper. It has good food and drink on-site.

Hedland Harbour Cafe CAFE $

(08-9173 2630; www.facebook.com/hedlandharbourcafe; 5 Wedge St; mains $10-20; 4am-4pm Mon-Tue, 4.30am-8pm Wed-Sun;) A favourite with early risers and dock workers, this friendly cafe serves up smashed avo with poached eggs, brekkie burritos, kebabs, grilled red emperor and chips, and other tasty fare. Good coffee and smoothies too.

Pilbara Room Restaurant AUSTRALIAN $$

(08-9173 1044; www.porthedland.wa.hospitalityinns.com.au/pilbararoom; Hospitality Inn, Webster St; mains $15-27; 6.30-9am & 6-8.30pm;) The Pilbara Room is a solid local favourite for hearty cooked breakfasts, generous servings of surf 'n' turf in the evenings and more creative fare, such as panko-crumbed Camembert and super-fresh calamari Provençale. Dinner reservations are a good idea on weekends.

Esplanade Hotel MODERN AUSTRALIAN $$

(08-9173 9700; www.theesplanadeporthedland.com.au; 2-4 Anderson St; bar mains $20-30, restaurant mains $22-44; 5.30am-midnight;) There's an air of sophistication about this old hotel. Breakfast (until 11.30am) is good value, then the Empire Bar's all-day menu blends old classics with new (Vietnamese poached chicken salad, T-bone steak – the latter merely OK). There's an evening restaurant too, with surprises like Thai seafood curry. Our favourite features: the big courtyard, and bar events throughout the week.

Shopping

★ **Spinifex Hill Studios** ART

(08-9172 1699; www.spinifexhillstudio.com.au; 18 Hedditch St, South Hedland; 10am-4pm Tue-Fri, to 2pm Sun) Aboriginal art from Port Hedland and a considerable range of styles from Noongar, Banjima, Innawongka, Martu, Kariyarra, Nyiyaparli and Yamatji cultural groups from across the Pilbara, plus the Torres Strait Islands, are housed inside a striking building. Saturday is the best time to visit, with artists at work and coffee offered (a kind of 'open house'). Good to call before visiting.

Information

Port Hedland Visitor Centre (08-9173 1711; www.visitporthedland.com; 13 Wedge St; 9am-5pm Mon-Fri, to 2pm Sat;) This excellent centre sells books on travel and Aboriginal culture, publishes shipping times, arranges iron-ore plant tours, and helps with turtle monitoring (November to February). Aboriginal designs, stunning regional photos and iron ore are for sale. Salt-mine tours are soon to be available.

Getting There & Away

Port Hedland International Airport (www.porthedlandairport.com.au; Williamson Way) is about 12km south of town and has good connections. Virgin Australia and Qantas both fly to Perth several times daily, and Qantas also has a weekly direct flight to Brisbane. Virgin has handy weekend flights to Bali. Skippers Aviation (www.skippers.com.au) serves Karratha.

Integrity (1800 226 339; www.integritycoachlines.com.au; Wedge St) operates two weekly bus services from the visitor centre north to Broome ($129, 6½ hours). There are four services to/from Perth ($274 to $293, 21½ to 28½ hours) taking various routes, coastal and inland. The quickest journey runs from Port Hedland on Thursdays via Newman and Meekatharra.

Karijini National Park

08

The 15 narrow, breathtaking gorges, hidden pools and spectacular waterfalls of the 6275-sq-km **Karijini National Park** (https://parks.dpaw.wa.gov.au/park/karijini; admission per car $13) form one of WA's most impressive attractions. Nature lovers flock to this red slice of the Hamersley Range and its deep, dark chasms (the traditional lands of the Banyjima, Kurrama and Innawonga peoples), home to abundant wildlife and over 800 different plant species.

Kangaroos, snappy gums and wildflowers dot the spinifex plains, rock wallabies cling to sheer cliffs and endangered olive pythons lurk in giant figs above quiet pools. The park also contains WA's three highest peaks: Mt Meharry, Punurrunha (Mt Bruce) and Mt Frederick.

WORTH A TRIP

EAST PILBARA ARTS CENTRE

Newman, about 200km southeast of Karijini National Park, is the location of state-of-the-art **East Pilbara Arts Centre** (08-9175 1020; www.martumili.com.au; Newman Dr, Newman; 10am-4pm Mon-Fri). This gallery is home to one of WA's most successful art collectives, Martumili Artists, and is a beautiful setting in which to admire their acclaimed, vibrant art. The Martu people live in remote desert communities in the East Pilbara region, and are the traditional custodians of vast stretches of WA desert. For sale are authentic Aboriginal paintings, artefacts and woodcarvings.

Summer temperatures reach extremes in the park (frequently over 40°C), so carry plenty of water. Winter nights are cold. At any time of year, choose walks wisely, dress appropriately and never enter a restricted area without a certified guide.

Sights & Activities

★ **Hancock Gorge** GORGE

(Weano Rd) The trail through Hancock Gorge is one of the shortest (400m, 80 minutes return) but also one of the most challenging in the park. A steep descent (partly on ladders), scramble on uneven rocks and fording or swimming a submerged section of the gorge brings you to the sunny **Amphitheatre**. Follow the narrow, slippery **Spider Walk** to sublime **Kermits Pool**.

★ **Dales Gorge** GORGE

(Dales Rd;) From the Fortescue Falls car park, a trail descends steeply via a long staircase to stunning **Fortescue Falls** (the park's only permanent waterfall; about one hour return) and a photogenic swimming hole, behind which a leafy 300m stroll upstream reveals beautiful **Fern Pool**.

You can enjoy a 2km **gorge-rim trail** from the start of the Fortescue Falls track to Circular Pool lookout, with great views into Dales Gorge. The Circular Pool lookout is connected to Dales Campground by an easy walking trail.

★ **Fern Pool** NATURAL POOL

(Jubura) Swim quietly and with respect at this lovely, shady pool – it has special

Karijini National Park

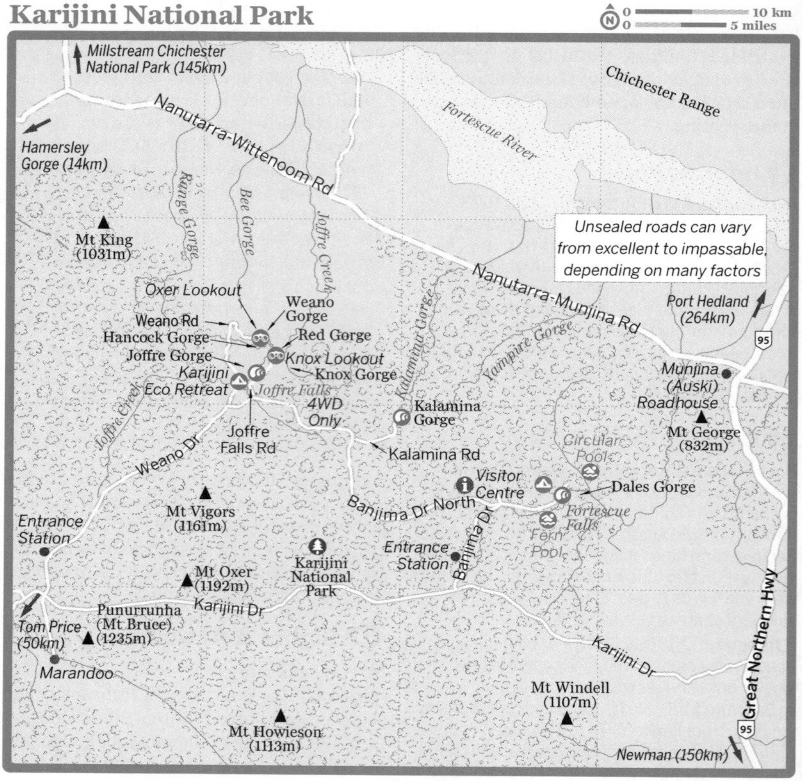

significance to the local Aboriginal people. It's a 300m (roughly 10-minute) walk upstream from Fortescue Falls.

★ Hamersley Gorge GORGE

(Hamersley Gorge Rd) Away in Karijini's northwest corner, this idyllic swimming hole and waterfall (400m; allow about an hour for the return walk) makes a lovely stop if you're heading north towards the coast or Millstream (it can't be accessed from Banjima Dr). It's about 67km from Tom Price: head north on Bingarn Rd for 26km, and turn right at the T-junction, carrying on another 41km (unsealed). Turn at the sign for Hamersley Gorge, not Hamersley Range.

Weano Gorge GORGE

(Weano Rd) The Upper Weano is dry, but the steep track winding down from the car park to the Lower Weano narrows until you reach the perfect, surreal bowl of **Handrail Pool** (150m, 30 minutes return). Hiking in the gorge itself may involve wading through cold water.

Oxer Lookout VIEWPOINT

(Weano Rd) The 13km drive (past the Karijini Eco Retreat) to the breathtaking Oxer Lookout is bumpy and unsealed, but it's worth it for the magnificent views of the junction of the Red, Weano, Joffre and Hancock Gorges some 130m below. The lookout is a short walk from the car park. Nearby is the Junction Pool Lookout with views of Hancock Gorge.

Joffre Gorge GORGE

(Joffre Falls Rd) When not trickling, **Joffre Falls** are spectacular, but the frigid pools below are perennially shaded. The Joffre Lookout is 10 minutes' walk from the parking area; there's a 3km-return trail down to the pool (about two hours there and back). There's also a walking track to the falls from the nearby Karijini Eco Retreat.

Kalamina Gorge GORGE
(Kalamina Gorge Rd) A wide, easy gorge where you can hike to the falls located upstream of a small, tranquil pool (3km, takes about two hours return). Access by 4WD or high-clearance AWD is best, as the road is severely corrugated.

Knox Gorge GORGE
(Joffre Falls Rd) Knox Lookout (300m; 15 minutes return) is best at sunrise or sunset. Descend from Knox Lookout into the gorge (2km; about three hours return) to several sunny swimming holes, fringed by native figs.

Punurrunha HIKING
(Mt Bruce; off Karijini Dr) Gorged out? Go and grab some altitude on WA's second-highest mountain (1235m), a superb ridge walk with fantastic views all the way to the summit. Start early, carry lots of water and allow six hours (9km return). The access road is off Karijini Dr, opposite Banjima Dr West.

Tours

★ **West Oz Active Adventure Tours** ADVENTURE
(☎0400 441 691; www.westozactive.com.au; Karijini Eco Retreat, Banjima Dr West; Joffre Gorge abseil $150; ⏲Apr-Oct) Based at Karijini Eco Retreat, this highly regarded company offers action-packed day trips through the restricted gorges of the park and combines hiking, swimming, floating on inner tubes, climbing, sliding off waterfalls and abseiling. All equipment and lunch provided. The minimum age for tours is 14.

★ **Flying Sandgroper** TOURS
(☎0438 913 713; www.flyingsandgroper.com.au; Karijini Eco Retreat, Weano Rd; 2-day Krijini package $425, 6-day Reef to Range tour $1265; ⏲Apr-Oct) The Flying Sandgroper's aim is to overcome the huge distances and costs of visiting the northwest, so offers multiday tours that take in Karijini (and Ningaloo too), with the choice of bus-in, bus-out and fly-in, fly-out packages, depending on your budget. It's affiliated with the excellent West Oz Active Adventure Tours, and based at Karijini Eco Retreat.

Sleeping

Dales Gorge Campground CAMPING GROUND $
(Dales Rd; camping per adult/child $11/3) Though somewhat dusty, this large Parks & Wildlife Service camping ground offers shady, spacious sites with nearby toilets, gas barbecues and picnic tables. Forget tent pegs – you'll be using rocks as anchors. It's first come, first served (no bookings). The camping ground is 17km on sealed road from the eastern entrance station.

★ **Karijini Eco Retreat** RESORT $$$
(☎08-9425 5591; www.karijiniecoretreat.com.au; Weano Rd; camping per person $20, eco cabin $199, deluxe tent r $349; P ❄) This 100% Aboriginal-owned retreat is a model for sustainable tourism, and the on-site **restaurant** (mains $18-39; ⏲7am-8pm) has fantastic food. The deluxe eco-tents have en suites; there are also cheaper tents, eco-cabins with shared bathrooms, and camping spaces. Access is via the sealed Banjima Dr West, with the final 3km on Weano Rd unsealed. Campers get access to hot showers and drinking water.

Information

Karijini Visitor Centre (☎08-9189 8121; https://parks.dpaw.wa.gov.au/park/karijini; Banjima Dr North; ⏲9am-4pm mid-Feb–mid-Dec) Aboriginal managed with excellent interpretive displays highlighting Banyjima, Yinhawangka and Kurrama cultures, as well as displays on park wildlife, good maps and walks information, a public phone, cold drinks, books on wildlife and Aboriginal art for sale, and really great air-con. In a separate building are toilets, plus showers ($4).

It's accessed via sealed road, 10km from the eastern entrance.

Getting There & Away

Bring your own vehicle or join a tour. Check out the excellent options from the Flying Sandgroper to make a visit more accessible.

The closest airports are Paraburdoo (101km) and Newman (201km).

Integrity (www.integritycoaches.com.au) operates a weekly bus service between Perth and Port Hedland along the coast, heading inland from Exmouth on Rte 136 and stopping at Paraburdoo and Tom Price, where you can pick up a tour to the park.

If driving between the park and Port Hedland, the only petrol stop along the way is at the **Auski Roadhouse** (Great Northern Hwy).

Getting Around

Karijini Dr is a sealed road stretching about 115km between Tom Price in the west and the Great Northern Hwy (Rte 95) in the east. The turn-off on Rte 95 is 160km northwest of Newman, and 300km south of Port Hedland.

WORTH A TRIP

MILLSTREAM CHICHESTER NATIONAL PARK

Among the arid, spinifex-covered plateaus and basalt ranges between Karijini and the coast, the tranquil waterholes of the Fortescue River form cool, lush oases in the 2400-sq-km **Millstream Chichester National Park** (https://parks.dpaw.wa.gov.au/park/millstream-chichester; admission per car $13), the traditional lands of the Yinjibarndi people. As well as a lifeline for local flora and fauna – which includes nearly 100 reptile species and around 150 bird species – the park is one of the most important Aboriginal sites in WA.

There are two main areas of the park: **Millstream** sits west of the Karratha–Tom Price Rd, and is home to the unmanned visitor centre, plus the park camping grounds – including the excellent **Miliyanha Campground** (camping per adult/child $13/2.20; ⏲ year-round) – and Deep Reach pool. In the park's north, east off the Karratha–Tom Price Rd, are the rolling hills, rocky peaks and escarpments of the **Chichester Range**.

Both sections of the park can be accessed from the Karratha–Tom Price Rd: the road through the Chichester Range begins 100km south of Karratha. Millstream's turn-off is about 120km south of Karratha. BYO vehicle, or join a tour from Karratha with Ngurrangga Tours (p201).

Millstream Trails

Clifftop Walk (600m return) Three viewpoints overlooking the Fortescue River, accessible from Millstream Rd.

Wetland Walk Gentle, compacted gravel loop (750m) that meanders through Millstream wetlands.

Warrungunha Trail (8km; 2½ hours return) Trail connecting the Millstream Homestead to the Cliff Lookout, passing through riverine woodland and grassland; gentle inclines.

Red Roo Trail (7.5km one way; three hours) Millstream Homestead to the Deep Reach Pool car park via the Cliff Lookout; gentle inclines and large section suitable for cyclists.

Stargazers to Deep Reach Pool (5km return; two hours) Easy, straightforward walk.

Jirndarwurrunha Pool A short stroll from the visitor centre, beautiful lily- and palm-fringed Jirndarwurrunha is deeply significant to the Aboriginal Yindjibarndi owners (no swimming).

Chichester Range Trails

Python Pool (100m) Very short, flat trail along dry creek to reach the pool.

Mt Herbert (600m return; 25 minutes) Panoramic views reachable via some short, steep sections, plus stairs.

Chichester Range Camel Trail (8km; three hours one way) Rugged trail with steep sections that passes Cameleers Lookout (2.4km; 1½ hours return) and McKenzie Spring (4.5km; 2½ hours return).

Banjima Dr, the park's main thoroughfare, connects with Karijini Dr at two entrance stations. The **eastern entrance station** (Banjima Dr) is closest to the visitor centre and Dales Gorge; the **western entrance station** (Weano Rd) is closest to Karijini Eco Retreat.

Hamersley Gorge is in a third, less-visited part of the park, accessed via an unsealed road near the west entrance to the park.

The east and west access roads are sealed, but Banjima Dr North is unsealed for most of its 29km length, and is recommended for 4WDs only as it is very bumpy. If you're in a 2WD, keep to the asphalt and use Karijini Dr to move between the park's east and west sections (it's longer, but far safer).

From Banjima Dr West, Weano Rd heads north to Karijini Eco Retreat and an area of gorge lookouts and trails. This road is unsealed and somewhat bumpy.

Take extra care driving, and avoid driving at night.

Broome & the Kimberley

Includes ➡

Broome 212
Dampier Peninsula.. 222
Derby 224
Devonian Reef National Parks 227
Gibb River Road 228
Great Northern Highway 230
Kununurra 233
Purnululu National Park & Bungle Bungle Range 236

Best Places to Eat

- ➡ Aarli (p219)
- ➡ Neaps Bistro (p226)
- ➡ PumpHouse (p236)
- ➡ Whale Song Cafe (p224)
- ➡ Jalangurru Mayi Cafe (p232)

Best Places to Stay

- ➡ McAlpine House (p218)
- ➡ Beaches of Broome (p218)
- ➡ Goombaragin Eco Retreat (p223)
- ➡ Home Valley (p230)
- ➡ Desert Rose (p226)

Why Go?

Australia's last frontier is a wild land of remote, spectacular scenery spread over huge distances, with a severe climate, a sparse population and minimal infrastructure. Larger than 75% of the world's countries, the Kimberley is hemmed by impenetrable coastline and unforgiving deserts. In between lie vast boab-studded spinifex plains, palm-fringed gorges, desolate mountains and magnificent waterfalls.

Aboriginal culture runs deep across the region, from the Dampier Peninsula, where neat communities welcome travellers to Country, to distant Mitchell Plateau, where ancient Wandjina and Gwion Gwion stand vigil over sacred waterholes.

Swashbuckling Broome (home to iconic Cable Beach, camel-tinged sunsets and amber-hued watering holes) and practical Kununurra (with its irrigation miracle) bookend the region. Both are great places to unwind, find a job and meet other travellers.

When to Go

Broome

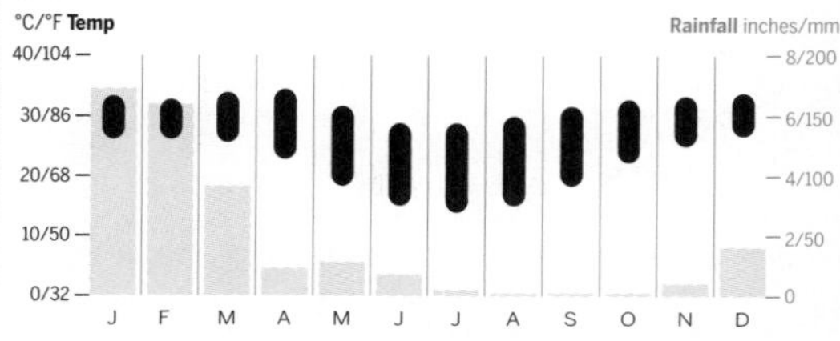

Apr Fly over thundering Mitchell and King George Falls.

May Broome's at its greenest right before the tourist tide.

Sep & Oct Hit Purnululu and the Gibb River Road as the season winds down.

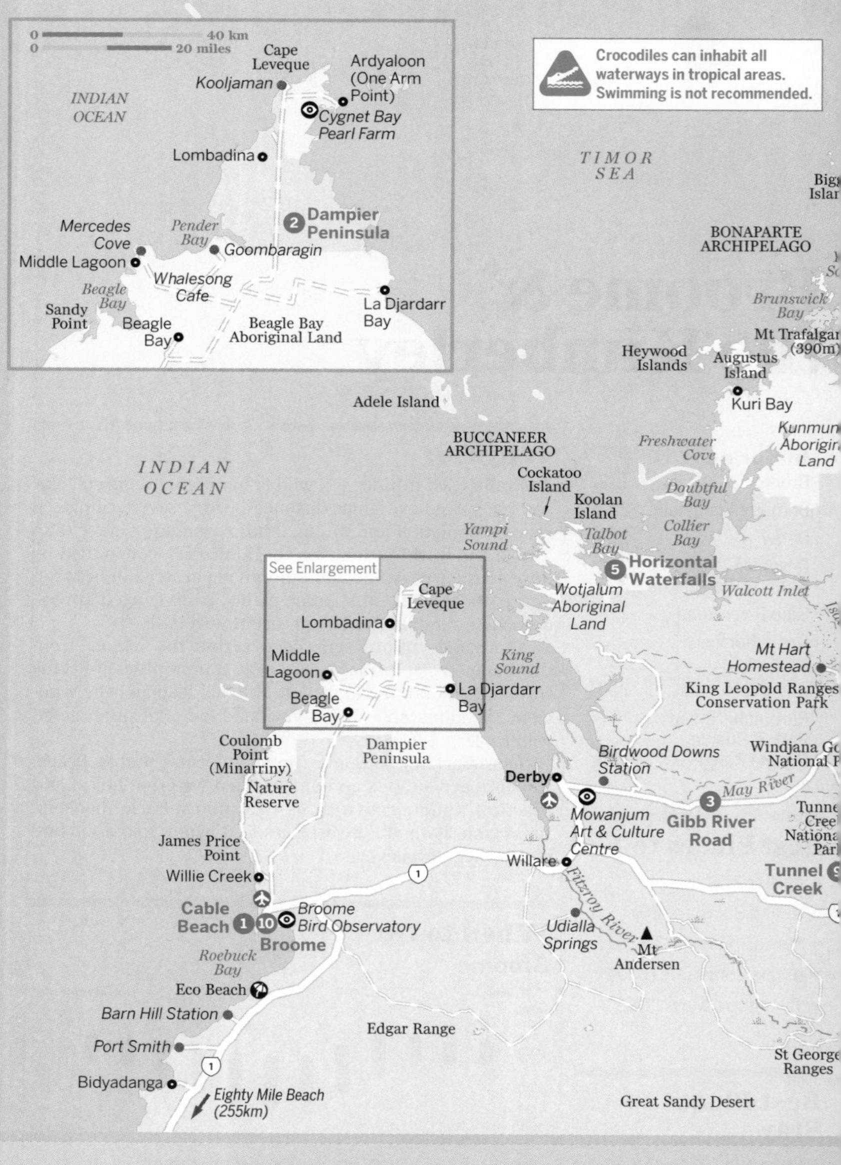

Broome & the Kimberley Highlights

1 Cable Beach (p212) Taking a camel ride at sunset along Broome's Cable Beach.

2 Dampier Peninsula (p222) Learning about traditional culture with Aboriginal communities on this pristine peninsula.

3 Gibb River Road (p228) Tackling the notorious Gibb River Road on a 4WD adventure.

4 Mitchell & King George Falls (p234) Flying over the stunning Mitchell and King George Falls after the Wet.

5 Horizontal Waterfalls (p226) Riding the wild

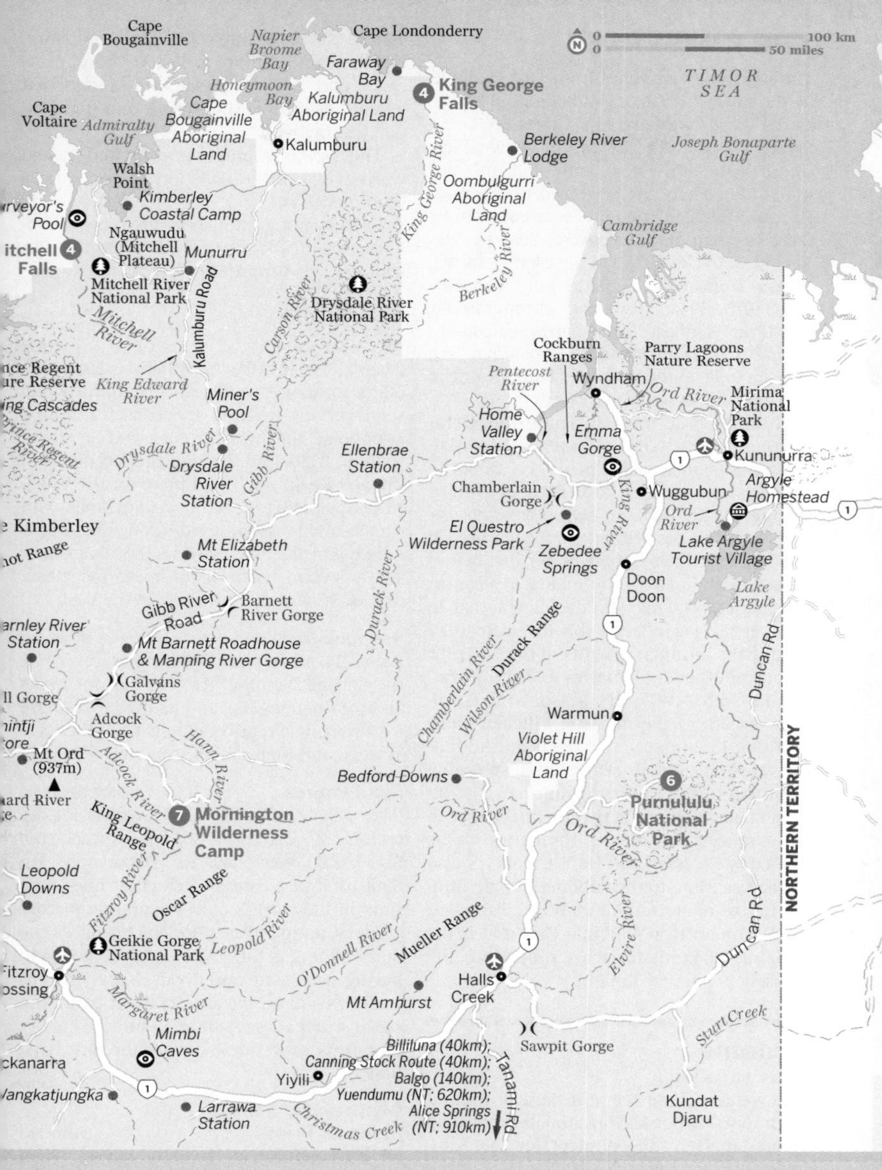

and intriguing 'horizontal waterfalls'.

6 Purnululu National Park (p236) Losing yourself among the ancient beehive domes of this national park.

7 Mornington Wilderness Camp (p229) Seeing incredible gorges and wildlife.

8 Aboriginal art (p225) Immersing yourself in Aboriginal art.

9 Tunnel Creek (p227) Trekking through the bowels of the earth at Tunnel Creek.

10 Lurujarri Dreaming Trail (p215) Following this trail to James Price Point and beyond.

THE KIMBERLEY

The Big Empty stretches from Port Hedland to the cosmopolitan big-smoke of Broome, as the Great Northern Hwy skirts the Great Sandy Desert. It's 609km of willy-willies (mini dust whirlwinds) and sand and not much else. There are only two roadhouses, **Pardoo** (08-9176 4916; www.pardoo.com.au; Great Northern Hwy; unpowered/powered sites $24/30, s/d/f $80/100/130; 24hr;), 148km from Port Hedland and **Sandfire** (08-9176 5944; www.facebook.com/sandfire.rh; Great Northern Hwy; unpowered/powered sites $20/30, dongas from $50; 7am-7pm;), 288km, so keep the tank full. The coast, wild and unspoilt, is never far away.

Heading east from Broome, the Great Northern Hwy (GNH) traverses the flat, scrubby Roebuck plains before crossing the (sometimes) mighty Fitzroy River at **Willare Bridge** (08-9191 4775; www.willareroadhouse.com; campsites per person from $16, dongas s/d $95/120; fuel 6am-8pm;), just before Derby. Boab-lined Derby makes a pleasant overnight stop while you decide whether to take on the legendary Gibb River Road or sample the bitumen delights of the GNH for the next 900-odd kilometres to Kununurra.

The Gibb (4WD, dry season only) provides access to the majestic Mitchell Falls, far-flung Kalumburu and the beautiful hidden gorges, eroded ranges and sweeping savannah of the Kimberley interior. The bitumen, all-weather GNH runs further south and connects the remote Kimberley towns of Fitzroy Crossing and Halls Creek. It's also the access route to the sublime Bungle Bungle Range of Purnululu National Park and the Devonian Reef National Park and is the jumping-off point for trips south into the sparsely populated Tanami.

Broome

08 / POP 16,500

Like a paste jewel set in a tiara of natural splendours, Broome clings to a narrow strip of pindan (red-soil country) on the Kimberley's far-western edge, at the base of the pristine Dampier Peninsula. Surrounded by the aquamarine waters of the Indian Ocean and the creeks, mangroves and mudflats of Roebuck Bay, this Yawuru Country is a good 2000km from the nearest capital city.

Cable Beach, with its luxury resorts, hauls in the tourists during high (dry) season (April to October), with romantic notions of camels, surf and sunsets. Magnificent, sure, but there's a lot more to Broome than postcards, and tourists are sometimes surprised when they scratch the surface and find pindan just below.

The Dry is a great time to find casual work, while in the Wet (low season) prices plummet.

Each evening, the whole town collectively pauses, drinks in mid-air, while the sun slinks slowly towards Madagascar.

Sights

★Cable Beach BEACH

(Map p216;) WA's most famous landmark offers turquoise waters and beautiful white sand curving away to the sunset. Clothing is optional north of the rocks, while south, walking trails lead through the red dunes of **Minyirr Park**, a spiritual place for the Yawuru people. Cable Beach is synonymous with camels and an evening ride along the sand is a highlight for many visitors. Locals in their 4WDs swarm north of the rocks for sunset drinks. Stingers are common in the Wet.

Roebuck Bay Lookout VIEWPOINT

(Map p214; cnr Frederick St & Dampier Tce;) At the end of Dampier Tce this lookout has a view of Roebuck Bay and its mangroves and features interpretative panels from the local Yawuru and high school students.

Sun Pictures HISTORIC BUILDING

(Map p214; 08-9192 1077; www.sunpictures.com.au; 27 Carnarvon St; movies adult/child $17.50/12.50, history tour $5; hours vary;) Sink back in a canvas deck chair under the stars in the world's oldest operating picture gardens, dating from 1916. The history of the Sun building is the history of Broome itself; having witnessed war, floods, low-flying aircraft (it's still on the airport flight path) and racial segregation. A short 15-minute history tour runs on request during the Dry (ring first).

Gantheaume Point & Dinosaur Prints VIEWPOINT

() Beautiful at dawn or sunset when the pindan cliffs turn scarlet and the Indian Ocean brilliant turquoise, this peaceful lookout holds a 135-million-year-old secret. Nearby lies one of the world's most varied collections of dinosaur footprints, impossible to find except at very low tides. Grab the map from the visitor centre (p221) and beware of slippery rocks. Look out for the ospreys returning with fish to their nests on the lighthouse.

WWII Flying Boat Wrecks HISTORIC SITE

FREE On a very low tide (<1.3m) it's possible to walk out across the mudflats from **Town Beach** (Map p214; P) to the wrecks of Catalina and Dornier flying boats attacked by Japanese 'Zeroes' during WWII. The planes had been evacuating refugees from Java and many still had passengers aboard. Over 60 people and 15 flying boats (mostly Dutch and British) were lost. Only six wrecks are visible, with the rest in deep water.

Bungalow GALLERY

(Map p214; 08-9192 6118; www.shortstgallery.com; 3 Hopton St, Town Beach; 10am-3pm Mon-Sat, shorter hours wet season) Short Street Gallery's Hopton St stock room at Town Beach holds a stunning collection of canvases from across the Kimberley and beyond.

Broome Bird Observatory NATURE RESERVE

(08-9193 5600; www.broomebirdobservatory.com; Crab Creek Rd; by donation, campsites per person $18, unit with shared bathroom s/d/f $45/60/85, chalets $140; 8am-4pm; P) The RAMSAR-recognised tidal mudflats of Roebuck Bay are a vital staging post for thousands of migratory birds, coming from as far away as Siberia. In a peaceful coastal setting 25km from Broome, the 'Bird Obbie' offers quiet walking trails, secluded bush campsites and a choice of low-key rooms. There are a number of tours ($70, 2½ hours) and courses ($1400, five days) available as well as volunteering opportunities. Hardcore twitchers shouldn't miss the daily 6pm bird count.

Old Convent Heritage Centre MUSEUM

(Map p214; 08-9192 3950; https://heritage.ssjg.org.au; 9 Barker St; $5 donation; 9am-1pm Mon-Fri, 10am-1pm Sat Feb-Nov; P) An amazing archival collection of photographs spanning over 100 years of interaction between the Sisters of St John of God with the people of the Kimberley. Housed in the heritage-listed Old Convent built in 1926 by a Japanese shipwright.

Nagula Jarndu Women's Resource Centre ARTS CENTRE

(0499 330 708; www.nagulajarndu.com.au; 3/12 Gregory St; 9am-4pm Mon-Fri; P) Beautiful screen- and block-printed textiles and other crafts are on show (and sale!) at this studio/gallery run by Yawuru women. Enter via Pembroke Rd.

BROOME'S CEMETERIES

Mute testament to Broome's multicultural past are its cemeteries. The most striking is the **Japanese Cemetery** (Port Dr) with 919 graves (mostly pearl divers) while nearby, the **Chinese Cemetery** (Frederick St) contains over 90 tombs. The small **Muslim Cemetery** (Frederick St) honours Malay pearl divers and Afghan cameleers.

A few kilometres southeast, the small **Pioneer Cemetery** (Map p214; P) overlooks Roebuck Bay at Town Beach.

Reddell Beach BEACH

(P) For a blistering sunset without tourists, camels or 4WDs, pull into any of the turn-offs along Kavite Rd between Gantheaume Point and the port and watch the pindan cliffs turn into molten lava. The beach is a favourite dog-walking spot, but it's strictly experienced swimmers only in the water due to the strong currents.

Malcolm Douglas Wilderness Park WILDLIFE RESERVE

(08-9193 6580; www.malcolmdouglas.com.au; Broome Hwy; adult/child/family $35/20/90; 2-5pm; P) Visitors enter through the jaws of a giant crocodile at this 30-hectare animal refuge 16km northeast of Broome. The park is home to dozens of crocs (don't miss the 3pm feeding), as well as kangaroos, cassowaries, emus, dingoes, jabirus and numerous other birds.

Broome Museum MUSEUM

(Map p214; 08-9192 2075; www.broomemuseum.org.au; 67 Robinson St; adult/child $12/8; 10am-4pm Mon-Fri, to 1pm Sat & Sun dry season, to 1pm daily wet season; P) Discover Cable Beach and Chinatown's origins through exhibits devoted to the area's pearling history and WWII bombing in this quirky museum, occupying the former Customs House.

Short Street Gallery GALLERY

(Map p214; 08-9192 2658; www.shortstgallery.com.au; 7 Short St; 10am-3pm Mon-Fri, 11am-3pm Sat) Dating from the early 1900s and known originally as Hanoe's Cottage, this typical Broome-style corrugated-iron building with louvred verandahs now houses small exhibitions of contemporary Aboriginal artworks.

Broome

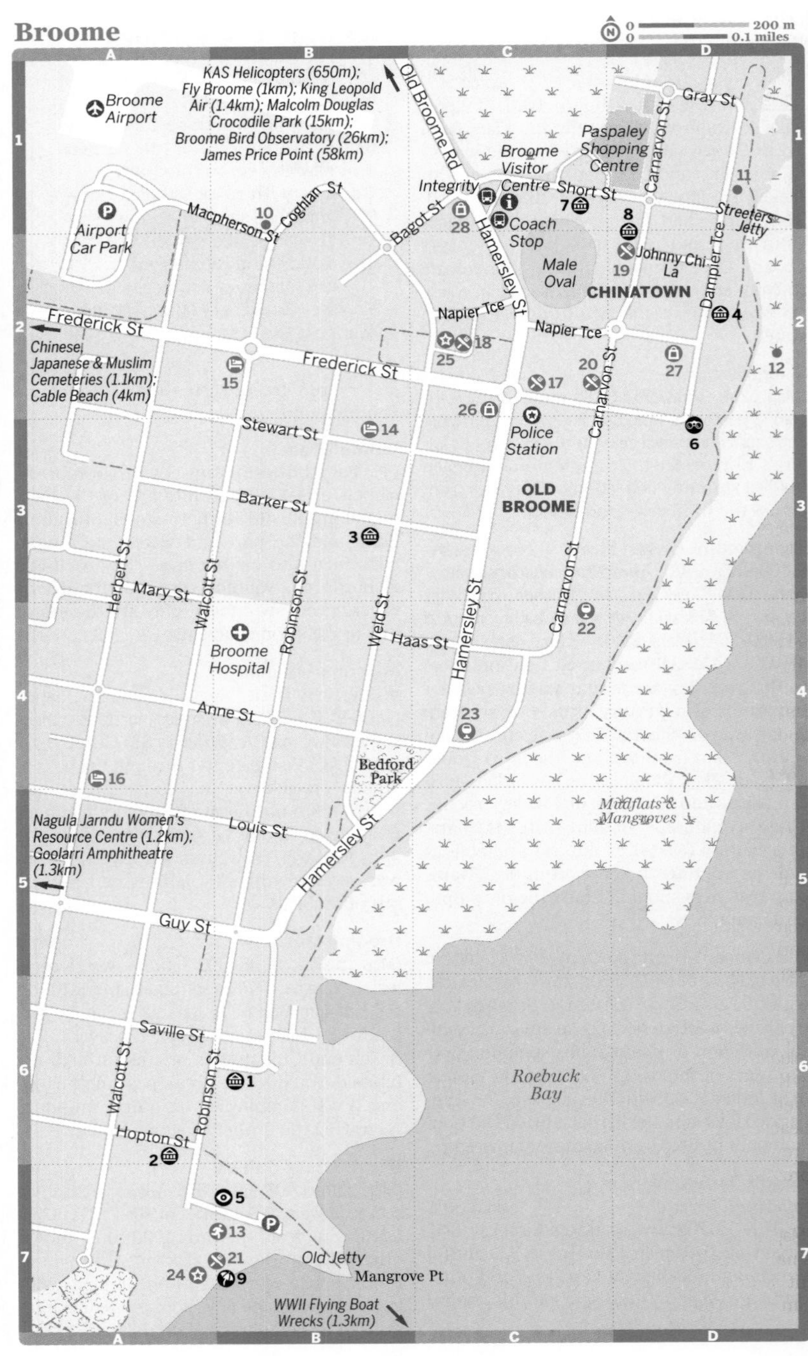

KAS Helicopters (650m); Fly Broome (1km); King Leopold Air (1.4km); Malcolm Douglas Crocodile Park (15km); Broome Bird Observatory (26km); James Price Point (58km)
Broome Airport
Airport Car Park
Old Broome Rd
Macpherson St
Coghlan St
Bagot St
Integrity
Broome Visitor Centre
Coach Stop
Paspaley Shopping Centre
Short St
Gray St
Carnarvon St
Streeters Jetty
Hamersley St
Male Oval
Johnny Chi La
CHINATOWN
Dampier Tce
Napier Tce
Frederick St
Chinese, Japanese & Muslim Cemeteries (1.1km); Cable Beach (4km)
Stewart St
Police Station
OLD BROOME
Barker St
Herbert St
Walcott St
Mary St
Robinson St
Weld St
Haas St
Broome Hospital
Anne St
Bedford Park
Mudflats & Mangroves
Nagula Jarndu Women's Resource Centre (1.2km); Goolarri Amphitheatre (1.3km)
Louis St
Guy St
Saville St
Roebuck Bay
Hopton St
Old Jetty
Mangrove Pt
WWII Flying Boat Wrecks (1.3km)

Broome

Sights
1 Broome Museum B6
2 Bungalow A6
3 Old Convent Heritage Centre B3
4 Pearl Luggers D2
5 Pioneer Cemetery B7
6 Roebuck Bay Lookout D3
7 Short Street Gallery C1
8 Sun Pictures D2
9 Town Beach B7

Activities, Courses & Tours
10 Broome Aviation B1
11 Jetty to Jetty D1
12 Narlijia Cultural Tours D2
13 Water Park B7

Sleeping
14 Broome Town B&B B3
15 Kimberley Klub B2
16 McAlpine House A4

Eating
17 Aarli C2
18 Good Cartel C2
19 Green Mango D2
20 Lockup C2
21 Town Beach Cafe B7

Drinking & Nightlife
22 Bay Club C4
23 Matso's Broome Brewery C4

Entertainment
24 Town Beach Night Markets A7
25 Twin Cinema C2

Shopping
26 Courthouse Markets C2
27 Kimberley Bookshop D2
28 Magabala Books C1

Pearl Luggers MUSEUM
(Map p214; ☎08-9192 0000; www.pearlluggers.com.au; 31 Dampier Tce; 90min tour adult/child/family $30/15/75; ⏲tours 11.30am & 3pm) FREE This compact museum provides an insight into Broome's tragic pearling past, evoking the diver experience with genuine artefacts. You can also wander over two of the last surviving luggers, named *Sam Male* and *DMcD*.

Activities

Odyssey Expeditions DIVING
(☎0428 382 505; www.odysseyexpeditions.com.au; 8-day tour from $3800; ⏲Sep-Oct) Runs several eight-day, live-aboard diving tours from Broome each spring to the Rowley Shoals Marine Park (p218). You need to be an experienced diver with your own gear (though some gear may be hired in Broome).

Turtle Monitoring WILDLIFE
(☎08-9195 5500; www.roebuckbay.org.au/volunteer-activities/turtle-monitoring; Cable Beach; ⏲Nov-Feb; 👪) Stuck in Broome over the Wet? Volunteers walk 4km along Cable Beach (p212) in the morning and record the previous night's turtle activity. Free training provided.

Water Park WATER PARK
(Map p214; ⏲9am-5pm, closed Tue; 👪) The small water park at Town Beach (p213) is a hit with kids. And with their parents who can retire to the nearby cafe. Free entry.

Tours

★ **Lurujarri Dreaming Trail** WALKING
(☎Frans 0423 817 925; www.goolarabooloo.org.au; adult/student $1600/900; ⏲hours vary May-Aug; 👪) This incredible 82km walk follows a section of ancient songline north along the coast from Gantheaume Point (p212; Minyirr) to Coulomb Point (Minarriny). The Goolarabooloo organise several guided nine-day walking trips each dry season, staying at traditional campsites. There is a strong emphasis on sharing Aboriginal culture with activities like spear-making, bush-tucker hunting, fishing, mud-crabbing and native jewellery making.

★ **Jetty to Jetty** WALKING
(Map p214; www.yawuru.com; 👪) This self-guided walking tour from the local Yawuru people comes with a fantastic audio accompaniment (download the free Jetty to Jetty smartphone app), taking you past 13 points of historical and cultural significance between Chinatown's Streeter's Jetty and the Old Jetty at Town Beach (p213). The 2.8km walk (with stops) should take around two hours.

★ **Astro Tours** TOURS
(☎0417 949 958; www.astrotours.net; adult/child $95/75; ⏲Apr-Oct) Fascinating after-dark two-hour stargazing tours held by the entertaining and (incredibly!) self-taught Greg Quicke, at a 'dark site' 20 minutes from Broome. Book online early as the tours are extremely popular. Self-drive and save $20.

Cable Beach

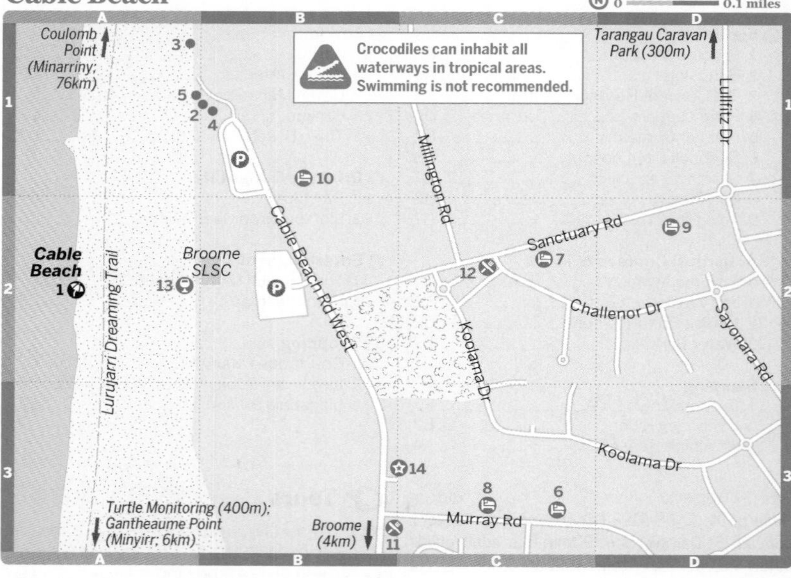

Cable Beach

Top Sights
1 Cable Beach ... A2

Activities, Courses & Tours
2 Broome Camel Safaris ... B1
3 Fat Bike ... A1
4 Red Sun Camels ... B1
5 Sundowner Camel Tours ... A1

Sleeping
6 Bali Hai Resort & Spa ... C3
7 Beaches of Broome ... C2
8 Broome Beach Resort ... C3
9 Cable Beach Backpackers ... D2
10 Cable Beach Club Resort ... B1

Eating
11 Cable Beach General Store & Cafe ... B3
12 Zookeepers Store ... C2

Drinking & Nightlife
13 Broome SLSC ... A2

Entertainment
14 Diver's Tavern ... C3

Narlijia Cultural Tours CULTURAL
(Map p214; ☎08-9195 0232; www.toursbroome.com.au; Chinatown; adult/child mangroves $75/35, history $55/25, Minyirr $95/65; ⊙May–mid-Oct;) Yawuru local Bart Pigram runs short (two- to three-hour) informative cultural tours around the mangroves and historical buildings of Chinatown and Minyirr.

Broome Adventure Company KAYAKING
(☎0419 895 367; www.broomeadventure.com.au; 3hr trip adult/child $85/65; ⊙Mar-Dec;) Glide past turtles, hidden beaches and sea caves on these eco-certified coastal kayaking trips.

KAS Helicopters SCENIC FLIGHTS
(Kimberley Air Supply; ☎08-9191 1886; www.kashelicopters.com.au; Gus Winckel Rd, Charter Aircraft Base; 30min/3hr/4hr tours per person from $289/639/1044) Unique tours with 'land anywhere' helicopters that offer seldom-visited locations like landing on top of the spectacular Edgar Range in the Great Sandy Desert ($1044), or a romantic lunch for two on an isolated beach ($639). Also fly from Derby (in season).

Fly Broome SCENIC FLIGHTS
(☎0455 502 965; www.flybroome.com.au; Gus Winckel Rd, Charter Aircraft Base; half-day tour $605) Flies a loop over the Dampier Peninsula and

Buccaneer Falls to the Horizontal Waterfalls, then lands at Cape Leveque for an inclusive meal and swim at Kooljaman (p223).

Fat Bike CYCLING
(Map p216; ☎0419 895 367; www.broomefatbikes.com.au; Cable Beach; 90min ride adult/child $69/55; ⏲sunset Mar-Nov) Camels passé? Ride off into the blazing Cable Beach sunset on these fat puppies from the Broome Adventure folks.

Broome Aviation SCENIC FLIGHTS
(Map p214; ☎08-9192 1369; www.broomeaviation.com.au; Unit 1, 2 Macpherson St; half-/full-day flights from $645/1180) Half-day flights to Cape Leveque and the Horizontal Falls (p226) from Broome. Full-day tours add on the Devonian Reef National Parks, Bell Gorge (p228) and Mt Hart, Mitchell Falls or even the Bungle Bungles ($1620).

King Leopold Air SCENIC FLIGHTS
(☎08-9193 7155; www.kingleopoldair.com.au; 9 Gus Winckel Rd; half-/full-day tours from $610/1140) Flights over the Dampier Peninsula (half day) and to Mitchell Falls or Devonian Reef National Parks (full day). Also has a 30-minute flight over Broome's beaches (per person two passengers/three to five passengers $240/150).

Snubfin Dolphins WILDLIFE
(Broome Whale Watching; ☎08-9192 8163; www.broomewhalewatching.com.au; ⏲3hr tour adult/child $105/75) Three-hour catamaran tours of Yawuru Nagulagun (Roebuck Bay Marine Park) searching for snubfin dolphins, turtles, dugongs and rays. Choice of morning or sunset tour. Also runs whale-watching tours in season (from $120 April to September).

Broome Historical Walking Tours WALKING
(☎0408 541 102; www.broomehistoricalwalkingtours.com; adult/child $50/30; ⏲twice daily Mon-Fri Apr-Nov (minimum 2 people)) This fabulous 1½-hour walking tour examines the Broome of yesteryear through site visits and photographs – from WWII back to the pearling days – with raconteur Wil telling some fabulous stories. The tour price includes admission to Broome Museum (p213). Wil also guides walks out to the flying boats on appropriate low tides (adult/child $55/45).

Kimberley Birdwatching BIRDWATCHING
(☎0429 706 800; www.kimberleybirdwatching.com.au; half-/full-day tours from $90/300) Join ornithologist George Swann on his informative Broome nature tours. Overnight and customised trips are also available, including a 10-day sailing expedition to Ashmore Reef ($6600).

Hovercraft Tours TOURS
(☎08-9193 5025; www.broomehovercraft.com.au; Port Dr; adult/child dinosaur $136/96, sunset $196/124, flying boats $196/124) Skim over tidal flats to visit historical sights, dinosaur footprints and, on very low tides, the wrecks of flying boats (p213) sunk during WWII. The sunset tour includes sparkling wine.

Festivals & Events

Broome Pride LGBT
(www.broomepride.com; ⏲Mar) Drag queens on camels and riotous cabaret feature as Broome gets its glitter on around the same time as Sydney's famous Mardi Gras.

Kullarri Naidoc Week CULTURAL
(www.goolarri.com; ⏲late Jun–mid-Jul) Celebration of Aboriginal and Torres Strait Islander culture.

A Taste of Broome PERFORMING ARTS
(☎08-9195 5333; www.goolarri.com; Goolarri Amphitheatre, Blackman St, Old Broome; general/VIP $35/70; ⏲Jul-Sep; 👪) Indigenous flavours, dance and music caress the senses at this ticket-only event held monthly from July to September. VIP tickets include premium seating and a tasting platter.

Broome Race Round SPORTS
(www.broometurfclub.com.au; Broome Racecourse; ⏲Aug) Locals and tourists frock up and

CAMEL TOURS

It's a feisty business, but at last count there were three (handily colour-coded) camel-tour operators running at Cable Beach offering similar trips:

Broome Camel Safaris (Map p216; ☎0419 916 101; www.broomecamelsafaris.com.au; adult/child morning $65/45, afternoon $40/30, sunset $90/70; 👪) Blue blankets.

Red Sun Camels (Map p216; ☎1800 184 488; www.redsuncamels.com.au; adult/child morning $70/50, afternoon $45/30, sunset $95/70) Red blankets.

Sundowner Camel Tours (Map p216; ☎0477 774 297; www.sundownercameltours.com; adult/child afternoon $45/30, sunset $90/60) Yellow blankets.

OFF THE BEATEN TRACK

ROWLEY SHOALS MARINE PARK

These three **coral atolls** lie approximately 300km from Broome in the Indian Ocean, on the edge of Australia's continental shelf, and have a reputation for some of the best diving in the country. Protected by a marine park, there are over 600 species of fish and 200-plus different varieties of coral. At a good 12-hour cruise from land, the shoals only see a minute number of visitors each year. Several Broome operators offer multi-night cruises for experienced divers.

party hard for the Kimberley Cup, Ladies' Day and Broome Cup horse races.

Opera Under the Stars MUSIC
(08-9195 2200; www.operaunderthestars.com.au; Mangrove Hotel, 47 Carnarvon St; Aug) Opera al fresco, one night only at the Mangrove Hotel. Bookings usually open in May, and tickets go quickly.

Corrugated Lines LITERATURE
(www.facebook.com/corrugatedlines; Aug) Three-day festival of the written (and spoken) word with various workshops and talks around town.

Shinju Matsuri Festival of the Pearl CULTURAL
(www.shinjumatsuri.com.au; Aug/Sep;) Broome's homage to the pearl includes a week of parades, food, art, concerts, fireworks and dragon-boat races.

Mango Festival FOOD & DRINK
(www.facebook.com/broomemangofestival; last weekend Nov) Three days of mango madness in late November, including quizzes, music, alcoholic beverages and anything else vaguely fruit related.

Sleeping

★ **Beaches of Broome** HOSTEL $
(Map p216; 1300 881 031; www.beachesofbroome.com.au; 4 Sanctuary Rd, Cable Beach; dm $32-45, motel d without/with bathroom $145/185;) More resort than hostel, its spotless, air-conditioned rooms are complemented by shady common areas, a poolside bar and a modern self-catering kitchen. Dorms come in a variety of sizes (and include female-only rooms) and the motel rooms are beautifully appointed. Both the continental breakfast and wi-fi are free. Scooter and bike hire available.

Tarangau Caravan Park CARAVAN PARK $
(08-9193 5084; www.tarangaucaravanpark.com; 16 Millington Rd, Cable Beach; unpowered/powered sites $40/50; office 8.30am-5pm;) A quieter alternative to the often noisy Cable Beach caravan parks, Tarangau has pleasant, grassy sites 1km from the beach.

Kimberley Klub HOSTEL $
(Map p214; 08-9192 3233; www.kimberleyklub.com; 62 Frederick St; dm $30-36, s $60-85, d $110-140;) Handy to the airport, this rambling, relaxed hostel is a great place to meet other travellers, hook-up lifts and find that job. There's a plethora of room options, poolside bar, games room, massive kitchen, an excellent noticeboard and organised activities most nights.

Cable Beach Backpackers HOSTEL $
(Map p216; 1800 655 011; www.cablebeachbackpackers.com; 12 Sanctuary Rd, Cable Beach; dm from $29;) Party-central for the under-30s, there's never a dull moment at this popular hostel a short splash from Cable Beach (p212). There's a tropical courtyard, large communal kitchen, pool and on-site bar. Beds are cheaper by the week and out of high season.

★ **McAlpine House** B&B $$$
(Map p214; 08-9192 0588; www.mcalpinehouse.com.au; 55 Herbert St; d $185-485;) Lord McAlpine made this stunning house, a former pearl master's lodge, his Broome residence during the '80s. Now renovated to its former glory, there are lovely airy rooms, open communal areas, shady tropical verandahs and a lush canopy of mango trees, tamarind and frangipanis. Escape from the heat by the pool, or travel back through time in the library.

Bali Hai Resort & Spa SPA HOTEL $$$
(Map p216; 08-9191 3100, cafe 08-9191 3160; www.balihairesort.com; 6 Murray Rd, Cable Beach; r from $338; cafe 5.30pm-late Wed-Sun, breakfast 8-11am Sat & Sun;) Lush and tranquil, this beautiful small resort has gorgeously decorated studios and villas, each with individual outside dining areas and open-roofed bathrooms. The emphasis is on relaxation and the on-site spa offers a range of exotic therapies. There's also an Asian-themed cafe (mains $29 to $42) showcas-

ing fresh Western Australian produce. The off-season prices are a bargain.

Broome Town B&B B&B $$$

(Map p214; ☎08-9192 2006; www.broometown.com.au; 15 Stewart St, Old Broome; r $285; P❄📶🏊) This delightful, boutique-style B&B epitomises Broome-style architecture, with high-pitched roofs, wooden louvres, jarrah floors, tasteful rooms, an open communal guest lounge and lots of tropical shade.

Broome Beach Resort APARTMENT $$$

(Map p216; ☎08-9158 3300; www.broomebeachresort.com; 4 Murray Rd, Cable Beach; 1-/2-/3-bedroom apt $295/360/385; P❄📶🏊) Great for families and groups, these large, modest apartments surround a central pool and are within easy walking distance of Cable Beach (p212). Much cheaper if you stay three-plus days.

Cable Beach Club Resort HOTEL $$$

(Map p216; ☎08-9192 0400; www.cablebeachclub.com; Cable Beach Rd; r from $469; P❄📶🏊) Broome does Bali in Cable Beach's original upmarket resort as honeymooners, package tourists and A-listers rub shoulders among the lush gardens, airy pavilions and Eastern symbolism primo-situated just beyond the waves. A village unto itself, there are numerous swimming pools, bars, restaurants, spas and other facilities to keep you close.

Eating

Lockup CAFE $

(Map p214; ☎08-9193 5633; 22 Carnarvon St; breakfast $7-13; ⏲7am-2pm Mon-Sat, 4.30-7pm Fri; ✎👪) Great coffee, cheap breakfasts and wholesome Southeast Asian–inspired lunches feature at this mostly outdoors licensed cafe on the site of an old jail. Enter via the narrow entrance behind the big boab.

Cable Beach General Store & Cafe CAFE $

(Map p216; ☎08-9192 5572; www.cablebeachstore.com.au; cnr Cable Beach & Murray Rds; burgers $11-17; ⏲6am-8pm; 📶👪) Cable Beach unplugged – a typical Aussie corner shop with egg breakfasts, barramundi burgers, pies, internet and no hidden charges. You can even play a round of minigolf (adult/child/family $8/6/20).

★**Good Cartel** CAFE $$

(Map p214; ☎0499 335 949; 3 Weld St; breakfast $7-25, burgers $12.50-20; ⏲5am-2pm; ✎👪🐾) *The* hippest place in town to grab a great coffee, healthy juice and Mexican-themed brekkies. Locals queue for its fabled lunchtime burgers. Follow the line of cars behind the Twin Cinema (p221) in the business park. Doggies are more than welcome as the cafe is active in rehabilitating strays. Find it on Facebook (search for Good Cartel Broome).

★**Aarli** TAPAS $$

(Map p214; ☎08-9192 5529; www.theaarli.com.au; 6 Hamersley St, enter via Frederick St; share plates $14-22, mains $20-38, breakfast $13-21; ⏲8am-late; ✎) Ask any Broome local where they love eating and most will say the Aarli, with its wonderful outdoor relaxed dining and the share plates that Broome does so well. Drop in for some quick tapas (Med-Asian fusion) or a main meal, or while away the afternoon working through the excellent wine list. Also open for breakfast (8am to noon).

Green Mango CAFE $$

(Map p214; ☎08-9192 5512; http://greenmangobroome.com; Shop 2/12 Carnarvon St, Chinatown; breakfast $14-25, lunch $11-23; ⏲kitchen 7am-2pm; ✎👪) This great healthy brunch choice in Broome's Chinatown has a wide selection of juices, smoothies and salads, as well as more traditional breakfast fare.

Zookeepers Store CAFE $$

(Map p216; ☎08-9192 0015; www.zks.com.au; 2 Challenor Dr, Cable Beach; breakfast $5-26, dinner $25-44, kids meals $6-12; ⏲7am-noon Tue &

STAIRCASE TO THE MOON

The reflections of a rising full moon rippling over exposed mudflats at low tide create the optical illusion of a golden stairway to the moon. Between April and October Broome buzzes around the full moon, with everyone eager to see the spectacle. At Town Beachthere's a lively evening market (p221) with food stalls and people bring fold-up chairs, although the small headland at the end of Hamersley St has a better view.

While Roebuck Bay parties like nowhere else, this phenomenon happens across the Kimberley and Pilbara coasts – anywhere with some east-facing mudflats. Other good viewing spots are **One Arm Point** at Cape Leveque, **Cooke Point** in Port Hedland, **Sunrise Beach** at Onslow, **Hearson Cove** near Dampier and the lookout at **Cossack**. Most visitor centres publish the dates on their websites.

WORTH A TRIP

MANARI ROAD – BROOME'S NORTHERN BEACHES

The beaches, headlands and red pindan cliffs along Manari Rd are one of Broome's best-kept secrets, frequented mainly by anglers, locals and adventurous travellers looking for something more than just Broome-time. Leaving the Cape Leveque Rd just 15km from the Great Northern Hwy, unsealed, sandy and sometimes corrugated Manari Rd runs roughly northwest through **Goolarabooloo Country**, parallel to the coastal **Lurujarri Songline** (an oral memory map of stories, song and dance describing the landscape and handed down from generation to generation).

Just 5km along you'll reach the turn-off to **Willie Creek** where there's a **pearl farm** (Wirrkinymirri; 08-9192 0000; www.williecreekpearls.com.au; Willie Creek Rd; tours adult/child/family from $75/40/190; cafe 11am-3pm Apr-Sep; P) in a stunning location on a mangrove-lined inlet; the 7.5km sandy access track feels quite remote as you skirt a wide salt lake. Various tours are available and there's a cafe for lunch, but don't swim, as there are salties (saltwater crocodiles) in the creek.

Back on Manari Rd, there are bush campsites (no facilities, maximum three-night stay) at **Barred Creek** (Nuwirrar; Manari Rd; campsites free; P), **Quandong Point** (Kardilakan; Manari Rd; campsites free;), James Price Point (p222) and **Coulomb Point** (Minarinny; Manari Rd; campsites free;), where there is a nature reserve. You can swim at the beaches here, fish off the reefs and wander the rock platforms at low tide looking for dinosaur footprints and plant fossils, but don't take anything away other than rubbish.

Conventional vehicles should make it to James Price Point, in the middle of the Songline. Its crumbling, crimson pindan cliffs, once home to the proud warrior **Walmadan**, have in more recent years become both an icon and the frontline of the Kimberley's environmental movement. Whether or not you plan on camping, don't miss this spectacular location. Especially at sunset!

For more information about the area, see www.goolarabooloo.org.au and www.environskimberley.org.au.

Wed, to 2pm & 5.30-9pm Thu-Mon;) Fans of deconstructed-hipsterism will love the breakfasts, vegos the wide and varied earth fodder and parents the thoughtful cheese-and-Vegemite toasties.

Wharf Restaurant SEAFOOD $$$
(08-9192 5800; www.facebook.com/thewharfrestaurantbroome; 401 Port Dr, Port; mains $36-120; 11am-late) Settle back for a long, lazy seafood lunch with waterside ambience and the chance of a whale sighting. OK, it's pricey and the service fluctuates, but the wine's cold, the sea stunning and the chilli crab and barramundi wings both sensational. Just wait until after 2pm to order oysters (when they become half-price).

Drinking & Nightlife

Bay Club BAR
(Mangrove Hotel; Map p214; 08-9192 1303; www.mangrovehotel.com.au; 47 Carnarvon St; mains $17-39; 11am-10pm;) The Mangrove Hotel's casual outdoor bar is perfect for a few early bevvies while contemplating Roebuck Bay. Sophisticated, healthy bistro meals and live music complement excellent Staircase to the Moon (p219) viewing. On Sundays, kids will enjoy the bouncing castle.

Matso's Broome Brewery PUB
(Map p214; 08-9193 5811; www.matsos.com.au; 60 Hamersley St; share plates $8-36, mains $23-38; 7am-midnight;) Get yourself a Chango (50/50 chilli/mango beer) and a half-kilo bucket of prawns, then kick back to the lazy afternoon music on the shady verandah at Broome's finest brewery.

Broome SLSC CLUB
(Surf Club; Map p216; 08-9193 7327; www.broomeslsc.com; Cable Beach foreshore; bar 5-7pm Fri & Sun May-Oct;) The cheapest drink in town also has the best view. Travellers are welcome to sink a couple of stubbies on the lawn and watch that flaming Indian Ocean sunset. Don't miss the Sunday morning sausage sizzle (sausages $2).

Entertainment

Other than the pubs, which occasionally host travelling bands and people-watching (ie anywhere in Cable Beach), entertainment options are limited to Sun Pictures (p212) and its modern sibling **Twin Cinema** (Map p214; 08-9192 3199; www.broomemovies.com.au; 3 Weld St; adult/child/family $17.50/12.50/55; 10am-midnight or end of last movie;).

Town Beach Night Markets MARKET
(Map p214; www.broomemarkets.com.au/markets; full moon Apr-Oct, Thu evenings Jun-Sep;) Food, crafts and live music every Thursday night at Town Beach (p213) June and September and over Staircase to the Moon (p219) nights between April and October.

Diver's Tavern LIVE MUSIC
(Map p216; 08-9193 6066; www.diverstavern.com.au; Cable Beach Rd; 11am-midnight) Diver's pumps most nights and if you're camped anywhere nearby, you'll know it. The Sunday Session jams are legendary.

Shopping

Kimberley Bookshop BOOKS
(Map p214; 08-9193 7169; www.kimberleybooks.com.au; 3 Napier Tce; 9.30am-4.30pm Mon-Fri, to 2pm Sat;) Extensive range of books on Broome and the Kimberley for every age group.

Magabala Books BOOKS
(Map p214; 08-9192 1991; www.magabala.com; 1 Bagot St; 9am-4.30pm Mon-Fri;) Brilliant Indigenous publishers showcasing Kimberley storytelling with a selection of novels, social history books, biographies and children's literature.

Courthouse Markets MARKET
(Map p214; www.broomemarkets.com.au; Hamersley St; 8am-1pm Sat year-round, Sun Apr-Oct;) Local arts, crafts, music, hawker food and general hippy gear.

Information

Broome Hospital (08-9194 2222, emergency 000; Robinson St, Old Broome; 24hr;) Emergency department. There's a **clinic** (08-9192 2022; www.broomemedical.com.au; 2/26 Robinson St; 8am-8pm Mon-Wed, to 5pm Thu & Fri, 8.30-11.30am Sat) next door for less serious cases.

Broome Visitor Centre (Map p214; 08-9195 2200; www.visitbroome.com.au; 1 Hamersley St; 8.30am-4.30pm Mon-Sat, to 3pm Sun, shorter hours during wet season) Great for info on road conditions, Staircase to the Moon (p219) viewing, dinosaur footprints (p212), WWII wrecks (p213), tide times and souvenirs. Books accommodation and tours for businesses registered with it and is also the long-haul coach stop. It's on the roundabout entering town, opposite Male Oval.

Getting There & Away

Unless you're on a long-haul road trip, the easiest way into Broome is by air. **Broome Airport** (Map p214; 08-9194 0600; www.broomeair.com.au; Macpherson St) is centrally located and serviced by **Qantas** (13 13 13; www.qantas.com.au), **Skippers** (1300 729 924; www.skippers.com.au), **Virgin** (13 67 89; www.virginaustralia.com) and **Airnorth** (08-8920 4001; www.airnorth.com.au). A **shuttle** (Airport Shuttle; 08-9192 5252; www.broometaxis.com; Broome/Cable Beach hotels $10/15) service meets flights and drops off passengers at most Broome hotels and Cable Beach resorts.

Long-distance **Integrity** (Map p214; 08-9274 7464; www.integritycoachlines.com.au; Visitor Centre) coaches run to Perth and **Greyhound** (1300 473 946; www.greyhound.com.au) to Darwin while a local bus (p227) services Derby. All services arrive/depart from the coach stop outside the visitor centre.

Britz (08-9192 2647; www.britz.com; 10 Livingston St; minimum 5-day hire van/4WD from $1000/1600) hires campervans, motorhomes and rugged 4WDs, the latter being essential for the Gibb River Road.

Getting Around

Broome's attractions are fairly spread out; don't underestimate distances or the heat. Most hostels will rent out bicycles and/or scooters.

Broome Broome (08-9192 2210; www.broomebroome.com.au; 3/15 Napier Tce; scooter/car/4WD per day from $35/75/185) The only rental-car company prepared to offer unlimited kilometres. Scooter hire is $35 per day.

Broome Cycles (08-9192 1871; www.broomecycles.com.au; 2 Hamersley St; day/week mountain bikes $30/100, fat bikes $60/400, deposit $150; 8.30am-5pm Mon-Fri, to 2pm Sat) Hires mountain bikes out by the day ($30) or week ($100) from Chinatown and from a trailer at **Cable Beach** (0409 192 289; cnr Cable Beach & Sanctuary Rds; 9am-noon May-Oct) when in season.

Town Bus Service (08-9193 6585; www.broomebus.com.au; adult $4, 24hr pass $15; 7.23am-6.23pm dry season, 8.53am-5.53pm Mon-Sat, from 10.53am Sun wet season;) Links Town Beach, Chinatown and Cable Beach every 30 minutes during the Dry and every hour during the Wet.

For a taxi, try **Broome Taxis** (13 10 08), **Chinatown Taxis** (1800 811 772) or **Pearl Town Taxis** (13 13 30).

Dampier Peninsula

08

Stretching north from Broome, the red pindan of the Dampier Peninsula ends abruptly above deserted beaches, secluded mangrove bays and cliffs burnished crimson by the setting sun. This remote and stunning Country is home to thriving Aboriginal settlements of the Ngumbarl, Jabirr Jabirr, Nyul Nyul, Nimanburu, Bardi Jawi and Goolarabooloo peoples. Access is via the rough, 215km-long Cape Leveque Rd.

The Manari Road (p220) turn-off, home to Broome's northern beaches and bush campsites, is reached after 15km.

Always book ahead when visiting Aboriginal communities, ideally directly with the community hosts, though the Broome Visitor Centre (p221) may help; check if permits and/or payments are required. Look for the informative booklet *Ardi–Dampier Peninsula Travellers Guide* ($5). You need to be self-sufficient, but limited supplies are available.

Sights

★James Price Point BEACH

(Walmadan; Manari Rd; P) FREE The striking red pindan cliffs of Walmadan (named for the proud warrior who once lived here) are worth a visit even if you're not camping; they're 35km from Cape Leveque Rd. Right in the middle of the Lurujarri Songline, this important cultural site of the Goolarabooloo people has been the scene of past environmental protests. Bush campsites (three-night maximum) sit on the bluff overlooking the stunning cliffs and mesmerising Indian Ocean.

Pender Bay BAY

Exquisitely remote, this pristine bay is an important calving ground for humpback whales and many can be seen offshore from May to November. The easiest access is from either Whale Song Cafe (p224), if open, or via the small Pender Bay campground, between Mercedes Cove and Whale Song, where clifftop vantage points provide exceptional viewing. Simple bush campsites (and an amenity block) are available.

Cape Leveque (Kooljaman) BEACH

(day access per person $10;) Spectacular Cape Leveque, right on the tip of the Dampier Peninsula, has stunning red cliffs and gorgeous white beaches perfect for swimming and snorkelling. Access is via Kooljaman resort, where there are plenty of accommodation options.

Beagle Bay Church CHURCH

(08-9192 4913; by donation; P) Around 110km from Broome, Beagle Bay is notable for the extraordinarily beautiful mother-of-pearl altar at Beagle Bay church, built by Pallottine monks in 1918. Fuel is available at the community shop (weekdays only).

Tours

Cape Leveque Tour BUS

(Broome Transit; 08-9192 5252; www.broometransittours.com.au; $240) This full-day tour of Cape Leveque takes in Beagle Bay, Kooljaman, Cygnet Bay, Ardyaloon and Gumbanan. Tours pick up from Broome accommodation around 6am, returning by 7pm.

Ngarlan Yarnin' HISTORY

(0438 118 578; Beagle Bay; 2 people/family $25/40; tours 9am, 10.30am, noon, 1.50pm & 5pm Mon-Sat) Mena Lewis, a local Nyul Nyul and Bardi woman, holds fascinating one-hour storytellings on the history of the Sacred Heart Church, Beagle Bay and the community itself. Cash only.

Brian Lee Tagalong Tours TOURS

(08-9192 4970; www.brianleetagalong.com.au; Kooljaman; adult/child $98/45) Tag along (in your own 4WD) with Bardi traditional owner Brian Lee as he reveals the culture and history surrounding Hunters Creek, where you'll get a chance to fish and hunt for mud crabs.

Festivals & Events

Ardi Festival CULTURAL

(hours vary Jun-Sep) Annual celebration of Ardi culture featuring music, food and art at the **Lombadina community** (08-9192 4936; www.lombadina.com; entry per car $10, campsites $50, s/d/cabin $100/170/220; office 8am-noon & 1-4pm Mon-Fri; P). Check the dates with the Lombadina community as the timing of this fledgling festival varies each year. Drug and alcohol free.

Sleeping & Eating

Pender Bay Campground CAMPGROUND $

(0429 845 707; www.facebook.com/penderbayescape; Pender Bay; day use/campsites per person $10/15;) Clifftop vantage points provide exceptional views of Pender Bay and migrating whales. There are simple bush campsites, an amenity block, and Andrew, who is a font

WORTH A TRIP

FAR-FLUNG LUXURY

Suddenly come into a small fortune? Then consider one of the *exotique* luxury wilderness camps hidden away along the rugged, inhospitable Kimberley coastline. With guest numbers kept to an absolute minimum, you can expect full five-star service.

Faraway Bay (0419 918 953; www.farawaybay.com.au; per person per night (minimum 3 nights) $1000; Mar-Oct;) Faraway by name and location, all meals and activities are included at this bush camp on the wild Kimberley coast. En-suite cabins with stunning views and private outdoor showers sit above a remote bay.

Kimberley Coastal Camp (0417 902 006; www.kimberleycoastalcamp.com.au; Admiralty Gulf; per person from $990) Pick (and pay for) activities such as fishing, yoga, rock-art tours and cooking lessons at this exclusive camp on the eastern side of Admiralty Gulf near Mitchell Falls.

Berkeley River Lodge (08-9169 1330; www.berkeleyriver.com.au; Berkeley River; villa $2850; Apr-Sep;) Twenty luxury air-con villas sit on top of a dune above the pristine coastline of Joseph Bonaparte Gulf.

El Questro Homestead (08-9169 1777; www.elquestro.com.au; r all-inclusive $2000-3100;) Not on the coast, but perched literally on the cliff-edge of Chamberlain Gorge on El Questro Station, these luxury rooms come with incredible views, gourmet meals and guided tours around the property.

of knowledge about the environmental challenges facing the Dampier Peninsula.

Gumbanan CAMPGROUND $
(0499 330 169; www.gumbananwildernessretreat.com.au; near One Arm Point; campsites per person $15, safari tent d/f $120/140;) On a beautifully unspoiled mangrove coast, this small outstation between Cape Leveque and **Ardyaloon** (Bardi; 08-9192 4930; per person $15, child free; office 8am-noon & 1.30-4pm Mon-Thu, 8am-noon & 1.30-3pm Fri) offers quiet, unpowered sites and simple safari tents. Immerse yourself in traditional Bardi culture with spear-making ($85), mud-crabbing ($95) or damper (camp bread)-making ($40) courses.

Smithy's Seaside Adventures CAMPGROUND $
(0429 086 388; https://youcamp.com/view/smithys-seaside-adventures; Embalgun; campsites $50; May-Sep;) Will and Colleen run this laid-back campground at the end of the road, 200m past Whale Song Cafe (p224), right on Pender Bay. Choose from a variety of Aboriginal cultural tours and interactions. Amenities are basic.

★ **Goombaragin Eco Retreat** RESORT $$
(0429 505 347; www.goombaragin.com.au; Pender Bay; campsites per person $18, tent with/without bathroom $175/80, chalets $220; Apr-Oct;) With a superb location overlooking the scarlet pindan cliffs and turquoise waters of Pender Bay, this eco-retreat offers several unpowered campsites, a range of safari tents and a self-contained chalet. There's a nightly communal get-together around the fire and regular pizza nights.

Mercedes Cove CABIN $$
(08-9192 4687; www.mercedescove.com.au; Pender Bay; eco-tents/cabins $150/300; Apr-Sep;) On a stunning, secluded cove near **Middle Lagoon** (Nature's Hideaway; 08-9192 4002; www.middlelagoon.com.au; campsites per person $20-22, cabins $150-300, day use $10;), Mercedes offers a chilled glamping experience with beautifully appointed eco-tents and air-con cabins, all with amazing Indian Ocean views. It's the perfect spot for whale watching, beachcombing, fishing and birdwatching. A minimum stay (two/three nights) applies for weekends/long weekends.

Kooljaman RESORT $$
(08-9192 4970; www.kooljaman.com.au; entry per adult $10, unpowered/powered sites $50/55, dome tents $90, beach shelters $120, cabin with/without bathroom $200/170, safari tents from $310;) Ecotourism award-winner Kooljaman offers a range of accommodation from grassy campsites and budget dome tents to driftwood beach shelters, cabins and hilltop safari tents with superb views. On-site restaurant **Raugi's** (lunch $16-29, BBQ packs $25; 7.30-10am, 11.30am-2pm & 6-10pm Apr-Oct, 11.30am-2pm Nov-Mar;) overlooks Western Beach and

the smaller **Dinka's Cafe** (snacks $3.50-7.50; 8am-4pm Mar-Sep;) is on the eastern side, or you can order takeaway BBQ packs.

Cygnet Bay Pearl Farm RESORT $$
(08-9192 4283; www.cygnetbaypearlfarm.com.au; Cygnet Bay; powered sites/safari tents/pearlers' shacks from $45/195/290, tours adult/child from $65/35;) In Bardi Jawi Country, and overlooking incredible Cygnet Bay, this historic pastoral lease and pearl farm offers a range of accommodation from camping and safari tents to air-conditioned pearlers' shacks. There are various cruises and cultural tours among the legendary tides of King Sound and an on-site restaurant and bar (lunch $18 to $32, buffet dinner $37.50).

Whale Song Cafe CAFE $$
(08-9192 4000; www.whalesongcafe.com.au; Munget, Pender Bay; light meals $13-29, campsites adult/child $20/10; 8.30am-4pm Jun-Aug;) This exquisitely located eco-cafe overlooking Pender Bay serves fabulous organic mango smoothies, homemade gourmet pizzas and the best coffee on the peninsula. There's a tiny bush campground with stunning views, a funky outdoor shower and not a caravan in sight. Telstra mobile reception available.

Getting There & Away

There is currently no public transport to the Dampier Peninsula though check with Broome Visitor Centre (p221) for the latest update. Without your own 4WD you'll have to take a tour.

Derby

08 / POP 3600

Late at night while Derby (dur-bee) sleeps, the boabs cut loose and wander around town, the marauding mobs flailing their many limbs in battle against an army of giant, killer croc-people emerging from the encircling mudflats... If only.

There *are* crocs hiding in the mangroves, but you're more likely to see birds (over 200 different varieties), while the boabs are firmly rooted along the two main parallel drags, Loch and Clarendon Sts. Derby, sitting on **King Sound**, is the West Kimberley's administrative centre and home to various Indigenous groups (eg Nykina, Dambimangari, Worrorra, Wunumbal) who comprise 50% of the population. Tours depart here for the Horizontal Waterfalls (p226) and Buccaneer Archipelago, and it's also the western terminus of the Gibb River Road (p228).

Sights

★**Norval Gallery** GALLERY
(0458 110 816; www.facebook.com/norvalgallery derby; 1 Sutherland St; hours vary) Kimberley art legends Mark and Mary Norval have set up an exciting gallery in an old tin shed on the edge of town. Featuring striking artworks, exquisite jewellery, decent coffee and 5000 vinyl records, a visit here is a delight to the senses. Note, they may be moving to the other end of town in the near future.

Jetty LANDMARK
(Jetty Rd;) Check out King Sound's colossal 11.5m tides from the circular jetty, 2km northwest of town, a popular fishing, crabbing, bird-spotting and staring-into-the-sunset haunt. Yep, there are crocs in the mangroves.

Kimberley School of the Air SCHOOL
(Marmion St; $10; hours vary;) Fascinating look at how school is conducted over the radio for children on remote stations. Currently open only on Thursdays, so check times with the visitor centre (p227) first.

Wharefinger Museum MUSEUM
(cnr Elder & Loch Sts; by donation;) Grab the key from the visitor centre (p227) and have a peek inside the nearby museum, with its atmospheric shipping and aviation displays.

Activities

Derby Wetlands BIRDWATCHING
(Conway St) The wetlands (aka sewerage ponds) are a likely place to spot migratory waders and local raptors.

Joonjoo Botanical Trail WALKING
This 2.3km trail, opposite the Gibb River Road turn-off, has neat interpretive displays from the local Nyikina people.

Tours

★**Horizontal Falls Seaplane Adventures** SCENIC FLIGHTS
(08-9192 1172; www.horizontalfallsadventures.com.au; 6hr tours from Derby/Broome $775/850) Flights to Horizontal Waterfalls (p226) land on Talbot Bay before transferring to high-powered speedboats for an adrenaline-packed ride through both sets of falls. There's also an overnight-stay option from $895.

Kimberley Dreamtime Adventure Tours CULTURAL
(08-9191 7280; www.kdatjarlmadangah.wordpress.com; adult/child 2 days from $492/350, 3 days from $710/565; Apr-Oct) Aboriginal-owned

THE KIMBERLEY'S ART SCENE

The Indigenous art of the Kimberley is unique. Encompassing powerful and strongly guarded Wandjina, prolific and enigmatic Gwion Gwion (Bradshaws), bright tropical coastal X-rays, subtle and sombre bush ochres and topographical dots of the western desert, every work sings a story about Country.

To experience it firsthand, visit some of these Aboriginal-owned cooperatives; most are accessible by 2WD.

Mowanjum Art & Culture Centre (☎08-9191 1008; www.mowanjumarts.com; Gibb River Rd; ⏰9am-5pm daily dry season, closed Sat & Sun wet season, closed Jan) FREE This incredible gallery, shaped like a Wandjina image, features work by Mowanjum artists. Just 4km along the Gibb River Road from Derby.

Waringarri Aboriginal Arts Centre (p233) Excellent Kununurra gallery-studio featuring abstract ochre works.

Warmun Arts (☎08-9168 7496; www.warmunart.com.au; Warmun; ⏰8am-4pm Mon-Fri; P) Between Kununurra and Halls Creek, Warmun artists create beautiful works using ochres to explore Gija identity.

Laarri Gallery (☎08-9191 7195; www.fitzroycrossingtourism.com.au/yiyili/laarri-gallery; Yiyili; ⏰9am-4pm school days Mar-Nov; P 👪) This tiny not-for-profit gallery located in the back of the Yiyili community school depicts local history through interesting contemporary-style art. It's 120km west of Halls Creek and 5km from the Great Northern Hwy. Phone ahead.

Mangkaja Arts (p232) Respected Fitzroy Crossing gallery where desert and river tribes interact, producing unique acrylics, prints and baskets.

Yarliyil Gallery (☎08-9168 6723; http://yarliyil.com.au; Great Northern Hwy; ⏰9am-5pm Mon-Fri; P) Great Halls Creek gallery showcasing talented local artists as well as some of the Kundat Djaru (Ringer Soak) mob.

Warlayirti Artists Centre (☎08-9168 8960; www.balgoart.org.au; Balgo; ⏰9am-5pm Mon-Fri) This Balgo centre, 255km down the Tanami Rd, is a conduit for artists around the area and features bright acrylic dot-style works as well as lithographs and glass works. Phone first, before leaving the highway.

Bidyadanga Community Art Centre (☎08-9192 4885; www.desertriversea.com.au/art-centres/bidyadanga-community-art-centre; Bidyadanga Rd, Bidyadanga; ⏰9am-1pm Mon-Thu) South of Broome, this intriguing centre brings together both desert and coastal influences in WA's largest remote community.

Nagula Jarndu Women's Resource Centre (p213) Don't miss the incredible printed fabrics at this Broome women's centre.

Marnin Studio (p232) Famous for their carved boab-nuts, the women at this Fitzroy Crossing studio also hand-print paper and silk scarves.

For more information, look up www.desertriversea.com.au and download the *Kimberley Aboriginal Art Trail* map, or find it in a visitor centre.

If time's short, wander through the Short Street Gallery's Bungalow (p213) in Hopton St, Broome, for a sample of the different Kimberley styles.

and -operated cultural tours based in Nyikina Mangala Country on Mt Anderson Station, 126km southeast of Derby. Camp under the stars, ride camels, fish, hunt, walk and learn about Aboriginal culture. Pick-ups from Broome, Willare or Derby.

Uptuyu CULTURAL

(☎0400 878 898; www.uptuyu.com.au; Oongkalkada Wilderness Camp, Udialla Springs; 2 nights, 1 full day (incl 3 activities) per person with/without transfers $990/760) Down in Nyikina Country on the Fitzroy River, 50km from the Great Northern Hwy, Neville and Jo run 'designer' cultural tours taking in wetlands, rock art, fishing and Aboriginal communities along the Fitzroy and further afield. Your stay includes two nights in a luxury eco-tent, all meals and a choice of activities.

HORIZONTAL WATERFALLS

One of the most intriguing features of the Kimberley coastline is the phenomenon known as **horizontal waterfalls** (Talbot Bay). Despite the name, the falls are simply tides gushing through narrow coastal gorges in the Buccaneer Archipelago, north of Derby. What creates such a spectacle are the huge tides, often varying up to 11m. The water flow reaches an astonishing 30 knots as it's forced through two narrow gaps 20m and 10m wide – resulting in a 'waterfall' reaching 4m in height.

Many tours leave Derby (and some Broome) each Dry, by air, sea or a combination of both. It's become *de rigueur* to 'ride' the tide change through the gorges on a high-powered speedboat. There is a risk element involved and accidents have occurred. Scenic flights are the quickest and cheapest option and some seaplanes will land and transfer passengers to a waiting speedboat for the adrenalin hit. If you prefer to be stirred, not shaken, then consider seeing the falls as part of a longer cruise through the archipelago. Book tours at the Derby and Broome visitor centres.

The traditional Dambimangari owners recognise that the falls are a tourist attraction, but ask you don't travel through them on the tide change, in respect to the Wongudd (creator snake), said to be the tide itself.

Windjana Tours CULTURAL
(08-9193 1502; www.windjana.com.au; adult/child $230/95; Tue, Thu & Sun Apr-Sep, also Fri Jun-Aug) Full-day cultural tours to Windjana Gorge and Tunnel Creek from Derby. Lunch and refreshments are included. May still run during the Wet (dependent on numbers and road conditions). Pick-up from visitor centre.

Festivals & Events

★**Boab Festival** MUSIC, CULTURAL
(www.derbyboabfestival.org.au; Jul;) Concerts, mud footy, horse and mud-crab races, poetry readings, art exhibitions and street parades. Try to catch the Long Table dinner out on the mudflats.

Sleeping

Kimberley Entrance Caravan Park CARAVAN PARK $
(08-9193 1055; www.kimberleyentrancecaravanpark.com; 2 Rowan St; unpowered/powered sites $36/40;) Not all sites are shaded, though there's always room. Amenities are basic but clean. Expect insects so close to the mudflats.

★**Desert Rose** B&B $$
(0428 332 269; twobrownies@bigpond.com; 4 Marmion St; d $225;) Book ahead for the best sleep in town, with spacious, individually styled rooms, a nice shady pool, leadlight windows and a sumptuous breakfast. Host Anne is a font of local information.

Derby Lodge MOTEL $$
(08-9193 2924; www.derbylodge.com.au; 15-19 Clarendon St; r/apt $150/210;) Choose between neat, clean motel rooms or self-contained apartments with cooking facilities. The on-site **Neaps Bistro** (08-9191 1263; www.facebook.com/neapsbistro; mains $19-38; 7-11am & 6-9pm Mon-Sat, 7-11am Sun;) does the best food in Derby.

Spinifex Hotel RESORT $$
(08-9191 1233; www.spinifexhotel.com.au; 6 Clarendon St; donga/motel r $120/225;) Rising phoenix-like from the ashes of the old Spini, this sleek resort has corporate-class rooms (some with kitchenettes) and an on-site restaurant (mains $22 to $42). Peak season brings outdoor live music.

Eating

Sampey Meats DELI $
(08-9193 2444; www.sampeymeats.com.au; 59 Rowan St; 8.30am-5pm Mon-Fri, 8am-noon Sat) Carnivores can stock up for the Gibb with homemade jerkies, biltong and succulent vacuum-sealed steaks.

HighTide Cafe CAFE $
(08-9193 2361; www.facebook.com/hightidecafederby; 2/59 Rowan St; breakfast $8-22, lunch $12-24; 7am-3pm Mon-Fri, to noon Sat;) Filling breakfasts, homemade pies and quiches, tasty salads and affordable light lunches complement great coffee at this local near the campground.

Jila Gallery ITALIAN $$
(08-9193 2560; www.jilacafe.com.au; 18 Clarendon St; pizzas $20-28, mains $24-34; 6pm-late Tue-Sat;) Jila's fortunes fluctuate with its chefs, who turn out wood-fired pizzas, homemade pastas and wonderful cakes, all in a shady, al fresco setting. Last orders 8.30pm.

Information

Derby Visitor Centre (08-9191 1426; www.derbytourism.com.au; 30 Loch St; 8.30am-4.30pm Mon-Fri, 9am-3pm Sat & Sun dry season) Helpful centre with the low-down on road conditions, accommodation, transport and tour bookings. Buses leave from here.

Getting There & Away

Charter and sightseeing flights use Derby Airport (DRB), just past the Gibb turn-off. Scheduled commercial services to Perth ceased in 2016 but may be reinstated; if so, they will leave from Curtin Airport (DCN), 40km away.

All buses depart from the visitor centre.

Derby Bus Service (08-9193 1550; www.derbybus.com.au; 30 Loch St; one way/return $50/80; Mon, Wed & Fri) Leaves early for Broome (2½ hours), stopping at Willare Roadhouse (and anywhere else along the way if you ask the driver), returning the same day.

Greyhound (1300 473 946; www.greyhound.com.au; 30 Loch St) Broome ($64, 2½ hours), Darwin ($289, 25 hours), Fitzroy Crossing ($72,three hours) and Kununurra ($144, 12 hours) daily (except Sundays).

Devonian Reef National Parks

08

Three national parks with three stunning gorges were once part of a western 'great barrier reef' in the Devonian era, 350 million years ago. Windjana Gorge and Tunnel Creek National Parks are accessed via the unsealed Fairfield-Leopold Downs Rd (linking the Great Northern Hwy with the Gibb River Road), while Geikie Gorge National Park is 22km northeast of Fitzroy Crossing.

Sights

★Tunnel Creek NATIONAL PARK

(per car $13; dry season; P) Sick of the sun? Then cool down underground at Tunnel Creek, which cuts through a spur of the Napier Range for almost 1km. It was famously the hideout of Jandamarra (a Bunuba man who waged an armed guerrilla war against the police and white settlers for three years before he was killed). In the Dry, the full length is walkable by wading partly through knee-deep water; watch out for bats and bring good footwear and a strong torch.

Geikie Gorge NATIONAL PARK

(Darngku; Apr-Dec; P) Don't miss this magnificent limestone gorge, 20km north of Fitzroy Crossing by sealed road. The self-guided trails are sandy and hot, so take one of the informative boat cruises run by either Parks & Wildlife staff or local Bunuba guides.

Windjana Gorge NATIONAL PARK

(per car $13, campsites adult/child $13/3; dry season) The sheer walls of the Napier Range soar 100m above the Lennard River in this gorge sacred to the Bunuba people. Contracting in the Dry to a series of pools, scores of freshwater crocodiles line the riverbank, hence swimming is not recommended. Bring plenty of water for the sandy 7km return walk from the campground.

Tours

Bungoolee Tours CULTURAL

(08-9191 5355; www.bungoolee.com.au; 2hr tour adult/child $60/30, smoking ceremony $25, full-day tour adult/child $235/150; 2hr tour 10am & 2pm Mon, Wed & Fri, full-day tour 8am Tue, Thu & Sat dry season) Bunuba lawman Dillon Andrews runs informative two-hour Tunnel Creek tours explaining the story of Jandamarra. Also available is a traditional 'Welcome to Country' smoking ceremony ($25) and a full-day tour to both Tunnel Creek and Windjana Gorge from Fitzroy Crossing. Book through the Fitzroy Crossing visitor centre (p232).

Darngku Heritage Tours CRUISE

(0417 907 609; www.darngku.com.au; adult/child 2hr tour $100/80, 3hr $120/90, half-day $200/165; Apr-Dec;) Local Bunuba guides introduce Aboriginal culture and bush tucker on these amazingly informative cruises through Geikie (Darngku) Gorge. A shorter one-hour cruise (adult/child $55/15) operates during the shoulder seasons (April and October to December).

Geikie Gorge Boat Tour CRUISE

(08-9191 5121; https://parksandwildlife.rezdy.com/154373/geikie-gorge-boat-tour; 1hr tour adult/child $50/14; cruises from 8am May-Oct) Parks & Wildlife staff run regular wildlife-spotting boat trips up the gorge with local Bunuba guides.

Getting There & Away

You'll need your own vehicle to visit the three parks. Geikie Gorge is easily accessed from Fitzroy Crossing, but if you only have a 2WD, check the condition of Fairfield-Leopold Downs Rd first – for Windjana Gorge and Tunnel Creek – where there's at least one permanent creek crossing. Otherwise, consider taking a day tour from Derby or Fitzroy Crossing.

Gibb River Road

08

Cutting a brown swath through the scorched heart of the Kimberley, the legendary Gibb River Road ('the Gibb' or GRR) provides one of Australia's wildest outback experiences. Stretching some 660km between Derby and Kununurra, the largely unpaved road is an endless sea of red dirt, big open skies and dramatic terrain. Rough, sometimes deeply corrugated side roads lead to remote gorges, shady pools, distant waterfalls and million-acre cattle stations. Rain can close the road at any time and it's permanently closed during the Wet. This is true wilderness with minimal services, so good planning and self-sufficiency are vital.

A high-clearance 4WD is mandatory, with two spare tyres, tools, emergency water (20L minimum) and several days' food in case of breakdown. Britz (p221) in Broome is a reputable hire outfit. Fuel is limited and expensive, mobile phone coverage is minimal and temperatures can be life-threatening.

Tours

Adventure Tours DRIVING
(1300 654 604; www.adventuretours.com.au; from $2195) Ten-day Gibb River Road camping tours catering for a younger crowd.

Wundargoodie Aboriginal Safaris CULTURAL
(0429 928 088; www.wundargoodie.com.au; 1707 Great Northern Hwy; tag-along per vehicle per day from $250; Apr-Sep;) These insightful Aboriginal-run 4WD tag-along tours (ie you bring your own vehicle) showcase local culture and rock art in the remote East Kimberley. It also runs all-inclusive women-only tours on demand, camping at special sites and sharing experiences with Aboriginal women from various communities.

Kimberley Adventure Tours DRIVING
(1800 171 616; www.kimberleyadventures.com.au; 9-day tour $2195) Small-group camping tours from Broome up the Gibb, with the nine-day tour continuing to Purnululu and Darwin. Also offers the reverse direction, starting in Darwin.

Kimberley Wild Expeditions DRIVING
(1300 738 870; www.kimberleywild.com.au; tours $245-4295) Consistent award winner. Tours from Broome range from one ($245) to 15 days ($4295) on the Gibb River Road and beyond.

Information

For tourist info head to the Derby (p227) and Kununurra (p236) visitor centre websites. The visitor centres also sell the *Gibb River & Kalumburu Roads* guide ($5).

An **Uunguu Visitor Pass** (UVP; www.wunambalgaambera.org.au; entry per person $45) (UVP) is required to visit Mitchell Falls and Munurru.

Mainroads Western Australia (p231) Highway and Gibb River Road conditions. Has a useful *Driving the Gibb River Road* downloadable brochure.

Parks & Wildlife Service (www.dpaw.wa.gov.au) Park permits, camping fees and information. Consider a Holiday Pass ($46) if visiting more than three parks in one month (does not cover Mitchell Falls).

Shire of Derby/West Kimberley (08-9191 0999; www.sdwk.wa.gov.au) Side-road conditions and closures for the Western and Central Gibb.

Shire of Wyndham/East Kimberley (08-9168 4100; www.swek.wa.gov.au) Kalumburu/Mitchell Falls road conditions.

Getting There & Away

Plan your fuel stops (note opening times carefully!) and carry extra supplies. Unleaded petrol is only available at Mt Barnett Roadhouse and Drysdale River Station, while diesel is available at both and also Imintji Store and Mt Hart Homestead. If you get stuck, you might be able to buy a few litres from one of the stations, but don't count on it.

Western Gibb

Heading east from Derby, the first 100-odd kilometres of the Gibb River Road are now sealed. Don't miss Mowanjum Art & Culture Centre (p225), only 4km along.

The Windjana Gorge (p227) turn-off at 119km is your last chance to head back to the Great Northern Hwy. Windjana is an easy 22km off the Gibb and is a popular camp site. Back on the GRR, the scenery improves after crossing the **Lennard River** into Napier Downs Station as the **King Leopold Ranges** loom ahead. Just after **Inglis Gap** is the Mount Hart Wilderness Lodge turn-off and another 7km brings the narrow **Lennard River Gorge**.

Despite its name, **March Fly Glen**, 204km from Derby, is a pleasant, shady picnic area ringed by pandanus and frequented by blue-faced honeyeaters. Don't miss stunning **Bell Gorge** (per car $13), with its waterfall and plunge pool. Refuel (diesel only), grab an ice cream and check your email at Imintji Store.

WORTH A TRIP

MITCHELL FALLS & DRYSDALE RIVER

In the Dry, Kalumburu Rd is normally navigable as far as **Drysdale River Station** (08-9161 4326; www.drysdaleriver.com.au; campsites per person $12-16, d from $150; 8am-5pm Apr-Sep, lunch 11am-2pm, dinner from 5pm; P ❄), 59km from the Gibb River Road.

The **Mitchell Plateau (Ngauwudu)** turn-off is 160km from the Gibb, and within 6km a deep, rocky ford crosses the **King Edward River**, which is formidable early in the season. You're now on **Wunambal Gaambera Country** and the first of two rock-art shelters is on the left, with the second just after the nearby **Munurru Campground** (campsites per adult/child $8/3; P), both to the right.

From the Kalumburu Rd it's a very rough 87km, past lookouts and forests of *Livistona* palms to the dusty campground at **Mitchell River National Park** (www.dpaw.wa.gov.au; entry per person $45, campsites adult/child $11/3; dry season; P). The park contains the stunning, multi-tiered **Mitchell Falls (Punamii-unpuu)**, which can be seen on a lovely three-hour return walk passing inviting, shady waterholes and incredible Aboriginal rock art.

Sleeping

Imintji Campground CAMPGROUND $
(08-9191 7699; www.imintji.com; Gibb River Rd; campsites per person $19; May-Oct; P) Community-run refurbished campground with shady sites and modern facilities, 500m west of the **community store** (08-9191 7227; 8am-5pm dry season, shorter hours wet season;).

Silent Grove CAMPGROUND $
(campsites adult/child $13/3; P) Nineteen kilometres from the Gibb, on the road to Bell Gorge, this sheltered, somewhat dusty Parks & Wildlife campground in the King Leopold Ranges is popular with groups.

Mount Hart Wilderness Lodge RESORT $
(08-9191 4645; www.mounthart.com.au; campsites adult/child $18/10, r or safari tent per person incl dinner & breakfast $295; dry season) Below Inglis Gap, a 50km track heads deep into the King Leopold Ranges Conservation Park to the privately run Wilderness Lodge, once the old Mt Hart Homestead. There's grassy (unpowered) campsites, wildlife, swimming holes and pleasant gorges.

Central Gibb

Heading east from Imintji, it's only 25km to the Mornington turn-off and another 5km further to the entrance of **Charnley River Station** (08-9191 4646; www.australianwildlife.org; campsites per person $20, entry per vehicle $25;). If heading across the wild, lonely savannah to exquisite Mornington Wilderness Camp, call first using the radio at the Gibb. Back on the GRR, most of the cattle you pass are from **Mount House Station**. Cross the **Adcock**, wave to Nev and Leonie as you pass **Over the Range Repairs** (08-9191 7887; overtherangetyres@gmail.com; 8am-5pm dry season), then drop down to **Galvans Gorge** (Gibb River Rd) FREE at the 286km mark.

Fuel up at **Mt Barnett Roadhouse** (08-9191 7007; www.facebook.com/mtbarnettroadhouse; 8am-5pm dry season, shorter hours wet season), 300km from Derby, and get your camping permit if choosing to stay at nearby **Manning River Gorge** (7km behind Mt Barnett Roadhouse; campsites per person $22.50, gorge day access $8; dry season;), though there are better options further east. There's free camping on the **Barnett River** (29km east of Mt Barnett Roadhouse; campsites free;) at the 329km mark, and if you've still got daylight, consider pushing on to historic Mt Elizabeth Station (p230); turn off at the 338km mark.

Sleeping

★ Mornington Wilderness Camp WILDLIFE RESERVE
(08-9191 7406; www.australianwildlife.org/mornington-wilderness-camp; entry per vehicle $25, campsites per adult/child $20/10, full-board safari tents s/d $335/600; May–mid-Oct;) Part of the Australian Wildlife Conservancy, the superb Mornington Wilderness Camp is as remote as it gets, lying on the Fitzroy River, an incredibly scenic 95km drive across the savannah from the Gibb's 247km mark. Nearly 400,000 hectares are devoted to conserving the Kimberley's endangered fauna and there's excellent canoeing, swimming, birdwatching and bushwalking.

Choose from shady campsites with gas BBQs or spacious raised tents (including full board) with verandahs and bathrooms. The bar and restaurant offer full dinner ($60), BBQ packs ($25) and the best cheese platter ($25) this side of Margaret River. Vegetarians are well-catered for. **Sir John Gorge** in the late afternoon sun is sublime. Call ahead using the radio provided at the Gibb turn-off.

Bachsten Creek Bush Camp CAMPGROUND **$**
(☎08-9191 1547; www.bushtracksafaris.com.au/bushcamp/bachsten.html; Munja Track, via Mt Elizabeth; campsites per adult/child $18/9, cabins d $120; ⏲dry season) You've often heard of 'the middle of nowhere'; well this is it, a lovely shady campground on the edge of Bachsten Creek, 1km off the fabled **Munja Track** (☎08-9191 4644; www.mtelizabethstationstay.com.au; per vehicle $150, key deposit $50; ⏲dry season) and 145km from Mt Elizabeth. There's a handful of cabins, BBQ pits, a camp kitchen, showers and swimming nearby. Many travellers prefer staying here, visiting Walcott Inlet as a day trip.

Mt Elizabeth Station FARMSTAY **$**
(☎08-9191 4644; www.mtelizabethstationstay.com.au; campsites per person $22, r per person with/without meals $220/135, gorge pass day/overnight $20/15; ⏲dry season; 📶) Around 338km from Derby is the turn-off to historic Mt Elizabeth Station. Run by the Lacy family for generations, and now owned by Chinese interests, the 200,000-hectare working cattle property is a good base for exploration to nearby gorges, waterfalls and Aboriginal rock art. Wallabies frequent the camp site and the home-style, three-course dinners ($50 – book ahead) hit the spot.

Eastern Gibb

At 406km from Derby you reach the Kalumburu turn-off. Head right on the Gibb River Road and 70km later call in for scones at historic **Ellenbrae Station** (☎08-9161 4325; www.ellenbraestation.com.au; Gibb River Rd; campsites per person $17.50, cabins from $155, scones $4.50; ⏲dry season; P). Continue through spectacular country, crossing the mighty **Durack River** then climbing though the **Pentecost Ranges** to 579km where there are panoramic views of the Cockburn Ranges, Cambridge Gulf and Pentecost River. Shortly after is the turn-off to the lovely **Home Valley Station** (☎08-9161 4322; www.homevalley.com.au; Gibb River Rd; campsites per person $21, eco-tent d from $165, homestead d from $295; ⏲May-Oct; ❄@📶🏊).

Soon after Home Valley, at 589km from Derby, you'll cross the infamous **Pentecost River** – take care as water levels are unpredictable and saltwater crocs lurk nearby. El Questro Wilderness Park looms on the right. The last section of the Gibb River Road is sealed. The turn-off to beautiful **Emma Gorge** (⏲Apr-Sep; P👪) is 10km past El Questro. You'll cross **King River** 630km from Derby and, at 647km, you'll finally hit the Great Northern Hwy – turn left for Wyndham (48km) and right to Kununurra (53km).

Sleeping

El Questro Wilderness Park PARK
(☎08-9169 1777; www.elquestro.com.au; adult permit per day/week $12/20; ⏲dry season; 👪) This vast 400,000-hectare former cattle station turned international resort incorporates scenic gorges (**Amelia**, **El Questro**) and **Zebedee Springs** (⏲7am-noon; P). **Boat tours** (adult/child from $65/33; ⏲3pm) explore Chamberlain Gorge or you can hire your own boat ($100). There are shady campsites and air-con bungalows at **El Questro Station Township** (☎08-9169 1777; www.elquestro.com.au; campsites per person $22-30, station tent d $175, bungalow d from $339; ❄📶) and also an outdoor bar and upmarket steakhouse (mains $28 to $44).

Great Northern Highway

☎08

One of the Kimberley's best-kept secrets is the vast subterranean labyrinth of **Mimbi Caves** (☎08-9191 5355; www.mimbicaves.com.au; Mt Pierre Station; P👪), 90km southeast of Fitzroy Crossing, located within Mt Pierre Station on Gooniyandi land. Stay at their wonderful **Jarlarloo Riwi** (Mimbi Caves Campground; ☎08-9191 5355; www.mimbicaves.com.au; Mt Pierre Station; campsites per adult/child/family $18/15/48; P) campground at the base of the scenic **Emmanuel Range** or keep heading east 50km to **Larrawa Station** (Bush Camp; ☎08-9191 7025; www.larrawabushcamp.com; Great Northern Hwy; campsites per person $10; ⏲Apr-Sep; @🐾), a pleasant overnight stop with hot showers, basic campsites and shearers' rooms. Another 30km towards Halls Creek is tiny Yiyili with its Laarri Gallery (p225).

Pushing on from Halls, the scenery becomes progressively more interesting and just after the **Ord River** bridge you'll pass the Purnululu National Park (p236) turn-off

OFF THE BEATEN TRACK

KALUMBURU

Kalumburu, Western Australia's most northerly settlement, is a picturesque mission nestled beneath giant mango trees and coconut palms on the King Edward River. There's some interesting rock art nearby and the odd WWII bomber wreck. Only opened to non-Indigenous tourists in 2018, the stunning hour-glass **Wongalala Falls** (www.facebook.com/kalumburutourism; Kalumburu access permit $50; dry season) empty into a large, perfectly circular plunge pool, 20km from Kalumburu. You can stay at the **Kalumburu Mission** (08-9161 4333; www.kalumburumission.org.au; campsites per adult/child $20/8, donga s/d $125/175;), which has a small **museum** (Fr Thomas Gill Museum; $10; 11am-1pm), or obtain a permit from the Kalumburu Aboriginal Community (KAC) office to camp at **Honeymoon Bay** (08-9161 4378; www.facebook.com/honeymoonbay-wa; campsites per person $15;) or **McGowan Island** (Sunset Beach; 08-9161 4748; www.facebook.com/mcgowanssunsetbeachcampingwa; campsites per person $20;), 20km further out on the coast – the end of the road.

You'll need a permit from the **Department of Aboriginal Affairs** (DAA; 1300 651 077; www.dplh.wa.gov.au) in Broome to visit Kalumburu and a **Kalumburu Aboriginal Community** (08-9161 4300; www.kalumburu.org) visitors' permit ($50 per vehicle, valid for seven days) upon entry, available from the **Community Resource Centre** (CRC, Visitor Centre; 08-9161 4627; www.kalumburu.org; hours vary;). Alcohol is banned at Kalumburu. BYO 4WD.

at 108km. Warmun (162km) has a roadhouse and an amazing gallery (p225) in the nearby community. **Doon Doon Roadhouse** (08-9167 8004; Doon Doon; 6am-8pm), 91km from Warmun and 60km from the Victoria Hwy junction, is the only other blip on the landscape and your last chance to refuel before Kununurra or Wyndham. If heading to **Wuggubun** (08-9161 4040; campsites per vehicle $30; Apr-Sep;), the signposted turn-off is 4km south of the highway junction, just before Card Creek (if heading north).

Tours

Luridgii Tours DRIVING

(Junama; 08-9168 2704; www.luridgiitours.com.au; Doon Doon; per vehicle $250) Be personally guided through the gorges, thermal pools and Dreaming stories of Miriuwung Country by the traditional owners on these 4WD cultural tag-alongs (you drive your own vehicle). Tours depart from Doon Doon Roadhouse on the Great Northern Hwy and there is an overnight camping option ($50 per vehicle). BYO food.

Girloorloo Tours CULTURAL

(08-9191 5355; www.mimbicaves.com.au; 2hr tour adult/child $80/40; 8am, 10am & 2pm Mon-Thu, 8am Fri, 8am & 10am Sat Apr-Sep;) Aboriginal-owned Girloorloo Tours runs trips to the remarkable Mimbi Caves, a vast subterranean labyrinth housing Aboriginal rock art and impressive fish fossils. The tours include an introduction to local Dreaming stories, bush tucker and traditional medicines. Book through Fitzroy Crossing or Halls Creek visitor centres.

Getting There & Away

The Great Northern Hwy (GNH) is sealed and services are spaced at manageable distances. Always carry extra water, because if your vehicle breaks down, you may need to spend the night in it before help arrives.

Aviair (08-9166 9300; www.aviair.com.au; adult one way $325) For Kununurra from Halls Creek.

Greyhound (p221) Links the towns on the GNH with Broome and Darwin.

Mainroads Western Australia (MRWA; 13 81 38; www.mainroads.wa.gov.au) For road conditions.

Skippers (1300 729 924; www.skippers.com.au) Flies to Broome from Fitzroy Crossing and Halls Creek.

Fitzroy Crossing

08 / POP 1300

Gooniyandi, Bunuba, Walmajarri, Nyikina and Wangkajungka peoples populate the small settlement of Fitzroy Crossing where the Great Northern Hwy crosses the mighty Fitzroy River. There's little reason to stay other than that it's a good access point for the Devonian Reef National Parks and has some fine art and craft studios.

OFF THE BEATEN TRACK

DUNCAN ROAD

Snaking its way east from Halls Creek before eventually turning north and playing hide and seek with the Northern Territory (NT) border, Duncan Rd is a much more singular driving experience than the heavily touristed Gibb River Road. Unsealed for its entire length (445km), it receives only a trickle of travellers, but those who make the effort are rewarded with stunning scenery, beautiful gorges, tranquil billabongs and breathtakingly lonely campsites.

Technically no harder than the Gibb, all creek crossings are concrete-lined and croc-free. It also makes a nice loop if you've come down the Great Northern Hwy to Purnululu and want to return to Kununurra and/or the NT. There are no services on the entire Duncan, so carry fuel for at least 500km. Enquire at Halls Creek or Kununurra (p236) visitor centres about road conditions.

Sights

Mangkaja Arts GALLERY
(08-9191 5833; www.mangkaja.com; 8 Bell Rd; 11am-4pm Mon-Fri) This Fitzroy Crossing gallery is where desert and river tribes interact, producing unique acrylics, prints and baskets.

Marnin Studio ARTS CENTRE
(Marninwarntikura Women's Resource Centre; 08-9191 5284; www.mwrc.com.au; Lot 284, Balanijangarri Rd; 8.30am-4.30pm Mon-Fri) Marnin is the Walmajarri word for women and this studio uses crafts such as boab-nut painting, textile printing and bush-nut jewellery-making to bind together the women of the various local language groups.

Sleeping & Eating

Fitzroy River Lodge RESORT $$
(08-9191 5141; www.fitzroyriverlodge.com.au; Great Northern Hwy; campsites per person $21, tent/motel d $210/265, studios $375-530; bar noon-8.30pm, restaurant 5.30-8.30pm; P @) Across the river from town, Fitzroy River Lodge has comfortable motel rooms, safari tents, exclusive Riverview studios and grassy campsites. The friendly bar offers decent counter meals ($22 to $38) from noon to 8.30pm, while the deck of the **Riverside Restaurant** (dinner only, mains $32 to $42) is perfect for that much-needed sundowner.

★ **Jalangurru Mayi Cafe** CAFE $$
(08-9191 5124; www.facebook.com/jalangurrumayi; 75 Emmanuel Way; meals $6.50-23; 7am-2pm Tue-Sat) Nourishing, healthy, paleo food is the mantra behind Jalangurru Mayi ('good mood'), which eschews refined ingredients and sugars, a smart move in a town where diabetes is a growing problem. Easily the best brunch option between Broome and Kununurra, seriously good coffee complements wholesome breakfasts, lunches, salad bowls and gluten-free cakes. Offers free training to community members.

Crossing Inn PUB
(08-9191 5080; www.crossinginn.com.au; Skuthorpe Rd) For a true outback beer experience, sink a cold one at the Kimberley's oldest pub. There's also a small camping area (unpowered/powered sites $38/44) and some adequate, though overpriced rooms (from $195, continental breakfast included). Friday nights can be rowdy.

Information

Visitor Centre (08-9191 5355; www.fitzroycrossingtourism.com.au; 8am-4pm Mon-Fri, to noon Sat) Can arrange accommodation and book tickets to Geikie Gorge (p227) and Mimbi Caves (p230). **Greyhound** (1300 473 946; www.greyhound.com.au) bus stop and public library are also here.

Halls Creek

08 / POP 1600

On the edge of the Great Sandy Desert, Halls Creek is a small services town with communities of Kija, Jaru and Gooniyandi peoples. The excellent visitor centre can book tours to the Bungle Bungles and tickets for Mimbi Caves (p230). Across the highway, Yarliyil Gallery (p225) is definitely worth a look. The town regularly suffers water shortages.

Sights

Sawpit Gorge GORGE
(Duncan Rd) Great bushwalking, swimming and secluded campsites await the traveller prepared to cross the rocky Albert Edward Range to this gorge 50km from Halls Creek.

Palm Springs OASIS
(Lugangarna; Duncan Rd) FREE Soak your weary, corrugations-bashed body in this beau-

tiful, permanent pool on the Black Elvire River, 45km from Halls Creek. Free, 24-hour camping allowed.

China Wall LANDMARK
(Duncan Rd) Amateur geologists will marvel at this vein of white quartzite sticking out of the red dirt and spinifex, 6km from Halls Creek.

Tours

Northwest Regional Airlines SCENIC FLIGHTS
(08-9168 5211; www.facebook.com/northwestregional; Halls Creek Airport; flights per person 2/3/4 passengers from $580/390/295) Scenic flights from Halls Creek over **Wolfe Creek Meteorite Crater** (Kandimalal; https://parks.dpaw.wa.gov.au/park/wolfe-creek-crater; Tanami; P) FREE and the Bungle Bungles (p236).

Sleeping & Eating

Zebra Rock Mine CAMPGROUND $
(Wetland Safaris; 0400 767 650; www.zebrarockmine.com.au; Duncan Rd, NT; unpowered sites per adult $10, safari tent $25; Apr-Sep; P) The only formal accommodation on Duncan Rd is 10km from the Victoria Hwy and is technically in the Northern Territory. Travellers love the rustic vibe, and the sunset birdwatching tour ($120) is not to be missed. There's also a small cafe and gift shop. It is 2WD accessible if coming from the north.

Kimberley Hotel HOTEL $$
(08-9168 6101; www.kimberleyhotel.com.au; Roberta Ave; r from $230; P) Comfortable rooms are complemented by a lovely pool, shady terrace bar and a kitchen open most of the day (mains $18 to $38, pizzas $20 to $25).

Halls Creek Motel MOTEL $$
(08-9168 9600; www.hallscreekmotel.com.au; r from $200; P) Right on the highway, there's a variety of well-equipped rooms, from budget to deluxe with spa. **Russian Jack's** (mains $25-44, kids $20; 5-8.30pm) opens for dinner.

★ **Cafe Mungarri in the Park** CAFE $
(0477 552 644; 2 Hall St; toastie/curry $10/14; 7.30am-3pm Mon-Sat) The nicest coffee option in Halls Creek, Mungarri serves up cheap, simple wraps, toasted sandwiches and fresh juices on a shady verandah in the same building as the visitor centre.

Information

Visitor Centre (08-9168 6262; www.hallscreektourism.com.au; 2 Hall St; 8am-4pm) This great local resource can book tours and arrange art-gallery visits, as well as tickets for the Mimbi Caves (p230). There's free wi-fi in the council precinct outside.

Kununurra

08 / POP 6000

On Miriwoong Country near the Northern Territory border, Kununurra is a relaxed oasis set among farmland growing superfoods, and tropical fruit and sandalwood plantations, all thanks to the Ord River irrigation scheme. With good transport and communications, excellent services and well-stocked supermarkets, it's every traveller's favourite slice of civilisation between Broome and Darwin.

Kununurra is also the departure point for most East Kimberley tours, and with all that fruit, there's plenty of seasonal work. Note that NT time is 90 minutes ahead of WA.

Sights

Kelly's Knob VIEWPOINT
(Kelly Rd) The best view in Kununurra is from this rock outcrop on the town's northern edge. Great for sunrise or sunset.

Mirima National Park NATIONAL PARK
(per car $13) Like a mini Bungle Bungles, the eroded gorges of Hidden Valley are home to brittle red peaks, spinifex, boab trees and abundant wildlife. Several walking trails lead to lookouts; early morning or dusk are the best times for sighting fauna.

Waringarri Aboriginal Arts Centre GALLERY
(08-9168 2212; www.waringarriarts.com.au; 16 Speargrass Rd; gallery tour adult/child $55/25; 8.30am-4.30pm Mon-Fri year-round, 10am-2pm Sat dry season only) This excellent gallery-studio hosts local artists working with ochres in a unique abstract style. It also represents artists from Kalumburu. A 90-minute artist-led gallery tour runs Tuesday to Thursday mornings.

Ngamoowalem Conservation Reserve NATURE RESERVE
(P) FREE Immediately west of Kununurra, stretching to Parry Lagoons (p238), is an area containing many hidden gorges, pools and springs culturally significant to the Miriwoong people. While most of the pools are seasonal and accessible by 4WD only,

Molly Spring (Galjiba) is a refreshingly permanent pool only 2.5km from the Victoria Hwy and normally open to most vehicles all year. The pandanus-ringed pool is at the bottom of a small, quartzite cliff.

Kununurra Historical Society Museum MUSEUM
(08-9169 3331; www.kununurra.org.au; Coolibah Dr; gold coin donation; noon-5.30pm Mon-Fri) Old photographs and newspaper articles document Kununurra's history, including the story of a wartime Wirraway aircraft crash and the subsequent recovery mission. The museum is opposite the country club exit. It's open whenever the gate is open.

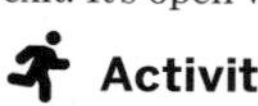

Activities

Go Wild ADVENTURE SPORTS
(1300 663 369; www.gowild.com.au; 3-day canoe trips $220) Self-guided multiday canoe trips from Lake Argyle along the Ord River, overnighting at riverside campsites. Canoes, camping equipment and transport are provided; BYO food and sleeping bag. It also runs group caving, abseiling and bushwalking trips.

Yeehaa Trail Rides HORSE RIDING
(0417 957 607; www.facebook.com/yeehaatrailrides; Boab Park; 1/6½hr rides $70/220) Trail rides and tuition to suit all skill levels, 8km from Kununurra. The sunset ride to Elephant Rock ($120, 2½ hours) is the perfect introduction to the Kimberley.

Tours

Waringarri Art & Culture Tours CULTURAL
(www.waringarriarts.com.au/tours; Mirima tours adult/child $85/45, On Country adult/child half-day $255/155, full-day $375/200; 10am-12.30pm Tue & Thu, 3-5.30pm Mon & Wed;) The Waringarri (p233) mob run informative 2½-hour art and culture tours around Mirima National Park (p233; including a stunning Sunset Tour) and longer 'On Country' tours at local sites with traditional custodians. All tours include a Welcome to Country, Dreaming stories and bush tucker.

Helispirit SCENIC FLIGHTS
(1800 180 085; www.helispirit.com.au; East Kimberley Regional Airport; 18/30/42min flights ex Bellbird $299/399/499) The Kimberley's largest chopper outfit offers scenic flights over the Bungle Bungles from Bellbird (inside the park) and Warmun ($425, 45 minutes). It also arranges flights over Mitchell Falls, Kununurra, King George Falls, Lake Argyle and anywhere else in the Kimberley.

Kimberley Air Tours SCENIC FLIGHTS
(08-9168 2653; www.kimberleyairtours.com.au; East Kimberley Regional Airport; half-/full-day $485/1120) Operates float-plane tours of Lake Argyle ($250), Bungle Bungle flyovers ($375), both locations ($485) and full-day Mitchell Falls tours ($1120). Also flies out of Broome.

Sunset BBQ Cruises CRUISE
(Kununurra Cruises; 08-9168 2882; www.kununurracruises.com.au; adult/child $95/65; May-Aug) Popular sunset BBQ dinner cruises on **Lake Kununurra** (Diversion Dam; P) and the Ord River. Complimentary drinks and all transfers included.

Triple J Tours CRUISE
(08-9168 2682; www.triplejtours.com.au; adult/child from $185/145; Apr-Oct) Triple J cruises the 55km Ord River between Kununurra and Lake Argyle Dam (dry season only).

Kingfisher Tours SCENIC FLIGHTS
(08-9148 2630; www.kingfishertours.net; East Kimberley Regional Airport; per person from $199) Various flights around the Bungles, Cambridge Gulf, Kalumburu and majestic Mitchell and King George Falls.

Festivals & Events

Ord Valley Muster CULTURAL
(08-9168 1177; www.ordvalleymuster.com.au; May;) For 10 days each May, Kununurra hits overdrive with a collection of sporting, charity and cultural events culminating in a large outdoor concert under the full moon on the banks of the Ord River.

CUSTOMS REGULATIONS

Western Australia has strict quarantine laws and there is a permanent 24-hour checkpoint on the Victoria Hwy Northern Territory border 42km outside Kununurra where any fresh produce (including honey) will be confiscated. Most travellers coming from NT have one last big cook-up at the rest area just before the checkpoint. Check www.agric.wa.gov.au/exporting-western-australia/quarantine-information-private-travellers for further info.

WORTH A TRIP

LAKE ARGYLE

Enormous Lake Argyle, where barren red ridges plunge spectacularly into the deep blue water of the dammed Ord River, is Australia's second-largest reservoir. Holding the equivalent of 18 Sydney Harbours, it provides Kununurra with year-round irrigation and important wildlife habitats for migratory waterbirds, freshwater crocodiles and isolated marsupial colonies.

Lake Argyle Cruises (08-9168 7687; www.lakeargylecruises.com; Lake Argyle Rd; adult/child morning $70/45, sunset $95/60, kayaks from $25/15;) Various (some seasonal) cruises take in the lake's highlights; the sunset ones are the most popular. Also hires kayaks and paddleboards.

Argyle Homestead (08-9167 8088; Lake Argyle Rd; adult/child/family $4/2.50/10; 8am-4pm Apr-Sep; P) Relocated when the waters rose, this former home of the pioneering Durack pastoral family (who at one time controlled over 15,000 sq km of the East Kimberley) is now a museum.

Lake Argyle Village (08-9168 7777; www.lakeargyle.com; Lake Argyle Rd; unpowered/powered sites $35/44, cabins from $259; P) Superbly located high above the lake, Lake Argyle Village offers grassy campsites, a variety of cabins and hearty meals from its licensed bistro. Don't miss a swim in the stunning infinity pool.

Sleeping

Hidden Valley Tourist Park CARAVAN PARK $
(08-9168 1790; www.hiddenvalleytouristpark.com; 110 Weaber Plains Rd; unpowered/powered sites $32/42, cabin d $140;) Under the looming crags of Mirima National Park (p233), this relaxed campground has nice grassy sites and is popular with seasonal workers and road-trippers. The self-contained cabins are good value.

Lakeside Resort CARAVAN PARK $
(08-9169 1092; www.lakeside.com.au; Casuarina Way; unpowered/powered sites from $35/40, r from $205;) At the edge of Lily Creek Lagoon, this leafy van park has a good range of standard and deluxe rooms (all with complimentary continental brekky) and various campsites. The on-site bistro is a hit and you can hire a **boat** (per hr $98) to play with on the lagoon.

★ **Wunan House** B&B $$
(08-9168 2436; www.wunanhouse.com; 167 Coolibah Dr; r from $155; P) Aboriginal-owned and -run, this immaculate B&B offers light, airy rooms, all with en suites and TVs. There's free wi-fi, off-street parking and an ample continental breakfast.

Freshwater APARTMENT $$
(08-9169 2010; www.freshwaterapartments.net.au; 19 Victoria Hwy; studios $228, 1-/2-/3-bedroom apt $272/366/433; P) Exquisite, fully self-contained units with exotic open-roofed showers surround an inviting figure-of-eight tropical pool. Once here, you won't want to leave.

Kimberley Croc Motel MOTEL $$
(08-9168 1411; www.kimberleycrocmotel.com.au; 2 River Fig Ave; budget/standard/deluxe d from $99/143/169; P) The old Croc lodge is now a sleek motel, offering a variety of renovated budget (basically four-bed dorms), standard, deluxe (garden or balcony) and pet-friendly rooms, all with en suites and kitchenettes. Add on the central location, mandatory pool, guests' kitchen and free wi-fi and you have a winner.

Eating & Drinking

★ **Wild Mango** CAFE $
(08-9169 2810; www.wildmangocafe.com.au; 20 Messmate Way; breakfast $7-25, lunch $15-19; 7am-4pm Mon-Fri, to 1pm Sat & Sun;) Hip and healthy offerings include breakfast burritos, succulent salads, mouth-watering pancakes, chai smoothies, real coffee and homemade gelato. The entrance is on Konkerberry Dr.

Ivanhoe Cafe CAFE $$
(0427 692 775; www.facebook.com/ivanhoecafe; Ivanhoe Rd; breakfast $9-23, lunch $12-24; 8am-2pm Wed-Mon Apr-Sep;) Grab a table under the leafy mango trees and tuck into tasty wraps, salads, tasting plates, dips and

healthy burgers, all made from fresh, local produce. Don't miss the signature mango smoothie. Vegan friendly.

★**PumpHouse** MODERN AUSTRALIAN **$$$**
(☎08-9169 3222; www.thepumphouserestaurant.com; Lot 3005, Lakeview Dr; mains lunch $21-27, dinner $29-44; ⊙4.30pm-late Tue-Fri, 8am-late Sat & Sun; P ☜) Idyllically situated on Lake Kununurra (p234), the PumpHouse creates succulent dishes featuring quality local ingredients. Watch the catfish swarm should a morsel slip off the verandah, or just have a beer and watch the sunset. There's also an excellent wine list.

Shopping

Artlandish ART
(☎08-9168 1881; www.artlandish.com; cnr Papuana St & Konkerberry Dr; ⊙9am-4pm Mon-Fri, to 1pm Sat) Stunning collection of Kimberley ochres and Western Desert acrylics to suit all price ranges.

Information

Parks & Wildlife Service (☎08-9168 4200; www.dpaw.wa.gov.au; Lot 248, Ivanhoe Rd; ⊙8.30am-4.30pm Mon-Fri) For park permits and publications.

Visitor Centre (☎1800 586 868; www.visitkununurra.com; Coolibah Dr; ⊙8.30am-4.30pm Apr-Sep, shorter hours Oct-Mar) Can help find accommodation, tours and seasonal work.

Getting There & Away

Airnorth (TL; ☎1800 627 474; www.airnorth.com.au; East Kimberley Regional Airport) flies to Broome and Darwin daily and to Perth on Saturdays. **Virgin Australia** (VA; ☎13 67 89; www.virginaustralia.com.au) has four flights a week to Perth.

Greyhound (☎1300 473 946; www.greyhound.com.au; 5 Messmate Way) buses depart the **BP Roadhouse** (☎08-9169 1188; 5 Messmate Way; ⊙24hr) Sunday to Friday for Broome ($171, 13 hours) via Halls Creek ($108, four hours), Fitzroy Crossing ($125, eight hours) and Derby ($146, 11 hours). The Darwin ($150, 10½ hours) via Katherine ($112, six hours) service runs Monday to Saturday.

Avis (☎08-9168 1999), **Budget** (☎08-9168 2033) and **Thrifty** (☎1800 626 515, 08-9169 1911) have offices at the East Kimberley Regional Airport. **Ordco** (Weaber Plains Rd, near Mills Rd; ⊙24hr) local co-op sells the cheapest diesel in Kununurra; for unleaded try **CGL** (3 Bandicoot Dr; ⊙24hr).

Purnululu National Park & Bungle Bungle Range

☎08

The bizarre, ancient, eroded sandstone domes of the Unesco World Heritage–listed Purnululu National Park will take your breath away. Known colloquially as the **Bungle Bungles**, these remote rocky ranges are recognised as the finest example of cone karst sandstone in the world.

The park is a microcosm of fauna and flora and several easy walks lead out of the baking sun into cool, shady palm-fringed gorges. Sunsets here are sublime. Facilities in the park are refreshingly minimal and visitors must be totally self-sufficient. Temperatures can be extreme. Rangers are in attendance during the high season when the small visitor centre (p238) opens. There are two large, basic bush campgrounds at either end of the park.

Access is by a rough, unsealed, flood-prone 4WD-only track from the Great Northern Hwy north of Halls Creek, or by air on a package tour from Kununurra or Warmun.

Sights

★**Purnululu National Park** NATIONAL PARK
(per car $13; ⊙Apr-Nov; P) Looking like a packet of half-melted Jaffas, World Heritage Purnululu is home to the incredible ochre and black striped 'beehive' domes of the Bungle Bungle Range.

The distinctive rounded rock towers are made of sandstone and conglomerates moulded by rainfall over millions of years. Their stripes are the result of oxidised iron compounds and algae. To the local Kidja people, *purnululu* means sandstone, with Bungle Bungle possibly a corruption of 'bundle bundle', a common grass.

Over 3000 sq km of ancient country contains a wide array of wildlife, including over 130 bird species. Rangers are based here from April to November and the park is closed outside this time.

You'll need a high-clearance 4WD for the 52km twisting, rough road from the highway to the visitor centre (p238) near Three Ways junction; allow 2½ hours. There are five deep creek crossings and the turn-off is 53km south of Warmun. Kurrajong and Walardi camps have fresh water and toilets. Book campsites online via www.parkstay.dpaw.wa.gov.au.

Purnululu National Park

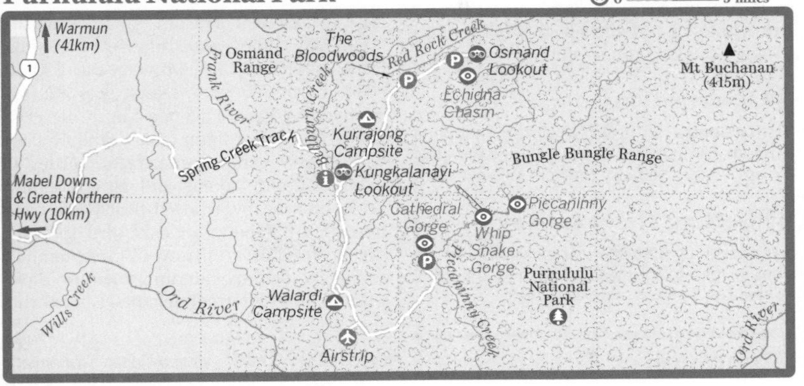

Kungkalanayi Lookout VIEWPOINT
(P) Sunsets and sunrises are spectacular from this hill near Three Ways. Mobile-phone reception from the top.

Piccaninny Gorge GORGE
This 30km return trek (two to three days) from the southern car park to a remote and pristine gorge is best suited for experienced hikers. There are plenty of opportunities for further exploration in the upper gorge. Take plenty of water and go early in the season. You must register at the visitor centre (p238) first.

Echidna Chasm GORGE
(P) Look for tiny bats high on the walls above this palm-fringed, extremely narrow gorge in the northern park. The entrance is fringed by *Livistona* palms. Allow one hour for the 2km return walk.

Cathedral Gorge GORGE
(P) Aptly named, this immense and inspiring circular cavern is an easy 2km (return) stroll from the southern car park.

Tours

Most Kimberley tour operators include Purnululu in multiday tours. You can also pick up tours at Warmun Roadhouse, Halls Creek and Mabel Downs. Helicopters will get you closer than fixed-wing flights.

Bungle Bungle Guided Tours WALKING
(1800 899 029; www.bunglebungleguidedtours.com.au; Bellburn Airstrip, Purnululu; adult/child from $299/149) Aboriginal-run half-day walking tours to Cathedral Gorge and Echidna Chasm and a full-day helicopter ride/hike ($997) to Piccaninny Gorge. Tours depart from the park airstrip at Bellburn and can be linked up with scenic flights from Kununurra, Warmun and Halls Creek.

Sleeping

Kurrajong Campsite CAMPGROUND $
(campsites per person $13; Apr-Nov; P) In the northern end of Purnululu National Park, there are dusty campsites with water, toilets and the odd picnic table, and thankfully no generators.

Walardi Campsite CAMPGROUND $
(campsites per person $13; Apr-Nov; P) Fresh water, toilets and some generator-free areas in the southern park.

Mabel Downs CAMPGROUND $
(Bungle Bungle Caravan Park; 08-9168 7220; www.bunglebunglecaravanpark.com.au; unpowered/powered sites $35/50, safari tents with/without bathroom $250/150, cabin $300; Apr-Sep;) Situated just 1km from the highway, outside Purnululu National Park, so don't expect much privacy. Tents are jammed between helicopters and ridiculously long trailers. Breakfast and dinner ($35) are available and for those without wheels, a **Bungle Bungle Expeditions** (08-9168 7220; www.bunglebungleexpeditions.com.au; 1-day bus tour adult/child $315/160, helicopter tour from $295) bus day tour will set you back $315.

Bungle Bungle Savannah Lodge LODGE $$$
(1800 682 213; www.bbsl.com.au; cabins incl breakfast & dinner standard/superior per person $230/269, self-catered d standard/superior $300/434; mid-Apr–Sep; P) Two grades of cabins, both with or without meals, are

available on Bellburn Creek in the middle of Purnululu National Park. If you cannot live without a hot shower, this is the place to stay. Standard cabins share a verandah.

Information

Visitor Centre (08-9168 7300; 8am-noon & 1-4pm Apr-Sep) Pay for your permit and grab a map. If it's closed, use the honesty envelopes.

Getting There & Away

If you haven't got a high-clearance 4WD, consider taking a tour instead. You can fly in from Kununurra, Warmun and Halls Creek.

Wyndham

08 / POP 900

A gold-rush town that has fallen on leaner times, Wyndham is scenically nestled between rugged hills and the **Cambridge Gulf**, on Balanggarra Country, some 100km northwest of Kununurra. Sunsets are superb from the spectacular **Five Rivers Lookout** (P) on Mt Bastion (325m) overlooking the King, Pentecost, Durack, Forrest and Ord Rivers entering the Cambridge Gulf.

A giant 20m croc greets visitors entering town. The historic port precinct is 5km further and contains a small **museum** (Old Courthouse, Port Precinct; 10am-2pm dry season) and pioneer graveyard, and is the northern terminus of the 3200km Great Northern Hwy, the longest road with a name in Australia.

Sights

Parry Lagoons Nature Reserve NATURE RESERVE

(P) FREE Migratory birds from as far away as Siberia visit these amazing Ramsar-listed wetlands, 25km from Wyndham. There's a bird hide and boardwalk at **Marlgu Billabong** and an excellent sunset view from **Telegraph Hill**. Nearby Parry Creek Farm has a small campground and raised rooms overlooking a billabong, perfect for birdwatching.

Festivals & Events

Wyndham Races SPORTS

(0419 826 435; wyndhamturfclub@gmail.com; Wyndham Racecourse; Aug) One of the oldest continual country race meetings in Australia provides a chance to dress up and have some fun with the locals.

Sleeping & Eating

★**Parry Creek Farm** FARMSTAY $

(08-9161 1139; www.parrycreekfarm.com.au; Parry Creek Rd; unpowered/powered sites $30/50, r $140, cabin $250; dry season; P) Surrounded by Parry Lagoons Nature Reserve, 25km from Wyndham, this tranquil farm with grassy campsites attracts hordes of wildlife. Comfy rooms and air-con cabins are connected by a raised boardwalk overlooking a billabong for easy bird spotting. The licensed cafe (open April to September) serves excellent barramundi, wood-fired pizzas and other gourmet delights. Ring ahead.

Wyndham Caravan Park CARAVAN PARK $

(08-9161 1064; www.wyndhamcaravanpark.com; 9 Baker St; unpowered/powered sites $30/38, donga/cabin $99/154; P) Laid-back park with shady, grassy campsites.

Rusty Wheelbarrow B&B $$

(0408 902 887; www.therustywheelbarrow.com.au; Lot 1293, Great Northern Hwy; s/d $140/160; P) Set on a 4-hectare block 5km from town this boutique B&B is a smart choice. Beautiful, elevated rooms, all with en suites, open onto a common airy breezeway. Both continental and cooked breakfasts are available, there's plenty of fresh fruit and you can even purchase a BBQ pack should you feel like dining in.

Croc Cafe & Bakery BAKERY $

(0457 826 616; 12 Great Northern Hwy; pies from $6; 7am-2pm;) Billed as WA's 'most northern bakery', the quirky selection of pies include crocodile and barramundi, best enjoyed under the courtyard mango trees. Find it on Facebook.

Entertainment

Wyndham Outdoor Picture Gardens OUTDOOR CINEMA

(0438 611 264; www.wyndhampicturegardens.com.au; 1 Civic Way; per person $4; from 6pm, every 2nd Sat Apr-Oct;) Australia's second-oldest outdoor 'picture garden' airs films on alternate Saturdays during the Dry.

Getting There & Away

Greyhound (p236) drops passengers 56km away at the Victoria Hwy junction; you'll need to arrange a pick-up prior to arrival. There's no taxi service in Wyndham.

Understand West Coast Australia

HISTORY 240

This is an ancient land, with 200 years of European lawlessness, hardship, boom and bust laid over the top. West Coast Australia has seen it all.

LOCAL PRODUCE, WINE & CRAFT BEER 248

Taste your way around West Coast Australia's stylish wineries, raffish craft breweries and local food producers.

MINING & THE ENVIRONMENT 253

Demand from Asia's mega-economies has shaped Western Australia's economic, demographic and physical landscapes in recent years – but at what price?

INDIGENOUS ART IN WESTERN AUSTRALIA . . . 258

Explore the key styles across West Coast Australia, with tips on where to experience the best examples and how to make an ethical purchase.

History

Western Australia's history is one of hardship, boom, bust and boom again. People had lived here for 40,000 years before Dutchman Dirk Hartog sighted the shores of WA in 1616. The British later settled Perth in 1829, sparking conflict with its Noongar inhabitants. WA first boomed with the 1880s discovery of gold, then suffered through wars and depression, before the nickel boom of the 1960s. The state's prosperity and its immense mineral wealth remain inextricably linked as the years tick by.

First Arrivals

People first arrived on the northern shores of Australia at least 40,000 years ago. As they began building shelters, cooking food and developing an oral history, they left behind signs of their activities: layers of carbon – the residue of their ancient fires – deep in the soil; piles of shells and fish bones marking the places where they hunted and ate; and on rock walls across WA, paintings and etchings. These artworks tell stories of the Dreaming, that spiritual dimension where the earth and its people were created and the law was laid down.

Contrary to popular belief, Australia's Aboriginal people, especially those who lived in the north, were not entirely isolated from the rest of the world. Until 6000 years ago, they were able to travel and trade across a bridge of land that connected Australia to New Guinea. Even after white occupation, the Aboriginal people of the northern coasts regularly hosted Macassan fisherfolk from Sulawesi, with whom they traded, socialised and occasionally had children.

When European sailors first stumbled on the coast of 'Terra Australis', the entire continent was occupied by hundreds of Aboriginal groups, living in their own territories and maintaining their own distinctive languages and traditions. The fertile Swan Valley around Perth, for example, is the customary homeland of about a dozen groups of Noongar people, each speaking a distinctive dialect.

The prehistory of Australia is filled with tantalising mysteries. In the Kimberley, scholars and amateur sleuths are fascinated by the so-called Bradshaw paintings. These enigmatic and mystical stick figures are thou-

TIMELINE

pre-40,000 BC

First humans arrive on the shores of Australia.

4000 BC

Aboriginal communities from northwestern Australia trade and interact with Macassan fisherfolk from Sulawesi.

AD1616

Dutch explorer Dirk Hartog lands on an island in Shark Bay, marking his visit with a pewter plate on which he inscribed a record of his visit.

sands of years old. Because they look nothing like the artwork of any other Aboriginal group, the identity of the culture that created them is the subject of fierce debate.

Meanwhile, there are historians who claim the Aboriginal peoples' first contact with the wider world occurred when a Chinese admiral, Zheng He, visited Australia in the 15th century. Others say that Portuguese navigators mapped the continent in the 16th century.

Early Dutch Exploration

Most authorities believe that the first person to travel any great distance to see Aboriginal Australia was a Dutchman named Willem Janszoon. In 1606 he sailed the speedy little ship *Duyfken* out of the Dutch settlement at Batavia (modern Jakarta) to scout for the Dutch East India Company, and found Cape York (the pointy bit at the top of Australia), which he thought was an extension of New Guinea.

Ten years later, another Dutch ship, the *Eendracht,* rode the mighty Atlantic trade winds, bound for the 'spice islands' of modern Indonesia. But the captain, Dirk Hartog, misjudged his position, and stumbled onto the island (near Gladstone) that now bears his name. Hartog inscribed the details of his visit onto a pewter plate and nailed it to a post. In 1697, the island was visited by a second Dutch explorer, named Willem de Vlamingh, who swapped Hartog's plate for one of his own.

Today Western Australia, the largest state in the country, is also the most sparsely populated, being home to just over 10% of the population.

Other Dutch mariners were not so lucky. Several ships were wrecked on the uncharted western coast of the Aboriginal continent. The most infamous of these is the *Batavia*. After the ship foundered in the waters off modern Geraldton in 1629, the captain, Francisco Pelsaert, sailed a boat to the Dutch East India Company's base at Batavia. While his back was turned, some crewmen unleashed a nightmare of debauchery, rape and murder on the men, women and children who had been on the ship. When Pelsaert returned with a rescue vessel, he executed the murderers, sparing only two youths whom he marooned on the beach of the continent they knew as New Holland. Some experts believe the legacy of these boys can be found in the sandy hair and Dutch-sounding words of some local Aboriginal peoples. The remains of the *Batavia* and other wrecks are now displayed at the Western Australian Museum in Geraldton and in the WA Shipwrecks Museum in Fremantle, where you can also see de Vlamingh's battered old plate.

The Dutch were businessmen, scouring the world for commodities. Nothing they saw on the dry coasts of this so-called 'New Holland' convinced them that the land or its native people offered any promise of profit. When another Dutchman named Abel Tasman charted the western and southern coasts of Australia in 1644, he was mapping not a commercial opportunity but a maritime hazard.

1629

Debauchery, rape and murder break out while the *Batavia* is shipwrecked at the Houtman Abrolhos Islands. All but two crew are subsequently executed at senior merchant Francisco Pelsaert's behest.

1644

Dutchman Abel Tasman charts the western and southern coasts of Australia.

1697

Willem de Vlamingh replaces Hartog's pewter plate with his own.

1826

The British army establishes a military post in Albany, on the southern coast.

In Came the Brits

Today the dominant version of Australian history is written as though Sydney is the only wellspring of Australia's identity. But when you live in Western Australia, history looks very different. In Sydney, white history traditionally begins with Captain James Cook's epic voyage of 1770, in which he mapped the east coast. But Cook creates little excitement in Albany, Perth or Geraldton – places he never saw.

Cook's voyage revealed that the eastern coastline was fertile, and he was particularly taken with the diversity of plant life at the place he called 'Botany Bay'. Acting on Cook's discovery, the British government decided to establish a convict colony there. The result was the settlement of Sydney in 1788 – out of which grew the great sheep industry of Australia.

By the early 19th century, it was clear that the Dutch had no inclination to settle WA. Meanwhile, the British were growing alarmed by the activities of the French in the region. So on Christmas Day 1826, the British army warned them off by establishing a lonely military outpost at Albany, on the strategically important southwestern tip of the country.

The founding of Perth is most famously depicted in George Pitt Morison's painting *The Foundation of Perth* (1829). It is often erroneously credited as an authentic record of the ceremony rather than a historical reconstruction.

The Founding of Perth

The challenge to Aboriginal supremacy in the west began in 1829, when a boatload of free immigrants arrived with all their possessions in the territory of the Noongar people. This group was led by Captain James Stirling – a swashbuckling and entrepreneurial naval officer – who had investigated the coastal region two years earlier. Stirling had convinced British authorities to appoint him governor of the new settlement, and promptly declared all the surrounding Aboriginal lands to be the property of King George IV. Such was the foundation of Perth.

Stirling's glowing reports had fired the ambitions of English adventurers and investors, and by the end of the year, 25 ships had reached the colony's port at Fremantle. Unlike their predecessors in Sydney, these settlers were determined to build their fortunes without calling on government assistance and without the shame of using convict labour.

Frontier Conflict

As a cluster of shops, houses and hotels rose on the banks of the Swan River, settlers established sheep and cattle runs in the surrounding country. This led to conflict with Aboriginal people, following a pattern that was tragically common throughout the Australian colonies. The Aboriginal people speared sheep and cattle – sometimes for food, sometimes as an act of defiance. In the reprisals that resulted, people on both sides were killed, and by 1832 it was clear that Aboriginal people were organising a violent resistance. Governor Stirling declared that he would

1829

Led by Captain James Stirling, a boatload of free immigrants land in the territory of the Noongar people, near present-day Perth Governor Stirling declares all surrounding lands to be the property of King George IV.

1834

The Battle of Pinjarra occurs after Stirling leads a punitive expedition against the Noongar. It is reported that 25 to 30 Aboriginal people are shot, with Stirling's camp suffering one fatality.

1840–41

An Aboriginal man called Wylie and explorer Edward Eyre make a staggering journey across the Nullarbor Plain to Albany from South Australia.

1850

Shiploads of male convicts start to arrive in Fremantle. They go on to build key historical buildings such as Fremantle Prison, Government House, today's Fremantle Arts Centre and Perth Town Hall.

retaliate with such 'acts of decisive severity as will appal them as people for a time and reduce their tribe to weakness'.

In October 1834, Stirling showed he was a man of his word. He led a punitive expedition against the Noongar, who were under the leadership of the warrior Calyute. In the Battle of Pinjarra, the governor's forces shot, according to the *Perth Gazette,* 25 to 30 people and suffered one fatality themselves. This display of official terror had the desired effect. The Noongar ended their resistance and the violence of the frontier moved further out.

Many of the first ships to bring convicts to WA were whalers. Human cargo would be unloaded, then the ships continued whaling.

The Deployment of Convicts

Aboriginal resistance was not the only threat to the survival of this most isolated outpost of the British Empire. The arid countryside, the loneliness and the cost of transport also took their toll. When tough men of capital could make a fortune in the east, there were few good reasons to struggle against the frustrations of the west, and most of the early settlers left. Two decades on, there were just 5000 Europeans holding out on the western edge of the continent. Some of the capitalists who had stayed began to rethink their aversion to using cheap prison labour.

In 1850 – just as the practice of sending British convicts to eastern Australia ended – shiploads of male convicts started to arrive in Fremantle harbour.

Exploration & Gold

Meanwhile, several explorers undertook journeys into the remote Aboriginal territories, drawn in by dreams of mighty rivers and rolling plains of grass 'further out'. Their thirsty ordeals mostly ended in disappointment. But the pastoralists did expand through much of the southwestern corner of WA, while others took up runs on the rivers of the northwest and in the Kimberley.

Built by convicts between 1861 and 1868, the Fremantle Arts Centre was once a lunatic asylum and then a poorhouse, or 'women's home'. Today this Gothic building is a thriving arts centre, which is well worth a visit.

Perhaps the most staggering journey of exploration was undertaken by an Aboriginal man called Wylie and the explorer Edward Eyre, who travelled from South Australia, across the vast, dry Nullarbor Plain, to Albany.

By the 1880s, the entire European population of this sleepy western third of Australia was not much more than 40,000 people. In the absence of democracy, a network of city merchants and large squatters exercised political and economic control over the colony.

The great agent of change was gold. The first discoveries were made in the 1880s in the Kimberley and the Pilbara, followed by huge finds in the 1890s at Coolgardie and Kalgoorlie, in hot, dry country 600km inland from Perth. So many people were lured by the promise of gold that the population of the colony doubled and redoubled in a single decade. But

1860s	1880s–90s	1890	1893
With no democracy, a network of city merchants and squatters exercises control over the colony.	Gold changes everything. The first discoveries are in the Kimberley and the Pilbara, followed by massive finds in Coolgardie and Kalgoorlie.	Representative government is formed. Bushman John Forrest is the first elected premier.	The Education Act, allowing white parents to bar Aboriginal children from schools, is followed by a policy of removing 'half-caste' children from their parents. These children become known as the stolen generations.

the easy gold was soon exhausted, and most independent prospectors gave way to mining companies who had the capital to sink deep shafts. Soon the miners were working not for nuggets of gold but for wages. Toiling in hot, dangerous conditions, these men banded together to form trade unions, which remained a potent force in the life of WA throughout the following century.

The Golden Pipeline to Kalgoorlie

The year 1890 also saw the introduction of representative government, a full generation after democracy had arrived in the east. The first elected premier was a tough, capable bushman named John Forrest, who borrowed courageously in order to finance vast public works to encourage immigrants and private investors. He was blessed with the services of a brilliant civil engineer, CY O'Connor. O'Connor oversaw the improvement of the Fremantle harbour, and built and ran the state's rail system. But O'Connor's greatest feat was the construction of a system of steam-powered pumping stations along a mighty pipeline to drive water uphill, from Mundaring Weir in the Perth Hills to the thirsty goldfields around distant Kalgoorlie.

Kim Scott's *Benang* (1999), which won the Miles Franklin Award in 2000, is a confronting but rewarding read about the assimilation policies of the 20th century and the devastating effect they had on Aboriginal Australia.

By the time Forrest opened the pipeline, O'Connor was dead. His political enemies had defamed him in the press and in parliament, falsely accusing him of incompetence and corruption. On 10 March 1902, O'Connor rode into the surf near Fremantle and shot himself. Today, the site of his anguish is commemorated by a haunting statue of him on horseback, which rises out of the waves at South Beach.

Ironically, just as the water began to flow, the mining industry went into decline. But the 'Golden Pipeline' continues to supply water to Kalgoorlie, where gold is once again being mined, on a Herculean-scale unimaginable a century ago. Today you can visit the No 1 Pump Station at Mundaring Weir and follow O'Connor's Golden Pipeline as a motorist from Perth to Kalgoorlie, where you can visit the rather astonishing Super Pit.

The Stolen Generations

At the turn of the century, the lives of many Aboriginal people became more wretched. The colony's 1893 Education Act empowered the parents of white schoolchildren to bar any Aboriginal child from attending their school, and it was not long before Aboriginal children were completely excluded from state-run classrooms. In the following decade, the government embarked on a policy of removing so-called 'half-caste' children from their parents, placing them with white families or in government institutions. The objective of the policy was explicit. Full-blood Aboriginal people were to be segregated, in the belief that they were doomed

1901
WA and the other colonies are federated to form the nation of Australia.

1914
Over 200,000 Australians are killed or wounded in WWI.

1933
Two-thirds of the voting population votes to secede from the rest of the country. Although never enacted, secession remains topical to this day.

1939
WWII begins. Several towns in WA's north, including Broome, are bombed during the war. Fremantle is turned into an Allied naval base, and a US submarine refuelling base is established at Exmouth.

to extinction, while half-caste children were expected to marry whites, thereby breeding Aboriginal people out of existence. These policies inflicted great suffering and sorrow on the many Aboriginal peoples who were recognised in the 1990s as the stolen generations.

Wars & the Great Depression

On 1 January 1901, WA and the other colonies federated to form the nation of Australia. This was not a declaration of independence: this new Australia was a dominion within the British Empire. It was as citizens of the empire that thousands of Australian men volunteered to fight in the Australian Imperial Force when WWI broke out in 1914. They fought in Turkey, Sinai and in Europe – notably on the Somme. More than 200,000 of them were killed or wounded over the terrible four years of the war. Today, in cities and towns across the state, you will see war memorials that commemorate their service.

Though mining, for the time being, had ceased to be an economic force, farmers were developing the lucrative WA wheat belt, which they cultivated with the horse-drawn stump-jump plough, one of the icons of Australian frontier farming. At the same time, a growing demand for wool and beef and the expansion of dairy farming added to the state's economic growth.

Nevertheless, many people were struggling to earn a living – especially those ex-soldiers who were unable to shake off the horrors they had endured in the trenches. In 1929, the lives of these 'battlers' grew even more miserable when the cold winds of the Great Depression blew through the towns and farms of the state. So alienated did Western Australians feel from the centres of power and politics in the east that, in 1933, two-thirds of them voted to secede from the rest of Australia. Although the decision was never enacted, it expressed a profound sense of isolation from the east that is still a major factor in the culture and attitudes of the state today.

In 1939, Australians were once again fighting a war alongside the British, this time against Hitler in WWII. But the military situation changed radically in December 1941 when the Japanese bombed the American fleet at Hawaii's Pearl Harbor. The Japanese swept through Southeast Asia and, within weeks, were threatening Australia. Over the next two years they bombed several towns in the north of the state, including Broome, which was almost abandoned.

It was not the British but the Americans who came to Australia's aid. As thousands of Australian soldiers were taken prisoner and suffered in the torturous Japanese prisoner-of-war camps, Western Australians opened their arms to US servicemen. Fremantle was transformed into an Allied naval base for operations in the Indian Ocean, while a US

Largely set in WA, *Gallipoli* (1981; directed by Peter Weir, screenplay by David Williamson) is an iconic Australian film about WWI, exploring naivety, social pressure to enlist and, ultimately, the utter futility of the Gallipoli campaign.

1963
Development of the gargantuan Ord River Irrigation Scheme to fertilise the desert.

1967
Australia's Indigenous people are recognised as Australian citizens and granted the right to vote.

1970
The Indian Pacific train completes its first transcontinental journey from Sydney to Perth. It remains one of the world's great train journeys.

1979
The Skylab space station crashes in the state's remote southeastern sector. Remnants are now at the Esperance Museum.

submarine-refuelling base was established at Exmouth. In New Guinea and the Pacific, Americans and Australians fought together until the tide of war eventually turned in their favour.

When *Australia II* won the America's Cup in 1983, Australian Prime Minister Bob Hawke opined, 'Any boss who sacks a worker for not turning up today is a bum'.

Postwar Prosperity

When WWII ended, the story of modern WA began to unfold. Under the banner of 'postwar reconstruction', the federal government set about transforming Australia with a policy of assisted immigration, designed to populate Australia more densely as a defence against the 'hordes' of Asia. Many members of this new workforce found jobs in the mines, where men and machines turned over thousands of tonnes of earth in search of the precious lode. On city stock exchanges, the names of such WA mines as Tom Price, Mt Newman and Goldsworthy became symbols of development, modernisation and wealth. Now, rather than being a wasteland that history had forgotten, the west was becoming synonymous with ambition, and a new spirit of capitalist pioneering. As union membership flourished, labour and capital entered into a pact to turn the country to profit. In the Kimberley, the government built the gigantic Ord River Irrigation Scheme, which boasted that it could bring fertility to the desert – and which convinced many Western Australians that engineering and not the environment contained the secret of life. There was so much country it hardly seemed to matter that salt was starting to poison the wheat belt or that mines scoured the land.

In 1952, the British exploded their first nuclear bomb on the state's Monte Bello Islands. And when opponents of the test alleged that nuclear clouds were drifting over Australia, the government scoffed. The land was big – and anyway, it needed a strong, nuclear-armed ally for protection in the Cold War world.

WESTERN AUSTRALIA IN BLACK & WHITE

Like other Aboriginal Australians in the rest of the country, the 70,000 or so who live in WA are the state's most disadvantaged group. Many live in deplorable conditions; outbreaks of preventable diseases are common, and infant mortality rates are higher than in many developing countries. Aboriginal employment in the resources sector is slowly increasing, but the mining boom has not alleviated Aboriginal social and economic disadvantage to any large degree.

In 1993, the federal government recognised that Aboriginal people with an ongoing association with their traditional lands were the rightful owners, unless those lands had been sold to someone else. Despite this recognition, the issue of racial relations in WA remains a problematic one, and racial intolerance is still evident in many parts of the state.

1980s

The state becomes known as WA Inc, a reference to its image as a giant corporation intent on speculation and profit.

1983

Entrepreneur Alan Bond funds the racing yacht *Australia II*, which wins the America's Cup with its secret winged keel. Bond is later jailed for corporate fraud.

1987

Sleepy Fremantle is transformed for Australia's first defence of the America's Cup. Australia loses 5-0 to the United States.

1990s

Aboriginal rock art, featuring distinctive stick-like images, is found in the Kimberley. Known as the Bradshaw paintings, these could be among the earliest figurative paintings ever executed.

This spirit of reckless capitalism reached its climax in the 1980s when the state became known as 'WA Inc' – a reference to the state as a giant corporation in which government, business and unions had lost sight of any value other than speculation and profit. The embodiment of this brash spirit was an English migrant named Alan Bond, who became so rich he could buy anything he pleased. In 1983 he funded a sleek new racing yacht called *Australia II* in its challenge for the millionaire's yachting prize, the America's Cup. Equipped with a secret – and now legendary – winged keel, the boat became the first non-American yacht to win the race. It seemed as though everyone in Australia was cheering on the day Bond held aloft the shining silver trophy.

But in the 1990s, legal authorities began to investigate the dealings of Bond and other players in WA Inc. Bond found himself in court and spent four years in jail after pleading guilty to Australia's biggest corporate fraud. He died in 2015.

Before he went bankrupt and was convicted of corporate fraud, Alan Bond's wealth was estimated at $265 million by *Business Review Weekly* in 2008.

A New Century

Throughout the early 21st century, WA's mining boom made the state one of the most dynamic parts of the country. Real-estate prices skyrocketed, and the populations of Perth and key mining areas such as the Pilbara grew faster than those of east-coast Australia. Substantial South African and British communities grew in Perth, with many New Zealanders and Irish immigrants also working in the mining and resources sector.

From late 2014, however, signs became evident that the vital Chinese economy fuelling the mining boom was definitely slowing down, causing a weakening in the Australian currency, lessening employment opportunities and reducing the stock-market value of the resources sector. As well, the construction phase of WA's resources industry was largely complete, with roads, ports and railways all in place to better accommodate industry and exports.

With the weakening of the Australian dollar, some relief emerged for the growing tourism sector, and a general easing of salaries in the resources sector eased the pressure for those Perth and WA residents not earning a mine-worker's salary.

Going ahead, WA is still firmly focused on the benefits of the resources sector, but agricultural exports to nearby mega-Asian economies such as China, Indonesia and Vietnam are also growing in importance.

The chill winds blowing through Australia's economy cannot be ignored, but WA's energy and resilience will continue to be vital drivers for the nation's eventual economic re-emergence and strengthening.

1990s

The stolen generations are formally recognised.

1998

One of Australia's most infamous trade union battles is waged in Fremantle between the Maritime Union and the Patrick Corporation (a stevedore company).

2000s

WA experiences huge economic growth due to the mining boom, albeit with a reduction in vital Chinese demand from late 2014.

2018

The West Coast Eagles win the AFL Grand Final – the fourth time they've won the national competition since they were founded in 1986.

Local Produce, Wine & Craft Beer

Regional produce and local wines are highlights of Western Australia, and leisurely, outdoor eating is best experienced in the vineyard restaurants of the Margaret River, Great Southern and Swan Valley wine regions. Select spots up north – Geraldton, Kalbarri, Carnarvon, Kununurra and Broome – also include some local foodie gems. For the best of WA's excellent craft beer scene, focus on Fremantle, the Swan Valley and Margaret River.

Regional Produce

WA's superb regional produce includes marron (small freshwater crayfish unique to the southwest), crayfish (rock lobster, from the Turquoise Coast in particular), McHenry Hohnen beef (Margaret River) and barramundi (the Kimberley). Much of WA's best produce is also available at supermarkets and delicatessens. Look out for Browne's iced coffee and yoghurts, Harvey Fresh products (good fresh orange juice) and excellent chilli mussels.

Perth's leading chefs celebrate the state's produce by showcasing Manjimup truffles, Mt Barker chicken and Shark Bay scallops. Top-end spots in the central city include Wildflower (p81) and Balthazar (p82), while Mount Lawley has Must Winebar (p86) and St Michael 6003 (p86). Excellent midrange cafes and restaurants include Petition Kitchen (p81) in the city, Henry Summer (p83) and Bivouac Canteen & Bar (p82) in Northbridge, Pinchos (p87), Duende (p87) and Sayers (p87) in Leederville, and Mrs S (p83), **Tarts** (Map p67; ☎08-9328 6607; www.tartscafe.com.au; 212 Lake St, Highgate; mains $11-25; ⏰7am-3.30pm Mon-Fri, to 4.30pm Sat & Sun) and Sayers Sister (p83) in Mount Lawley. In Fremantle, Bread in Common (p88), Ootong & Lincoln (p88) and Manuka Woodfire Kitchen (p88) are all outstanding.

> Tipping is not required in WA restaurants, though 10% is appreciated if you've had a positive experience and your waiter was a good'un.

Regional dining highlights include Margaret River winery restaurants, Neaps Bistro (p226) in Derby, Yarri (p134) in Dunsborough, PumpHouse (p236) in Kununurra, Market Eating House (p129) in Bunbury, Loose Goose (p168) in Esperance, Aarli (p219) tapas in Broome, the excellent Karijini Eco Retreat Restaurant (p207), and Flic's Kitchen (p108) in Mandurah.

West Coast Wine & the Cellar Door

Wine is a big deal in WA, with the focus firmly on the quality end of the market. The Margaret River region has over 95 wineries producing just 3% of Australia's grapes, but this accounts for over 20% of the country's premium wines.

The first wineries were established in the southwest in the 1960s: Vasse Felix was a notable early player. Because the southwest has always focused on low-yield, quality output, it wasn't as influenced by the oversupply problems that beset the Australian wine industry in 2005 and 2006. Fortuitous combinations of rain and warm weather also produced consistently excellent Margaret River vintages from 2007 to 2013. Since then it's been steady-as-she-goes for Margaret River, with the region maintaining its annual crush output while many other Australian regions have dropped away.

Aside from Margaret River, other key wine areas are the Swan Valley, the Great Southern (Frankland, the Porongurups, Denmark, Mt Barker), Pemberton and the Geographe region. The Perth Hills also have some small, boutique producers.

BYO – bringing your own beer or wine to the restaurant – is a widely accepted and budget-friendly practice. You might be charged 'corkage' (how quaint) of anywhere from $5 to $20 a bottle (or sometimes per person) – restaurants have to make a profit somehow!

Margaret River

WA's best wineries are in Margaret River (www.margaretriver.com/eat-drink/wineries), 250km southwest of Perth. The climate is defined by cooling ocean breezes, producing Margaret River's distinctively elegant and rich wines.

Margaret River also produces many blends of semillon and sauvignon blanc grapes. These very popular fruity wines are not Margaret River's very best, but they are often the most affordable. Cape Mentelle (p137) and Cullen Wines (p144) make good examples. Cullen Wines is also renowned for its organic and sustainable approach to winemaking.

Smaller cellar doors to explore around Margaret River include:

Ashbrook (p142) A friendly family-owned operation.
Thompson Estate (p142) With a spectacular tasting room.
Stella Bella (p137) Excellent wines and wonderfully designed labels.
Stormflower Vineyard (p141) Organic with highly regarded cabernet shiraz.

The slightly cooler Geographe region nearby features wineries of varying quality. Many people come to visit Capel Vale (p130), a winery with a 30-year history of winemaking excellence, particularly with chardonnay, shiraz and, more recently, merlot.

Great Southern & Pemberton

Wines from the low-key Great Southern region (www.greatsouthernwine.asn.au) are flavoursome, powerful and elegant – shiraz, cabernet sauvignon, riesling and sauvignon blanc do especially well. The region stretches from Frankland southeast to Albany, then west again to Denmark, with Mt Barker, in the middle.

In Frankland, **Alkoomi** (Map p158; ☎08-9841 2027; www.alkoomiwines.com.au; 225 Stirling Tce; ⏲11am-5pm Mon-Sat) is still a family-run business, and produces great cabernet sauvignon and riesling. Ferngrove produces an honest chardonnay, an excellent shiraz and a brilliant cabernet sauvignon–shiraz blend called 'the Stirlings'. Frankland Estate is one of the key wineries that has helped revitalise riesling.

BEST FOR VEGETARIANS

Raw Kitchen (p89) Vegan, vegetarian and virtuous flavours in Fremantle.

Little Concept (p88) Lots of raw and vegan options and fortifying teas in Fremantle.

Kakulas Bros (p82) Natural products and ingredients abound at this iconic Perth delicatessen.

Veggie Mama (Map p67; ☎08-9227 1910; www.facebook.com/veggiemama01; cnr Beaufort & Vincent Sts, Mount Lawley; mains $10-20; ⏲8am-6pm Mon, to 8pm Tue, to 9pm Wed-Sat, to 7pm Sun; 📶✍) 🌿 Funky decor and flavour-packed food in Perth's Mount Lawley neighbourhood.

Maleeya's Thai Cafe (p163) Zingy flavours crafted from the on-site herb garden in Porungurup.

Local Produce & Wineries

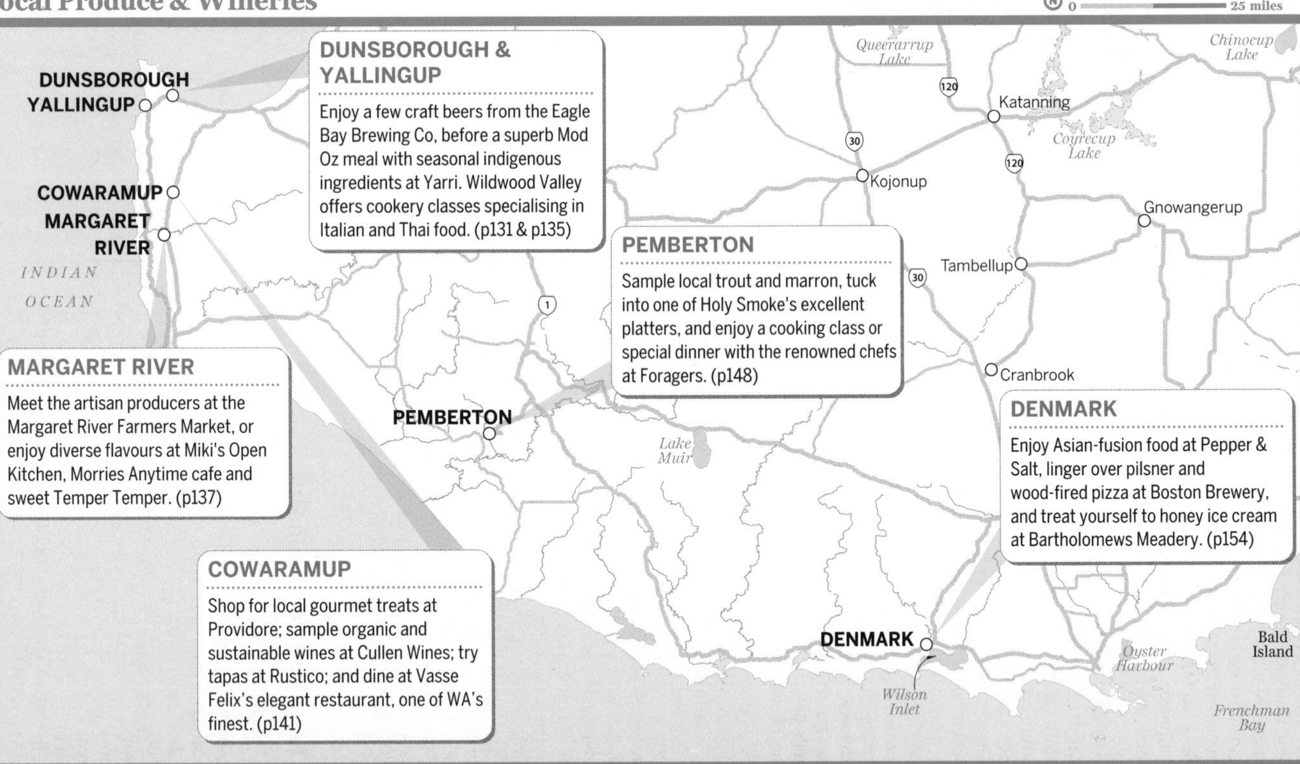

In Mt Barker and the nearby Porongurup range, riesling and shiraz are consistently great performers; also try the lean, long-flavoured cabernet sauvignon. Two of the best are Plantagenet Wines (p161), the Great Southern region's first winery, and Poacher's Ridge (p161), a regular on lists of Australia's best wineries. West Cape Howe Wines (p161), just west of Mt Barker, is another five-star winery winner.

Further south, in Denmark and Albany, are some of Australia's most esteemed wine names. Must-visit Albany wineries include Montgomery's Hill (p160), Wignalls Wines (p160) and the excellently named Oranje Tractor (p160), an organic operator doing some good things with sparkling wines. In Denmark, try Moombaki Wines (p156), Harewood Estate (p156) and Singlefile Wines (p156) – just three of the many cellar doors in this booming region.

Between Margaret River and the Great Southern region, you'll hit Pemberton. Its cool-ish climate produces cooler wine styles – pinot noir, merlot and chardonnay, in particular.

Wine for Dudes (p139) has excellent Margaret River wine tours led by a winemaker. Around the Great Southern, hook up with Denmark Wine Lovers Tour (p155). For the Swan Valley, try d'Vine Wine Tours (p114), which also runs tours to the Perth Hills wineries.

Swan Valley

The Swan Valley (www.swanvalley.com.au/eat-and-drink) may once have aspired to take on mighty Margaret River, but now the region's true merit lies in its proximity to Perth and its small clutch of winery-restaurants – not the wines per se. It's hotter than down south, so long, languid outdoor-dining opportunities are the norm. Sandalford Wines (p113) is one of the region's big-ticket producers, hosting concerts on the lawns and with an excellent bistro. You can also get here by ferrry up the river from the city.

Houghton (p113) is the area's best winery, and the Houghton Classic White, a blend of white-wine grapes that drinks like a mix of tropical, zesty fruits, is the Swan Valley's most ubiquitous wine. Others of note include **Pinelli Estate Wines** (☎08-9377 7733; www.pinellirestaurant.com.au; 114 Benara Rd, Caversham; mains $18-42; ⏰11.30am-2.30pm Thu-Sun & 5.30pm-late Thu-Sat) and RiverBank Estate (p114), both of which are great for lunch.

Perth Hills

Just 30 minutes form Perth, the Perth Hills is a very low-key wine region, with a dozen small-time boutique producers around the Bickley Valley. But the Hills' proximity to the city makes it prime terrain for naughty weekends away! Stop by Brookside Vineyard (p110) for tastings and a lovely lunch, with further sippings at nearby **Plume Estate** (☎08-9293 5808; www.facebook.com/plume-estate-vineyard-797329867024101; 91 Glenisla Rd, Bickley; ⏰11am-5pm Sat & Sun). See www.experienceperthhills.com.au/wineries for more.

In central Perth, Lalla Rookh (p81) is a classy wine bar with an excellent selection of WA wines. Swallow (p91) in Maylands and nearby Must Winebar (p91) are also outstanding.

Then There's the Beer

WA's leading blue-collar beers are Emu Bitter (EB) and Swan Draught. They're both pretty bland – focus instead on exploring the craft-beer scene, which is booming. In Fremantle and the southwest in particular, local microbreweries abound; the Swan Valley is also a top spot.

In Fremantle, visit the Norfolk Hotel (p92) and the **Monk** (Map p70; ☎08-9336 7666; www.themonk.com.au; 33 South Tce; ⏰11am-late) for blackboards full of ever-changing brews. Freo also has the iconic Little Creatures (p92), now owned by a multinational company but still tasting great with its hoppy Pale Ale. A few pints on the deck here as the sun sets is a quintessential WA experience.

In the Swan Valley, the best craft breweries are Homestead (p114) at Mandoon Estate, Feral Brewing Company (p114) and **Mash** (☎08-9296 5588; www.mashbrewing.com.au; 10250 West Swan Rd, Henley Brook;

⏲11am-5pm Sun-Thu, to 9pm Fri & Sat). Mash also has an outlet in Bunbury. There's also the raffish **Iron Bark Brewery** (☎08-9377 4400; www.ironbarkbrewery.com.au; 55 Benara Rd, Caversham; ⏲11am-4pm Mon & Tue, 10.30am-5pm Wed-Fri, to 6pm Sat & Sun), right next door to the progressive (and equally raffish) **Funk Cider** (☎08-9377 4884; www.funkcider.com.au; 55 Benara Rd, Caversham; ⏲11am-5.30pm Mon-Fri, 10am-6.30pm Sat, to 5.30am Sun).

For information and tasting notes about WA wines, check out www.mrwines.com.

Continuing south, the Margaret River region is a definite craft-beer hotspot, and a guided tour with Margaret River Brewery Tours (p139) will get you to the best of the breweries. Denmark's Boston Brewery (p156) and Pemberton's Jarrah Jacks (p150) are both worth visiting, and good beers and ciders are crafted at the Cidery (p147) in Bridgetown. Along Caves Rd west of the Margaret River township, you'll find a burgeoning number of brewers, including Cheeky Monkey (p143), the rustic Bootleg Brewery (p143) and Beer Farm (p143), and the excellent Caves Road Collective (p143), which also does cider.

Up north, the only craft brewery you'll find is Matso's (p220) in Broome.

Mining & the Environment

If you fly into Perth, you'll notice one thing straight away: despite the recent cooling of mining-sector activity, the fly-in, fly-out (FIFO) lifestyle remains ubiquitous. Large clutches of workers nonchalantly board their flights to remote mines and oil and gas plants every few hours. Some will be wearing their fluorescent orange or yellow 'high-vis' vests, required attire on-site and an understated badge of honour at Perth Airport (less understated are their rampant tattoos – Perth is a seriously inked city!).

A few years ago, many construction workers were also part of this airborne ebb and flow, but now that massive infrastructure projects are largely completed in Western Australia's north, this movement mainly comprises mining workers. Contraction of the vital Chinese economy since 2014 has slowed Australia's exports of iron ore considerably, causing the Aussie dollar to devalue and the Australian economy to weaken – but mining is still the biggest game in town out west.

Against this backdrop of growth and opportunity, the boom's effect on the environment remains a source of concern for many in WA and across the country.

How It All Got Started

Really, mining is old news – this is a frontier land founded on mining money. Although in the 1800s WA was quietly focused on acquiring more modest fortunes from wheat, meat and wool, in 1892 gold was discovered in Coolgardie, and in 1893 it was uncovered again in Kalgoorlie. And so the economic transformation began. Today, gold mining is still going strong, albeit with incrementally diminishing returns. In Kalgoorlie you can visit the Super Pit, an open-pit gold mine the size of 35 football fields sunk 600m into the ground. Copper, nickel, oil and gas are also steady sources of income for the state, with uranium mining (slated for Wiluna, in the midwest) a current aspiration.

But iron ore has been the recent multi-billion-dollar blockbuster industry. Karara mine in the midwest, for example, sits on just under $100 billion worth of iron ore. All this magnetite dug up out of the ground, later to become iron ore, is expected to generate around $3 billion per year in export revenue. Most of it goes to China, but the demand has slowed in recent years, sending a chill through the entire Australian economy.

Foreign investment remains big business. And while such major investment has now been criticised for exposing the state to the capricious

WA'S GREEN BATTLES

1970s
Environmentalists take on and defeat the Albany whaling industry.

1980s
Clashes with loggers over the old-growth jarrah, karri and wandoo forests in the southwest.

2000s
Development of a $200 million marina resort at Ningaloo Reef is prevented.

2013
Development of a massive liquefied natural gas (LNG) hub around James Price Point was halted after successful lobbying by the Wilderness Society.

2017
The WA government's policy of culling sharks, which ran from 2014–17 in response to several fatal shark attacks, is abandoned after public protest.

fortunes of the Chinese economy, the boom would never have occurred without it. For an iron-ore mine, for example, about $1 billion must be available upfront just to develop the extraction machinery. These biscuits are just too big for the Australian economy alone.

The 'four weeks on, one week off' fly-in, fly-out schedule on the mines is referred to as the 'Divorce Roster'. Light-hearted, yes, but a real problem: with broken families increasingly commonplace, the social toll of the WA mining boom will play out for many decades to come.

Life in the Mines

Mining life remains outside the field of vision for most travellers. The Pilbara gold-mining town of Telfer – considered the most remote town in WA – is a good example. Life here is altogether different to that in the leafy western suburbs of Perth. Telfer is less a traditional country town (main street, quiet pub, maybe a community town hall) and more a giant mine plus attendant camp, purpose-built for its hundreds of workers.

Mobile Workforce

In an effort to accommodate a workforce that periodically grows and shrinks, Telfer has been dismantled and rebuilt a few times by mining companies over the years. But by the mid-1990s it was discovered that it was cheaper to simply fly the entire workforce in and out rather than continually build and reconstruct permanent accommodation. Under the new plan, those flown in would work for a sustained period of time (say, four weeks), then have a week or two off back home – in Perth, on Australia's east coast, in New Zealand, or even in Bali. The company would then be able to draw from a broader, more skilled labour force, and workers would no longer need to contemplate the unattractive lifestyle of living permanently in the middle of nowhere. As this business model was adopted across the state, the FIFO work culture was born.

Environmentalist Tim Flannery's *The Future Eaters* (1994) is a highly readable overview of evolution in Australia's ecology. Covering the last 120 million years of history, Flannery offers insightful thoughts on how the environment has shaped Australia's human cultures.

Setting up Camp

The fly-in, fly-out lifestyle is perhaps nowhere more prevalent than in Karratha, once a sleepy, nondescript town but today hosting a large FIFO population, relatively expensive food and accommodation shortages. The recent slowing of WA's resources sector has now brought Karratha's accommodation prices to a more realistic level, and there's a better sense of community here as a few more families commit to the town long term.

Woodside, a major oil and gas producer, has set up camp here, exploring for gas off the north coast. The pace of expansion has been so speedy that there wasn't time to build brick-and-tile homes for the workers. And so today in Karratha, bolted onto the original small town centre, are a number of suburbs composed of 'dongas' – makeshift, moveable, one-person accommodation units. A typical donga in Gap Ridge, the main suburb, has a single bed, a TV, a shower and a toilet carved into a shipping container–like box home. Meals are taken in the 'wet mess', much like a mess hall.

Karratha locals have for some time been voicing concerns that an entire FIFO population parties in their town without regard for the community. Places like Gap Ridge are home to an almost entirely young, moneyed, male population, and this has created a pattern of influx and change in Karratha that is echoed in other mining towns across the state. Many labourers are away from home and family, and have considerable funds to sink into beer and good times. A Woodside proposal to build a more permanent 700-berth miners' camp on the edge of Karratha was rejected by the local council in 2018 – so it seems, for the moment at least, that the good-time donga life will continue.

Graham Pizzey and Frank Knight's *Field Guide to the Birds of Australia* is the definitive tome on WA's birds – full colour, splendidly detailed, accessible and portable.

Such social shifts have not gone unnoticed by politicians. One initiative rolled out since the peak of the boom is 'Royalties for Regions' – putting money back into regional areas such as Karratha, which had not been able to easily build much-needed infrastructure despite the boom. Mobile-phone coverage is now being expanded on the remote highways.

Work Hard, Play Hard

Drinking has long been a tenet of Australian culture, but clocked-off FIFO workers focus particularly keenly on playing hard. Throughout the global financial crisis (or 'GFC' in Australian parlance), letting off steam over a few beers simply continued apace for many. But as iron ore and nickel prices have fallen in recent years, it is perhaps those holding the mantra 'work hard, play hard' most closely to their hearts who have been found to be the most vulnerable to economic wobbles. Many young workers have limited education and have been earning big sums from a young age. For some, the upkeep of their lifestyle (jet skis, cars, houses) has always been contingent on a mining salary that did not waver. Now that the economy has inevitably slowed, some workers are struggling to unearth a plan B.

Boomtown 2050, by landscape architect Richard Weller, is a nicely packaged book about how a rapidly growing town like Perth could be developed – sustainably.

Aboriginal Workforce in Mining

Employment of Aboriginal Australians within the mining industry is very low. Some argue that training programs for Aboriginal Australians – attempts to settle Australia's most disadvantaged into the Western working life – have not proved effective. In 2008 mining magnate Andrew 'Twiggy' Forrest, who the *Financial Review* named as one of Australia's 10 richest people in 2017, boldly promised support for 50,000 jobs for Aboriginal Australians. This government-backed program, called GenerationOne, is also one of the most high-profile attempts by a key mining figure to not only change employment patterns but also speak frankly about the lack of opportunity afforded to Aboriginal communities across the state.

Uptake of GenerationOne opportunities was initially slow – just 10,000 positions by 2012 – but ever-committed to the cause, in 2014 Forrest also released *Creating Parity,* an Australian government-sponsored review of Aboriginal jobs and training. Public submissions were invited on the report's recommendations, but some ideas – such as a cashless 'Healthy Welfare Card' promoted to aid family budgeting and minimise access to drugs and alcohol – came under criticism from Aboriginal and welfare rights advocacy groups. Undaunted, and bolstered by the announcement of 5000 new GenerationOne jobs in 2017, Forrest announced a new initiative in 2018: a vocational training and employment centre at Perth's Acacia Prison for Aboriginal men. WA has disturbingly high incarceration rates for Aboriginal males – something approaching one in 12 Aboriginal men is in prison across the state.

Forrest's ongoing philanthropy, for all its idealism, is at least a push in the right direction. The tension between income and cost of living in WA has eased – Perth's real estate prices fell by 5% in 2018 as the mining boom continued to cool – but it is now more widely acknowledged that the gap between the resource boom–driven 'haves' and 'have nots' is a problem that won't go away quickly.

Mt Augustus (715m), on the central west coast, is the largest rock in the world, twice the size and three times as old as the more famous Uluru in the Northern Territory.

Footprints & Flashpoints

James Price Point is an expanse of wilderness along the Kimberley coast 60km north of Broome. A multinational consortium and the WA state government were proposing a liquefied natural gas (LNG) station here – the biggest in the world. In 2013, eight years after first proposing the development, Woodside Petroleum Ltd announced that the refineries were not economically viable, which was a significant victory for environmental groups seeking to protect the largely pristine Kimberley coastline.

Aside from its dinosaur fossils, the proposed area is a playground for dolphins, dugongs and breeding bilbies. Humpback whales breed and calve along the coastline, and the rainforest backing the coast harbours

Keep your eyes peeled for the banded anteater, aka the numbat, a critically endangered native marsupial. There are only around 1500 of these tiny, light-footed and incredibly shy creatures left in the wild, almost all of them in WA. Numbats are solitary creatures who only venture outside of their neatly delineated territories to mate. Singular dietary requirement: termites.

a multitude of plant species. Not least, this is traditional Aboriginal land. Woodside negotiating a native title deed this size would have marked a historic achievement.

James Price Point became a leading symbol of tensions between the growing financial fortunes of the state and the less easily quantified value of an untouched landscape. Not only were business interests, traditional land owners, politicians and environmentalists in fierce disagreement with each other, but divisions *within* these groups ran deep, despite the amendment of the project to utilise floating offshore LNG rigs. For locals in nearby Broome, 'whose side you're on' became common knowledge, and this lack of anonymity provided a further source of strain.

Following lobbying by the Wilderness Society and environmental-impact studies, the Supreme Court of Western Australia overruled the WA Environment Minister and the WA Environmental Protection Authority to block the proposed Browse LNG plant at James Price Point.

Validating this decision, a 2016 University of Queensland study of the region's cretaceous footprints concluded that they are the world's largest dinosaur footprint collection, with 21 species represented, and contain the world's largest single dinosaur footprint. Further sauropod footprints were found here in 2017, measuring a massive 1.7m across – the record for 'world's biggest' was broken again.

Of course, local Aboriginal Jabirr Jabirr and Goolarabooloo people have always known about these footprints on the beach, representing the steps of Emu-man, their Dreaming ancestor who lives today in the land, the people and their stories. For the moment at least, it's this kind of liquid time, rather than liquid natural gas, that has won the day.

Other Environmental Issues

WA's environmental flashpoints are by no means limited to the footprint-dappled James Price Point. Other controversial sites slated for mining include the Burrup Peninsula in the Dampier Archipelago, which is the location of many petroglyphs (rock art), archaeological wonders thought to date from the last ice age (more than a few of which depict the extinct thylacine, aka the Tasmanian tiger). Although disruption to the works began in the 1960s, in 2007 Woodside Petroleum Ltd had several petroglyphs gingerly removed and fenced off in a separate area to better facilitate development. Some argue that the works are not discrete: that the disruption of one petroglyph compromises the entire site. Elsewhere

THE SAVE NINGALOO CAMPAIGN

Some locals still sport 'Save Ningaloo' bumper stickers on their cars. No one seems to pay much attention to the faded stickers these days, but they're a reminder of one of the most high-profile and fiercely contested environmental campaigns Western Australia has seen. 'Save Ningaloo', with its thousands of protesters, successfully blocked development of a massive marina resort (slated for 2003) on a loggerhead-turtle nesting ground. Comprising 280km of coral reef, and visited by species such as manta rays, whale sharks, dugongs, humpback whales and turtles, Ningaloo is one of the last healthy major reef systems in the world.

The area did nevertheless remain a site of interest for property developers and the resources sector, and in late 2012 BHP Billiton submitted a proposal to the state government to explore for liquefied natural gas some 5km from Ningaloo's perimeter.

This proposal was rejected and now BHP Billiton has joined with Australia's CSIRO (Commonwealth Scientific and Industrial Research Organisation) in a five-year marine research partnership.

in the state, uranium mines are under consideration, though to date no uranium has been exported from WA.

Meanwhile, groundwater has been utilised freely for decades; alternative water sources, using desalination plants, have been in place for some time. Old-growth forests, with their 1000-year-old karri trees, were logged until the 1990s; today scientists cite lowered rainfall in the southwest as the result of deforestation.

And, much like other major cities in Australia, Perth is subject to suburban sprawl. Because the mining boom drove much property development, the city now tails out across 100km, in new developments studded with affordable (read: cheaply built) housing. The environmental effects of the lifestyle out here are not immediately apparent, but may nevertheless prove significant. Many housing estates are divorced from public-transport routes, so people must always drive for their litre of milk, and Perth's roads are becoming increasingly congested. Many have long been calling for more high-density housing in and near central Perth.

From around April to June, the World Heritage–listed Ningaloo Reef hosts whales sharks that can grow up to 12m long. They're remarkably docile, but keep your distance: humanity owes them a little peace and quiet.

Looking Ahead

Going ahead, the balancing act between the economy and environmental issues remains at the very heart of WA society and politics, and the stakes have never been higher. Now that the Chinese economy's appetite for iron ore has eased, developers and the state government will be even more focused on tapping other rich veins of WA's resources sector. Inevitably, there will be more conflict between industrial interests and environmental advocates.

The boom has spawned a breed of mega-rich mining magnates whose influence extends well beyond resources into politics and the media, and they are eyeing further wilderness areas as sites for the development of new mines and gas plants, with all the costs and benefits they entail.

The resources boom may have slowed, but the ongoing tension between economic growth and environmental protection will continue to define Australia's most sprawling state for the foreseeable future.

In *The Weather Makers* (2005), Australian environmentalist Tim Flannery argues lucidly and passionately for the immediate need to address climate change. His follow-up *Atmosphere of Hope* (2016) offers further thoughts and solutions.

Indigenous Art in Western Australia

Experiencing the Aboriginal art of Western Australia creates an indelible link for travellers to this land of red dirt and desert expanses. Ancient rock art travels across the centuries, traditional designs and motifs inspire modern artists, and Aboriginal tour operators inform with stories of spirituality, bush tucker and 'country'.

Aboriginal art has impacted the broader Australian cultural landscape, and is now showcased at national and international events and celebrated as a significant part of Australian culture. It still retains the role of passing on knowledge, but today is also important for economic, educational and political reasons. Art has been used to raise awareness of issues such as health and has been a primary tool for the reconciliation process across Australia. In many Indigenous communities, art has become a major source of employment and income.

The Dreaming

All early Aboriginal art was based on the various clans' and nations' ancestral Dreaming – the Creation – when the earth's physical features were formed by the struggles between powerful supernatural ancestors such as the Rainbow Serpent, the Lightning Men and the Wandjina.

Rock Art

Although there is no word in Indigenous Australian languages for 'art', visual imagery is a fundamental part of Aboriginal culture and life: a connection between the past, present and future, and between Indigenous people and their traditional homelands. The earliest forms of Indigenous visual cultural expression were rock carvings (petroglyphs) and paintings on rock galleries, with the earliest engraved designs known to exist dating back at least 40,000 years – perhaps older. Some of Australia's oldest examples of engravings can be found in the Pilbara and in the Kimberley, where the focus is on the Wandjina, the ancestral creation spirits.

WHERE TO SEE ROCK ART

- Mulka's Cave (p112), near Wave Rock and Hyden.
- Burrup Peninsula, Pilbara with Ngurrangga Tours (p201).
- Mitchell Plateau in the Kimberley, especially Mitchell Falls (p229) and Munurru Campground (p229).
- Mt Elizabeth Station (p230) on the Gibb River Road.
- Some of the Wandjina and Gwion Gwion images hidden across the Kimberley are accessible from some stations on the Gibb River Road.

BEST NORTHERN GALLERIES

- Mowanjum Art & Culture Centre (p225), Gibb River Road
- Waringarri Aboriginal Arts Centre (p233), Kununurra
- East Pilbara Arts Centre (p205), Newman
- Spinifex Hill Studios (p204), Port Hedland
- Yinjaa-Barndi Gallery (p201), Rosebourne

Some Aboriginal rock paintings are believed to date back between 18,000 and 60,000 years and provide a record of changing environments and lifestyles over the millennia. For the local Aboriginal people, rock-art sites are a major source of traditional knowledge – they are historical archives in place of a written form.

The earliest hand or grass prints were followed by a naturalistic style, with large outlines of people or animals filled in with colour. Then came the dynamic style, in which motion was often depicted (a dotted line, for example, to show a spear's path through the air). In this era the first mythological beings appeared, with human bodies and animal heads. Following this were simple human silhouettes, and then the more recent X-ray style, displaying the internal organs and bones of animals.

Art of the Kimberley

The art of the Kimberley is perhaps best known for its images of the Wandjina, a group of ancestral beings who came from the sky and sea and were associated with fertility. They controlled the elements and were responsible for the formation of the country's natural features.

Wandjina images are found painted on rock as well as on more recent contemporary media; some of the rock images are more than 7m long. They generally appear in human form, with large black eyes, a nose but no mouth, a halo around the head (representative of both hair and clouds) and a black oval shape on the chest.

Each Wandjina traditionally has its own custodian family, and to ensure good relations between the Wandjina and the people, the images have to be retouched annually.

Another significant painting style found in the Kimberley is that of the Gwion Gwion figures. The Gwion Gwion figures are generally small and seem to depict ethereal beings engaged in ceremony or dance. It is believed that they pre-date the Wandjina paintings, though little is known of their significance or meaning.

Warlayirti Artists Centre (p225) in Balgo in the Kimberley is a successful Aboriginal art collective and supports artists from seven language groups. Balgo art started in the 1970s with canvas and paint introduced by missionaries and is now internationally acclaimed. Visitors are welcome but you must enquire in advance to arrange permits.

Western Desert Painting

Western Desert painting, also known as dot painting, is probably the most well known of Australia's Aboriginal painting styles. The style partly evolved from 'ground paintings', which formed the centrepiece of dances and songs. These were made from pulped plant material, with designs made on the ground. While dot paintings may look random and abstract, they depict Dreaming stories and can be read in many ways, including as aerial landscape maps. Many paintings feature the tracks of birds, animals and humans, often identifying the land's ancestral beings. Subjects may be depicted by the imprint they leave in the sand – a simple arc depicts a person (as that is the print left by someone sitting cross-legged), a coolamon (wooden carrying dish) is shown by an oval shape, a digging stick by a single line, and a campfire by a circle. Men or women are identified by the objects associated with them: digging sticks and coolamons for women, spears and boomerangs for men. Concentric

BEST CITY GALLERIES

- Art Gallery of Western Australia (p60), Perth
- Mossenson Galleries – Indigenart (p96), Perth
- Japingka (p96), Fremantle
- Aboriginal Art & Craft Gallery (p96), Perth

circles usually depict Dreaming sites, or places where ancestors paused in their journeys.

While these symbols are widely used, their meaning in each painting is known only by the artist and the people closely associated with them – either by clan or by the Dreaming – since different clans apply different interpretations to each painting. In this way, sacred stories can be publicly portrayed, as the deeper meaning is not revealed to uninitiated viewers.

Buying Aboriginal Art – Ethically

Around Perth you'll find plenty of commercial galleries selling gorgeous Aboriginal art from across WA and beyond. Unfortunately, some of these artworks feature designs that are illegally copied from Aboriginal people or are just plain fake, often made overseas by underpaid workers. Furthermore, some Aboriginal artists continue to be paid small sums for their work, only to find it being sold for top dollar in city galleries.

The Western Desert Mob is a coalition of artist cooperatives of the Ngaanyatjarra lands of Western Australia. Mediums include *punu*, the traditional art of woodcarving. Online, see www.westerndesertmob.com.au.

By making an informed choice and buying authentic artworks, you are supporting Aboriginal culture and helping to ensure that traditional expertise continues to be of economic and cultural benefit to Aboriginal artists and their communities.

Make sure what you're buying is the real deal and that your money goes to the right people: buy either directly from communities that have art collectives, or from galleries and outlets that are owned and operated, or supported, by Aboriginal communities. The **Indigenous Art Code** (www.indigenousartcode.org) lists galleries considered to observe ethical practices. Artworks themselves should also have a certificate of authenticity. Note, too, that haggling is not part of Aboriginal culture.

Survival Guide

DIRECTORY A–Z 262
Accessible Travel 262
Customs Regulations 262
Discount Cards 262
Electricity 262
Embassies & Consulates 262
Food 263
Health 263
Insurance 265
Internet Access 265
Legal Matters 265
LGBT+ Travellers 265
Maps 266
Money 266
Opening Hours 266
Post 266
Public Holidays 266
Safe Travel 267
Telephone 269
Time 269
Toilets 270
Tourist Information 270
Visas 270
Volunteering 270
Women Travellers 271
Work 271

TRANSPORT 272
GETTING THERE & AWAY 272
Entering the Country/Region 272
Air 272
Land 272
Sea 273
GETTING AROUND 273
Air 273
Bicycle 273
Bus 274
Car & Motorcycle 274
Local Transport 276
Train 276

Directory A–Z

Accessible Travel

Disability awareness in WA is excellent. Legislation requires that new accommodation meet accessibility standards, and discrimination by tourism operators is illegal. Many of the state's key attractions provide access for those with limited mobility and an increasing number are addressing the needs of visitors with visual or aural impairments. Contact attractions in advance to confirm the facilities.

Useful resources:

AccessPlus WA Deaf (Map p58; ☎08-9441 2655; www.wadeaf.org.au; 34 Dodd St, Wembley; ⊙9am-5pm Mon-Fri) Advice for travellers with hearing impairments.

Lonely Planet Download the free Accessible Travel guide from http://lptravel.to/AccessibleTravel.

National Public Toilet Map (www.toiletmap.gov.au) Lists more than 14,000 public toilets around Australia, including those with wheelchair access.

People with Disabilities WA (www.pwdwa.org) Website detailing WA's major disability service providers.

Tourism WA (www.westernaustralia.com) Website highlighting all accessible listings (accommodation, restaurants, tours etc).

VisAbility (☎08-9311 8202; www.visability.com.au) Support for people living with blindness and vision impairment.

Customs Regulations

For comprehensive information, contact the **Department of Immigration and Border Protection** (☎1300 363 263, 02-6275 6666; www.border.gov.au).

On arrival, declare all goods of animal or plant origin, as it's vital to protect Australia's unique environment and agricultural industries. If you fail to declare quarantine items on arrival, you risk an on-the-spot fine of over $200 or even prosecution and imprisonment. For more information contact the Australian Department of Agriculture (www.agriculture.gov.au/biosecurity).

Duty-free allowances:

Alcohol 2.25L

Cigarettes 50

Other goods Up to $900 value; or items for personal use that you will be taking with you when you leave.

Discount Cards

The most common card for discounts on accommodation, transport and some attractions in WA is the International Student Identity Card (www.isic.org), issued to full-time students aged 12 years and over. There's also an International Youth Travel Card (IYTC), issued to people between 12 and 30 years of age who are not full-time students: see www.isic.com.au/about/the-cards/youth-card-iytc.

Electricity

Embassies & Consulates

The principal diplomatic representations to Australia are in Canberra, but many countries are represented in Perth by consular staff.

Remember that while in Australia you are bound by

Australian laws. Your embassy will not be sympathetic if you end up in jail after committing a crime locally, even if such actions are legal in your own country.

Dutch Consulate (☎08-9486 1579; www.netherlandsworldwide.nl; 1139 Hay St, West Perth)

German Consulate (☎08-9321 2926; www.germanconsulperth.com; 1113 Hay St, West Perth)

Irish Consulate (☎08-6557 5802; www.consulateofirelandwa.com.au; 165/580 Hay St; ⏰by appointment 10.30am-2pm Mon-Fri)

New Zealand Consulate (☎08-9364 1700; www.mfat.govt.nz; 1 Sleat Rd, Applecross; ⏰8am-5pm Mon-Fri)

UK Consulate (☎08-9224 4700; www.british-consulate.org; level 12, 251 Adelaide Tce; ⏰9am-5pm Mon-Fri)

US Consulate (☎08-6144-5100; https://au.usembassy.gov/embassy-consulates/perth; 4th fl, 16 St Georges Tce; ⏰8.30am-4.30pm)

Food

With some skillful navigation and planning, eating is one of the pleasures of travelling around Western Australia. Tables should be booked in advance at Perth's high-end restaurants, but most cafes and pubs favour a more relaxed drop-in style of eating.

Cafes Many operate as dining options throughout the day, before morphing into bars after dark.

Pubs Throughout the region, pub meals are good value.

Vineyard restaurants and craft breweries Dining at the vineyards and craft breweries of Margaret River and the Swan Valley makes for a particularly enjoyable afternoon.

Farmers markets Excellent spots for good-value snacks and picking up local produce.

EATING PRICE RANGES

The following price ranges refer to a standard main course:

$ less than $15

$$ $15 to $32

$$$ more than $32

BOOK YOUR STAY ONLINE

For more accommodation reviews by Lonely Planet authors, check out http://lonelyplanet.com/hotels/. You'll find independent reviews, as well as recommendations on the best places to stay. Best of all, you can book online.

Health

Australia is a healthy country for travellers. Malaria and yellow fever are unknown, cholera and typhoid are unheard of, and animal diseases such as rabies and foot-and-mouth disease have yet to be recorded. The standard of hospitals and healthcare is high. Few travellers should experience anything worse than an upset stomach or a hangover.

Before You Go

Pack medications in their original, clearly labelled, containers. A signed and dated letter from your physician describing your medical conditions and medications, including generic names, is also a good idea. If carrying syringes or needles, be sure to have a physician's letter documenting their medical necessity.

HEALTH INSURANCE

Health insurance is essential for all travellers. You may prefer a policy that pays doctors or hospitals directly rather than requiring you to pay on the spot and claim later. If you have to claim later make sure you keep all documentation. Check that the policy covers ambulances and emergency medical evacuations by air.

RECOMMENDED VACCINATIONS

No particular vaccinations are needed, but the World Health Organization (www.who.int) recommends that all global travellers should be vaccinated against diphtheria, tetanus, measles, mumps, rubella, chickenpox and polio, as well as hepatitis B, regardless of their destination. While Australia has high levels of childhood vaccination coverage, outbreaks of these diseases do occur.

Proof of yellow-fever vaccination is required from travellers entering Australia within six days of having stayed overnight or longer in a yellow-fever-infected country. For a full list of these countries, see the websites of the World Health Organization (www.who.int/wer) or the Centers for Disease Control & Prevention (www.cdc.gov/travel).

MEDICAL CHECKLIST

- acetaminophen (paracetamol) or aspirin
- adhesive or paper tape
- antibacterial ointment in case of cuts or abrasions
- antibiotics (also bring any prescriptions)
- antidiarrhoeal drugs (eg loperamide)
- antihistamines (for hayfever and allergic reactions)
- anti-inflammatory drugs (eg ibuprofen)
- bandages, gauze, gauze rolls
- DEET-containing insect repellent for the skin

- iodine tablets or water filter (for water purification)
- oral rehydration salts
- permethrin-containing insect spray for clothing, tents and bed nets
- pocketknife
- scissors, safety pins, tweezers
- steroid cream or cortisone (for allergic rashes)
- sunscreen
- thermometer

RESOURCES

There's a wealth of travel health advice on the internet: Lonely Planet (www.lonely planet.com) is a good place to start.

World Health Organization (www.who.int/ith) Publishes *International Travel and Health*, revised annually and available free online.

MD Travel Health (www.redplanet.travel/mdtravelhealth) Provides complete travel-health recommendations for every country, updated daily.

In West Coast Australia

AVAILABILITY & COST OF HEALTHCARE

Like the rest of Australia, Western Australia has an excellent healthcare system: a mixture of privately run medical clinics and hospitals alongside public hospitals funded by the Australian government. There are also excellent specialised public health facilities for women and children in major centres.

You'll find general practitioners (GPs) working in most WA towns who are available for prebooked appointments, and hospitals with emergency departments in major centres.

Australia's Medicare system (www.medicareaustralia.gov.au) covers Australian residents for some healthcare costs and emergency care, with reciprocity for citizens of New Zealand, Belgium, UK, Netherlands, Sweden, Finland, Italy, Malta, Norway, Slovenia and Ireland. Online, see www.humanservices.gov.au/individuals/services/medicare. But even if you're not covered by Medicare, a short consultation with a local GP will usually only set you back around $70.

Over-the-counter medications are widely available at pharmacies. These include painkillers, antihistamines for allergies and skin-care products.

Some medications readily available over the counter in other countries are only available in Australia by prescription. These include the oral contraceptive pill, some medications for asthma and all antibiotics. If you take medication on a regular basis, bring an adequate supply and ensure you know the generic name, as brand names may differ.

ENVIRONMENTAL HAZARDS

Heat Exhaustion & Heatstroke

These are significant risks across WA. Heat exhaustion occurs when fluid intake does not keep up with fluid loss. Symptoms include dizziness, fainting, fatigue, nausea or vomiting. On observation, the skin is usually pale, cool and clammy. Treatment consists of rest in a cool, shady place and fluid replacement with water or diluted sports drinks.

Heatstroke is a severe form of heat illness that occurs after fluid depletion or extreme heat challenge from heavy exercise. This is a true medical emergency: heating of the brain leads to disorientation, hallucinations and seizures. Prevention is by maintaining an adequate fluid intake to ensure the continued passage of clear and copious urine, especially during physical exertion.

Hypothermia

During the winter months in the southern parts of Western Australia, hypothermia is a possible risk for bushwakers, surfers and bikers. Early signs include the inability to perform fine movements (such as doing up buttons), shivering and a bad case of the 'umbles' (fumbles, mumbles, grumbles, stumbles). The key elements of treatment include changing the environment to one where heat loss is minimised, changing out of any wet clothing, adding dry clothes with windproof and waterproof layers, adding insulation and providing fuel (water and carbohydrate) to allow shivering, which builds the internal temperature. In severe cases of hypothermia, shivering actually stops – this is a medical emergency requiring rapid evacuation in addition to the above measures.

INFECTIOUS DISEASES

The chance of a traveller to WA encountering any of these diseases is low, but here are the fundamentals.

Bat Lyssavirus

This disease is related to rabies and some deaths have occurred after bites. The risk is greatest for animal handlers and vets. Rabies vaccine is effective, but the risk to travellers is very low.

Dengue Fever

Also known as 'breakbone fever', because of the severe muscular pains that accompany the fever, this viral disease is spread by a species of mosquito that feeds primarily during the day. Most people recover in a few days, but more severe forms of the disease can occur, particularly in residents who are exposed to another strain of the virus (there are four types) in a subsequent season.

Giardiasis

Giardiasis is widespread in the waterways around Australia. Drinking untreated water from streams and lakes is not recommended. Water filters, and boiling or treating water with iodine, are effective in preventing the disease. Symptoms consist of intermittent bad-smelling diarrhoea, abdominal bloating and wind. Effective treatment is available (tinidazole or metronidazole).

Meningococcal Disease

This disease occurs worldwide and is a risk with prolonged, dormitory-style accommodation. A vaccine exists for some types of this disease, namely meningococcal A, C, Y and W. No vaccine is presently available for the viral type of meningitis.

Ross River Fever

The Ross River virus is widespread throughout Australia and is spread by mosquitoes living in marshy areas. In addition to fever, the disease causes headache, joint and muscular pains and a rash, before resolving after five to seven days.

Sexually Transmitted Diseases

STDs occur at rates similar to those in most other Western countries. Always use a condom with any new sexual partner. Condoms are readily available in chemists and through vending machines in many public places, including toilets.

Viral Encephalitis

Also known as the Murray Valley encephalitis virus, this is spread by mosquitoes and is most common in northern Australia, especially during the wet season (November to April). This potentially serious disease is normally accompanied by headache, muscle pains and light sensitivity. Residual neurological damage can occur and no specific treatment is available. However, the risk to most travellers is low.

Tap Water

Tap water is mainly safe to drink in WA, but a few small towns do have bore water, which you need to sterilise before drinking. Ask if you're not sure.

To prevent diarrhoea, avoid drinking from streams, rivers and lakes, or purify water before drinking. The simplest way to do this is to boil it thoroughly. Consider purchasing a water filter; read the specifications first, so that you know exactly what it removes from the water and what it doesn't. Simple filtering will not remove all dangerous organisms, so if you cannot boil water it should be treated chemically. Chlorine tablets will kill many pathogens, but not some parasites, such as giardia. Iodine is more effective and is available in tablet form, but remember that too much iodine can be harmful.

Insurance

Sign up for a travel-insurance policy covering theft, loss and medical problems.

Some policies exclude designated 'dangerous activities' such as scuba diving, parasailing or even bushwalking. Ensure your policy fully covers you for activities of your choice. Check you're covered for ambulances and emergency medical evacuations by air.

Third-party personal-injury insurance (p275) is included in vehicle registration costs, and comprehensive insurance is usually included when hiring a vehicle, though consider reducing your excess to offset costs in the event of an accident.

Worldwide travel insurance is available at www.lonelyplanet.com/bookings.

Internet Access

Internet cafes have virtually vanished across Australia with the arrival of smartphones and other internet-enabled mobile devices. Many backpacker hostels and public libraries offer wi-fi connections; in smaller towns visit community centres. At your accommodation, if wi-fi is not totally free, you might still get a certain amount of data gratis, then pay-per-use after that.

Legal Matters

Most travellers will have no contact with WA police or the legal system. If you do, it's most likely to be while driving.

Driving There's a significant police presence on WA roads – police have the power to stop your car, see your licence (you're required to carry it), check your vehicle for roadworthiness and insist that you take a breath test for alcohol (and sometimes illicit drugs).

Drugs First-time offenders caught with small amounts of illegal drugs are likely to receive a fine rather than go to jail, but the recording of a conviction against you may affect your visa status.

Visas If you remain in Australia beyond the life of your visa, you'll officially be an 'overstayer' and could face detention and then be prevented from returning to Australia for up to three years.

Arrested? It's your right to telephone a friend, lawyer or relative before questioning begins. Legal aid is available only in serious cases; for Legal Aid office info, see www.legalaid.wa.gov.au. However, many solicitors do not charge for an initial consultation.

LGBT+ Travellers

In general, Western Australians are open-minded about homosexuality, and in WA gay and lesbian people are protected by antidiscrimination legislation and share an equal age of consent with heterosexuals (16 years).

Perth has the state's only gay and lesbian venues and its small scene is centred around Northbridge. It's unlikely you'll experience any real problems, although the further away from the main centres, the more likely you are to experience overt homophobia.

Useful resources:

Living Proud (☎08-9486 9855, counselling 1800 184 527; www.livingproud.org.au) Information and counselling line.

Q Pages (www.qpages.com.au) Gay and lesbian business directory and what's-on listings.

Visit Gay Australia (www.galta.com.au) Lists WA members offering accommodation and tours.

Maps

Tourist information offices usually have serviceable town maps. For more detailed information, the **Royal Automobile Club of Western Australia** (RAC; ☎13 17 03; www.rac.com.au) has road maps available (including downloadable route maps). UBD publishes a handy *South West & Great Southern* book.

Hema Maps (www.hemamaps.com.au) Best for the north, especially the dirt roads. The website has a wealth of planning information and specialists apps and GPS navigation systems can be purchased.

Landgate (www.landgate.wa.gov.au) Statewide maps as well as topographical maps for bushwalking.

Money

ATMs

Bank branches with 24-hour ATMs can be found statewide. In the smallest towns there's usually an ATM in the local petrol station or the pub. Most ATMs accept cards from other banks and are linked to international networks.

Cash

The Australian dollar is made up of 100 cents; there are 5¢, 10¢, 20¢, 50¢, $1 and $2 coins, and $5, $10, $20, $50 and $100 notes.

Cash amounts equal to or in excess of the equivalent of A$10,000 (in any currency) must be declared on arrival or departure in Australia.

Changing foreign currency is usually no problem at banks throughout WA.

Credit & Debit Cards

Visa and MasterCard are widely accepted and a credit card is essential (in lieu of a large deposit) for car hire. With debit cards, any card connected to the international banking network (Cirrus, Maestro, Plus and Eurocard) will work. Diners Club and Amex are not as widely accepted.

Tipping

Tipping is not the cultural norm in WA, but around 10% is appropriate if you feel service in a restaurant has been exemplary. Many cafes have a tip jar on the counter for loose change and this is usually shared between all the staff.

Travellers Cheques

Travellers cheques have fallen out of fashion these days. Still, Amex, Thomas Cook and other well-known international brands are easily exchanged and are commission-free when exchanged at their bureaux; however, local banks charge hefty fees for the same service.

Opening Hours

Shops outside of Perth may close on weekends. Restaurants in vineyards and breweries are usually only open for lunch, though cafes are often open later for dinner. Most of Perth's city-centre shops and major shopping malls are open seven days per week, with extended hours on Friday.

Post

Australia Post (www.auspost.com.au) is the nationwide provider. Most substantial WA towns have a post office, or an Australia Post desk within a local shop. Services are reliable, but slower than they used to be (recent cost-saving cutbacks are to blame). Express Post delivers a parcel or envelope interstate within Australia by the next business day; otherwise allow four days for urban deliveries, longer for country areas.

Public Holidays

New Year's Day 1 January

Australia Day 26 January

Labour Day First Monday in March

Easter (Good Friday and Easter Monday) March/April

Anzac Day 25 April

Western Australia Day First Monday in June

Queen's Birthday Last Monday in September

Christmas Day 25 December

Boxing Day 26 December

School Holidays

The Christmas season is part of the summer school holidays (mid-December to late January), when transport and accommodation are often booked out, and there are long, restless queues at tourist attractions. There are three shorter (around two weeks) school-holiday periods during the year that shift slightly from year to year. Generally, they fall in mid-April, mid-July and late September to mid-October.

Safe Travel

Dangerous animals around WA include snakes, crocodiles, sharks and jellyfish – but if you exercise a bit of common sense, you're unlikely to encounter any of these. The state is generally a low-crime area, although care should be taken after midnight in central nightlife areas like Northbridge in Perth.

PRACTICALITIES

Newspapers Perth's daily paper is the *West Australian* (www.west.com.au), aka *The West;* the *Australian* and *Financial Review* are also widely available. There's also a Sunday tabloid called the *Sunday Times*.

Online See www.perthnow.com.au for breaking news, and www.xpressmag.com.au and www.scenestr.com.au/perth for live music and culture.

Radio Tune in to the ABC on the radio – pick a program and frequency from www.abc.net.au/radio.

TV Networks include the commercial-free ABC, multicultural SBS, and commercial TV stations Seven, Nine and Ten.

DVDs Those sold in Australia can be watched on players accepting region 4 DVDs (the same as Mexico, South America, Central America, New Zealand, the Pacific and the Caribbean). The USA and Canada are region 1 countries, and Europe and Japan are region 2.

Smoking Banned on public transport and planes, in cars carrying children, between the flags at patrolled beaches, within 10m of a playground and in government buildings. It's also banned within bars and clubs but permitted in some al fresco or courtyard areas.

Weights & Measures The metric system is used across Australia.

Animal Hazards

Australia is home to some seriously dangerous creatures. On land there are poisonous snakes and spiders, while the sea harbours deadly box jellyfish and white pointer sharks. The saltwater crocodile spans both environments.

In reality you're unlikely to see these creatures in the wild, much less be attacked by one. Far more likely is a hangover after a big night, or getting sunburned after not wearing sunscreen.

BOX JELLYFISH & MARINE SPECIES

There have been fatal encounters between swimmers and box jellyfish on the northern coast. Also known as the sea wasp or 'stinger', they have venomous tentacles that can grow up to 3m long. You can be stung any time, but from November to March you should stay out of the water unless you're wearing a 'stinger suit' (available from sporting shops).

If you are stung, first aid consists of washing the skin with vinegar to prevent further discharge of remaining stinging cells, followed by rapid transfer to a hospital; antivenin is widely available.

Marine spikes from sea urchins, stonefish, scorpion fish, catfish and stingrays can cause severe local pain. If this occurs, immediately immerse the affected area in water that's as hot as can be tolerated. Keep topping up with hot water until the pain subsides and medical care can be reached. The stonefish is found only in tropical Australia; antivenin is available.

CROCODILES

In northwest WA, saltwater crocodiles can be a real danger. They live around the coast, and are also found in estuaries, creeks and rivers, sometimes a long way inland. Observe safety signs or ask locals whether an inviting waterhole or river is croc-free before plunging in. The last fatality in WA caused by a saltwater crocodile was in 2018, and attacks occurred in 2006, 2012, 2015 and 2016.

INSECTS

For four to six months of the year, you'll have to cope with flies and mosquitoes in WA. Flies are more prevalent in the outback, where a humble fly net is effective. Repellents may also deter them.

Mozzies are a problem in summer, especially near wetlands in tropical areas, and some species are carriers of viral infections. Keep your arms and legs covered after sunset and use repellent.

The biting midge (sandfly) lives in WA's northern coastal areas. Locals often appear immune, but it's almost a rite of passage for those heading north to be covered in bites. Cover up at dusk.

Ticks and leeches are also common. For protection, wear loose-fitting clothing with long sleeves. Apply 30% DEET on exposed skin, repeated every three to four hours, and impregnate clothing with permethrin.

SHARKS

Between 2000 and 2019, there were 15 fatal shark attacks in WA, mostly involving surfers at remote beaches. Around popular coastal and city beaches, shark-spotting methods include nets, spotter planes, jet skis and surf lifesavers.

In early 2014 a three-month trial using baited lines was launched around Perth and southwest beaches, but while 68 sharks were caught and shot, none were great whites. Following protests from environmental and animal-rights groups, the catch-and-kill policy was discontinued after 2017. However, the WA Fisheries Department has the authority to trap and kill individual sharks deemed to be a risk to public safety.

SNAKES

There are many venomous snakes in the Australian bush, the most common being the dugite, brown snakes and tiger snakes. Unless you're interfering with one, or accidentally stand on it, it's extremely unlikely you'll be bitten.

Australian snakes have a reputation that is justified in terms of the potency of their venom, but unjustified in terms of the actual risk to travellers and locals. They are endowed with only small fangs, making it easy to prevent bites to the lower limbs (where 80% of bites occur) by wearing protective clothing (such as gaiters) around the ankles when bushwalking.

The bite marks are small and preventing the spread of toxic venom can be achieved by applying pressure to the wound and immobilising the area with a splint or sling before seeking medical attention. Application of an elastic bandage (you can improvise with a T-shirt) wrapped firmly, but not so tightly that circulation is cut off, around the entire limb – along with immobilisation – is a lifesaving first aid measure.

SPIDERS

The redback is the most common poisonous spider in WA. It's small and black with a distinctive red stripe on its body. Bites cause increasing pain at the site followed by profuse sweating and generalised symptoms. First aid includes application of ice or cold packs to the bite and transfer to hospital.

Hospitals have antivenin on hand for all common snake and spider bites, but it helps to know which type you've been bitten by.

Other Hazards

BUSHFIRES

Bushfires are a regular occurrence in WA, so in hot, dry and windy weather, be extremely careful with any naked flame. Even cigarette butts thrown out of car windows can start fires. On a total fire ban day it's forbidden even to use a camping stove in the open.

Bushwalkers should seek local advice before setting out. When a total fire ban is in place, delay your trip until the weather improves. If you're out in the bush and you see smoke, even a long distance away, take heed – bushfires move fast and change direction with the wind. Go to the nearest open space, downhill if possible. A forested ridge is the most dangerous place to be during a bushfire.

CRIME

Western Australia is a relatively safe place to visit, but you should still take reasonable precautions. Don't leave hotel rooms or cars unlocked, and don't leave valuables unattended and visible in cars.

In recent years there has been a spate of glassings (stabbings with broken glass) at Perth venues. If you see trouble brewing, it's best to walk away. Take due caution on the streets after dark, especially around hotspots such as Northbridge where many venues enforce lockouts in the early morning – that is, if you're not inside the venue before a certain time, you will not be able to gain entry.

There have also been reports of drinks spiked with drugs in Perth pubs and clubs. Authorities advise women to refuse drinks offered by strangers in bars and to drink bottled alcohol rather than drinks served in a glass.

DRIVING

Australian drivers are generally a courteous bunch, but rural 'petrolheads', inner-city speedsters and drink-drivers can pose risks. Open-road dangers can include wildlife, such as kangaroos (mainly at dusk and dawn); fatigue, caused by travelling long distances without the necessary breaks; and excessive speed. Driving on dirt roads can also be tricky for the uninitiated.

HYPOTHERMIA

More bushwalkers in Australia actually die of cold than in bushfires. Even in summer,

A BIT OF PERSPECTIVE

Despite the recent increase in fatal shark attacks in WA, statistically it's still very unlikely that visitors will be attacked. Blue-ringed octopus deaths are even rarer – only two in the last century – and there's only ever been one confirmed death from a cone shell. Jellyfish kill about two people annually, but you're still 100 times more likely to drown.

On land, snakes kill one or two people per year (about the same as bee stings, or less than one-thousandth of those killed on the roads). There hasn't been a recorded death from a tick bite for over 50 years, nor from spider bites in the last 20.

temperatures can drop below freezing at night and the weather can change very quickly. Exposure in even moderately cool temperatures can sometimes result in hypothermia.

OUTBACK TRAVEL

If you're keen to explore outback WA, it's important not to embark on your trip without careful planning and preparation. Travellers regularly encounter difficulties in the harsh outback conditions far from potential assistance, and trips occasionally prove fatal.

SWIMMING

Popular beaches are patrolled by surf lifesavers and flags mark out patrolled areas. Even so, WA's surf beaches can be dangerous places to swim if you aren't used to heavy surf. Undertows (or 'rips') are the main problem. If you find yourself being carried out by a rip, just keep afloat; don't panic or try to swim against the rip, which will exhaust you. In most cases the current will stop within a couple of hundred metres of the shore and you can then swim parallel to the shore for a short way to get out of the rip and swim back to land.

On the south coast, freak 'king waves' from the Southern Ocean can sometimes break on the shore with little or no warning, dragging people out to sea. In populated areas there are warning signs; in other areas be extremely careful.

People have been paralysed by diving into waves in shallow water and hitting a sandbar; look before you leap.

GOVERNMENT TRAVEL ADVICE

Government travel-health websites include the following:

Australia (www.smartraveller.gov.au)

Canada (www.hc-sc.gc.ca)

UK (www.nhs.uk/livewell/travelhealth)

USA (www.cdc.gov/travel)

Telephone

Australia's two main telecommunications companies are Telstra (www.telstra.com.au) and Optus (www.optus.com.au). Mobile (cell) services are provided by Telstra, Optus, Vodafone (www.vodafone.com.au) and Virgin (www.virginmobile.com.au).

Mobile Phones

- Australia's mobile networks service more than 90% of the population but leave vast tracts of the country uncovered, including much of inland WA.
- Perth and larger centres get good reception, but service in other areas can be haphazard or nonexistent.
- Telstra has the best coverage, especially in the more remote north, but if you're sticking to the southwest and northern tourist areas, coverage is largely similar, so shop around for a good deal from the four mobile operators.
- Australia's mobile network is compatible with most European phones, but generally not with the US or Japanese systems. The main service providers offer prepaid SIMs.

Phone Codes

0011 International calling prefix (the equivalent of 00 in most other countries).

61 Country code for Australia.

08 Area code for all of WA. If calling from overseas, drop the initial zero.

04 All numbers starting with 04 (such as 0410, 0412) are mobile-phone numbers. If calling from overseas, drop the initial zero.

190 Usually recorded information calls, charged at anything from 35¢ to $5 or more per minute (more from mobiles and public phones).

1800 Toll-free numbers; can be called free of charge from anywhere in the country, though they may not be accessible from certain areas or from mobile phones.

1800-REVERSE (738 3773) or 12 550 Dial to make a reverse-charge (collect) call from any public or private phone.

13 or 1300 Charged at the rate of a local call. The numbers can usually be dialled Australia-wide, but may be applicable only to a specific state or STD district.

Note: Telephone numbers beginning with 1800, 13 or 1300 cannot be dialled from outside Australia.

Time

Australia is divided into three time zones: the Western Standard Time zone (GMT/UTC plus eight hours) covers most of WA; Central Standard Time (plus 9½ hours) covers the Northern Territory, South Australia and parts of WA's Central Desert and Nullarbor regions near the border; and Eastern Standard Time (plus 10 hours) covering Tasmania, Victoria, New South Wales, the Australian Capital Territory and Queensland. So when it's noon in Perth, it's 1.30pm in Darwin and Adelaide, and 2pm in Sydney or Melbourne.

Daylight saving time – where clocks are put forward an hour – operates in most other states during the warmer months (October to March), but not in WA.

Toilets

There is no charge for using public toilets throughout Western Australia. The National Public Toilet Map (www.toiletmap.gov.au) lists more than 14,000 public toilets around Australia, including those with wheelchair access.

Tourist Information

For general statewide information, try the **Western Australian Visitor Centre** (Map p62; ☎08-9483 1111; www.wavisitorcentre.com.au; 55 William St; ⏰9am-5pm Mon-Fri, 9.30am-4pm Sat & Sun) in Perth, Tourism Western Australia (www.westernaustralia.com) or the Department of Parks & Wildlife (https://parks.dpaw.wa.gov.au).

Around WA, tourist offices with friendly staff (often volunteers) provide local knowledge, including info on road conditions.

Visas

All visitors to Australia need a visa – only New Zealand nationals are exempt, and even they receive a 'special category' visa on arrival. Visa application forms are available from Australian diplomatic missions overseas, travel agents or the website of the Department of Home Affairs (www.homeaffairs.gov.au).

eVisitor (651)

- Many European passport-holders are eligible for a free eVisitor visa, allowing visits to Australia for up to three months at a time within a 12-month period.
- eVisitor visas must be applied for online. They are electronically stored and linked to individual passport numbers, so no stamp in your passport is required.
- It's advisable to apply at least 14 days prior to the proposed date of travel to Australia.

Electronic Travel Authority (ETA; 601)

- Passport-holders from many of the European countries eligible for eVisitor visas, plus passport-holders from Brunei, Canada, Hong Kong, Japan, Malaysia, Singapore, South Korea and the USA, can apply for either a visitor ETA or business ETA.
- ETAs are valid for 12 months, with multiple stays of up to three months permitted.
- ETA visas cost $20; apply via travel agents worldwide, or online.

Visitor (600)

- Short-term Visitor visas have largely been replaced by the eVisitor and ETA. However, if you're from a country not covered by either, or you want to stay longer than three months, you'll need to apply for a Visitor visa.
- Standard Visitor visas allow one entry for a stay of up to three, six or 12 months, and are valid for use within 12 months of issue.
- Visitor visas cost from $355.

Work & Holiday (462)

- Nationals from 20-plus countries including Argentina, Bangladesh, Chile, China, Indonesia, Israel, Luxembourg, Malaysia, Peru, Poland, Portugal, San Marino, Singapore, the Slovak Republic, Slovenia, Spain, Thailand, Turkey, the USA, Uruguay and Vietnam who are aged between 18 and 30 can apply for a Work and Holiday visa prior to entry to Australia.
- Once granted, this visa allows the holder to enter Australia within three months of issue, stay for up to 12 months, leave and reenter Australia any number of times within those 12 months, undertake temporary employment to supplement a trip, and study for up to four months.
- The application fee is $450.

Working Holiday Maker (WHM; 417)

- Young visitors (aged 18 to 30) from Belgium, Canada, Cyprus, Denmark, Estonia, Finland, France, Germany, Hong Kong, Ireland, Italy, Japan, the Republic of Korea, Malta, the Netherlands, Norway, Sweden, Taiwan and the UK are eligible for a Working Holiday visa, which allows you to visit for up to 12 months and gain casual employment.
- Holders can leave and reenter Australia any number of times within those 12 months.
- Holders can only work for any one employer for a maximum of six months.
- Apply prior to entry to Australia (up to a year in advance) – you can't change from another tourist visa to a Working Holiday visa once you're in Australia.
- Conditions include having a return air ticket or sufficient funds ($5000) for a return or onward fare.
- The application fee is $450.
- Second Working Holiday visas can be applied for once you're in Australia, subject to certain conditions.

Visa Extensions

If you want to stay in Australia for longer than your visa allows, you'll need to apply for a new visa (usually a Visitor visa 600). Apply online at least two or three weeks before your visa expires.

Volunteering

Lonely Planet's *Volunteer: A Traveller's Guide to Making a Difference Around the World* provides useful information about volunteering.

Department of Parks & Wildlife (www.dpaw.wa.gov.au) Current and future opportunities at national parks all over WA. Online, click on the 'Get Involved' tab and then 'Volunteering Opportunities'. Opportunities vary enormously, from turtle tagging at Ningaloo Marine Park to feral-animal control at Shark Bay. Working with the dolphins at Monkey Mia is popular, but be aware that swimming with dolphins in the wild is considered by some to be disruptive to the habitat and behaviour of the animals.

Willing Workers on Organic Farms (www.wwoof.com.au) WWOOFing is where you do a few hours of work each day on a farm in return for bed and board. Most hosts are concerned to some extent with alternative lifestyles, and have a minimum stay of two nights. Join online for $70. You'll get a membership number and a booklet listing participating enterprises ($5 overseas postage).

Women Travellers

West Coast Australia is generally a safe place for women travellers, and the following sensible precautions all apply for men, as well as women.

Night-time Avoid walking alone late at night in any of the major cities and towns – keep enough money aside for a taxi back to your accommodation.

Pubs Be wary of basic pub accommodation unless it looks particularly well managed. Alcohol can affect people's behaviour and compromise safety.

Drink spiking Pubs in major cities sometimes post warnings about drugged or 'spiked' drinks. Play it cautious if someone offers you a drink in a bar.

Sexual harassment Unfortunately still a fairly big problem in Australia from street harassment to 'nice guys' on dating apps.

Hitching Hitching is never recommended for anyone, even when travelling in pairs. Exercise caution at all times.

Solo travel Most people won't bat an eyelid if you're female-identifying and travelling alone. Go forth and have the time of your life in Australia, without having to compromise just to have a buddy on the road.

Work

If you come to Australia on a tourist visa then you're not allowed to work for pay – but working for approved volunteer organisations in exchange for board is OK. If you're caught breaching your visa conditions, you can be expelled from the country and banned for up to three years. Those travellers who wish to work while in the country should investigate the Work & Holiday and Working Holiday Maker visas.

Resources

Backpacker accommodation, magazines and newspapers are good resources for local work opportunities.

Useful websites:

Adzuna (www.adzuna.com.au) Website for general employment; good for metropolitan areas.

Australian Jobsearch (www.jobsearch.gov.au) Government site offering a job database.

Career One (www.careerone.com.au) General employment site; good for metropolitan areas.

Department of Human Services (www.humanservices.gov.au) The Australian government employment service has information and advice on looking for work, training and assistance.

Gumtree (www.gumtree.com.au) Great classified site with jobs, accommodation and items for sale.

Harvest Trail (https://jobsearch.gov.au/harvest) Specialised recruitment search for the agricultural industry, including a 'crop list' detailing what you can pick and pack, when and where.

Job Shop (www.thejobshop.com.au) WA-based recruitment agency specialising in jobs for WA as well as the Northern Territory.

Seek (www.seek.com.au) General employment site, good for metropolitan areas.

Travellers at Work (www.taw.com.au) Excellent site for working travellers in Australia.

SEASONAL WORK

In Perth, plenty of temporary work is available in tourism and hospitality, administration, IT, nursing, childcare, factories and labouring. Outside Perth, travellers can easily get jobs in tourism and hospitality, plus a variety of seasonal work. Some places have specialised needs; in Broome, for example, there is lucrative work in pearling, on farms and boats.

INDUSTRY	TIME	REGION
grapes	Feb–Mar	Denmark, Margaret River, Mt Barker, Manjimup
apples/pears	Feb–Apr	Donnybrook, Manjimup
prawn trawlers	Mar–Jun	Carnarvon
bananas	Apr–Dec	Kununurra
bananas	year-round	Carnarvon
veggies	May–Nov	Kununurra, Carnarvon
tourism	May–Dec	Kununurra
flowers	Sep–Nov	Midlands
lobsters	Nov–May	Esperance, Cervantes

Transport

GETTING THERE & AWAY

Unless you're coming by land from other states in Australia, chances are you'll be touching down at Perth Airport. And, as you'll no doubt be told at some point, Perth is actually closer to Jakarta than Sydney.

Flights, tours and rail tickets can be booked online at www.lonelyplanet.com/bookings.

Entering the Country/Region

Global instability has resulted in increased security in Australian airports, in both domestic and international terminals. Customs procedures may be a little more time-consuming but are still straightforward.

Passport

If you have a current passport and visa, your entry into Western Australia should be straightforward.

Air

If you're coming to Australia from Europe, Asia or Africa, you'll find it quicker to fly directly to Perth Airport, rather than via the east-coast cities. If you do fly to the east coast first, there are frequent connecting flights to Perth from major cities. Port Hedland and Broome both welcome interstate flights, and there are weekend flights between Port Hedland and Bali.

Airports & Airlines

Perth Airport (☎08-9478 8888; www.perthairport.com; Airport Dr, Perth Airport) is the main international entry point. The following airlines offer interstate services between WA and the rest of the country (and fly internationally):

Jetstar (☎13 15 38; www.jetstar.com)

Qantas (☎13 13 13; www.qantas.com.au)

Tigerair Australia (☎1300 174 266; www.tigerair.com.au)

Virgin Australia (☎13 67 89; www.virginaustralia.com)

Other airlines flying into WA from overseas include:

Air Asia (D7;☎02-8188 2133; www.airasia.com)

Air Mauritius (☎1800 247 628; www.airmauritius.com)

Air New Zealand (NZ;☎13 24 76; www.airnewzealand.com.au)

Cathay Pacific (☎13 17 47; www.cathaypacific.com)

China Southern Airlines (☎1300 889 628; www.csair.com/en)

Emirates (☎1300 303 777; www.emirates.com)

Etihad (☎1300 532 215; www.etihad.com)

Garuda Indonesia (GA;☎08-9214 5100; www.garuda-indonesia.com)

Malaysia Airlines (☎13 26 27; www.malaysiaairlines.com)

Qatar Airways (☎1300 340 600; www.qatarairways.com)

Scoot (☎02-9009 0860; www.flyscoot.com)

Singapore Airlines (☎13 10 11; www.singaporeair.com)

South African Airways (☎1300 435 972; www.flysaa.com)

Thai Airways (☎1300 651 960; www.thaiairways.com)

Land

The nearest state capital to Perth is Adelaide, 2560km away by the shortest road route. To Melbourne it's at least 3280km, Darwin is around 4040km and Sydney is 3940km. Despite the vast distances, sealed roads cross the Nullarbor Plain from the eastern states to Perth, and then up the Indian Ocean coast and through the Kimberley to Darwin.

Bus

The only interstate bus is the regular **Greyhound** (☎1300 473 946; www.greyhound.com.au) service between Darwin and Broome (from $300, 24 hours), via Kununurra, Fitzroy Crossing and Derby.

DEPARTURE TAX

Departure tax is included in the price of a ticket.

CLIMATE CHANGE & TRAVEL

Every form of transport that relies on carbon-based fuel generates CO_2, the main cause of human-induced climate change. Modern travel is dependent on aeroplanes, which might use less fuel per kilometre per person than most cars but travel much greater distances. The altitude at which aircraft emit gases (including CO_2) and particles also contributes to their climate change impact. Many websites offer 'carbon calculators' that allow people to estimate the carbon emissions generated by their journey and, for those who wish to do so, to offset the impact of the greenhouse gases emitted with contributions to portfolios of climate-friendly initiatives throughout the world. Lonely Planet offsets the carbon footprint of all staff and author travel.

There's no bus link between Adelaide and Perth.

Car & Motorcycle

Driving to Perth from any other state is a *very* long journey, but it's a great way to see the country. Be aware that there are strict quarantine restrictions on fruit and vegetables when crossing the border into WA.

People looking for travelling companions for driving to WA from Sydney, Melbourne, Adelaide or Darwin frequently leave notices in backpacker hostels, or you can look for car-sharing options online:

- www.coseats.com
- www.gumtree.com.au
- www.shareyourride.net/carpool/australia

Hitching

Hitching is never entirely safe – we don't recommend it. Hitching to or from WA across the Nullarbor is definitely not advisable, as waits of several days are not uncommon.

Train

The only interstate rail link into WA is the famous *Indian Pacific*, run by **Great Southern Rail** (☎1800 703 357; www.greatsouthernrail.com.au), which travels 4352km to Perth from Sydney via Broken Hill, Adelaide and Kalgoorlie over four days and three nights. The journey includes a 478km stretch across the Nullarbor that's the longest straight section of train line in the world. Trains pull into East Perth station.

One-way adult fares for the full journey, including all food and drink and off-train excursions, start at $2239. A limited number of cars can also be transported; check online for details.

Sea

Unless you're sailing the high seas on a yacht, the only way to reach WA by water is on a scheduled cruise liner docking at Fremantle.

GETTING AROUND

Air

WA is huge: flying internally can save you many, many hours. Airlines that offer internal flights include:

Airnorth (☎1800 627 474; www.airnorth.com.au)

Alliance Airlines (☎1300 780 970; www.allianceairlines.com.au)

Qantas (☎13 13 13; www.qantas.com.au)

Rex (Rex;☎13 17 13; www.rex.com.au)

Skippers Aviation (☎1300 729 924; www.skippers.com.au)

Virgin Australia (☎13 67 89; www.virginaustralia.com)

Bicycle

Bicycle helmets are compulsory in WA, as are white front lights and red rear lights for riding at night.

If you're coming specifically to cycle, bring your own bike. Within WA you can load your bike onto a bus to skip the boring bits of the country. Book ahead so that you and your bike can travel on the same vehicle.

Suffering dehydration is a very real risk in WA and can be life-threatening. It can get very hot in summer, so take things slowly until you're used to the heat. A prudent plan is to start riding every day at sunrise, relax in the shade – bring your own shelter – during the heat of the day and then ride a few more hours in the afternoon. Always wear a hat and plenty of sunscreen, and drink *lots* of water.

Outback travel needs to be planned thoroughly, with the availability of drinking water the main concern. Those isolated water sources (bores, tanks, creeks) shown on your map may be dry or undrinkable, so you can't always depend on them. Also, don't count on getting water from private mine sites as many are closed to the public. Bring necessary spare parts and bike-repair knowledge. Check with locals (start at the visitor centres) if you're heading into remote areas, and always let someone know where you're headed before setting off.

A useful contacts for information on touring around WA, including suggested routes, road conditions and cycling maps, is the Cycle Touring Association of WA (www.ctawa.asn.au).

Bus

WA's bus network could hardly be called comprehensive, but it offers access to substantially more destinations than the railways. All long-distance buses are modern and well-equipped, with air-con and toilets. Bus companies offering services within WA:

Greyhound (☎1300 473 946; www.greyhound.com.au) To Broome from Darwin via Derby, Fitzroy Crossing and Halls Creek.

Integrity Coach Lines (☎08-9274 7464; www.integritycoachlines.com.au) North of Perth to Broome.

South West Coach Lines (☎08-9753 7700; www.southwestcoachlines.com.au) From Perth to all the major towns in the southwest – your best choice for Margaret River.

Transwa (☎1300 662 205; www.transwa.wa.gov.au) Services extending from Perth as far as Kalbarri, Geraldton, Kalgoorlie, Esperance and the southwest.

Car & Motorcycle

Providing the freedom to explore, travelling with your own vehicle is the best transport option in WA. With several people travelling together, costs can be contained, and if you don't have major mechanical problems, there are many benefits.

The climate is good for motorcycles for much of the year, and many small trails into the bush lead to perfect camping spots. Bringing your own motorcycle into Australia requires valid registration in the country of origin and a *Carnet de Passages en Douanes* (CPD), allowing the holder to import their vehicle without paying customs duty or taxes. Apply to the motoring organisation/association in your home country. You'll also need a rider's licence and a helmet. A fuel range of 350km will get you between most fuel stops around the state. The long, open roads are really made for large-capacity machines above 750cc.

The **Royal Automobile Club of Western Australia** (RAC; ☎13 17 03; www.rac.com.au) has useful advice on statewide motoring, including road safety, local regulations and buying/selling a car. It also offers car insurance to members, and membership can secure discounts on car rentals and motel accommodation.

Also popular are car-share sites (p273), especially for securing a lift to Broome, Perth, Denmark and Darwin.

Driving Licence

You can use your home country's driving licence in WA for up to three months, as long as it carries your photo for identification and is in English. Alternatively (or in addition to this), arrange an International Driving Permit (IDP) from your home country's automobile association and carry it along with your licence.

To travel through Aboriginal land in WA you need a permit. Applications can be lodged on the internet or in person via the **Department of Planning, Lands and Heritage** (Map p62; ☎08-6551 8002; www.dplh.wa.gov.au; Bairds Building, L2, 491 Wellington St, Perth; ⌚9am-5pm Mon-Fri).

Fuel

Fuel (predominantly unleaded and diesel) is available from service stations. Liquefied petroleum gas (LPG) is not always stocked at more remote roadhouses – if your car runs on gas, it's safer to have dual-fuel capacity.

Prices vary wildly in WA, even between stations in Perth. For up-to-date fuel prices, visit the government fuel-watch website (www.fuelwatch.wa.gov.au).

Distances between fill-ups can be vast in the outback, but there are only a handful of tracks where you'll require a long-range fuel tank or need to use jerry cans. However, if you are doing some back-road explorations, always calculate your fuel consumption, plan accordingly and carry a spare jerry can or two. Keep in mind that most small-town service stations are only open from 6am to 7pm and roadhouses aren't always open 24 hours. On main roads there'll be a small town or roadhouse roughly every 150km to 200km.

Hire

Competition between car-rental companies in Australia is fierce, so rates vary and special deals come and go. The main thing to remember when assessing your options is distance – if you want to travel widely, you need to weigh up the price difference between an unlimited-kilometres deal and one that offers a set number of kilometres free with a fee per kilometre over that set number.

Local firms are always cheaper than the big operators – sometimes half the price – but cheap car hire often comes with restrictions on how far you can take the vehicle away from the rental centre.

Some, but not all, car-rental companies offer one-way hires, so research this option before you arrive. It's worth investigating and combining with an internal flight if you're travelling to somewhere like Exmouth, Broome or Esperance. A significant premium is usually charged. There are sometimes good deals for taking a car or campervan from, say, Broome back to Perth, but you'll need to contact local rental companies closer to the time of rental.

You must be at least 21 years old to hire from most firms – if you're under 25, you may only be able to hire a small car or have to pay a surcharge. A credit card will be essential.

Renting a 4WD enables you to safely tackle routes

off the beaten track and get out to more remote natural wonders. Note that many standard rental cars aren't allowed off main roads, so always check insurance conditions carefully, especially the excess, as they can be onerous. Even for a 4WD, the insurance offered by most companies does not cover damage caused when travelling 'off-road', which basically means anything that is not a maintained bitumen or dirt road.

Insurance

In Australia, third-party personal-injury insurance is always included in the vehicle registration cost. This ensures that every registered vehicle carries at least minimum insurance. You'd be wise to extend that minimum to at least third-party property insurance as well – minor collisions with other vehicles can be surprisingly expensive.

If you're bringing your own car from within Australia, take out the most comprehensive roadside assistance plan you can. Think of it not as a matter of if your car will break down, but when. Having the top cover will offset your recovery costs considerably.

For hire cars, establish exactly what your liability is in the event of an accident. Rather than risk paying out thousands of dollars if you do have an accident, you can take out your own comprehensive insurance on the car, or (the usual option) pay an additional daily amount to the rental company for an 'insurance excess reduction' policy. This brings the amount of excess you must pay in the event of an accident down from between $2000 and $5000 to a few hundred dollars. However, check your travel-insurance policy as well as any insurance you have through your credit card before forking out the cash to reduce your excess, as excess reduction may be covered by a policy you already have. Alternatively, companies such as Tripcover and RAC offer excess-reduction policies that often cost much less than those offered by car-hire companies.

Be aware that if you're travelling on dirt roads, you may not be covered by insurance. Because of potential accidents with wildlife, some insurance policies may preclude driving after dusk. Also, most companies won't cover the cost of damage to glass (including the windscreen) or tyres. Always read the small print.

Purchase

If you're planning a stay of several months that involves lots of driving, buying a secondhand car will be much cheaper than renting. But remember that reliability is all-important. Breaking down in the outback is very inconvenient (and potentially dangerous) – the nearest mechanic can be a very expensive tow-truck ride away!

You'll probably get any car cheaper by buying privately online – via www.carsales.com.au, www.gumtree.com.au or www.drive.com.au – rather than through a car dealer. Buying through a dealer can include a guarantee, but this is not much use if you're buying a car in Perth for a trip to Broome.

There are local regulations to comply with when buying or selling a car in WA. Vehicles don't need a roadworthiness certificate to be bought or sold: it's up to the buyer to avoid buying a lemon. You might consider forking out some extra money for a vehicle appraisal before purchase. The **RAC** (☎13 17 03; www.rac.com.au) offers this kind of check in Perth and other large WA centres, and also offers extensive advice on buying and selling cars on its website.

It's also the buyer's responsibility to ensure that the car isn't stolen and that there's no money owing on it: check the car's details with the Australian government's Personal Property Securities Register (www.ppsr.gov.au).

See www.transport.wa.gov.au/licensing/my-vehicle.asp for info on transferring vehicle ownership post-purchase, which can be done online.

The beginning of winter (June) is a good time to start looking for a used motorbike. Local newspapers and the bike-related press have classified advertisement sections.

Fremantle has a number of secondhand car yards, including a cluster in North Fremantle on the Stirling Hwy.

Road Conditions

WA is not criss-crossed by multilane highways; there's not enough traffic and the distances are too great to justify them. All the main routes are well surfaced and have two lanes, but not far off the beaten track you'll find yourself on unsealed roads. Anybody seeing the state in reasonable detail can expect some dirt-road travelling. A 2WD car can cope with the major ones, but for serious exploration, plan on a 4WD.

Driving on unsealed roads requires special care – a car will perform differently when braking and turning on dirt. Under no circumstances exceed 80km/h on dirt roads; if you go faster, you won't have enough time to respond to a sharp turn, stock on the road, or an unmarked gate or cattle grid. Take it easy and take time to see the sights.

It's important to note that when it rains, some roads flood – a real problem up north during the wet season. Exercise extreme caution when it rains, especially at the frequent yellow 'Floodway' signs. If you come to a stretch of water and you're not sure of the depth or what could lie beneath it, pull up at the side of the road and walk through it (excluding known saltwater-crocodile areas, such as the Pentecost River crossing on the Gibb River Rd!). Even on major highways, if it has been raining, you can sometimes be driving through water 30cm or more deep for hundreds of metres at a time.

Mainroads (☎13 81 38; www.mainroads.wa.gov.au) provides statewide road-condition reports, updated daily (and more frequently if necessary).

Road Hazards

Travelling by car within WA means sometimes having to pass road trains. These articulated trucks and their loads (consisting of two or more trailers) can be up to 53.5m long, 2.5m wide and travel at around 100km/h. Overtaking them is tricky – once you commit to passing there's no going back. Exercise caution and pick your time, but don't get timid midmanoeuvre. Also, remember that it is much harder for the truck driver to control their giant-sized vehicle than it is for you to control your car.

WA's enormous distances can lead to dangerous levels of driver fatigue. Stop and rest every two hours or so – do some exercise, change drivers and/or have a coffee. The major routes have rest areas and many roadhouses offer free coffee for drivers; ask the RAC for maps that indicate rest stops.

Cattle, emus and kangaroos are common hazards on country roads, and a collision is likely to kill the animal and cause serious damage to your vehicle. Kangaroos are most active around dawn and dusk, and they travel in groups. If possible, plan your travel to avoid these times of the day. If you see a roo hopping across the road in front of you, slow right down – its friends are probably just behind it.

It's important to keep a safe distance behind the vehicle in front, in case it hits an animal or has to slow down suddenly. If an animal runs out in front of you, brake if you can, but don't swerve unless it is safe to do so. You're likely to come out of a collision with an emu better than a collision with a tree or another vehicle.

Always carry two spare tyres and at least 20L of water.

Road Rules

Driving in WA holds few surprises, other than those that hop out in front of your vehicle. Cars are driven on the left-hand side of the road (as in the rest of Australia). An important road rule is 'give way to the right' – if an intersection is unmarked, you must give way to vehicles entering the intersection from your right.

The speed limit in urban areas is generally 60km/h, unless signposted otherwise. The state speed limit is 110km/h, applicable to all roads in non-built-up areas, unless otherwise indicated. The police have radar speed traps and speed cameras, often in carefully concealed locations.

Oncoming drivers who flash their lights at you may be giving you a warning of a speed camera ahead – or they may be telling you that your headlights are not on. It's polite to wave back if someone does this. Don't get caught flashing your lights yourself, as it's illegal.

Seat belts are compulsory, and not using them incurs a fine. Children must be strapped into an approved safety seat. Talking on a handheld mobile phone while driving is illegal.

Drink-driving is a serious problem in WA, especially in country areas, and random breath tests are used to reduce the road toll. If you're caught driving with a blood-alcohol level of more than 0.05%, expect a hefty fine, a court appearance and the loss of your licence.

Local Transport

Perth has an efficient, fully integrated public transport system called **Transperth** (☎13 62 13; www.transperth.wa.gov.au) covering public buses, trains and ferries in a large area that reaches south to include Fremantle, Rockingham and Mandurah. Larger regional centres, including Bunbury, Busselton and Albany, have limited local bus services.

Taxis are available in most of the larger towns.

Train

The **Transperth** (☎13 62 13; www.transperth.wa.gov.au) local train network reaches as far south as Mandurah. Further afield, **Transwa** (☎1300 662 205; www.transwa.wa.gov.au) runs the following services from Perth into rural WA:

Australind (twice daily) Perth station to Pinjarra ($18.05, 1¼ hours) and Bunbury ($33.50, 2½ hours).

MerredinLink (daily) East Perth station to Toodyay ($18.05, 1¼ hours), Northam ($21.15, 1½ hours) and Merredin ($48.60, 3¼ hours).

Prospector (daily) East Perth to Kalgoorlie-Boulder ($891.80, 5¾ hours).

Behind the Scenes

SEND US YOUR FEEDBACK

We love to hear from travellers – your comments keep us on our toes and help make our books better. Our well-travelled team reads every word on what you loved or loathed about this book. Although we cannot reply individually to your submissions, we always guarantee that your feedback goes straight to the appropriate authors, in time for the next edition. Each person who sends us information is thanked in the next edition – the most useful submissions are rewarded with a selection of digital PDF chapters.

Visit **lonelyplanet.com/contact** to submit your updates and suggestions or to ask for help. Our award-winning website also features inspirational travel stories, news and discussions.

Note: We may edit, reproduce and incorporate your comments in Lonely Planet products such as guidebooks, websites and digital products, so let us know if you don't want your comments reproduced or your name acknowledged. For a copy of our privacy policy visit lonelyplanet.com/privacy.

WRITER THANKS

Charles Rawlings-Way

Boundless thanks to Tasmin for the gig, to Fleur for the inside running on Perth culture, and to all the helpful souls I met on the road in and around Perth who flew through my questions with the greatest of ease. Biggest thanks of all to Meg, who held the increasingly chaotic fort while I was busy scooting around in the sunshine ('Where's daddy?') – and made sure that Ione, Remy, Liv and Reuben were fed, watered, washed, schooled, tucked in and read to.

Fleur Bainger

Thrilled and grateful to be on board, I'm eager to thank both Tasmin and Charles for their endless patience with helping me learn the guidebook-writing ropes. Western Australia's epic scenery, passionate characters and inspiring produce also deserve gratitude; they constantly inspire me to share the word on this stunning, still relatively untouched part of the world.

Anna Kaminski

Huge thanks to Tasmin for entrusting me with a chunk of Western Australia, to fellow scribes Charles, Steve, Carolyn and Brett for the advice, and to everyone who's helped me along the way. In particular: John and Debbie in Geraldton; Barbara in Esperance; Anna in Meekatharra; my adoptive Wongutha family (Linden, Trevor and Marcia), plus Monica, Billy and Becky in Kalgoorlie; 'Capes' in Denham; Amy in Port Hedland; Maria, Kate and Michael in Denmark; Lyn in Norseman; and all the helpful visitor-centre staff and Aboriginal artists who've shared their work with me.

Tasmin Waby

Thanks to Jennifer Carey and the rest of the Australia writer crew for the encouragement to hit the road. Love to my beautiful daughters and their father for letting me take off in the middle of the British winter. Big clap to the excellent editors who knocked this sometimes scrappy work into shape. And Sir Ix, aka Nicholas Reed, for being there, as always.

Steve Waters

Big thanks to John and Jan for fireside hospitality; Lauren, James, Jane, Trish, Anika and the rest of MC for (more) gorge love; Marie for vino frenzies; Leonie and Mera for tea and bikkies; Ted for unruliness; Kaz for listening; Roz and Megan for caretaking; Vicky and Pippa for letting me trash their car; and Jennifer from the RACV for getting me out of Marla on Grand Final Day.

ACKNOWLEDGEMENTS

Climate map data adapted from Peel MC, Finlayson BL & McMahon TA (2007) 'Updated World Map of the Köppen-Geiger Climate Classification', *Hydrology and Earth System Sciences*, 11, 1633–44.

Cover photograph: Cape Leveque (Kooljaman), Liz Barker/Getty Images ©

THIS BOOK

This 10th edition of Lonely Planet's *West Coast Australia* guidebook was researched and written by Charles Rawlings-Way, Fleur Bainger, Anna Kaminski, Tasmin Waby and Steve Waters. The previous two editions were written by Steve, Brett Atkinson, Kate Armstrong and Carolyn Bain. This guidebook was produced by the following:

Destination Editor Tasmin Waby

Senior Product Editors Kate Chapman, Sandie Kestell, Anne Mason

Regional Senior Cartographer Julie Sheridan

Product Editor Kate Mathews

Book Designer Jessica Rose

Assisting Editors Sarah Bailey, Judith Bamber, Emma Gibbs, Carly Hall, Kellie Langdon, Lou McGregor, Anne Mulvaney, Charlotte Orr, Fionnuala Twomey

Assisting Cartographer Julie Dodkins

Cover Researcher Brendan Dempsey-Spencer

Thanks to Jennifer Carey, Laura Crawford, David Hodges, Dario Lepori, Virginia Moreno, Claire Naylor, Vicky Smith, Anna Tyler, Daisy van Amerom, Diana von Holdt and Branislava Vladisavljevic

Index

A

Aboriginal Australians 246
  art & culture 10, 26, 225, 258-60, **10**
  history 240-1, 242-3, 244-5, 258-60
  languages 17
  mining employment 255
Abrolhos, the 174
accessible travel 262
accommodation 18, 22-3, 263, *see also individual locations*
  stations 195
  wilderness camps 223
AC/DC 78
activities 42-7, *see also individual activities*
air travel 25, 272, 273
airlines 272, 273
airports 272
Albany 157-61, **158**
Alexander Morrison National Park 123
America's Cup 247
amusement parks 49
animals 14, 28, 267-8 *see also individual species*
aquariums
  Denham 180
  Ningaloo Interpretation Centre 192
  Perth 61
area codes 17
art galleries, *see* museums & galleries
ATMs 266
Augusta 144-5
Avon Valley 115, **110**

B

B&Bs 22
Badgingarra National Park 123
Balingup 147
bargaining 19
Barnett River 229
Batavia Coast 171-9
bathrooms 270
beaches 26
  Basin, the 102
  Bathers Beach 66
  Big Lagoon 182
  Bill's Bay 190
  Blue Haven 167
  Cable Beach 212, **216**, **13**
  Cape Leveque (Kooljaman) 222
  Cattle Well 182
  City Beach 61
  Cottesloe Beach 61, 81, **8-9**
  Floreat Beach 62
  Fourth Beach 167
  Gnaraloo Bay 185
  Granny's Beach 171
  Hearson's Cove 203
  James Price Point 222
  Le Grand Beach 166
  Leighton Beach 66
  Lucky Bay 166, **5**
  Manari Road 220
  Mandalay Beach 153
  Mettams Pool 61
  Northshore Beach 171
  Ocean Beach 154
  Point Quobba 185
  Red Bluff Beach 175
  Reddell Beach 213
  Salmon Beach 167
  Samson Beach 201
  Scarborough Beach 61
  Seaspray Beach 171
  Shell Beach 179
  South Beach 171
  Swanbourne Beach 62-3
  Trigg Beach 63
  Turquoise Bay 198
  Twilight Beach 167
  West Beach 167
  Wittecarra Beach 175
beer 26, 251-2, *see also* breweries
Bell Gorge 228, **12**
Bibbulmun Track 153, 159, **47**
bicycle travel *see* cycling, mountain biking
birdwatching
  books 254
  Broome 213, 217
  Derby 224
  Parry Lagoons Nature Reserve 238
  Penguin Island 106
  red-tailed tropicbirds 136
Blues at Bridgetown Festival 31
boat travel 273
boat trips
  Augusta 145
  Esperance 167
  Geikie Gorge 227
  Houtman Abrolhos Islands 174
  Kununurra 234
  Lake Argyle 235
  Mandurah Cruises 107
  Monkey Mia 183
  Nornalup Inlet 153
  Perth 72
  Pemberton 149
Bond, Alan 247
booking services 23
books
  architecture 255
  birdwatching 254
  diving 198
  ecology 254
  environmentalism 257
  roadmaps 266
box jellyfish 267
Bradshaw paintings 240-1
Bremer Bay 164-5
breweries 40-1, 251-2, *see also* beer, brewery tours
  Beer Farm 143
  Bootleg Brewery 143
  Boston Brewery 156
  Brewhouse 140
  Caves Road Collective 143
  Cheeky Monkey 143
  Colonial Brewing Co 140
  Eagle Bay Brewing Co 134
  Feral Brewing Company 114
  Froth Craft Brewery 194
  Homestead Brewery 114
  Little Creatures 92
  Lucky Bay Brewery 168
  Margaret River 143
  Matso's Broome Brewery 220
  Northbridge Brewing Company 91
  Three Rivers Brewing Company 108
  Whalebone Brewing Company 194-5
  Wilson Brewing Company 160
brewery tours 139
Bridgetown 146-7
Broome 12, 52, 212-21, **214**, **216**, **13**
  accommodation 209, 218-19
  activities 215
  climate 209
  drinking 220
  entertainment 220-1
  events 217-18
  festivals 217-18
  food 209, 219-20
  for children 50
  highlights 210-11
  information 221
  nightlife 220
  shopping 221
  sights 212-15
  tours 215-17

Map Pages **000**
Photo Pages **000**

Broome *continued*
travel seasons 209
travel to/from 221
travel within 221
budget 17
Bunbury 127-9, **128**
Bunbury Geographe 127-31
Bungle Bungle Range 236-8, **45**
bus travel 25, 272-3, 274
bushfires 268
bushwalking, *see* hiking
business hours 17, 266
Busselton 130-1
BYO 249

C

Cable Beach 212, **216**, **13**
Cambridge Gulf 238
camel tours
Broome 217
Perth 73
camping 22, 223
canoeing, *see also* kayaking
Kalbarri 176
Kununurra 234
Pemberton 149
canyoning 176, *see also* gorges
Cape Arid National Park 166
Cape Le Grand National Park 166
Cape Leveque (Kooljaman) 222
Cape Naturaliste 134-5
Cape Peron 182
Cape Range National Park 199-200
car rental 274-5
car travel 24-5, 268, 273, 274-6, *see also* driving routes
caravan parks 22
Carnarvon 183-5
Cathedral Gorge 237
caves 41
Crystal Cave 120
Giants Cave 142
Jewel Cave 145
Jingemia Cave 119
Lake Cave 141, **41**
Mammoth Cave 142
Mimbi Caves 230
Mulka's Cave 112
Ngilgi Cave 134-5
Stockyard Gully Caves 124
Caves Road 141-4
cell phones 16, 269
cemeteries
Broome 213
Fremantle Cemetery 78
Wadjemup Aboriginal Burial Ground 102
Cervantes 122-3
Charles Knife Canyon 199
Chichester Range 208
children, travel with 48-50
accommodation 22-3
cideries
Cheeky Monkey 143
Core Cider 110
Tangletoe Cidery 149
Wine Tree Cidery 108-9
cinemas
Broome 212, 221
Perth 93
Wyndham 238
climate 16, 29-31, *see also individual regions*
climbing 66
clothing 18
consulates 262-3
cooking classes
Cape Lodge 142
Gumbanan 223
Wildwood Valley Cooking School 135-6
coral 198
Coral Bay 190-1
Cossack 201
costs 17
Cottesloe Beach 61, 81, **8-9**
courses
Aboriginal culture 66
birdwatching 213
bush skills 223
cooking 135-6, 142, 223
diving 72, 190, 193
mountain biking 111
surfing 48, 72, 135, 137, 172
yoga 135
Cowaramup 141
credit cards 266
cricket 95
crocodiles 267, **14**
cultural centres
Bilya Koort Boodja 115
Walyalup Aboriginal Cultural Centre 66
currency 16
customs regulations 234, 262
cycling 25, 44, 273, *see also* bicycle travel, mountain biking
Broome 217
Geraldton 172
Kalbarri 175
Perth 66

D

Dales Gorge 205
Dampier 203
Dampier Archipelago 203
Dampier Peninsula 222-4
dangers, *see* safety
Darling Range 110-11, **110**
dengue fever 264
Denham 180-2
Denmark 154-7
Derby 224-7
Devonian Reef National Parks 227
dinosaur footprints 212-13, 256
Dirk Hartog Island National Park 181
disabilities, travellers with 262
distilleries
Great Southern Distillery 157-8
Illegal Tender Rum Co 171
Margaret River Distilling Company 137
Whipper Snapper Distillery 57
diving 28, 46
Albany 159
books 198
Broome 215
courses 72, 190, 193
Dunsborough 133
Esperance 167
Exmouth 196-7
Houtman Abrolhos Islands 174
Ningaloo Marine Park 198
Ningaloo Reef 190, 193
Perth 72
dolphin encounters
Broome 217
Bunbury 127-8
Mandurah 107
Monkey Mia 182-3
dolphins **11**
Dolphin Discovery Centre 127
Dongara 171-2
dot painting 259-60
Dreaming, the 258
drinks, *see also* breweries, cideries, distilleries, wineries
beer 26, 251-2
cider 21
wine 9, 26, 248-51
driving, *see* car travel
driving routes
Boranup Drive 142
Duncan Road 232
Gibb River Road 12, 228-30
Great Forest Trees Drive 148
Great Northern Highway 230-3
Great Ocean Drive 167
Karri Forest Explorer 150
Knoll Drive 153
Lesueur Scenic Drive 123
Manari Road 220
Mt Augustus National Park 185
Mt Shadforth Road 154
Scotsdale Road 154
Shark Bay Road World Heritage Drive 179-80
Shothole Canyon Road 200
Valley of the Giants Rd 153
Warlu Way 200-1
Dryandra Woodland 113
Drysdale River 229
Duncan Road 232
Dunsborough 131-4
Durack River 230
Dwellingup 108-9

E

Echidna Chasm 237
economy 255
El Questro Gorge 230
electricity 262
Ellen Peak 163
embassies 262-3
emergencies 17
Emmanuel Range 230
environmental issues 253-7
Esperance 166-8
etiquette 19
events 29-31
exchange rates 17
Exmouth 191-5, **192**
Exmouth region 195-7, **196**

Map Pages **000**
Photo Pages **000**

F

festivals 29-31
FIFO 254
films 130, 245
fishing 46, 167
Fitzgerald River National Park 165-6, **47**
Fitzroy Crossing 231-2, **2**
flowers 118, 123, 176
fly-in, fly-out 254
food 19, 27-8, 49, 248, 263, *see also individual locations*
  festivals 139
  vegetarian 249
Forrest, Andrew 'Twiggy' 255
Francois Peron National Park 182, **19**
Fremantle Doctor 77
Fremantle Festival 30
Frenchman Peak 166
fuel 274

G

galleries, *see* museums & galleries
Galvans Gorge 229
Gascoyne Coast 183-6
gay travellers 86, 265-6
Geikie Gorge 227
Geraldton 172-5, **173**
Gibb River Road 12, 228-30
gorges
  Amelia Gorge 230
  Bell Gorge 228, **12**
  Cathedral Gorge 237
  Charles Knife Canyon 199
  Dales Gorge 205
  Deep Gorge 203
  Echidna Chasm 237
  El Questro Gorge 230
  Galvans Gorge 229
  Geikie Gorge 227
  Hamersley Gorge 206
  Hancock Gorge 205, **14**
  Joffre Gorge 206
  Kalamina Gorge 207
  Knox Gorge 207
  Lennard River Gorge 228
  Mandu Mandu Gorge 199
  Piccaninny Gorge 237
  Sawpit Gorge 232
  Weano Gorge 206
  Windjana Gorge 227, **14**
  Yardie Creek Gorge 199
Great Northern Highway 230-3
Great Southern Rail 273
Great Southern wine region 249, 251
Green Head 124
Greenbushes 147
Guilderton 120-1
Guildford 112-13
Gwion Gwion art 259

H

Halls Creek 232-3
Hamelin Pool 179
Hamersley Gorge 206
Hancock Gorge 205, **14**
health 263-5
heat exhaustion 264
heatstroke 264
Hellfire Bay 166, **27**
hiking 13, 27, **13**
  Bibbulmun Track 153, 159, **47**
  Broome 215
  Cape Range National Park 199
  Cape to Cape Track 139, 142
  Chichester Range 208
  Fremantle Trails 71
  Hopetoun 166
  Kalbarri National Park 178-9, **42**
  Le Grand Coastal Trail 166
  Lurujarri Dreaming Trail 215
  Melaleuca Cycle-Walk Trail 175
  Millstream 208
  Mokare Heritage Trail 154
  Mt Augustus National Park 185
  Munda Biddi Trail 108
  Nornalup Trail 154
  Piccaninny Gorge 237
  Porongurup National Park 162, **162**
  Punurrunha 207
  Stirling Range National Park 163, **164-5**
  Wilson Inlet Trail 154
  Yaburara Heritage Trail 201
history 240-7
  Aboriginal Australians 240-1, 242-3, 244-5
  convicts 243
  environmentalism 253
  European explorers 241-2
  European settlement 242-3
  exploration 243
  gold 243-4
  Great Depression, the 245
  modern WA 246-7
  public works 244
  stolen generations 244-5
  WWI 245
  WWII 245-6
hitching 273
holidays 266
Hopetoun 166
horizontal waterfalls 226
horse riding 234
hostels 22
hotels 22
Houtman Abrolhos Islands 174
Hyden 111-12
hypothermia 264, 268-9

I

Indigenous art 10, 26, 225, 258-60, **10**
Indigenous culture 26
insects 267
insurance 265
  car 275
  health 263
internet access 265
internet resources 17
  accommodation 23
  car sharing 273
  children, travel with 50
  health 264
  travel advisories 269
  work 271
itineraries 32-7

J

Jarrahdale 109
Joffre Gorge 206
Johns, Joseph Bolitho 117
Jurien Bay 123-4

K

Kalamina Gorge 207
Kalbarri 175-8, **177**
Kalbarri National Park 178-9, **42**
Kalumburu 231
Karijini National Park 14, 205-8, **206**, **14**
Karratha 200-3
  mining industry 254
kayaking, *see also* canoeing
  Broome 216
  Denmark 154
  Dwellingup 109
  Exmouth 192-3
  Lake Argyle 235
  Ningaloo Reef 190, 198
  Perth 71
  Rottnest Island 103
  Shoalwater Islands Marine Park 106
Kimberley, the 52, 209-38, **210-11**
  accommodation 209
  climate 209
  food 209
  for children 50
  highlights 210-11
  travel seasons 209
King Edward River 229
King Leopold Ranges 228
King Sound 224
Kings Park Festival 31
kitesurfing 45, *see also* windsurfing
  Exmouth 197
  Geraldton 172
  Margaret River 138
Knox Gorge 207
Kununurra 233-6
Kwongan heathlands 123

L

Lake Argyle 235
lakes
  Lake Argyle 235
  Lake Kununurra 234
  Lake Monger 60
  Miaree Pool 200
  Pink Lake 178
Lancelin 121
languages 16, 17
Leeman 124
legal matters 265
Lennard River 228
Lennard River Gorge 228
Lesueur National Park 123
LGBT+ travellers 86, 265-6
lighthouses
  Cape Leeuwin Lighthouse 145
  Cape Naturaliste Lighthouse 135
  Vlamingh Head Lighthouse 196
  Wadjemup Lighthouse 102
Lucky Bay 166, **5**

M

Manari Road 220
Mandalay Beach 153
Mandu Mandu Gorge 199
Mandurah 107-8
mangos 218
Manjimup 147-8
maps 266
Marble Bar 202
Margaret River 137-41, **138**, **15**
Margaret River Gourmet Escape 31
Margaret River Pro 139
Margaret River region 38-41, 51, 125-50, **126**, **38**
  accommodation 125
  climate 125
  food 125, 249
  for children 49
  highlights 126
  travel seasons 125
Margaret River wine region 9, 39, 131-45, 249, **132**, **40**
marine reserves, *see also* national parks, nature reserves
  Hamelin Pool 179
  Monkey Mia Marine Reserve 10, 182-3, **11**
  Ningaloo Marine Park 11, 197-9, **11**
  Rowley Shoals Marine Park 218
  Shoalwater Islands Marine Park 106
markets
  Bunbury Farmers Market 129
  Fremantle 65
  Margaret River Farmers Market 140
  Perth 86
measures 267
medical services 264
Miaree Pool 200
Millstream Chichester National Park 208
Mimbi Caves 230
mining industry 253-7
Minyirr Park 212
Mirima National Park 233
Mitchell Falls 229
Mitchell Plateau 229
mobile phones 16, 269

Map Pages **000**
Photo Pages **000**

money 16, 17, 266
Monkey Mia Marine Reserve 10, 182-3, **11**
  for children 50
Moondyne Joe 117
Moora 119
motels 22
motorcycle travel 273, 274-6
mountain biking 44
  Dwellingup 109
  Margaret River 137, 138
  Pemberton 148
  Perth Hills 111
Mt Augustus 185
Mt Augustus National Park 185
Mt Barker 161-2
Mt Lesueur 123
Mt Welcome 201
Murujuga National Park 203
museums & galleries 225, 260
  Army Museum of WA 66
  Art Gallery of Western Australia 60
  ArtGeo Cultural Complex 130
  Augusta Historical Museum 145
  Bidyadanga Community Art Centre 225
  Broome Museum 213
  Bunbury Museum & Heritage Centre 127
  Bunbury Regional Art Gallery 127
  Bungalow 213
  Carnarvon Space & Technology Museum 184
  Comet Gold Mine Museum 202
  Courthouse Gallery 203-4
  East Pilbara Arts Centre 205
  Esperance Museum 167
  Fremantle Arts Centre 65
  Geraldton Regional Art Gallery (GRAG) 172
  Kununurra Historical Society Museum 234
  Laarri Gallery 225
  Mandurah Museum 107
  Mangkaja Arts 225, 232
  Marnin Studio 225
  Motor Museum of Western Australia 114
  Mowanjum Art & Culture Centre 225
  Museum of the Great Southern 157
  Nagula Jarndu Women's Resource Centre 213, 225
  National Anzac Centre 157
  New Museum for Western Australia 20
  New Norcia Museum & Art Gallery 118
  Newcastle Gaol Museum 117
  Ningaloo Interpretation Centre 192
  Norval Gallery 224
  Nostalgia Box 60
  Old Convent Heritage Centre 213
  Pearl Luggers 215
  Pemberton Fine Woodcraft Gallery 148
  Perth Institute of Contemporary Arts 60
  Petrichor Gallery 153
  Revolutions Transport Museum 113-14
  Rottnest Museum 102
  Scitech 61
  Shark Bay World Heritage Discovery Centre 180
  Short Street Gallery 213
  Tractor Museum 114
  WA Shipwrecks Museum 65
  Waringarri Aboriginal Arts Centre 225, 233
  Warlayirti Artists Centre 225
  Warmun Arts 225
  Western Australian Museum – Geraldton 172
  Western Australian Museum – Maritime 65
  Western Australian Museum – Perth 60
  Wharefinger Museum 224
  Yarliyil Gallery 225
  Yinjaa-Barndi Gallery 201
  York Motor Museum 116

N

Nambung National Park 122
Nannup 146
National Anzac Centre 157
national parks 45, *see also* marine reserves, nature reserves
  Alexander Morrison National Park 123
  Badgingarra National Park 123
  Beedelup National Park 150
  Cape Arid National Park 166
  Cape Le Grand National Park 166
  Cape Range National Park 199-200
  Devonian Reef National Parks 227
  Dirk Hartog Island National Park 181
  Esperance region 166
  Francois Peron National Park 182, **19**
  Geikie Gorge 227
  Kalbarri National Park 178-9, **42**
  Karijini National Park 14, 205-8, **206**, **14**
  Leeuwin-Naturaliste National Park 141
  Lesueur National Park 123
  Millstream Chichester National Park 208
  Mirima National Park 233
  Mitchell River National Park 229
  Mt Augustus National Park 185
  Murujuga National Park 203
  Nambung National Park 122
  Penguin Island 106
  Porongurup National Park 162-3, **162**
  Purnululu National Park 236-8, **237**, **45**
  Serpentine National Park 109
  Shoalwater Islands Marine Park 106
  Stirling Range National Park 163-4, **164-5**
  Stokes National Park 166
  Tathra National Park 123
  Torndirrup National Park 159
  Tuart Forest National Park 130
  Tunnel Creek 227

Walpole-Nornalup National Park 153
Watheroo National Park 119
Waychinicup National Park 159
West Cape Howe National Park 154
William Bay National Park 154
Windjana Gorge 227, **14**
Yalgorup National Park 108
Yanchep National Park 120
nature reserves, *see also* marine reserves, national parks
Broome Bird Observatory 213
Dampier Archipelago 203
Forest Discovery Centre 109
Lane Pool Reserve 109
Ngamoowalem Conservation Reserve 233-4
Parry Lagoons Nature Reserve 238
Valley of the Giants 153, **13**
New Norcia 118
newspapers 267
Ningaloo coast 52, 190-200, **188-9**
accommodation 187
climate 187
food 187
for children 50
highlights 188-9
travel seasons 187
Ningaloo Marine Park 11, 197-9, **11**
No 1 rabbit-proof fence 166
No 2 rabbit-proof fence 165
Nornalup 153-4
North West Cape 195-7, **196**
Northam 115-16

O

observatories 110
opening hours 17, 266
Optus Stadium 20, 95
Ord River 230
outback travel 269

P

parks & gardens
Hyde Park 60
Kings Park & Botanic Garden 60-1
Whiteman Park 113-14
pearl farms 220
Peel Region 107-9
pelicans 176
Pemberton 148-50
Pender Bay 222
penguins 106
Pentecost Ranges 230
Perth 9, 51, 54-99, **55**, **58-9**, **62-3**, **67**, **68-9**, **70**
accommodation 54, 75-80
activities 66-72
climate 54
drinking 89-93
entertainment 93-5
events 73-5
festivals 73-5
food 54, 80-9
for children 49, 61
highlights 55
history 56
information 96-7
itineraries 57
LGBT+ travellers 86
nightlife 89-93
shopping 95-6
sights 56-66, 91
tours 72-3
travel seasons 54
travel to/from 97-8
travel within 98-9
walking tour 74, **74**
Perth Festival 29
Perth Hills 110-11, **110**
wineries 251
Perth region 51, 100-24, **101**
accommodation 100
climate 100
food 100
for children 49
highlights 101
petrol 274
Piccaninny Gorge 237
Pilbara, the 52, 200-8, **188-9**
accommodation 187
climate 187
food 187
for children 50
highlights 188-9
travel seasons 187
pine trees 81
Pink Lake 178
Pinnacles Desert 15, 122-3, **15**
planning
accommodation 22-3
budgeting 17
calendar of events 29-31
children, travel with 48-50
internet resources 17
itineraries 32-7
repeat visitors 20-1
travel seasons 16
West Coast Australia basics 16-17
West Coast Australia's regions 51-2
Point Samson 201
population 21
Porongurup National Park 162-3, **162**
Port Denison 171-2
Port Hedland 203-5
post 266
produce 248-52
public holidays 266
public transport 25, 276
pubs 22
Punurrunha 207
Purnululu National Park 236-8, **237**, **45**

Q

Quobba Coast 185-6
quokkas 103, **12**

R

rabbit-proof fence 165, 166
radio 267
red-tailed tropicbirds 136
road conditions 275-6
road rules 276
rock art 258-9, **10**
Mitchell River National Park 229
Mt Augustus National Park 185
Mulka's Cave 112
Murujuga National Park 203
Yaburara Heritage Trail 201
Rockingham 106-7
Roebourne 201
Rottnest Island 12, 102-6, **104**, **44**
Rowley Shoals Marine Park 218

S

safety 267-9
driving 275-6
hitching 273
swimming 269
women travellers 271
sandalwood 161
Sawpit Gorge 232
scenic drives, *see* driving routes
Scott, Ronald Belford (Bon) 78
seasonal work 271
Serpentine National Park 109
Shark Bay 10, 179-83
Shark Bay Road 179-80
sharks 267-8
shipwrecks 46, 65
Batavia 65, 172, 241
HMAS *Perth* 159
Mandalay 153
Shoalwater Islands Marine Park 106
shopping 260, *see also* markets
silo art 115
skating 69, 71
skydiving
Perth 71
Rottnest Island 103
York 116
smoking 267
snakes 268
snorkelling 28, 46, *see also* diving
Coral Bay 190
Exmouth 193
Jurien Bay 123
Kalbarri 175
Ningaloo Marine Park 198
Ningaloo Reef 190
Purdy Point 190
Rottnest Island 102
south coast Western Australia 52, 151-68, **152**
accommodation 151
climate 151
food 151
highlights 152
travel seasons 151
Southern Forests 146-50
southwest Western Australia 38-41, 51, 125-50, **126**
accommodation 125
climate 125
food 125
for children 49
highlights 126
travel seasons 125
spiders 268

Staircase to the Moon
Broome 219
Port Hedland 203
stand-up paddleboarding
Albany 159
Margaret River 137
Stirling Range National Park 163-4, **164-5**
Stokes National Park 166
stolen generations 244-5
street art 91
Sunset Coast 120-1
surfing 15, 28, 39-40, 44-5, 48, **15**
classes 48, 72, 135, 137, 172
competitions 139
Denmark 154
Geraldton 172
Jakes Bay 175
Margaret River 137
Perth 72
Quobba Coast 185-6
Tombstones 186
Yallingup 135
Swan River 56
Swan Valley 112-15, **110**
Swan Valley wine region 113-15, 251
swimming 48, *see also* beaches
Pemberton 148, 149
Perth 68-9
Port Hedland 204
safety 269
Yallingup 135

T

Tathra National Park 123
telephone services 16, 269
television 267
time zones 16, 269
tipping 19, 266
toilets 270
Toodyay 117
Torndirrup National Park 159
tourist information 270
train rides 103, 114, 130
train travel 25, 273, 276
tram rides 114, 149
transport 24-5, 276
travel to/from West Coast Australia 272-3
travel within West Coast Australia 24-5, 273-6
trekking, *see* hiking
truffles 147
Tuart Forest National Park 130
Tunnel Creek 227
Turquoise Coast 121-4
turtles 196, 215
Two Peoples Bay 159

V

vacations 266
Valley of the Giants 153, **13**
vegetarian travellers 249
visas 16, 270
volunteering 182-3, 215, 270-1

W

WACA 95
walking, *see* hiking
Walpole 153-4
Walpole-Nornalup National Park 153
Wandjina 259
water parks 49
Wave Rock 111-12, **2**
Waychinicup National Park 159
Weano Gorge 206
weather 16, 29-31
websites, *see* internet resources
weights 267
West Cape Howe National Park 154
West Coast Australia basics 16-17
Western Desert Mob 260
Western Desert painting 259-60
whale sharks 198
whale watching 46, 49
Albany 158-9
Augusta 145
Bremer Bay 164
Conspicuous Cliffs 153
Dunsborough 133
Fitzgerald River National Park 165
wi-fi 265
Wildflower Way 118-20
wildflowers 118, 123, 176
wildlife 14, 28
wildlife reserves & sanctuaries 48, *see also* zoos
Barna Mia Nocturnal Animal Sanctuary 113
Broome Bird Observatory 213
Eagles Heritage 142
Malcolm Douglas Wilderness Park 213
Rainbow Jungle 175-6
William Bay National Park 154
Willie Creek 220
Windjana Gorge 227, **14**
windsurfing 28, 44-5
Margaret River 138
wine 9, 26, 248-51, *see also* wine tours, wineries
wine tours 251, *see also* wine, wineries
Denmark 155
Margaret River 139
Swan Valley 114
wineries 21, *see also* wine, wine tours
Albany 160
Ashbrook 142
Blind Corner 131, 133
Brookside Vineyard 110
Cape Mentelle 137
Capel Vale 130
Castle Rock Estate 162
Core Cider 110
Cullen Wines 144, **9**
Denmark 156
Duke's Vineyard 162
Geographe Bay 127
Great Southern wine region 249, 251
Harewood Estate 156
Houghton 113
Ironwood Estate Wines 162-3
Leeuwin Estate 144
Margaret River Regional Wine Centre 141
Margaret River wine region 9, 39, 131-45, 249, **132**, **40**
Montgomery's Hill 160
Moombaki Wines 156
Mountford Wines 149
Oranje Tractor 160
Perth Hills 251
Plantagenet Wines 161
Plume Estate 251
Poacher's Ridge 161
Rising Star 156
Rockcliffe Winery 156
Sandalford Wines 113
Singlefile Wines 156
Stella Bella 137
Stormflower Vineyard 141
Swan Valley wine region 113-15, 251
Thompson Estate 142
Vasse Felix 144
Voyager Estate 141
Watershed Premium Wines 144
West Cape Howe Wines 161
Wignalls Wines 160
Wine Tree Cidery 108-9
Zarephath Wines 162
women travellers 271
Wongalala Falls 231
Wongan Hills 119-20
work 271
WWOOFing 271
Wyndham 238

Y

Yalgorup National Park 108
Yallingup 135-7
Yanchep National Park 120
Yardie Creek Gorge 199
yoga 135
York 116

Z

zoos 48, *see also* wildlife reserves & sanctuaries
Bunbury Wildlife Park 127
Caversham Wildlife Park 113
Perth 57

Map Legend

Sights

- Beach
- Bird Sanctuary
- Buddhist
- Castle/Palace
- Christian
- Confucian
- Hindu
- Islamic
- Jain
- Jewish
- Monument
- Museum/Gallery/Historic Building
- Ruin
- Shinto
- Sikh
- Taoist
- Winery/Vineyard
- Zoo/Wildlife Sanctuary
- Other Sight

Activities, Courses & Tours

- Bodysurfing
- Diving
- Canoeing/Kayaking
- Course/Tour
- Sento Hot Baths/Onsen
- Skiing
- Snorkelling
- Surfing
- Swimming/Pool
- Walking
- Windsurfing
- Other Activity

Sleeping

- Sleeping
- Camping

Eating

- Eating

Drinking & Nightlife

- Drinking & Nightlife
- Cafe

Entertainment

- Entertainment

Shopping

- Shopping

Information

- Bank
- Embassy/Consulate
- Hospital/Medical
- Internet
- Police
- Post Office
- Telephone
- Toilet
- Tourist Information
- Other Information

Geographic

- Beach
- Gate
- Hut/Shelter
- Lighthouse
- Lookout
- Mountain/Volcano
- Oasis
- Park
- Pass
- Picnic Area
- Waterfall

Population

- Capital (National)
- Capital (State/Province)
- City/Large Town
- Town/Village

Transport

- Airport
- Border crossing
- Bus
- Cable car/Funicular
- Cycling
- Ferry
- Metro station
- Monorail
- Parking
- Petrol station
- Subway station
- Taxi
- Train station/Railway
- Tram
- Underground station
- Other Transport

Note: Not all symbols displayed above appear on the maps in this book

Routes

- Tollway
- Freeway
- Primary
- Secondary
- Tertiary
- Lane
- Unsealed road
- Road under construction
- Plaza/Mall
- Steps
- Tunnel
- Pedestrian overpass
- Walking Tour
- Walking Tour detour
- Path/Walking Trail

Boundaries

- International
- State/Province
- Disputed
- Regional/Suburb
- Marine Park
- Cliff
- Wall

Hydrography

- River, Creek
- Intermittent River
- Canal
- Water
- Dry/Salt/Intermittent Lake
- Reef

Areas

- Airport/Runway
- Beach/Desert
- Cemetery (Christian)
- Cemetery (Other)
- Glacier
- Mudflat
- Park/Forest
- Sight (Building)
- Sportsground
- Swamp/Mangrove

Tasmin Waby

Margaret River & the Southwest A London-born writer with Kiwi *whānau* who grew up in Australia, Tasmin loves cartography, starry night skies, and getting off the beaten track. When not on the road for Lonely Planet she lives in a narrow-boat and is planning her next adventure with her two school-aged kids. Her love affair with Western Australia is off the charts.

Steve Waters

Broome & the Kimberley Travel and adventure have always been Steve's life; he couldn't imagine a world without them. He's been using Lonely Planet guide-books for over 30 years in places as diverse as Iran, Central Asia, Kamchatka, Tuva, the Himalaya, Canada, Patagonia, the Australian Outback, Northeast Asia, Myanmar and the Sahara. Little wonder then that he finally got a gig with the company he was supporting! Steve has contributed to *Iran, Indonesia* and the past five editions of *West Coast Australia,* and come any September you're likely to find him in a remote gorge somewhere in the Kimberley.

Contributing Writer

Michael Cathcart is well known as a broadcaster on ABC Radio National and has presented history programs on ABC TV. He has also taught Australian history and culture at Deakin University and the University of Melbourne. Michael wrote the History chapter.

OUR STORY

A beat-up old car, a few dollars in the pocket and a sense of adventure. In 1972 that's all Tony and Maureen Wheeler needed for the trip of a lifetime – across Europe and Asia overland to Australia. It took several months, and at the end – broke but inspired – they sat at their kitchen table writing and stapling together their first travel guide, *Across Asia on the Cheap*. Within a week they'd sold 1500 copies. Lonely Planet was born.

Today, Lonely Planet has offices in Franklin, London, Melbourne, Oakland, Dublin, Beijing and Delhi, with more than 600 staff and writers. We share Tony's belief that 'a great guidebook should do three things: inform, educate and amuse'.

OUR WRITERS

Charles Rawlings-Way

Perth, Perth Region Charles is a veteran travel, food and music writer who has penned 40-something titles for Lonely Planet – including guides to Singapore, Toronto, Sydney, Tonga, New Zealand, the South Pacific and every state in Australia, including his native terrain of Tasmania and current homeland of South Australia – plus too many articles to recall. After dabbling in the dark arts of architecture, cartography, project management and busking for some years, Charles hit the road for Lonely Planet in 2005 and hasn't stopped travelling since. He's also the author of a bestselling rock biography on Glasgow band Del Amitri, *These Are Such Perfect Days*. Follow Charles on the socials @crawlingsway and www.facebook.com/chasrwmusic. Charles also wrote the Plan, Understand and Survival Guide chapters.

Fleur Bainger

Perth Having worn her first backpack to Europe when she was just 10 years old, Perth-based journalist Fleur Bainger gets a heck of a buzz from being a freelance travel and food writer. As Western Australia's weekly food reviewer for the *Sunday Times Magazine*, she's constantly on the hunt for Perth's best new eateries, while her weekly 'what's on' slot on 6PR talkback radio means she's always got the lowdown on events and openings around town. She's a Lonely Planet Local, a destination expert for the *Telegraph* (UK) and a regular contributor to *Australian Traveller*, *Escape*, ABC radio and more.

Anna Kaminski

South Coast WA, Monkey Mia & the Central West, Ningaloo Coast & the Pilbara

Originally from the Soviet Union, Anna grew up in Cambridge, UK. She graduated from the University of Warwick with a degree in Comparative American Studies, a background in the history, culture and literature of the Americas and the Caribbean, and an enduring love of Latin America. Her restless wanderings led her to settle briefly in Oaxaca and Bangkok and her flirtation with criminal law saw her volunteering as a lawyer's assistant in the courts, ghettos and prisons of Kingston, Jamaica. Anna has contributed to almost 30 Lonely Planet titles. When not on the road, Anna calls London home.

OVER PAGE MORE WRITERS

Published by Lonely Planet Global Limited
CRN 554153
10th edition – November 2019
ISBN 978 1 78701 389 6

10 9 8 7 6 5 4 3 2 1
Printed in Malaysia

What?

Who? When?

Tudors

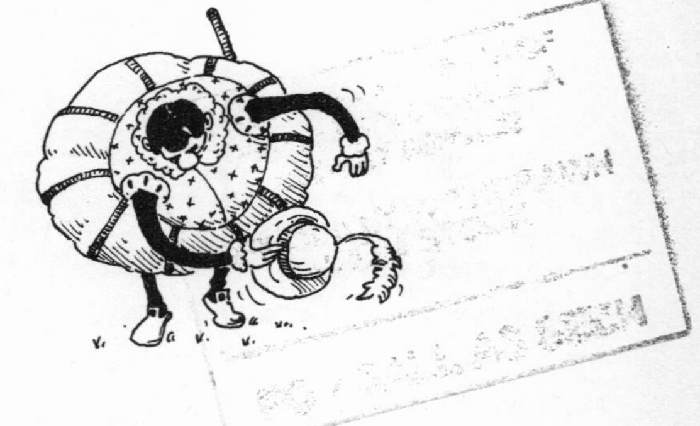

Produced by Fowke & Co. for Hodder Children's Books

Published by Hodder Children's Books 2003

0 340 85185 6

10 9 8 7 6 5 4 3 2

Hodder Children's Books
a division of Hodder Headline Limited
338 Euston Road
London NW1 3BH

Printed and bound in Great Britain by Bookmarque Ltd, Croydon
A Catalogue record for this book is available from the British Library

Who? What? When?

Tudors

By Bob Fowke

With drawings by the same

a division of Hodder Headline Limited

Plea for forgiveness

The Tudors were giants. They dragged England out of the Middle Ages and shoved it screaming and kicking through the gateway to the modern world. They took a country weakened by thirty years of civil war (the Wars of the Roses) and put it on the road to greatness.

Sometimes it seems that all Tudors were giants, not just the kings and queens. Tudor men and women circled the world, wrote some of the greatest plays ever written, established the first English-speaking colonies in North America, fought off the world's largest empire, changed their religion - and invented the flush toilet. No one book can tell more than a fraction of their story, but this book takes the most important bits, the bits you need to know about for your studies or simply if you want to grasp the basics of this incredible period. Pity the poor author who had to decide what those important bits are, and forgive him if he's left out anything or anyone whom you think should be in.

Bob Fowke